6th Edition

UNDERSTANDING COMPUTERS IN A CHANGING SOCIETY

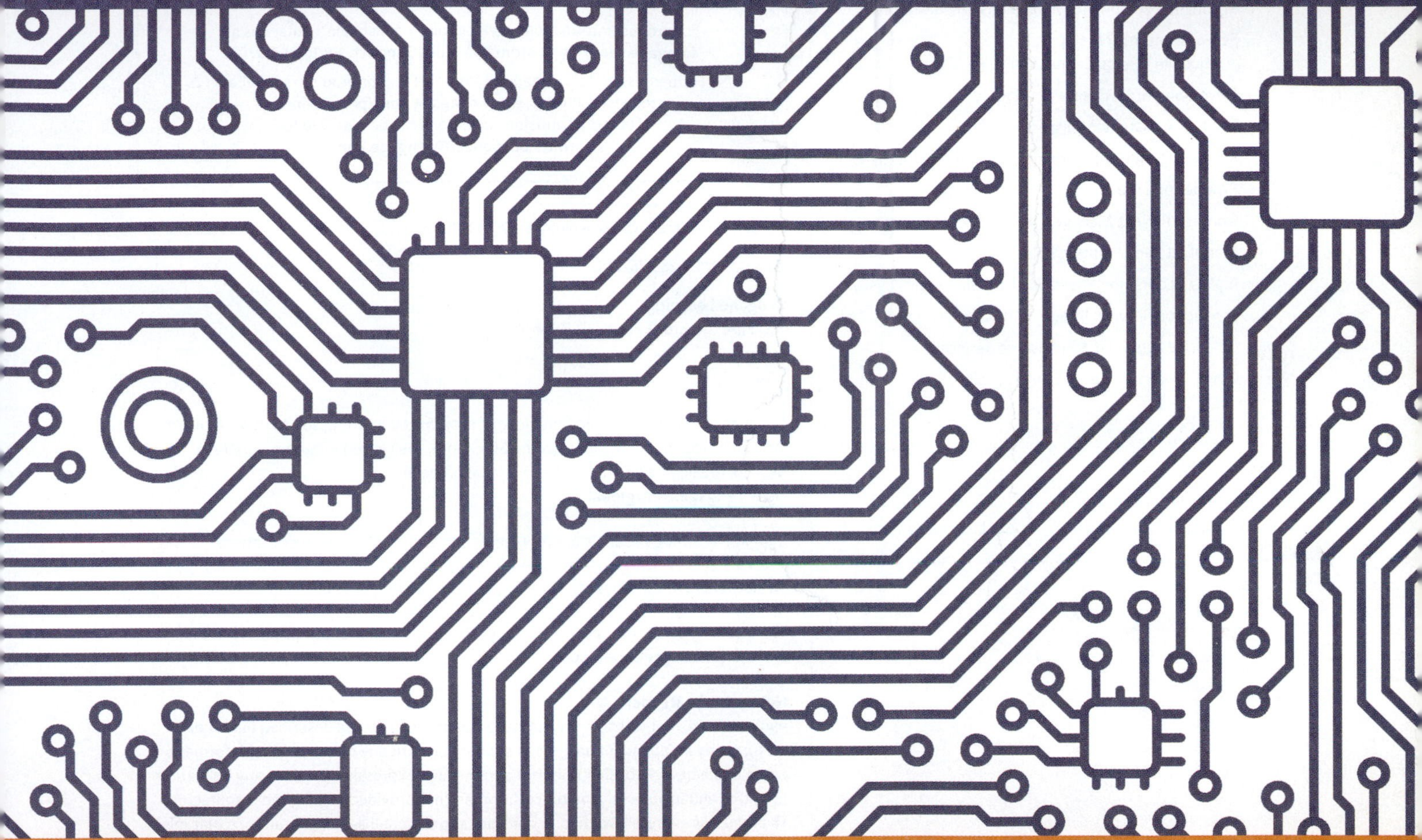

DEBORAH MORLEY

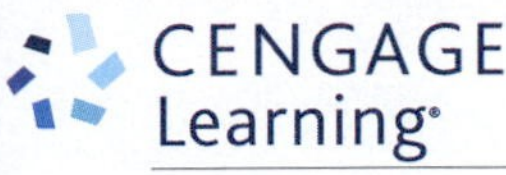

Australia • Brazil • Japan • Korea • Mexico • Singapore • Spain • United Kingdom • United States

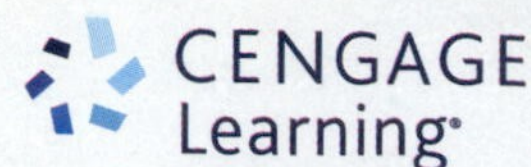

Understanding Computers in a Changing Society, 6th Edition
Deborah Morley

Vice President, General Manager: Dawn Gerrain

Product Director: Kathleen McMahon

Product Team Manager: Donna Gridley

Director, Development: Marah Bellegarde

Product Development Manager: Leigh Hefferon

Senior Content Developer: Michelle Ruelos Cannistraci

Developmental Editor: Pam Conrad

Product Assistant: Melissa Stehler

Marketing Manager: Gretchen Swann, Kristie Clark

Production Director: Patty Stephan

Content Project Manager: Jennifer Feltri-George

Manufacturing Planner: Fola Orekoya

Rights Acquisition Specialist: Christine Myaskovsky

Production Service: Integra Software Services Pvt. Ltd.

Cover Designer: GEX Publishing Services

Cover Image: ©Artens/Shutterstock

Library of Congress Control Number: 2013958042

ISBN-13: 978-1-285-76771-0

Cengage Learning
200 First Stamford Place, 4th Floor
Stamford, CT 06902
USA

Cengage Learning is a leading provider of customized learning solutions with office locations around the globe, including Singapore, the United Kingdom, Australia, Mexico, Brazil, and Japan. Locate your local office at:
www.cengage.com/global

Cengage Learning products are represented in Canada by Nelson Education, Ltd.

To learn more about Cengage Learning, visit **www.cengage.com**

Purchase any of our products at your local college store or at our preferred online store **www.cengagebrain.com**

Printed in the United States of America
1 2 3 4 5 6 7 18 17 16 15 14

PREFACE

In today's technology-oriented society, computers and technology impact virtually everyone's life. *Understanding Computers in a Changing Society, 6th Edition* is designed to ensure that students are current and informed in order to thrive in our technology-oriented, global society. With this new edition, students not only learn about relevant cutting-edge technology trends, but they also gain a better understanding of technology in general and the important issues surrounding technology today. This information gives students the knowledge they need to succeed in today's world.

This nontechnical, introductory text explains in straightforward terms the importance of learning about computers and other computing devices, the various types of devices and their components, the principles by which computers work, the practical applications of computers and related technologies, the ways in which the world is being changed by these technologies, and the associated risks and other potential implications of computers and related technologies. The goal of this text is to provide readers with a solid knowledge of computing fundamentals, an understanding of the impact of our technology-oriented society, and a framework for using this knowledge effectively in their lives.

KEY FEATURES

Just like its previous editions, *Understanding Computers in a Changing Society, 6th Edition* provides current and comprehensive coverage of important topics. Flexible organization and an engaging presentation, combined with a variety of learning tools associated with each chapter, help students master the important computing concepts they will encounter in school, on the job, and in their personal lives.

Currency and Accuracy

The state-of-the-art content of this book reflects the latest technologies, trends, and classroom needs. To reflect the importance of mobile computing today, the entire text has an increased emphasis on smartphones, media tablets, mobile apps, and the issues that surround them, such as mobile security. All topics and figures have been updated for currency and, to ensure the content is as accurate and up to date as possible, numerous **Industry Expert Reviewers** provided feedback and suggestions for improvements to the content in their areas of expertise. Throughout the writing and production stages, enhancements were continually made to ensure that the final product is as current and accurate as possible.

Comprehensiveness and Depth

Accommodating a wide range of teaching styles, *Understanding Computers in a Changing Society, 6th Edition* provides comprehensive coverage of traditional topics while also covering relevant, up-to-the-minute new technologies and important societal issues. This edition has an increased emphasis on mobile computing, cloud applications, and social media and includes the following new topics:

- New hardware developments, including smartphones, media tablets, smart watches, Google Glass, hybrid notebook-tablet computers, tiny PCs like the

Raspberry Pi and Chromecast, GPUs, immersion cooling systems, tablet and smartphone docks, personal 3D printers, projector phones, self-driving cars, self-healing devices, perceptual computing, gesture input, touch mice, eye tracking tablets, tablet storage devices, DNA data storage, and 4K (Ultra HD) Blu-ray Discs.

- New software developments and issues, including Windows 8, the Google Play store, mobile app builders, and the impact of cloud computing.
- New mobile applications, including Bring Your Own Device (BYOD), mobile ticketing, mobile data caps, group messaging, geofencing, Google Now, and mobile ergonomics.
- New networking technologies, including new and emerging Wi-Fi standards, the Internet of Things (IoT), Bluetooth Smart, software defined networking (SDN), and new Wi-Fi-enabled products such as smart thermostats, scales, and Wi-Fi locks.
- New security risks, including BYOD security issues, social media hacks, and scareware, ransomware, and chargeware.
- New security precautions, including digital tattoos and other emerging biometric systems, soft and hard tokens for OTPs/two-factor authentication, 3D Secure online purchase verification, wireless tethers for mobile devices, and proximity devices and apps to automatically lock and unlock a computer.
- New Web applications, including cloud printing, Internet monitors, virtual currency, social commerce, and social media integration.

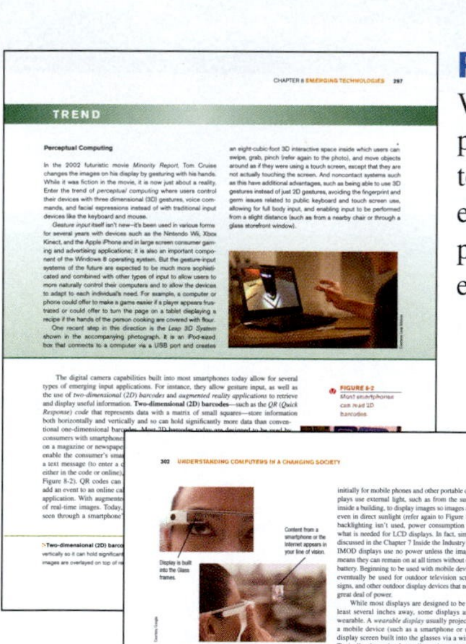
CHAPTER 8 EMERGING TECHNOLOGIES 297

TREND

Perceptual Computing

In the 2002 futuristic movie *Minority Report*, Tom Cruise changes the images on his display by gesturing with his hands. While it was fiction in the movie, it is now just about a reality. Enter the trend of *perceptual computing* where users control their devices with three dimensional (3D) gestures, voice commands, and facial expressions instead of with traditional input devices like the keyboard and mouse.

Gesture input itself isn't new—it's been used in various forms for several years with devices such as the Nintendo Wii, Xbox Kinect, and the Apple iPhone and in large screen consumer gaming and advertising applications; it is also an important component of the Windows 8 operating system. But the gesture-input systems of the future are expected to be much more sophisticated and combined with other types of input to allow users to more naturally control their computers and to allow the devices to adapt to each individual's need. For example, a computer or phone could offer to make a game easier if a player appears frustrated or could offer to turn the page on a tablet displaying a recipe if the hands of the person cooking are covered with flour.

One recent step in this direction is the *Leap 3D System* shown in the accompanying photograph. It is an iPod-sized box that connects to a computer via a USB port and creates an eight-cubic-foot 3D interactive space inside which users can swipe, grab, pinch (refer again to the photo), and move objects around as if they were using a touch screen, except that they are not actually touching the screen. And noncontact systems such as this have additional advantages, such as being able to use 3D gestures instead of just 2D gestures, avoiding the fingerprint and germ issues related to public keyboard and touch screen use, allowing for full body input, and enabling input to be performed from a slight distance (such as from a nearby chair or through a glass storefront window).

The digital camera capabilities built into most smartphones today allow for several types of emerging input applications. For instance, they allow gesture input, as well as the use of *two-dimensional (2D) barcodes* and *augmented reality applications* to retrieve and display useful information. **Two-dimensional (2D) barcodes**—such as the *QR (Quick Response) code* that represents data with a matrix of small squares—store information both horizontally and vertically and so can hold significantly more data than conventional one-dimensional barc… consumers with smartphone… on a magazine or newspape… enable the consumer's sma… a text message (to enter a c… either in the code or online)… Figure 8-2). QR codes can… add an event to an online ca… application. With augmente… of real-time images. Today,… seen through a smartphone'…

FIGURE 8-2 Most smartphones can read 2D barcodes.

Two-dimensional (2D) barc… vertically so it can hold significan… images are overlayed on top of r…

302 UNDERSTANDING COMPUTERS IN A CHANGING SOCIETY

Content from a smartphone or the Internet appears in your line of vision.
Display is built into the Glass frames.

FIGURE 8-8 Google Glass.

initially for mobile phones and other portable devices, IMOD displays use external light, such as from the sun or artificial light inside a building, to display images so images are bright and clear even in direct sunlight (refer again to Figure 8-7). And, because backlighting isn't used, power consumption is much less than what is needed for LCD displays. In fact, similar to the e-paper discussed in the Chapter 7 Inside the Industry box, devices using IMOD displays use no power unless the image changes, which means they can remain on at all times without draining the device battery. Beginning to be used with mobile devices, IMODs could eventually be used for outdoor television screens, large digital signs, and other outdoor display devices that normally consume a great deal of power.

While most displays are designed to be looked at from at least several inches away, some displays are designed to be wearable. A *wearable display* usually projects the image from a mobile device (such as a smartphone or media tablet) to a display screen built into the glasses via a wireless connection. Typically, the technology allows the user to see the image as if it is on a distant large screen display, and many wearable displays overlay the projected image on top of what the user is seeing in real time to provide augmented reality. For example, the *Google Glass* eyeglasses-based display shown in Figure 8-8 has a tiny display located where the right lens would be and users can see content projected on that screen in front of what they are seeing normally. Google Glass is typically connected (via Bluetooth) to a smartphone and then content (such as text messages, maps and directions, video calls, and Web pages) is streamed from that phone to the Google Glass display. Google Glass also has a built-in Web browser and can connect directly to a Wi-Fi hotspot when needed, has a touch-sensitive pad on the right side of the frame for input, and a bone-conductive audio output system so that audio output is heard only by the user. In addition to consumer wearable displays that have entertainment and productivity applications (such as being able to access GPS directions as needed or to monitor your e-mail during a meeting), there are also wearable displays designed for soldiers and other mobile workers.

ASK THE EXPERT

Josh Tinker, Product Planning Manager, Seagate Technology

Should my next computer have a magnetic hard drive or an SSD?

Your storage options for a new PC include traditional hard drives (HDDs), solid-state drives (SSDs), and the newer solid-state hybrid drives (SSHDs). Selecting what is right for you is a trade-off between price, performance, and capacity.

- SSDs have maximized PC performance and very good shock resistance, but are low capacity and pricey.
- HDDs have the lowest cost and high capacity but have average performance.
- SSHDs have SSD-like performance and high capacity, but have a small price premium.

Emerging Storage Devices

Improvements in magnetic disk technology are continuing to increase the data that can be stored on hard drives. Traditionally, the magnetic particles on a hard disk have been aligned horizontally, parallel to the hard disk's surface (referred to as *longitudinal magnetic recording*). To increase capacity and reliability, most new hard drives today use *perpendicular magnetic recording (PMR)*, in which the bits are placed upright to allow them to be closer together than is possible with a horizontal layout. For instance, PMR currently allows a recording density up to 1 *terabit per square inch* (*Tb/inch*^{2}), which results in internal hard drives with capacities up to about 4 TB of storage for a 3.5-inch

Readability

We remember more about a subject if it is made interesting and exciting, as well as presented in a straightforward manner. This book is written in a conversational, down-to-earth style—one designed to be accurate without being intimidating. Concepts are explained clearly and simply, without the use of overly technical terminology. More complex concepts are explained in an understandable manner and with realistic examples from everyday life.

Chapter Learning Tools

1. **Outline**, **Learning Objectives, and Overview**: For each chapter, an **Outline** of the major topics covered, a list of student **Learning Objectives**, and a **Chapter Overview** help instructors put the subject matter of the chapter in perspective and let students know what they will be reading about.
2. **Boldfaced Key Terms and Running Glossary**: Important terms appear in boldface type as they are introduced in the chapter. These terms are defined at the bottom of the page on which they appear and in the end-of-text glossary.
3. **Chapter Boxes**: In each chapter, a **Trend** box provides students with a look at current and upcoming technology trends; an **Inside the Industry** box provides insight into some of the practices and issues related to the computer industry; a **How It Works** box explains in detail how a technology or product works; and a **Technology and You** box takes a look at how computers and technology are used in everyday life.
4. **Ask the Expert Boxes**: In each chapter, three **Ask the Expert** boxes feature a question about a computing concept, a trend, or how computers

are used on the job or otherwise in the real world along with the response from an expert. Experts for this edition include a former Navy pilot, a guitarist from a rock band, and executives from notable companies like McDonald's, SONIC, ARM, Seagate, ACM, Rhapsody, The Computer Ethics Institute, Sony Animations, D-Link, GreenDisk, and Symantec.

TIP

Both Facebook and Twitter allow you to encrypt your connections—enable this option when you are using a public Wi-Fi hotspot to protect your account from hackers.

5. **Marginal Tips and Caution Elements**: **Tip** marginal elements feature time-saving tips or ways to avoid a common problem or terminology mistake, or present students with interesting additional information related to the chapter content. **Caution** elements warn of a possible problem students should avoid.

CAUTION CAUTION CAUTI

When upgrading your mobile phone, be c phone to others. Before disposing of or re settings to clear all personal data from the

6. **Illustrations and Photographs**: Instructive, current, full-color illustrations and photographs are used to illustrate important concepts. Figures and screenshots show the latest hardware and software and are annotated to convey important information.

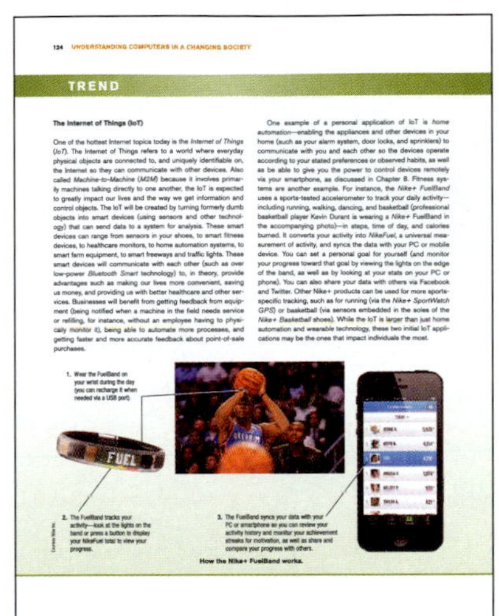
TREND

The Internet of Things (IoT)

How the Nike+ FuelBand works.

7. **Summary and Key Terms**: The end-of-chapter material includes a concise, section-by-section **Summary** of the main points in the chapter. The chapter's Learning Objectives appear in the margin next to the relevant section of the summary so that students are better able to relate the Learning Objectives to the chapter material. Every boldfaced key term in the chapter also appears in boldface type in the summary.

8. **Review Activities**: End-of-chapter **Review Activities** allow students to test themselves on what they have just read. A matching exercise of selected **Key Terms** helps students test their retention of the chapter material. A **Self-Quiz** (with the answers listed at the end of the book) consists of ten true-false and completion questions. Five additional easily graded matching and short-answer **Exercises** are included for instructors who would like to assign graded homework. Two short **Discussion Questions** for each chapter provide a springboard to jump-start classroom discussions.

9. **Projects**: End-of-chapter **Projects** require students to extend their knowledge by doing research and activities beyond merely reading the book. Organized into six types of projects (**Hot Topics**, **Short Answer/Research**, **Hands On**, **Ethics in Action**, **Presentation/Demonstration**, and **Balancing Act**), the projects feature explicit instructions so that students can work through them without additional directions from instructors and some require students to form an opinion about a current issue and discuss it in a classroom discussion or short paper. A special marginal icon denotes projects that require Internet access.

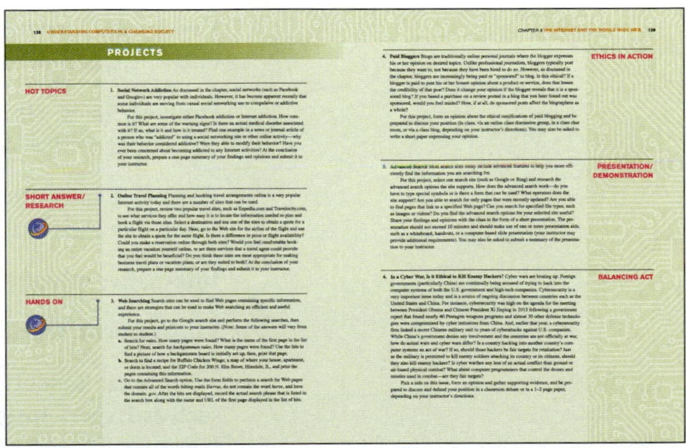
PROJECTS

HOT TOPICS

SHORT ANSWER/ RESEARCH

HANDS ON

ETHICS IN ACTION

PRESENTATION/ DEMONSTRATION

BALANCING ACT

References and Resources Guide

A **References and Resources Guide** at the end of the book brings together in one convenient location a collection of computer-related references and resources, including a **Computer History Timeline**, a **Guide to Buying a PC**, **A Look at Numbering Systems** feature, and a **Coding Charts** feature.

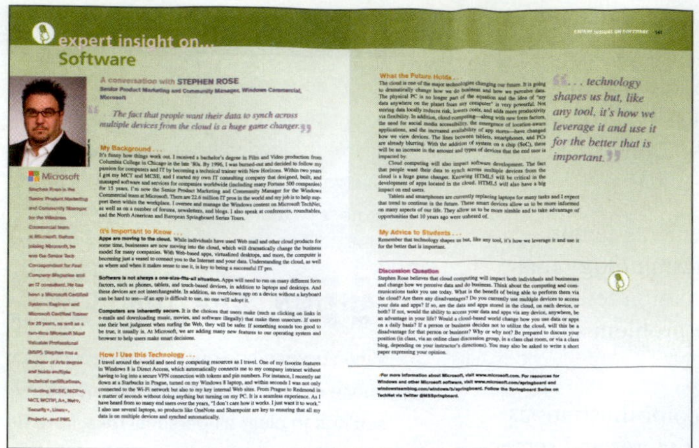

NEW and Updated Expert Insight Features

In the exciting **Expert Insight** feature located at the end of the first seven chapters, industry experts provide students with personal insights on topics presented in the book, including their personal experiences with technology, key points to remember, and advice for students. The experts, professionals from these major companies—**D-Link**, **Logitech**, **Microsoft**, **McAfee**, **eBay**, **ACM/Google**, and **Dell**—provide a unique perspective on the book's content and how the topics discussed in the text impact their lives and their industry, what it means for the future, and more!

Student and Instructor Support Materials

Understanding Computers in a Changing Society, 6th Edition is available with a complete package of support materials for instructors and students. Included in the package are **CourseMate**, the **Instructor Companion Site**, and, if access to SAM has been purchased, **SAM Computer Concepts** material is available.

CourseMate

The *Understanding Computers in a Changing Society, 6th Edition* includes **CourseMate**, which helps you make the grade. CourseMate includes:

- **Key Term Matching** and **Flashcards**—allow students to test their knowledge of selected chapter key terms.
- **Interactive Quiz**—allows students to test their retention of chapter concepts.
- **Global Technology Watch**—provides additional reading on the latest technology topics.
- **Beat the Clock**—allows students to test how ready they are for upcoming exams.
- **Crossword Puzzles**—incorporate the key terms from each chapter into an online interactive crossword puzzle.
- **Online Videos**—include several videos per chapter related to the topics in that chapter, as well as practical "How To" information related to chapter topics.
- **Further Exploration**—includes links to additional information about content covered in each chapter.
- **Interactive eBook**—includes highlighting, note taking, and search capabilities.
- **Engagement Tracker**—monitors student engagement in the course.
- **Additional Resources**—include additional resources that can be viewed or printed, such as **Expert Insights**; an **Online Study Guide**, **Online Summary**, and **Online Glossary** for each chapter; a **Guide to Buying a PC** and a **Computer History Timeline**; and more information about **Numbering Systems** and **Coding Charts**.

(Go to **cengagebrain.com** to access these resources.)

Instructor Companion Site

Everything you need for your course in one place! This collection of book-specific lecture and class tools is available online via **www.cengage.com/login**. Access and download PowerPoint presentations, images, Instructor's Manual, videos, and more.

Electronic Instructor's Manual

The **Instructor's Manual** is written to provide instructors with practical suggestions for enhancing classroom presentations. The Instructor's Manual provides: **Lecture Notes**, **Teacher Tips**, **Quick Quizzes**, **Classroom Activities**, **Discussion Questions**, **Key Terms**, a **Chapter Quiz**, and more!

Cengage Learning Testing Powered by Cognero

Cengage Learning Testing Powered by Cognero is a flexible, online system that allows you to:

- Author, edit, and manage test bank content from multiple Cengage Learning solutions
- Create multiple test versions in an instant
- Deliver tests from your LMS, your classroom, or wherever you want

PowerPoint Presentations

This book has **Microsoft PowerPoint presentations** available for each chapter. These are included as a teaching aid for classroom presentation, to make available to students on a network for chapter review, or to be printed for classroom distribution. Instructors can customize these presentations to cover any additional topics they introduce to the class. **Figure Files** for all figures in the textbook are also available online.

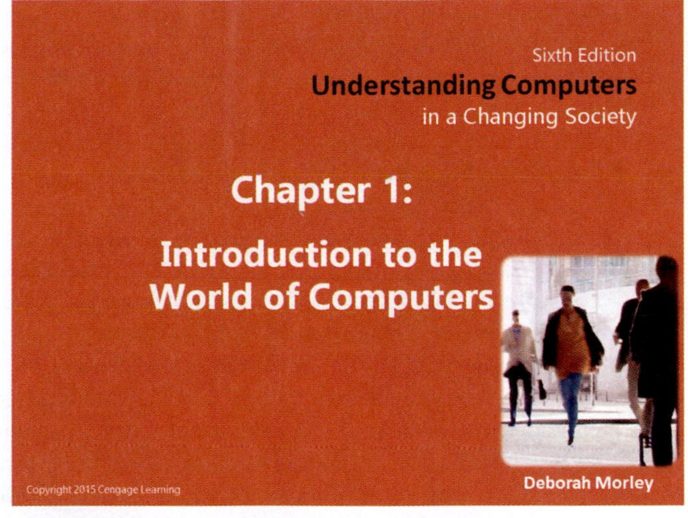

SAM: Skills Assessment Manager

SAM 2013 is designed to help bring students from the classroom to the real world. It allows students to train and test on important computer skills in an active, hands-on environment. SAM's easy-to-use system includes powerful interactive exams, training, and projects on the most commonly used Microsoft Office applications. SAM simulates the Office 2013 application environment, allowing students to demonstrate their knowledge and think through the skills by performing real-world tasks such as bolding text or setting up slide transitions. Add in live-in-the-application projects and students are on their way to truly learning and applying skills to business-centric documents.

Designed to be used with the New Perspectives Series, SAM includes handy page references, so students can print helpful study guides that match the New Perspectives Series textbooks used in class. For instructors, SAM also includes robust scheduling and reporting features.

ACKNOWLEDGMENTS

I would like to extend a special thank you to all of the industry professionals who provided their expertise for the **Expert Insight** features:

Daniel Kelley, Vice President, Marketing, D-Link Systems, Inc.
Ali Moayer, Senior Director of Engineering, Logitech
Stephen Rose, Senior Product Marketing and Community Manager, Windows Commercial, Microsoft
Greg Hampton, Vice President, Product Management, McAfee
Jim Griffith, Dean of eBay Education, eBay
Stuart Feldman, Past President of ACM and Vice President, Engineering, Google
Frank Molsberry, Sr. Principal Engineer and Security Technologist, Dell Inc.

In addition, I am very grateful to the numerous Industry Expert Reviewers that perform technical reviews and provide helpful suggestions each edition to ensure this book is as accurate and current as possible. I would also like to thank the Educational Reviewers who have helped to define and improve the quality of this text over the years. In particular, I would like to thank the following individuals:

Industry Expert Reviewers

Julie Anne Mossler, Director of Communications, Groupon; Alan Tringham, Senior Marketing Communications Manager, ARM; The Wi-Fi Alliance; Mike Hall, Corporate Communications, Seagate Technology; Kevin Curtis, CTO, InPhase Technologies; Sriram K. Peruvemba, Vice President, Marketing, E Ink Corporation; Jim Sherhart, Senior Director of Marketing, Data Robotics; Jack Dollard, Marketing, Mitek Systems; Joe Melfi, Director of Product Marketing for Cloud Solutions, D-Link Systems; Dave Gelvin, President, Tranzeo Wireless USA; Kevin Raineri, Director, Sales and Marketing, Innovative Card Technologies; Bill Shribman, Executive Producer, WGBH Interactive; Mike Markham, Vice President of Sales, Cadre Technologies; Renee Cassata, Marketing Manager, iDashboards; Russell T. Cross, Vice President of AAC Products, Prentke Romich Company; Dr. Kimberly Young, Director, The Center for Internet Addiction Recovery; Jason Taylor, Worldwide Director of Corporate Communications, MobiTV; Nicole Rodrigues, Public Relations Manager, MobiTV; Stephen Yeo, Worldwide Strategic Marketing Director, IGEL Technology; Bob Hirschfeld, Public Information Officer, Lawrence Livermore National Lab; Bryan Crum, Vice President of Communication, Omnilert, LLC; David Bondurant, MRAM Product Manager, Freescale Semiconductor, Inc.; Rick McGowan, Vice President & Senior Software Engineer, Unicode, Inc.; Margaret Lewis, Director of Commercial Solutions, AMD; Mark Tekunoff, Senior Technology Manager, Kingston Technology; Billy Rudock, Customer Service Staff Engineer, Seagate Technology; James M. DePuydt, Ph.D., Technology Director, Imation Corporation; Dan Bloom, Sr. PR Manager, SanDisk; Kevin Curtis, CTO, InPhase Technologies; Gail Levy, Director of Marketing, TabletKiosk; Novell Marketing; John McCreesh, Marketing Project Lead, OpenOffice.org; Jackson Dunlap, ESP Systems; Laura Abram, Director of Corporate Marketing, Dust Networks; Kevin Schader, Communications Director, ZigBee Alliance; Mauro Dresti, Linksys Product Marketing Manager; Lianne Caetano, Executive Director, WirelessHD, LLC; Brad Booth; Howard Frazier; Bob Grow; Michael McCormack; George Cravens, Technical Marketing, D-Link Systems; Christiaan Stoudt, Founder, HomeNetworkHelp.Info; Douglas M. Winneg, President, Software Secure, Inc.; Frank Archambeault, Director of Network Services, Dartmouth College; Adam Goldstein, IT Security Engineer, Dartmouth College; Ellen Young, Manager of Consulting Services, Dartmouth College; Becky Waring, Executive Editor, JiWire.com; Ellen Craw, General Manager, Ilium Software; Michael Behr, Senior Architect, TIBCO; Joe McGlynn, Director of Product Management, CodeGear; John Nash, Vice President of Marketing, Visible Systems; Josh Shaul, Director of Technology Strategy, Application Security, Inc.; Jodi Florence, Marketing Director, IDology, Inc.; Dr. Maressa Hecht Orzack, Director, Computer Addiction Services; Janice K. Mahon, Vice President of Technology Commercialization, Universal Display Corporation; Dr. Nhon Quach, Next Generation Processor Architect, AMD; Jos van Haaren, Department Head Storage Physics, Philips Research Laboratories; Terry O'Kelly, Technical Communications Manager, Memorex; Randy Culpepper, Texas Instruments RFID Systems; Aaron Newman, CTO and Co-Founder, Application Security Inc.; Alan Charlesworth, Staff Engineer, Sun Microsystems; Khaled A. Elamrawi, Senior Marketing Engineer, Intel Corporation; Timothy D. O'Brien, Senior Systems Engineer, Fujitsu Software; John Paulson, Manager, Product Communications, Seagate Technology; Omid Rahmat, Editor in Chief, Tom's Hardware Guide; Jeremy Bates, Multimedia Developer, R & L Multimedia Developers; Charles Hayes, Product Marketing Manager, SimpleTech, Inc.; Rick McGowan, Vice President & Senior Software Engineer, Unicode, Inc.; Russell Reynolds, Chief Operating Officer & Web Designer, R & L Multimedia Developers; Rob Stephens, Director, Technology Strategies, SAS; Dave Stow, Database Specialist, OSE Systems, Inc.

Educational Reviewers

Marc Forestiere, Fresno City College; Beverly Amer, Northern Arizona University; James Ambroise Jr., Southern University, Louisiana; Virginia Anderson, University of North Dakota; Robert Andree, Indiana University Northwest; Linda Armbruster, Rancho Santiago College; Michael Atherton, Mankato State University; Gary E. Baker, Marshalltown Community College; Richard Batt, Saint Louis Community College at Meremec; Luverne Bierle, Iowa Central Community College; Fariba Bolandhemat, Santa Monica College; Jerry Booher, Scottsdale Community College; Frederick W. Bounds, Georgia Perimeter College; James Bradley, University of Calgary; Curtis Bring, Moorhead State University; Brenda K. Britt, Fayetteville Technical Community College; Cathy Brotherton, Riverside Community College; Chris Brown, Bemidji State University; Janice Burke, South Suburban College; James Buxton, Tidewater Community College, Virginia; Gena Casas, Florida Community College, Jacksonville; Thomas Case, Georgia Southern University; John E. Castek, University of Wisconsin-La Crosse; Mario E. Cecchetti, Westmoreland County Community College; Jack W. Chandler, San Joaquin Delta College; Alan Charlesworth, Staff Engineer, Sun Microsystems; Jerry M. Chin, Southwest Missouri State University;

Edward W. Christensen, Monmouth University; Carl Clavadetscher, California State Polytechnic University; Vernon Clodfelter, Rowan Technical College, North Carolina; Joann C. Cook, College of DuPage; Laura Cooper, College of the Mainland, Texas; Cynthia Corritore, University of Nebraska at Omaha; Sandra Cunningham, Ranger College; Marvin Daugherty, Indiana Vocational Technical College; Donald L. Davis, University of Mississippi; Garrace De Groot, University of Wyoming; Jackie Dennis, Prairie State College; Donald Dershem, Mountain View College; John DiElsi, Marcy College, New York; Mark Dishaw, Boston University; Eugene T. Dolan, University of the District of Columbia; Bennie Allen Dooley, Pasadena City College; Robert H. Dependahl Jr.; Santa Barbara City College; William Dorin, Indiana University Northwest; Mike Doroshow, Eastfield College; Jackie O. Duncan, Hopkinsville Community College; John Dunn, Palo Alto College; John W. Durham, Fort Hays State University; Hyun B. Eom, Middle Tennessee State University; Michael Feiler, Merritt College; Terry Felke, WR Harper College; J. Patrick Fenton, West Valley Community College; James H. Finger, University of South Carolina at Columbia; William C. Fink, Lewis and Clark Community College, Illinois; Ronald W. Fordonski, College of Du Page; Connie Morris Fox, West Virginia Institute of Technology; Paula S. Funkhouser, Truckee Meadows Community College; Janos T. Fustos, Metropolitan State; Gene Garza, University of Montevallo; Timothy Gottleber, North Lake College; Dwight Graham, Prairie State College; Wade Graves, Grayson County College; Kay H. Gray, Jacksonville State University; David W. Green, Nashville State Technical Institute, Tennessee; George P. Grill, University of North Carolina, Greensboro; John Groh, San Joaquin Delta College; Rosemary C. Gross, Creighton University; Dennis Guster, Saint Louis Community College at Meremec; Joe Hagarty, Raritan Valley Community College; Donald Hall, Manatee Community College; Jim Hanson, Austin Community College; Sallyann Z. Hanson, Mercer County Community College; L. D. Harber, Volunteer State Community College, Tennessee; Hank Hartman, Iowa State University; Richard Hatch, San Diego State University; Mary Lou Hawkins, Del Mar College; Ricci L. Heishman, Northern Virginia Community College; William Hightower, Elon College, North Carolina; Sharon A. Hill, Prince George's Community College, Maryland; Alyse Hollingsworth, Brevard College; Fred C. Homeyer, Angelo State University; Stanley P. Honacki, Moraine Valley Community College; L. Wayne Horn, Pensacola Junior College; J. William Howorth, Seneca College, Ontario, Canada; Mark W. Huber, East Carolina University; Peter L. Irwin, Richland College, Texas; John Jasma, Palo Alto College; Elizabeth Swoope Johnson, Louisiana State University; Jim Johnson, Valencia Community College; Mary T. Johnson, Mt. San Antonio College; Susan M. Jones, Southwest State University; Amardeep K. Kahlon, Austin Community College; Robert T. Keim, Arizona State University; Mary Louise Kelly, Palm Beach Community College; William R. Kenney, San Diego Mesa College; Richard Kerns, East Carolina University, North Carolina; Glenn Kersnick, Sinclair Community College, Ohio; Richard Kiger, Dallas Baptist University; Gordon C. Kimbell, Everett Community College, Washington; Robert Kirklin, Los Angeles Harbor Community College; Judith A. Knapp, Indiana University Northwest; Mary Veronica Kolesar, Utah State University; James G. Kriz, Cuyahoga Community College, Ohio; Joan Krone, Denison University; Fran Kubicek, Kalamazoo Valley Community College; Rose M. Laird, Northern Virginia Community College; Robert Landrum, Jones Junior College; Shelly Langman, Bellevue Community College; James F. LaSalle, The University of Arizona; Chang-Yang Lin, Eastern Kentucky University; Linda J. Lindaman, Black Hawk College; Alden Lorents, Northern Arizona University; Paul M. Lou, Diablo Valley College; Deborah R. Ludford, Glendale Community College; Kent Lundin, Brigham Young University-Idaho; Barbara J. Maccarone, North Shore Community College; Wayne Madison, Clemson University, South Carolina; Donna L. Madsen, Kirkwood Community College; Randy Marak, Hill College; Gary Marks, Austin Community College, Texas; Kathryn A. Marold, Ph.D., Metropolitan State College of Denver; Cesar Marron, University of Wyoming; Ed Martin, Kingsborough Community College; Vickie McCullough, Palomar College; James W. McGuffee, Austin Community College; James McMahon, Community College of Rhode Island; William A. McMillan, Madonna University; Don B. Medley, California State Polytechnic University; John Melrose, University of Wisconsin—Eau Claire; Dixie Mercer, Kirkwood Community College; Mary Meredith, University of Southwestern Louisiana; Marilyn Meyer, Fresno City College; Carolyn H. Monroe, Baylor University; William J. Moon, Palm Beach Community College; Marilyn Moore, Purdue University; Marty Murray, Portland Community College; Don Nielsen, Golden West College; George Novotny, Ferris State University; Richard Okezie, Mesa Community College; Joseph D. Oldham, University of Kentucky; Dennis J. Olsen, Pikes Peak Community College; Bob Palank, Florissant Community College; James Payne, Kellogg Community College; Lisa B. Perez, San Joaquin Delta College; Savitha Pinnepalli, Louisiana State University; Delores Pusins, Hillsborough CC; Mike Rabaut, Hillsborough CC; Robert Ralph, Fayetteville Technical Institute, North Carolina; Herbert F. Rebhun, University of Houston-Downtown; Nicholas John Robak, Saint Joseph's University; Arthur E. Rowland, Shasta College; Kenneth R. Ruhrup, St. Petersburg Junior College; John F. Sanford, Philadelphia College of Textiles and Science; Kammy Sanghera, George Mason University; Carol A. Schwab, Webster University; Larry Schwartzman, Trident Technical College; Benito R. Serenil, South Seattle Community College; Allanagh Sewell, Southeastern Louisiana University; Tom Seymour, Minot State University; John J. Shuler, San Antonio College, Texas; Gayla Jo Slauson, Mesa State College; Harold Smith, Brigham Young University; Willard A. Smith, Tennessee State University; David Spaisman, Katherine Gibbs; Elizabeth Spooner, Holmes Community College; Timothy M. Stanford, City University; Alfred C. St. Onge, Springfield

Technical Community College, Massachusetts; Michael L. Stratford, Charles County Community College, Maryland; Karen Studniarz, Kishwaukee College; Sandra Swanson, Lewis & Clark Community College; Tim Sylvester, Glendale Community College; Semih Tahaoglu, Southeastern Louisiana University; Jane J. Thompson, Solano Community College; Sue Traynor, Clarion University of Pennsylvania; William H. Trueheart, New Hampshire College; James D. Van Tassel, Mission College; James R. Walters, Pikes Peak Community College; Joyce V. Walton, Seneca College, Ontario, Canada; Diane B. Walz, University of Texas at San Antonio; Joseph Waters, Santa Rosa Junior College, California; Liang Chee Wee, University of Arizona; Merrill Wells, Red Rocks Community College; Fred J. Wilke, Saint Louis Community College; Charles M. Williams, Georgia State University; Roseanne Witkowski, Orange County Community College; David Womack, University of Texas, San Antonio; George Woodbury, College of the Sequoias; Nan Woodsome, Araphoe Community College; James D. Woolever, Cerritos College; Patricia Joann Wykoff, Western Michigan University; A. James Wynne, Virginia Commonwealth University; Robert D. Yearout, University of North Carolina at Asheville; Israel Yost, University of New Hampshire; and Vic Zamora, Mt. San Antonio College.

I would also like to thank the people on the Cengage team—their professionalism, attention to detail, and enormous enthusiasm make working with them a pleasure. In particular, I'd like to thank Donna Gridley, Michelle Ruelos Cannistraci, Jennifer Feltri-George, Christine Myaskovsky, and Pam Conrad for all their ideas, support, and tireless efforts during the design, writing, rewriting, and production of this book. I would also like to thank Marissa Falco for the interior design and GEX Publishing Services for the cover design. I want to thank Sreejith Govindan and Integra for all their help managing the production of the book. Thanks also to Kathleen McMahon.

I am also very appreciative of the numerous individuals and organizations that were kind enough to supply information and photographs for this text and the many organizations, as well as Daniel Davis of Tinkernut.com, that generously allowed us to use their content for the Online Videos, which can be found on CourseMate.

I sincerely hope you find this book interesting, informative, and enjoyable to read.

Deborah Morley

BRIEF CONTENTS

CONTENTS

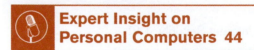

6th Edition

UNDERSTANDING COMPUTERS

IN A CHANGING SOCIETY

chapter 1

Introduction to the World of Computers

After completing this chapter, you will be able to do the following:

1. Explain why it is essential to learn about computers today and discuss several ways computers are integrated into our business and personal lives.
2. Define a computer and describe its primary operations.
3. List some important milestones in computer evolution.
4. Identify the major parts of a personal computer, including input, processing, output, storage, and communications hardware.
5. Define software and understand how it is used to instruct the computer what to do.
6. List the six basic types of computers, giving at least one example of each type of computer and stating what that computer might be used for.
7. Explain what a network, the Internet, and the World Wide Web are, as well as how computers, people, and Web pages are identified on the Internet.
8. Describe how to access a Web page and navigate through a Web site.
9. Discuss the societal impact of computers, including some benefits and risks related to their prominence in our society.

outline

OVERVIEW

Computers and other forms of technology impact our daily lives in a multitude of ways. We encounter computers in stores, restaurants, and other retail establishments. We use computers and the Internet regularly to obtain information, experience online entertainment, buy products and services, and communicate with others. Many of us carry a mobile phone or other mobile device with us at all times so we can remain in touch with others on a continual basis and can access Internet information as we need it. We also use these devices to pay for purchases, play online games with others, watch TV and movies, and much, much more.

Businesses also use computers extensively, such as to maintain employee and customer records, manage inventories, maintain online stores and other Web sites, process sales, control robots and other machines in factories, and provide business executives with the up-to-date information they need to make decisions. The government uses computers to support our nation's defense systems, for space exploration, for storing and organizing vital information about citizens, for law enforcement and military purposes, and for other important tasks. In short, computers and computing technology are used in an endless number of ways.

Understanding Computers in a Changing Society is a guide to computers and related technology, how they are being used in the world today, and their impact on our society. It will provide you with an introduction to computer concepts and terminology and give you a solid foundation for future computer-related courses. It will also provide you with the basic knowledge you need to understand and use computers in school, on the job, and in your personal life, as well as give you an understanding of the various societal issues related to technology, such as security and privacy issues, ethical considerations, and environmental concerns.

Chapter 1 is designed to help you understand what computers are, how they work, and how people use them. It introduces the important terms and concepts that you will encounter throughout this text and in discussions about computers with others, as well as includes an overview of the history of computers. It also takes a brief look at how to use a computer to perform basic tasks and to access resources on the Internet and the World Wide Web in order to provide you with the knowledge, skills, and tools you need to complete the projects and online activities that accompany this textbook. The chapter closes with an overview of the societal impact of computers. ■

TIP

Most of the computer concepts introduced in this chapter are discussed in more detail in subsequent chapters of this text.

COMPUTERS IN YOUR LIFE

Computers today are used in virtually every aspect of most individuals' lives—at home, at school, at work, and while on the go. The next few sections provide an overview of the importance of computers and some of the most common computer-related activities that individuals may encounter every day.

Why Learn About Computers?

Fifty years ago, computers were used primarily by researchers and scientists. Today, computers are an integral part of our lives. Experts call this trend *pervasive computing*, in which few aspects of daily life remain untouched by computers and computing technology. With pervasive computing—also referred to as *ubiquitous computing*—computers are found virtually everywhere and computing technology is integrated into an ever-increasing number of devices to give those devices additional functionality, such as enabling them to communicate with other devices on an ongoing basis. Because of the prominence of computers in our society, it is important to understand what a computer is, a little about how a computer works, and the implications of living in a computer-oriented society.

Prior to about 1980, computers were large and expensive, and few people had access to them. Most computers used in organizations were equipped to do little more than carry out high-volume processing tasks, such as issuing bills and keeping track of inventories. The average person did not need to know how to use a computer for his or her job, and it was uncommon to have a computer at home. Furthermore, the use of computers generally required a lot of technical knowledge and the use of the *Internet* was reserved primarily for researchers and educational institutions. Because there were few good reasons or opportunities for learning how to use computers, the average person was unfamiliar with them.

TIP

More than half of all U.S. mobile phone users today are *smartphone* users; that is, their mobile phones include Internet capabilities and the ability to run mobile programs or *apps*.

Beginning in the early 1980s, things began to change. *Microcomputers*—inexpensive *personal computers* that you will read about later in this chapter—were invented and computer use increased dramatically. The creation of the *World Wide Web* (*WWW*) in the late 1980s and the graphical *Web browser* in the early 1990s started the trend of individuals buying and using computers for personal use. Today, *portable computers* and *mobile phones* have brought personal computing to a whole new level—nearly 90% of all U.S. households have a computer or mobile phone, and most individuals use some type of computer on the job. Whether you become a teacher, attorney, doctor, engineer, restaurant manager, salesperson, professional athlete, musician, executive, or skilled tradesperson, you will likely use a computer to obtain and evaluate information, to facilitate necessary on-the-job tasks, and to communicate with others. Today's computers are very useful tools for these purposes; they are also taking on new roles in our society, such as delivering entertainment on demand. In fact, computers and the traditional communications and entertainment devices that we use every day—such as telephones, televisions, gaming devices, and home entertainment systems—are *converging* into single units with multiple capabilities. For instance, you can check your *e-mail* (electronic messages), watch videos, and view other Internet content on your living room TV; you can make telephone calls via your personal computer; and you can view Internet content and watch TV on your *smartphone* or other *mobile device* (see Figure 1-1). As a result of this *convergence* trend, the computer is no longer an isolated productivity tool; instead, it is an integral part of our daily lives.

FIGURE 1-1
Convergence.
Many devices today include computing or Internet capabilities.

Courtesy Netflix

TELEVISIONS
Can be used to access Web pages, e-mail, streaming movies, and other Internet content, in addition to viewing TV content.

Used with permission from Microsoft Corporation

SMARTPHONES
Can be used to access Internet content, play music and games, take photos, watch TV shows, and more, in addition to making phone calls.

Just as you can learn to drive a car without knowing much about car engines, you can learn to use a computer without understanding the technical details of how a computer works. However, a little knowledge gives you a big advantage. Knowing something about cars can help you make wise purchasing decisions and save money on repairs. Likewise, knowing something about computers can help you buy the right one for your needs, get the most efficient use out of it, be able to properly *upgrade* it as your needs change, and have a much higher level of comfort and confidence along the way. Therefore, basic **computer literacy**—knowing about and understanding computers and their uses—is an essential skill today for everyone.

>**Computer literacy.** The knowledge and understanding of basic computer fundamentals.

Computers in the Home

Home computing has increased dramatically over the last few years as computers and Internet access have become less expensive and as a vast array of online consumer activities have become available. Use of the Internet at home to look up information, exchange e-mail, shop, watch TV and videos, download music and movies, research products, pay bills and manage bank accounts, check news and weather, store and organize *digital photos*, play games, make vacation plans, and so forth is now the norm for many individuals (see Figure 1-2). Many individuals also use a computer at home for work-related tasks, such as to review work-related documents or check work e-mail from home.

As the Internet, wireless technology, and devices such as computers, televisions, mobile phones, *digital video recorders* (*DVRs*), and *gaming consoles* continue to converge, the computer is also becoming a central part of home entertainment. *Wireless networking* allows the use of computers in virtually any location and both online and offline content to be sent wirelessly from one device to another. Both voice and video telephone calls can be made over your Internet connection, and your TV can display Internet content.

Computing technologies also make it possible to have *smart appliances*—traditional appliances (such as refrigerators, thermostats, or ovens) with some type of built-in computer or communications technology that allows them to be controlled by the user via a smartphone or the Internet, to access and display Internet information, or to perform other computer-related functions. *Smart homes*—homes in which household tasks (such as watering the lawn, turning the air conditioning on or off, making coffee, monitoring the security of the home and grounds, and managing home entertainment content) are controlled by a main computer in the home or by the homeowner remotely via a smartphone—have arrived, and they are expected to be the norm in less than a decade. Some believe that one primary focus of smart appliances and smart homes will be energy conservation—for instance, the ability to perform tasks (such as running the dishwasher and watering the lawn) during nonpeak energy periods and to potentially transfer waste heat from one appliance (such as an oven) to another appliance (such as a dishwasher) as needed.

REFERENCE
Retrieving information, obtaining news, viewing recipes, shopping online, and exchanging e-mail are popular home computer activities.

PRODUCTIVITY
Home computers are frequently used for editing and managing digital photos and home videos, creating and editing work-related documents, paying bills, and other productivity tasks.

ENTERTAINMENT
Home computers and gaming consoles are becoming a central hub for entertainment, such as the delivery of photos, videos, music, games, TV shows, instant messages, and social networking updates.

FIGURE 1-2
Computer use at home.

Computers in Education

Today's youth can definitely be called the *computing generation*. From *handheld gaming devices* to mobile phones to computers at school and home, most children and teens today have been exposed to computers and related technology all their lives. Although the amount of computer use varies from school to school and from grade level to grade level, most students today have access to computers at school—and some schools have completely integrated computers into the curriculum, such as by adopting *e-book* (electronic) textbooks that run on school-owned portable computers, or allowing students to bring in devices to use in class (referred to as *BYOD* or *Bring Your Own Device*). Many schools (particularly college campuses) today also have *wireless hotspots* that allow students to connect their personal computers or mobile devices wirelessly to the Internet from anywhere on campus. Today, students at all levels are typically required to use a computer to some extent as part of their normal coursework—such as for preparing papers, practicing skills, doing Internet research, accessing Internet content (for instance, class *Web pages* or their campus *YouTube* channel), or delivering presentations—and some colleges require a computer for enrollment.

Computers are also used to facilitate *distance learning*—an alternative to traditional classroom learning in which students participate, typically at their own pace, from their current location (via their computers and Internet connections) instead of physically going to class. Consequently, distance learning gives students greater flexibility to schedule class time around

© Goodluz/Shutterstock.com

COMPUTER LABS AND CLASSROOMS
Many schools today have computers and Internet access available in the classroom and/or a computer lab for student use.

© iStockphoto.com/sturti

CAMPUS WIRELESS HOTSPOTS
Many students can access the Internet from anywhere on campus to do research, check e-mail, and more, via a campus hotspot.

Denver Makle, 7th Army JMTC

DISTANCE LEARNING
With distance learning, students—such as these U.S. Army soldiers—can take classes from home or wherever they happen to be at the moment.

FIGURE 1-3
Computer use in education.

their personal, family, and work commitments, as well as allows individuals located in very rural areas or stationed at military posts overseas to take courses when they are not able to attend classes physically. Some examples of computer use in education are shown in Figure 1-3.

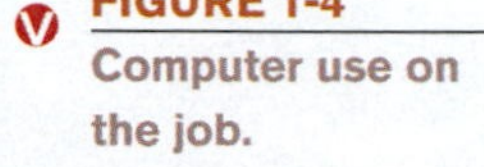

FIGURE 1-4
Computer use on the job.

Computers on the Job

Although computers have been used on the job for years, their role is continually evolving. Computers were originally used as research tools for computer experts and scientists and then as productivity tools for office workers. Today, computers are used by all types of employees in all types of businesses—including corporate executives, retail store clerks, traveling sales professionals, artists and musicians, engineers, police officers, insurance adjusters, delivery workers, doctors and nurses, auto mechanics and repair personnel, and professional athletes. In essence, the computer has become a universal tool for on-the-job decision making, productivity, and communications (see Figure 1-4). Computers are also used extensively for access control at many businesses and organizations, such as *authentication systems* that allow only authorized individuals to enter an office building, punch in or out of work, or access the company network via an access card or a fingerprint or hand scan, as shown in Figure 1-4 and discussed in detail in Chapter 4. In addition to jobs that require the use of computers by employees, many new jobs have been created simply because computers exist, such as jobs in electronics manufacturing, online retailing, Internet applications, and technology-related computer support.

© iStockphoto.com/sturti

DECISION MAKING
Many individuals today use a computer to help them make on-the-job decisions.

© Monkey Business Images/Shutterstock.com

PRODUCTIVITY
Many individuals today use a computer to perform on-the-job tasks efficiently and accurately.

© iStockphoto.com/fstop123

OFF-SITE COMMUNICATIONS
Many individuals use portable computers or mobile devices to record data, access data, or communicate with others when they are out of the office.

Courtesy Ingersoll Rand

AUTHENTICATION
Many individuals are required to use authentication systems to punch in and out of work, access facilities, or log on to company computers.

TECHNOLOGY AND YOU

Restaurant iPad Ordering Systems

You may have used your iPad or other device to place a pickup order at your local eatery; you may also have had a server use an iPad to take your order at a restaurant. Nice innovations, but guess what's next? Placing your order yourself at a restaurant using an iPad.

This new trend of using iPads and *e-menus* to have customers place their orders in restaurants is growing rapidly. In addition to enabling customers to place their orders at their convenience without waiting for a server, it also allows the restaurant to provide more resources to customers (such as photographs of menu items, pairing suggestions for appetizers and drinks, and so forth). The overall goal is to allow customers to control their dining experience from the time they are seated until they choose to pay the check. And, yes, they pay via the iPad as well (see the credit card reader at the top right of the iPad shown in the accompanying photo).

iPad ordering systems work especially well for restaurants that offer customized menu items. For example, Stacked, one of the first large-scale adopters of restaurant iPad ordering systems, offers typical American food (such as pizza, burgers, and salads) at its Southern California restaurants but everything on the menu is customizable—customers choose from a wide variety of ingredients, toppings, and sauces. The iPad systems enable customers to build their selections, adding or removing ingredients, until they are satisfied with the order (the price adjusts as they change their selections). This allows customers to build their orders at a comfortable pace without having to remember them until a server arrives, or having to make that many decisions with a server waiting.

More than 7,000 e-menu-enabled iPads are also arriving at airport restaurants in three airports in North America. They will be used not only for placing orders but also for providing travelers with free access to Facebook, Twitter, e-mail, games, news, and flight updates while they wait (for security purposes, all personal information is wiped from the device as soon as the home button is pressed).

The two biggest risks for restaurants introducing iPad ordering systems is customer acceptance (most offer assistance from servers if the customer desires to help alleviate any customer concerns about using the devices) and technology issues. To avoid network or Internet outage issues, some restaurants are implementing redundant systems, such as multiple routers that can be used if the main router goes down or a 4G Internet connection that the system can use to access the Internet via a cellular connection if the main Internet source goes down.

Courtesy of Square, Inc.

Computers are also used extensively by military personnel for communications and navigational purposes, as well as to control missiles and other weapons, identify terrorists and other potential enemies, and perform other necessary national security tasks. To update their computer skills, many employees in all lines of work periodically take computer training classes or enroll in computer certification programs.

Computers on the Go

In addition to using computers in the home, at school, and on the job, most people encounter and use all types of computers in other aspects of day-to-day life. For example, it is common for consumers to use *consumer kiosks* (small self-service computer-based stations that provide information or other services to the public, including those used for ATM transactions, bridal registries, ticketing systems, and more), *point-of-sale (POS) systems* (such as those found at most retail stores to check customers out—see the Technology and You box for a look at how you may soon be using iPads to order at restaurants), and *self-checkout systems* (which allow retail store customers to scan their purchases and pay

© iStockphoto.com/JohnnyGreig

PORTABLE DEVICES
Many people today carry a portable computer or smartphone with them at all times or when they travel in order to remain in touch with others and to access Internet resources.

Courtesy RedBox

CONSUMER KIOSKS
Electronic kiosks are widely available to view conference or gift registry information, print photographs, order products or services, and more.

Courtesy Intel

MOBILE PAYMENT SYSTEMS
Allow individuals to pay for purchases using a smartphone or other device.

Courtesy Ingersoll Rand

CONSUMER AUTHENTICATION SYSTEMS
Allow only authorized members, such as theme park annual pass holders as shown here, access to facilities.

FIGURE 1-5
Computer use while on the go.

for them without a salesclerk) while in retail stores and other public locations. Individuals may also need to use a computer-based consumer authentication system to gain access to a local health club, theme park, or other membership-based facility (see Figure 1-5).

In addition, many individuals carry a *portable computer* or *mobile device* with them on a regular basis to remain electronically in touch with others and to access information (such as stock quotes, driving directions, airline flight updates, movie times, news headlines, and more) as needed while on the go. These portable devices are also commonly used to watch TV, download and listen to music, access *Facebook* pages and other *social networking sites*, and perform other mobile entertainment options. Smartphones can also be used to pay for products and services (refer again to Figure 1-5), as well as remotely deposit checks, transfer money to others, pay bills electronicially, and perform other *mobile banking* applications. *GPS* (*global positioning system*) capabilities are frequently built into smartphones, cars, and other devices to provide individuals with driving directions and other navigational aids while traveling or hiking.

WHAT IS A COMPUTER AND WHAT DOES IT DO?

A **computer** can be defined as a programmable, electronic device that accepts data, performs operations on that data, presents the results, and stores the data or results as needed. The fact that a computer is *programmable* means that a computer will do whatever the instructions—called the *program*—tell it to do. The programs used with a computer determine the tasks the computer is able to perform.

The four operations described in this definition are more technically referred to as *input*, *processing*, *output*, and *storage*. These four primary operations of a computer can be defined as follows:

- **Input**—entering data into the computer.
- **Processing**—performing operations on the data.

>Computer. A programmable, electronic device that accepts data input, performs processing operations on that data, and outputs and stores the results. **>Input.** The process of entering data into a computer; can also refer to the data itself. **>Processing.** Performing operations on data that has been input into a computer to convert that input to output.

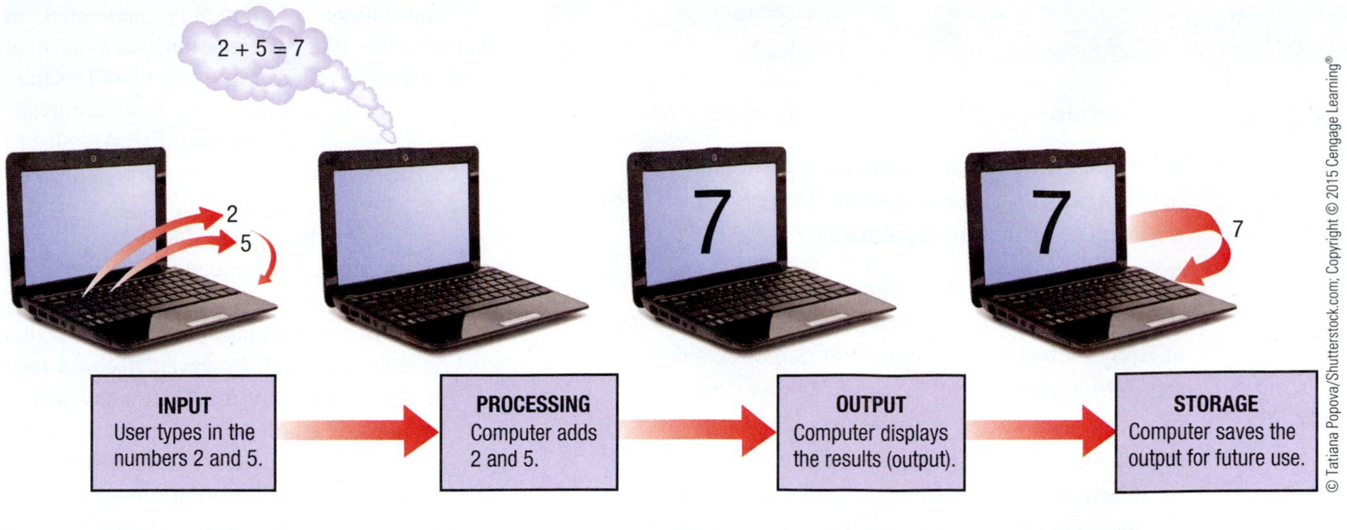
2 + 5 = 7
2
5
7
7
7
INPUT
User types in the numbers 2 and 5.
PROCESSING
Computer adds 2 and 5.
OUTPUT
Computer displays the results (output).
STORAGE
Computer saves the output for future use.

FIGURE 1-6
The information processing cycle.

- **Output**—presenting the results.
- **Storage**—saving data, programs, or output for future use.

For example, assume that you have a computer that has been programmed to add two numbers. As shown in Figure 1-6, input occurs when data (in this example, the numbers 2 and 5) is entered into the computer, processing takes place when the computer program adds those two numbers, and output happens when the sum of 7 is displayed on the computer screen. The storage operation occurs any time the data, a change to a program, or the output is saved for future use.

For an additional example, look at a supermarket *barcode reader* to see how it fits this definition of a computer. First, the grocery item being purchased is passed over the barcode reader—input. Next, the description and price of the item are looked up—processing. Then, the item description and price are displayed on the cash register and printed on the receipt—output. Finally, the inventory, ordering, and sales records are updated—storage.

This progression of input, processing, output, and storage is sometimes referred to as the *IPOS cycle* or the *information processing cycle.* In addition to these four primary computer operations, today's computers almost always perform **communications** functions, such as sending or retrieving data via the Internet, accessing information located in a shared company database, or exchanging data or e-mail messages with others. Therefore, communications—technically an input or output operation, depending on which direction the information is going—is often considered the fifth primary computer operation.

Data vs. Information

As just discussed, a user inputs **data** into a computer, and then the computer processes it. Almost any kind of fact or set of facts can become computer data, such as the words in a letter to a friend, the numbers in a monthly budget, the images in a photograph, the notes in a song, or the facts stored in an employee record. When data is processed into a meaningful form, it becomes **information**.

>**Output.** The process of presenting the results of processing; can also refer to the results themselves. >**Storage.** The operation of saving data, programs, or output for future use. >**Communications.** The transmission of data from one device to another. >**Data.** Raw, unorganized facts. >**Information.** Data that has been processed into a meaningful form.

ASK THE EXPERT

Courtesy Sony Pictures Imageworks

Rob Bredow, CTO, Sony Pictures Imageworks

What position might a college student graduating with a computer degree qualify for at Sony Pictures Imageworks?

We employ a number of talented engineers (typically computer science or computer engineering majors) at Sony Pictures Imageworks whose specialties range from developing completely new computer graphics techniques to focusing on our high performance networking and disk configurations. A recent graduate with experience in computer graphics rendering might, for example, help write shaders to simulate the lighting in the surface of a new challenging material like skin or cloth used for both animated and live-action films. We recently hired an engineer who first joined us as an intern and, because of her enthusiastic attitude and technical abilities, is now on the front lines of our Linux support team deploying new hardware and supporting artists working on our films. In summary, a great attitude—along with strong computer, math, and engineering skills—are qualities we love to see in our technology teams at Sony Pictures Imageworks.

Information is frequently generated to answer some type of question, such as how many of a restaurant's employees work less than 20 hours per week, how many seats are available on a particular flight from Los Angeles to San Francisco, or what is Hank Aaron's lifetime home run total. Of course, you don't need a computer system to process data into information; for example, anyone can go through time cards or employee files and make a list of people who work a certain number of hours. If this work is done by hand, however, it could take a lot of time, especially for a company with a large number of employees. Computers, however, can perform such tasks almost instantly, with accurate results. *Information processing* (the conversion of data into information) is a vital activity today for all computer users, as well as for businesses and other organizations.

Computers Then and Now

The basic ideas of computing and calculating are very old, going back thousands of years. However, the computer in the form in which it is recognized today is a fairly recent invention. In fact, personal computers have only been around since the late 1970s. The history of computers is often referred to in terms of *generations*, with each new generation characterized by a major technological development. The next sections summarize some early calculating devices and the different computer generations.

Precomputers and Early Computers (before approximately 1946)

Based on archeological finds, such as notched bones, knotted twine, and hieroglyphics, experts have concluded that ancient civilizations had the ability to count and compute. The *abacus* is considered by many to be the earliest recorded calculating device; it was used primarily as an aid for basic arithmetic calculations. Other early computing devices include the *slide rule*, the *mechanical calculator*, and Dr. Herman Hollerith's *Punch Card Tabulating Machine and Sorter.* This latter device (see Figure 1-7) was the first electromechanical machine that could read *punch cards*—special cards with holes punched in them to represent data. Hollerith's machine was used to process the 1890 U.S. Census data and it was able to complete the task in two and one-half years, instead of the decade it usually took to process the data manually. Consequently, this is considered to be the first successful case of an information processing system replacing a paper-and-pen-based system. Hollerith's company eventually became *International Business Machines (IBM)*.

First-Generation Computers (approximately 1946–1957)

The first computers were enormous, often taking up entire rooms. They were powered by thousands of *vacuum tubes*—glass tubes that look similar to large light bulbs—which needed replacing constantly, required a great deal of electricity, and generated a lot of heat. *First-generation computers* could solve only one problem at a time because they needed to be physically rewired with cables to be reprogrammed (see Figure 1-7), which typically took several days (sometimes even weeks) to complete and several more days to check before the computer could be used. Usually paper punch cards and paper tape were used for input, and output was printed on paper.

Two of the most significant examples of first-generation computers were *ENIAC* and *UNIVAC*. ENIAC, shown in Figure 1-7, was the world's first large-scale, general-purpose computer. Although it was not completed until 1946, ENIAC was developed during World War II to compute artillery-firing tables for the U.S. Army. Instead of the 40 hours required for a person to compute the optimal settings for a single weapon under a single set of conditions using manual calculations, ENIAC could complete the same calculations in less than two minutes. UNIVAC, released in 1951, was initially built for the U.S. Census Bureau and was used to analyze votes in the 1952 U.S. presidential election. Interestingly, its correct prediction of an Eisenhower victory only 45 minutes after the polls closed was not publicly aired because the results were not trusted. However, UNIVAC became the first computer to be mass produced for general commercial use.

Second-Generation Computers (approximately 1958–1963)

The second generation of computers began when the *transistor*—a small device made of *semiconductor* material that acts like a switch to open or close *electronic circuits*—started to replace the vacuum tube. Transistors allowed *second-generation computers* to be smaller, less expensive, more powerful, more energy-efficient, and more reliable than first-generation computers. Typically, programs and data were input on punch cards and *magnetic tape*, output was on punch cards and paper printouts, and magnetic tape (see Figure 1-7) was used for storage. *Hard drives* and *programming languages* (such as *FORTRAN* and *COBOL*) were developed and implemented during this generation.

PRECOMPUTERS AND EARLY COMPUTERS
Dr. Herman Hollerith's Punch Card Tabulating Machine and Sorter is an example of an early computing device. It was used to process the 1890 U.S. Census data.

FIRST-GENERATION COMPUTERS
First-generation computers, such as ENIAC shown here, were large and bulky, used vacuum tubes, and had to be physically wired and reset to run programs.

SECOND-GENERATION COMPUTERS
Second-generation computers, such as the IBM 1401 mainframe shown here, used transistors instead of vacuum tubes so they were smaller, faster, and more reliable than first-generation computers.

THIRD-GENERATION COMPUTERS
Third-generation computers used integrated circuits, which allowed the introduction of smaller computers such as the IBM System/360 mainframe shown here.

FOURTH-GENERATION COMPUTERS
Fourth-generation computers, such as the original IBM PC shown here, are based on microprocessors. Most of today's computers fall into this category.

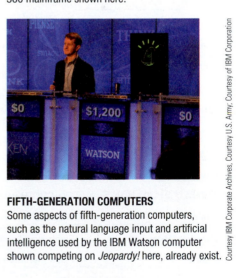

FIFTH-GENERATION COMPUTERS
Some aspects of fifth-generation computers, such as the natural language input and artificial intelligence used by the IBM Watson computer shown competing on *Jeopardy!* here, already exist.

Courtesy IBM Corporate Archives, Courtesy U.S. Army; Courtesy of IBM Corporation

FIGURE 1-7
A brief look at computer generations.

Third-Generation Computers (approximately 1964–1970)

The replacement of the transistor with *integrated circuits* (*ICs*) marked the beginning of the third generation of computers. Integrated circuits incorporate many transistors and electronic circuits on a single tiny silicon *chip*, allowing *third-generation computers* to be even smaller and more reliable than computers in the earlier computer generations. Instead of punch cards and paper printouts, *keyboards* and *monitors* were introduced for input and output; hard drives were typically used for storage. An example of a widely used third-generation computer is shown in Figure 1-7.

TIP

For a more detailed timeline regarding the development of computers, see the "Computer History Timeline" located in the References and Resources Guide at the end of this book.

Fourth-Generation Computers (approximately 1971–present)

A technological breakthrough in the early 1970s made it possible to place an increasing number of transistors on a single chip. This led to the invention of the *microprocessor* in 1971, which ushered in the fourth generation of computers. In essence, a microprocessor contains the core processing capabilities of an entire computer on one single chip. The original *IBM PC* (see Figure 1-7) and *Apple Macintosh* computers, and most of today's traditional computers, fall into this category. *Fourth-generation computers* typically use a keyboard and *mouse* for input, a monitor and *printer* for output, and *hard drives*, *flash memory media*, and *optical discs* for storage. This generation also witnessed the development of *computer networks*, *wireless technologies*, and the Internet.

Fifth-Generation Computers (now and the future)

Fifth-generation computers are most commonly defined as those that are based on *artificial intelligence*, allowing them to think, reason, and learn (see one example in Figure 1-7). Some aspects of fifth-generation computers—such as voice and touch input and *speech recognition*—are being used today. In the future, fifth-generation computers are expected to be constructed differently than they are today, such as in the form of *optical computers* that process data using light instead of electrons, tiny computers that utilize *nanotechnology*, or as entire general-purpose computers built into desks, home appliances, and other everyday devices.

Hardware

The physical parts of a computer (the parts you can touch and discussed next) are called **hardware**. The instructions or programs used with a computer—called *software*—are discussed shortly. Hardware components can be *internal* (located inside the main box or *system unit* of the computer) or *external* (located outside the system unit and connected to the system unit via a wired or wireless connection). There are hardware devices associated with each of the five computer operations previously discussed (input, processing, output, storage, and communications), as summarized in Figure 1-8 and illustrated in Figure 1-9. Both hardware and software are discussed in more detail in Chapter 2.

FIGURE 1-8 Common hardware listed by operation.

INPUT	PROCESSING
Keyboard	CPU
Mouse	**OUTPUT**
Microphone	Monitor/display screen
Scanner	Printer
Digital camera	Speakers
Digital pen/stylus	Headphones/headsets
Touch pad/touch screen	Data projector
Gaming controller	**STORAGE**
Fingerprint reader	Hard drive
COMMUNICATIONS	CD/DVD/Blu-ray disc
Modem	CD/DVD/Blu-ray drive
Network adapter	Flash memory card
Router	Flash memory card reader
	USB flash drive

Input Devices

An *input device* is any piece of equipment that is used to input data into the computer. The input devices shown in Figure 1-9 are a *keyboard*, *mouse*, and *microphone*. Other common input devices include *scanners*, *digital cameras*, *digital pens* and *styluses*, *touch pads* and *touch screens*, *fingerprint readers*, and *gaming controllers*.

Processing Devices

The main *processing device* for a computer is the *central processing unit* (*CPU*). The CPU is located inside the system unit and performs the calculations and comparisons needed for processing;

>**Hardware.** The physical parts of a computer system, such as the keyboard, monitor, printer, and so forth.

FLASH MEMORY CARD READER
Reads and writes flash memory cards.
DVD DRIVE
Reads and writes CD and DVD discs.
HARD DRIVE
Located inside the system unit; stores programs and most data.
SYSTEM UNIT
Case that contains the CPU, memory, power supply, storage devices, and all other internal hardware.
MONITOR
Lets you see your work as you go; the primary output device.
PRINTER
Produces printed copies of computer output.
MICROPHONE
Captures spoken input.
SPEAKERS
Produce audio output.
ROUTER
Connects devices so they can share an Internet connection and data.
USB PORTS
Connect external devices that use the USB interface.
MODEM
Connects the computer to the Internet.
KEYBOARD
Used to type instructions into the computer; a primary input device.
CD AND DVD DISCS
Used to deliver programs and store large multimedia files.
MOUSE
Used to make on-screen selections; a primary input device.
FLASH MEMORY CARDS
Used to store digital photos, music files, and other content.
USB FLASH DRIVE
Used to store documents, digital photos, music files, and other content to be moved from one PC to another.

FIGURE 1-9
Typical computer hardware.

it also controls the computer's operations. For these reasons, the CPU is often considered the "brain" of the computer. Also involved in processing are various types of *memory* that are located inside the system unit and used to store data and instructions while the CPU is working with them, as well as additional processors such as the *graphics processing unit* (*GPU*).

Output Devices

An *output device* accepts processed data from the computer and presents the results to the user, most of the time on the display screen (*monitor*), on paper (via a *printer*), or through a *speaker.* Other common output devices include *headphones* and *headsets* (used to deliver audio output to a single user) and *data projectors* (used to project computer images onto a projection screen).

Storage Devices

Storage devices (such as *DVD drives* and *flash memory card readers*) are used to store data on or access data from *storage media* (such as *DVD discs* and *flash memory cards*). Some storage hardware (such as a *hard drive* or a *USB flash drive*) includes both a storage device and storage medium in a single piece of hardware. Storage devices are used to save data, program settings, or output for future use; they can be installed inside the computer, attached to the computer as an external device, or accessed remotely through a network or wireless connection.

Communications Devices

Communications devices allow users to communicate electronically with others and to access remote information via the Internet or a home, school, or company computer network. Communications hardware includes *modems* (used to connect a computer to the Internet), *network adapters* (used to connect a computer to a computer network), and *routers* (used to create a small network so a variety of devices can share an Internet connection and data). A variety of modems and network adapters are available because there are different types of Internet and network connections—a modem used to connect to the Internet via a wireless connection and that also contains a built-in wireless router is shown in Figure 1-9. Communications hardware is discussed in more detail in Chapter 2; connecting to the Internet is covered in Chapter 3.

Software

The term **software** refers to the programs or instructions used to tell the computer hardware what to do. Software is traditionally purchased on a CD or DVD or is downloaded from the Internet; in either case, the software typically needs to be *installed* on a computer before it can be used. Software can also be run directly from the Internet (via Web pages) without being installed on your computer; this is referred to as *cloud software, Web-based software*, *Software as a Service* (*SaaS*), and *cloud computing* and is discussed in more detail in Chapter 2.

Computers use two basic types of software: *system software* and *application software.* The differences between these types of software are discussed next.

System Software

The programs that allow a computer to operate are collectively referred to as *system software.* The main system software is the **operating system**, which starts up the computer and controls its operation. Common operating system tasks include setting up new hardware, allowing users to run other software, and allowing users to manage the documents stored on their computers. Without an operating system, a computer cannot function. Common *desktop operating systems* designed for personal computers are *Windows*, *Mac OS*, and *Linux*; *mobile operating systems* used with mobile phones and other mobile devices include *Android*, *iOS*, and *Windows Phone*.

To use a computer, first turn on the power to the computer by pressing the power button, and then the computer will begin to **boot**. During the *boot process*, part of the computer's operating system is loaded into memory, the computer does a quick diagnostic of itself, and then it launches any programs—such as security software—designated to run each time the computer starts up. You may need to supply a password to *log on* to your computer or a computer network to finish the boot process.

Once a computer has booted, it is ready to be used and waits for input from the user. Most software today uses a variety of graphical objects (such as *icons, buttons,* and *tiles*) that are selected with the mouse (or with a finger or stylus for a computer that supports touch or pen input) to tell the computer what to do. For instance, the **Windows desktop** (the basic workspace for computers running the Windows operating system; that is, the place where documents, folders, programs, and other objects are displayed when they are being used), along with some common graphical objects used in Windows and many other software programs, is shown in Figure 1-10.

TIP

While the original release of Windows 8 did not include the traditional *Windows Start button,* it was reinstated in Windows 8.1 but displays the Start screen instead of the Start menu.

>Software. The instructions, also called computer programs, that are used to tell a computer what it should do. **>Operating system.** The main component of system software that enables a computer to operate, manage its activities and the resources under its control, run application programs, and interface with the user. **>Boot.** To start up a computer. **>Windows desktop.** The background work area displayed on the screen for computers running Microsoft Windows.

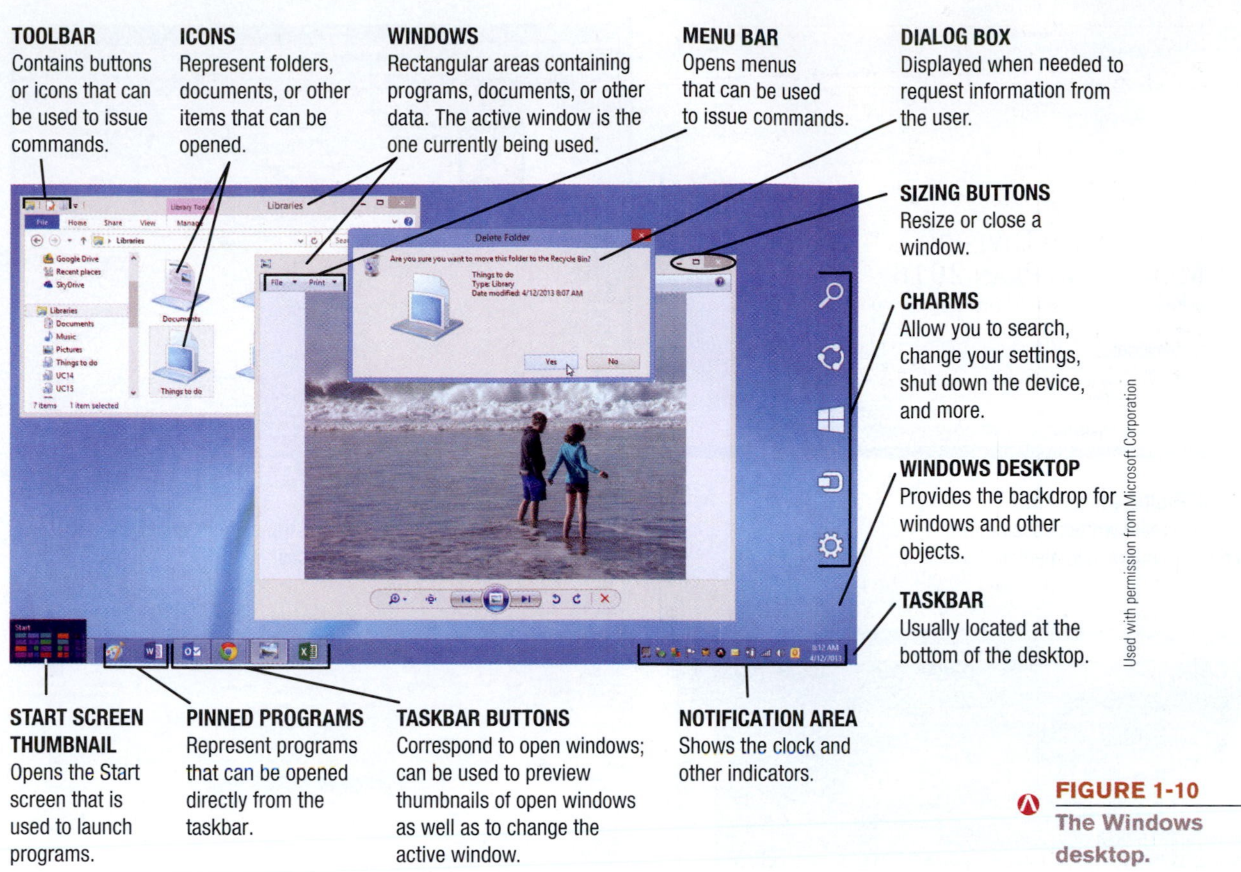

TOOLBAR
Contains buttons or icons that can be used to issue commands.
ICONS
Represent folders, documents, or other items that can be opened.
WINDOWS
Rectangular areas containing programs, documents, or other data. The active window is the one currently being used.
MENU BAR
Opens menus that can be used to issue commands.
DIALOG BOX
Displayed when needed to request information from the user.
SIZING BUTTONS
Resize or close a window.
CHARMS
Allow you to search, change your settings, shut down the device, and more.
WINDOWS DESKTOP
Provides the backdrop for windows and other objects.
TASKBAR
Usually located at the bottom of the desktop.
START SCREEN THUMBNAIL
Opens the Start screen that is used to launch programs.
PINNED PROGRAMS
Represent programs that can be opened directly from the taskbar.
TASKBAR BUTTONS
Correspond to open windows; can be used to preview thumbnails of open windows as well as to change the active window.
NOTIFICATION AREA
Shows the clock and other indicators.

FIGURE 1-10
The Windows desktop.

Application Software

Application software (see Figure 1-11) consists of programs designed to allow people to perform specific tasks using a computer, such as creating letters (*word processing software*), preparing budgets (*spreadsheet software*), managing inventory and customer databases (*database software*), playing games (*gaming software*), watching videos or listening to music (*multimedia software*), editing digital photographs (*image editing software*), viewing Web pages (*Web browsers*), and exchanging e-mail (*e-mail programs*). Application software can be sold as individual stand-alone programs; related programs are sometimes bundled together into a *software suite*, such as the popular *Microsoft Office* and *Google Docs* software suites. Application software is launched via the operating system, such as by using the *Windows Start screen* for Windows 8 computers (or the *Windows Start menu* for older versions of Windows).

There are also application programs that help users write their own programs in a form the computer can understand using a *programming language* like *BASIC*, *Visual Basic*, *COBOL*, *C++*, *Java*, or *Python*. Some languages are traditional programming languages for developing applications; others are designed for use with Web pages or multimedia programming. For overall Web page development, *markup languages*—such as *Hypertext Markup Language (HTML)* and *Extensible Hypertext Markup Language (XHTML)*—can be used. Markup languages use text-based *tags* embedded into Web pages to indicate where and how the content of a Web page should be displayed. *Scripting languages* (such as *JavaScript* or *VBScript*), as well as the most recent version of HTML (*HTML5*), are often used to create interactive Web pages.

TIP

Application software programs are also referred to as *apps*.

>**Application software.** Programs that enable users to perform specific tasks on a computer, such as writing letters or playing games; also called *apps*.

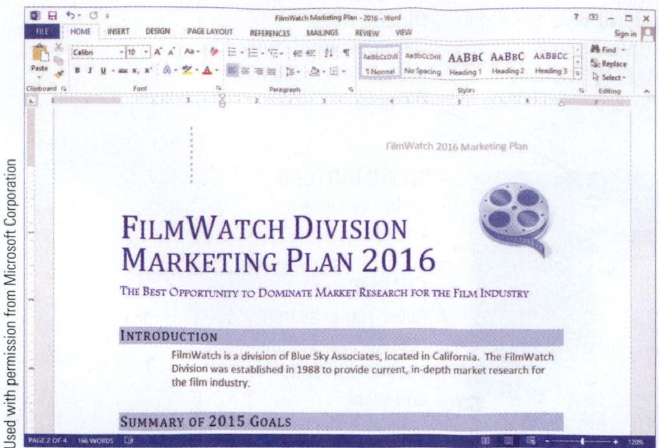

Used with permission from Microsoft Corporation

WORD PROCESSING PROGRAMS
Allow users to create written documents, such as reports, letters, and memos.

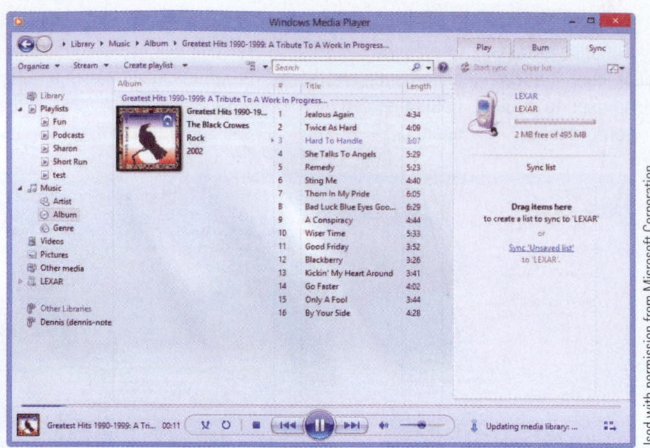

Used with permission from Microsoft Corporation

MULTIMEDIA PROGRAMS
Allow users to play music or videos and transfer content to and from CDs, DVDs, and portable devices.

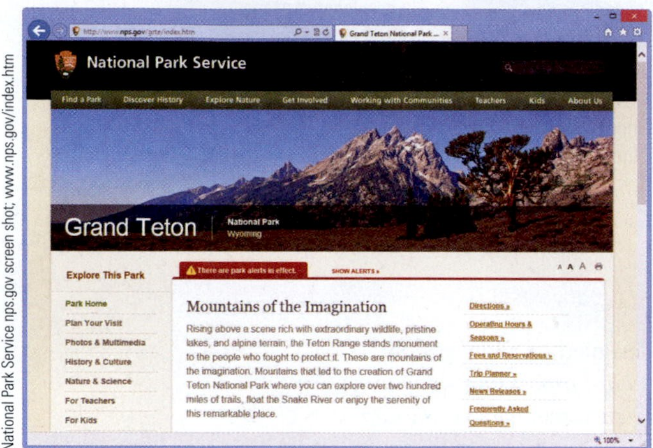

National Park Service nps.gov screen shot; www.nps.gov/index.htm

WEB BROWSERS
Allow users to view Web pages and other information located on the Internet.

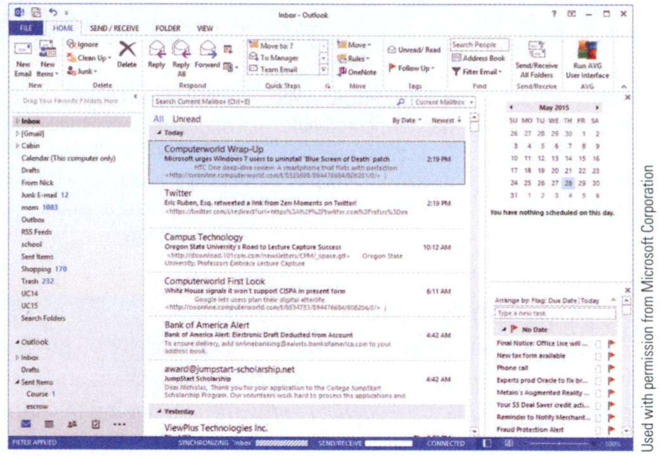

Used with permission from Microsoft Corporation

E-MAIL PROGRAMS
Allow users to compose, send, receive, and manage electronic messages; some also include calendars, to-do lists, and other features.

FIGURE 1-11
Examples of application software.

Computer Users and Professionals

In addition to hardware, software, data, and *procedures* (the predetermined steps to be carried out in particular situations), a computer system includes people. *Computer users*, or *end users*, are the people who use computers to perform tasks or obtain information. Anyone who uses a computer is a computer user, including an accountant electronically preparing a client's taxes, an office worker using a word processing program to create a letter, a supervisor using a computer to check and see whether or not manufacturing workers have met the day's quotas, a parent e-mailing his or her child's teacher, a college student researching a topic online, a doctor updating a patient's electronic medical record, a child playing a computer game, and a person shopping online.

Programmers, on the other hand, are computer professionals who write the programs that computers use. Other *computer professionals* include *systems analysts* (who design computer systems to be used within their companies), *computer operations personnel* (who are responsible for the day-to-day computer operations at a company, such as maintaining systems or troubleshooting user-related problems), and *security specialists* (who are responsible for securing the company computers and networks against *hackers* and other intruders who are discussed in more detail in Chapter 4).

COMPUTERS TO FIT EVERY NEED

The types of computers available today vary from the tiny computers embedded in consumer products, to the mobile devices that do a limited number of computing tasks, to the powerful and versatile *desktop* and *portable computers* found in homes and businesses, to the superpowerful computers used to control the country's defense systems. Computers are generally classified in one of six categories, based on size, capability, and price.

- *Embedded computers*—tiny computers embedded into products to perform specific functions or tasks for that product.
- *Mobile devices*—mobile phones, small tablets, and other small personal devices that contain built-in computing or Internet capabilities.
- *Personal computers*—fully functioning portable or desktop computers that are designed to be used by a single individual at a time.
- *Servers*—computers that host data and programs available to a small group of users.
- *Mainframe computers*—powerful computers used to host a large amount of data and programs available to a wide group of users.
- *Supercomputers*—extremely powerful computers used for complex computations and processing.

In practice, classifying a computer into one of these six categories is not always easy or straightforward. For example, some high-end personal computers today are as powerful as servers, and some personal computers today are the size of a mobile phone or smaller (see the Trend box). In addition, new trends impact the categories. For example, small tablet devices (often called *mobile tablets*, *media tablets*, or just *tablets*) are typically considered mobile devices because they are only slightly larger than a mobile phone, are typically used primarily for viewing Web content and displaying *multimedia* content instead of general-purpose computing, and usually run a mobile operating system. However, larger, more powerful tablet computers running a desktop operating system are typically considered personal computers. So even though the distinction between some of the categories (particularly mobile devices and personal computers) is blurring, these six categories are commonly used today to refer to groups of computers designed for similar purposes.

FIGURE 1-12
Embedded computers. This car's embedded computers control numerous features, such as notifying the driver when a car enters his or her blind spot.

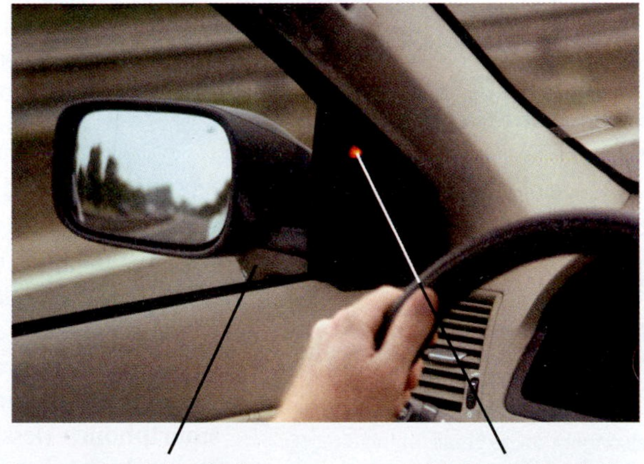

A camera located under the mirror detects moving vehicles in the driver's blind spot.

A light indicates that a moving vehicle is in the driver's blind spot.

Embedded Computers

An **embedded computer** is a tiny computer embedded into a product designed to perform specific tasks or functions for that product. For example, computers are often embedded into household appliances (such as dishwashers, microwaves, ovens, coffeemakers, and so forth), as well as into other everyday objects (such as thermostats, answering machines, treadmills, sewing machines, DVD players, and televisions), to help those appliances and objects perform their designated tasks. Typically, cars also use many embedded computers to assist with diagnostics, to notify the user of important conditions (such as an underinflated tire or an oil filter that needs changing), to control the use of the airbag and other safety devices (such as cameras that alert a driver that a vehicle is in his or her blind spot—see Figure 1-12—or

>**Embedded computer.** A tiny computer embedded in a product and designed to perform specific tasks or functions for that product.

TREND

Tiny PCs

Computers have shrunk again. Forget tiny notebooks or even media tablets if you want portability—today's newest tiny PCs are the size of a USB flash drive.

Some of these new computers actually do look just like a USB flash drive; others are just a small circuit board, sometimes enclosed in a case. Whatever their appearance, the idea is similar—you connect them to a display device and an input device (if needed) and you are good to go.

These emerging tiny PCs are designed to connect in different ways and have different capabilities. For example, Google's *Chromecast* (shown in the accompanying photo) plugs directly into an HDTV using its built-in HMDI connector. After connecting Chromecast, you can stream online content (such as videos, movies, and music) via Wi-Fi from your smartphone, tablet, or laptop to that HDTV. The *Raspberry Pi* tiny PC can connect to an HDTV via HDMI, as well as to a standard TV via RCA jacks. Instead of being used in conjunction with another device like Chromecast, however, the Raspberry Pi is a stand-alone computer that can be used with USB input devices (such as a keyboard and mouse) and connects to the Internet via an Ethernet port. Another tiny stand-alone PC is the *Cstick Cotton Candy*. This device, the size of a USB flash drive, can connect to another computer or an HDTV via its built-in HDMI and USB ports, to peripheral devices via USB or Bluetooth, and to the Internet via Wi-Fi.

The flexibility of these devices and the apps that can be used with them vary from device to device, based on the operating system used (most use a version of Linux or Android, though Chromecast uses Chrome) and the amount of storage available (devices with a USB port typically support USB flash drives or hard drives for additional storage if needed). But for turning a TV at any location into your own personal computer, gaming device, or video player, tiny PCs are definitely the way to go.

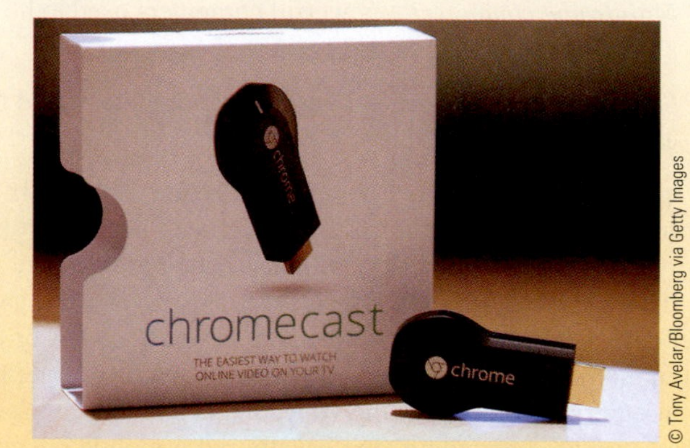

© Tony Avelar/Bloomberg via Getty Images

auto braking systems that engage when a front collision is imminent), to facilitate the car's navigational or entertainment systems, and to help the driver perform tasks. Embedded computers are designed for specific tasks and specific products and so cannot be used as general-purpose computers.

> **TIP**
> More than half of all U.S. adults carry an Internet-enabled mobile device with them to provide Internet access while on the go.

> **TIP**
> Larger smartphones that can also function as small tablets are sometimes referred to as *phablets*.

Mobile Devices

A **mobile device** is loosely defined as a very small (typically pocket-sized) device that has built-in computing or Internet capability. Mobile phones are the most common type of mobile device and can typically be used to make telephone calls, send *text messages* (short text-based messages), view Web pages, take digital photos, play games, download and play music, watch TV shows, and access calendars and other personal productivity features. Mobile phones that include computing and Internet capabilities (such as the one in Figure 1-13) are called **smartphones** (less capable mobile phones are sometimes referred to as *feature phones*). Handheld gaming devices (such as the *Nintendo 3DS*), *portable digital media players* (such as the *iPod Touch*), *smart watches*, and other personal devices that include Internet capabilities can also be referred to as mobile devices. As previously mentioned, **media tablets** (such as the

>**Mobile device.** A very small device that has built-in computing or Internet capability. >**Smartphone.** A mobile device based on a mobile phone that includes Internet capabilities and can run mobile apps. >**Media tablet.** A mobile device, usually larger than a smartphone, that is typically used to access the Internet and display multimedia content.

one shown in Figure 1-13) designed for Web browsing, playing movies and other multimedia content, gaming, and similar activities are also typically considered mobile devices. Mobile devices are almost always powered by a rechargeable battery system and typically include wireless connectivity to enable the device to connect to a wireless hotspot or to a *cellular provider* for Internet access.

Today's mobile devices typically have small screens and some, but not all, have keyboards. Because of this, mobile devices are most appropriate for individuals wanting continual access to e-mail, brief checks of Web content (such as doing a quick Web search, checking movie times or weather forecasts, looking up driving directions, or getting updates from Web sites like Facebook), and music collections rather than for those individuals wanting general Web browsing and computing capabilities. This is beginning to change, however, as mobile devices continue to grow in capabilities, as wireless communications continue to become faster, and as mobile input options (such as voice and touch input, and mobile keyboards) continue to improve. For instance, many mobile devices can perform Internet searches and other tasks via voice commands, some can be used to pay for purchases while you are on the go, many can view virtually any Web content, and some can view and edit documents stored in a common format, such as *Microsoft Office* documents. For a look at how tech clothing can be used to organize your mobile devices while you are on the go, see the Inside the Industry box.

Courtesy HTC

SMARTPHONES

Courtesy Amazon

MEDIA TABLETS

FIGURE 1-13
Mobile devices.

Personal Computers (PCs)

A **personal computer** (**PC**) or **microcomputer** is a small computer designed to be used by one person at a time. Personal computers are widely used by individuals and businesses today and are available in a variety of shapes and sizes, as discussed next.

TIP

For tips on buying a personal computer, see the "Guide to Buying a PC" in the References and Resources Guide located at the end of this book.

CAUTION CAUTION CAUTION CAUTION CAUTION CAUTION CAUT

Because many mobile devices and personal computers today are continually connected to the Internet, securing those devices against *computer viruses* and *hackers*—as introduced later in this chapter and discussed in detail in Chapter 4—is essential for both individuals and businesses.

FIGURE 1-14
Desktop computers.

Desktop Computers

Conventional personal computers that are designed to fit on or next to a desk (see Figure 1-14) are often referred to as **desktop computers**. Desktop computers can use a *tower case* (designed to sit vertically, typically on the floor), a *desktop case* (designed to be placed horizontally on a desk's surface), or an *all-in-one case* (designed to incorporate the monitor and system unit into a single piece of hardware).

TOWER COMPUTERS

ALL-IN-ONE COMPUTERS

Courtesy Dell Inc.; Courtesy Lenovo

>**Personal computer (PC).** A type of computer based on a microprocessor and designed to be used by one person at a time; also called a **microcomputer**. >**Desktop computer.** A personal computer designed to fit on or next to a desk.

INSIDE THE INDUSTRY

Tech Clothing

The extreme popularity of mobile phones, portable digital media players, media tablets, and other mobile devices has led to the need to easily and securely carry these devices with you while on the go. While a single device can typically just go in your pocket, individuals carrying multiple devices may find it easier to use *tech clothing.*

Similar to the way many backpacks today have built-in pockets for portable digital media players along with internal channels to run earbud cords, clothing manufacturers are increasingly designing products with mobile devices in mind, such as including clear pouches for storing and using devices while on the go. The jacket shown in the accompanying illustration goes a step further—it has 24 pockets, including some clear pockets to hold devices as they are being used and a pocket large enough to hold an iPad, as well as a wire management system to organize earbuds and other cords. To use this jacket, first put your devices in the appropriate pockets and then run your cables through the appropriate internal channels—the devices then can be used in the normal fashion. Other items, such as keys, a wallet, a digital camera, or airline tickets, can also be stored securely in a pocket. In addition to just helping you carry your devices, using a tech jacket or vest also has additional advantages. For instance, your devices cannot be accidentally dropped and they are safe from thieves as long as you are wearing the garment. If you are traveling by air, a tech garment can simplify your airport security experience and prevent you from losing or forgetting items at the security checkpoint because you can just take off the garment and have it examined as a single item. So, with tech clothing, at least in the area of mobile devices, you can take it with you.

Scottevest

REGULAR APPEARANCE

X-RAY VIEW

Desktop computer systems typically cost between $300 and $1,500 and usually conform to one of two standards or *platforms*: *PC-compatible* or *Mac*. PC-compatible computers (sometimes referred to as *Windows PCs* or *IBM-compatible PCs*) evolved from the original IBM PC—the first personal computer widely accepted for business use. They are made by companies such as Dell, Hewlett-Packard, NEC, Acer, Lenovo, Fujitsu, and Gateway and typically run the Microsoft Windows operating system, although some run an alternative operating system (such as Linux). Mac computers are made by Apple and use the Mac OS operating system. Windows, Linux, and Mac computers all use different software. Although PC-compatible computers are by far the most widely used in the United States, the Mac is traditionally the computer of choice for artists, designers, and others who require advanced graphics capabilities. Extra powerful desktop computers designed for computer users running graphics, music, film, architecture, science, and other powerful applications are sometimes referred to as *workstations*.

ASK THE EXPERT

Courtesy of Jack in the Box, Inc.

Michael Verdesca, Vice President and Chief Information Officer, Jack in the Box Inc.

How long will it be until paying for fast-food purchases by mobile phone is the norm?

The technology exists today to allow for the payment of fast-food purchases by mobile phone and it's being used in Europe and Japan. Though it's being tested in the United States, there are still some hurdles, primarily the adoption of the technology by cell phone providers and retailers, and consumers' willingness to use it. Another hurdle is consumers' concerns about the technology being secure. It will likely be a few years before there is widespread use.

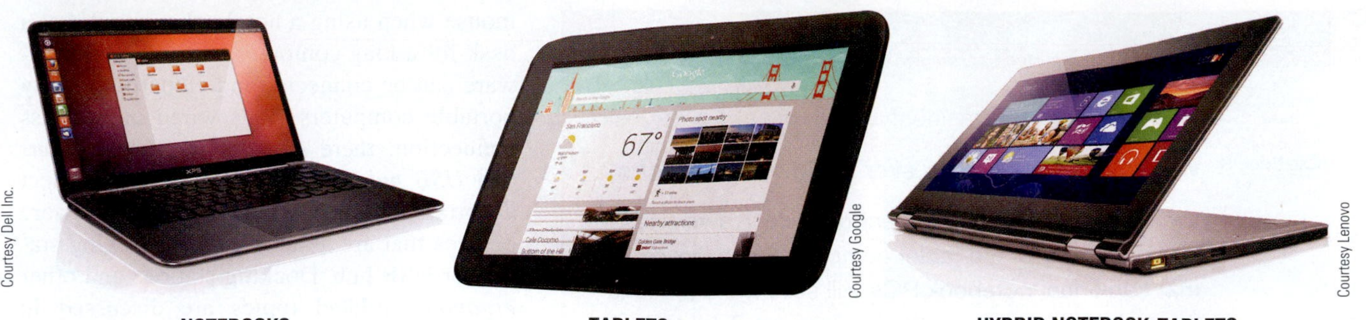

FIGURE 1-15
Portable computers.

Portable Computers

Portable computers are fully functioning computers designed to be carried around easily. This portability makes them very flexible. They can be used at home or in the office; they can also be used at school, while on vacation, at off-site meetings, and other locations. Like mobile devices, portable computers are designed to be powered by rechargeable batteries so they can be used while on the go. While portable computers are essential for many workers, such as salespeople who need to make presentations or take orders from clients off-site, agents who need to collect data at remote locations, and managers who need computing and communications resources as they travel, they are typically also the computer of choice today for students and for individuals buying a new home computer. In fact, portable computers now outsell desktop computers in the United States. Portable computers are available in a variety of configurations, as discussed next and shown in Figure 1-15.

- **Notebook computers** (also called **laptop computers**) are about the size of a paper notebook and open to reveal a screen on the top half of the computer and a keyboard on the bottom. They are typically comparable to desktop computers in features and capabilities. Very thin and very light notebooks are often referred to as *subnotebooks* or *ultraportables*; ultraportables conforming to Intel's standards can be marketed as *Ultrabooks*.
- **Tablet computers** are typically about the size of a notebook computer and are designed to be used with a digital pen/stylus or touch input. Unlike notebooks, they don't have a physical keyboard but they typically can use an on-screen or attached keyboard as needed.
- **Hybrid notebook-tablet computers** (also called *convertible tablets*) can function as either a notebook or a tablet computer. Some (such as the one in Figure 1-15) have a display screen that folds shut to resemble a tablet; others are designed to separate the display from the keyboard when a tablet is needed.
- **Netbooks** are similar to notebook computers but are smaller and have more limited features, such as relying on cloud software and external DVD drives.

It is important to realize that while a portable computer offers the convenience of mobility, it typically isn't as comfortable to use for a primary home or work computer as a desktop computer is, without additional hardware. For instance, many individuals find it more convenient to connect and use a conventional monitor, keyboard, and

TIP

Tablets are expected to outsell laptops by 2016.

TIP

Computers that allow pen or touch input—such as tablet computers—are convenient in crowded situations, as well as in places where the clicking of a keyboard would be annoying to others.

TIP

Portable computers (typically netbooks) that run the Chrome operating system are often referred to as *Chromebooks*.

>Portable computer. A small personal computer, such as a notebook or tablet, that is designed to be carried around easily.
>Notebook computer. A fully functioning portable computer that opens to reveal a screen and keyboard; also called a **laptop computer**.
>Tablet computer. A portable computer about the size of a notebook that is designed to be used with a digital pen. **>Hybrid notebook-tablet computer.** A portable computer designed to function as both a notebook and a tablet PC. **>Netbook.** A computer that is smaller and has more limited features than a notebook computer.

ASK THE EXPERT

Courtesy of TabletKiosk

Martin Smekal, President and Founder, TabletKiosk

Will tablet computers ever replace notebooks?

While we have seen a tremendous rise in awareness and popularity of the tablet computer, we believe that traditional notebook PCs will still have a place in the mobile device market going forward. Tablets and tablet PCs are incredibly effective and ergonomically advantageous for mobility purposes, but there will still be certain applications where a more traditional computer with an integrated keyboard makes sense. In the end, it will come down to what is the right tool for the application. That said, there will likely be applications where it makes sense to replace today's notebook with a more mobile-friendly tablet computing solution. We see some portion of market share held today by notebooks shifting in favor of the tablet and tablet PC market over time.

mouse when using a notebook computer at a desk for a long computer session. This hardware can be connected individually to many portable computers via a wired or wireless connection; there are also *docking stations* and *USB hubs* that can be used to connect a portable computer easily to the hardware devices that are attached to the docking station or USB hub. Docking stations and other *ergonomic*-related topics are discussed in more detail in Chapter 7.

Thin Clients and Internet Appliances

Most personal computers today are sold as stand-alone, self-sufficient units that are equipped with all the necessary hardware and software needed to operate independently. In other words, they can perform input, processing, output, and storage without being connected to a network, although they can be networked if desired. In contrast, a device that must be connected to a network to perform processing or storage tasks is referred to as a *dumb terminal.* Two types of personal computers that may be able to perform a limited amount of independent processing but are designed to be used with a network are *thin clients* and *Internet appliances.*

TIP

Virtually any device (such as a smartphone) being used to access a company network or cloud resource can also be referred to as a "thin client" while it is being used for that purpose.

A **thin client** is designed to utilize a company network for much of its processing capabilities. Instead of using local hard drives for storage, programs are typically accessed from and data is stored on a *network server.* The main advantage of thin clients over desktop computers is lower cost because hardware needs to be replaced less frequently, and costs are lower for computer maintenance, power, and air conditioning. Additional benefits include increased security (because data is not stored on the computer) and easier maintenance (because all software is located on a central server). Disadvantages include having limited or no local storage (although this is an advantage for companies with highly secure data that need to prevent data from leaving the facility) and not being able to function as a stand-alone computer when the network is not working. Thin clients are used by businesses to provide employees with access to network applications; they are also used in school computer labs (such as the one shown in Figure 1-16).

Ordinary devices that can be used for accessing the Internet can be called **Internet appliances** (sometimes referred to as *Internet-enabled devices*). Some Internet appliances (such as *smart TVs* and the *smart refrigerator* shown in Figure 1-16) use apps to deliver news, sports scores, weather, music, and other Web-based information. Gaming consoles (such as the *Nintendo Wii*, the *Xbox 360* shown accessing a Web page in Figure 1-16, and the *Sony PlayStation 3*) that can be used to view Internet content, in addition to their gaming abilities, can also be classified as Internet appliances when they are used to access the Internet.

>**Thin client.** A personal computer designed to access a network for processing and data storage, instead of performing those tasks locally.

>**Internet appliance.** A device that can be used to access the Internet.

Courtesy Spoon River College

THIN CLIENTS

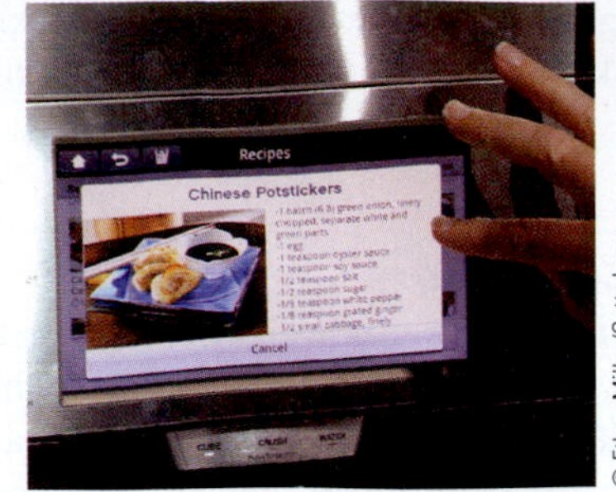
© Ethan Miller/Getty Images

SMART FRIDGES

Used with permission from Microsoft Corporation

INTERNET-ENABLED GAMING CONSOLES

FIGURE 1-16
Thin clients and Internet appliances.

Servers

A **server**—also sometimes called a *midrange server, minicomputer,* or *midrange computer*—is a computer used to host programs and data for a small network. Typically larger, more powerful, and more expensive than a desktop computer, a server is usually located in an out-of-the-way place and can serve many users at one time. Users connect to the server through a network, using their desktop computer, portable computer, thin client, or a dumb terminal consisting of just a monitor and keyboard (see Figure 1-17). Servers are often used in small- to medium-sized businesses (such as medical or dental offices), as well as in school computer labs. There are also special *home servers* designed for home use, which are often used to *back up* (make duplicate copies of) the content located on all the computers in the home automatically and to host music, photos, movies, and other media to be shared via a *home network.*

One trend involving servers (as well as the *mainframe computers* discussed next) today is **virtualization**—creating *virtual* (rather than actual) versions of a computing resource. *Server virtualization* uses separate server environments that, although physically located on the same computer, function as separate servers and do not interact with each other. For instance, all applications for an organization can be installed in virtual environments on one or more physical servers instead of using a separate server for each application. Using a separate server for each application often wastes resources because the servers are typically not used to full capacity—one estimate is that only about 10% of server capability is frequently utilized. With virtualization, companies can fulfill their computing needs with fewer servers, which results in lower costs for hardware and server management, as well as lower power and cooling costs. Consequently, one of the most significant appeals of server virtualization today is increased efficiency.

With the wide use of portable computers and mobile devices in the workplace, *desktop virtualization* is a growing trend. Desktop virtualization separates the user's desktop environment from his or her physical computer so that each user's desktop (stored on a central server) can be delivered to that individual via any authorized device; the user interacts with the virtual desktop in the same way he or she would interact with

FIGURE 1-17
Servers. Servers are used to host data and programs on a small network, such as a school computer lab or medical office network.

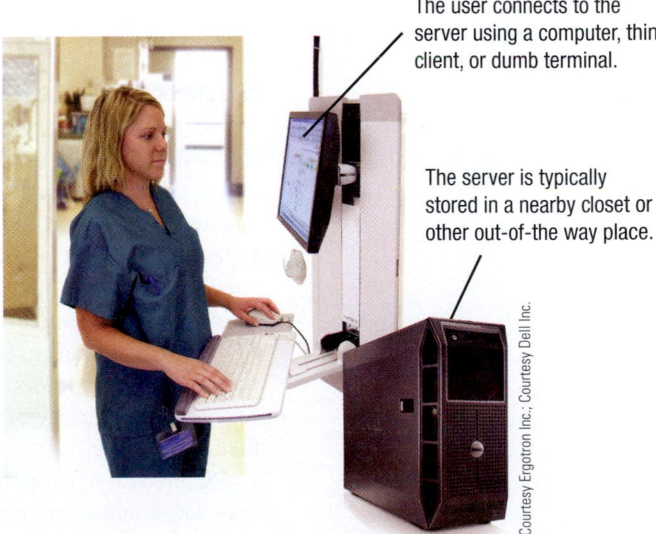

The user connects to the server using a computer, thin client, or dumb terminal.
The server is typically stored in a nearby closet or other out-of-the way place.

Courtesy Ergotron Inc.; Courtesy Dell Inc.

>**Server.** A computer used to host programs and data for a small network. >**Virtualization.** Creating virtual (rather than actual) versions of a computing resource, such as several separate environments that are located on a single server but function as different servers.

a physical desktop. Desktop virtualization adds flexibility to where and how each worker performs daily tasks. Virtualization is also used in other computing areas, such as networking and storage.

Mainframe Computers

A **mainframe computer** is a powerful computer used by many large organizations—such as hospitals, universities, large businesses, banks, and government offices—that need to manage large amounts of centralized data. Larger, more expensive, and more powerful than servers, mainframes can serve thousands of users connected to the mainframe via personal computers, thin clients, or dumb terminals, in a manner similar to the way users connect to servers. Mainframe computers are typically located in climate-controlled *data centers* (see Figure 1-18) and are connected to the rest of the company computers via a computer network. During regular business hours, a mainframe typically runs the programs needed to meet the different needs of its wide variety of users. At night, it commonly performs large processing tasks, such as payroll and billing. Today's mainframes are sometimes referred to as *high-end servers* or *enterprise-class servers* and they usually cost at least several hundred thousand dollars each.

FIGURE 1-18
Mainframe computers. Mainframes are used to perform large processing tasks for businesses.

Courtesy of IBM Corporation

One issue facing businesses today is the high cost of electricity to power and cool the mainframes, servers, and personal computers used in an organization. Consequently, making the computers located in a business—particularly mainframes and servers—more energy efficient is a high priority today. Virtualization is often used today to utilize a company's mainframes more efficiently. Another current focus for mainframes today is ensuring they can handle new and emerging needs (such as having the computational power to process data from *smart meters* and other new technology and having the ability to run mobile and social networking applications) for businesses that want to offer these apps but want to have the power and security of a mainframe.

Supercomputers

Some applications require extraordinary speed, accuracy, and processing capabilities—for example, sending astronauts into space, controlling missile guidance systems and satellites, forecasting the weather, exploring for oil, breaking codes, and designing and testing new products. **Supercomputers**—the most powerful and most expensive type of computer available—were developed to fill this need. Some relatively new supercomputing applications include hosting extremely complex Web sites (such as search sites and social networking sites) and *three-dimensional applications* (such as 3D medical imaging, 3D image projections, and 3D architectural modeling). Unlike mainframe computers, which typically run multiple applications simultaneously to serve a wide variety of users, supercomputers generally run one program at a time, as fast as possible.

Conventional supercomputers can cost several million dollars each. They tend to be very large and contain a large number of CPUs. For example, the *Titan* supercomputer shown in Figure 1-19 occupies 4,352 square feet of floor space and contains 299,008

>Mainframe computer. A computer used in large organizations (such as hospitals, large businesses, and colleges) that need to manage large amounts of centralized data and run multiple programs simultaneously. **>Supercomputer.** The fastest, most expensive, and most powerful type of computer.

CPUs. This supercomputer is being installed at the U.S. Department of Energy Oak Ridge National Laboratory and is expected to be used for a variety of scientific research, including climate change and astrophysics; its speed is expected to give researchers unparalleled accuracy in their simulations and facilitate faster research breakthroughs. At 17.59 *petaflops* (quadrillions of *floating point operations* or calculations *per second*) at the present time and expected to surpass 20 petaflops when completed, Titan is one of the fastest computers in the world.

Courtesy of Oak Ridge National Laboratory

FIGURE 1-19
The Titan supercomputer. Supercomputers are used for specialized situations in which immense processing speed is required.

COMPUTER NETWORKS AND THE INTERNET

A **computer network** is a collection of computers and other devices that are connected together to enable users to share hardware, software, and data, as well as to communicate electronically with each other. Computer networks exist in many sizes and types. For instance, home networks are commonly used to allow home computers to share a single printer and Internet connection, as well as to exchange files. Small office networks enable workers to access company records stored on a *network server*, communicate with other employees, share a high-speed printer, and access the Internet (see Figure 1-20). School networks allow students and teachers to access the Internet and school resources, and large corporate networks often connect all of the offices or retail stores in the corporation, creating a network that spans several cities or states. Public wireless networks—such as those available at some coffeehouses, restaurants, public libraries, and parks—provide Internet access to individuals via their portable computers and mobile devices; mobile telephone networks provide Internet access and communications capabilities to smartphone users. Most computers today connect to a computer network.

What Are the Internet and the World Wide Web?

The **Internet** is the largest and most well-known computer network in the world. It is technically a network of networks because it consists of thousands of networks that can all access each other via the main *backbone* infrastructure of the Internet. Individual users connect to the Internet by connecting their computers or other devices to servers belonging to an **Internet service provider (ISP)**—a company that provides Internet access, usually for a fee. ISPs (which include conventional and mobile telephone companies like AT&T, Verizon, and Sprint; cable providers like Comcast and Time Warner; and stand-alone ISPs like NetZero and EarthLink) function as gateways or onramps to the Internet, providing Internet access to their subscribers. ISP servers are continually connected to a larger network, called a *regional network*, which, in turn, is connected to one of the major high-speed networks within a country, called a *backbone network.* Backbone networks within a country are connected to each other and to backbone networks in other countries. Together they form one enormous network of networks—the Internet. Tips for selecting an ISP are included in Chapter 3.

Millions of people and organizations all over the world are connected to the Internet. The most common Internet activities today are exchanging e-mail messages

>**Computer network.** A collection of computers and other hardware devices that are connected together to share hardware, software, and data, as well as to communicate electronically with one another. >**Internet.** The largest and most well-known computer network, linking millions of computers all over the world. >**Internet service provider (ISP).** A business or other organization that provides Internet access to others, typically for a fee.

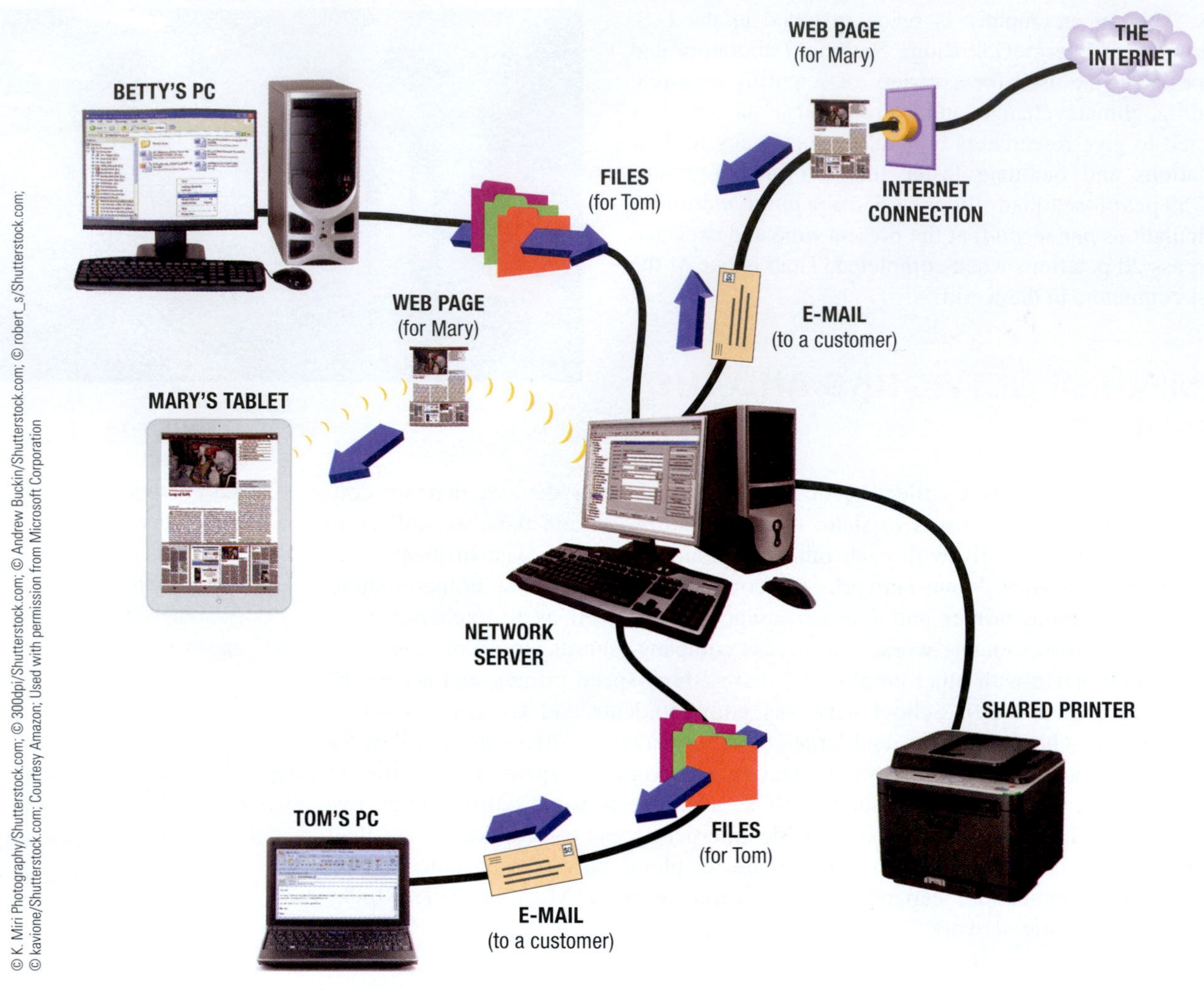

FIGURE 1-20
Example of a computer network.

and accessing content located on *Web pages.* While the term *Internet* refers to the physical structure of that network, the **World Wide Web (WWW)** refers to one resource—a collection of documents called **Web pages**—available through the Internet. A group of Web pages belonging to one individual or company is called a **Web site**. Web pages are stored on computers (called **Web servers**) that are continually connected to the Internet; they can be accessed at any time by anyone with a computer (or other Web-enabled device) and an Internet connection. A wide variety of information is available via Web pages, such as company and product information, government forms and publications, maps, telephone directories, news, weather, sports results, airline schedules, and much, much more. You can also use Web pages to shop, bank, trade stock, and perform other types of online financial transactions; access *social media* like *Facebook* and *Google+* social networking sites and *blogs*; and listen to music, play games, watch television shows, and perform other entertainment-oriented activities (see Figure 1-21). Web pages are viewed using a **Web browser**, such as *Internet Explorer (IE)*, *Chrome*, *Safari*, *Opera*, or *Firefox*.

TIP

Although some people use the terms *Internet* and *Web* interchangeably, technically the Web—the collection of Web pages available over the Internet—is only one resource available via the Internet.

>World Wide Web (WWW). The collection of Web pages available through the Internet. **>Web page.** A document, typically containing hyperlinks to other documents, located on a Web server and available through the World Wide Web. **>Web site.** A collection of related Web pages usually belonging to an organization or individual. **>Web server.** A computer that is continually connected to the Internet and hosts Web pages that are accessible through the Internet. **>Web browser.** A program used to view Web pages.

LOOKING UP INFORMATION

ACCESSING SOCIAL NETWORKS

WATCHING VIDEOS, TV SHOWS, AND MOVIES

FIGURE 1-21
Some common Web activities.

Accessing a Network or the Internet

To access a local computer network (such as a home network, a school or company network, or a public wireless hotspot), you need to use a network adapter (either built into your computer or attached to it) to connect your computer to the network. With some computer networks you need to supply logon information (such as a *username* and a password) to *log on* to a network. Once you are connected to the network, you can access network resources, including the network's Internet connection. If you are connecting to the Internet without going through a computer network, your computer needs to use a modem to connect to the communications media (such as a telephone line, cable connection, or wireless signal) used by your ISP to deliver Internet content. Network adapters and modems are discussed in more detail in Chapter 2.

Most Internet connections today are *direct* (or *always-on*) *connections*, which means the computer or other device being used to access the Internet is continually connected to the ISP's computer. With a direct connection, you only need to open your Web browser to begin using the Internet. With a *dial-up connection*, however, you must start the program that instructs your computer to dial and connect to the ISP's server via a telephone line, and then open a Web browser, each time you want to access the Internet.

To request a Web page or other resource located on the Internet, its **Internet address**—a unique numeric or text-based address—is used. The most common types of Internet addresses are *IP addresses* and *domain names* (to identify computers), *URLs* (to identify Web pages), and *e-mail addresses* (to identify people).

>**Internet address.** An address that identifies a computer, person, or Web page on the Internet, such as an IP address, domain name, or e-mail address.

IP Addresses and Domain Names

IP addresses and their corresponding **domain names** are used to identify computers available through the Internet. IP (short for *Internet Protocol*) addresses are numeric, such as *207.46.197.32*, and are commonly used by computers to refer to other computers. A computer that hosts information available through the Internet (such as a Web server hosting Web pages) usually has a unique text-based domain name (such as *microsoft.com*) that corresponds to that computer's IP address in order to make it easier for people to request Web pages located on that computer. IP addresses and domain names are unique; that is, there cannot be two computers on the Internet using the exact same IP address or exact same domain name. To ensure this, specific IP addresses are allocated to each network (such as a company network or an ISP) to be used with the computers on that network, and there is a worldwide registration system for domain name registration. When a domain name is registered, the IP address of the computer that will be hosting the Web site associated with that domain name is also registered; the Web site can be accessed using either its domain name or corresponding IP address. When a Web site is requested using its domain name, the corresponding IP address is looked up using one of the Internet's *domain name system* (*DNS*) *servers* and then the appropriate Web page is displayed. While today's IP addresses (called *IPv4*) have four parts separated by periods, the newer *IPv6* addresses have six parts separated by colons in order to have significantly more unique addresses. The transition from IPv4 to IPv6 is necessary because of the vast number of devices connecting to the Internet today.

ORIGINAL TLDS	INTENDED USE
.com	Commercial businesses
.edu	Educational institutions
.gov	Government organizations
.int	International treaty organizations
.mil	Military organizations
.net	Network providers and ISPs
.org	Noncommercial organizations

NEWER TLDS	INTENDED USE
.aero	Aviation industry
.biz	Businesses
.fr	French businesses
.info	Resource sites
.jobs	Employment sites
.mobi	Sites optimized for mobile devices
.name	Individuals
.pro	Licensed professionals
.uk	United Kingdom businesses

FIGURE 1-22
Sample top-level domains (TLDs).

Domain names typically reflect the name of the individual or organization associated with that Web site and the different parts of a domain name are separated by a period. The far right part of the domain name (which begins with the rightmost period) is called the *top-level domain* (*TLD*) and traditionally identifies the type of organization or its location (such as *.com* for businesses, *.edu* for educational institutions, *.jp* for Web sites located in Japan, or *.fr* for Web sites located in France). The part of the domain name that precedes the TLD is called the *second-level domain name* and typically reflects the name of a company or an organization, a product, or an individual. There were seven original TLDs used in the United States; additional TLDs and numerous two-letter *country code TLDs* have since been created (see some examples in Figure 1-22) and more are in the works. More than 250 million domain names are registered worldwide.

TIP

Only the legitimate holder of a trademarked name (such as Microsoft) can use that trademarked name as a domain name (such as microsoft.com); trademarks are discussed in detail in Chapter 6.

Uniform Resource Locators (URLs)

Similar to the way an IP address or a domain name uniquely identifies a computer on the Internet, a **Uniform Resource Locator** (**URL**) uniquely identifies a specific Web page (including the *protocol* or standard being used to display the Web page, the Web server hosting the Web page, the name of any folders on the Web server in which the Web page file is stored, and the Web page's filename, if needed).

>**IP address.** A numeric Internet address used to uniquely identify a computer on the Internet. >**Domain name.** A text-based Internet address used to uniquely identify a computer on the Internet. >**Uniform Resource Locator (URL).** An Internet address (usually beginning with http://) that uniquely identifies a Web page.

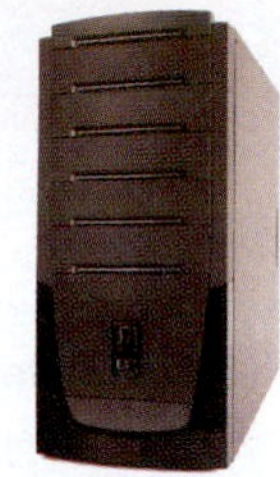

Web page URLs usually begin with http:// (for nonsecure Web pages) or https:// (for secure Web pages).
This part of the URL identifies the Web server hosting the Web page.
Next comes the folder(s) in which the Web page is stored, if necessary.
This is the Web page document that is to be retrieved and displayed.
https:// twitter.com / jobs / index.html
Come join the flock
Open positions

FIGURE 1-23
A Web page URL.

The most common Web page protocols are *Hypertext Transfer Protocol* (*http://*) for regular Web pages or *Secure Hypertext Transfer Protocol* (*https://*) for *secure Web pages* that can safely be used to transmit sensitive information, such as credit card numbers. *File Transfer Protocol* (*ftp://*) is sometimes used to upload and download files. The *file extension* used in the Web page filename indicates the type of Web page that will be displayed (such as *.html* and *.htm* for standard Web pages created using HTML or XHTML). For example, looking at the URL for the Web page shown in Figure 1-23 from right to left, we can see that the Web page is called *index.html*, is stored in a folder called *jobs* on the Web server associated with the *twitter.com* domain, and is a secure Web page because the *https://* protocol is being used.

TIP

Be sure that any Web page used to send sensitive data (such as your Social Security number or credit card information) is secure. Look for a URL that starts with *https* instead of *http* and a locked padlock icon on the Address bar.

E-Mail Addresses

To contact people using the Internet, you often use their **e-mail addresses**. An e-mail address consists of a **username** (an identifying name), followed by the @ symbol, followed by the domain name for the computer that will be handling that person's e-mail (called a *mail server*). For example,

jsmith@cengage.com
maria_s@cengage.com
sam.peterson@cengage.com

are the e-mail addresses assigned respectively to jsmith (John Smith), maria_s (Maria Sanchez), and sam.peterson (Sam Peterson), three hypothetical employees at Cengage Learning, the publisher of this textbook. Usernames are typically a combination of the person's first and last names and sometimes include periods, underscores, and numbers, but cannot include blank spaces. To ensure a unique e-mail address for everyone in the world, usernames must be unique within each domain name. So, even though there could be a *jsmith* at Cengage Learning using the e-mail address *jsmith@cengage.com* and a *jsmith* at Stanford University using the e-mail address *jsmith@stanford.edu*, the two e-mail addresses are unique. It is up to each organization with a registered domain name to ensure that one—and only one—exact same username is assigned to its domain. Using e-mail addresses to send e-mail messages is discussed later in this chapter; other forms of online communications—such as text messaging and chat—are covered in Chapter 3. For a look at how online communications are being used to help keep college students safe, see the How It Works box.

TIP

You can also communicate directly with your friends via social networking sites, such as Facebook and Twitter, and mobile phone text messages.

>**E-mail address.** An Internet address consisting of a username and computer domain name that uniquely identifies a person on the Internet.
>**Username.** A name that uniquely identifies a user on a specific computer network.

HOW IT WORKS

Campus Emergency Notification Systems

Recent emergencies, such as school shootings and dangerous weather, have increased attention on ways organizations can quickly and effectively notify a large number of individuals. Following the Virginia Tech tragedy in 2007, which involved a shooting rampage lasting about two hours and killing more than 30 individuals, the *Higher Education Opportunity Act* was signed into law. The law provides grants and other assistance to colleges and universities to create an emergency communications system that can be used to contact students when a significant emergency or dangerous situation emerges. In response, colleges across the United States are implementing emergency notification systems to notify students, faculty, staff, and campus visitors of an emergency, severe weather condition, campus closure, or other critical event.

Because nearly all college students in the United States today have mobile phones, sending emergency alerts via text message is a natural option. To be able to send a text message to an entire campus typically requires the use of a company that specializes in this type of mass communications. One such company is *Omnilert*, which has systems installed in more than 800 colleges and universities around the country. With the Omnilert campus notification system—called *e2Campus*—the contact information of the students, faculty, and staff to be notified is entered into the system and then the individuals can be divided into groups, depending on the types of messages each individual should receive. Individuals can also opt in to alerts via text message. When an alert needs to be sent, an administrator sends the message (via a mobile phone or computer) and it is distributed to the appropriate individuals (see the accompanying illustration). In addition to text messages, alerts can also be sent simultaneously and automatically via virtually any voice or text communications medium, such as voice messages, e-mail messages, RSS feeds, instant messages, Twitter feeds, Facebook pages, school Web pages, personal portal pages, desktop pop-up alerts, TTY/TDD devices, digital signage systems (such as signs located inside dorms and the student union), indoor and outdoor campus public address (PA) systems, information hotlines, and more.

To facilitate campus emergency notification systems, some colleges now require all undergraduate students to have a mobile phone. Some campuses also implement other useful mobile services, such as tracking campus shuttle buses, participating in class polls, accessing class assignments and grades, and texting tips about suspicious activities or crimes to campus security. An additional safety feature available at some schools is the ability to use the phones to activate an alert whenever a student feels unsafe on campus; these alerts automatically send the student's physical location (determined via the phone's GPS coordinates) to the campus police so the student can be located quickly.

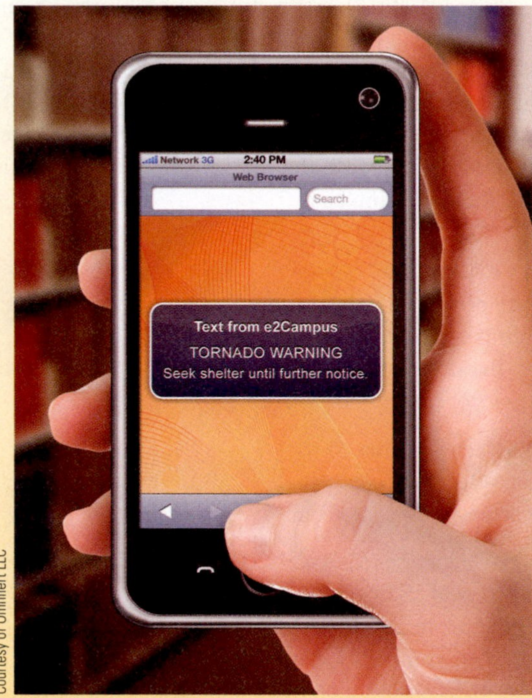

Courtesy of Omnilert LLC

Pronouncing Internet Addresses

Because Internet addresses are frequently given verbally, it is important to know how to pronounce them. A few guidelines are listed next, and Figure 1-24 shows some examples of Internet addresses and their proper pronunciations.

- If a portion of the address forms a recognizable word or name, it is spoken; otherwise, it is spelled out.
- The @ sign is pronounced *at*.
- The period (.) is pronounced *dot*.
- The forward slash (/) is pronounced *slash*.

TYPE OF ADDRESS	SAMPLE ADDRESS	PRONUNCIATION
Domain name	berkeley.edu	berkeley dot e d u
URL	microsoft.com/windows/ie/default.asp	microsoft dot com slash windows slash i e slash default dot a s p
E-mail address	president@whitehouse.gov	president at white house dot gov

FIGURE 1-24 **Pronouncing Internet addresses.**

Surfing the Web

Once you have an Internet connection, you are ready to begin *surfing the Web*—that is, using a Web browser to view Web pages. The first page that your Web browser displays when it is opened is your browser's starting page or *home page*. Often this is the home page for the Web site belonging to your browser, school, or ISP. However, you can use your browser's customization options to change the current home page to any page that you plan to visit regularly. From your browser's home page, you can move to any Web page you desire, as discussed next.

TIP

The *home page* for a Web site is the starting page of that particular site; the *home page* for your browser is the Web page designated as the first page you see each time the browser is opened.

Using URLs and Hyperlinks

To navigate to a new Web page for which you know the URL, type that URL in the browser's *Address bar* (shown in Figure 1-25) and press Enter. Once that page is displayed, you can use the *hyperlinks*—graphics or text linked to other Web pages—located on that page to display other Web pages. In addition to Web pages, hyperlinks can also be linked to other types of files, such as to enable Web visitors to view or download images, listen to or download music files, view video clips, or download software programs.

The most commonly used Web browsers include Internet Explorer (shown in Figure 1-25), Chrome (shown in Figure 1-26), Safari, and Firefox. Most browsers today include *tabbed browsing* (which allows you to have multiple Web pages open at the same time and to drag a tab to move that window), the ability to search for Web pages using the Address bar, and tools for *bookmarking* and revisiting Web pages, as discussed shortly. Browsers today also typically include security features to help notify you of possible threats as you browse the Web, *download managers* to help you manage your downloaded files, and *crash recovery* features, such as the ability to open the last set of Web pages that

FIGURE 1-25 **Surfing the Web with Internet Explorer.** URLs, hyperlinks, and favorites can be used to display Web pages.

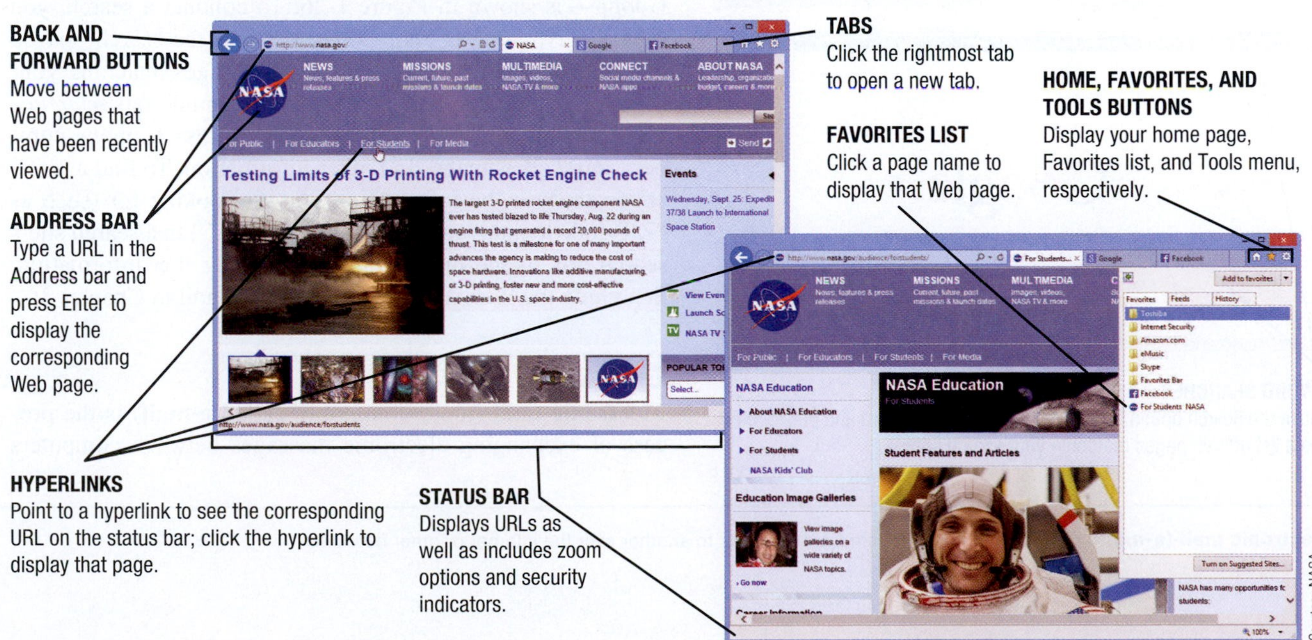
BACK AND FORWARD BUTTONS
Move between Web pages that have been recently viewed.
ADDRESS BAR
Type a URL in the Address bar and press Enter to display the corresponding Web page.
HYPERLINKS
Point to a hyperlink to see the corresponding URL on the status bar; click the hyperlink to display that page.
STATUS BAR
Displays URLs as well as includes zoom options and security indicators.
TABS
Click the rightmost tab to open a new tab.
FAVORITES LIST
Click a page name to display that Web page.
HOME, FAVORITES, AND TOOLS BUTTONS
Display your home page, Favorites list, and Tools menu, respectively.
Testing Limits of 3-D Printing With Rocket Engine Check
NASA Education
Student Features and Articles

TIP

If you get an error message when typing a URL, first check to make sure you typed it correctly. If it is correct, edit the URL to remove any folder or filenames and press Enter to try to load the home page of that site.

TIP

If you accidentally close a browser window in Chrome, open a new tab and redisplay the page using the *Recently closed* list at the bottom of the window.

were open before you accidentally closed your browser or before the browser or computer *crashed* (stopped working). In any browser, you can use the Back button to return to a previous page and the Home button to display your browser's home page. To print the current Web page, click the Tools button in Internet Explorer and select *Print* from the displayed menu.

Using Favorites and the History List

All Web browsers have a feature (usually called *Favorites* or *Bookmarks* and accessed via a Favorites or Bookmarks menu, button, or bar) that you can use to save Web page URLs. Once a Web page is saved as a favorite or a bookmark, you can redisplay that page without typing its URL—you simply select its link from the Favorites or Bookmarks list (refer again to Figure 1-25). You can also use this feature to save a group of tabbed Web pages to open the entire group again at a later time. Web browsers also maintain a *History list*, which is a record of all Web pages visited during the period of time specified in the browser settings; you can revisit a Web page located on the History list by displaying the History list and selecting that page.

Most Web browsers today allow you to delete, move into folders, and otherwise organize your favorites/bookmarks, as well as to search your favorites/bookmarks or History list to help you find pages more easily. In Windows 8, you can also *pin* (lock) a Web page to keep it handy—drag the site's icon on the left of the Address bar to pin a site to the Windows taskbar; use the Tools menu to add the site to your Start screen.

Because many individuals use multiple devices (such as a personal computer and a smartphone) to surf the Web today, it is becoming more common to want to *sync* your browser settings (such as bookmarks, history, passwords, and so forth) across all of your devices. Most browsers today have synching capabilities; typically an online account (such as your Google account for Chrome or your SkyDrive account for Internet Explorer) is used to securely sync the devices.

FIGURE 1-26
The Google search site displayed in the Chrome browser.

OTHER SEARCHES
Use these options to search for images, maps, videos, news, video, products for sale, and more, as well as access your Gmail, Google Drive, or Google Calendar.

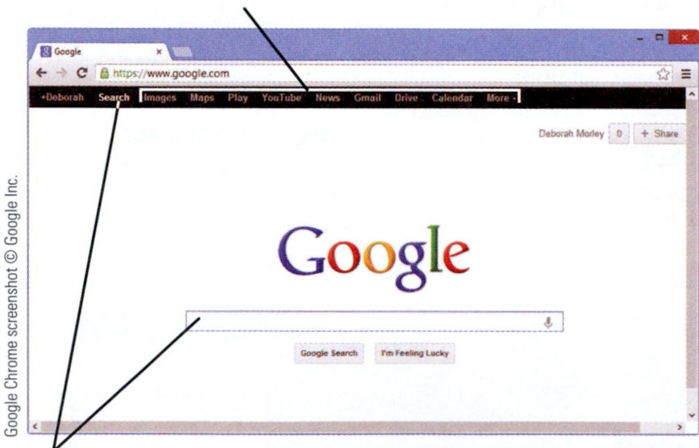

KEYWORD SEARCHES
Because the Search option is selected, type keywords here and press Enter to see a list of Web pages matching your search criteria.

Searching the Web

People typically turn to the Web to find specific types of information. There are a number of special Web pages, called *search sites*, available to help you locate what you are looking for on the Internet. One of the most popular search sites—*Google*—is shown in Figure 1-26. To conduct a search, you typically type one or more *keywords* into the search box on a search site, and a list of links to Web pages matching your search criteria is displayed. There are also numerous *reference sites* available on the Web to look up addresses, phone numbers, ZIP codes, maps, and other information. To find a reference site, type the information you are looking for (such as "ZIP code lookup" or "topographical maps") in a search site's search box to see links to sites containing that information. Searching the Web is discussed in more detail in Chapter 3.

E-Mail

Electronic mail (more commonly called **e-mail**) is the process of exchanging electronic messages between computers

>**Electronic mail (e-mail).** Electronic messages sent from one user to another over the Internet or other network.

over a network—usually the Internet. E-mail is one of the most widely used Internet applications—Americans alone send billions of e-mail messages daily and use of *mobile e-mail* (e-mail sent via a mobile device) is growing at an astounding rate. You can send an e-mail message from any Internet-enabled device (such as a personal computer or mobile device) to anyone who has an Internet e-mail address. As illustrated in Figure 1-27, e-mail messages travel from the sender's device to his or her ISP's *mail server*, and then through the Internet to the mail server being used by the recipient's ISP. When the recipient's computer retrieves new e-mail (typically on a regular basis as long as the computer is powered up, connected to the Internet, and the e-mail program is open), it is displayed on the computer he or she is using. In addition to text, e-mail messages can include attached files, such as documents, photos, and videos.

E-mail can be sent and received via an *e-mail program*, such as *Microsoft Outlook* or *Mac OS X Mail*, installed on the computer being used (sometimes referred to as *conventional e-mail*) or via a Web page belonging to a Web mail provider such as *Gmail* or *Outlook.com* (typically called *Web mail*). Using an installed e-mail program is convenient for individuals who use e-mail often and want to have copies of sent and received e-mail messages stored on their computer. To use an installed e-mail program, however, it must first be set up with the user's name, e-mail address, incoming mail server, and outgoing mail server information. Web mail does not require this setup and a user's e-mail can be accessed from any device with an Internet connection by just displaying the appropriate Web mail page and logging on. Consequently, Web-based e-mail is more flexible than conventional e-mail because it can be accessed easily from any computer or other device with an Internet connection. However, Web mail is typically slower than conventional e-mail and messages can only be viewed when the user is online and logged on to his or her Web mail account, unless an e-mail program is used to download the e-mail messages to a computer.

Web-based e-mail is typically free and virtually all ISPs used with personal computers include e-mail service in their monthly fee. Mobile e-mail may require a fee, depending on the data plan being used. Other types of mobile communications, such as text messages and multimedia messages that typically use the *Short Message Service (SMS)* and *Multimedia Message Service (MMS)* protocols, respectively, may also incur a fee. Messaging and other types of online communications that can be used in addition to e-mail are discussed in Chapter 3.

FIGURE 1-27
How e-mail works.

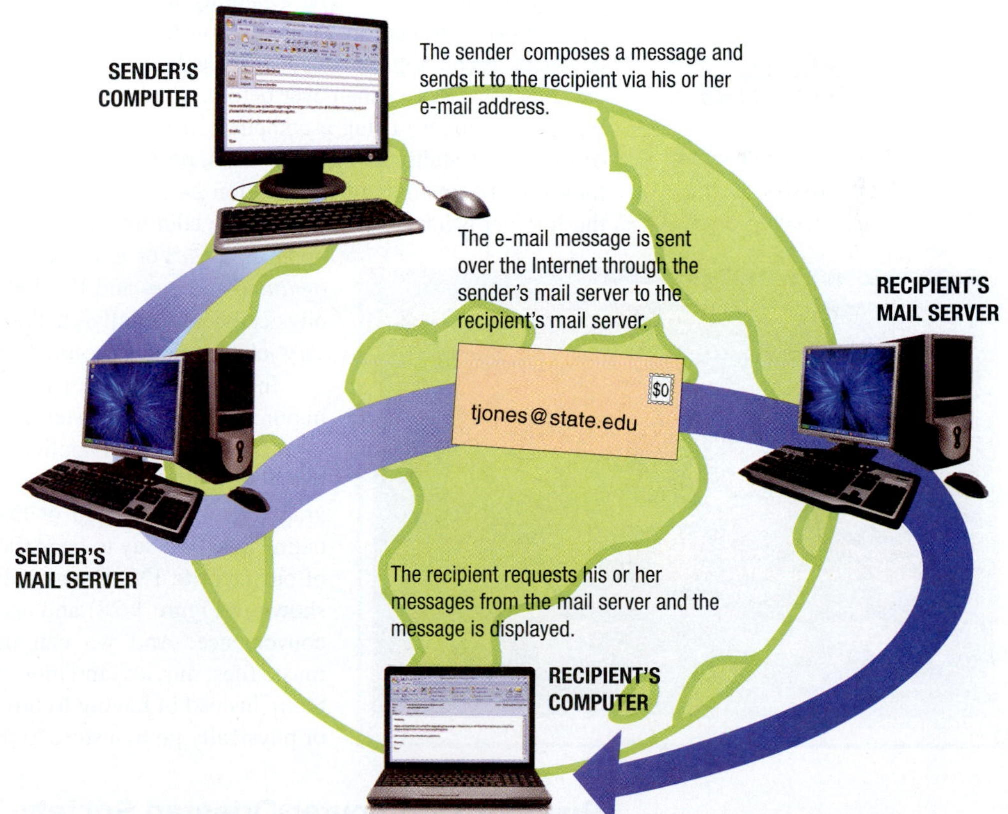
SENDER'S COMPUTER
The sender composes a message and sends it to the recipient via his or her e-mail address.
The e-mail message is sent over the Internet through the sender's mail server to the recipient's mail server.
RECIPIENT'S MAIL SERVER
$0
tjones@state.edu
SENDER'S MAIL SERVER
The recipient requests his or her messages from the mail server and the message is displayed.
RECIPIENT'S COMPUTER

COMPUTERS AND SOCIETY

The vast improvements in technology over the past decade have had a distinct impact on daily life, both at home and at work. Computers have become indispensable tools in our personal and professional lives, and related technological advancements have changed the way our everyday items—cars, microwaves, coffeepots, toys, exercise bikes, telephones, televisions, and more—look and function. As computers and everyday devices become smarter, they tend to do their intended jobs faster, better, and more reliably than before, as well as take on additional capabilities. In addition to affecting individuals, computerization and technological advances have changed society as a whole. Without computers, banks would be overwhelmed by the job of tracking all the transactions they process, moon exploration and the space shuttle would still belong to science fiction, and some scientific advances—such as DNA analysis and gene mapping—would be nonexistent. In addition, we as individuals are getting accustomed to the increased automation of everyday activities, such as shopping and banking, and we depend on having fast and easy access to information via the Internet and rapid communications via e-mail and messaging. In addition, many of us would not think about making a major purchase without first researching it online. In fact, it is surprising how fast the Internet and its resources have become an integral part of our society. But despite all its benefits, *cyberspace* has some risks. Some of the most important societal implications related to computers and the Internet are introduced next; many of these issues are covered in more detail in later chapters of this text.

Benefits of a Computer-Oriented Society

The benefits of having such a computer-oriented society are numerous, as touched on throughout this chapter. The capability to virtually design, build, and test new buildings, cars, and airplanes before the actual construction begins helps professionals create safer end products. Technological advances in medicine allow for earlier diagnosis and more effective treatment of diseases than ever before. The benefit of beginning medical students performing virtual surgery using a computer instead of performing actual surgery on a patient is obvious. The ability to shop, pay bills, research products, participate in online courses, and look up vast amounts of information 24 hours a day, 7 days a week, 365 days a year via the Internet is a huge convenience. In addition, a computer-oriented society generates new opportunities. For example, technologies—such as *speech recognition software* and Braille input and output devices—enable physically- or visually-challenged individuals to perform necessary job tasks and to communicate with others more easily.

CBS Broadcasting Inc.

FIGURE 1-28
Episodes of many television shows are available online to be viewed at the user's convenience.

In general, technology has also made a huge number of tasks in our lives go much faster. Instead of experiencing a long delay for a credit check, an applicant can get approved for a purchase, loan, or credit card almost immediately. Documents and photographs can be e-mailed or faxed in mere moments, instead of taking at least a day to be mailed physically. We can watch many of our favorite TVs shows online (such as the *Survivor* episode shown in Figure 1-28) and access up-to-the-minute news at our convenience. And we can download information, programs, music files, movies, and more on demand when we want or need them, instead of having to order them and then wait for delivery or physically go to a store to purchase the desired items.

Risks of a Computer-Oriented Society

Although there are a great number of benefits from having a computer-oriented society and a *networked economy*, there are risks as well. A variety of problems have emerged from our extensive computer use, ranging from stress and health concerns, to the proliferation of *spam* (unsolicited e-mails) and *malware* (harmful programs that can be installed on our computers without our knowledge), to security and privacy issues, to legal and ethical dilemmas. Many of the security and privacy concerns stem from the fact that so much of our personal business takes place online—or at least ends up as data in a computer database somewhere—and the potential for misuse of this data is enormous. Another concern is the repercussions of collecting such vast amounts of information electronically. Some people worry about creating a "Big Brother" situation, in which the government or another organization is watching everything that we do. Although the accumulation and distribution of information is a necessary factor of our networked economy, it is one area of great concern to many individuals. And some Internet behavior, such as downloading music or movies from an unauthorized source or viewing pornography on an office computer, can get you arrested or fired.

Security Issues

One of the most common online security risks today is your computer becoming infected with a malware program, such as a *computer virus*—a malicious software program designed to change the way a computer operates. Malware often causes damage to the infected computer, such as erasing data or bogging down the computer so it does not function well. It can also be used to try to locate sensitive data on your computer (such as Web site passwords or credit card numbers) and send that data to the malware creator or to take control of your computer to use as part of a *botnet* (a network of computers used without their owners' knowledge) for criminal activities. Malware is typically installed by downloading a program that secretly contains malware or by clicking a link on a Web page or in an e-mail message that then installs malware. In addition to computers, malware and other security threats are increasingly being directed toward smartphones and other mobile devices. To help protect your computer or mobile device, never open an e-mail attachment from someone you do not know or that has an executable *file extension* (the last three letters in the filename preceded by a period), such as *.exe*, *.com*, or *.vbs*, without checking with the sender first to make sure the attachment is legitimate. You should also be careful about what files you download from the Internet. In addition, it is crucial to install *security software* on your computer and mobile devices and to set up the program to monitor your devices on a continual basis (see Figure 1-29). If a virus or other type of malware attempts to install itself on your computer or mobile device (such as through an e-mail message attachment or a Web link), the security program will block it. If malware does find its way onto your computer or mobile device, the security program will detect it during a regular scan, notify you, and attempt to remove it.

FIGURE 1-29
Security software. Security software is crucial for protecting your computer and mobile devices from malware and other threats.

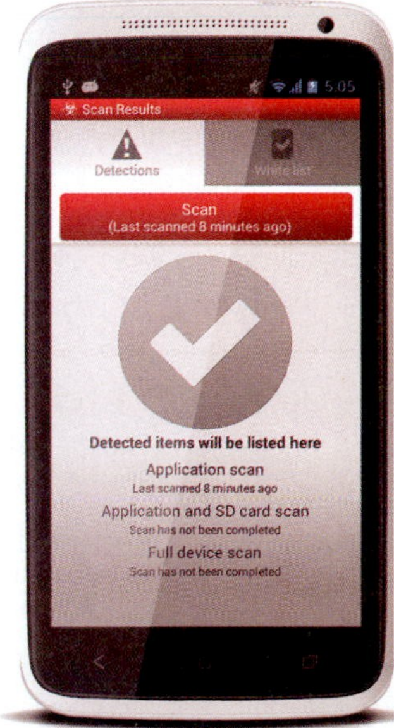

Courtesy Bullguard

Another ongoing security problem is *identity theft*—in which someone else uses your identity, typically to purchase goods or services. Identity theft can stem from personal information discovered from offline means—like discarded papers or stolen mail—or from information found online, stolen from an online database, or obtained via a malware program. *Phishing*—in which identity thieves send fraudulent e-mails to people masquerading as legitimate businesses to obtain Social Security numbers or other information needed for identity theft—is also a major security issue today. Common security concerns and precautions, such as protecting your computer from malware and protecting yourself against identity theft and phishing schemes, are discussed in detail in Chapter 4.

Privacy Issues

Some individuals view the potential risk to personal privacy as one of the most important issues regarding our networked society. As more and more data about our everyday activities is collected and stored on devices accessible via the Internet, our privacy is at risk because the potential for privacy violations increases. Today, data is collected about practically anything we buy online or offline, although offline purchases may not be associated with our identity unless we use a credit card or a membership or loyalty card. At issue is not that data is collected—with virtually all organizations using computers for recordkeeping, that is unavoidable—but rather how the collected data is used and how secure it is. Data collected by businesses may be used only by that company or, depending on the businesses' *privacy policy*, may be shared with others. Data shared with others often results in spam, which is considered by many to be a violation of personal privacy. Privacy concerns and precautions are discussed in detail in Chapter 5.

CAUTION CAUTION CAUTION CAUTION CAUTION CAUTION CAUT

Using your primary e-mail address when shopping online or signing up for a sweepstake or other online activity will undoubtedly result in spam being sent to that e-mail address. Use a *throw-away e-mail address* (a free e-mail address from Gmail or another free e-mail provider that you can change easily) for these activities instead to help protect your privacy and cut back on the amount of spam delivered to your regular e-mail account.

Differences in Online Communications

There is no doubt that e-mail and other online communications methods have helped speed up both personal and business communications and have made them more efficient (such as avoiding the telephone tag problem). As you spend more and more time communicating online, you will probably notice some differences between online communications methods (such as e-mail and social networking updates) and traditional communications methods (such as telephone calls and written letters). In general, online communications tend to be much less formal and, in fact, many people compose and send e-mail messages quickly, without taking the time to reread the message content or check the spelling or grammar. However, you need to be careful not to be so casual—particularly in business—that your communications appear unprofessional or become too personal with people you do not know.

To help in that regard, a special etiquette—referred to as *netiquette*—has evolved to guide online behavior. A good rule of thumb is always to be polite and considerate of others and to refrain from offensive remarks. This holds true whether you are asking a question via a company's e-mail address, posting a message on someone's Facebook page, or messaging a friend. With business communications, you should also be very careful with your grammar and spelling to avoid embarrassing yourself. Some specific guidelines for proper online behavior are listed in Figure 1-30.

Another trend in online communications is the use of abbreviations and *emoticons*. Abbreviations or *acronyms*, such as BTW for "by the way," are commonly used to save time in all types of communications today. They are being used with increased frequency in text messaging and e-mail exchanged via mobile phones to speed up the text entry process. Emoticons are illustrations of faces showing smiles, frowns, and other expressions that are created with keyboard symbols—such as the popular :-) smile emoticon—and allow people to add an emotional tone to written online communications. Without these symbols, it is sometimes difficult to tell if the person who sent the online communication is serious or joking because you cannot see the individual's face or hear his or her tone of voice.

FIGURE 1-30
Netiquette. Use these netiquette guidelines and common sense when communicating online.

RULE	EXPLANATION
Use descriptive subject lines	Use short, descriptive subject lines for e-mail messages and online posts. For example, "Question regarding MP3 downloads" is much better than a vague title, such as "Question."
Don't shout	SHOUTING REFERS TO TYPING YOUR ENTIRE E-MAIL MESSAGE OR ONLINE POST USING CAPITAL LETTERS. Use capital letters only when it is grammatically correct to do so or for emphasizing a few words.
Watch what you say	Things that you say or write online can be interpreted as being sexist, racist, or in just general bad taste. Also check spelling and grammar—typos look unprofessional and nobody likes wading through poorly written materials.
Don't spam your contacts	Don't hit *Reply All* to an e-mail when a simple *Reply* will do. The same goes for forwarding e-mail chain letters, *retweeting* every joke you run across, or sending every funny YouTube video you find—to everyone you know.
Be cautious	Don't give out personal information—such as your real name, telephone number, or credit card information—to people you meet online.
Think before you send or post	Once you send an e-mail or text message or post something online, you lose control of it. Don't include content (such as compromising photos of yourself) that you would not want shared with others, and don't tag people in photos that are unflattering to them. In addition, don't e-mail or post anything if emotions are running high—wait until you calm down.

While most people would agree that using abbreviations and emoticons with personal communications is fine, they are not usually viewed as appropriate for formal business communications.

The Anonymity Factor

By their very nature, online communications lend themselves to *anonymity.* Because recipients usually do not hear senders' voices or see their handwriting, it is difficult to know for sure who the sender is. Particularly on *forums* (online discussions in which users post messages and respond to other posts), in *virtual worlds* (online worlds that users can explore), and other online activities where individuals use made-up names instead of real names, there is an anonymous feel to being online.

Being anonymous gives many individuals a sense of freedom, which makes them feel able to say or do anything online. This sense of true freedom of speech can be beneficial. For example, a reserved individual who might never complain about a poor product or service in person may feel comfortable lodging a complaint by e-mail. In online discussions, many people feel they can be completely honest about what they think and can introduce new ideas and points of view without inhibition. Anonymous e-mail is also a safe way for an employee to blow the whistle on a questionable business practice, or for an individual to tip off police to a crime or potential terrorist attack.

But, like all good things, online anonymity can be abused. Using the Internet as their shield, some people use rude comments, ridicule, profanity, and even slander to attack people, places, and things they do not like or agree with. Others may use multiple online identities (such as multiple usernames on a message board) to give the appearance of increased support for their points of view. Still others may use multiple identities to try to manipulate stock prices (by posting false information about a company to drive the price down, for instance), to get buyers to trust an online auction seller (by posting fictitious positive feedback about themselves), or to commit other illegal or unethical acts.

It is possible to hide your true identity while browsing or sending e-mail by removing personal information from your browser and e-mail program or by using privacy software that acts as a middleman between you and Web sites and hides your identity, as discussed in more detail in Chapter 5. But, in fact, even when personal information is removed, ISPs and the government may still be able to trace communications back to a particular computer when a crime has occurred, so it is difficult—perhaps impossible—to be completely anonymous online.

FIGURE 1-31

Snopes.com. This Web site can be used to check out online rumors.

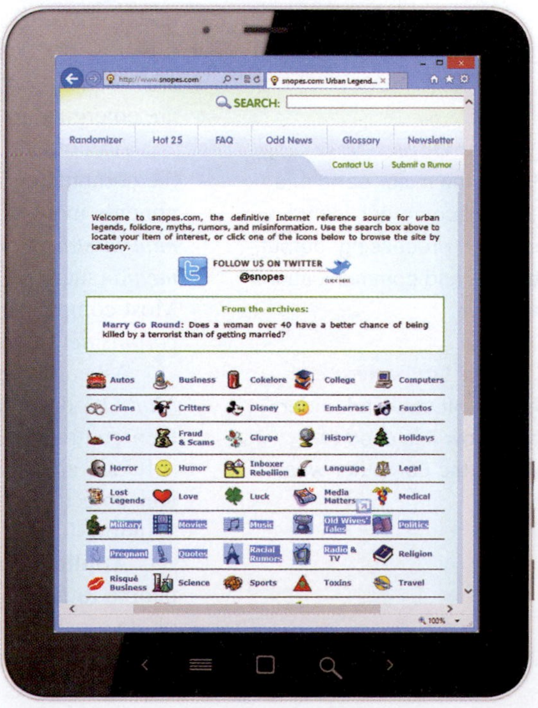

Information Integrity

The Web contains a vast amount of information on a wide variety of topics. While much of the information is factual, other information may be misleading, biased, or just plain wrong. As more and more people turn to the Web for information, it is crucial that they take the time to determine if the information they obtain and pass on to others is accurate. There have been numerous cases of information intended as a joke being restated on a Web site as fact, statements being quoted out of context (which changed the meaning from the original intent), and hoaxes circulated via e-mail. Consequently, use common sense when evaluating what you read online, and double-check information before passing it on to others.

One way to evaluate online content is by its source. If you obtain information from a news source that you trust, you should feel confident that the accuracy of its online information is close to that of its offline counterpart. For information about a particular product, go to the originating company. For government information, government Web sites are your best source for fact checking. There are also independent Web sites (such as the *Snopes* Web site shown in Figure 1-31) that report on the validity of current online rumors and stories.

SUMMARY

COMPUTERS IN YOUR LIFE

Chapter Objective 1: Explain why it is essential to learn about computers today and discuss several ways computers are integrated into our business and personal lives.

Computers appear almost everywhere in today's world, and most people need to use a computer or a computerized device frequently on the job, at home, at school, or while on the go. **Computer literacy**, which is being familiar with basic computer concepts, helps individuals feel comfortable using computers and is a necessary skill for everyone today.

Computers abound in today's homes, schools, workplaces, and other locations. Most students and employees need to use a computer for productivity, research, or other important tasks. Individuals often use computers at home and/or carry portable computers or mobile devices with them to remain in touch with others or to use Internet resources on a continual basis. Individuals also frequently encounter computers while on the go, such as *consumer kiosks* and *point-of-sale* (*POS*) *systems.*

WHAT IS A COMPUTER AND WHAT DOES IT DO?

Chapter Objective 2: Define a computer and describe its primary operations.

A **computer** is a *programmable* electronic device that accepts **input**; performs **processing** operations; **outputs** the results; and provides **storage** for data, programs, or output when needed. Most computers today also have **communications** capabilities. This progression of input, processing, output, and storage is sometimes called the *information processing cycle.*

Data is the raw, unorganized facts that are input into the computer to be processed. Data that the computer has processed into a useful form is called **information**. Data can exist in many forms, representing text, graphics, audio, and video.

Chapter Objective 3: List some important milestones in computer evolution.

One of the first calculating devices was the *abacus.* Early computing devices that predate today's computers include the *slide rule*, the *mechanical calculator*, and Dr. Herman Hollerith's *Punch Card Tabulating Machine and Sorter. First-generation computers*, such as *ENIAC* and *UNIVAC*, were powered by *vacuum tubes*; *second-generation computers* used *transistors*; and *third-generation computers* were possible because of the invention of the *integrated circuit* (*IC*). Today's *fourth-generation computers* use *microprocessors* and are frequently connected to the *Internet* and other *networks. Fifth-generation computers* are emerging and are, at the present time, based on *artificial intelligence.*

Chapter Objective 4: Identify the major parts of a personal computer, including input, processing, output, storage, and communications hardware.

A computer is made up of **hardware** (the actual physical equipment that makes up the computer system) and **software** (the computer's programs). Common hardware components include the *keyboard* and *mouse* (*input devices*), the *CPU* (a *processing device*), *monitors/display screens* and *printers* (*output devices*), and *storage devices* and *storage media* (such as *CDs*, *DVD drives, hard drives, USB flash drives*, and *flash memory cards*). Most computers today also include a *modem*, *network adapter*, or other type of *communications device* to allow users to connect to the Internet or other network.

Chapter Objective 5: Define software and understand how it is used to instruct the computer what to do.

All computers need *system software*, namely an **operating system** (usually *Windows*, *Mac OS*, or *Linux*), to function. The operating system assists with the **boot** process, and then controls the operation of the computer, such as to allow users to run other types of software and to manage their files. Most software programs today use a variety of graphical objects that are selected to tell the computer what to do. The basic workspace for Windows' users is the **Windows desktop**.

Application software (also called *apps*) consists of programs designed to allow people to perform specific tasks or applications, such as word processing, Web browsing, photo touch-up, and so on. Software programs are written using a *programming language.* Programs are written by *programmers*; *computer users* are the people who use computers to perform tasks or obtain information.

COMPUTERS TO FIT EVERY NEED

Embedded computers are built into products (such as cars and household appliances) to give them added functionality. **Mobile devices** are small devices (such as *mobile phones* and **media tablets**) with computing or Internet capabilities; an Internet-enabled mobile phone is called a **smartphone**.

Small computers used by individuals at home or work are called **personal computers (PCs)** or **microcomputers**. Most personal computers today are either **desktop computers** or **portable computers** (**notebook computers**, **laptop computers**, **tablet computers, hybrid notebook-tablet computers,** and **netbooks**) and typically conform to either the *PC-compatible* or *Mac* standard. **Thin clients** are designed solely to access a network; **Internet appliances** are ordinary devices that can be used to access the Internet.

Medium-sized computers, or **servers**, are used in many businesses to host data and programs to be accessed via the company network. A growing trend is **virtualization**, such as creating separate virtual environments on a single server that act as separate servers or delivering each users' desktop to his or her device. The powerful computers used by most large businesses and organizations to perform the information processing necessary for day-to-day operations are called **mainframe computers**. The very largest, most powerful computers, which typically run one application at a time, are **supercomputers**.

Chapter Objective 6:
List the six basic types of computers, giving at least one example of each type of computer and stating what that computer might be used for.

COMPUTER NETWORKS AND THE INTERNET

Computer networks are used to connect individual computers and related devices so that users can share hardware, software, and data as well as communicate with one another. The **Internet** is a worldwide collection of networks. Typically, individual users connect to the Internet by connecting to computers belonging to an **Internet service provider (ISP)**—a company that provides Internet access, usually for a fee. One resource available through the Internet is the **World Wide Web (WWW)**—an enormous collection of **Web pages** located on **Web servers**. The starting page for a **Web site** (a related group of Web pages) is called the *home page* for that site. Web pages are viewed with a **Web browser**, are connected with *hyperlinks*, and can be used for many helpful activities.

To access a computer network, you need some type of *modem* or *network adapter.* To access the Internet, an Internet service provider (ISP) is also used. **Internet addresses** are used to identify resources on the Internet and include numerical **IP addresses** and text-based **domain names** (used to identify computers), **Uniform Resource Locators** or **URLs** (used to identify Web pages), and **e-mail addresses** (a combination of a **username** and domain name that is used to send an individual e-mail messages).

Web pages are displayed by clicking hyperlinks or by typing appropriate URLs in the browser's *Address bar. Favorites/Bookmarks* and the *History list* can be used to redisplay a previously visited Web page and *search sites* can be used to locate Web pages matching specified criteria. **Electronic mail (e-mail)** is used to send electronic messages over the Internet.

Chapter Objective 7:
Explain what a network, the Internet, and the World Wide Web are, as well as how computers, people, and Web pages are identified on the Internet.

Chapter Objective 8:
Describe how to access a Web page and navigate through a Web site.

COMPUTERS AND SOCIETY

Computers and devices based on related technology have become indispensable tools for modern life, making ordinary tasks easier and quicker than ever before and helping make today's worker more productive than ever before. In addition to the benefits, however, there are many risks and societal implications related to our heavy use of the Internet and the vast amount of information available through the Internet. Issues include privacy and security risks and concerns (such as *malware*, *identity theft*, *phishing*, and *spam*), the differences in online and offline communications, the anonymity factor, and the amount of unreliable information that can be found on the Internet.

Chapter Objective 9:
Discuss the societal impact of computers, including some benefits and risks related to their prominence in our society.

REVIEW ACTIVITIES

KEY TERM MATCHING

a. computer

b. hardware

c. Internet

d. processing

e. software

f. storage

g. supercomputer

h. tablet computer

i. Uniform Resource Locator (URL)

j. Web site

Instructions: Match each key term on the left with the definition on the right that best describes it.

1. ________ A collection of related Web pages usually belonging to an organization or individual.

2. ________ An Internet address, usually beginning with http://, that uniquely identifies a Web page.

3. ________ A programmable, electronic device that accepts data input, performs processing operations on that data, and outputs and stores the results.

4. ________ A portable computer about the size of a notebook that is designed to be used with a digital pen.

5. ________ Performing operations on data that has been input into a computer to convert that input to output.

6. ________ The operation of saving data, programs, or output for future use.

7. ________ The fastest, most expensive, and most powerful type of computer.

8. ________ The instructions, also called computer programs, that are used to tell a computer what it should do.

9. ________ The largest and most well-known computer network, linking millions of computers all over the world.

10. ________ The physical parts of a computer system, such as the keyboard, monitor, printer, and so forth.

SELF-QUIZ

Instructions: Circle **T** if the statement is true, **F** if the statement is false, or write the best answer in the space provided. **Answers for the self-quiz are located in the References and Resources Guide at the end of the book.**

1. **T F** A mouse is one common input device.

2. **T F** Software includes all the physical equipment in a computer system.

3. **T F** A computer can run without an operating system if it has good application software.

4. **T F** One of the most common types of home computers is the server.

5. **T F** An example of a domain name is *microsoft.com.*

6. ________ is the operation in which data is entered into the computer.

7. A(n) ________ computer is a portable computer designed to function as both a notebook and a tablet PC.

8. ________ is frequently used with servers today to create several separate environments on a single server that function as separate servers.

9. Electronic messages sent over the Internet that can be retrieved by the recipient at his or her convenience are called ________.

10. Write the number of the term that best matches each of the following descriptions in the blank to the left of its description.

a. ________ Allows access to resources located on the Internet.

b. ________ Supervises the running of all other programs on the computer.

c. ________ Enables users to perform specific tasks on a computer.

d. ________ Allows the creation of application programs.

1. Application software
2. Operating system
3. Programming language
4. Web browser

EXERCISES

1. For the following list of computer hardware devices, indicate the principal function of each device by writing the appropriate letter—I (input device), O (output device), S (storage device), P (processing device), or C (communications device)—in the space provided.

a. CPU ________	**d.** Keyboard ________	**g.** Speakers ________
b. Monitor ________	**e.** Hard drive ________	**h.** DVD drive ________
c. Mouse ________	**f.** Modem ________	**i.** Microphone ________

2. Supply the missing words to complete the following statements.

a. The Internet is an example of a(n) ________, a collection of computers and other devices connected together to share resources and communicate with each other.

b. The starting page for a Web site is called the site's ________.

c. For the e-mail address *jsmith@cengage.com*, *jsmith* is the ________ and *cengage.com* is the ________ name.

d. The e-mail address pronounced *bill gee at microsoft dot com* is written ________.

3. What are three differences between a desktop computer and a portable computer?

4. List two reasons why a business may choose to network its employees' computers.

5. If a computer manufacturer called Apex created a home page for the Web, what would its URL likely be? Also, supply an appropriate e-mail address for yourself, assuming that you are employed by that company.

DISCUSSION QUESTIONS

1. There is usually a positive side and a negative side to each new technological improvement. Select a technology you use every day and consider its benefits and risks. What benefits does the technology provide? Are there any risks involved and, if so, how can they be minimized? If you chose not to use this technology because of the possible risks associated with it, how would your life be affected? Who should determine if the benefits of a new technology outweigh the potential risks? Consumers? The government?

2. The ubiquitous nature of mobile phones today brings tremendous convenience to our lives, but will misuse of new improvements to this technology result in the loss of that convenience? For instance, camera phones are now banned in many fitness centers, park restrooms, and other similar facilities because some people have used them inappropriately to take compromising photos, and mobile phones are banned in many classrooms because of the disruption of constant text messaging and the use of the phone by dishonest students to cheat on exams. Do you think these reactions to mobile phone misuse are justified? Is there another way to ensure the appropriate use of mobile phones without banning their use for all individuals? Should there be more stringent consequences for those who use technology for illegal or unethical purposes?

PROJECTS

HOT TOPICS

1. **Mobile TV** As discussed in this chapter, TV is one of the newest entertainment options available for smartphones. From live TV to video clips and movies, mobile TV is taking off.

   For this project, investigate the mobile TV options available today. Find at least two services and compare features, such as cost, compatibility, channels, and programming. Do your selected services offer live TV, video-on-demand, or both? If you have a smartphone, are any of the services available through your mobile provider? Are there currently Web sites where mobile users can view episodes of TV shows for free, like personal computer users can? What is the current status of the push by the *Open Mobile Video Coalition* to have a free mobile TV standard across the United States? Have you ever watched TV on a smartphone? If so, how do you rate your experience and would you do it again? If not, would you want to watch TV on a smartphone? Do you think mobile TV is the wave of the future? Why or why not? At the conclusion of your research, prepare a one-page summary of your findings and opinions and submit it to your instructor.

SHORT ANSWER/ RESEARCH

2. **Buying a New PC** New personal computers are widely available directly from manufacturers, as well as in retail, computer, electronic, and warehouse stores. Some stores carry only standard configurations as set up by the manufacturers; others allow you to customize a system.

   For this project, assume that you are in the market for a new personal computer. Give some thought to the type of computer (such as desktop, notebook, or tablet computer) that best fits your lifestyle and the tasks you wish to perform (such as the application programs you wish to use, how many programs you want to use at one time, and how fast you desire the response time to be). Make a list of your hardware and software requirements (refer to the "Guide to Buying a PC" in the References and Resources Guide at the end of this book, if needed), being as specific as possible. By researching newspaper ads, manufacturer Web sites, and/or systems for sale at local stores, find three systems that meet your minimum requirements. Prepare a one-page comparison chart, listing each requirement and how each system meets or exceeds it. Also include any additional features each system has, and information regarding the brand, price, delivery time, shipping, sales tax, and warranty for each system. On your comparison sheet, mark the system that you would prefer to buy and write one paragraph explaining why. Turn in your comparison sheet and summary to your instructor, stapled to copies of the printed ads, specifications printed from Web sites, or other written documentation that you collected during this project.

HANDS ON

3. **The Internet** The Internet and World Wide Web are handy tools that can help you research topics covered in this textbook, complete many of the projects, and perform the online activities available via the textbook's Web site that are designed to enhance your learning and help you prepare for exams on the content covered in this textbook.

   For this project, find an Internet-enabled computer on your campus, at home, or at your public library and perform the following tasks, then submit your results and printout to your instructor. (Note: Some of the answers will vary from student to student.)

   a. Open a browser and the Google search site. Enter the search terms *define: Internet* to search for definitions of that term. Click on one result to display the definition. Use your browser's *Print* option to print the page.

   b. Click your browser's *Back* button to return to the Google home page. Use your browser's Bookmark or Favorites feature to bookmark the page. Close your browser.

   c. Reopen your browser and use its Bookmark or Favorites feature to redisplay the Google home page.

   d. Google yourself to see if you can find any information online. On your printout from part a, indicate how many hits were returned for this search and if any on the first page of hits really contained information about yourself.

ETHICS IN ACTION

4. **Gossip Sites** A recent trend on college campuses today is the use of campus gossip sites, where students can post campus-related news, rumors, and basic gossip. These sites were originally set up to promote free speech and to allow participants to publish comments anonymously without repercussions from school administrators, professors, and other officials. However, they are now being used to post vicious comments about others. What do you think of campus gossip sites? Is it ethical to post a rumor about another individual on these sites? How would you feel if you read a posting about yourself on a gossip site? School administrators cannot regulate the content because the sites are not sponsored or run by the college, and federal law prohibits Web hosts from being liable for the content posted by its users. Is this ethical? What if a posting leads to a criminal act, such as a rape, murder, or suicide? Who, if anyone, should be held responsible?

   For this project, form an opinion about the ethical ramifications of gossip Web sites and be prepared to discuss your position (in class, via an online class discussion group, in a class chat room, or via a class blog, depending on your instructor's directions). You may also be asked to write a short paper expressing your opinion.

PRESENTATION/ DEMONSTRATION

5. **Online Education** The amount of distance learning available through the Internet and World Wide Web has exploded in the last couple of years. A few years ago, it was possible to take an occasional course online—now, an entire college degree can be earned online.

   For this project, look into the online education options available at your school and two other colleges or universities. Compare and contrast the programs in general, including whether or not the institution is accredited, the types of courses available online, whether or not an entire certificate or degree can be earned online, and the required fees. Next, select one online course and research it more closely. Find out how the course works in an online format—including whether or not any face-to-face class time is required, whether assignments and exams are submitted online, which software programs are required, and other course requirements—and determine if you would be interested in taking that course. Share your findings with the class in the form of a short presentation. The presentation should not exceed 10 minutes and should make use of one or more presentation aids, such as a whiteboard, handouts, or a computer-based slide presentation (your instructor may provide additional requirements). You may also be asked to submit a summary of the presentation to your instructor.

BALANCING ACT

6. **Should Social Media Activity Cost You a Job?** When you apply for a new job, there's a good chance that the company will take a look at your social media activity, such as your Facebook page, blog activity, and even Craigslist listings. In fact, many companies now require job applicants to pass a social media background check before offering them a job. Companies are trying to protect themselves by looking for such things as racist remarks and illegal activities, as well as get a feel for whether or not an individual would be a good fit for the company. But should individuals have to risk losing a job if they post a photo of themselves in a racy Halloween costume or make an offhand comment that an employer may misinterpret? What if a company denies you a job based on inaccurate information or information they wouldn't be allowed to ask in a job interview, such as information relating to your age, race, gender, religion, and so forth? And what if someone else posts and tags a questionable photo of you—should a potential employer be able to use that or other third-party information to make a decision about your future? To be safe, should job applicants have to abstain from social media activity in order to protect themselves, even though such sites are typically viewed as places to casually interact with others on personal free time? Or is everything a potential employer finds online fair game?

   Pick a side on this issue, form an opinion and gather supporting evidence, and be prepared to discuss and defend your position in a classroom debate or in a 1–2 page paper, depending on your instructor's directions.

expert insight on...

Personal Computers

Courtesy of D-Link Systems

D-Link
Building Networks for People

Daniel Kelley is the Vice President of Marketing for D-Link Systems, Inc. and is responsible for connectivity solutions tailored for home and business users. He has more than 15 years of professional marketing experience and holds a Bachelor of Arts degree in communications. As a result of Daniel's leadership and thriving marketing programs, many of the programs initiated in North America, including the implementation of numerous social media campaigns hosted on D-Link's social media platforms, have been adopted worldwide.

A conversation with DANIEL KELLEY

Vice President, Marketing, D-Link Systems, Inc.

"Putting a full-fledged computer with virtually unlimited potential into one's pocket has changed how we interact with information and with others in ways we're still discovering."

My Background . . .

As the Vice President of Marketing for D-Link Systems, Inc., I am responsible for the overall marketing and branding of the company and its products. My focus is on creating demand and loyalty from customers through a range of disciplines including advertising, sponsorships, press relations, social media, and channel marketing. Although I hold a degree in communications, which helped launch my career in marketing, I attribute most of my skills to real-world marketing experience and constantly challenging myself to learn and stay on top of the latest marketing tactics, platforms, and trends.

It's Important to Know . . .

The evolution from the first massively-sized computers to today's small devices, such as the iPhone, has created a major shift in the industry. Once the average consumer could get a powerful PC in his or her home, it started what we now view as the natural integration of technology in our daily lives. Putting a full-fledged computer with virtually unlimited potential into one's pocket has changed how we interact with information and with others in ways we're still discovering.

Software is the interactive way a customer sees and uses a device, such as a PC, tablet, or phone. Software—in the form of applications (or apps)—allows us to utilize the hardware of the machine itself in ways that are seemingly unending.

Social media's influence will continue to grow and impact how we communicate. The noticeable shift from customers trusting impersonal third-party reviews of products and services to those of friends, family members, and others via social media sites is changing the way businesses market themselves and communicate with customers. We've also seen a rapid adoption of short video platforms such as Vine and Instagram, which is a key indicator that individuals are looking to capture and share more video for not only entertainment but also for everyday interactions.

How I Use this Technology . . .

Growing up, I always had an interest in all things creative and spent much of my time drawing, painting, and doing other creative projects. I carried this interest through my education, learning design graphics, animation, video, and Web development programs. The knowledge of these programs and my eye for design helps me provide direction on creative projects and allows me to dive in and give more specific examples or direction as needed. Today, I also use a laptop, tablet, and my smartphone every day to work and communicate with others from home, the office, and while traveling. My most used app is Catch, which helps me create and keep track of notes and ideas across all of my devices.

What the Future Holds . . .

One of the trends I personally find the most interesting is the rapid evolution of wearable technology. With the introduction of Google Glass and wellness-focused products such as FitBit, I see a very rapid adoption of new solutions designed to integrate technology with our clothing and accessories, which will lead to an entirely new way of interacting with information in our daily lives. We've become empowered in ways never dreamed of just decades ago, with endless information and new communication vehicles at our fingertips, and we've seen a rapid and dramatic shift from face-to-face conversations and phone calls to texting, e-mail, and social media as preferred ways to communicate. This shift will continue to accelerate, with video calls and video messages becoming a primary communication medium. However, we have to be careful we don't become more isolated and detached from others in public social situations so we can continue to interact positively with each other in the future.

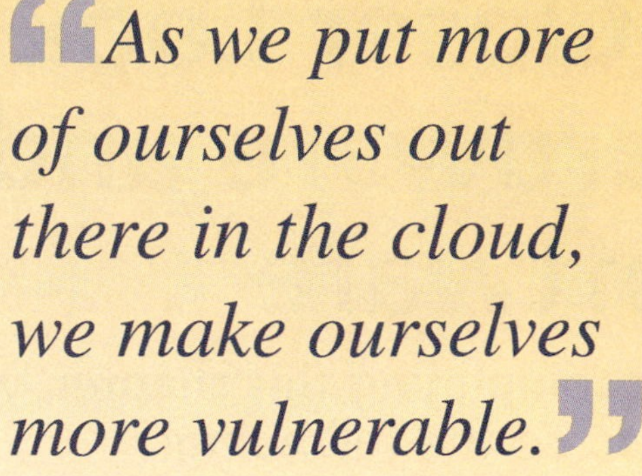
"As we put more of ourselves out there in the cloud, we make ourselves more vulnerable."

Another concern for the future is privacy. As we put more of ourselves out there in the cloud, we make ourselves more vulnerable. With any new technology or service, there are going to be those looking to exploit it and cause harm to others for personal gain and we've seen how private information doesn't necessarily remain private. This should encourage individuals to protect themselves as much as possible, such as using strong online passwords and just using common sense when determining what to share online.

I'm hoping that one of the biggest impacts of technology in the future is in the medical field or solving big problems like world hunger. Technology advancements, such as the use of 3D printers to create live tissue that can be used for replacing lost body parts, can have a very positive impact on our health and wellness. This same 3D printing technology has the potential to create a large food supply (utilizing protein "ink" from meal worms, for instance) for third-world countries where food is desperately needed. As much as technology advances our entertainment and social interaction, I am more interested to see how it can actually improve how we take care of those in need.

My Advice to Students . . .

Jump in with both feet. Take things apart, build things, and constantly learn new things through education and resources such as the Internet and books. We are living in a truly remarkable time where opportunities abound in the tech field, and those who apply themselves and commit to learning, trying, and doing will have an upper hand for building a career or leading the next wave of where tech can take us.

Discussion Question

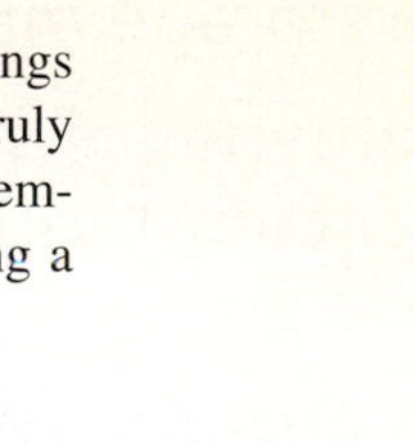

Daniel Kelley views wearable technology as one of the most interesting trends evolving today. Think about the tasks you use your mobile phone and personal computer for today. Could they be performed using a wearable mobile device, such as Google Glass or perhaps a wearable smartphone? If not, what changes would need to be made in the future in order to perform these tasks using a wearable device? Is the wearable mobile device the computer of the future? Be prepared to discuss your position (in class, via an online class discussion group, in a class chat room, or via a class blog, depending on your instructor's directions). You may also be asked to write a short paper expressing your opinion.

>For more information about D-Link, visit the official Web site at dlink.com. D-Link also communicates through social sites (facebook.com/dlink and twitter.com/dlink), and has a resource center located at resource.dlink.com.

chapter 2

A Closer Look at Hardware and Software

After completing this chapter, you will be able to do the following:

1. Understand how data is represented to a computer.
2. Identify several types of input devices and explain their functions.
3. Explain the functions of the primary hardware components found inside the system unit, namely the motherboard, the CPU, and memory.
4. List several output devices and explain their functions.
5. Understand the difference between storage and memory, as well as between a storage device and a storage medium.
6. Name several types of storage systems and explain the circumstances under which they are typically used.
7. Describe the purpose of communications hardware.
8. Understand basic software concepts and commands.

outline

OVERVIEW

When you hear the phrase "computer system," you probably picture hardware—a desktop or notebook computer, a printer, or maybe a smartphone. But a computer system involves more than just hardware. As you already know from Chapter 1, computers need software in order to function. It is the software that tells the hardware what to do and when to do it. Computers also need data input, which is used to begin the information processing cycle.

This chapter opens with a discussion of data and how it is represented to a computer. Next, we take a closer look at the hardware that makes up a computer system. Because it is not possible to mention all of the hardware products available today, a sampling of the most common hardware products used for input, processing, output, storage, and communications is covered in this chapter. Although a complete discussion of software is also beyond the scope of this book, the chapter concludes with a brief look at some basic software concepts and operations.

The basic hardware and software concepts and terminology covered in this chapter are important for all computer users to understand. In addition, these concepts will provide you with a solid foundation for discussing the important societal issues featured throughout this text. Many of you will apply this chapter's content to conventional personal computers—such as desktop and portable computers. However, it is important to realize that the principles and procedures discussed in this chapter apply to other types of computers as well, such as those embedded in toys, consumer devices, household appliances, cars, and other devices, and those used with mobile devices, servers, mainframes, and supercomputers. ■

DIGITAL DATA REPRESENTATION

Virtually all computers today—such as the embedded computers, mobile devices, personal computers, servers, mainframes, and supercomputers discussed in Chapter 1—are *digital computers*. Most digital computers are *binary computers*, which can understand only two states, usually thought of as *off* and *on* and represented by the digits 0 and 1. Consequently, all data processed by a binary computer must be in binary form (0s and 1s) and those 0s and 1s can be represented in a variety of ways, such as with an open or closed circuit or two different types of magnetic alignment on a storage medium (see Figure 2-1). Fortunately, the computer takes care of translating input into the form needed by the computer being used and then, after processing, translates and outputs the resulting information into a form that can be understood by the user.

FIGURE 2-1
Ways of representing 0 and 1. Binary computers recognize only two states—off and on—usually represented by 0 and 1.

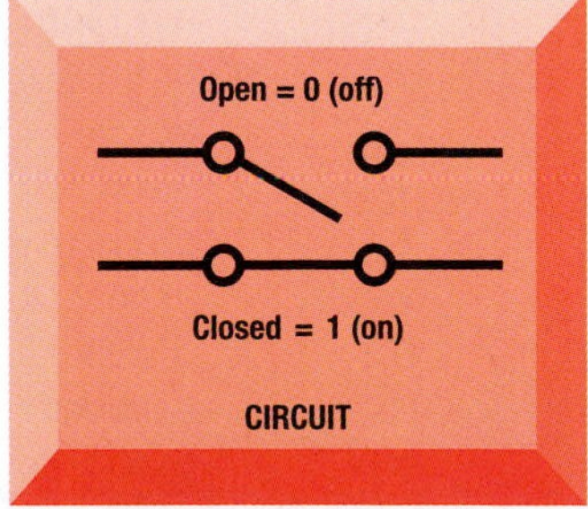

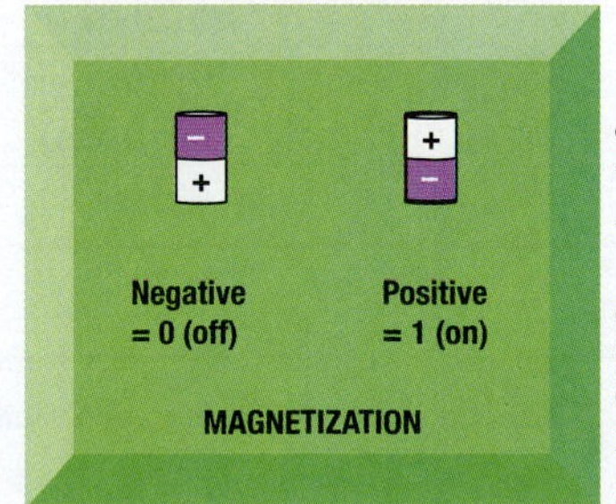

Bits and Bytes

The 0s and 1s used to represent data can be represented in a variety of ways, such as with an open or closed circuit, the absence or presence of an electronic charge, the absence or presence of a magnetic spot or depression on a storage medium, and so on.

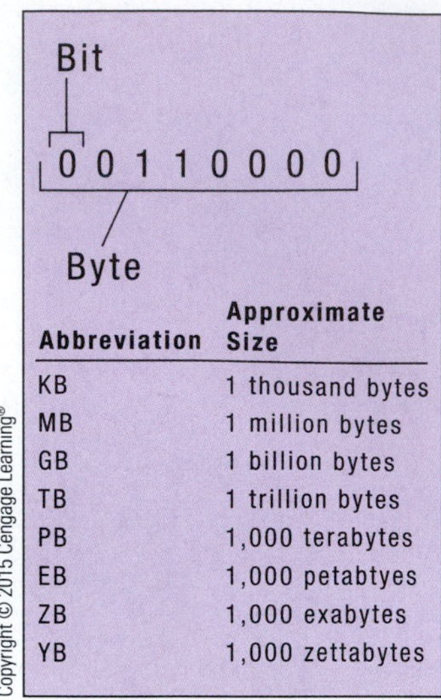

Abbreviation	Approximate Size
KB	1 thousand bytes
MB	1 million bytes
GB	1 billion bytes
TB	1 trillion bytes
PB	1,000 terabytes
EB	1,000 petabtyes
ZB	1,000 exabytes
YB	1,000 zettabytes

FIGURE 2-2
Bits and bytes. Document size, storage capacity, and memory capacity are all measured in bytes.

Regardless of their physical representations, these 0s and 1s are commonly referred to as *bits*, a computing term derived from the phrase *binary digits*. A **bit** is the smallest unit of data that a binary computer can recognize. Therefore, the input you enter via a keyboard, the software program you use to play your music collection, the term paper stored on your USB flash drive, and the digital photos located on your mobile phone are all just groups of bits. Consequently, binary can be thought of as the computer's "native language."

A bit by itself typically represents only a fraction of a piece of data. Consequently, large numbers of bits are needed to represent a written document, computer program, digital photo, music file, or virtually any other type of data. Eight bits grouped together are collectively referred to as a **byte**. It is important to be familiar with this concept because *byte* terminology is frequently used in a variety of computer contexts, such as to indicate the size of a document or digital photo, the amount of memory a computer has, or the amount of room left on a storage medium. Because these quantities often involve thousands or millions of bytes, prefixes are commonly used in conjunction with the term *byte* to represent larger amounts of data (see Figure 2-2). For instance, a **kilobyte (KB)** is equal to 1,024 bytes, but it is usually thought of as approximately 1,000 bytes; a **megabyte (MB)** is about 1 million bytes; a **gigabyte (GB)** is about 1 billion bytes; a **terabyte (TB)** is about 1 trillion bytes; and a **petabyte (PB)** is about 1,000 terabytes (2^{50} bytes). Therefore, 5 KB is about 5,000 bytes, 10 MB is about 10 million bytes, and 2 TB is about 2 trillion bytes.

Numbering Systems and Coding Systems

A *numbering system* is a way of representing numbers. The numbering system we commonly use is called the **decimal numbering system** because it uses 10 symbols—the digits 0, 1, 2, 3, 4, 5, 6, 7, 8, and 9—to represent all possible numbers. Numbers greater than nine, such as 21 and 683, are represented using combinations of these 10 symbols. The **binary numbering system** uses only two symbols—the digits 0 and 1—to represent all possible numbers. Consequently, binary computers use the binary numbering system to represent numbers and perform math computations.

In both numbering systems, the position of each digit determines the power, or exponent, to which the *base number* (10 for decimal or 2 for binary) is raised. In the decimal numbering system, going from right to left, the first position or column (the ones column) represents 10^0 or 1; the second column (the tens column) represents 10^1 or 10; the third column (the hundreds column) represents 10^2 or 100; and so forth. Consequently, 101 represents "one hundred one" in the decimal number system, but it equals "five" ($1 \times 2^2 + 0 \times 2^1 + 1 \times 2^0$ or $4 + 0 + 1$ or 5) using the binary number system. For more information about numbering systems and some examples of converting between numbering systems, see the "A Look at Numbering Systems" section in the References and Resources Guide at the end of this book.

To represent text-based data, special fixed-length binary *coding systems*—namely, *ASCII* and *Unicode*—were developed. These codes represent all characters that can appear in text data, including numeric characters, alphabetic characters, and special characters such as the dollar sign ($) and period (.). **ASCII (American Standard Code for Information Interchange)** is the coding system traditionally used with personal computers. ASCII is a 7-digit (7-bit) code, although there are several different 8-bit *extended* versions of ASCII that contain additional symbols not included in the 7-bit ASCII code, such as to represent non-English characters, graphics symbols, and mathematical symbols. The extended ASCII character sets (see some examples in Figure 2-3) represent each character as a unique combination of 8 bits (1 byte), which allows 256 (2^8) unique combinations. Therefore, an 8-bit code (like extended ASCII) can represent 256 characters.

FIGURE 2-3
Some extended ASCII code examples.

CHARACTER	ASCII
0	00110000
1	00110001
2	00110010
3	00110011
4	00110100
5	00110101
A	01000001
B	01000010
C	01000011
D	01000100
E	01000101
F	01000110
+	00101011
!	00100001
#	00100011

>**Bit.** The smallest unit of data a digital computer can recognize; represented by a 0 or a 1. >**Byte.** A group of 8 bits. >**Kilobyte (KB).** Approximately 1 thousand bytes (1,024 bytes to be precise). >**Megabyte (MB).** Approximately 1 million bytes. >**Gigabyte (GB).** Approximately 1 billion bytes. >**Terabyte (TB).** Approximately 1 trillion bytes. >**Petabyte (PB).** Approximately 1,000 terabytes. >**Decimal numbering system.** The numbering system that represents all numbers using 10 symbols (0–9). >**Binary numbering system.** The numbering system that represents all numbers using just two symbols (0 and 1). >**ASCII (American Standard Code for Information Interchange).** A fixed-length, binary coding system used to represent text-based data for computer processing on many types of computers.

Unlike ASCII, which is limited to only the Latin alphabet used with the English language, **Unicode** is a universal international coding standard designed to represent text-based data written in any ancient or modern language, including those with different alphabets, such as Chinese, Greek, Hebrew, Amharic, Tibetan, and Russian (see Figure 2-4). Unicode uniquely identifies each character using 0s and 1s, no matter which language, program, or computer platform is being used. It is a longer code, consisting of 1 to 4 bytes (8 to 32 bits) per character, and can represent over one million characters, which is more than enough unique combinations to represent the standard characters in all the world's written languages, as well as thousands of mathematical and technical symbols, punctuation marks, and other symbols and signs. The biggest advantage of Unicode is that it can be used worldwide with consistent and unambiguous results.

FIGURE 2-4
Unicode. Many characters, such as these, can be represented by Unicode but not by ASCII.

INPUT HARDWARE

As discussed in Chapter 1, *input* is the process of entering data into a computer. An **input device** is any piece of hardware that is used to perform data input. Traditional input devices include the *keyboard* and *mouse*, but there are also many other types of input devices in use today.

> **TIP**
>
> For more examples of ASCII and Unicode, as well as the *EBCDIC* coding system used primarily with mainframe computers, see the "Coding Charts" section in the References and Resources Guide at the end of this book.

Keyboards

Most computers today are designed to be used with a **keyboard**—a device used to enter characters at the location on the screen marked by the *insertion point* or *cursor* (typically a blinking vertical line). An *integrated keyboard* is built into a device, a *wired keyboard* is connected via a cable to the computer's *system unit* (typically via a *USB port*), and a *wireless keyboard* is powered by batteries and connected via a wireless networking connection (such as *Bluetooth*). Most keyboards today contain standard alphanumeric keys along with a variety of special keys for specific purposes. However, the order and layout of the keys on a mobile device may be different from the order and layout on a conventional keyboard, and the keyboard layout may vary from device to device.

Virtually all desktop computers include a keyboard. Notebook and netbook computers usually have a keyboard that is similar to a desktop keyboard, but it is typically smaller, contains fewer keys (it often has no numeric keypad, for instance), and the keys are typically placed somewhat closer together. Because of the increasing amount of data entered into mobile devices today, most mobile devices have either an integrated keyboard (such as a *slide-out keyboard* that can be revealed when needed and hidden when not in use) or an *on-screen keyboard* (that can be used with *pen* or *touch input*, as discussed shortly). Some mobile devices can also connect to a *portable keyboard*, or to a *keyboard dock* or *keyboard folio* that contains a keyboard, for easier data entry. A mobile device with a slide-out keyboard is shown in Figure 2-5; a typical desktop keyboard is shown in Figure 2-6.

FIGURE 2-5
Slide-out keyboards.

Courtesy Sprint

Pointing Devices

In addition to a keyboard, most computers today are used in conjunction with some type of **pointing device**. Pointing devices are used to select and manipulate objects, to input certain types of data (such as handwritten data or edits to

>Unicode. An international coding system that can be used to represent text-based data in any written language. **>Input device.** A piece of hardware that supplies input to a computer. **>Keyboard.** An input device containing numerous keys that can be used to input letters, numbers, and other symbols. **>Pointing device.** An input device that moves an on-screen pointer, such as an arrow, to allow the user to select objects on the screen.

FUNCTION KEYS
Perform a different command or function in each program designed to use them.
BACKSPACE KEY
Erases one character to the left of the insertion point.
INSERT KEY
Toggles between inserting text and typing over text in many programs.
DELETE KEY
Deletes one character to the right of the insertion point.
ALPHANUMERIC KEYS
Usually arranged in the same order as the keys on a standard typewriter.
TAB KEY
Moves to the next tab location.
CAPS LOCK KEY
Turns all caps on or off.
PAGE UP AND PAGE DOWN KEYS
Move up or down one page or screen in most programs.
WINDOWS KEY
Opens the Windows Start screen or menu.
NUMERIC KEYPAD
Used to efficiently enter numerical data.
CONTROL AND ALTERNATE KEYS
Used in combination with other keys to enter commands into the computer.
SPACE BAR
Enters a blank space.
SHIFT KEY
Produces uppercase letters and symbols on the upper part of certain keys when the Caps Lock key is not on.
ARROW KEYS
Move the cursor around a document without disturbing existing text.
ENTER KEY
Used to enter commands into the computer, end paragraphs, and insert blank lines in documents.

Courtesy Logitech

FIGURE 2-6
A typical desktop keyboard.

TIP

Some keys on a keyboard, like the Caps Lock and Number Lock keys, are *toggle* keys, which are pressed once to turn the feature on and again to turn the feature off. If you ever find yourself typing in all caps or the numeric keypad does not work, check the status of these keys.

images), and to issue commands to the computer. Two of the most common pointing devices are the *mouse* and the *pen/stylus*, which are used to *click* screen objects and perform *pen input*, respectively; a common pointing device that uses *touch input* is the *touch screen*.

Mice

The **mouse** is the most common pointing device for a desktop computer. It typically rests on the desk or other flat surface close to the user's computer, and it is moved across the surface with the user's hand in the appropriate direction to point to and select objects on the screen. As it moves, an on-screen *mouse pointer*—usually an arrow—moves accordingly. Once the mouse pointer is pointing to the desired object on the screen, the buttons on the mouse are used to perform actions on that object (such as to open a hyperlink or to resize an image). Most mice today are *optical mice* or *laser mice* that track movements with light. Mice are used to start programs; open, move around, and edit documents; draw or edit images; and more. There are also mice that support two-dimensional gestures, such as *touch mice* designed for Windows 8 devices. Instead of buttons, these mice include a touch surface on top of the mouse in order to support *finger swipes* and other movements for convenient navigation. Some of the most common mouse operations are described in Figure 2-7. Similar to keyboards, mice today typically connect via a USB port or via a wireless connection.

>**Mouse.** A common pointing device that the user slides along a flat surface to move a pointer around the screen and clicks its buttons to make selections.

Pens/Styluses

Many devices today, including computers, media tablets, and smartphones, can accept *pen input*; that is, input by writing, drawing, or tapping on the screen with a penlike device called a **stylus**. Sometimes, the stylus (also called a *digital pen*, *electronic pen*, or *tablet pen*) is simply a plastic device with no additional functionality; other times, it is a pressure-sensitive device that transmits the pressure applied by the user to the device that the stylus is being used with in order to allow more precise input. These more sophisticated styluses are typically powered by the device that they are being used with, have a smooth rounded tip so they don't scratch the screen, and contain buttons to perform actions such as erasing content or right-clicking.

POINT
Move the mouse until the mouse pointer is at the desired location on the screen.

CLICK
Press and release the left mouse button. (To right-click, click the right mouse button; to double-click, click the left mouse button twice, in rapid succession.)

SCROLL WHEEL/BUTTON
If your mouse has a wheel or button on top, use it to scroll through the displayed document.

DRAG-AND-DROP
When the mouse pointer is over the appropriate object, press and hold down the left mouse button, drag the object to the proper location on the screen by moving the mouse, and then drop the object by releasing the mouse button.

SWIPE AND TAP
If your mouse supports gestures, swipe the surface with your fingers to scroll, flip, and zoom; tap on the mouse to click.

FIGURE 2-7
Common mouse operations.

The idea behind pen-based input and *digital writing* in general is to make using a computer or other device as convenient as writing with a pen, while adding the functionality that pen input can provide (such as converting handwritten pen input to editable typed text). In addition to supporting handwritten input (referred to as *inking*), digital pens can also be used to navigate through a document and issue commands to the computer. Pens can also be used to provide easier touch input for mobile device users who wear gloves in the winter or who have a device with a screen that is too small to have accurate touch input via a finger.

Although their capabilities depend on the type of device and software being used, pen input can be used with a variety of computers and mobile devices today (see Figure 2-8). Most often, pens are used with mobile devices and tablet computers to input handwritten text and sketches, as well as to manipulate objects (such as to select an option from a menu, select text, or resize an image). They can also be used with desktop or notebook computers if the device supports pen input and they are used increasingly for photography, graphic design, animation, industrial design, document processing, and healthcare applications. Depending on the software being used, handwritten input can be stored as an image, stored as handwritten characters that can be recognized by the computer, or converted to editable, typed text. For the latter two options, software with *handwriting recognition* capabilities

FIGURE 2-8
Examples of digital pen use.

SMARTPHONES

DESKTOP COMPUTERS

SIGNATURE CAPTURE DEVICES

>**Stylus.** An input device that is used to write electronically on the display screen.

> **TIP**
>
> Extensive touch input works the best with hybrid notebook-tablet computers, mobile devices, and other devices that can be held in a more horizontal position.

must be used. The use of handwriting recognition technology in conjunction with *digital forms* (forms that are filled out using a computer or other digital device and a digital pen instead of on paper) is growing rapidly and is expected to continue to grow as companies increasingly move toward digital records and digital documents, such as *electronic health records (EHRs)*. Other devices that use digital pens are *graphics tablets* (flat, touch-sensitive tablets used in conjunction with a digital pen to transfer input drawn or written on the graphics tablet to the connected computer) and *signature capture devices* (devices used to electronically record signatures for deliveries and to authorize credit card purchases).

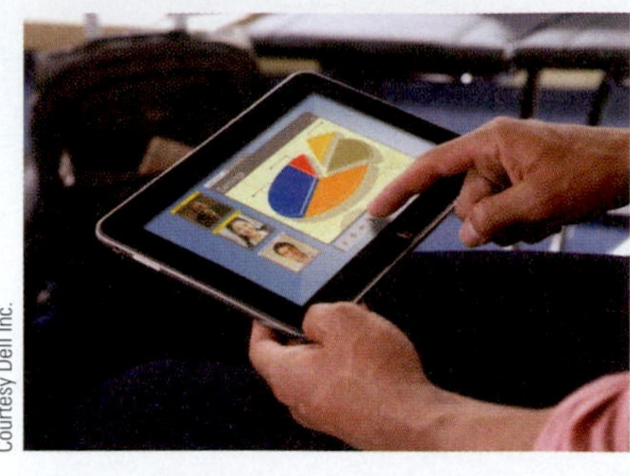

Courtesy Dell Inc.

Courtesy Dell Inc.

TOUCH SCREENS
Commonly found on mobile devices (left) and increasingly being used with many types of computers today (right).

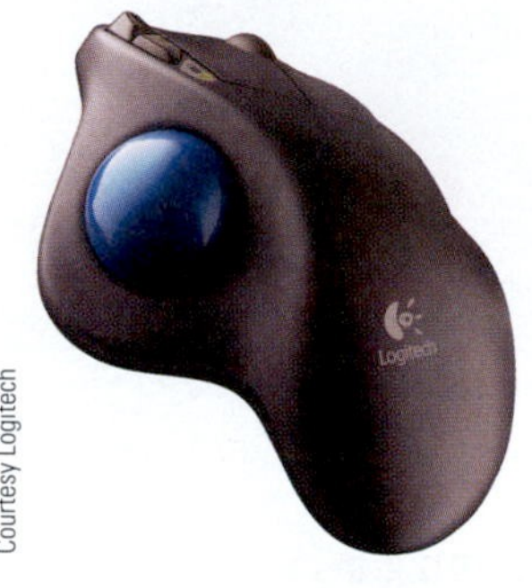

Courtesy Logitech

TRACKBALLS
An alternative to a mouse that some individuals find easier to use.

© byggarn.se/Shutterstock.com; Courtesy Logitech

TOUCH PADS
Commonly found on notebook and netbook computers (left); also available as stand-alone devices (right).

FIGURE 2-9
Examples of other common pointing devices.

Touch Screens

Touch screens allow the user to touch the screen with his or her finger to select commands or otherwise provide input to the computer associated with the touch screen (see Figure 2-9). Touch screens are common on portable computers, as well as on smartphones and other mobile devices to provide easy input. Many touch screens today are *multi-touch*; that is, they can recognize input from more than one finger at a time. Touch screens are also used in consumer kiosks and other point-of-sale (POS) systems, and they are useful for on-the-job applications (such as factory work) where it might be impractical to use a keyboard or mouse. While touch screens make many devices today more convenient for the majority of individuals to use, there is also concern that these devices are not accessible to blind individuals and users with limited mobility; accessibility and pointing devices designed for users with limited mobility are discussed in detail in Chapter 7.

Other common pointing devices include the following (refer again to Figure 2-9):

- *Control buttons* and *wheels*—used to select items and issue commands such as on portable digital media players and handheld gaming devices.
- *Trackballs*—have a ball on top, which is rotated to move an on-screen pointer, and buttons, which are clicked to make selections.
- *Touch pads*—rectangular pads across which a fingertip or thumb slides to move the on-screen pointer; the most common pointing device for notebook and netbook computers, though stand-alone touch pads are available.
- *Gaming devices*—*joysticks*, *gamepads*, *steering wheels*, *guitars*, and other input devices used with computer games and gaming consoles like the Wii, Xbox, and PlayStation.

>**Touch screen.** A display device that is touched with the finger to issue commands or otherwise provide input to the connected device.

Scanners, Readers, and Digital Cameras

Some input devices are designed either to convert data that already exists in physical form to digital form or to capture data initially in digital form. Three of the most common types of these input devices—*scanners*, *readers*, and *digital cameras*—are discussed next.

Scanners and Readers

There are various types of scanners and readers that can be used to capture data from a *source document* (a document containing data that already exists in physical form, such as a photograph, check, or product label) and convert it into input that the computer can understand. Capturing data electronically from a source document is widely used today because it can save a great deal of time and is much more accurate than inputting that data manually.

A **scanner**, more officially called an *optical scanner*, captures the image of a usually flat object (such as a printed document or photograph) in digital form and then transfers that data to a computer. Typically, the entire document (including both text and images) is input as a single image that can be resized, inserted into other documents, posted on a Web page, e-mailed to someone, printed, or otherwise treated like any other graphical image. The text in the image, however, cannot be edited unless *optical character recognition* (*OCR*) software is used in conjunction with the scanner to input the scanned text as individual text characters.

Scanners are frequently used by individuals to input printed photographs and other personal documents into a computer. Businesses are increasingly using scanners to convert paper documents into electronic format for archival or document processing purposes. The most common type of scanner is the *flatbed scanner* (see Figure 2-10), which is designed to scan flat objects one page at a time. *Portable scanners* are designed to capture text and other data while on the go. They are typically powered by batteries, the scanned content is stored in the scanner, and the content is transferred to a computer (via a cable or a wireless connection) when needed. The quality of scanned images is indicated by *resolution*, which is usually measured in the number of *dots per inch* (*dpi*) and can be specified when an item is scanned; the resolution can also be reduced if needed (such as to *compress* an image to reduce its file size before posting it on a Web page) using an *image editing program*. A higher resolution results in a better image but also results in a larger file size. A higher

FIGURE 2-10
Scanners and readers transform data from physical form to digital form.

FLATBED SCANNERS
Used to input photos, sketches, slides, book pages, and other relatively flat documents into the computer.

PORTABLE BARCODE READERS
Used to read barcodes when portability is needed.

STATIONARY RFID READERS
Used to read RFID tags, such as to automatically open ski lift entry gates for valid lift ticket holders at a ski resort in Utah (left) and to process payments via RFID-enabled credit cards (right).

>**Scanner.** An input device that reads printed text and graphics and transfers them to a computer in digital form.

FIGURE 2-11 Common types of barcodes.

resolution is needed, however, if the image is to be enlarged significantly or if only one part of the image is to be extracted and enlarged.

A **barcode** is an *optical code* that represents data with bars of varying widths or heights (see Figure 2-11). Barcodes are read with **barcode readers**, which use either light reflected from the barcode or imaging technology to interpret the bars contained in the barcode as the numbers or letters they represent. Two of the most familiar barcodes are *UPC* (*Universal Product Code*)—the barcode found on packaged goods in supermarkets and other retail stores—and *ISBN* (*International Standard Book Number*)—the type of barcode used with printed books. Businesses and organizations can also create and use custom barcodes to fulfill their unique needs. For instance, shipping organizations (such as FedEx, UPS, and the U.S. Postal Service) use custom barcodes to mark and track packages; hospitals use custom barcodes to match patients with their charts and medicines; researchers use custom barcodes to tag and track the migration habits of animals; and law enforcement agencies use custom barcodes to mark evidence. *Fixed barcode readers* are frequently used in point-of-sale (POS) systems; *portable barcode readers* (such as the one shown in Figure 2-10) are also available. Newer *two-dimensional* (*2D*) *barcodes*, such as *QR codes* (refer again to Figure 2-11), store more data than traditional barcodes and are designed to be read by smartphones for consumer applications. For a look at how barcodes are being used in a new trend—mobile ticketing—see the Technology and You box.

Radio frequency identification (*RFID*) is a technology that can store, read, and transmit data located in *RFID tags*. **RFID tags** contain tiny chips and radio antennas and can be attached to objects, such as products, ID cards, assets, shipping containers, and more. The data in RFID tags is read by **RFID readers** and can be unique so that each item containing an RFID tag can be individually identified. Whenever an RFID-tagged item is within range of an RFID reader (from 2 inches up to 300 feet or more, depending on the type of tag and the radio frequency being used), the tag's built-in antenna allows the information located within the RFID tag to be sent to the reader. Because RFID tags are read by radio waves (not by light like barcodes), the tags only need to be within range (not within line of sight) of a reader. This enables RFID readers to read the data stored in many RFID tags at the same time and read them through cardboard and other materials. In addition, RFID chips can be updated during the life of a product (such as to record information about a product's origin, shipping history, and the temperature range the item has been exposed to) and that information can be read when needed (such as at a product's final destination). RFID can also be used in conjunction with GPS to include location information. Consequently, RFID can be used for many different purposes, including for tracking the movement of the items the tags are attached to, for tracking the movement of inventory pallets and shipping containers during transit, for ticketing applications, and as part of a *mobile payment system*. *Handheld RFID readers* look similar to handheld barcode readers, *stationary RFID readers* are in a fixed location, and *portal RFID readers* can be used to read all the RFID tags inside a shipping box or palette when it passes through the portal.

TIP

Capture QR codes found in advertisements, magazines, or other printed material with your smartphone to easily access the associated resources, such as to enter a contest, watch a video, *Like* a Facebook page, or download a coupon.

Despite all its advantages, RFID growth in the retail industry has been slower than initially expected. This is primarily because of cost constraints and a number of privacy and security issues, such as concerns that others might be able to read the data contained in an RFID tag attached to your clothing, passport, or other personal item, or they might be able to make fraudulent charges via your smartphone. Privacy advocates are concerned about linking RFID tag data with personally identifiable data contained in corporate databases, such as to track consumer movements or shopping habits. As of now, no long-term solution to this issue has been reached. However, precautions against fraudulent use—such as using high-frequency tags that need to be within a few inches of the reader and requiring a PIN code, signature, or other type of authorization when an RFID credit card or mobile

>**Barcode.** A machine-readable code that represents data as a set of bars. >**Barcode reader.** An input device that reads barcodes.
>**RFID tag.** A device containing a tiny chip and a radio antenna that is attached to an object so it can be identified using RFID technology.
>**RFID reader.** A device used to read RFID tags.

TECHNOLOGY AND YOU

Mobile Ticketing

A new trend is *mobile ticketing*. Mobile ticketing goes beyond just using your smartphone or other mobile device to locate and purchase tickets that are then mailed to you. From concerts to sporting events to transportation to movie tickets, you can now use your mobile device as your actual admission ticket.

To buy a mobile ticket, you typically use a mobile app, such as an individual app for a particular application or organization (such as the *Fandango app* for movie tickets) or a generalized app (such as *StubHub*) for tickets to sporting events, concerts, and more. In either case, you use the app to make the applicable selections (such as the desired event, date, time, and seat location) and pay, and then your tickets are either sent to your smartphone or media tablet via e-mail or text message, or you use a link to download them. Typically, mobile tickets have a barcode on them; to enter the venue, you just display the ticket on your device, an attendant scans it, and you're in. For example, the *mobile boarding pass* shown in the accompanying photo allows you to use your smartphone or media tablet as your airline boarding pass at airport security checkpoints or at the gate during boarding.

There are also Web sites (such as *MogoTix*) that allow you to easily sell and distribute mobile tickets to custom events, such as a fundraiser or conference. You just publish an event (including details, ticket prices, and payment options) on the ticketing Web site and you're in business!

© robert_s/Shutterstock.com; Courtesy American Airlines

payment system is used—are being developed. Currently, a price limit (such as $25) for completely automated purchases (without a signature or other authorization), similar to many credit card purchase today, is being debated as a compromise between convenience and security.

Biometric readers read *biometric data* (measurable biological characteristics, such as an individual's fingerprint, hand geometry, face, iris, or voice) in order to identify or authenticate individuals, as discussed in more detail in Chapter 4. Biometric readers can be stand-alone or built into a computer or mobile device (see Figure 2-12); they can also be built into another piece of hardware, such as a keyboard, an external hard drive, or a USB flash drive. Other types of readers include *optical mark readers* (*OMRs*), which input data from special forms to score or tally exams, questionnaires, ballots, and so forth; *optical character recognition* (*OCR*) *readers*, which are used to read *optical characters* printed on documents, such as invoices and utility bills; and *magnetic ink character recognition* (*MICR*) *readers*, which are used to read the MICR-encoded bank and account information on checks, in order to sort and process the checks.

FIGURE 2-12

Biometric readers. This device has fully integrated iris, face, fingerprint, and voice biometric capabilities.

Fingerprint reader

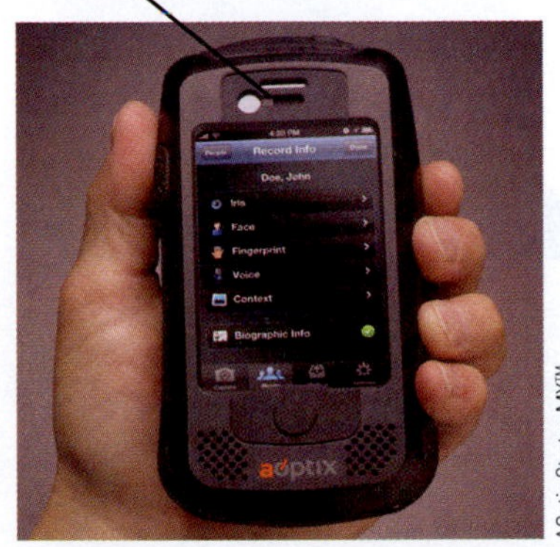

AOptix Stratus MX™

Digital Cameras

Digital cameras work much like conventional film cameras, but instead of recording images on film they record them on a digital storage medium, such as a *flash memory card*, built-in *hard drive*, or *DVD disc*. Digital cameras are usually designated either as

> **Biometric reader.** A device used to input biometric data, such as an individual's fingerprint or voice. > **Digital camera.** An input device that takes pictures and records them as digital images.

Courtesy Sony Electronics Inc.; ©MaszaS/Shutterstock.com; Courtesy Kingston Technology Company, Inc.

Virtually all digital cameras let you display and erase images.

Most cameras use removable storage media in addition to, or instead of, built-in storage.

CONSUMER DIGITAL STILL CAMERAS
Typically store photos on flash memory media.

Courtesy Sony Electronics Inc.

CONSUMER DIGITAL CAMCORDERS
Typically store video on a built-in hard drive (as in this camera) or on DVD discs.

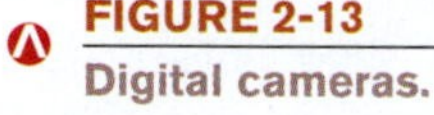

FIGURE 2-13
Digital cameras.

still cameras (which take individual still photos) or *video* cameras (which capture moving video images), although many cameras today take both still images and video. In addition to stand-alone still and video cameras (see Figure 2-13), digital camera capabilities are integrated into many portable computers and mobile devices today.

Digital still cameras are available in a wide variety of sizes and capabilities, such as inexpensive point-and-shoot digital cameras designed for consumers, professional digital cameras with removable lenses, and digital cameras integrated into mobile phones and other mobile devices. The primary appeal of digital still cameras is that the images are immediately available for viewing or printing, instead of having to have the film developed first as was the case with conventional film cameras. Digital still cameras most often use flash memory cards for storage; the number of digital photos that can be stored at one time depends on the capacity of the card being used, as well as the photo resolution being used. Photos taken with a digital camera are typically transferred to a computer or printer via the flash memory card containing the images or by connecting the camera to the computer or printer using a wired or wireless connection. Once the photos have been transferred to a computer, they can be retouched with image editing software; saved, printed, or posted to a Web page; or burned onto a CD or DVD disc, just like any other digital image. The images on the storage medium can be deleted at any time to make room for more photos.

Digital video cameras include *digital camcorders* (such as the one shown in Figure 2-13) and small digital video cameras used in conjunction with computers and other devices. Both types of digital video cameras are commonly used by individuals and businesses today to capture or transmit video images. Digital video cameras can also be used for identification purposes, such as in conjunction with face recognition technology to authorize access to a secure facility or computer resource, as discussed in more detail in Chapter 4. Digital camcorders are similar to conventional *analog* camcorders, but they store images on digital media—typically on built-in hard drives or rewritable DVDs for conventional-sized camcorders or flash memory for pocket-sized camcorders. Once a video is recorded, it can be transferred to a computer, edited with software as needed, or saved to a DVD or other type of storage medium. It can also be *compressed* (made smaller), if needed, and then uploaded to video sharing sites, such as YouTube. Some digital video cameras today can take high-definition (HD) video. Video cameras used with personal computers—commonly called *webcams* or *PC cams*—are typically used to transmit still or video images over the Internet (such as during a *videoconference* or *video phone call*) or to broadcast images continually to a Web page.

TIP

Photos or videos taken on a device with a built-in camera (such as a smartphone) are typically stored on the device's internal storage.

TIP

Some digital cameras, flash memory cards, and smartphones (with the appropriate app) can upload photos and videos as they are taken to a photo sharing Web site via a *Wi-Fi* connection.

Other Input Devices

Other input devices include *microphones* or *headsets* (used for voice input, such as issuing commands or dictating documents to a computer (via *speech recognition software*), placing phone calls via a computer (referred to as *Voice over IP* or *VoIP*), or recording spoken voice for a *podcast* (a recorded audio file that is distributed via the Internet). Music can be input into a computer via a CD, a DVD, or a Web download. For original compositions, microphones, *keyboard controllers*, and *guitar controllers* can be used. Once the music is input into the computer, it can be saved, modified, played, inserted into other programs, or burned to a CD or DVD. *Adaptive input devices* (designed for users with a physical disability) and *ergonomic hardware* (designed to lessen the physical impact of computer use) are discussed in detail in Chapter 7; types of emerging input devices are covered in Chapter 8.

PROCESSING HARDWARE AND OTHER HARDWARE INSIDE THE SYSTEM UNIT

The **system unit** is the main case of a computer or mobile device. It houses the *processing hardware* for that device, as well as a few other components, such as storage devices, the power supply, and cooling fans. The system unit for a desktop computer often looks like a rectangular box, as in Figure 2-14. The system units for all-in-one computers, notebooks, tablets, and mobile devices are much smaller and are usually combined with the device's display screen to form a single piece of hardware. However, these system units typically have components that are similar to those found in a desktop computer. As shown in Figure 2-14, a system unit contains one or more *processors*, several types of *memory*, interfaces to connect external *peripheral devices* (such as printers), and other components all interconnected through the *motherboard*. These components are discussed in detail in the next few sections.

The Motherboard

A *circuit board* is a thin board containing *computer chips*—very small pieces of silicon or other semiconducting material—and other electronic components. The main circuit board inside the system unit is called the **motherboard**. As shown in Figure 2-14, the

FIGURE 2-14
Inside a typical system unit. The system unit houses the CPU, memory, and other important pieces of hardware.

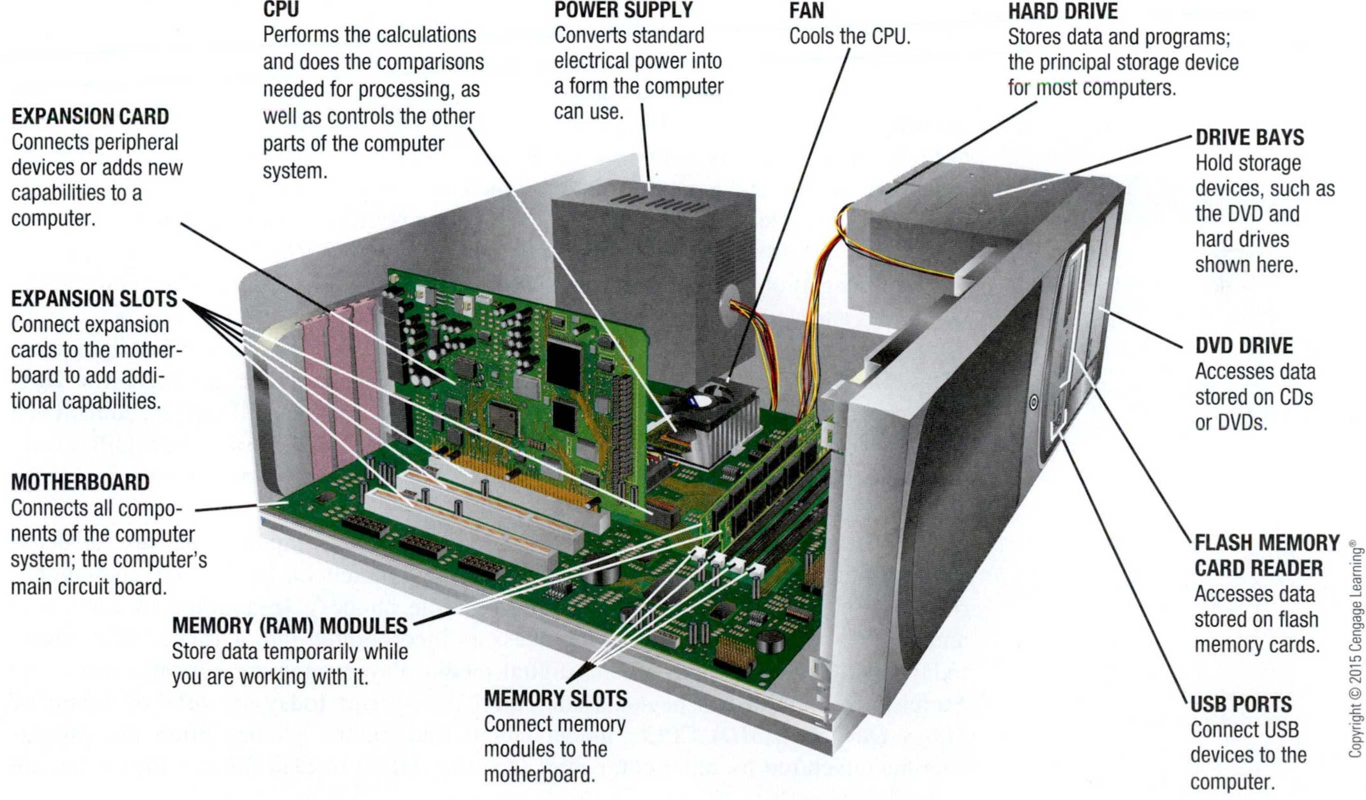

CPU
Performs the calculations and does the comparisons needed for processing, as well as controls the other parts of the computer system.
POWER SUPPLY
Converts standard electrical power into a form the computer can use.
FAN
Cools the CPU.
HARD DRIVE
Stores data and programs; the principal storage device for most computers.
EXPANSION CARD
Connects peripheral devices or adds new capabilities to a computer.
DRIVE BAYS
Hold storage devices, such as the DVD and hard drives shown here.
EXPANSION SLOTS
Connect expansion cards to the motherboard to add additional capabilities.
DVD DRIVE
Accesses data stored on CDs or DVDs.
MOTHERBOARD
Connects all components of the computer system; the computer's main circuit board.
FLASH MEMORY CARD READER
Accesses data stored on flash memory cards.
MEMORY (RAM) MODULES
Store data temporarily while you are working with it.
MEMORY SLOTS
Connect memory modules to the motherboard.
USB PORTS
Connect USB devices to the computer.

>**System unit.** The main box of a computer that houses the CPU, motherboard, memory, and other devices. >**Motherboard.** The main circuit board of a computer, located inside the system unit, to which all computer system components connect.

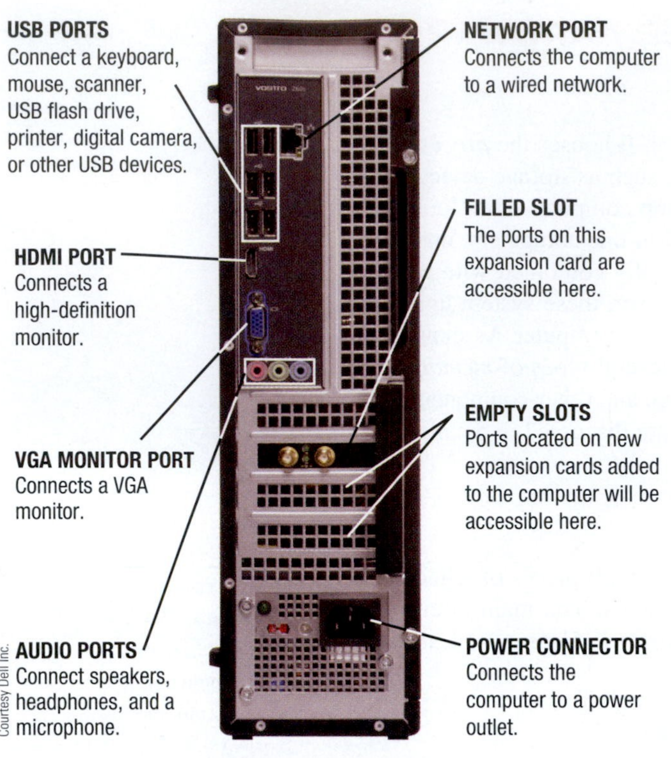

USB PORTS
Connect a keyboard, mouse, scanner, USB flash drive, printer, digital camera, or other USB devices.
HDMI PORT
Connects a high-definition monitor.
VGA MONITOR PORT
Connects a VGA monitor.
AUDIO PORTS
Connect speakers, headphones, and a microphone.
NETWORK PORT
Connects the computer to a wired network.
FILLED SLOT
The ports on this expansion card are accessible here.
EMPTY SLOTS
Ports located on new expansion cards added to the computer will be accessible here.
POWER CONNECTOR
Connects the computer to a power outlet.
Courtesy Dell Inc.

FIGURE 2-15
Ports are used to connect external devices to the motherboard.

motherboard has a variety of chips and boards attached to it; in fact, all devices used with a computer need to be connected in one way or another to the motherboard. To accomplish this, a variety of *ports*—special connectors exposed through the exterior of the system unit case—are either built into the motherboard or are created via an *expansion card* inserted into an *expansion slot* on the motherboard. These ports are used to connect *external* devices (such as monitors, keyboards, mice, and printers) to the computer. *Wireless external devices* connect to the motherboard either via a *wireless transceiver* that plugs into a port on the computer or via wireless networking technology (such as *Bluetooth*) built into the motherboard.

The most common ports for a desktop computer are shown in Figure 2-15. Portable computers have ports similar to desktop computers, but they often have fewer of them. Smartphones and other mobile devices have a more limited amount of expandability, such as a USB port, an HDMI port, or a flash memory card slot.

TIP

The most universal port is the *USB port*, used to connect a variety of input, output, and storage devices. When buying a new computer, be sure it has several USB ports.

Processors

Computers and mobile devices today contain one or more **processors** (such as *CPUs* and *GPUs*), which consist of a variety of circuitry and components that are packaged together and connected directly to the motherboard. The primary processor is the **central processing unit** (**CPU**)—also called the **microprocessor** when talking about personal computers—and it does the vast majority of the processing for a computer. The CPU contains an *arithmetic/logic unit* (*ALU*), which performs arithmetic (addition, subtraction, multiplication, and division) involving integers and logical operations (such as comparing two pieces of data to see if they are equal or determining if a specific condition is true or false). Arithmetic requiring decimals is usually performed by the *floating point unit* (*FPU*). Together, the ALU and FPU are the part of the CPU that computes. The *control unit* coordinates and controls the operations and activities taking place within the CPU, such as retrieving data and instructions and passing them on to the ALU for execution. The most recent CPU designs often also include the **graphics processing unit** (**GPU**) inside the CPU package. The GPU takes care of the processing needed to display images (including still images, animations, and video)—and particularly 3D images—on the screen. (For a look at how GPUs were used to create the new *Transformers: The Ride 3D* at Universal Studios, see the Inside the Industry box.)

CPUs are typically designed for a specific type of computer, such as for desktop computers, servers, portable computers (like notebook and tablet computers), or mobile devices (like media tablets and mobile phones). In addition to computers and mobile devices, there are also processors incorporated into a variety of products today, such as TVs, smart meters, digital media players, gaming consoles, cars, and exercise machines. Most personal computers and servers today use *Intel* or *Advanced Micro Devices* (*AMD*) CPUs; media tablets and mobile phones often use processors manufactured by other companies (such as ARM) instead. Most CPUs today are

>**Processor.** A chip (such as the CPU or GPU) that performs processing functions. >**Central processing unit (CPU).** The chip located on the motherboard of a computer that performs most of the processing for a computer. >**Microprocessor.** A central processing unit (CPU) for a personal computer. >**Graphics processing unit (GPU).** The chip that does the processing needed to display images on the screen; can be located on the motherboard, inside the CPU, or on a video graphics board.

INSIDE THE INDUSTRY

GPUs and *Transformers: The Ride 3D* at Universal Studios

At the Universal Studios Hollywood theme park, passengers can take a ride through a Transformers battlescape, thanks to the new *Transformers: The Ride 3D* ride. A motion platform, a 2,000 foot-long track, 14 huge screens (some of which curve around the audience), and 34 projectors fitted with custom 3D lenses are used to create the realistic experience, which is helped by motion that is synchronized with the action and a 14-channel audio system built into the ride vehicle. But the star of the show is the ride's impressive photorealistic 3D images.

The *Transformers: The Ride 3D* imagery uses *4K resolution*, which is four times greater than the typical movie. The images took two years to create at Industrial Light and Magic (ILM) and were more difficult to create than initially expected due to their 3D nature, the 4K resolution, and the fact that the images had to be associated with the proper perspective for each of the screens. According to Chick Russell, show producer at Universal Studios, "We were using every single server and computer that ILM had. This was the most complex project ILM ever worked on."

One key, according to Jeff White, the visual effects supervisor at ILM, was being able to see the 3D animations play back in real time as they were being developed (see the accompanying photo)—for that, they relied on the speed of NVIDIA's Quadro GPUs. Considering every robot in the ride is over a million polygons, a lot of rendering power is needed to pull that off and the GPUs delivered.

Total cost: $40 million. Result: The most technically advanced ride that Universal Studios has ever produced.

Courtesy NVIDIA

multi-core CPUs; that is, CPUs that contain the processing components or *cores* of multiple independent processors on a single CPU. For example, **dual-core CPUs** contain two cores and **quad-core CPUs** contain four cores. Up until just a few years ago, most CPUs designed for desktop computers had only a single core, and a common way to increase the amount of processing performed by the CPU was to increase the speed of the CPU. However, heat constraints are making it progressively more difficult to continue to increase CPU speed, so CPU manufacturers today are focusing on multi-core CPUs to increase the amount of processing that a CPU can do in a given time period. One measurement of the *processing speed* for a CPU is *CPU clock speed*, which is rated in *megahertz* (*MHz*) or *gigahertz* (*GHz*). A CPU with a higher CPU clock speed means that more instructions can be processed per second than the same CPU with a lower CPU clock speed. For instance, a *Core i7* processor running at 3.0 GHz would be faster than a Core i7 running at 2.4 GHz, if all other components remain the same. Although CPU clock speed is an important factor in computer performance, other factors (such as the number of cores, the amount of memory, and the speed of external storage devices) greatly affect the overall processing speed of the computer. As a result, computers today are typically classified less by CPU clock speed and more by the computer's overall processing speed or performance.

TIP

Increasingly, CPU manufacturers are integrating other features (such as graphics and networking capabilities) into processors. A processor that contains all the necessary capabilities for a single device is sometimes referred to as a *system-on-a-chip* (*SoC*).

>Multi-core CPU. A CPU that contains the processing components or core of more than one processor in a single CPU. **>Dual-core CPU.** A CPU that contains two separate processing cores. **>Quad-core CPU.** A CPU that contains four separate processing cores.

FIGURE 2-16
CPUs. CPUs today typically have multiple cores.

Multi-core CPUs (such as the Intel quad-core CPU designed for desktop computers that is shown in Figure 2-16) allow computers to work simultaneously on more than one task at a time, such as burning a DVD while surfing the Web, as well as to work faster within a single application if the software is designed to take advantage of multiple cores. Another benefit of multi-core CPUs is that they typically experience fewer heat problems than *single-core CPUs* because each core typically runs slower than a single-core CPU, although the total processing power of the multi-core CPU is greater. In addition to heat reduction, goals of CPU manufacturers today include creating CPUs that are as energy-efficient as possible (in order to reduce power consumption and increase battery life) and that use materials that are not toxic when disposed of (in order to lessen the *e-waste* impact of computers, as discussed in detail in Chapter 7).

Memory

Memory refers to chip-based storage. When the term *memory* is used alone, it refers to chip-based storage—typically **random access memory** or **RAM**—that is located inside the system unit to store data on a short-term, temporary basis. In contrast, the term *storage* refers to the amount of long-term storage available to a computer—usually in the form of the computer's hard drive or removable storage media (such as CDs, DVDs, flash memory cards, and USB flash drives, all discussed later in this chapter), but it can also be in the form of chip-based internal storage, especially in mobile devices. RAM is used to store the essential parts of the operating system while the computer is running, as well as the programs and data that the computer is currently using. RAM is **volatile**, which means its content is lost when the computer is shut off. Data in RAM is also deleted when it is no longer needed, such as when the program using that data is closed. If you want to retrieve a document at a later time, you need to save the document on a storage medium before closing it. There are several forms of *nonvolatile RAM* (*NVRAM*) under development that may be a possibility for the future; these and other types of emerging processing hardware are discussed in more detail in Chapter 8.

TIP

With devices that use embedded memory chips instead of memory modules, you typically cannot expand or replace the RAM.

Like the CPU, RAM consists of circuits etched onto chips. While smartphones and other mobile devices typically use *embedded memory chips*, the memory chips for servers and personal computers are typically arranged onto circuit boards called *memory modules* (see Figure 2-17), which, in turn, are plugged into the motherboard. RAM capacity is measured in bytes and most personal computers sold today have 2 to 8 GB of RAM. It is important for a computer to have sufficient RAM because more RAM allows more applications to run at one time and the computer to respond more quickly when a user switches from task to task.

In addition to RAM, computer users should be aware of four other types of computer memory. Two of these—*cache memory* and *registers*—are volatile like RAM; the other two—*read-only memory* (*ROM*) and *flash memory*—are *nonvolatile*.

FIGURE 2-17
RAM memory modules.

>**Random access memory (RAM).** Chips connected to the motherboard that provide a temporary location for the computer to hold data and program instructions while they are needed. >**Volatile.** A characteristic of memory or storage in which data is not retained when the power to the computer is turned off.

Cache memory is a special group of very fast memory chips located on or close to the CPU. Cache memory is used to speed up processing by storing the data and instructions that may be needed next by the CPU in handy locations. Cache memory level numbers indicate the order in which the various caches are accessed by the CPU when it requires new data or instructions. *Level 1 (L1) cache* (which is the fastest type of cache but typically holds less data than other levels of cache) is checked first, followed by *Level 2 (L2) cache*, followed by *Level 3 (L3) cache* if it exists. If the data or instructions are not found in cache memory, the computer looks for them in RAM, which is slower than cache memory. If the data or instructions cannot be found in RAM, then they are retrieved from the hard drive—an even slower operation. Typically, more cache memory results in faster processing. Most multi-core CPUs today have some cache memory (such as L1 and L2 cache) dedicated to each core; they may also use a larger shared cache memory (such as L3 cache, as shown in Figure 2-16) that can be accessed by any core as needed.

ASK THE EXPERT

ARM Courtesy of ARM

James Bruce, Lead Mobile Strategist, ARM

Why does a smartphone need a dual-core processor?

Dual core processors allow smartphones to deliver increased performance, while delivering better battery life. The reason for this is that the tasks that run on a smartphone have widely different performance needs; for instance, compare writing an SMS text message with playing a 3D game.

To provide this scalability of performance and power in today's advanced chip manufacturing processes such as 28 nm (1 nm = 1 billionth of a meter), it is better to have multiple smaller cores versus one large monolithic core. With dual-core processors, you can switch one core off for tasks such as SMS (to save power), and then you can switch both cores on when maximum performance is needed.

Registers are another type of high-speed memory built into the CPU. Registers are used by the CPU to temporarily store data and intermediary results during processing. Registers are the fastest type of memory used by the CPU, even faster than Level 1 cache. Generally, the more data a register can contain at one time, the faster the CPU performs.

ROM (*read-only memory*) consists of nonvolatile chips that permanently store data or programs. Like RAM, these chips are attached to the motherboard inside the system unit, and the data or programs are retrieved by the computer when they are needed. An important difference, however, is that you can neither write over the data or programs in ROM chips (which is the reason ROM chips are called *read-only*), nor destroy their contents when you shut off the computer's power. Traditionally, ROM was used to store permanent instructions used by a computer (referred to as *firmware*); ROM is increasingly being replaced with *flash memory*, as discussed next, for any data that may need to be updated during the life of the computer.

TIP

To avoid confusion, when you are referring to the amount of room on your hard drive, use the proper term—*storage* space, not *memory*.

Flash memory is a type of nonvolatile memory into which data can be stored and retrieved. Flash memory chips have begun to replace ROM for storing system information, such as a computer's *BIOS* (*basic input/output system*)—the sequence of instructions the computer follows during the boot process. By storing this information in flash memory instead of in ROM, it can be updated as needed. Similarly, firmware for personal computers and other devices (such as mobile phones and networking hardware) are now typically stored in flash memory that is embedded in the device so the firmware can be updated over the life of the product. In addition to built-in flash memory chips that are used only by the computer, computers and storage devices can include built-in flash memory chips designed to be used by the user for storage purposes, as discussed shortly.

TIP

Product descriptions for media tablets and other devices that use built-in flash memory for storage sometimes refer to that storage as memory—it's important for shoppers to realize that this quantity refers to storage, not RAM.

OUTPUT HARDWARE

Output hardware consists of all the devices that are used to produce the results of processing—usually, output is displayed on a computer screen, printed on paper, or presented as audio output. Hardware devices that produce output are called **output devices**. The most common output devices are discussed next; types of emerging output devices are discussed in Chapter 8.

MEDIA TABLETS

SMART WATCHES

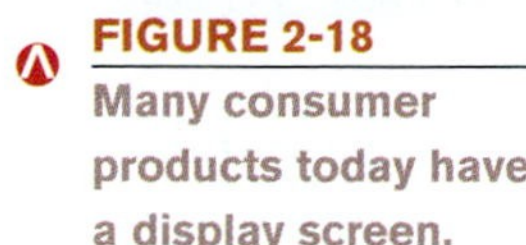
FIGURE 2-18
Many consumer products today have a display screen.

Display Devices

A **display device**—the most common form of output device—presents output visually on some type of screen. The display device for a desktop computer is more formally called a **monitor**; the display device for a notebook, netbook, tablet, mobile phone, or other device for which the screen is built into the device is typically called a **display screen**. In addition to being used with computers and mobile devices (see Figure 2-18), display screens are also built into handheld gaming devices, home entertainment devices (like remote controls, televisions, and portable DVD players), and kitchen appliances. They are also an important component in *digital photo frames* (stand-alone or wall-mounted photo frames that display digital photos, which are typically transferred to the frame via a flash memory card or a wireless networking connection), *e-book readers* or *e-readers* (which display e-books), portable digital media players, smart watches, and other consumer products. A *data projector* is a display device that projects computer output onto a wall or projection screen for a large group presentation; *digital signage systems* display digital signs (such as for billboards, restaurant menus, and advertising signs in retail stores) whose content can be changed throughout the day as needed.

The *CRT monitor* used to be the norm for desktop computers. CRTs use *cathode-ray tube* technology to display images; as a result, they are large, bulky, and heavy like conventional televisions. While CRT monitors are still in use, most computers today (as well as most television sets) use the thinner and lighter *flat-panel display* technology. Flat-panel display technology is also used in the display screens integrated into mobile phones and consumer electronics. Flat-panel displays form images by manipulating electronically charged chemicals or gases sandwiched between thin panes of glass or other transparent material. Flat-panel displays consume less power than CRTs. They also take up less desk space, which makes it possible to use multiple monitors working together to increase the amount of data the user can view at one time. To use multiple monitors, you must have the necessary hardware to support this feature, such as an appropriate monitor port. Multiple displays can be used with both desktop and portable computers; typically, you will use the displays to *extend* your desktop as in Figure 2-19, instead of duplicate it.

Regardless of the technology used, the screen of a display device is divided into a fine grid of small areas or dots called **pixels** (from the phrase *picture element*). A pixel is the smallest colorable area in an electronic image. The number of pixels used on a display screen determines the *screen resolution*, which affects the amount of information that can be displayed on the screen at one time. When a higher resolution is selected, such as 1,600 pixels horizontally by 900 pixels vertically for a standard computer monitor (written as 1,600 × 900 and read as *1600 by 900*), more information can fit on the screen, but everything will be displayed smaller than with a lower resolution, such as 1,280 × 768. The screen resolution on many computers today can be changed by users to match their preferences and the software being used. On Windows computers, display options are changed using the Control Panel. When multiple monitors are used, typically the screen resolution of each display can be set independently of the others. Very high-resolution monitors are available for special applications, such as viewing digital X-rays.

TIP

Flat-panel displays typically use *digital signals*, which allow for sharper images.

>**Output device.** A piece of hardware that presents the results of processing in a form the user can understand. >**Display device.** An output device that contains a viewing screen. >**Monitor.** A display device for a desktop computer. >**Display screen.** A display device built into a notebook computer, netbook, or other device. >**Pixel.** The smallest colorable area in an electronic image, such as a scanned image, a digital photograph, or an image displayed on a display screen.

Display devices today are typically *color displays*, which form colors by mixing combinations of three colors—red, green, and blue. Screen size is usually measured diagonally from corner to corner, in a manner similar to the way TV screens are measured. As discussed earlier in this chapter, it is increasingly common for monitors and display screens to support touch input. Touch screen displays are commonly used with personal computers, as well as with consumer kiosks, portable gaming devices, mobile phones, media tablets, smart TVs, and other consumer devices.

©iStockphoto.com/gl0ck; Used with permission from Microsoft Corporation

FIGURE 2-19
Multiple monitors. Can be used to extend a desktop, which can increase productivity.

Printers

Instead of the temporary, ever-changing soft copy output that a monitor produces, **printers** produce *hard copy*; that is, a permanent copy of the output on paper. Most desktop computers are connected to a printer; portable computers can use printers as well. Printers designed to be connected to a single computer are referred to as *personal printers*; *network printers* are designed to be shared by multiple users via a home or an office network.

Printers produce images through either impact or nonimpact technologies. *Impact printers*, like old ribbon typewriters, have a print mechanism that actually strikes the paper to transfer ink to the paper. Most printers today are *nonimpact printers*, meaning they form images without the print mechanism actually touching the paper. Impact printers, such as the older *dot-matrix printers*, are primarily used today for producing multipart forms, such as invoices, packing slips, and credit card receipts. Nonimpact printers usually produce higher-quality images and are much quieter than impact printers. Both impact and nonimpact printers form images with dots, similar to the way monitors display images using pixels. Because of this, printers are very versatile and can print text in virtually any size, as well as print photos and other graphical images. Printers can be *color printers* (see Figure 2-20) or *black-and-white printers*; color printers either apply all of the colors in one pass or go through the entire printing process multiple times, applying one color during each pass. In addition, printer quality is measured in dots per inch (dpi) and printer speed is measured in *pages per minute* (*ppm*). Most personal printers today connect to a computer via a USB connection; many also have the option of connecting via a wired or wireless networking connection as well. In addition, some personal printers can receive data to be printed via a flash memory card or directly from a digital camera. Network printers connect directly to a network and can be used by any device on that network, or via the Internet if *cloud printing* is available and enabled. The two most common types of printers today are *laser printers* and *ink-jet printers*, both of which are nonimpact printers.

© Paul Broadbent/Shutterstock.com

FIGURE 2-20
Color printing. Requres multiple cartridges or cartridges that contain multiple colors.

Laser Printers

Laser printers are the standard for business documents and come in both personal and network versions; they are also available as both color and black-and-white printers. To print a document, the laser printer first uses a laser beam to charge the appropriate locations on a drum to form the page's image, and then *toner powder* (powdered ink) is released from a *toner cartridge* and sticks to the drum. The toner is then transferred to a piece of

TIP

Printers that offer more than just printing capabilities (such as printing, copying, scanning, and faxing) are referred to as *multifunction devices* (*MFD*) or *all-in-ones*.

>**Printer.** An output device that produces output on paper. >**Laser printer.** An output device that uses toner powder and technology similar to that of a photocopier to produce images on paper.

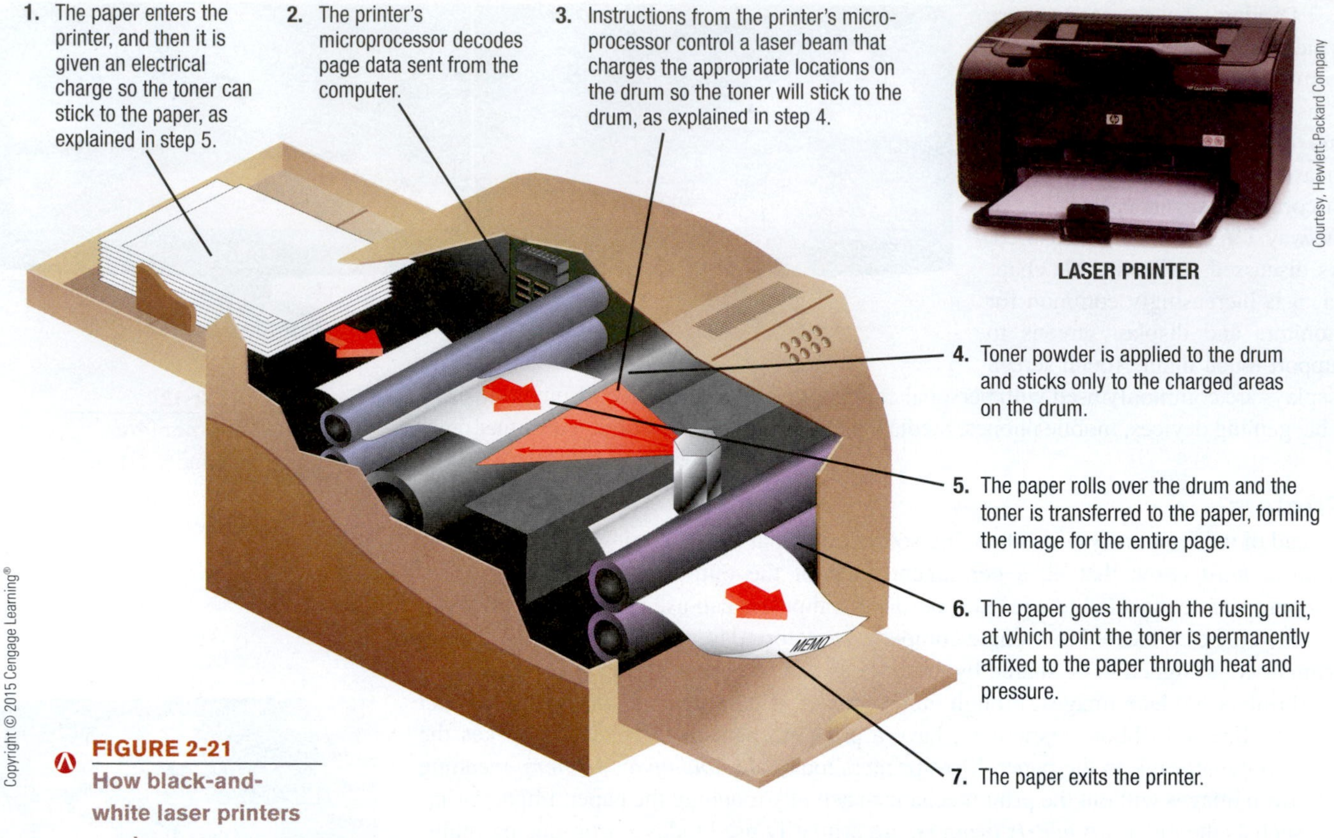

1. The paper enters the printer, and then it is given an electrical charge so the toner can stick to the paper, as explained in step 5.
2. The printer's microprocessor decodes page data sent from the computer.
3. Instructions from the printer's microprocessor control a laser beam that charges the appropriate locations on the drum so the toner will stick to the drum, as explained in step 4.
LASER PRINTER
Courtesy, Hewlett-Packard Company
4. Toner powder is applied to the drum and sticks only to the charged areas on the drum.
5. The paper rolls over the drum and the toner is transferred to the paper, forming the image for the entire page.
6. The paper goes through the fusing unit, at which point the toner is permanently affixed to the paper through heat and pressure.
7. The paper exits the printer.
MEMO

FIGURE 2-21
How black-and-white laser printers work.

paper when the paper is rolled over the drum, and a heating unit fuses the toner powder to the paper to permanently form the image (see Figure 2-21). Laser printers print one entire page at a time and are typically faster and have better quality output than *ink-jet printers*, discussed next. Common print resolutions for laser printers are between 600 and 2,400 dpi; common speeds for laser printers range from about 10 to 70 ppm.

TIP

To save money, buy *recharged* (refilled) toner or ink cartridges to replace your printer cartridge when it runs out of toner or ink powder. Recharged cartridges typically cost about one-third less than new cartridges and last at least as long.

Ink-Jet Printers

Ink-jet printers form images by spraying tiny drops of liquid ink from one or more *ink cartridges* onto the page, one printed line at a time (see Figure 2-22). Some printers print with one single-sized ink droplet; others print using different-sized ink droplets and using multiple nozzles or varying electrical charges for more precise printing. The printhead for ink-jet printers typically travels back and forth across the page, which is one reason why ink-jet printers are slower than laser printers (ink-jet printers print up to about 30 ppm). Because they are relatively inexpensive, have good-quality output, and can print in color, ink-jet printers are often the printer of choice for home use. With the use of special photo paper, most ink-jet printers can also print photograph-quality digital photos. Ink-jet printers are typically less expensive than laser printers, although the cost of the replaceable ink cartridges can add up, especially if you do a lot of color printing.

Special-Purpose Printers

Although both laser and ink-jet printers can typically print on a variety of media—including sheets of labels, envelopes, transparencies, photo paper, and even fabric—in addition to

>**Ink-jet printer.** An output device that sprays droplets of ink to produce images on paper.

various sizes of paper, some printers are designed for a particular purpose. For instance, *photo printers* are color printers designed to print photographs; *barcode printers* enable businesses and other organizations to print custom barcodes on price tags, shipping labels, and other documents for identification or pricing purposes; *portable printers* are small, lightweight printers that can be used on the go, such as with a notebook computer or mobile device; *wide-format ink-jet printers* are designed to produce charts, drawings, maps, blueprints, advertising banners, and other large documents; and *3D printers* form output in layers using molten plastic during a series of passes to build a 3D version of the desired output.

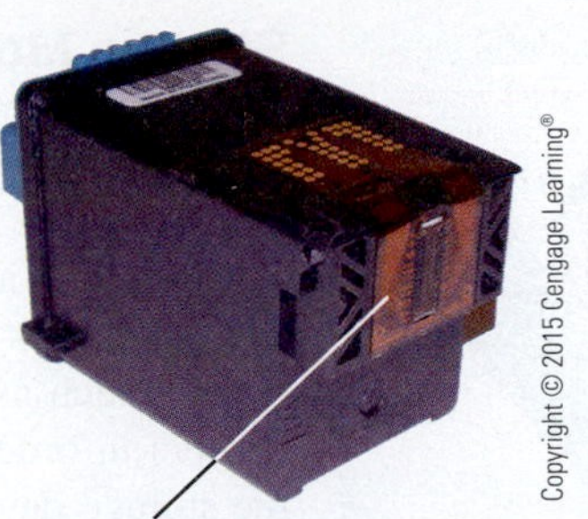

Each ink cartridge is made up of multiple tiny ink-filled firing chambers; to print images, the appropriate color ink is ejected through the appropriate firing chamber.

INK-JET PRINTER

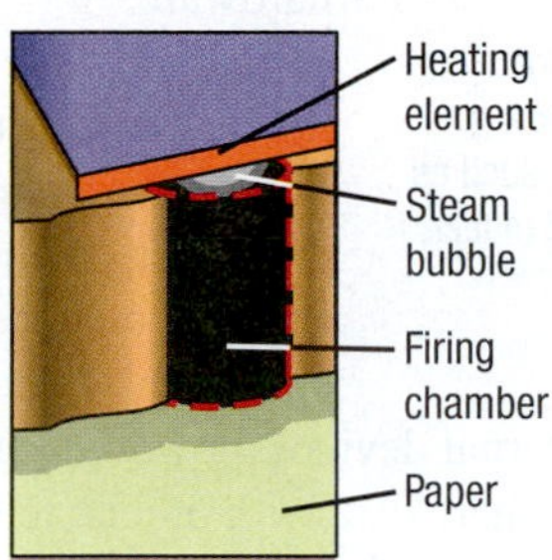

1. A heating element makes the ink boil, which causes a steam bubble to form.

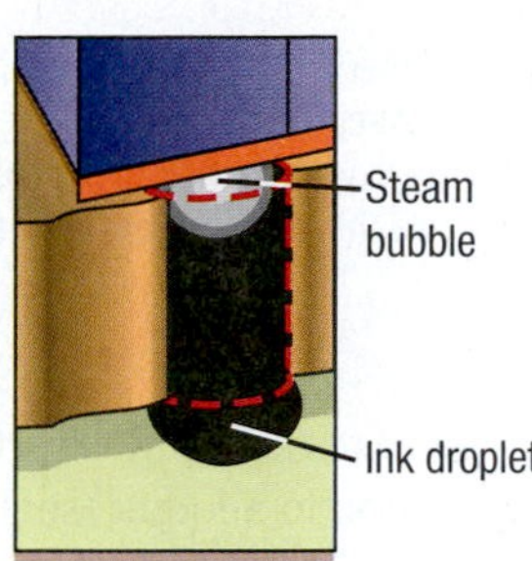

2. As the steam bubble expands, it pushes ink through the firing chamber.

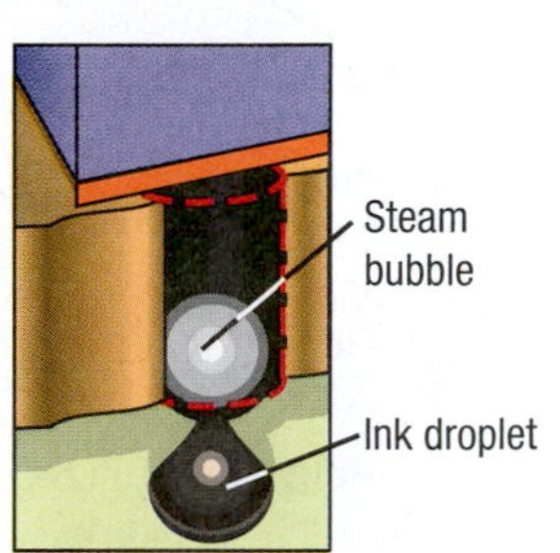

3. The ink droplet is ejected onto the paper and the steam bubble collapses, pulling more ink into the firing chamber.

FIGURE 2-22
How ink-jet printers work.

Other Output Devices

Other types of output devices include **computer speakers**, such as those that connect to a computer and provide audio output for computer games, music, video clips and TV shows, videoconferencing, and other applications. *Headphones* can be used instead of speakers when you don't want the audio output to disturb others (such as in a school computer lab or public library). *Headsets* are headphones with a built-in microphone and are often used for dictating, making phone calls, or participating in videoconferences using a computer; wireless headsets are commonly used in conjunction with mobile phones. Even smaller than headphones are the *earphones* and *earbuds* often used with portable digital media players, handheld gaming devices, and other mobile devices.

TIP

Emerging types of output devices (such as *wireless displays*, *cloud printing*, *3D printers*, and *Google Glass*) are discussed in Chapter 8.

STORAGE HARDWARE

Unlike RAM, which is volatile and holds data only temporarily, *storage systems* are non-volatile and are used anytime you want to save a document for future use. The basic characteristics of storage systems are discussed first, followed by a look at the most common types of storage systems.

Storage System Characteristics

All storage systems have specific characteristics, such as having both a *storage device* and a *storage medium*, the *portability* and *volatility* of the system, and the type of storage technology used.

> **Computer speakers.** Output devices connected to computers that provide audio output.

The letter C is usually assigned to the first hard drive.
CD/DVD drives are usually assigned letters after the hard drives, such as D in this example.
Any storage devices attached to the computer via USB ports are typically assigned next, such as E for this USB flash drive.
Other letters, beginning with F in this example, are used for any other storage devices attached to the computer, such as via this built-in flash memory card reader.
© AS-kom/Shutterstock.com

FIGURE 2-23 **Storage device identifiers.** To keep track of storage devices in an unambiguous way, the computer system assigns letters of the alphabet or names to each of them.

Storage Media and Storage Devices

There are two parts to any storage system: the **storage medium** and the **storage device**. A storage medium is the hardware where data is actually stored (for example, a *DVD* or a *flash memory card*); a storage medium is inserted into its corresponding storage device (such as a *DVD drive* or a *flash memory card reader*) in order to be read from or written to. Often the storage device and storage medium are two separate pieces of hardware (that is, the storage medium is *removable*), although with some systems—such as a *hard drive* or most *USB flash drives*—the two parts are permanently sealed together to form one piece of hardware.

Storage devices can be *internal* (located inside the system unit), *external* (plugged into an external port on the system unit), or *remote* (located on another computer, such as a network server or Web server). Internal devices have the advantage of requiring no additional desk space and are usually faster than their external counterparts. External devices, however, can be easily transported from one location to another (such as to share data with others, to transfer data between a work computer and a home computer, or to take digital photos to a photo store). They can also be removed from the computer and stored in a secure area (such as for backup purposes or to protect sensitive data). Remote devices are accessed over a network. Some remote storage devices, such as those accessed via the Internet, have the additional advantage of being accessible from any computer with an Internet connection. Regardless of how storage devices are connected to a computer, letters of the alphabet and/or names are typically assigned to each storage device so that the user can identify each device easily when it needs to be used (see Figure 2-23).

> **TIP**
>
> Although most computers today typically do not include a *floppy drive* (an older type of removable storage device not widely used today), the drive letters A and B are still often reserved for floppy drives so you may not have a drive A or B on your computer.

Type of Storage Technology Used

Data is stored *magnetically* or *optically* on many types of storage media. With magnetic storage systems, such as conventional hard drives, data is stored magnetically on the storage medium, which means the data (0s and 1s) is represented using different magnetic alignments. The storage device can change the magnetic alignment when needed, so data can be written to the medium, deleted from the medium, or rewritten to the medium. Optical storage media (such as CDs and DVDs) store data optically using laser beams. On some optical media, the laser burns permanent marks to represent 0s and 1s into the surface of the medium so the data cannot be erased or rewritten. With *rewritable* optical media, the laser changes the reflectivity of the medium to represent 0s and 1s but it does not permanently alter the disc surface so the reflectivity of the medium can be changed back again as needed. Consequently, the data stored on a rewritable optical disc can be changed.

Some storage systems use a combination of magnetic and optical technology. Others use a different technology altogether, such as *flash memory storage systems* that represent data using *electrons*. Some of the most widely used storage systems are discussed in the next few sections.

>Storage medium. The part of a storage system, such as a DVD disc, where data is stored. **>Storage device.** A piece of hardware, such as a DVD drive, into which a storage medium is inserted to be read from or written to.

Hard Drives

With the exception of computers designed to use only network storage devices (such as thin clients and some Internet appliances), virtually all personal computers come with a **hard drive** that is used to store most programs and data. *Internal hard drives* (those located inside the system unit) are not designed to be removed, unless they need to be repaired or replaced. *External hard drives* typically connect to a computer via an external port (such as a USB or FireWire port) and are frequently used for additional storage (such as for digital photos, videos, and other large multimedia files), to move files between computers, and for backup purposes. Hard drives are also incorporated into other consumer products, such as mobile phones, portable digital media players, digital video recorders (DVRs), gaming consoles, digital camcorders, and more, though some mobile devices today use only flash memory chips for internal storage.

Courtesy Apricorn

FIGURE 2-24
Encrypted hard drives. The data stored on this external hard drive is accessed via a fingerprint scanner.

For security purposes, both internal and external hard drives today are available with built-in *encryption* that automatically encrypts (essentially scrambles) all data stored on the hard drive and limits access to the hard drive to only authorized users, typically via a *password* or *fingerprint scan* (see Figure 2-24). Encryption, passwords, and *fingerprint readers* are discussed in detail in Chapter 4.

Magnetic Hard Drives

A **magnetic hard drive** (the traditional type of hard drive) contains metal *hard disks* or *platters* that are coated with a magnetizable substance. These hard disks are permanently sealed inside the hard drive case, along with the *read/write heads* used to store (*write*) and retrieve (*read*) data and an *access mechanism* used to move the read/write heads in and out over the surface of the hard disks (see Figure 2-25). The surface of a hard disk is organized into *tracks* (concentric rings) and pie-shaped groups of *sectors* (small pieces of a track). The read/write heads magnetize particles a certain way on the disk surface to represent the data's 0s and 1s. The particles retain their magnetic orientation until the orientation

FIGURE 2-25
Magnetic hard drives.

2.5-INCH HARD DRIVE LOCATED INSIDE A NOTEBOOK COMPUTER

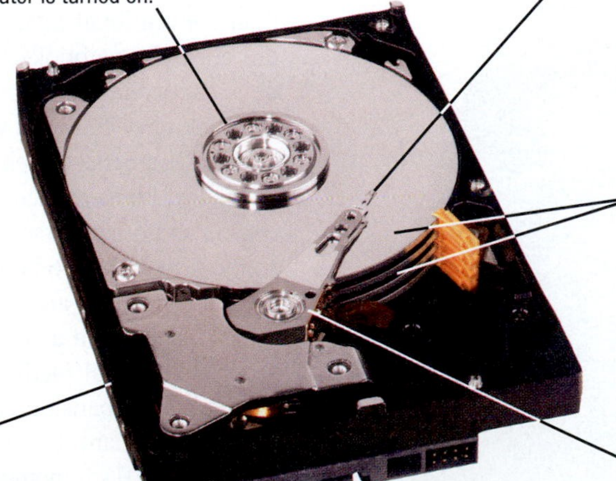

MOUNTING SHAFT
The mounting shaft spins the hard disks at a speed of several thousand revolutions per minute while the computer is turned on.

READ/WRITE HEADS
There is a read/write head for each hard disk surface, and they move in and out over the disks together.

HARD DISKS
There are usually several hard disk surfaces on which to store data. Most hard drives store data on both sides of each disk.

SEALED DRIVE
The hard disks and the drive mechanism are hermetically sealed inside a case to keep them free from contamination.

ACCESS MECHANISM
The access mechanism moves the read/write heads in and out together between the hard disk surfaces to access required data.

INSIDE A 3.5-INCH HARD DRIVE

Courtesy of Hitachi Global Storage Technologies; Courtesy Western Digital

>**Hard drive.** The primary storage system for most computers; used to store most programs and data used with a computer.

>**Magnetic hard drive.** A hard drive consisting of one or more metal magnetic disks permanently sealed, along with an access mechanism and read/write heads, inside its drive.

is changed again, so data can be stored, rewritten to the disk, and deleted as needed. The computer uses a *file system* to record where each document (called a *file*) is physically stored on the hard drive and what *filename* the user has assigned to it. When the user requests a document (always by filename), the computer uses its file system to retrieve it.

Hard drives designed for desktop computers (sometimes referred to as *desktop hard drives*) typically use 2.5-inch or 3.5-inch hard disks and notebook hard drives typically use 2.5-inch hard disks. Portable digital media players, mobile phones, and other mobile devices that include a magnetic hard drive typically use tiny 1.5-inch or smaller hard drives instead. Regardless of the size, one hard drive usually contains a stack of several hard disks; if so, there is a read/write head for each hard disk surface (top and bottom), and these heads move in and out over the disk surfaces simultaneously.

TIP

Some computers today use two types of drives for efficiency—such as a smaller SSD (for the operating system and important applications) and a larger magnetic hard drive (for data storage and lesser-used applications).

CAUTION CAUTION CAUTION CAUTION CAUTION CAUTION CAUT

Because you never know when a head crash or other hard drive failure will occur—there may be no warning whatsoever—be sure to *back up* the data on your hard drive on a regular basis. Backing up data—that is, creating a second copy of important files—is critical not only for businesses but also for individuals and is discussed in more detail in Chapter 5.

Solid State Drives (SSDs) and Hybrid Hard Drives

Solid-state drives (SSDs) are hard drives that use flash memory technology instead of spinning hard disk platters and magnetic technology (see Figure 2-26); consequently, SSDs have no moving parts and data is stored as electrical charges on the *flash memory media* located within the SSDs. These characteristics mean that SSDs (along with the other types of flash memory storage systems discussed later in this chapter) are not subject to mechanical failures like magnetic hard drives and are, therefore, more resistant to shock and vibration. They also consume less power, generate less heat, make no noise, and are much faster than magnetic hard drives. Consequently, SSDs are an especially attractive option for portable computers and mobile devices. Although previously too expensive for all but specialty applications, prices of SSDs (also sometimes called *flash memory hard drives*) have fallen significantly over the past few years (although they are still significantly more expensive per GB than conventional magnetic hard drives) and they are becoming the norm for netbooks, mobile devices, and other very portable devices. In addition to cost, another disadvantage of SSDs is that flash memory cells can wear out with repeated use.

FIGURE 2-26
Solid-state drives (SSDs).

Transcend
Data is stored in flash memory chips located inside the drive; unlike magnetic drives, there are no moving parts.

Courtesy Transcend Information USA

SSDs are most often 2.5-inch drives so they can easily be used instead of conventional magnetic hard drives in notebooks, netbooks, and other personal computers (most come with a bracket so the drive can also be used in a 3.5-inch drive bay of a desktop computer). There are also smaller 1.8-inch SSDs available that can be used when a smaller physical size is needed, such as for a portable digital media player or mobile phone. SSDs are also available as expansion card drives. SSDs capacities between 128 GB and 1 TB are the most common today. **Hybrid hard drives** include both flash memory and a magnetic hard drive—this combination is less expensive than an SSD, can extend the battery life of portable computers and mobile devices, and can allow encryption or other security measures to be built into the drive.

>**Solid-state drive (SSD).** A hard drive that uses flash memory media instead of metal magnetic hard disks. >**Hybrid hard drive.** A hard drive that contains both a large amount of flash memory and magnetic hard disks.

Internal vs. External Hard Drives

Internal hard drives are permanently located inside a computer's system unit and typically are not removed unless there is a problem with them. Virtually all computers have at least one internal hard drive (either a magnetic hard drive or an SSD) that is used to store programs and data. *External hard drives* are commonly used for transporting a large amount of data from one computer to another (by moving the entire hard drive to another computer), for backup purposes, and for additional storage. Today, because of their large capacity, full-sized external hard drives (which are typically magnetic hard drives that hold between 1 TB and 4 TB, though 1 TB SSD external drives are now available) are often used by individuals to store their digital photos, digital music, home movies, recorded TV shows, and other multimedia content to be distributed to the computers and entertainment devices located in the home. While full-sized external hard drives can be moved from computer to computer when needed, *portable hard drives* are smaller external hard drives specifically designed for that purpose (see Figure 2-27). Unlike full-sized external hard drives (which typically need to be plugged into a power outlet to be used), portable hard drives are typically powered via the computer they are being used with instead. Portable magnetic hard drives typically hold up to 2 TB; the capacity of portable SSD hard drives at the present time is smaller—up to 256 GB. Most external desktop and portable hard drives connect to the computer via a USB connection. However, some can connect via a wired or wireless networking connection instead.

TIP

To determine how large an external drive you need, consider the following: Each 100 GB will hold up to approximately 20,000 photos, 7.5 hours of video, or 25,000 songs.

FIGURE 2-27
External hard drives.

Courtesy Western Digital

FULL-SIZED EXTERNAL HARD DRIVES
Are about the size of a 5 by 7-inch picture frame, but thicker; this drive contains two magnetic hard drives, which hold 6 TB total.

Courtesy Transcend Information USA

PORTABLE HARD DRIVES
Are about the size of a credit card, but thicker; this SSD drive holds 256 GB.

Optical Discs and Drives

Data stored on **optical discs** (such as *CDs*, *DVDs*, and *Blu-ray Discs* (*BDs*)) is stored and read *optically*; that is, using laser beams. Optical discs are thin circular discs made out of molded *polycarbonate substrates*—essentially a type of very strong plastic—that are topped with layers of other materials and coatings used to store data and protect the disc. Data can be stored on one or both sides of an optical disc, depending on the disc design, and some types of discs use multiple recording layers on each side of the disc to increase capacity. To keep data organized, optical discs are divided into tracks and sectors like magnetic disks but use a single grooved spiral track beginning at the center of the disc (see Figure 2-28) instead of a series of concentric tracks. Data is written to an optical disc in one of two ways. With *read-only optical discs* like movie, music, and software CDs and DVDs, the surface of the disc is molded or stamped appropriately to represent the data. With *recordable* or *rewritable optical discs* that can be written to using an *optical drive* such as a *DVD drive*, the reflectivity of the disc is changed using a laser to represent the data. In either case, the disc is read with a laser and the computer interprets the reflection of the laser off the disc surface as 1s and 0s.

TIP

Use the term *disks* when referring to magnetic media; use the term *discs* when referring to optical media.

To accomplish this with molded or stamped optical discs, tiny depressions (when viewed from the top side of the disc) or bumps (when viewed from the bottom) are created on the disc's surface. These bumps are called *pits*; the areas on the disc that are not changed are called *lands*. Although many people think that each individual pit and land represents a 1 or 0, that is not completely accurate—it is the transition between a pit and land that represents a 1. When the disc is read, the amount of laser light reflected back from the disc changes when the laser reaches a transition between a pit and a land. When the optical drive detects a transition, it is interpreted

>**Optical disc.** A type of storage medium read from and written to using a laser beam.

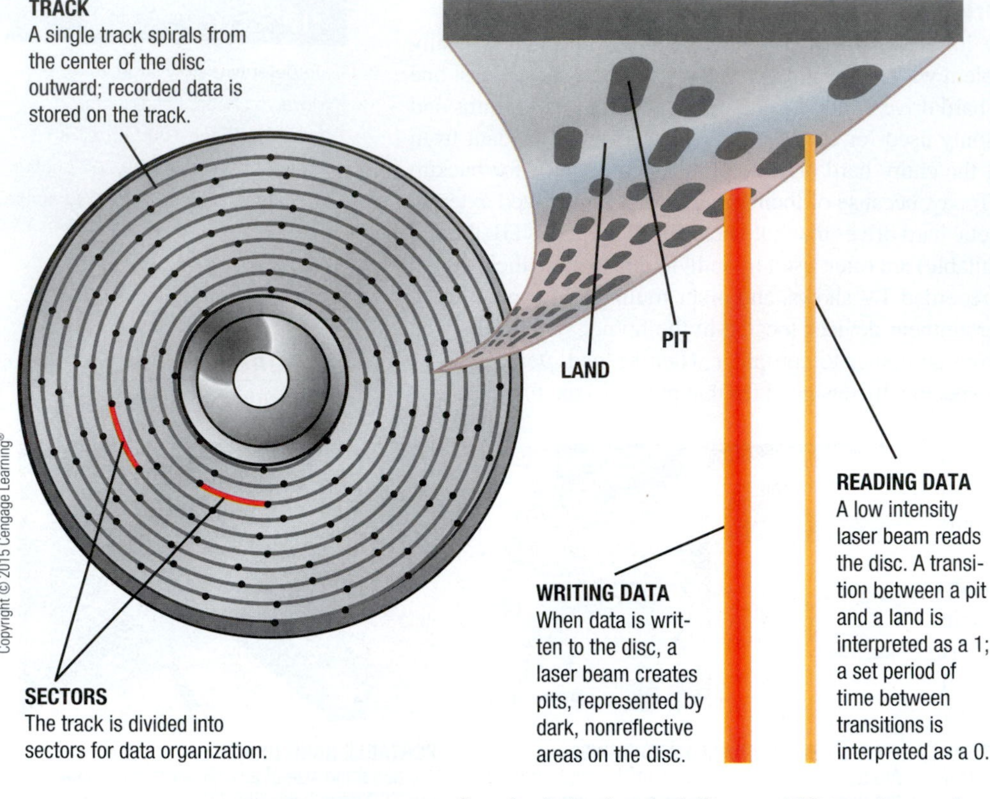
TRACK
A single track spirals from the center of the disc outward; recorded data is stored on the track.
LAND
PIT
SECTORS
The track is divided into sectors for data organization.
WRITING DATA
When data is written to the disc, a laser beam creates pits, represented by dark, nonreflective areas on the disc.
READING DATA
A low intensity laser beam reads the disc. A transition between a pit and a land is interpreted as a 1; a set period of time between transitions is interpreted as a 0.

FIGURE 2-28
How recorded optical discs work.

as a 1; no transition for a specific period of time indicates a 0.

With a disc that is recorded using a DVD drive, the recording laser beam changes the reflectivity of the appropriate areas on the disc to represent the data stored there—dark, nonreflective areas are pits; reflective areas are lands, as illustrated in Figure 2-28. As with molded or stamped discs, the transition between a pit and a land represents a 1 and no transition for a specific distance along the track represents a 0. Different types of optical discs use different types of laser beams. Conventional **CD discs** use *infrared* lasers; conventional **DVD discs** use *red* lasers, which allow data to be stored more compactly on the same size disc; and high-definition **Blu-ray Discs (BDs)** use *blue-violet lasers*, which can store data even more compactly on a disc.

Standard-sized optical discs are 120-mm (approximately 4½-inch) discs (see Figure 2-29). Smaller 80-mm (approximately 3-inch) *mini discs* typically use either that smaller form factor or are surrounded by clear material to be the same physical size as a standard disc to better fit in optical disc drives. Because the track starts at the center of the disc and the track just stops when it reaches an outer edge of the disc, optical discs theoretically can be made into a variety of sizes and shapes—such as a heart, an irregular shape, or a hockey-rink shape appropriate for *business card CDs*—but an ongoing patent battle has resulted in these custom shapes not being available by any CD or DVD manufacturer at the present time.

One of the biggest advantages of optical discs is their large capacity. Standard-sized CD discs normally hold 700 MB (though some hold 650 MB), standard-sized DVD discs hold 4.7 GB, and standard-sized BD discs hold 25 GB. To further increase capacity, many discs are available as *dual-layer discs* (also called *double-layer discs*) that store data in two layers on a single side of the disc, so the capacity is approximately doubled. Discs can also be *double sided*, which doubles the capacity; however, the disc must be turned over to access the second side. Double-sided discs are most often used with movies and other prerecorded content, such as to store a *widescreen version* of a movie on one side of a DVD disc and a *standard version* on the other side. Small optical discs have a smaller storage capacity than their larger counterparts: typically, single-layer, single-sided 3-inch mini CD, DVD, and BD discs hold about 200 MB, 1.4 GB, and 7.5 GB, respectively, and business-card-sized CD and DVD discs hold about 50 MB and 325 MB, respectively.

TIP

Blu-ray Discs containing *4K* (*Ultra HD*) movies became available in 2013.

As with magnetic disks, researchers are continually working to increase the capacity of optical discs without increasing their physical size. For instance, the new BD standard (*BDXL*), which uses more layers to boost capacity, supports capacities up to 128 GB, large enough to support *4K* (*Ultra HD*) versions of movies.

>CD disc. A low capacity (typically 700 MB) optical disc that is often used to deliver music and software, as well as to store user data. **>DVD disc.** A medium capacity (typically 4.7 GB or 8.5 GB) optical disc that is often used to deliver software and movies, as well as to store user data. **>Blu-ray Disc (BD).** A high-capacity (typically 25 GB or 50 GB) disc that is often used to deliver high-definition movies, as well as to store user data.

Courtesy Adobe

STANDARD 120 MM (4.7 INCH) SIZED DISC

Copyright © 2015 Cengage Learning®

MINI 80 MM (3.1 INCH) SIZED DISC

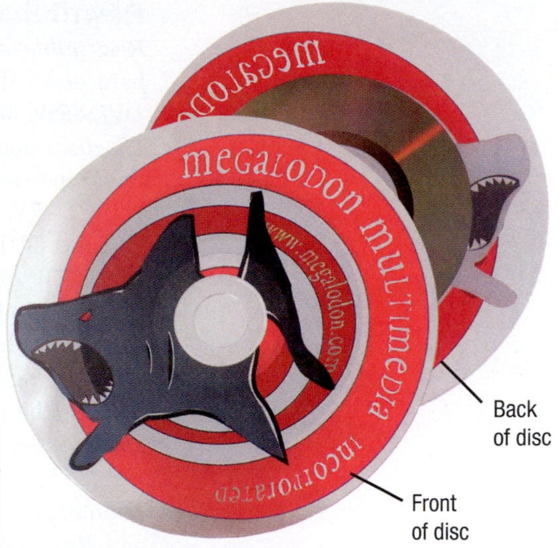

Courtesy Megaladon

MINI 80 MM (3.1 INCH) SIZED DISC (with a clear background to be standard size)

FIGURE 2-29
Optical discs are available in a variety of sizes, appearances, and capacities.

Read-Only Discs: CD-ROM, DVD-ROM, and BD-ROM Discs

CD-ROM (*compact disc read-only memory*) *discs* and *DVD-ROM* (*digital versatile disc read-only memory*) *discs* are *read-only optical discs* that come prerecorded with commercial products, such as software programs, clip art and other types of graphics collections, music, and movies. For high-definition content (such as feature films), *BD-ROM* (*Blu-ray Disc read-only memory*) *discs* are available. There are also additional read-only disc formats for specific gaming devices, such as the proprietary discs used with the Wii, Xbox, and PlayStation gaming consoles. The data on a read-only disc cannot be erased, changed, or added to because the pits that are molded into the surface of the disc when the disc is produced are permanent.

Recordable Discs: CD-R, DVD-R, DVD+R, and BD-R Discs

Recordable optical discs (also sometimes called *write-once discs*) can be written to, but the discs cannot be erased and reused. Recordable CDs are referred to as *CD-R discs*. Single-layer recordable DVDs are called either *DVD-R discs* or *DVD+R discs*, depending on the standard being used, and dual-layer recordable DVDs are called *DVD+R DL* and *DVD-R DL discs*. Recordable BD discs are also available in single-layer, dual-layer, and XL discs (*BD-R discs*, *BD-R DL discs*, and *BD-R XL*, respectively). The capacities of recordable optical discs are the same as the read-only formats. Recordable optical discs are written to using an appropriate optical drive, such as a *CD-R drive* for CD-R discs or a *DVD-R drive* for DVD-R discs, although optical drives are usually *downward-compatible*, meaning that they can be used with lower formats, such as using a DVD-R drive to burn a CD-R disc.

Recordable CDs are commonly used for backing up files, sending large files to others, and creating custom music CDs (for example, from MP3 files legally downloaded from the Internet or from songs located on a music album purchased on CD). DVD-Rs can be used for similar purposes when more storage space is needed, such as for backing up large files and for storing home movies, digital photos, and other multimedia files. BD-R discs can be used when an even greater amount of storage is needed, such as very large backups or high-definition multimedia files. Because of their widespread use of CDs and DVDs, most personal computers today come with an internal optical drive; one exception is netbooks, which typically do not include an optical drive. An *external optical drive* that connects via a USB port (see Figure 2-30) can be used with these computers whenever an optical drive is temporarily needed.

FIGURE 2-30
External optical drives. Can be connected as needed, typically via a USB port, such as to the netbook shown here.

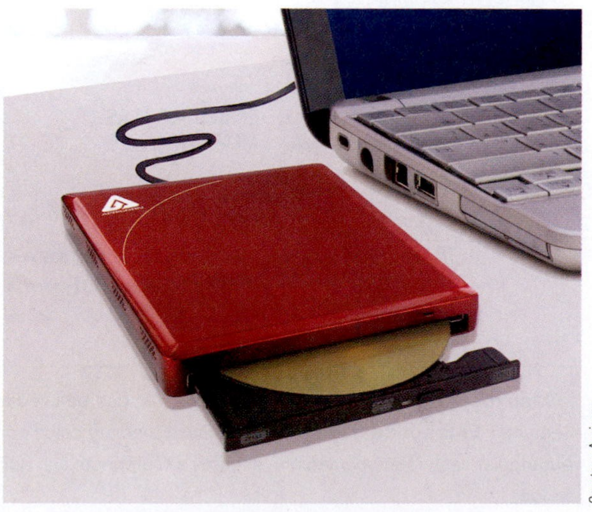
Courtesy Apricorn

Rewritable Discs: CD-RW, DVD-RW, DVD+RW, and BD-RE Discs

Rewritable optical discs can be written to, erased, and overwritten just like magnetic hard disks. The most common types of rewritable optical media are *CD-RW*, *DVD-RW*, *DVD+RW*, and *BD-RE discs*; BD-RE discs are also available as dual-layer discs (*BD-RE DL discs* and XL discs (*BD-RE XL*)). The capacities of rewritable discs are the same as their read-only and recordable counterparts.

CD-RW discs can be written to using a *CD-RW drive* and can be read by most CD and DVD drives. DVD-RW and DVD+RW discs are recorded using a *DVD-RW* or *DVD+RW drive*, respectively, and can be read by most DVD drives. BD-RE discs are recorded and read by *rewritable Blu-ray Disc drives*. Instead of permanently altering the surface of the disc, rewritable optical discs use *phase change* technology and a heating and cooling process to make the appropriate areas of the disc nonreflective to function as pits (the reflective areas function as lands). To erase the disc, the heating and cooling process is used to change the areas to be erased back to their original reflective state. The capacities of rewritable discs are the same as their read-only and recordable counterparts.

Rewritable optical discs are used for many of the same purposes as recordable optical discs. However, they are particularly appropriate for situations in which data written to the optical disc can be erased at a later time so the disc can be reused (such as for transferring large files from one computer to another or temporarily storing TV shows recorded on your computer that you will later watch using your living room TV and DVD player).

Flash Memory Storage Systems

Flash memory is a chip-based storage medium that represents data using electrons. It is used in a variety of storage systems, such as the SSDs and hybrid hard drives already discussed and the additional storage systems discussed next. Flash memory media are rewritable and have a longer expected life than magnetic media, though they are typically more expensive per MB.

Courtesy Apple Inc.; Courtesy of SanDisk Corporation

MEDIA TABLET
Contains 64 GB of embedded flash memory.

EMBEDDED FLASH MEMORY

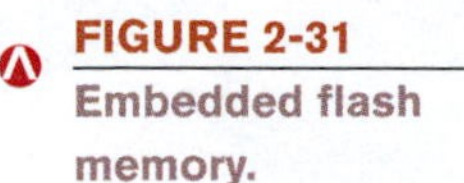

FIGURE 2-31
Embedded flash memory.

Embedded Flash Memory

Embedded flash memory refers to flash memory chips embedded into products. Because flash memory media are physically very small, they are increasingly being embedded directly into a variety of consumer products—such as portable digital media players, digital cameras, handheld gaming devices, media tablets, mobile phones, and even sunglasses and wristwatches—to provide built-in data storage. While embedded flash memory can take the form of small SSDs or memory cards, it is increasingly being implemented with small stand-alone chips, such as the one shown in Figure 2-31.

Flash Memory Cards and Readers

One of the most common types of flash memory media is the **flash memory card**—a small card containing one or more flash memory chips, a controller chip, other electrical components, and metal contacts to connect the card to the device or reader being used. Flash memory cards are available in a variety of formats, such as *CompactFlash* (*CF*), *Secure Digital* (*SD*), *Secure Digital High Capacity* (*SDHC*), *xD Picture Card* (*xD*),

>**Flash memory.** Nonvolatile memory chips that can be used for storage by the computer or user; can be built into a computer or a storage medium. >**Embedded flash memory.** Flash memory chips embedded into products, such as consumer devices. >**Flash memory card.** A small, rectangular flash memory medium, such as a CompactFlash (CF) or Secure Digital (SD) card; often used with digital cameras and other portable devices.

XQD, and *Memory Stick* (*MS*) (see Figure 2-32). These formats are not interchangeable, so the type of flash memory card used with a device is determined by the type of flash media card that device can accept. Flash memory cards come in a variety of capacities; one of the most widely used types of flash memory media—Secure Digital (SD)—is also available in different physical sizes. For instance, standard-sized SD cards are often used in digital cameras and computers; the smaller *miniSD* and *microSD* (about one-half and one-quarter the size of a standard SD card, respectively) are designed to be used with mobile phones and other mobile devices. When more storage space is needed, higher capacity *miniSDHC* and *microSDHC* cards can be used; adapters can be used with mobile-sized flash memory cards in order to use them in a larger, but compatible, memory card slot (such as the *microSD-to-SD adapter* shown in Figure 2-32).

FIGURE 2-32
Some flash memory cards, readers, and adapters.

Flash memory cards are the most common type of storage media for digital cameras, portable digital media players, mobile phones, and other portable devices. Flash memory cards can also be used to store data for a personal computer, as needed, as well as to transfer data from a portable device (such as a digital camera, media tablet, or smartphone) to a computer. Consequently, most personal computers and many mobile devices today come with a *flash memory card reader* capable of reading flash memory cards; an external flash memory card reader (such as the ones shown in Figure 2-32) that typically connects via a USB port can be used when the destination device doesn't have a built-in reader. The capacity of flash memory cards is continually growing and is up to 256 GB at the present time with even higher capacity cards expected in the near future.

USB Flash Drives

USB flash drives (sometimes called *USB flash memory drives*, *thumb drives*, or *jump drives*) consist of flash memory media integrated into a self-contained unit that connects to a computer or other device via a standard USB port and is powered via that port. USB flash drives are designed to be very small and very portable (see Figure 2-33). In order to be appropriate for a wide variety of applications, USB flash drives are available in a variety of configurations—including those designed to be attached to backpacks or worn on a lanyard around the neck; those built into pens, necklaces, wristbands, or wristwatches; those thin enough to fit easily into a wallet; and those made into custom shapes for promotional or novelty purposes. To read from or write to a USB flash drive, you just plug it into a USB port. If the USB flash drive is being used with a computer, it

FIGURE 2-33
USB flash drives.
Are often used to store data and transfer files from one device to another.

>**USB flash drive.** A small storage device that plugs into a USB port and contains flash memory media.

HOW IT WORKS

More Storage for Your Tablet

For many users, the internal storage capacity (typically less than 64 GB) of a media tablet just doesn't cut it. While minimizing the built-in flash memory of these devices is necessary to keep the cost and size down, many users want more. While some users connect their device to a desktop or notebook computer to transfer content (movies, music, photos, and more) to and from their mobile devices, there is another, easier option—going wireless.

A number of new storage products are emerging that connect directly to your devices (including tablets, smartphones, and computers) via Wi-Fi so you don't have to worry about cables or how to connect to a device that doesn't have a USB port. Sizes and configurations vary widely—from the 32 GB Kingston SSD *Wi-Drive* to the 1TB Seagate *Wireless Plus* magnetic hard drive (shown in the accompanying photograph) that can hold up to 500 high-definition movies. These hard drives typically have built-in Wi-Fi capabilities and data can be transferred in both directions (such as to stream a movie from the hard drive to your tablet or smart TV, or to transfer photos or videos taken with your phone to the hard drive). Unlike cloud storage, these hard drives can be used in locations (such as while traveling in a car or an airplane) where you don't have Internet access and, because these hard drives are accessed locally, you can play back full HD video without any buffering or stuttering. The Wireless Plus even allows up to eight devices to access the hard drive at one time and it has a 10-hour battery life, which makes it even more useful while you are on the go.

To use one of these wireless hard drives with your mobile device, you need to download the appropriate media app from your app store (such as the *App Store* for iPad and iPhone users or *Google Play* for Andriod users) and launch it. You should then have quick and easy wireless access to the hard drive. You can also connect these hard drives to your computer, if you wish, via Wi-Fi.

While carrying an extra device with you may be inconvenient at times, until 1 TB mobile devices come along, it works.

Courtesy of Seagate Technology LLC

> **TIP**
>
> To avoid data loss when you are finished using a USB flash drive on a Windows PC, first double-click the *Safely Remove Hardware and Eject Media icon* in the system tray, and then stop the drive before removing it from the USB port.

is assigned a drive letter by the computer, just like any other type of attached drive, and files can be read from or written to the USB flash drive until it is unplugged from the USB port. The capacity of most USB flash drives today ranges from about 4 GB to 1 TB. USB flash drive use has become commonplace for individuals, students, and employees to transport files from one computer to another, as well as to quickly back up important files.

In addition to providing basic data storage and data portability, USB flash drives can provide additional capabilities. For instance, they can be used to lock a computer and to issue Web site passwords; they can also include *biometric features*—such as a built-in fingerprint reader—to allow only authorized individuals access to the data stored on the USB flash drive or to the computer with which the USB flash drive is being used.

Other Types of Storage Systems

Two additional types of storage systems that are frequently used are *network/cloud storage systems* and *smart cards*. Types of emerging storage systems are discussed in Chapter 8.

Network and Cloud Storage Systems

Remote storage refers to using a storage device that is not connected directly to the user's computer; instead, the device is accessed through a local network or through the Internet. Using a remote storage device via a local network (referred to as **network storage**) works in much the same way as using *local storage* (the storage devices and media that are directly attached to the user's computer). To read data from or write data to a remote storage device (such as a hard drive being accessed via a network), the user just selects it (see Figure 2-34) and then performs the necessary tasks in the normal fashion. Network storage is common in businesses; it is also used by individuals with home networks for backup purposes or to share files with another computer in the home. For a look at how you can use network storage to extend the storage or your media tablet and other device with limited internal storage, see the How It Works box.

Remote storage services accessed via the Internet are often referred to as **cloud storage** or **online storage**. Cloud storage can be provided either as a stand-alone service or as part of a cloud computing service. For instance, most cloud applications (such as *Google Docs*, the *Flickr* photo sharing service, and social networking sites like *Facebook*) provide online storage for these services. There are also sites whose primary objective is to allow users to store documents online, such as *Box*, *Dropbox*, *Google Drive*, or Microsoft *SkyDrive* (see Figure 2-34). As shown in this figure, cloud storage sites are typically password protected and allow users to share uploaded files or folders with others via an e-mail message or a link to the shared content. The ability to store documents online (or "in the cloud") is growing in importance as more and more applications are becoming cloud based and as individuals increasingly want access to their files from anywhere with any Internet-enabled device, such as a portable computer, media tablet, or smartphone.

Cloud storage is also increasingly being used for backup purposes. In fact, some sites have an automatic backup option that uploads the files in designated folders on your computer to your cloud account at regular specified intervals, as long as your computer is connected to the Internet. Many Web sites providing cloud storage to individuals offer the service for free (for instance, SkyDrive gives each

TIP

If you choose to sync your files with your cloud storage account, any files you delete from your cloud account will typically be deleted from the cloud folder on your computer, so be sure to back up those files to another location first if you will still need them.

FIGURE 2-34
Cloud storage.

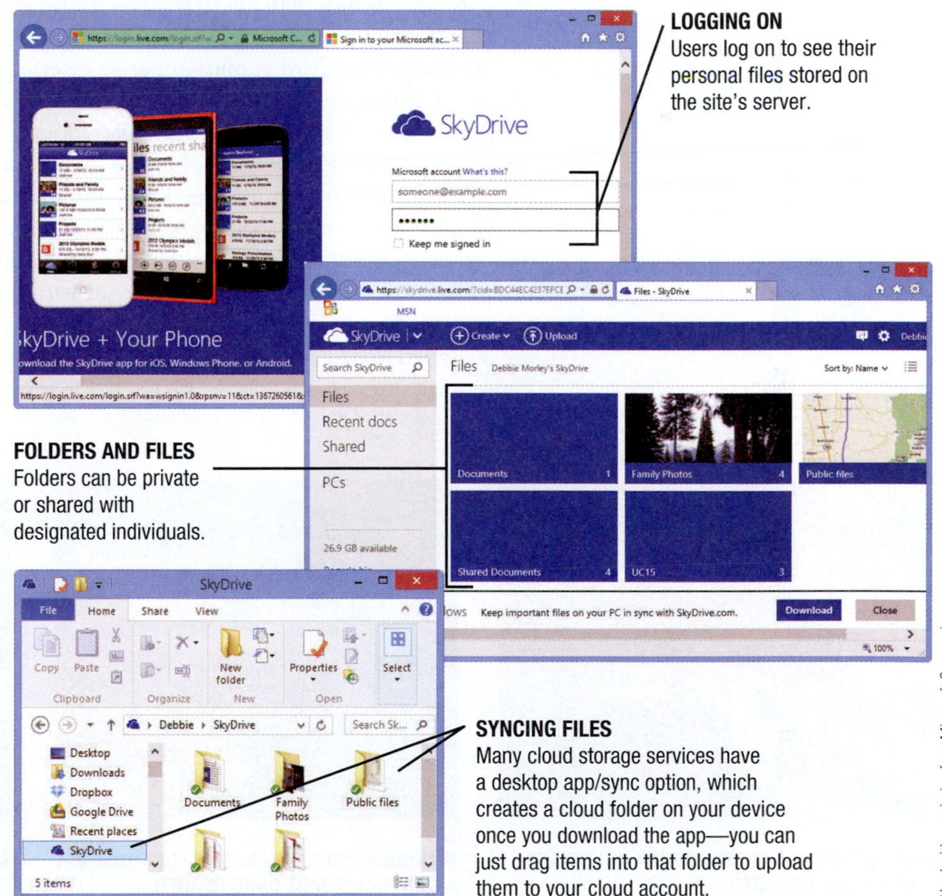

>**Network storage.** Refers to using a storage device that is accessed through a local network. >**Cloud storage.** Refers to using a storage device that is accessed via the Internet; also called **online storage**.

individual 7 GB of free storage space); others charge a small fee, such as $10 per month for 25 to 100 GB of storage space.

TIP

The SIM cards used with mobile phones today are a special type of smart card.

Smart Cards

A **smart card** is a credit card-sized piece of plastic that has built-in computer circuitry and components—typically a processor, memory, and storage. Smart cards today store a relatively small amount of data (typically 64 KB or less) that can be used for payment or identification purposes. For example, a smart card can store a prepaid amount of *digital cash*, which can be used for purchases at a smart card-enabled vending machine or computer—the amount of cash available on the card is reduced each time the card is used. Smart cards are also commonly used worldwide for national and student ID cards (for example, Bangladesh recently implemented a smart card ID program for workers headed to other countries to prevent employment fraud), credit and debit cards, and cards that store identification data for accessing facilities or computer networks. Although these applications have used conventional *magnetic stripe* technology in the past, the processor integrated into a smart card can perform computations—such as to authenticate the card, encrypt the data on the card to protect its integrity, and secure it against unauthorized access—and can allow data to be added to the card or modified on the card as needed. Smart cards can also store the identifying data needed to accelerate airport security and to link patients to the *electronic health records* (*EHRs*) increasingly being used by hospitals.

To use a smart card, it must either be inserted into a *smart card reader* (if it is the type of card that requires contact) or placed close to a smart card reader (if it is a *contactless* card) built into or attached to a computer, door lock, ATM machine, vending machine, or other device (see Figure 2-35). Once a smart card has been verified by the card reader, the transaction—such as making a purchase or unlocking a door—can be completed. For an even higher level of security, some smart cards today store biometric data in the card and use that data to authenticate the card's user before authorizing the smart card transaction (biometrics, encryption, and other security procedures are discussed in more detail in Chapter 4). An emerging trend is the use of *mobile smart cards*—smart microSD cards that are designed to add smart card capabilities to any computer or mobile device that contains a microSD slot.

FIGURE 2-35
Smart cards.

LOGGING ONTO A COMPUTER VIA A CONTACT SMART CARD READER

MAKING A VENDING MACHINE PURCHASE VIA A CONTACT SMART CARD READER

ACCESSING A SECURE FACILITY VIA A CONTACTLESS SMART CARD READER

Photos by HID Global Corporation

>**Smart card.** A credit card-sized piece of plastic containing a chip and other circuitry that can store data.

Evaluating Your Storage Alternatives

Storage alternatives are often compared by weighing a number of product characteristics and cost factors. Some of these product characteristics include speed, compatibility, storage capacity, convenience, and the portability of the media. Keep in mind that each storage alternative normally involves trade-offs. For instance, most systems with removable media are slower than those with fixed media, and external drives are typically slower than internal ones. Although cost is a factor when comparing similar devices, it is often not the most compelling reason to choose a particular technology. For instance, although USB flash drives are relatively expensive per GB compared with optical discs and external hard drives, many users find them essential for transferring files between work and home or for taking presentations or other files with them as they travel. For drives that use a USB interface, the type of USB port is also significant. For example, storage devices that connect via a USB port adhering to the original *USB 1.0* standard transfer data at up to 12 *Mbps* (millions of bits per second)—*USB 2.0* devices are about 40 times faster and *USB 3.0* devices are about 10 times as fast as USB 2.0 devices.

With so many different storage alternatives available, it is a good idea to research which devices and media are most appropriate for your personal situation. In general, most computer users today need a hard drive (for storing programs and data), some type of optical drive (for installing programs, backing up files, and sharing files with others), and a flash memory card reader (for transferring photos, music, and other content between portable devices and the computer). Virtually all computer users today will also need at least one convenient free USB port to be used to connect external hard drives, USB flash drives, printers, mice, and other USB-based hardware, as well as USB devices that contain storage media, such as digital cameras and portable digital media players.

TIP

If you will be transferring music, digital photos, and other multimedia data on a regular basis between your devices, be sure to select and use the flash memory media that are compatible with those devices.

COMMUNICATIONS HARDWARE

Most computers today include *communications hardware* to enable the user to communicate with others over a network or the Internet. The type of **communications device** used depends on the device being used (desktop computer, notebook computer, or media tablet, for instance), as well as the *communication standard* (such as *Ethernet* for wired networks, *Wi-Fi* or *WiMAX* for wireless networks, *Bluetooth* for short-range wireless connections, or a *cellular standard* for a mobile phone) being used. Common communications devices include *network adapters*, *modems*, *cabling*, and other networking hardware as discussed next; emerging communications standards and devices are discussed in more detail in Chapter 8.

ASK THE EXPERT

Courtesy McDonald's Corporation

Jim Sappington, Senior Vice President, Chief Information Officer, McDonald's Corporation

How has the emergence of Wi-Fi affected companies such as McDonald's?

The emergence of Wi-Fi has fueled our customers' expectations of having immediate access to information. Our customers and employees love the convenience and relevance of McDonald's "hotspots." Through wireless connectivity, Wi-Fi is creating a more modern and relevant experience for our customers. The ability to conveniently check e-mail, Facebook, or browse the Internet can be a deciding factor in choosing a place to eat—a trend we don't see ending anytime soon.

>**Communications device.** A piece of hardware that allows one device to communicate with other devices via a network or the Internet.

Network Adapters and Modems

A **network adapter**, also called a **network interface card** (**NIC**) when it is in the form of an expansion card, is used to connect a computer to a network. A **modem** (derived from the terms *modulate* and *demodulate*) is used to connect a computer to a network over telephone lines. However, in everyday use, the term *modem* is also used to refer to any device that connects a computer to a *broadband Internet connection*, such as a *cable modem* used for cable Internet service. As a result, there are a number of different types of modems in use today, each matching a particular type of Internet connection, such as *conventional dial-up*, *cable*, *fixed wireless*, and *DSL* (the types of Internet services that utilize these modems are discussed in detail in Chapter 3).

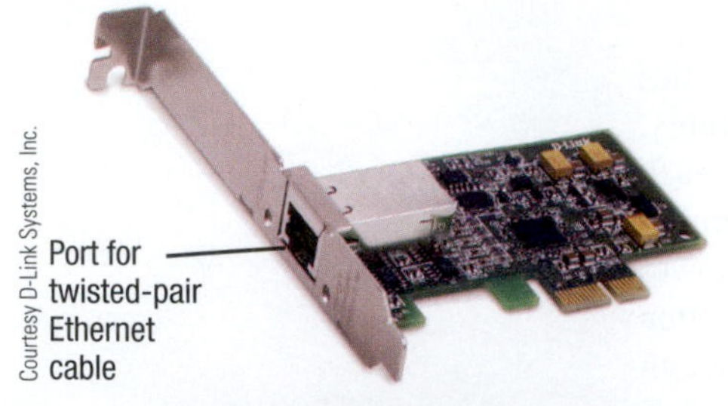
Courtesy D-Link Systems, Inc.
Port for twisted-pair Ethernet cable

PCI EXPRESS GIGABIT ETHERNET ADAPTERS FOR DESKTOP COMPUTERS

Courtesy NETGEAR
Connects to USB port

MICRO USB WI-FI ADAPTERS FOR DESKTOP OR NOTEBOOK COMPUTERS

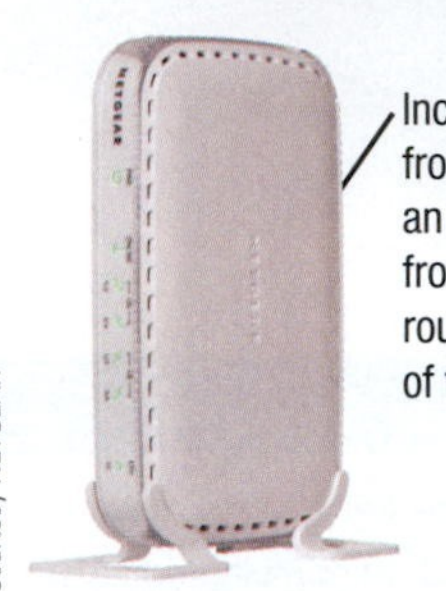
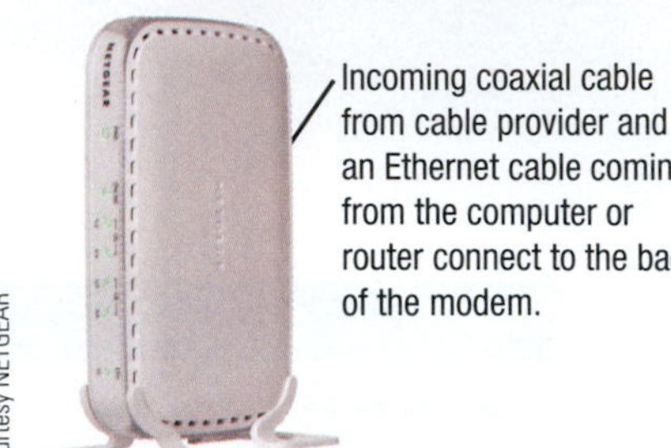
Courtesy NETGEAR
Incoming coaxial cable from cable provider and an Ethernet cable coming from the computer or router connect to the back of the modem.

ETHERNET CABLE MODEMS

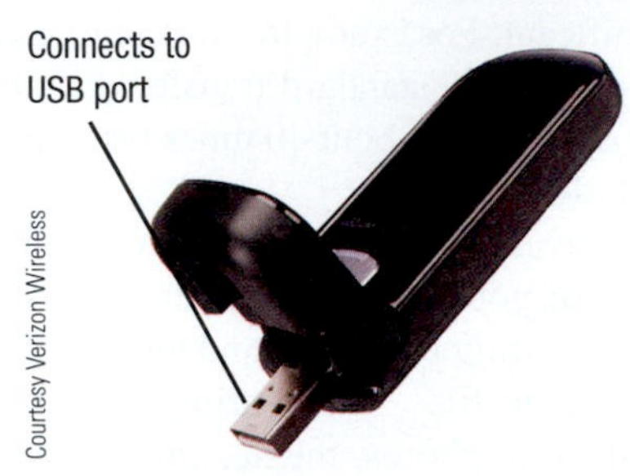
Courtesy Verizon Wireless
Connects to USB port

USB 4G CELLULAR MODEMS FOR DESKTOP OR NOTEBOOK COMPUTERS

FIGURE 2-36
Network adapters and modems.

Most computers and mobile devices today come with a network adapter and/or modem built in to the device, typically as a network interface card (NIC), as a chip included on the motherboard, or as circuitry built directly into the CPU. The type of network adapter and modem used depends on the type of network (such as Ethernet, Wi-Fi, or cellular) and Internet access being used. For instance, to connect a computer to an Ethernet network, an Ethernet network adapter is used. To connect a computer to a cable Internet connection, typically both a cable modem (such as the NETGEAR modem shown in Figure 2-36) and an Ethernet network adapter are used. To connect a computer to a cellular, Wi-Fi, or WiMAX network, a cellular, Wi-Fi, or WiMAX network adapter, respectively, is used. Some examples of network adapters and modems are shown in Figure 2-36. When a new type of networking connectivity is needed (such as wanting to use a newer Wi-Fi standard or switching to a different type of Internet connection), an external adapter or modem can be obtained. The network adapter or modem needs to be for the appropriate type of network, as well as support the type of networking media (such as the type of networking cable or *wireless signal*) being used.

FIGURE 2-37
Wireless routers.
Enable devices to connect to each other and to an Internet connection.

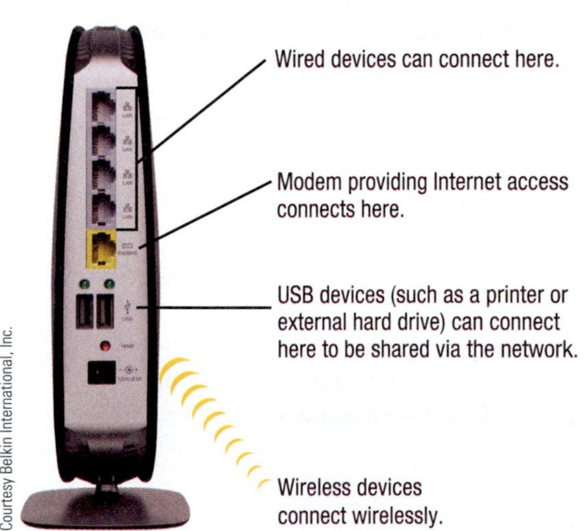
Courtesy Belkin International, Inc.
Wired devices can connect here.
Modem providing Internet access connects here.
USB devices (such as a printer or external hard drive) can connect here to be shared via the network.
Wireless devices connect wirelessly.

Other Networking Hardware

To connect the devices on a network together, typically a central device is needed. This device can be a *hub*, *switch*, or *router* for wired networks; networks designed for wireless users typically use a *wireless access point* or *wireless router* instead (a Wi-Fi wireless router is shown in Figure 2-37). To increase the range of a network, *repeaters*, *range extenders*, and *antennas* can be used. To connect the wired devices to the network, *cabling* (typically *twisted-pair*, *coaxial cable*, or *fiber-optic cable*) is used.

>Network adapter. A network interface, such as an expansion card or external network adapter. **> Network interface card (NIC).** An expansion card through which a computer can connect to a network. **>Modem.** A device that enables a computer to communicate over analog networking media, such as to connect that computer to the Internet via telephone lines.

SOFTWARE BASICS

As discussed in Chapter 1, all computers need an operating system (such as Windows, Linux, or Mac OS) in order to function. The operating system is used to boot the computer, control its operation, and allow users to run application software or apps—the programs used to perform specific tasks on the computer. Although features and capabilities vary from program to program, most software programs today use similar basic features and operations. While covering how to use specific software programs is beyond the scope of this book, an understanding of basic software concepts and operations is an important part of becoming familiar with computers. An overview of booting a computer, using the Windows user interface, and some common types of application software was included in Chapter 1. Other important software basics—including software ownership rights, installation options, common software commands, and the concept of *file management*— are discussed in the remainder of this chapter.

TIP

Ownership rights for original creative works are referred to as *copyrights* and are discussed in more detail in Chapter 6.

Software Ownership Rights

The *ownership rights* of a software program specify the allowable use of that program. After a software program is developed, the developer (typically an individual or an organization) holds the ownership rights for that program and decides whether or not the program can be sold, shared with others, or otherwise distributed. When a software program is purchased, the buyer is not actually buying the software. Instead, the buyer is acquiring a **software license** that permits him or her to use the software. This license specifies the conditions under which a buyer can use the software, such as the number of computers on which it may be installed. In fact, many software licenses permit the software to be installed on only one computer. In addition to being included in printed form inside the packaging of most software programs, the licensing agreement is usually displayed and must be agreed to by the end user at the beginning of the software installation process.

There are four basic categories of software: *commercial software* (software that is developed and sold for a profit), *shareware* (software that is distributed on the honor system), *freeware* (software that is given away free of charge), and *public domain software* (software that is not copyrighted). In addition, software that falls into any of these four categories can also be *open source software*, which are programs made up of source code that is available to the general public. An open source program can be copyrighted, but individuals and businesses are allowed to modify the program and redistribute it—the only restrictions are that changes must be shared with the open source community and the original copyright notice must remain intact.

ASK THE EXPERT

Courtesy Tucows

Stacy Reed, Software Librarian and Editor, Tucows

Why should an individual or business pay for shareware?

Ethically and legally, it's the right thing to do. Software publishers offer trial versions of their software for free because it allows users ample opportunity to evaluate the software to ensure it meets their needs. After the trial period expires, you should either uninstall the software or pay for the full version so the developer can continue to provide technical support and product enhancements. Some software may disable or cripple functionality after the trial has ended; others may remind you to pay by displaying nag screens, watermarks, or advertisements. Though there are sneaky ways to circumvent licensing, doing so is copyright infringement and it is illegal. Conviction could include jail time and/or fines for each infringement and, if you or your company willfully profit from stolen software, you stand to face maximum penalties—in some countries, that could mean hundreds of thousands of dollars in fines per instance or several years in prison.

> **Software license.** An agreement, either included in a software package or displayed on the screen when the software is installed or launched, that specifies the conditions under which the program can be used.

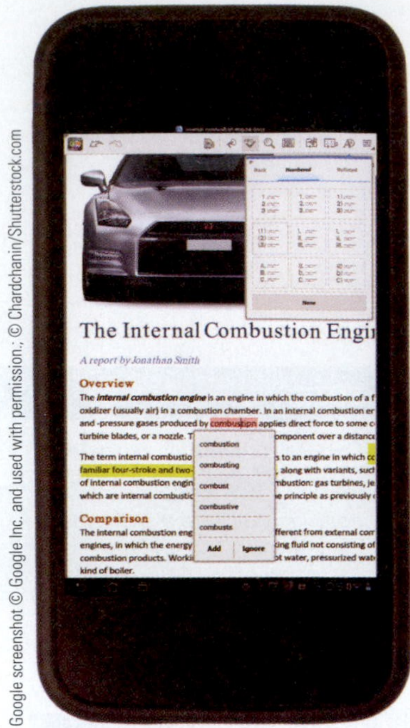

FIGURE 2-38
Mobile software.

Desktop vs. Mobile Software

Notebook computers, tablet computers, netbooks, and other portable computers typically run the same application software as desktop computers. However, smartphones and other mobile devices (such as iPads and other media tablets) typically require *mobile software* (also called *mobile apps*); that is, software specifically designed for a specific type of smartphone or other mobile device, such as an Apple or Android device. A wide range of apps is available today. For instance, there are mobile versions of popular programs like Word or PowerPoint, games and other entertainment apps, business and reference tools, calendars and communications apps, location-based apps, financial and banking apps, health and fitness apps, Web browsers, and more. In fact, there are approximately one million Android apps available via the *Google Play* store and the Apple *App Store*, which has over 900,000 apps, hit its 50 billionth download in mid 2013. In addition to having a more compact, efficient appearance than *desktop software*, many mobile apps include features for easier data input, such as an on-screen keyboard, a phrase list, voice input capabilities, or handwriting recognition capabilities. Some mobile apps are designed to be compatible with popular desktop software, such as *Microsoft Office* or *Google Docs* (see Figure 2-38), to facilitate sharing documents between the two platforms. Many apps are available free of charge or for a minimal cost, such as 99 cents. For a look at a new trend in creating mobile apps (*mobile app builders*), see the Trend box.

Installed vs. Cloud Software

Software also differs in how it is accessed by the end user. It can be **installed software** that is installed on and run from the end user's computer (or installed on and run from a network server in a network setting), or it can be **cloud software** that is accessed by the end user over the Internet. Installed desktop software can be purchased in physical form (such as on a CD or DVD) or downloaded from the Internet (see Figure 2-39); mobile software is almost always downloaded from an *app store*, such as the App Store or Google Play. Cloud software (also referred to as *Software as a Service* (*SaaS*) and *cloudware*) is delivered on demand via the Web to wherever the user is at the moment, provided he or she has an Internet connection (and has paid to use the software if a payment is required). The use of cloud software is growing rapidly and research firm IDC estimates that the the enterprise SaaS market alone will exceed $67 billion by 2016. Typically, documents created using cloud software are stored online.

FIGURE 2-39
Installed software.
Is often purchased via the Internet.

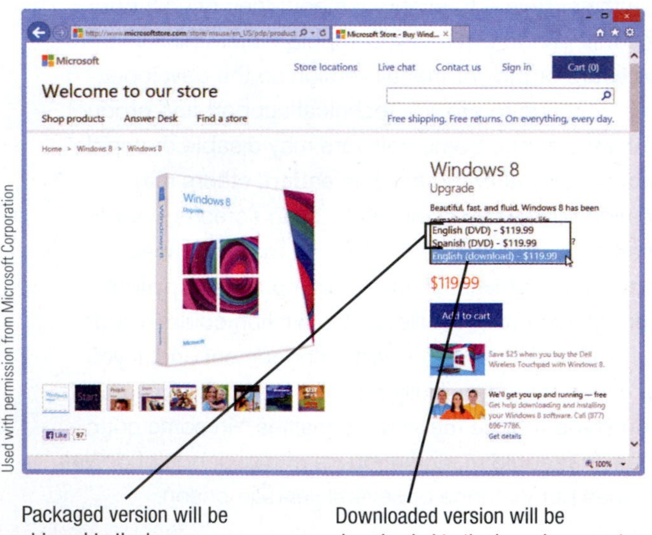

One advantage of cloud software over installed software is that the programs and your documents can be accessed from any computer with an Internet connection regardless of the type of computer or operating system used; some can also be accessed via a smartphone, media tablet, or other type of Internet-enabled mobile devices. This makes cloud software especially appropriate for applications like shared scheduling and collaboration applications that are time-critical because documents and other data can be shared regardless of an individual's location or device. Some potential disadvantages of cloud software are that online applications tend to run more slowly than applications stored on a local hard drive, that many online applications have a limit regarding the file size of the documents you create, and that the cost may eventually exceed the cost of buying a similar installed software program. In addition, you cannot access cloud software and your

>Installed software. Software that must be installed on a computer in order to be used. **>Cloud software.** Software that is delivered on demand via the Web; also referred to as *Software as a Service* (*SaaS*) and *cloudware*.

TREND

Mobile App Builders

Have an idea for a mobile app? Now you can create it easily using the growing collection of mobile app development tools. Many of the tools are designed to be code-free, though some allow you to download the finished source code so you can control it and modify it as needed. Commonly, the finished app can be adapted to deploy on the various platforms you want to use, such as iOS and Android mobile apps, a Web app, and a desktop app.

While some of these *mobile app builders* are not appropriate for complex apps, most can be used to quickly and easily write personal apps, simple games, or apps that coordinate with your Web site. One example of a Web-based mobile app builder is *appsbar* (see the accompanying illustration), which allows you to build and publish apps for free. To get started, you select the type of app you want to create (such as business, music, or social networking) and then you create the pages of the app, previewing and modifying them as you go along (a wizard helps you add buttons, forms, maps, and more). Once you are satisfied with your app, appsbar tests it to identify any potential problems that would prevent publication. Once the app meets publication requirements, it is then submitted to the major app markets for publication. While appsbar only works with apps that will be available for free, it is an easy way for individuals and small businesses to get their apps created and available to the world.

Courtesy of APPSBAR

data if the server on which they reside goes down or if you are in a location with no Internet access, such as while traveling or in a rural area. To eliminate this last concern, a growing trend is for online applications to also function, at least in part, offline. For instance, Google Docs includes offline capabilities so that users can access the Google Docs applications and their documents locally on their computers, when needed. Edits are stored locally on the computer when a user is offline and, when the user reconnects to the Internet, the changes are synchronized with the documents stored on the Google Docs servers.

Common Software Commands

Application programs today have a number of concepts and commands in common. For example, many programs allow you to create a new document (such as a letter, drawing, house plan, or greeting card) and then *save* it. To reopen the document at a later time, you use the *open* command; to print the document, you use the *print* command. One of the greatest advantages of using software instead of paper and pencil to create documents is that you can make changes without erasing or recreating the entire document because the document is created in RAM and then saved on a storage medium, instead of being created directly on paper. Consequently, the document can be retrieved, modified, saved, and printed as many times as needed. Many programs also include tools to help you as you create documents, such as a *spelling and grammar check* feature to locate and help you correct possible spelling and grammar errors in your documents, and a *styles* feature that allows you to apply a common format to a series of documents or a group of similar headings within a single document.

Toolbars, Menus, Keyboard Shortcuts, and the Ribbon

Most commands in an application program are issued through *menus*, *keyboard shortcuts*, or *command buttons* located on a *toolbar* or *Ribbon*. As shown in Figure 1-10 in Chapter 1, the *menu bar* appears at the top of many windows and contains text-based lists (menus),

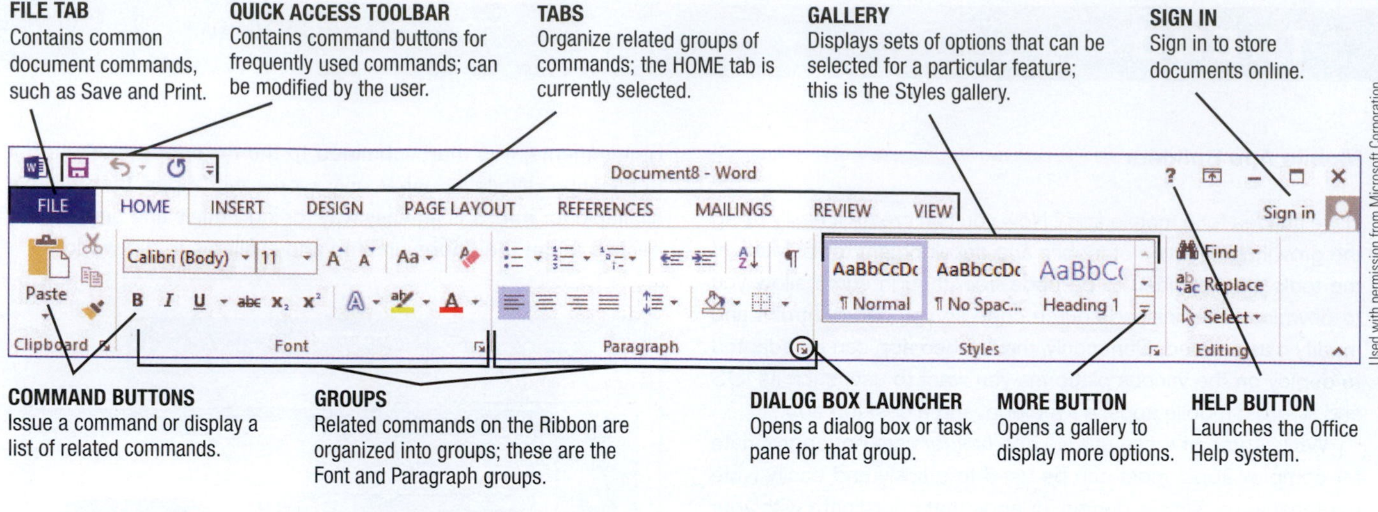
FILE TAB
Contains common document commands, such as Save and Print.
QUICK ACCESS TOOLBAR
Contains command buttons for frequently used commands; can be modified by the user.
TABS
Organize related groups of commands; the HOME tab is currently selected.
GALLERY
Displays sets of options that can be selected for a particular feature; this is the Styles gallery.
SIGN IN
Sign in to store documents online.
Document8 - Word
FILE
HOME
INSERT
DESIGN
PAGE LAYOUT
REFERENCES
MAILINGS
REVIEW
VIEW
Sign in
Paste
Calibri (Body)
11
AaBbCcDc
AaBbCcDc
AaBbC
¶ Normal
¶ No Spac...
Heading 1
Find
Replace
Select
Clipboard
Font
Paragraph
Styles
Editing
COMMAND BUTTONS
Issue a command or display a list of related commands.
GROUPS
Related commands on the Ribbon are organized into groups; these are the Font and Paragraph groups.
DIALOG BOX LAUNCHER
Opens a dialog box or task pane for that group.
MORE BUTTON
Opens a gallery to display more options.
HELP BUTTON
Launches the Office Help system.

FIGURE 2-40
The Microsoft Office Ribbon.

TIP

Right-click a command button on the Ribbon and select *Add to Quick Access Toolbar* to add that command to your Quick Access toolbar.

which provide access to commands that can be selected to perform actions in that program. Many programs also have toolbars—sets of *icons* or command buttons that are clicked with the mouse to issue commands. *Keyboard shortcuts* are key combinations that correspond to specific commands, such as Ctrl+S for the Save command (this keyboard shortcut is issued by holding down the Ctrl key and pressing the S key).

The **Ribbon** is a tool in recent versions of Microsoft Office starting with Office 2007. The Ribbon (see Figure 2-40) consists of *tabs*, which contain *groups* of related commands for the program being used. For convenience, most programs have a *HOME tab* that contains the most frequently used commands in that program. In addition to the standard Ribbon tabs that are available whenever the program is open, additional *contextual tabs* are displayed as needed, depending on the action being taken. For instance, selecting a picture or other graphic in Word displays the *PICTURE TOOLS tab* that contains commands you might use to edit a picture, such as to crop, resize, rotate, or recolor it. Clicking a command button on the Ribbon either carries out that command or displays a *gallery* of choices from which the user can select the desired action. The *FILE tab* replaces the Microsoft Office Button and the File menu used in older versions of Office and opens the *Backstage view*, which contains commands commonly used with all documents, such as to open, save, print, send, and publish a document.

Editing a Document

Editing a document refers to changing the content of the document, such as adding or deleting text. Most application programs that allow text editing have an *insertion point* that looks like a blinking vertical line on the screen and shows where the next change will be made to the document currently displayed on the screen. To insert text, just start typing and the text will appear at the insertion point location. To delete text, press the Delete key to delete one character to the right of the insertion point or press the Backspace key to delete one character to the left of the insertion point. If the insertion point is not in the proper location for the edit, it must be moved to the appropriate location in the document by using the arrow keys on the keyboard or by pointing and clicking with the mouse. To select an object or block of text, click the object or drag the mouse over the text. Usually, once an object or some text is selected, it can be manipulated, such as to be moved, deleted, copied, or *formatted*.

>**Ribbon.** A feature found in recent versions of Microsoft Office that uses tabs to organize groups of related commands. >**Editing.** Changing the content of a document, such as inserting or deleting words.

Formatting a Document

While editing changes the actual content of a document, **formatting** changes the appearance of the document. One common type of formatting is changing the appearance of selected text in a document. You can change the *font face* or *typeface* (a named collection of text characters that share a common design, such as Calibri or Times New Roman), *font size* (which is measured in *points*), *font style* (such as bold, italic, or underline), and *font color*. Other common types of formatting include changing the *line spacing* or *margins* of a document; adding *page numbers*; and adding *shading* or *borders* to a paragraph, image, or other item.

TIP

When selecting font size in a document, 72 points equals one-inch-tall text.

Working with Files and Folders

It is important for software users to understand the concepts of *files* and *folders* and be able to work with them quickly and efficiently. Anything (such as a program, letter, digital photograph, or song) stored on a storage medium is referred to as a **file**. Data files are also often called *documents*. When a document that was just created (such as a memo or letter in a word processing program) is saved, it is stored as a new file on the storage medium designated by the user. During the storage process, the user is required to give the file a name, called a **filename**; that filename is used to retrieve the file later.

To keep files organized, related documents are often stored in **folders** (also called *directories*) located on the storage medium. For example, one folder might contain memos to business associates while another might hold a set of budgets (see Figure 2-41). To organize files further, you can create *subfolders* (*subdirectories*) within a folder. For instance, you might create a subfolder within the *Budgets* subfolder for each fiscal year. In Figure 2-41, both *Budgets* and *Memos* are subfolders inside the *My Documents* folder; the *Budgets* subfolder contains two additional subfolders (*Current year* and *Next year*).

File management programs (such as *Windows Explorer* and *File Explorer* for Windows users) allow you to perform file management tasks, such as searching for a file or viewing the files stored on a storage medium, as well as copying, moving, deleting, and renaming folders and files. For instance, you can see the folders and files stored on your hard drive, USB flash drive, or any other storage medium by clicking the appropriate letter or name for that medium in the File Explorer window, and then selecting the desired folder if needed. You can copy a file or folder by selecting the desired item, issuing the *Copy* command (such as by using the File Explorer's Home tab or by pressing Ctrl+C), displaying the location where you want the copy to go, and then issuing the *Paste* command (such as by pressing Ctrl+V). You can delete an item by selecting it and pressing the Delete key on the keyboard. You can also create new folders (click the *New Folder* button shown in Figure 2-41 or right-click inside a folder and select *New Folder*), and you can move files from one folder to another as needed.

TIP

To *restore* (undelete) a file or folder deleted from your computer's hard drive, open your computer's *Recycle Bin* and restore the file to its original location.

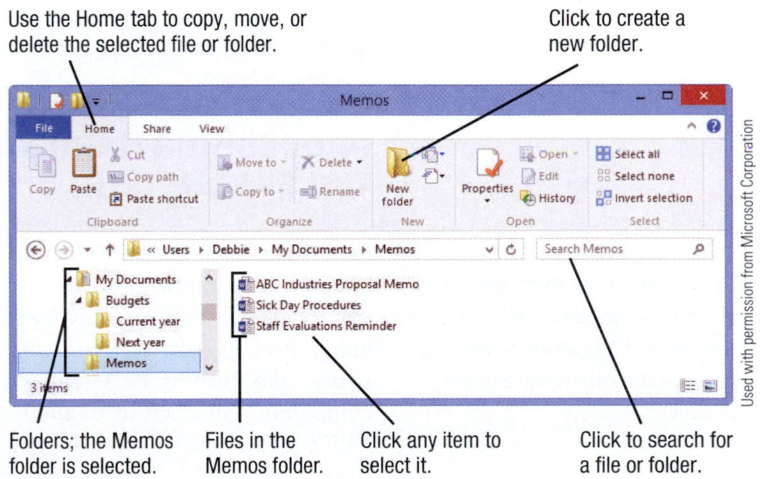

FIGURE 2-41
File Explorer.

>**Formatting.** Changing the appearance of a document, such as changing the margins or font size. >**File.** Something stored on a storage medium, such as a program, a document, or an image. >**Filename.** A name given to a file by the user; it is used to retrieve the file at a later time. >**Folder.** A named place on a storage medium into which the user can place files in order to keep the files stored on that medium organized.

SUMMARY

DIGITAL DATA REPRESENTATION

Chapter Objective 1: Understand how data is represented to a computer.

Data must be represented appropriately (using 0s and 1s) in order to be used by a computer. A single 0 or 1 is called a **bit**; 8 bits together is referred to as a **byte**. A **kilobyte** (**KB**) equals 1,024 bytes, a **megabyte** (**MB**) is about 1 million bytes, a **gigabyte** (**GB**) is about 1 billion bytes, a **terabyte** (**TB**) is about 1 trillion bytes, and a **petabyte** (**PB**) is about 1,000 terabytes. To represent numbers and do mathematical operations, computers use the **binary numbering system** instead of the **decimal numbering system** that people are accustomed to using; for representing characters, coding systems, such as **ASCII** (**American Standard Code for Information Interchange**) and **Unicode**, are used.

INPUT HARDWARE

Chapter Objective 2: Identify several types of input devices and explain their functions.

An **input device** is any piece of hardware that is used to input data into a computer. Two of the most common input devices are the **keyboard** and **mouse**. While a keyboard is designed to enter input by pressing keys, a mouse is a **pointing device** that is used to select objects and commands on the screen. Another common pointing device is the **stylus** (also called an *electronic pen* or *digital pen*), which is used with computers and other devices to input handwritten data and select options. **Touch screens** are touched with the finger to select commands or provide input. Other pointing devices include *graphics tablets*, *gaming devices*, *buttons* and *wheels*, and *touch pads*.

To input data that already exists, a **scanner** (either *flatbed* or *handheld*) can be used. When used with *optical character recognition* (*OCR*) software, the computer system recognizes scanned text characters and stores them digitally so they can be manipulated by the computer. If not, the scanned data is input as an image. Other types of scanners or readers include **barcode readers** (used to read **barcodes** on consumer products and other objects), **RFID readers** (used to read **RFID tags**), and **biometric readers** (used to read *biometric data* belonging to an individual). **Digital cameras** (both *still* and *video cameras*) are used to capture images in digital form and record images on some type of digital storage medium. *Microphones*, *headsets*, and *MIDI* devices can be used for input, as well.

PROCESSING HARDWARE AND OTHER HARDWARE INSIDE THE SYSTEM UNIT

Chapter Objective 3: Explain the functions of the primary hardware components found inside the system unit, namely the motherboard, the CPU, and memory.

Processing hardware is located inside the **system unit**, along with other important components. The **motherboard** or *system board* is the main *circuit board* for a personal computer. All hardware used with a computer must be connected to the motherboard, either directly or via a *port*. Every computer has at least one **processor** (usually a **central processing unit** (**CPU**))—also called a **microprocessor** when referring to personal computers—attached to its motherboard that performs the processing for the computer. CPUs today are often **multi-core CPUs**, such as **dual-core** (two cores) and **quad-core** (four cores) **CPUs**. The **graphics processing unit** (**GPU**) performs the processing needed to display images on the screen; it can be located on the motherboard, inside the CPU, or on a video graphics board. The term *memory* is usually used to refer to **random access memory** (**RAM**)—groups of chips that are also attached to the motherboard and provide temporary storage for the computer to use. RAM is **volatile**, so all data in RAM is erased when the power to the computer goes off. Other types of memory used by the computer include *cache memory*, *registers*, *read-only memory* (*ROM*), and *flash memory*.

OUTPUT HARDWARE

Output devices present the result of processing to the user, usually in the form of a **display device**—also called a **monitor** or a **display screen**—or a **printer**. The common types of monitors are *CRTs* and *flat-panel displays*. Monitors form images using **pixels**, and the number of pixels used to display an image determines the *screen resolution*.

The most widely used printers today are **laser printers** (the standard for business documents) and **ink-jet printers** (used in homes and for inexpensive color printouts). Specialty printers, such as *photo printers*, *barcode printers*, and *portable printers* are also available. Other output devices include **computer speakers**, *headphones*, and *headsets*.

Chapter Objective 4:
List several output devices and explain their functions.

STORAGE HARDWARE

Storage systems make it possible to save programs, data, and processing results for later use. All storage systems have a **storage medium** (which holds the data) and a **storage device** (which reads from and writes to the medium). Data is stored either *magnetically* or *optically* on most storage media. Storage devices can be *internal*, *external*, or *remote*. They are typically assigned letters by the computer, which are used to identify the drive.

Chapter Objective 5:
Understand the difference between storage and memory, as well as between a storage device and a storage medium.

Hard drives are used in most computers to store programs and data. Conventional hard drives are **magnetic hard drives**; a newer type of hard drive that uses flash memory instead of magnetic disks is the **solid-state drive** (**SSD**). Hard drives can be *internal* or *external*; external hard drives can be full-sized or portable. **Hybrid hard drives** are a combination of a magnetic hard drive and an SSD, designed to provide increased performance while reducing power consumption.

Optical discs (such as **CD discs**, **DVD discs**, and **Blu-ray Discs** (**BDs**)) store data *optically* using laser beams, and they can store data much more densely than magnetic disk technology. Optical discs can be *read-only*, *recordable*, or *rewritable*.

Chapter Objective 6:
Name several types of storage systems and explain the circumstances under which they are typically used.

Flash memory storage systems use nonvolatile memory chips and so have no moving parts. **Flash memory cards** are commonly used with a variety of devices, and come in many formats. **USB flash drives** connect to a computer via a USB port and are a convenient method of transferring files between computers; **embedded flash memory** is built directly into a product. Other possibilities for storage include **network storage**—storage accessed through the Internet (**cloud storage** or **online storage**) or another network—and **smart cards** (that contain small amounts of data, such as digital cash or personal data, for a variety of purposes).

COMMUNICATIONS HARDWARE

Communications devices, such as **network adapters**, **network interface cards** (**NICs**), and **modems**, enable users to communicate with others over a network. Other networking hardware (such as *hubs*, *routers*, *wireless access points*, and *cabling*) is used to connect the devices on a network; *repeaters*, *range extenders*, and *antennas* can be used to extend the range of a network.

Chapter Objective 7:
Describe the purpose of communications hardware.

SOFTWARE BASICS

A program's **software license** explains the allowable use of the program. Most software today is *commercial*, *shareware*, *freeware*, or *public domain* and can be either **installed software** or **cloud software**. **Editing** refers to making changes to the content of a document; **formatting** refers to changing its appearance. To issue commands to a software program, user interface tools such as *menus*, *keyboard shortcuts*, *toolbar buttons*, and the **Ribbon** are used. Anything stored on a storage medium (such as a document, a program, or an image) is called a **file** and is given an identifying **filename** by the user. To keep files organized, related documents can be stored inside **folders**. Users can open, copy, move, and delete files and folders, using a *file management program*, such as *File Explorer.*

Chapter Objective 8:
Understand basic software concepts and commands.

REVIEW ACTIVITIES

KEY TERM MATCHING

a. byte

b. central processing unit (CPU)

c. file

d. keyboard

e. laser printer

f. modem

g. motherboard

h. optical disc

i. software license

j. USB flash drive

Instructions: Match each key term on the left with the definition on the right that best describes it.

1. ________ A device that enables a computer to communicate over analog networking media, such as to connect that computer to the Internet via telephone lines.
2. ________ A group of 8 bits.
3. ________ An agreement, either included in a software package or displayed on the screen when the software is installed or launched, that specifies the conditions under which a buyer of the program can use it.
4. ________ An input device containing numerous keys that can be used to input letters, numbers, and other symbols.
5. ________ An output device that uses toner powder and technology similar to that of a photocopier to produce images on paper.
6. ________ A small storage device that plugs into a USB port and contains flash memory media.
7. ________ A type of storage medium read from and written to using a laser beam.
8. ________ Something stored on a storage medium, such as a program, a document, or an image.
9. ________ The chip located on the motherboard of a computer that performs most of the processing for a computer.
10. ________ The main circuit board of a computer, located inside the system unit, to which all computer system components connect.

SELF-QUIZ

Instructions: Circle **T** if the statement is true, **F** if the statement is false, or write the best answer in the space provided. **Answers for the self-quiz are located in the References and Resources Guide at the end of the book.**

1. **T F** A storage medium that can hold 256 GB can hold about 256 billion characters.
2. **T F** A mouse is an example of a pointing device.
3. **T F** An ink-jet printer normally produces a better image than a laser printer.
4. **T F** A hybrid hard drive contains both magnetic hard disks and optical discs.
5. **T F** Changing the font size in a document is an example of a formatting operation.
6. A(n) ________ can be used to convert flat printed documents, such as a drawing or photograph, into digital form.
7. A CPU with four separate processing cores is referred to as a(n) ________ CPU.
8. Secure Digital (SD) cards are one type of ________ storage medium.
9. Files can be stored inside ________ to keep them organized.
10. Match each input device to its input application, and write the corresponding number in the blank to the left of the input application.

a. ________ Pen-based computing	**1.** Keyboard
b. ________ Consumer kiosk	**2.** Stylus
c. ________ Text-based data entry	**3.** RFID tag
d. ________ Secure facility access	**4.** Biometric reader
e. ________ Tracking goods	**5.** Touch screen

EXERCISES

1. Number the following terms from 1 to 6 to indicate their size from smallest to largest.

   a. ________ Petabyte b. ________ Kilobyte c. ________ Byte

   d. ________ Terabyte e. ________ Gigabyte f. ________ Megabyte

2. For the following list of hardware devices, write the appropriate abbreviation (I, P, O, S, or C) in the space provided to indicate whether each device is used for input (I), processing (P), output (O), storage (S), or communications (C).

   a. ________ Biometric reader f. ________ Display device

   b. ________ Modem g. ________ USB flash drive

   c. ________ Speaker h. ________ Microphone

   d. ________ Photo printer i. ________ Hard drive

   e. ________ CPU j. ________Network adapter

3. Supply the missing words to complete the following statements.

   a. The smallest piece of data (a 0 or 1) that can be represented by a computer is called a(n) __________.

   b. ________ is an international coding system that can be used to represent text-based data in any written language.

   c. A(n) ________ optical disc can hold either 25 GB or 50 GB and is designed for high-definition content, such as movies.

4. List one personal or business application that you believe is more appropriate for a dot-matrix printer, instead of another type of printer, and explain why.

5. Which types of storage media would be appropriate for someone who needed to exchange large (5 MB to 75 MB) files with another person? List at least three different types, stating under what specific conditions each might be the most appropriate type of storage medium to use.

DISCUSSION QUESTIONS

1. People send their digital photos over the Internet in different ways. For instance, digital photos are often e-mailed to others, posted on Facebook pages and other social networking sites, and uploaded to a server (such as one belonging to Snapfish, Walmart, or Costco) in order to order prints, enlargements, or other photo-based items. If you have ever sent photos over the Internet, were you concerned about someone other than the intended recipient intercepting or viewing your photo files? If you have ever uploaded files to a processing service for printing, did you check to see if the Web server being used was secure? Should individuals be concerned about sending their personal photos over the Internet? There are a number of advantages, but are there privacy risks, as well?

2. The choice of an appropriate input device for a product is often based on both the type of device being used and the target market for that device. For instance, a device targeted to college students and one targeted to older individuals may use different input methods. Suppose that you are developing a device to be used primarily for Internet access that will be marketed to senior citizens. What type of hardware would you select as the primary input device? Why? What are the advantages and disadvantages of your selected input device? How could the disadvantages be minimized?

PROJECTS

HOT TOPICS

1. **Tablet Storage** As discussed in the chapter How It Works box, most media tablets have a limited amount of storage and limited ways to connect additional storage.

   For this project, select a specific media tablet and determine how much internal storage it has and what type of connectivity it offers. Next, determine two options for expanding the storage for that tablet and locate at least one product for each option. Determine the amount of storage that can be added via your options, as well as the cost. If you owned this tablet, would you want to use either of your selected options for additional storage? Why or why not? At the conclusion of your research, prepare a one- to two-page summary of your findings and opinions and submit it to your instructor.

SHORT ANSWER/ RESEARCH

2. **Adding Memory** Adding additional RAM to a computer is one of the most common computer upgrades. Before purchasing additional memory, however, it is important to make sure that the purchased memory is compatible with the computer.

   For this project, select a computer (such as your own computer, a school computer, or a computer at a local store) and then determine (by looking at the computer or asking an appropriate individual—such as a lab aide in the school computer lab or a salesperson at the local store) the following: manufacturer and model number, CPU, current amount of memory, total memory slots, and the number of available memory slots. (If you look inside the computer, be sure to unplug the power cord first and do not touch any components inside the system unit.) Once you have the necessary information, call a local store or use your information and a memory supplier's Web site to determine the appropriate type of memory needed for your selected computer. What choices do you have in terms of capacity and configuration? Can you add just one memory module, or do you have to add memory in pairs? Can you keep the old memory modules, or do they have to be removed? At the conclusion of your research, prepare a one-page summary of your findings and recommendations and submit it to your instructor.

HANDS ON

3. **Keyboarding Speed Test** Although voice and other alternative means of input are emerging, most data input today is still performed via the keyboard. Proper keyboarding technique can help increase speed and accuracy. Online keyboarding tests can help to evaluate your keyboarding ability.

   For this project, find a site (such as **Typingtest.com**) that offers a free online typing test and test your keyboarding speed and accuracy. At the conclusion of the test, rate your keyboarding ability and determine whether a keyboarding course or tutor program, or just keyboarding practice, will help you improve if your score is not at least 20 correct words per minute (cwpm). Take the test one more time to see if your speed improves now that you are familiar with how the test works. If your speed is fast, but accuracy is low, take the test once more, concentrating on accuracy. If you still test less than 20 cwpm, locate a free typing tutor program or Web site and evaluate it to see if it would help you to increase your speed and accuracy. At the conclusion of this task, prepare a short summary of your experience, including the typing test site used and your best score.

ETHICS IN ACTION

4. **Lost and Found** Portable computers, mobile phones, USB flash drives, and other portable devices are lost all the time today. They can be dropped out of a pocket or bag, inadvertently left on a table, and so forth. If the owner has identifying information (name, phone number, or e-mail address, for instance) printed on the device, the individual who finds the device can attempt to return it to the owner. But what if there is no identifying information clearly visible on the device? Should the finder look at the contents of the device to try to determine the owner? If the device is lost in a location where there is a responsible party (such as an airplane or a restaurant), the finder can turn over the device to that authority (such as a flight attendant or manager). But, is it ethical for the responsible party to look at the contents in order to identify the owner? If you lost a device, would you want someone to look at the contents to try to determine your identity? Why or why not? Is looking at the contents on a found device ever ethical? Should it be illegal?

   For this project, form an opinion about the ethical ramifications of lost devices and be prepared to discuss your position (in class, via an online class discussion group, in a class chat room, or via a class blog, depending on your instructor's directions). You may also be asked to write a short paper expressing your opinion.

PRESENTATION/ DEMONSTRATION

5. **Compatibility** Files created by an application program are often upward compatible but not always downward compatible. For example, a *.docx* file created in Microsoft Word 2013 cannot be opened in Word 2003, but a Word 2003 *.doc* file can be opened in Word 2013. Most application programs feature a "Save As" option that can be used to save a file in one of several formats.

   For this project, select one widely used software program and determine in which file formats the program can save documents and which file formats the program can open. If there are older versions of the program, are documents upward compatible? Downward compatible? Research *plain text* (*.txt*), *Portable Document Format* (*PDF*), and the *Rich Text Format* (*.rtf*) and determine their purposes, the programs in which documents saved in each of these formats can be opened, and any disadvantages for using these formats. Have you ever experienced a compatibility problem with a document? If so, how was the problem resolved? Share your findings with the class in the form of a short presentation. The presentation should not exceed 10 minutes and should make use of one or more presentation aids, such as a whiteboard, handouts, or a computer-based slide presentation (your instructor may provide additional requirements). You may also be asked to submit a summary of the presentation to your instructor.

BALANCING ACT

6. **Should Printers Be Used to Print Body Parts?** Researchers are looking to ink-jet printers and 3D printers as a means to create body parts for the future. Possibilities include replacement joints, blood vessels, skin, muscles, organs, and implants. Instead of ink, these printers print with living cells. It is looking like this technology will eventually be feasible, but do we want it to be? Possible advantages include quickly printing new skin on a burn victim's wound, printing new organs on demand when needed, and creating custom implants from the patient's cells so they won't be as easily rejected. But what about the ethical ramifications, such as selling manufactured body parts or surgeons adding extra body parts (such as an extra ear or arm) on demand for a fashion statement or for added productivity? What if replacing our failing organs as needed leads to virtual immortality—will we end up an overcrowded society of essentially mutants? Or are the potential benefits worth the risks?

   Pick a side on this issue, form an opinion and gather supporting evidence, and be prepared to discuss and defend your position in a classroom debate or in a 1–2 page paper, depending on your instructor's directions.

expert insight on...

Hardware

Courtesy Logitech

Logitech

Ali Moayer is a Senior Director at Logitech and the head of engineering for developing audio/ video communications products for the Unified Communications (UC) market. He has worked on many innovative ideas and designs, many of which were patented. Ali has more than 30 years of engineering experience and holds a Bachelor of Science degree in Electrical Engineering and an MBA in Technology Management.

A conversation with ALI MOAYER

Senior Director of Engineering, Logitech

“*. . . augmented reality technology in products such as Google Glass will transform the way we look at the world and interact with each other.*”

My Background . . .

I have been curious about technology from my childhood. I studied engineering and technology management in college and then started my career developing office messaging and networking equipment. I am now a Senior Director of Engineering in the Logitech for Business (LFB) group. As part of my responsibilities, I am the head of engineering for developing audio/video communications products for the Unified Communications (UC) market; my group also develops webcams and security cameras for the electronics retail market. Throughout my career, my college background, together with my work experiences developing medical imaging instruments, video cameras, and a wide variety of computer peripherals, has helped me be successful in the computer hardware industry. I also believe that my ability to understand electronics and consumer needs has been a contributing factor in my success in developing some of the best-in-class products for the PC peripheral market.

It's Important to Know . . .

The importance of input/output devices. Interface devices used with computers, such as audio/ video capture and playback control devices and human interface control devices like mice and touch screens, are essential for providing a good user experience. We will continue to see computer interfaces enhanced with voice and gesture recognition, as well as new interfaces evolving to enable the human-to-machine interface to be more natural and intuitive.

Hardware will continue to shrink in size while increasing in capabilities. Computation power and memory capacity in devices will continue to increase and hardware systems will have access to remote sensors and robots. In addition, expect to see products that accommodate organic shapes with forms that no longer have to be rigid.

Our interactions with smart devices will intensify. We will rely on smart devices to act as our intelligent personal assistant and we will start to expect much more from computers to relieve us from mundane tasks. In addition, augmented reality technology in products such as Google Glass will transform the way we look at the world and interact with each other. However, before wearable products become mainstream, the industry will need to break technology barriers in the areas of miniature electronics, very low energy devices, and wireless connectivity.

How I Use this Technology . . .

Like most people, I use computer systems for my personal life and, in fact, feel detached from our world if I don't have my smartphone next to me. I use audio/video communications tools, such as Skype and FaceTime, with my computing devices to enable me to have closer relationships with people around the world. I also use my smartphone to capture audio/video clips and pictures to share on social networking sites, as well as to read the latest news and conduct business over interactive Web sites. At home, I am starting to build electronic control systems that will be accessed with my phone to make my home smarter and more energy efficient, and I imagine that we will all have smart digital homes in the near future that will save us money and make our lives easier.

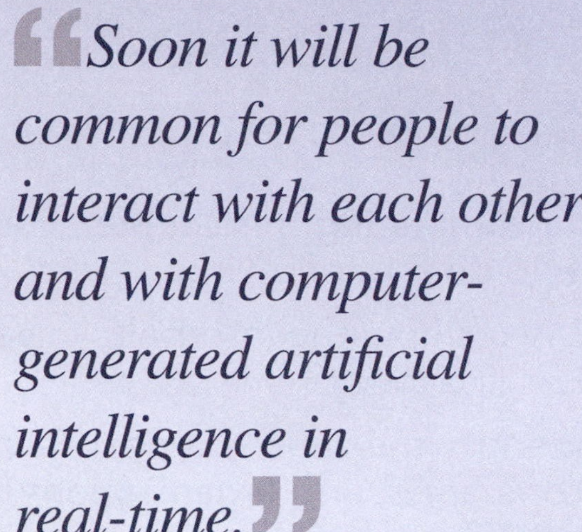
Soon it will be common for people to interact with each other and with computer-generated artificial intelligence in real-time.

What the Future Holds . . .

Electronic systems will continue to expand in many sectors, such as wearable electronics, mobile phones and personal computers, smart home and business appliances, robotics, and Internet servers. The intelligence and capabilities of these systems will grow rapidly and be challenged with being energy efficient, compact, and low cost. Audio, video, and control interfaces for home and business appliances will improve and Internet servers will provide analytic capabilities for making decisions and monitoring and controlling our environment, in addition to storing, searching, and exchanging data.

Another difference in the future will be in the intelligence and fluidity of the interactions between users and computers. The Internet initially provided access to stored data and services that were provided by large organizations. Now the majority of information is authored and shared by individuals but is still in a pre-recorded or stored form. Soon it will be common for people to interact with each other and with computer-generated artificial intelligence in real-time.

One ongoing risk for the future is privacy. Our personal information is now mostly in the form of digital records, and our lives are being tracked by electronic sensors and cameras all over the world. We all need to understand that our private data can be accessed easily by hackers and we should try our best to secure it with passwords, data encryption, and firewalls. We should also all be careful not to post sensitive information about our personal lives and our family members on social networking websites, and should become educated about the "social engineering" techniques that criminals are increasingly using. Unfortunately, hackers have become creative in manipulating people as the human interactions shift more toward electronic systems and we all should do what we can to protect ourselves.

My Advice to Students . . .

Participate in as many hands-on projects or internship programs that your time allows. This will help you to learn valuable problem-solving techniques, as well as retain the knowledge that you gain in school.

Discussion Question

Ali Moayer believes that we will rely on smart devices to act as our intelligent personal assistant and relieve us from mundane tasks in the near future. Think about the routine tasks that you need to do on a daily basis—which tasks could be performed by a smart device? Are there any tasks that you wouldn't feel comfortable trusting to that device? If so, what technological improvements would need to be made in order for you to assign those tasks to your device? Would a more natural and intuitive human-to-computer interface make a difference? Are there some routine tasks that you don't see ever being turned over to your computer? Be prepared to discuss your position (in class, via an online class discussion group, in a class chat room, or via a class blog, depending on your instructor's directions). You may also be asked to write a short paper expressing your opinion.

>For more information about Logitech, visit www.logitech.com.

chapter 3

The Internet and the World Wide Web

After completing this chapter, you will be able to do the following:

1. Discuss how the Internet evolved and what it is like today.
2. Identify the various types of individuals, companies, and organizations involved in the Internet community and explain their purposes.
3. Describe device and connection options for connecting to the Internet, as well as some considerations to keep in mind when selecting an ISP.
4. Understand how to search effectively for information on the Internet and how to cite Internet resources properly.
5. List several ways to communicate over the Internet, in addition to e-mail.
6. List several useful activities that can be performed via the Web.
7. Discuss censorship and privacy and how they are related to Internet use.

outline

OVERVIEW

With the prominence of the Internet in our personal and professional lives today, it is hard to believe that there was a time not too long ago that few people had even heard of the Internet, let alone used it. But technology is continually evolving and, in fact, it is only relatively recently that it has evolved enough to allow the use of multimedia applications—such as downloading music and movies, watching TV and videos, and playing multimedia interactive games—over the Internet to become everyday activities. Today, the Internet and the World Wide Web are household words, and, in many ways, they have redefined how people think about computers, communications, and the availability of news and information.

Despite the popularity of the Internet, however, many users cannot answer some important basic questions about it. What makes up the Internet? Is it the same thing as the World Wide Web? How did the Internet begin, and where is it heading? What is the most effective way to use the Internet to find specific information? This chapter addresses these types of questions and more.

Chapter 3 begins with a discussion of the evolution of the Internet, followed by a look at the many individuals, companies, and organizations that make up the Internet community. Next, the chapter covers different options for connecting to the Internet, including the types of devices, Internet connections, and ISPs that are available today. Then, one of the most important Internet skills you should acquire—efficient Internet searching—is discussed. To help you appreciate the wide spectrum of resources and activities available over the Internet, we also take a brief look at some of the most common applications available via the Internet. The chapter closes with a discussion of a few of the important societal issues that apply to Internet use. ■

EVOLUTION OF THE INTERNET

The **Internet** is a worldwide collection of separate, but interconnected, networks accessed daily by millions of people using a variety of devices to obtain information, disseminate information, access entertainment, or communicate with others. While *Internet* has become a household word only during the past two decades or so, it has actually operated in one form or another for much longer than that.

From ARPANET to Internet2

The roots of the Internet began with an experimental project called *ARPANET*. The Internet we know today is the result of the evolution of ARPANET and the creation of the *World Wide Web (WWW)*.

>**Internet.** The largest and most well-known computer network, linking millions of computers all over the world.

ARPANET

The U.S. Department of Defense *Advanced Research Projects Agency* (*ARPA*) created **ARPANET** in 1969. One objective of the ARPANET project was to create a computer network that would allow researchers located in different places to communicate with each other. Another objective was to build a computer network capable of sending or receiving data over a variety of paths to ensure that network communications could continue even if part of the network was destroyed, such as in a nuclear attack or by a natural disaster.

Initially, ARPANET connected four supercomputers and enabled researchers at a few dozen academic institutions to communicate with each other and with government agencies. As the project grew during the next decade, students were granted access to ARPANET as hundreds of college and university networks were connected to it. These networks consisted of a mixture of different computers so, over the years, protocols were developed for tying this mix of computers and networks together, for transferring data over the network, and for ensuring that data was transferred intact. Additional networks soon connected to ARPANET, and this *internet*—or network of networks—eventually evolved into the present day *Internet*.

The Internet infrastructure today can be used for a variety of purposes, such as researching topics of interest; exchanging e-mail and other messages; participating in videoconferences and making telephone calls; downloading software, music, and movies; purchasing goods and services; watching TV and video online; accessing computers remotely; and sharing files with others. Most of these activities are available through the primary Internet resource—the *World Wide Web* (*WWW*).

The World Wide Web

In its early years, the Internet was used primarily by the government, scientists, and educational institutions. Despite its popularity in academia and with government researchers, the Internet went virtually unnoticed by the public and the business community for over two decades because 1) it required a computer and 2) it was hard to use (see the left image in Figure 3-1). As always, however, computer and networking technology improved and new applications quickly followed. Then, in 1989, a researcher named *Tim Berners-Lee* proposed the idea of the **World Wide Web** (**WWW**). He envisioned the World Wide Web as a way to organize information in the form of pages linked together through selectable text or images (which are today's hyperlinks) on the screen. Although the introduction of Web pages did not replace all other Internet resources (such as e-mail and collections of downloadable files), it became a popular way for researchers to provide written information to others.

In 1993, a group of professors and their students at the University of Illinois *National Center for Supercomputing Applications* (*NCSA*) released the *Mosaic* Web browser. Soon after,

FIGURE 3-1
Using the Internet: Back in the "old days" versus now.

EARLY 1990s
Even at the beginning of the 1990s, using the Internet for most people meant learning how to work with a cryptic sequence of commands. Virtually all information was text-based.

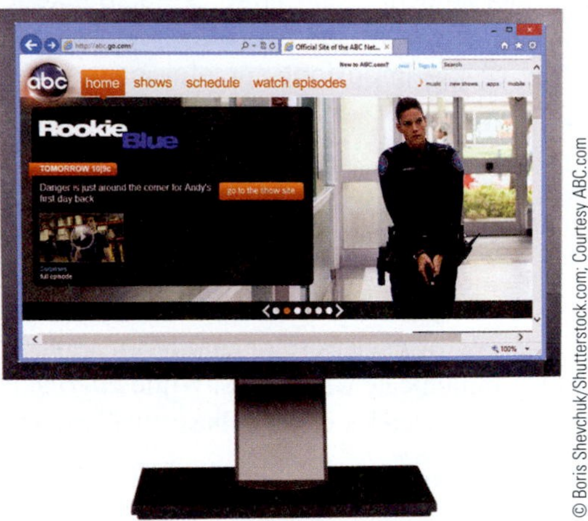

TODAY
Today's Web organizes much of the Internet's content into easy-to-read pages that can contain text, graphics, animation, video, and interactive content that users access via hyperlinks.

>**ARPANET.** The predecessor to the Internet, named after the Advanced Research Projects Agency (ARPA), which sponsored its development.
>**World Wide Web (WWW).** The collection of Web pages available through the Internet.

use of the World Wide Web began to increase dramatically because Mosaic's *graphical user interface* (*GUI*) and its ability to display images on Web pages made using the World Wide Web both easier and more fun than in the past. Today's Web pages are a true multimedia, interactive experience (see the *Rookie Blue* Web site shown in Figure 3-1). They can contain text, graphics, animation, sound, video, and three-dimensional virtual reality objects.

A growing number of today's Web-based applications and services are referred to as *Web 2.0* applications. Although there is no precise definition, Web 2.0 generally refers to applications and services that use the Web as a platform to deliver rich applications that enable people to collaborate, socialize, and share information online. Some Web 2.0 applications (such as cloud computing) have been discussed in previous chapters; others (such as *social networking sites*, *RSS feeds*, *podcasts*, *blogs*, and *wikis*) are covered later in this chapter.

Although the Web is only part of the Internet, it is by far the most widely used part. Today, most companies regard their use of the Internet and their World Wide Web presence as indispensable competitive business tools, and many individuals view the Internet—and especially the Web—as a vital research, communications, and entertainment medium.

One remarkable characteristic of both the Internet and World Wide Web is that they are not owned by any person or business, and no single person, business, or organization is in charge. Web pages are developed by individuals and organizations, and are hosted on Web servers owned by individuals, schools, businesses, or other entities. Each network connected to the Internet is privately owned and managed individually by that network's administrator, and the primary infrastructure that makes up the *Internet backbone* is typically owned by communications companies, such as telephone and cable companies. In addition, the computers and other devices used to access the Internet belong to individuals or organizations. So, while individual components of the Internet are owned by individuals and organizations, the Internet as a whole has no owner or network administrator. The closest the Internet comes to having a governing body is a group of organizations that are involved with issues such as establishing the protocols used on the Internet, making recommendations for changes, and encouraging cooperation between and coordinating communications among the networks connected to the Internet.

ASK THE EXPERT

Courtesy McDonald's Corporation

Jim Sappington, Senior Vice President, Chief Information Officer, McDonald's Corporation

How important is it for a business to have a Web site today if it doesn't sell products and services online?

At McDonald's, our online presence is about extending the McDonald's experience to our customers. Our Web sites (www.aboutmcdonalds.com and www.mcdonalds.com) allow our customers another channel to engage with our brand without ever entering a restaurant. Through our Web sites, customers can find promotions and nutritional information on all of our products. On the Open for Discussion blog, customers are talking about McDonald's corporate sustainability efforts. In addition, customers can download podcasts about food safety.

For McDonald's, our Web sites allow us the opportunity to connect with our customers on topics that are important to them and in the way that they want to connect. In addition, in some parts of the world you can order off the menu located on our Web site and have it delivered to your door. As our customers demand even more convenience and control over the "ordering process," this may become even more prevalent, and mobile, in the future.

Internet2

Internet2 is a consortium of researchers, educators, and technology leaders from industry, government, and the international community that is dedicated to the development of revolutionary Internet technologies. Internet2 uses high-performance networks linking over 200 member institutions to deploy and test new network applications and technologies. Internet2 is designed as a research and development tool to help develop technologies that ensure the Internet in the future can handle tomorrow's applications, and it is now being used to deploy advanced applications and technologies that might not be possible otherwise with today's Internet. Much of Internet2 research is focused on speed. In fact,

TIP

Ethernet and other networking standards are discussed in Chapter 8.

the Internet2 backbone network was recently upgraded to support 8.8 Tbps. This network is the first national network to use *100 Gigabit Ethernet* over its entire footprint; it will be used to support high bandwidth applications, such as telemedicine and distance learning, to schools, libraries, hospitals, and other organizations.

The Internet Community Today

The Internet community today consists of individuals, businesses, and a variety of organizations located throughout the world. Virtually anyone with a computer or other Web-enabled device can be part of the Internet, either as a user or as a supplier of information or services. Most members of the Internet community fall into one or more of the following groups.

Users

Users are people who use the Internet to retrieve content or perform online activities, such as to look up a telephone number, read the day's news headlines or top stories, browse through an online catalog, make an online purchase, download a music file, watch an online video, make a phone call, or send an e-mail message. According to the Pew Internet & American Life Project, more than 80% of U.S. adults (and 95% of all U.S. teens) are Internet users, using the Internet at work, home, school, or another location. The availability of low-cost computers, low-cost or free Internet access (such as at libraries, schools, and other public locations), smartphones, and bundled pricing for obtaining Internet service in conjunction with telephone and/or television service has helped Internet use begin to approach the popularity and widespread use of telephones and TVs.

Internet Service Providers (ISPs)

Internet service providers (**ISPs**) are businesses or other organizations (see some examples in Figure 3-2) that provide Internet access to others, typically for a fee. ISPs (sometimes called *wireless ISPs* or *WISPs* when referring to ISPs that offer service via a wireless network) include most communications and media companies, such as conventional and wireless phone providers, cable providers, and satellite providers. Some ISPs (such as cable and cellular phone companies) offer Internet service over their private networks; other ISPs provide Internet service over the regular telephone lines or the airwaves. While many ISPs (such as AT&T and EarthLink) provide service nationwide, others provide service to a more limited geographical area. Regardless of their delivery method and geographical coverage, ISPs are the onramp to the Internet, providing their subscribers with access to the World Wide Web, e-mail, and other Internet resources. In addition to Internet access, some ISPs provide proprietary online services available only to their subscribers. A later section of this chapter covers ISPs in more detail, including factors to consider when selecting an ISP.

FIGURE 3-2 Companies that provide Internet access today include telephone, cable, and satellite companies.

Internet Content Providers

Internet content providers supply the information that is available through the Internet. Internet content providers can be commercial businesses, nonprofit organizations, educational institutions, individuals, and more. Some examples of Internet content providers are listed next.

- A photographer who posts samples of her best work on a Web page.
- An individual who publishes his opinion on various subjects to an online journal or *blog*.

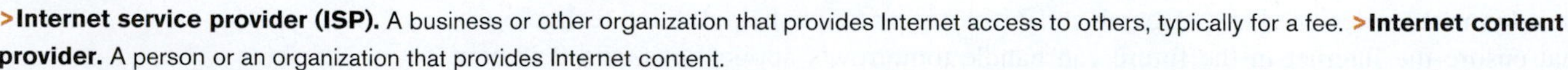

>Internet service provider (ISP). A business or other organization that provides Internet access to others, typically for a fee. **>Internet content provider.** A person or an organization that provides Internet content.

- A software company that creates a Web site to provide product information and software downloads.
- A national news organization that maintains an online site to provide up-to-the-minute news, feature stories, and video clips.
- A television network that develops a site for its TV shows, including episode summaries, cast information, and links to watch past episodes online.

Application Service Providers (ASPs) and Web Services

Application service providers (**ASPs**) are companies that manage and distribute Web-based software services to customers over the Internet. Instead of providing access to the Internet like ISPs do, ASPs provide access to software applications via the Internet. In essence, ASPs rent access to software programs to companies or individuals—typically, customers pay a monthly or yearly fee to use each application. As discussed in Chapter 2, this software can be called *cloud software*, *Software as a Service* (*SaaS*), and *cloudware*. Common ASP applications for businesses include office suites, collaboration and communications software, accounting programs, and e-commerce software.

One type of self-contained business application designed to work over the Internet or a company network is a **Web service**. A Web service can be added to Web pages to provide a service that would otherwise not be feasible (such as the inclusion of mapping information on a Web site or in a Web application using Microsoft's *MapPoint .NET Web service*). For example, Web developers for secure Web sites (such as Zappos.com, shown in Figure 3-3) can use a new Web service by Amazon to allow their customers to log onto those secure Web sites by using their Amazon, Facebook, or Google account logon information. A Web service can also be used to provide a service via a user's computer and the Internet. For instance, the *FedEx QuickShip Web service* allows users to create a shipment to any Microsoft Outlook contact from within Microsoft Outlook. It is important to realize that Web services are not stand-alone applications—they are simply a standardized way of allowing different applications and computers to share data and processes via a network so they can work together with other Web services and be used with many different computer systems. A company that provides Web services is sometimes referred to as a *Web services provider*.

FIGURE 3-3
Web services. This Web service enables Web developers to use Amazon's authentication system for users.

Clicking this button logs a Zappos.com customer in via an Amazon Web service and the customer's Amazon account.

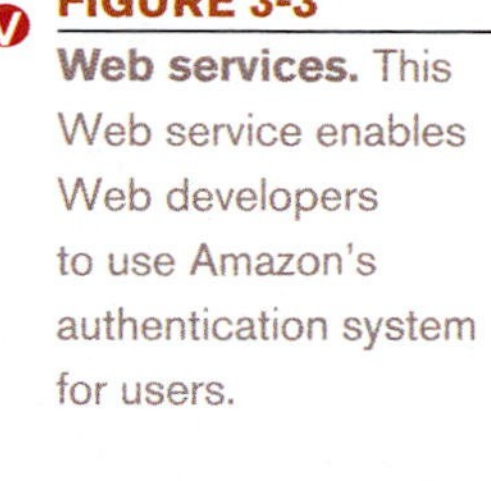

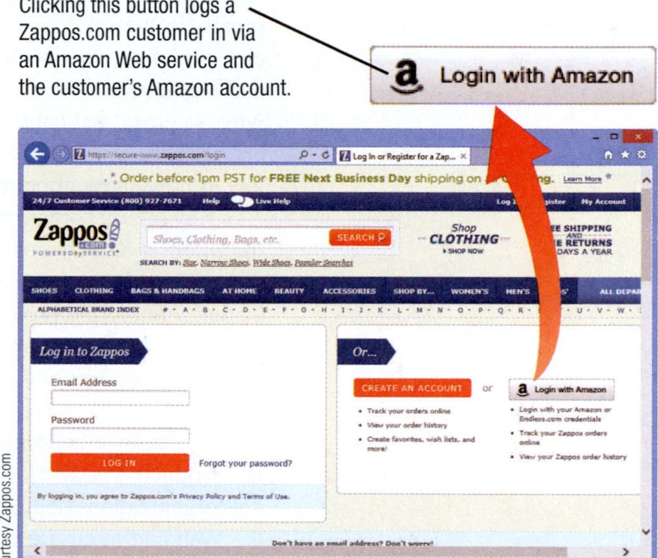

Courtesy Zappos.com

Infrastructure Companies

Infrastructure companies are the enterprises that own or operate the paths or "roadways" along which Internet data travels, such as the Internet backbone and the communications networks connected to it. Examples of infrastructure companies include conventional and mobile phone companies, cable companies, and satellite Internet providers.

Hardware and Software Companies

A wide variety of hardware and software companies make and distribute the products used with the Internet and Internet activities. For example, companies that create or sell the software used in conjunction with the Internet (such as Web browsers, e-mail programs, e-commerce

>**Application service provider (ASP).** A company that manages and distributes software-based services over the Internet. >**Web service.** A self-contained business application that operates over the Internet.

and multimedia software, and Web development tools) fall into this category. So, too, do the companies that make the hardware (network adapters, modems, cables, routers, servers, computers, and smartphones, for instance) that is used with the Internet.

The Government and Other Organizations

Many organizations influence the Internet and its uses. Governments have the most visible impact; their laws can limit both the information made available via Web servers located in a particular country and the access individuals residing in that country have to the Internet. For example, in France, it is illegal to sell items or post online content related to racist groups or activities; in China, there are tight controls imposed on what information is published on Web servers located in China, as well as on the information available to its citizens. And in the United States, anything illegal offline (illegal drugs, child pornography, and so forth) is also illegal online.

Legal rulings also can have a large impact on the communications industry in general. For example, the 1968 *Carterfone Decision* allowed companies other than AT&T to utilize the AT&T infrastructure and the 1996 *Telecommunications Act* deregulated the entire communications industry so that telephone companies, cable TV and satellite operators, and firms in other segments of the industry were free to enter each other's markets. In addition to making these types of decisions, the Federal Communications Commission (FCC) also greatly influences the communications industry through its ability to allocate radio frequencies (which are used with most types of wireless communications) and to implement policies and regulations related to interstate and international communications via radio, television, wire, satellite, and cable. The ability of the government to approve or block potential mergers between communications companies and to break apart companies based on antitrust law to prevent monopolies also impacts the Internet and communications industry.

Key Internet organizations are responsible for many aspects of the Internet. For example, the *Internet Society* provides leadership in addressing issues that may impact the future of the Internet. It also oversees the groups responsible for Internet infrastructure standards, such as determining the protocols that can be used and how Internet addresses are constructed, as well as facilitating and coordinating Internet-related initiatives around the world. *ICANN* (*Internet Corporation for Assigned Names and Numbers*) coordinates activities related to the Internet's naming system, such as IP address allocation and domain name management. For instance, it reviews nominations for new top-level domains and determines which new TLDs to introduce. The *World Wide Web Consortium* (*W3C*) is an international community of over 450 organizations dedicated to developing new protocols and specifications to be used with the Web and to ensure its interoperability. In addition, many colleges and universities support Internet research and manage blocks of the Internet's resources.

Myths About the Internet

Because the Internet is so unique in the history of the world—and its content and applications keep evolving—several widespread myths about it have surfaced.

Myth 1: The Internet Is Free

This myth stems from the fact that there has traditionally been no cost associated with accessing online content—such as news and product information—or with e-mail exchange, other than what the Internet users pay their ISPs for Internet access. And many people—such as students, employees, and consumers who opt for free Internet service or use free access available at public libraries or other public locations—pay nothing for Internet access. Yet it should also be obvious that someone, somewhere, has to pay to keep the Internet up and running.

Businesses, schools, public libraries, and most home users pay Internet service providers flat monthly fees to connect to the Internet. In addition, businesses, schools, libraries, and other large organizations might have to lease high-capacity communications lines (such as from a telephone company) to support their high level of Internet traffic.

Mobile users who want Internet access while on the go typically pay hotspot providers or wireless providers for this access. ISPs, phone companies, cable companies, and other organizations that own part of the Internet infrastructure pay to keep their parts of the Internet running smoothly. ISPs also pay software and hardware companies for the resources they need to support their subscribers. Eventually, most of these costs are passed along to end users through ISP fees. ISPs that offer free Internet access typically obtain revenue by selling on-screen ads that display on the screen when the service is being used.

Another reason the idea that the Internet is free is a myth is the growing trend of subscription or per-use fees to access Web-based resources. For instance, downloadable music and movies are very common today (see Figure 3-4) and some journal or newspaper articles require a fee to view them online. In fact, many newspapers and magazines have moved entirely online and most charge a subscription fee to view the level of content that was previously published in a print version. In lieu of a mandatory fee, some Web sites request a donation for use of the site. Many experts expect the use of fee-based Internet content to continue to grow at a rapid pace.

Courtesy Netflix, Inc.

FIGURE 3-4

Fee-based Web content. The use of fee-based Web content, such as streaming movies via Netflix as shown here, is growing.

Myth 2: Someone Controls the Internet

As already discussed, no single group or organization controls the Internet. Governments in each country have the power to regulate the content and use of the Internet within their borders, as allowed by their laws. However, legislators often face serious obstacles getting legislation passed into law—let alone getting it enforced. Making governmental control even harder is the "bombproof" design of the Internet itself. If a government tries to block access to or from a specific country or Web site, for example, users can use a third party (such as an individual located in another country or a different Web site) to circumvent the block. This occurred in Iran when the Iranian government blocked access to social networking sites after the 2009 elections—some Iranian citizens were able to send and read Twitter updates via third-party sites.

Myth 3: The Internet and the World Wide Web Are Identical

Because you can now use a Web browser to access most of the Internet's resources, many people think the Internet and the Web are the same thing. Even though in everyday use many people use the terms *Internet* and *Web* interchangeably, they are not the same thing. Technically, the Internet is the physical network, and the Web is the collection of Web pages accessible over the Internet. A majority of Internet activities today take place via Web pages, but there are Internet resources other than the Web that are not accessed via a Web browser. For instance, files can be uploaded and downloaded using an *FTP (File Transfer Protocol) program* and conventional e-mail can be accessed using an e-mail program.

GETTING SET UP TO USE THE INTERNET

Getting set up to use the Internet typically involves three decisions—determining the type of device you will use to access the Internet, deciding which type of connection is desired, and selecting the Internet service provider to be used. Once these determinations have been made, your computer can be set up to access the Internet.

> **TIP**
>
> Many people use multiple devices to access the Internet; according to Cisco, there will be nearly three times as many Internet-enabled devices than people in the world by 2017.

Type of Device

The Internet today can be accessed using a variety of devices. The type of device used depends on a combination of factors, such as the devices available to you, if you need

INSIDE THE INDUSTRY

Mobile Data Caps

Mobile data use has increased tremendously recently as individuals are watching TV and videos, downloading music and movies, playing online multiplayer games, participating in video phone calls, and otherwise performing high-bandwidth activities using their smartphones and media tablets. This has created the issue of wireless carriers potentially running out of bandwidth available for customers, resulting in outages or delays. In response, many wireless carriers have implemented *data caps* and have eliminated unlimited data plans (though many plans still have unlimited talk and texts). With a data cap, customers either temporarily lose high-speed Internet access (such as being slowed down from 4G to 2G speeds—called *data throttling*) or are charged an additional fee if they exceed their download limit (often 2 GB per month).

One explanation for the increased data usage is speed—4G data speeds are significantly faster than 3G service and the results (such as faster Web pages and smoother streaming videos) make it easier for users to go through a large amount of bandwidth in a relatively short period of time. One potential solution under consideration by wireless carriers is allowing content providers or app developers to pay carriers so that their services don't count against a customer's monthly data limit—essentially buying traffic for their content. However, the Internet is designed for all content and services to be treated equally. Because this solution would give larger companies an unfair advantage over upstarts, it is viewed by some as a *net neutrality* issue.

So how do you avoid the expensive or annoying ramifications associated with going over your data cap? The best way is to not go over your limit in the first place. To help with this, use Wi-Fi for large downloads instead of your cellular connection. It is also prudent to monitor your data usage to make sure you stay under your data cap (you can also use this information to decide if you need to consider upgrading to a higher plan if your usage is typical but still over your data cap). Some smartphones have an option for viewing your total data usage for the current billing period, as well as usage per app or Web site to help you see where you are using the most data.

Another useful tool is third-party apps designed to help you monitor your bandwidth usage. One such app is *Onavo Extend*, shown in the accompanying illustration. It gives you a breakdown of consumption by app, so you know your worst bandwidth offenders. As a bonus, it compresses your incoming data by up to 500% so you can do up to five times more with your data plan without going over. Five times more data for free? It's about time!

Courtesy Onavo Mobile Ltd.

access just at home or while on the go, and what types of Internet content you want to access. Some possible devices are shown in Figure 3-5 and discussed next.

Personal Computers

Most users who have access to a personal computer (such as a desktop or notebook computer) at home, work, or school will use it to access the Internet. One advantage of using personal computers for Internet access is that they have relatively large screens for viewing Internet content and keyboards for easier data entry. They can also be used to view or otherwise access virtually any Web page content, such as graphics, animation, music, games, and videos. In addition, they typically have a large hard drive and are connected to a printer so Web pages, e-mail messages, and downloaded files can be saved and/or printed easily.

TIP

According to market research firm IDC, more people will access the Internet through their mobile devices than through their personal computers by 2015.

Smartphones, Media Tablets, and Other Mobile Devices

Smartphones and other mobile devices are increasingly being used to view Web page content, exchange e-mail and other messages, and download music and other online content. In fact, mobile Web use—or *wireless Web*, as it is sometimes called—is one of the fastest

Courtesy Viewsonic Corporation

PERSONAL COMPUTERS

Courtesy Groupon

SMARTPHONES

Courtesy Yahoo!® Connected TV

SMART TVS

FIGURE 3-5
A variety of devices can be used to access the Internet.

growing uses of the Internet today (more than half of American adults now own smartphones). While smartphones are convenient to use on the go, they typically have a relatively small display screen; media tablets typically have a larger screen size for easier viewing. As discussed in Chapter 2, some mobile devices include a built-in or slide-out keyboard for easier data entry; others utilize pen, voice, or touch input instead.

Gaming Devices and Televisions

Another option is using a gaming device (such as a gaming console or handheld gaming device) to access Web content, in addition to using that device to play games. For instance, the Sony PlayStation, Sony PSP, Nintendo Wii, and Nintendo 3DS all have Web browsers that can be used to access Web content. Smart TVs have built-in Internet capabilities in order to display Web pages and other Web content (such as interactive polls and other show-specific information, social networking updates, and shopping opportunities, as shown in Figure 3-5) without any additional hardware. It is estimated that 400 million households worldwide will have smart TVs by 2016.

Type of Connection and Internet Access

In order to use the Internet, you need to connect a computer or other device to it. Typically, this occurs by connecting the device you are using to a computer or a network (usually belonging to your ISP, school, or employer) that is connected continually to the Internet. As discussed in Chapter 2, communications hardware is used to connect one device to another device. Most types of Internet connections today are *broadband* or high-speed connections. In fact, 90% of all home Internet connections in the United States are broadband connections, according to a recent study. As applications requiring high-speed connections continue to grow in popularity, access to broadband Internet speeds is needed in order to take full advantage of these applications. For instance, high-definition video, video chat, video-on-demand (VOD), and other multimedia applications all require broadband connections (see Figure 3-6). For a look at an issue related to the increased use of multimedia Internet content—*mobile data caps*—see the Inside the Industry box.

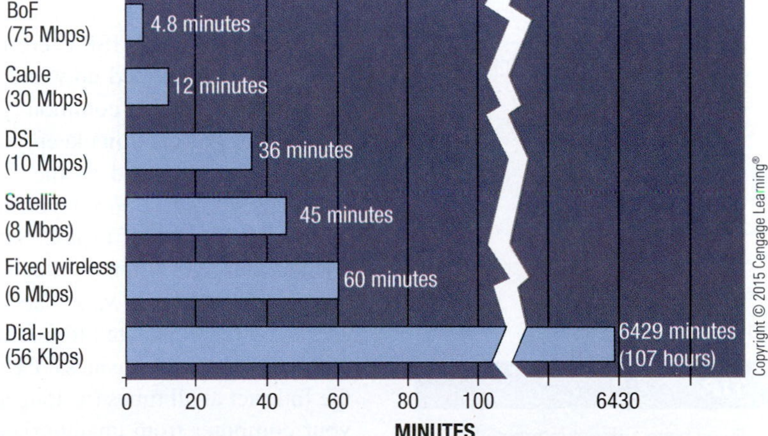

Copyright © 2015 Cengage Learning®

FIGURE 3-6
Approximate time to download a 2.7 GB (about 2-hour HD) movie using different home Internet options.

The difference between *dial-up* and *direct* Internet connections is discussed next, followed by an overview of the most common types of Internet connections used for personal use today; these types of Internet connections are also summarized in Figure 3-7. Many providers today offer bundles (such as cable TV, telephone, and Internet service) to lower an individual's overall total cost for the services. Similar to the mobile data caps discussed in the Inside the Industry box, some home broadband Internet services have data caps (you typically either

TYPE OF INTERNET CONNECTION	AVAILABILITY	APPROXIMATE MAXIMUM SPEED*	APPROXIMATE MONTHLY PRICE
Conventional dial-up	Anywhere there is telephone service	56 Kbps	Free–$20
Cable	Virtually anywhere cable TV service is available	3–100 Mbps	$30–110
DSL	Within 3 miles of a switching station that supports DSL	1–25 Mbps	$20–65
Satellite	Anywhere there is a clear view of the southern sky and where a satellite dish can be mounted and receive a signal	5–15 Mbps	$40–100
Fixed wireless	Selected areas where service is available	1–12 Mbps	$35–75
Broadband over fiber (BoF)	Anywhere fiber has been installed to the building	15–150 Mbps	$45–130
Mobile wireless (3G/4G)	Virtually anywhere cellular phone service is available	1–30 Mbps	Varies greatly; often bundled with mobile phone service

* Download speed; most connections have slower upload speeds.

FIGURE 3-7
Typical home Internet connection options.

are throttled down significantly or are charged an additional fee when you go over your limit), while others offer unlimited Internet.

Dial-Up vs. Direct Connections

While some Internet connections are *dial-up connections* (in which your computer dials up and connects to your ISP's computer only when needed), most are *direct* (or *always-on*) *connections* (in which you have a continuous connection to your ISP).

Dial-up connections work over standard telephone lines. To connect to the Internet, your computer dials its modem and then connects to a modem attached to a computer belonging to your ISP via the telephone lines. While you are connected to your ISP, your computer can access Internet resources. To end your Internet session, you disconnect from your ISP. One advantage of a dial-up connection is security. Because you are not continually connected to the Internet, it is much less likely that anyone (such as a *hacker*, as discussed in Chapter 4) will gain access to your computer via the Internet, either to access the data located on your computer or, more commonly, to use your computer in some type of illegal or unethical manner. However, dial-up connections are significantly slower than other types of connections; they are also inconvenient because you have to instruct your computer to dial up your ISP every time you want to connect to the Internet. Also, your telephone line will be tied up while you are accessing the Internet, unless you have a second phone line. The most common type of dial-up Internet service is *conventional dial-up*.

Direct connections keep you continually connected to your provider and, therefore, continually connected to the Internet. With a direct connection (such as *cable*, *DSL*, *satellite*, or *fixed wireless*), you access the Internet simply by opening a Web browser, such as Internet Explorer, Chrome, Safari, or Firefox. Direct Internet connections are broadband connections, are often available in different *tiers* (which means you have a choice of speeds and the price varies accordingly), are commonly used in homes and businesses, and are often connected to a LAN to share the Internet connection with multiple devices within the home or business. Because direct connections keep your computer connected to the Internet at all times (as long as your computer is powered up), it is important to protect your computer from unauthorized access or hackers. Consequently, all computers with a direct Internet connection should use a *firewall* program. Firewall programs block access to a computer from outside computers and enable each user to specify which programs on his or her computer are allowed to have access to the Internet. Firewalls, as well as other network and Internet security precautions, are discussed in more detail in Chapter 4.

TIP

If you have a direct Internet connection, leave your e-mail program open to retrieve your e-mail on a continual basis.

>**Dial-up connection.** A type of Internet connection in which the computer or other device must dial up and connect to a service provider's computer via telephone lines before being connected to the Internet. >**Direct connection.** A type of Internet connection in which the computer or other device is connected to the Internet continually.

Conventional Dial-Up

Conventional dial-up Internet access uses a *conventional dial-up modem* connected to a standard telephone jack with regular twisted-pair telephone cabling. Conventional dial-up Internet service is most often used with home computers for users who don't need, or do not want to pay for, broadband Internet service. Advantages include inexpensive hardware, ease of setup and use, and widespread availability (including remote areas). The primary disadvantage is slow connection speed—a maximum of 56 Kbps.

> **TIP**
>
> Before using a dial-up access number to connect to the Internet, verify that it is a local telephone number; if it is not, you will incur long-distance charges.

Cable

Cable Internet access uses a direct connection and is the most widely used type of home broadband connection, with over half of the home broadband market. Cable connections are very fast (typically between 15 and 50 Mbps, though faster services up to 100 Mbps are available in some areas for a premium fee) and are available wherever cable TV access is available, provided the local cable provider supports Internet access. Consequently, cable Internet is not widely available in rural areas. Cable Internet service requires a *cable modem.*

DSL

DSL (Digital Subscriber Line) Internet access is a type of direct connection that transmits via standard telephone lines, but it does not tie up your telephone line. DSL requires a *DSL modem* and is available only to users who are relatively close (within three miles) to a telephone switching station and who have telephone lines capable of handling DSL. DSL speeds are slower than cable speeds and the speed of the connection degrades as the distance between the modem and the switching station gets closer to the three-mile limit. Consequently, DSL is usually only available in urban areas. Download speeds can be up to about 25 Mbps, but are more typically between 1 and 15 Mbps.

Satellite

Satellite Internet access uses a direct connection, but it is slower and more expensive than cable or DSL access (between 5 and 15 Mbps, though around 10 Mbps is typical) and almost always has a data cap. However, it is often the only broadband option for rural areas. In addition to a *satellite modem*, it requires a *transceiver satellite dish* mounted outside the home or building to receive and transmit data to and from the satellites being used. Installation requires an unobstructed view of the southern sky (to have a clear line of sight between the transceiver and appropriate satellite), and performance might degrade or stop altogether during very heavy rain or snowstorms.

FIGURE 3-8
WiMAX towers. This tower is installed at the peak of Whistler Mountain in British Columbia.

Courtesy Tranzeo Wireless USA

Fixed Wireless

Fixed wireless Internet access uses a direct connection and is similar to satellite Internet in that it uses wireless signals, but it uses radio transmission towers (either stand-alone towers like the one shown in Figure 3-8 or transmitters placed on existing cell phone towers) instead of satellites. Fixed wireless Internet access requires a modem and, sometimes, an outside-mounted transceiver. Fixed wireless companies typically use *WiMAX* technology to broadcast the wireless signals to customers. Speeds are typically up to about 12 Mbps, though the speed depends somewhat on the distance between the

---

>**Conventional dial-up Internet access.** Dial-up Internet access via standard telephone lines. >**Cable Internet access.** Fast, direct Internet access via cable TV lines. >**DSL (Digital Subscriber Line) Internet access.** Fast, direct Internet access via standard telephone lines. >**Satellite Internet access.** Fast, direct Internet access via the airwaves and a satellite dish. >**Fixed wireless Internet access.** Fast, direct Internet access available in some areas via the airwaves.

TIP

Using a media tablet in conjunction with a mobile wireless data plan is growing at an astounding rate—from 20 million in 2012, to 40 million in 2013, to an estimated 165 million by 2017.

tower and the customer, the types and number of obstacles in the path, and the type and speed of the connection between the wireless transmitter and the Internet.

Broadband over Fiber (BoF)

A relatively new type of very fast direct connection available to homes and businesses in areas where there is fiber-optic cabling available all the way to the building is generically called **broadband over fiber (BoF)** or **fiber-to-the-premises (FTTP) Internet access**, with other names being used by individual providers, such as Verizon's *fiber-optic service (FiOS)*. These fiber-optic networks are most often installed by telephone companies in order to upgrade their overall infrastructures and, where installed, are used to deliver telephone and TV service in addition to Internet service. Where available, download speeds for BoF service typically range between 15 Mbps and 150 Mbps, though some areas offer speeds as fast as 1 Gbps. BoF requires a special networking terminal installed at the building to convert the optical signals into electrical signals that can be sent to a computer or over a LAN.

Mobile Wireless

Mobile wireless Internet access is the type of direct connection most commonly used with smartphones and media tablets to keep them connected to the Internet via a cellular network, even as they are carried from place to place. Some mobile wireless services can be used with computers as well as with mobile devices. To add Internet access to a mobile device, typically a *data plan* is needed. The speed of mobile wireless depends on the cellular standard being used—*3G networks* typically have speeds between 1 and 4 Mbps; *4G networks* are often between 3 and 15 Mbps, with speeds up to 30 Mbps available in some areas. Costs for mobile wireless Internet access vary widely, with some packages (typically 4G WiMAX services) including unlimited Internet, some charging by the number of minutes of Internet use, and some charging by the amount of data transferred. A growing trend is *prepaid* and *pay as you go plans*, in which you purchase service month to month (or day to day), instead of committing to a lengthy contract.

Wi-Fi Hotspots

While not typically used for primary home Internet access, another option for Internet access is a **Wi-Fi hotspot**—a location with a direct Internet connection and a wireless access point that allows users to connect wirelessly (via Wi-Fi) to the hotspot to use its Internet connection (see Figure 3-9). Public Wi-Fi

FIGURE 3-9
Wi-Fi hotspots. Hotspots are used to wirelessly connect to the Internet via the Internet connection belonging to a business, city, school, or other organization.

© iStockphoto.com/LuckyBusiness

COFFEEHOUSES AND OTHER PUBLIC LOCATIONS
Often fee-based, though some are available for free.

© iStockphoto.com/YanLev

HOTELS AND CONFERENCE CENTERS
Often free for guests.

© Burlingham/Shutterstock.com

HOSPITALS, BUSINESSES, AND OTHER ORGANIZATIONS
Usually designed for employees but are sometimes also available free to visitors.

© iStockphoto.com/CEFutcher

COLLEGE CAMPUSES
Usually designed for students and faculty; sometimes used directly in class, as shown here.

>**Broadband over fiber (BoF) Internet access.** Very fast, direct Internet access via fiber-optic networks; also referred to as **fiber-to-the-premises (FTTP) Internet access**. >**Mobile wireless Internet access.** Internet access via a mobile phone network. >**Wi-Fi hotspot.** A location that provides wireless Internet access to the public.

hotpots are widely available today, including at many coffeehouses and restaurants; at hotels, airports, and other locations frequented by business travelers; and in or nearby public areas such as libraries, subway stations, and parks. Some public Wi-Fi hotspots are free; others charge per hour, per day, or on a subscription basis. College campuses also typically have Wi-Fi hotspots to provide Internet access to students; many businesses and other organizations have Wi-Fi hotspots for use by employees in their offices, as well as by employees and guests in conference rooms, waiting rooms, lunchrooms, and other on-site locations.

TIP

Unlike most home Internet connections, mobile wireless service is typically tied to a particular device, though *family plans* are often available to give discounted rates for additional devices and mobile hotspots and *tethering* can often be used to share a single connection temporarily when needed.

Selecting an ISP and Setting Up Your Computer

Once the type of Internet access to be used is determined, the final steps to getting connected to the Internet are selecting an ISP and setting up your system. While this discussion is geared primarily toward a home Internet connection used with a personal computer, some of the concepts apply to business or mobile users as well.

Selecting an ISP

The type of device used (such as a personal computer or mobile device), the type of Internet connection and service desired (such as cable Internet or mobile wireless), and your geographical location (such as metropolitan or rural) will likely determine your ISP options. The pricing and services available often vary within a single ISP, as well as from one ISP to the next. The questions listed in Figure 3-10 can help you narrow your ISP choices and determine the questions you want answered before you decide on an ISP and a service package. A growing trend is for ISPs to offer a number of *tiers*; that is, different combinations of speeds and/or data caps for different prices so users requiring faster service or a more generous data plan can get it, but at a higher price.

Setting Up Your Computer

The specific steps for setting up your computer to use your selected type of Internet connection depend on the type of device, the type of connection, and the ISP you have chosen to use. Some types of Internet connections, such as satellite and broadband over fiber, require professional installation, after which you will be online; with other types, you can install the necessary hardware (typically a modem that connects to your computer or wireless router via an *Ethernet cable*) yourself (mobile device setup usually doesn't require any additional hardware). You will usually need to select a username and your desired payment method at some point during the ordering or setup process; this username is typically used in your e-mail address that will be associated with that Internet service.

After one computer is successfully connected to the Internet, you may need to add additional hardware to connect other computers and devices that you want to be able to access the Internet.

FIGURE 3-10
Choosing an ISP.
Some questions to ask before making your final selection.

AREA	QUESTIONS TO ASK
Services	Is the service compatible with my device?
	Is there a monthly bandwidth limit? If so, do I have a choice of tiers?
	How many e-mail addresses can I have?
	What is the size limit on incoming and outgoing e-mail messages and attachments?
	Do I have a choice between conventional and Web-based e-mail?
	Are there any special member features or benefits?
	Does the service include Web site hosting?
Speed	How fast are the maximum and usual downstream (ISP to my PC) speeds?
	How fast are the maximum and usual upstream (my PC to ISP) speeds?
	How much does the service slow down under adverse conditions, such as high traffic or poor weather?
Support	Is telephone technical support available?
	Is Web-based technical support (such as via e-mail) available?
	Is there ever a charge for technical support?
Cost	What is the monthly cost for the service? Is it lower if I prepay a few months in advance? Are different tiers available?
	Is there a setup fee? If so, can it be waived with a long-term agreement?
	What is the cost of any additional hardware needed, such as modem or transceiver? Can the fee be waived with a long-term service agreement?
	Are there any other services (telephone service, or cable or satellite TV, for instance) available from this provider that can be combined with Internet access for a lower total cost?

For instance, to share a broadband connection, you can connect other computers directly to the modem (via an Ethernet cable or Wi-Fi connection) if the modem contains a built-in switch or wireless router. If the modem does not include switching or wireless routing capabilities, you will need to connect a switch or wireless router to the modem (typically via an Ethernet cable) and then connect your devices to the switch or router in order to share the Internet connection with those devices.

SEARCHING THE INTERNET

> **TIP**
>
> Change the home page of your browser to your favorite search site to view that page automatically whenever you open your browser or click its Home button.

Most people who use the Internet turn to it to find specific information. For instance, you might want to find out the lowest price of the latest *Star Trek* DVD, the flights available from Los Angeles to New York on a particular day, a recipe for clam chowder, the weather forecast for the upcoming weekend, a video of the last presidential inaugural address, or a map of hiking trails in the Grand Tetons. The Internet provides access to a vast array of interesting and useful information, but that information is useless if you cannot find it when you need it. Consequently, one of the most important skills an Internet user can acquire today is how to search for and locate information on the Internet successfully. Basic Internet searching was introduced in Chapter 1, but understanding the various types of search sites available and how they work, as well as some key searching strategies, can help you perform more successful and efficient Internet searches. These topics are discussed next.

Search Sites

Search sites (such as *Google*, *Bing*, *Yahoo! Search*, *Ask.com*, and so forth) are Web sites designed specifically to help you find information on the Web. Most search sites use a **search engine**—a software program—in conjunction with a huge database of information about Web pages to help visitors find Web pages that contain the information they are seeking. Search site databases are updated on a regular basis; for example, Google estimates that its entire index is updated about once per month. Typically, this occurs using small, automated programs (often called *spiders* or *web crawlers*) that use the hyperlinks located on Web pages to *crawl* (jump continually) from page to page. At each Web page, the spider program records important data about the page into the search site's database, such as the page's URL, its title, the keywords that appear frequently on the page, and the keywords and descriptive information added to the page's code by the Web page author when the page was created. Spider programs can be tremendously fast, visiting millions of pages per day. In addition to spider programs, search site databases also obtain information from Web page authors who submit Web page URLs and keywords associated with their Web sites to the search site. The size of the database used varies with each particular search site, but typically includes information collected from several billion Web pages. Designing a Web site so it is classified properly by search sites and is listed in the search results when appropriate keywords are typed is referred to as *search engine optimization* (*SEO*).

> **TIP**
>
> If you are using Chrome, you can do a *voice search* by clicking the microphone icon next to the Google search box and speaking your desired search terms; many smartphone search apps support voice search as well.

To begin a search using a search site, type the URL for the desired search site in the Address bar of your browser (alternately, many Web browsers allow you to type search terms in the Address bar instead of a URL and the search will be performed using whichever search site is specified as the default search site). Most search sites today are designed for *keyword searches*; some sites allow *directory searches* as well. These two types of searches are discussed next. In addition, as the ability to search becomes more and more important, new types of searching are being developed. One

>Search site. A Web site designed to help users search for Web pages that match specified keywords or selected categories. **>Search engine.** A software program used by a search site to retrieve matching Web pages from a search database.

emerging possibility is *real-time search engines* that search the Web live, instead of relying on a search site database (one such service—called *MyLiveSearch*—is currently in development). Another emerging search site—*ChaCha Search*—uses human guides that you can chat with via the ChaCha Search page if you can't find the information you are looking for.

Keyword Search

The most common type of Internet search is the **keyword search**—that is, when you type appropriate **keywords** (one or more key terms) describing what you are looking for into a search box. The site's search engine then uses those keywords to return a list of Web pages (called *hits*) that match your search criteria; you can view any one of these Web pages by clicking its corresponding hyperlink (see Figure 3-11). Search sites differ in determining how close a match must be between the specified search criteria and a Web page before a link to that page is displayed, so the number of hits from one search site to another may vary. To reduce the number of hits displayed, good search strategies (discussed shortly) can be used. Search sites also differ with respect to the order in which the hits are displayed. Some sites list the most popular sites (usually judged by the number of Web pages that link to it) first; others list Web pages belonging to organizations that pay a fee to receive a higher rank (typically called *sponsored links*) first.

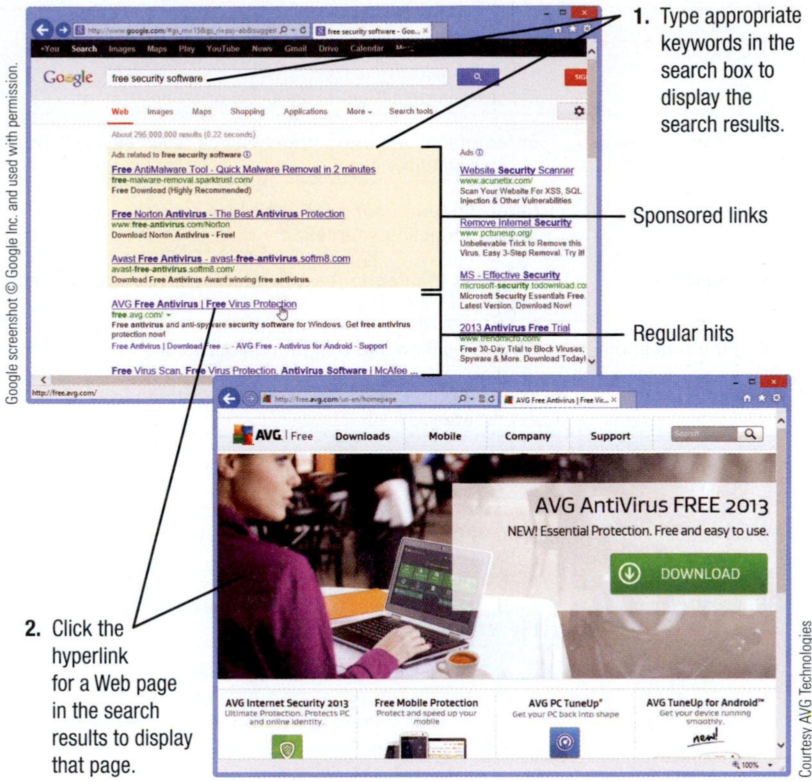

FIGURE 3-11
Using a search site.

The keyword search is the most commonly used search type. It is used not only on conventional search sites like the Google search site shown in Figure 3-11, but also on many other Web sites. For instance, many types of Web pages include a keyword search box like the one shown in Figure 3-12 so visitors can search that Web site to find information (such as items for sale via the site or specific documents or Web pages located on that site). These Web site searches are typically powered by search engine technology, such as by *Google Site Search* or the open source *Lucene* search application.

FIGURE 3-12
Web page keyword searches. Allow users to search the Web site for the desired content.

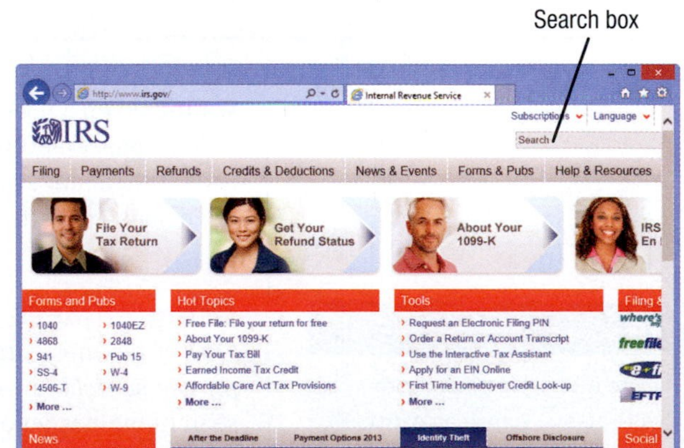

Directory Search

An alternate type of Internet search available on some search sites is the **directory search**, which uses lists of categories instead of a search box. To perform a directory search, click the category that best matches what you are looking for in order to display a list of more specific subcategories within the main category. You can then click specific subcategories to drill down to more specific topics until you see hyperlinks to Web pages matching the information you are looking for.

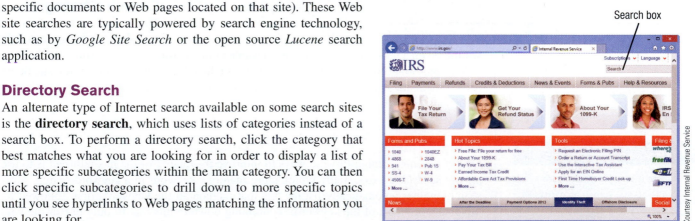

>**Keyword search.** A type of Internet search where keywords are typed in a search box to locate information on the Internet. >**Keyword.** A word typed in a search box on a search site or other Web page to locate information related to that keyword. >**Directory search.** A type of Internet search where categories are selected to locate information on the Internet.

FUNCTION	EXPLANATION
Calculator	Enter a mathematical expression or a conversion to see the result.
Currency converter	Enter an amount and currency types (such as *10 Euro in USD*) to see the corresponding value.
Dictionary	Enter the term *define* followed by a term to view definitions for that term from online sources.
Earthquakes	Enter the term *earthquake* to see recent earthquake activity around the world.
Flight information	Enter an airline and a flight number to see status information.
Movie showtimes	Enter the term *movie* followed by a ZIP Code to view movies showing in that area.
Number search	Enter a UPS, FedEx, or USPS tracking number; an area code; or a UPC code to view the associated information.
Sports scores	Enter a team name or league name to see scores, schedules, and other information.
Sunrise/sunset	Enter the term *sunrise* or *sunset* followed by a city name to see the time of the sunrise or sunset in that city.
Street maps	Enter an address to find a map to that location.
Time	Enter the term *time* followed by a city name to see the current time in that city.
Weather	Enter the term *weather* followed by a city name or ZIP Code to view the weather for that location.
Yellow pages	Enter a type of business and city name or ZIP Code to view businesses in that local area.

EXAMPLES:

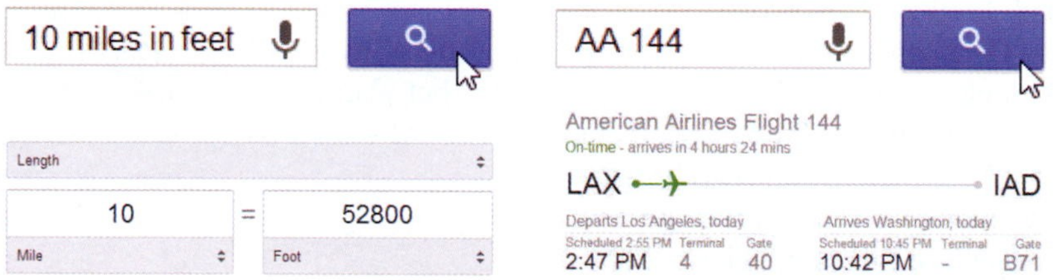

FIGURE 3-13
Google search tools.

Search Site Tools

Many search sites contain a variety of tools that can be used to find specific types of information. For instance, many search sites include links next to the search box that allow you to search for items other than Web pages, such as music files, videos, images, maps, news articles, products for sale—even files on your computer. Google is one of the most versatile search sites at the present time and is continually adding new search options. In addition to the options just listed, Google allows a variety of special searches to be conducted by typing specific search criteria in its search box to find other useful information, such as to quickly track a shipped package, look up a telephone number, check on the status of an airline flight, or make a calculation or conversion. Some examples of search tools that can be performed using the Google search box are listed in Figure 3-13.

Search Strategies

There are a variety of strategies that can be used to help whittle down a list of hits to a more manageable number (some searches can return billions of Web pages). Some search strategies can be employed regardless of the search site being used; others are available only on certain sites. Some of the most useful search strategies are discussed next.

> **TIP**
> If there is an uncommon word that relates to your search, use it to help improve your results.

Using Phrases

One of the most straightforward ways to improve the quality of the hits returned is to use *phrase searching*—essentially typing more than one keyword in a keyword search. Most search engines automatically list the hits that include all the keywords first, followed by hits matching most of the keywords, continuing down to hits that fit only one of the keywords. To force this type of sorting, virtually all search engines allow you to use some type of character—often quotation marks—to indicate that you want to search for the entire phrase together. Because search options vary from site to site, it is best to look for a search tips link on the search site you are using; the search tips should explain all of the search options available for that site. Examples of the results based on different search phrases to find Web pages about hand signals used with dogs and conducted at two search sites are listed in Figure 3-14. Notice that while the last two search phrases shown in Figure 3-14

SEARCH PHRASE USED	SEARCH SITE	NUMBER OF PAGES FOUND	TITLE OF FIRST TWO NONSPONSORED PAGES FOUND*
dogs	Google	1,420,000,000	Dogs – Wikipedia, the free encyclopedia Dog: Dog Breeds, Adoption, Bringing a Dog Home and Care
	Bing	53,200,000	Dog – Wikipedia, the free encyclopedia Dog Supplies | Dog Accessories & Dog Products – Dog.com
hand signals	Google	26,300,000	Hand Signals – Wikipedia, the free encyclopedia California Driver Handbook – Safe Driving Practices
	Bing	17,400,000	Hand Signals – Wikipedia, the free encyclopedia Hand Signs Part 1
dog hand signals	Google	1,830,000	DDEAF Training Hand Signs – Deaf Dog Education Action Fund Dog Training Hand Signals – Dog Training Excellence
	Bing	6,500,000	How to Teach a Dog Hand Signals | eHow.com Dog Training Hand Signals, A Different Type of Communication
"dog hand signals"	Google	51,500	DDEAF Training Hand Signs – Deaf Dog Education Action Fund Utilize Dog Hand Signals in Your Training: Dog Obedience Training
	Bing	6,490	How to Teach a Dog Hand Signals | eHow.com Dog Training Hand Signals, A Different Type of Communication

* Highlighted entries indicate Web pages about dog hand signals.

FIGURE 3-14
Examples of phrase searching. Using different search phrases and different search sites can significantly change the search results.

both returned relevant (and similar) Web pages, the number of Web pages found varied dramatically (thousands of pages versus millions).

Using Boolean Operators

To further specify exactly what you want a search engine to find, *Boolean operators*—most commonly AND, OR, and NOT—can often be used in keyword searches. For example, if you want a search engine to find all documents that cover *both* the Intel and AMD microprocessor manufacturers, you can use the search phrase *Intel AND AMD* if the search engine supports Boolean operators. If, instead, you want documents that discuss *either* of these companies, the search phrase *Intel OR AMD* can be used. On the other hand, if you want documents about microprocessors that are cataloged with no mention of Intel, *microprocessors NOT Intel* can be used. Just as with other operators, the rules for using Boolean operators might vary from search site to search site (for instance, Google automatically assumes the AND operator as the default operator any time more than one search term is listed and Google uses a minus sign (–) instead of the word *NOT*). Be sure to check the search tips for the search site that you are using to see what operators can be used on that site. Some search sites also include an *Advanced Search* option that helps you specify Boolean conditions and other advanced search techniques using a fill-in-the-blank form.

Using Multiple Search Sites

Most users have a favorite search site that they are most comfortable using. However, as illustrated in Figure 3-14, different search sites can return different results. It is important to realize that sometimes a different search site might perform better than the one you use regularly. If you are searching for something and are not making any progress with one search site, then try another search site.

TIP

When searching, be efficient—if an appropriate Web page is not included among the first page or two of hits, redo the search using more specific criteria, a different search site, or a different search strategy.

Using Appropriate Keywords, Synonyms, Variant Word Forms, and Wildcards

When choosing the keywords to be used with a search site, it is important to select words that represent the key concept you are searching for. For example, if you want to find out about bed and breakfasts located in the town of Leavenworth, Washington, a keyword phrase (such as *Leavenworth Washington bed and breakfast*) should return appropriate

FIELD TYPE	EXAMPLE	EXPLANATION
Title	title: "tax tips"	Searches for Web pages containing the words "tax tips" in the page title.
Text	text: "tax tips"	Searches for Web pages containing "tax tips" in the text of the page.
Site	forms site:irs.gov	Searches for Web pages associated with the keyword "forms" that are located only on the irs.gov Web site.
Domain	tax tips site:*.gov	Searches for Web pages associated with the keywords "tax tips" that are located on government Web sites (they can have anything for the first part of the domain name, but must have a .gov TLD).

FIGURE 3-15
Field searching. Field searches limit search results to just those pages that match specific field criteria, in addition to any specified search criteria.

TIP

To search for a search term and its synonyms at the same time in Google, type the tilde symbol (~) immediately in front of your search term, such as *~bed and breakfast* to have Google search for *bed and breakfast*, as well as automatically also search for *hotels*, *motels*, and other synonymous terms.

results. If your initial search does not produce the results you are hoping for, you can try *synonyms*—words that have meanings similar to other words. For example, you could replace *bed and breakfast* with *hotel* or *lodging*. To use synonyms in addition to the original keywords, Boolean operators can be used, such as the search phrase *"bed and breakfast" OR hotel OR lodging AND Leavenworth AND Washington*.

Variant—or alternate—word forms are another possibility. Try to think of a different spelling or form of your keywords if your search still does not work as desired. For example, *bed and breakfast* could be replaced or supplemented with the variants *bed & breakfast* and *B&B*, and the *hand signals* keywords used in Figure 3-14 could be replaced with the variants *hand signal* and *hand signaling*. Using alternative spellings is a form of this strategy, as well. Another strategy that is sometimes used with keywords is the *wildcard* approach. A wildcard is a special symbol that is used in conjunction with a part of a word to specify the pattern of the terms you want to search for. For instance, the asterisk wildcard (*) is used to represent one or more letters at the asterisk location, so on many sites searching for *hand sign** would search for *hand sign*, *hand signal*, *hand signals*, *hand signaling*, and any other keywords that fit this specific pattern.

Using Field Searches

Another strategy that can be used when basic searching is not producing the desired results is *field searching*. A field search limits the search to a particular search characteristic (or *field*), such as the page title, URL, page text, top-level domain, or Web site (see Figure 3-15). When a field search is performed, only the hits associated with the Web pages that match the specified criteria in the specified field are displayed. You can also use field searching in conjunction with regular search terms, such as to search for a particular keyword on just Web sites that use a specific domain. Many, but not all, search engines support some type of field searching. Check the search tips for the particular search site you are using to see if it has that option.

Evaluating Search Results

Once a list of Web sites is returned as the result of a search, it is time to evaluate the sites to determine their quality and potential for meeting your needs. Two questions to ask yourself before clicking a link in the search results are as follows:

- Does the title and listed description sound appropriate for the information you are seeking?
- Is the URL from an appropriate company or organization? For example, if you want technical specifications about a particular product, you might want to start with information on the manufacturer's Web site. If you are looking for government publications, stick with government Web sites.

After an appropriate Web page is found, the evaluation process is still not complete. To determine if the information can be trusted, you should evaluate both the author and the source to decide if the information can be considered reliable and whether or not it is biased. Be sure to also check for a date to see how up to date the information is—many online

TYPE OF RESOURCE	CITATION EXAMPLE
Web page article (magazine)	Dvorak, J. (2013, June 3). The Google assumption engine. *PC Magazine.* Retrieved from http://www.pcmag.com/article2/0,2817,2419867,00.asp
Web page article (journal)	Dickens, C. (2013, June). Health literacy and nursing: An update. *American Journal of Nursing, 113(6),* 52–57. Retrieved from http://journals.lww.com/ajnonline/Fulltext/2013/06000/Health_Literacy_and_Nursing___An_Update.29.aspx
Web page article (not appearing in a periodical)	Elias, P. (2013, June 01). Judge orders Google to turn over data to FBI. Retrieved from http://www.nbcnews.com/technology/judge-orders-google-turn-over-data-fbi-6C10157219
Web page content (not an article)	*Security 101 - Internet Security Glossary / Norton.* (n.d.) Retrieved from http://us.norton.com/security-101
E-mail (cited in text, not reference list)	M. Rodriquez (personal communication, March 28, 2014)

FIGURE 3-16
Citing Web sources. These examples follow the American Psychological Association (APA) citation guidelines.

articles are years old. If you will be using the information in a report, paper, or other document in which accuracy is important, try to verify the information with a second source.

Citing Internet Resources

According to the online version of the Merriam-Webster Dictionary, the term *plagiarize* means "to steal and pass off the ideas or words of another as one's own" or to "use another's production without crediting the source." To avoid plagiarizing Web page content, you need to credit Web page sources—as well as any other Internet resources—when you use them in papers, on Web pages, or in other documents.

The guidelines for citing Web page content are similar to those for written sources. In general, the author, date of publication, and article or Web page title are listed along with a "Retrieved" statement listing the URL of the Web page used to retrieve the article. Some citation examples based on the guidelines obtained from the *American Psychological Association* (*APA*) Web site are shown in Figure 3-16. If in doubt when preparing a research paper, check with your instructor as to the style manual (such as APA, *Modern Language Association* (*MLA*), or *Chicago Manual of Style*) he or she prefers you to follow and refer to that guide for direction.

BEYOND BROWSING AND E-MAIL

In addition to basic browsing and e-mail (discussed in Chapter 1), there are a host of other activities that can take place via the Internet. Some of the most common of these Web-based applications are discussed next.

Other Types of Online Communications

Many types of online communications methods exist. E-mail, discussed in Chapter 1, is one of the most common; other types of online communications are discussed in the next few sections. While the programs that supported the various types of online communications discussed next were originally dedicated to a single task, today's programs can typically be used for a variety of types of online communications. For instance, the *Skype* online communications program shown in Figure 3-17 can be used to exchange *instant messages* (*IMs*), make voice and video calls via *Voice over Internet Protocol* (*VoIP*), and exchange files with your online contacts; the Gmail Web mail service can be used to exchange instant messages and make voice and video calls (using Google's *Hangouts* communications app), in addition to sending

FIGURE 3-17
Skype. This app can be used for a variety of online communications.

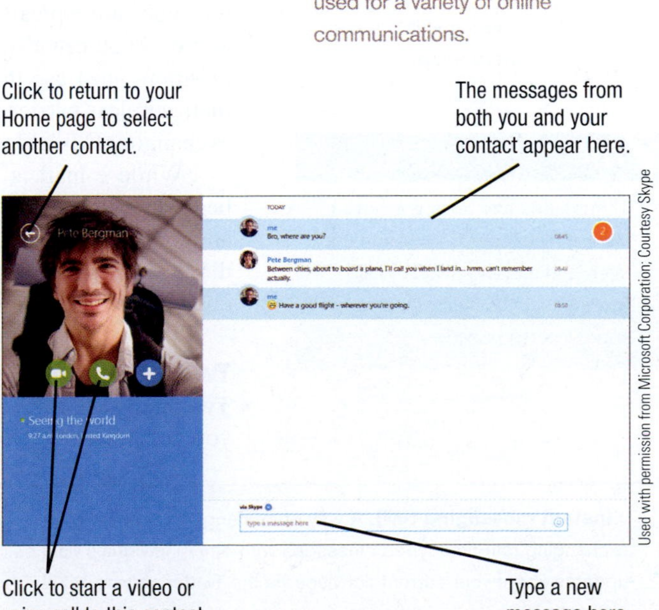
Click to return to your Home page to select another contact.
The messages from both you and your contact appear here.
Pete Bergman
Click to start a video or voice call to this contact.
Type a new message here.

> **TIP**
> Many IM apps today offer basic features (such as IMs, voice calls, and video calls between two individuals) for free; more advanced features may require a fee.

and receiving e-mail messages. Some e-mail programs (such as Microsoft Outlook) can also display your contact's social networking updates. This online communications convergence trend is found in both personal and business applications; in business, it is referred to as *unified communications* (*UC*). With UC, all of a business's communications (such as e-mail, instant messaging, videoconferencing, customer service center communications, and telephone calls via both in-office landlines and mobile phones) are tied together and work with a single unified mailbox and interface—often via a cloud UC provider.

Instant Messaging (IM) and Text Messaging

Instant messaging (**IM**), also commonly referred to as **chat**, allows you to exchange real-time typed messages with people on your *contact list* or *buddy list*—a list of individuals (such as family, friends, and business associates) that you specify or with whom you have already exchanged messages. Instant messages (IMs) can be sent via computers and smartphones via *messaging programs* or *apps* (such as *AIM*, *Yahoo! Messenger*, the Skype program shown in Figure 3-17, or the *WhatsApp* mobile app shown in Figure 3-18) or via Web pages (such as TV show Web sites and social networking sites like Facebook and Google+) that support instant messaging. Originally a popular communications method among friends, IM has also become a valuable business tool.

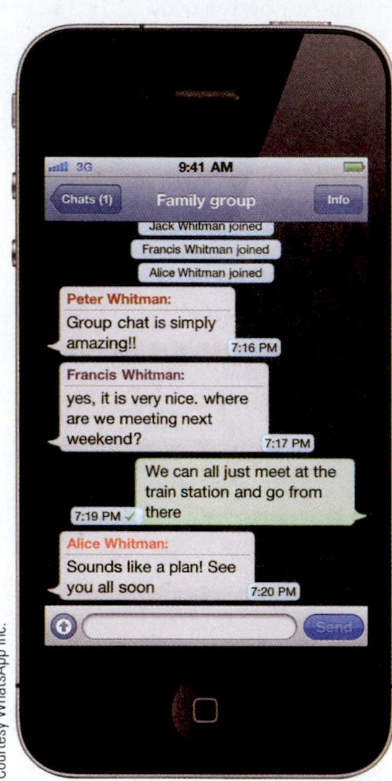

Courtesy WhatsApp Inc.

FIGURE 3-18
Group messaging. Works the same as traditional IM, just with more people.

In order to send an IM, you must be signed in to your IM service. You can then select a contact and send an IM, which then appears immediately on your contact's device. You can also typically engage in other types of activities with your contact via the IM program, such as sending a photo or file, starting a voice or video conversation, or starting a *group call* or *conversation* (refer again to Figure 3-18). Instant messaging capabilities are also often integrated into Web pages, such as to ask questions of a customer service representative or to start a conversation with one of your friends via a social networking site.

Because IM applications typically display the status of your buddies (such as if they are online or if they have set their status to "Busy" or "In a meeting"), IM is an example of an application that uses *presence technology*—technology that enables one computing device to identify the current status of another device. Presence technology is increasingly being integrated into devices and applications and is discussed in more detail in Chapter 5. For a look at a growing presence application—*geofencing*—see the How It Works box.

Text messaging is a form of messaging frequently used by mobile phone users. Also called *Short Message Service* or *SMS*, text messaging is used to send short (less than 160 character) text-based messages via a cellular network. If the messages also include photos, audio, or video, *Multimedia Message Service* or *MMS* is used instead. In either case, the messages are typically sent to the recipient via his or her mobile phone number or e-mail address (you can also send text messages to a mobile phone from your computer's e-mail program—just use the recipient's mobile phone number and the appropriate domain for their wireless carrier such as *111-555-0000@txt.att.net*). Individuals may incur a fee for exchanging IMs and text messages, if these services are not included in their wireless plan.

> **TIP**
> Though IMs and texts are similar, instant messages go through the Web and an IM provider, while text messages usually go through your wireless provider.

While e-mail is still important for business online communications, messaging is beginning to replace e-mail for personal communications—particularly with teenagers and other individuals who carry a moble phone with them at all times. According to the director of engineering at Facebook, "The future of messaging is more real time, more conversational, and more casual."

Twittering and Social Networking Updates

Twittering refers to posting short (up to 140 character) updates (called *tweets*) about what you are doing or thinking about at any moment to the *Twitter* social network. The updates

---

>**Instant messaging (IM).** A way of exchanging real-time typed messages with other individuals; also called **chat**. >**Text messaging.** A way of exchanging real-time typed messages with other individuals via a cellular network and, typically, cell phones. >**Twittering.** Sending short status updates about your current activities via the Twitter service.

HOW IT WORKS

Geofencing

Using your smartphone's location to deliver Web content—sometimes referred to as *geobrowsing*—is nothing new. Some geobrowsing applications and services (such as *Foursquare*) allow you to broadcast your current location to friends or *check in* to share your current location with friends; others (such as *Eventful*) are designed to find entertainment and live events that are close to your current location.

Location-based marketing and *geofencing* take geobrowsing one step further by enabling developers to deliver ads, offers, and other marketing resources to users based on their current physical location. For instance, a business could set up *geofences* (prescribed geographical areas) so it is notified when a customer is close to a particular store location, as well as when the customer enters and exits the store, in order to send appropriate messages and offers to that customer via his or her smartphone. Google recently released tools to help developers create these types of applications—the tools can determine more accurate locations faster and without draining the smartphone's battery; can determine if the user is walking, cycling, or driving; and can set up location-based triggers when someone enters or exists a geofenced area.

While *mobile marketing* is a common use for geofencing, the same technology can be used by individuals for geofences they set up for themselves (such as the geofence shown being added in the accompanying illustration). For example, you can use a geofencing app to turn off your Wi-Fi when you are out of range of a network (for security reasons and to save your battery) or an app to remind you of tasks you need to accomplish when you enter or exit a specific geofence. And a new *Nearby* service from Wikipedia displays Wikipedia articles based on people's current location in hopes that these individuals will upload photos and otherwise update content using their smartphones. Geofencing possibilities are growing and appear to be only limited by developers' imaginations.

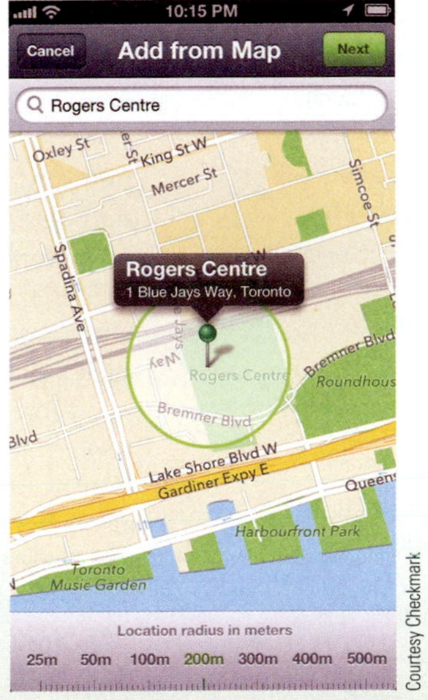

Creating a geofence from a map location.

can be sent via text message or the Twitter Web site. Individuals see the tweets of people they *follow* on their Twitter home page; they can view other tweets by searching Twitter for key terms or *hashtags* (key terms used on Twitter and that are preceded by the symbol #), as shown in Figure 3-19. You can also send *direct messages* to one of your followers, which are then seen only by you and the recipient.

Features similar to Twitter tweets (generally referred to as *status updates*) are available on some social networking sites (most notably, Facebook) to keep your friends up to date on your current activities, as discussed shortly. The use of Twitter and status updates is changing the way some people communicate online. Twitter is used today to get updates on the weather, to ask for assistance with problems or to conduct information searches—even for personal safety purposes. For instance, as shown in Figure 3-19, the U.S. State Department uses Twitter to issue traveling advisories. Increasingly, people turn to Twitter to comment on newsworthy events—such as terrorist attacks, natural disasters, and breaking news—as they occur.

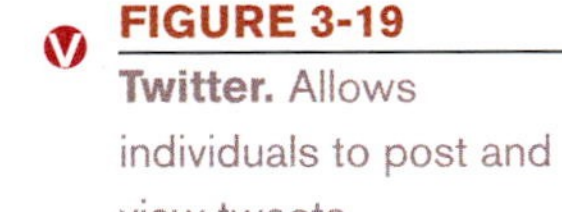

FIGURE 3-19
Twitter. Allows individuals to post and view tweets.

Forums

For asking questions of, making comments to, or initiating discussions with a large group of individuals, **forums** (also called *discussion groups* and *message boards*) can be used. Forums are Web pages designed to facilitate written discussions on specific subjects, such as TV shows, computers, movies, investing, gardening, music, photography, or politics. They typically have a *moderator* who monitors the forum to remove inappropriate posts. When a participant posts a message, it is displayed for anyone accessing the forum to read and respond to. Messages are usually organized by topics (called *threads*); participants can post new messages in response to an existing message and stay within that thread, or they can start a new thread. Forum participants do not have to be online at the same time so participants can post and respond to messages at their convenience.

TIP

Some VoIP providers (such as Vonage) provide an app that enables you to make calls from anywhere, using your smartphone, a Wi-Fi connection, and your home VoIP account.

Voice over Internet Protocol (VoIP)

Internet telephony is the original industry term for the process of placing telephone calls over the Internet. Today, the standard term for placing telephone calls over the Internet or any other type of data network is **Voice over Internet Protocol** (**VoIP**) and it can take many forms. At its simplest level, VoIP calls can take place from computer to computer, such as by starting a voice conversation with an online contact using a messaging program and a headset or microphone. Computer-to-computer calls (such as via the popular Skype service shown in Figure 3-17, as well as via messaging programs that support voice calls) are generally free. Often calls can be received from or made to conventional or mobile phones for a small fee, such as 2 cents per minute or $2.99 per month for unlimited calling for domestic calls.

More permanent VoIP setups (sometimes referred to as *digital voice* or *broadband phone*) are designed to replace conventional landline phones in homes and businesses. VoIP is offered through some ISPs, such as cable, telephone, and wireless providers; it is also offered through dedicated VoIP providers, such as *Vonage*. Permanent VoIP setups require a broadband Internet connection and a *VoIP phone adapter* that goes between a conventional phone and a broadband router, as shown in Figure 3-20. Once your phone calls are routed through your phone adapter and router to the Internet, they travel to the recipient's phone, which can be another VoIP phone, a mobile phone, or a landline phone. VoIP phone adapters are typically designed for a specific VoIP provider. With these more permanent VoIP setups, most users switching from landline phone service can keep their existing telephone number.

The biggest advantage of VoIP is cost savings, such as unlimited local and long-distance calls for as little as $25 per month, or basic cable and VoIP services bundled together for about $50 per month. One of the biggest disadvantages of VoIP at the present time is that it does not function during a power outage or if your Internet connection (such as your cable connection for cable Internet users) goes down.

FIGURE 3-20
Voice over IP (VoIP). Permanent VoIP setups allow telephone calls to be placed via a broadband Internet connection using a conventional telephone.

1. A conventional phone is plugged into a VoIP adapter, which is connected to a broadband modem.
2. Calls coming from the VoIP phone travel over the Internet to the recipient's phone.

Web Conferences and Webinars

The term *videoconferencing* refers to the use of computers or mobile devices, video cameras, microphones, and other communications technologies to conduct real-time,

>**Forum.** A Web page that enables individuals to post messages on a particular topic for others to read and respond to; also called a *discussion group* or *message board.* >**Voice over Internet Protocol (VoIP).** The process of placing telephone calls via the Internet.

face-to-face meetings between people in different locations. Videoconferencing that takes place via the Internet is often called *Web conferencing* or *online conferencing*. **Web conferences** typically take place via a personal computer or mobile device (see Figure 3-21) and are used by businesses and individuals. As previously discussed, many free messaging programs or services (such as Skype, Google Hangouts, and *Apple FaceTime*) support video phone calls. While some of these programs support group calls and other more advanced features, business Web conferences that require multiple participants or other communications tools (such as a shared whiteboard or the ability for attendees to share the content on their computer screens) may need to use a *Web conferencing service* (such as *WebEx*) or a premium service from Skype or another messaging service instead. Business Web conferencing is often used for meetings between individuals located in different geographical locations, as well as for employee training, sales presentations, customer support, and other business applications.

Courtesy Cisco Systems

FIGURE 3-21
Web conferencing. Allows individuals to talk with and see each other in real time.

Webinars (Web seminars) are similar to Web conferences, but typically have a designated presenter and an audience. Although interaction with the audience is usually included (such as question-and-answer sessions), a Webinar is typically more one-way communication than a Web conference. A completely one-way presentation (such as a recorded Webinar played back on demand) is sometimes referred to as a *Webcast*.

Social Networking/Social Media

A **social networking site** can be loosely defined as any site that creates a community of individuals who can communicate with and/or share information with one another; the collection of social networking sites and other communications channels used to transmit or share information with a broad audience is referred to as **social media**. Some examples of social networking sites are *MySpace*, *Facebook*, and *Google+* that allow users to post information about themselves for others to read; *Meetup* that connects people in specific geographic areas with common hobbies and interests; *Flickr* and *Fotki* and other photo sharing sites; *Pinterest* that allows individuals to share ideas and snippets from Web pages, organized by topic; and *YouTube* and other video sharing sites. Social networking can be performed via personal computers, though the use of *mobile social networking*—social networks accessed with a smartphone or other mobile device—is more common today, making social networking a real-time, on-the-go activity. Some reasons for this include that

ASK THE EXPERT

THROW THE FIGHT **Ryan Baustert,** Guitarist, Throw the Fight

Courtesy Throw the Fight www.facebook.com/throwthefight, www.throwthefight.com.

What impact has the Internet and social networking sites had on your band's success?

The Internet has had a major impact on us. The best marketing is when the distance between artist and audience is short and direct. Due to sites like MySpace, Purevolume, and Facebook, we are able to stay better connected and interact with our fans on a more personal level. We can also gauge how our music is received by peoples' reactions and comments online.

It's much easier to promote shows, tours, and album releases, as well. More recently, with the explosion of Twitter, we can go one step further and give fans more insight into what is going on in our lives behind the scenes. This, in turn, helps us build brand loyalty.

>**Web conference.** A face-to-face meeting taking place via the Web; typically uses video cameras and microphones to enable participants to see and hear each other. >**Webinar.** A seminar presented via the Web. >**Social networking site.** A site that enables a community of individuals to communicate and share information. >**Social media.** The collection of social networking sites and other communications channels used to transmit or share information with a broad audience.

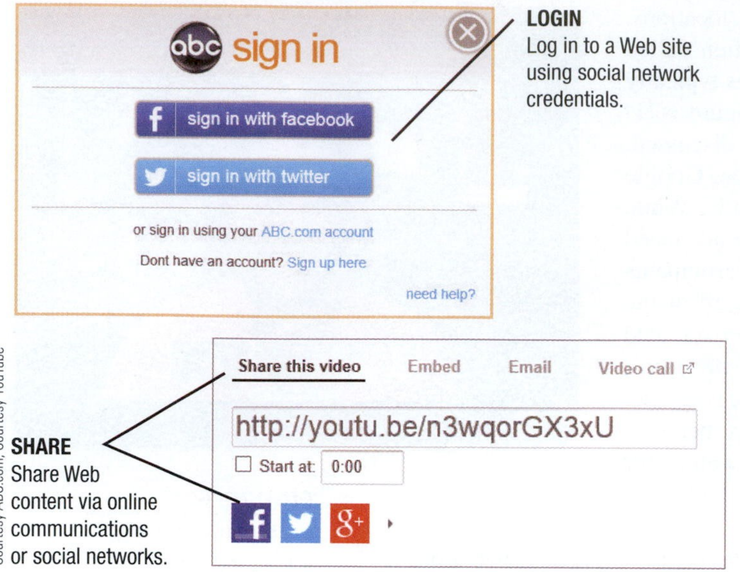

Courtesy ABC.com; Courtesy YouTube

FIGURE 3-22

Social networks are integrated into many Web sites.

most individuals carry a mobile phone with them all the time, many individuals like to communicate with others via the Web while they are on the go, and smartphones enable location applications to be integrated into the social networking experience.

Social networking is also increasingly being integrated with other online activities. For instance, you can exchange messages or have video calls with your friends from within Google+ or Facebook; you can share YouTube videos via an e-mail message, a video call, or one of your social networking pages from a YouTube video page; and you can view your friends' Facebook updates in Skype. In addition, many Web sites include *Like* buttons on their site to allow a visitor to Like the business's Facebook page, Like content (such as a video) on the business's Web site, or share content from the business's Web site on the visitor's Facebook page. A Web site can also integrate an *Activity Feed* to show visitors Likes and comments about the site made by the visitor's *Facebook friends*. In addition, a Web site can allow visitors to easily log in to its Web site using the visitor's logon credentials from Facebook or another social network (see Figure 3-22).

Social networking sites are used most often to communicate with existing friends. Facebook (shown in Figure 3-23), for instance, allows you to post photos, videos, music, status updates, and other content for your *Facebook friends* (individuals you have chosen to communicate with via Facebook) to view. You can also chat with your Facebook friends who are currently online, and *Like* or comment on the posts shown on your friends' Facebook pages or in the *news feed* on your Facebook page. For privacy purposes, you can limit access to your Facebook page to the individuals you identify (such as just to your Facebook friends).

FIGURE 3-23

Social networking sites. Allow individuals to exchange posts, photos, videos, messages, and more with their friends.

Courtesy Facebook; Courtesy Throw the Fight www.facebook.com/throwthefight, www.throwthefight.com.

In addition to being used to communicate with existing friends, social networking sites are also used to learn about individuals you currently don't know. For instance, college-bound students can use social media to meet other incoming freshmen before the school year starts, "facestalk" (view the profiles of) other students in their graduating class, look up the profiles of their dorm roommates, find fellow students with common interests, and more—all before actually setting foot on campus. They are also used to share information during natural disasters, such as New Yorkers sharing transportation updates and gas station availability via Twitter during the power outages following Hurricane Sandy.

In addition to being used for personal use, social networking sites today are also viewed as a business marketing tool. For instance, Twitter, Facebook, and YouTube are often used by businesses, political candidates, emerging musicians, and other professionals or professional organizations to increase their online presence. There are also business social networking sites designed for business networking. Some of these sites (such as *LinkedIn*) are used for recruiting new employees, finding new jobs, building professional contacts, and other business activities. Others (such as *StartupNation*) are designed to help entrepreneurs connect with business owners and resources, and exchange ideas. Other specialized social networking sites include sites designed for children (these usually work in a manner similar to Facebook, but they have safeguards in place to prevent personal information from being posted, to monitor language, and so forth) and families (such as to exchange messages, view online tasks lists, and access a shared family calendar).

When using a social networking site, adults and children should be cautious about revealing too much personal information via these sites, both for personal safety reasons and to prevent the information from being used in personalized, targeted *spear phishing* attacks, discussed in Chapter 4. In addition, social networking content is increasingly being monitored by colleges (to find inappropriate behavior by students and to research college applicants) and employers (to find unprofessional behavior by current employees and to research potential job candidates). Because of this, all individuals should be careful about the types of photos and other content they post online. There have been numerous cases over the past few years of students being disciplined or not admitted to a college, and individuals being fired or not hired, due to content posted to a social networking site. Consequently, it is a good idea for individuals to take a close look at their online posts and photos and remove anything that might be potentially embarrassing if viewed by current or future employers, a future partner, or other people important to them now or in the future.

TIP

Social media today is also used by law enforcement. For instance, investigators hunting for the second bomber in the 2013 Boston Marathon attack used the suspects' social networking sites, as well as posts and videos uploaded by witnesses, in the search.

Another emerging issue is what happens to social networking content when someone dies unexpectedly because family members and heirs cannot access the sites without logon information or access to the deceased's e-mail for password recovery purposes. In response, some special services have emerged to help individuals store information about their online assets (such as logon information) and to designate a beneficiary—the person designated to receive that information or to whom the account ownership will be transferred upon the individual's death. Some services can also distribute e-mail messages to designated individuals when the member dies, as well as update the person's bio or change his or her status update to one predesignated by the member. An alternative is for individuals to leave the necessary online contact and access information, as well as instructions regarding how to notify online friends and sites, with a trusted friend or relative who is instructed to use the information only in the event of the individual's death.

Online Shopping and Investing

Online shopping and *online investing* are examples of *e-commerce*—online financial transactions. It is very common today to order products, buy and sell stock, pay bills, and manage financial accounts online. However, because *online fraud*, *credit card fraud*, and *identity theft* (a situation in which someone gains enough personal information to pose as another person) are continuing to grow at a rapid pace, it is important to be cautious when participating in online financial activities. To protect yourself, use a credit card or *online payment service* (such as *PayPal*) whenever possible when purchasing goods or services online so that any fraudulent activities can be disputed. Also, be sure to enter your payment information only on a *secure Web page* (look for a URL that begins with *https* instead of *http*) and don't perform any financial transactions via a public Wi-Fi hotspot. Online financial accounts should also be protected with *strong user passwords* that are changed frequently. Internet security and strong passwords are discussed in detail in Chapter 4.

Online Shopping and Online Auctions

Online shopping is commonly used to purchase both physical products (such as clothing, books, DVDs, shoes, furniture, and more) and downloadable products (such as software, movies, music, and e-books) via Web pages. Typically, shoppers locate the items

>**Online shopping.** Buying products or services over the Internet.

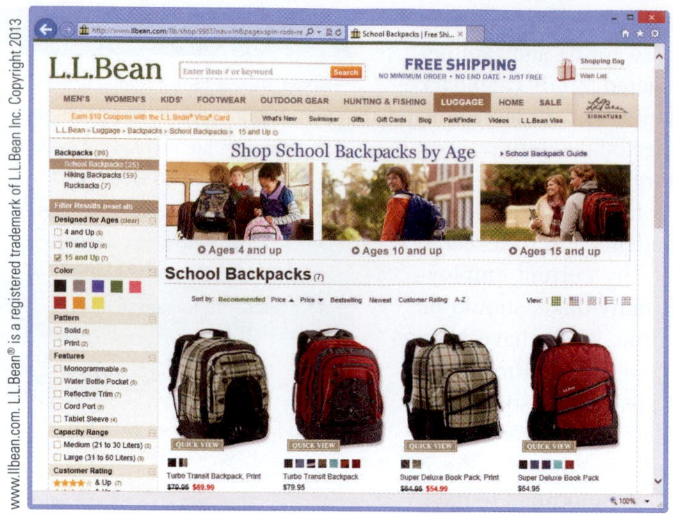

www.llbean.com. L.L.Bean® is a registered trademark of L.L.Bean Inc. Copyright 2013

FIGURE 3-24
Online shopping. Allows you to purchase goods and services online.

they would like to purchase using an online shopping site (such as the L.L. Bean Web site shown in Figure 3-24), and then they add those items to their online *shopping carts* or *shopping bags*. The site's *checkout* process—including supplying the necessary billing and shipping information—is then used to complete the sale. After the payment is processed, the item is either shipped to the customer (if it is a physical product), or the customer is given instructions on how to download it (if it is a downloadable product). Forrester Research predicts that U.S. online sales will reach approximately $370 billion by 2017.

Online auctions are one of the most common ways to purchase items online from other individuals. Sellers list items for sale on an auction site (such as *eBay*) and pay a small listing fee if required, and then pay a commission to the auction site if the item is sold. Individuals can visit the auction site and enter bids on auction items until the end of the auction. At that time, the person with the highest bid is declared the successful bidder (provided the minimum selling price, if one was established, was met) and arranges payment for and delivery of the item directly with the seller. Another common way to purchase items from other individuals is via online classified ads, such as those posted on the popular *Craigslist* site.

Online Banking and Online Investing

Many banks today offer **online banking** as a free service to their customers to enable customers to check balances on all their accounts (such as checking, credit cards, mortgage, and investment accounts), view cashed checks and other transactions, transfer funds between accounts, pay bills electronically, and perform other activities related to their bank accounts. Online banking is continually growing and can be performed via a computer or a mobile device. In fact, most banks today allow users to view balances, transfer funds, make remote check deposits, and more via a mobile Web site, mobile banking app, or text message (see Figure 3-25).

FIGURE 3-25
Mobile banking.

Courtesy Ally Bank

Buying and selling stocks, bonds, mutual funds, and other types of securities is referred to as **online investing**. Although it is common to see stock quote capabilities on many search and news sites, trading stocks and other securities requires an *online broker*. The biggest advantages of online investing include lower transaction fees and the ability to quickly buy or sell stock when desired, without having to make a phone call—a convenience for those investors who do a lot of trading. Common online investing services include the ability to order sales and purchases; access performance histories, corporate news, and other useful investment information; and set up an *online portfolio* that displays the status of the stocks you specify. On some Web sites, stock price data is delayed 20 minutes; on other sites, real-time quotes are available. Like other Web page data, stock price data is current at the time it is retrieved via a Web page, but it may not be updated (and you will not see current quotes, for instance) until you reload the Web page using your browser's Refresh or Reload toolbar button.

>**Online auction.** An online activity where bids are placed for items, and the highest bidder purchases the item. >**Online banking.** Performing banking activities via the Web. >**Online investing.** Buying and selling stocks or other types of investments via the Web.

Online Entertainment

There are an ever-growing number of ways to use the Web for entertainment purposes, such as listening to music, watching TV and videos, and playing online games. Some applications can be accessed with virtually any type of Internet connection; others are only practical with a broadband connection. Many online entertainment applications require the use of a *media player program* or *plug-in* (such as *QuickTime Player* or *Silverlight*) to deliver multimedia content.

Online Music

There are a number of options available today for **online music**, such as listening to live radio broadcasts via an *online radio station*, watching music videos on *MTV.com* or *Yahoo! Music*, listening to or downloading music on demand via a monthly *online music subscription service*, or downloading music from *online music stores*, such as the *iTunes Music Store* or *Amazon MP3*. Music can be listened to or downloaded via a computer, mobile phone, or portable digital media player. Music files downloaded to your computer can be played from your computer's hard drive; they can also be copied to a CD to create a custom music CD or transferred to a portable digital media player or mobile phone provided the download agreement does not preclude it. Most online music is accessed via a mobile device and online subscription services are viewed as the fastest growing online music market. In fact, Juniper Research predicts the number of mobile online music subscribers will hit 178 million users by 2015.

Online TV, Videos, and Movies

Watching TV shows, videos, and movies online is another very popular type of online entertainment (see Figure 3-26). **Online videos** (such as news videos and movie trailers, videos posted to Web sites belonging to businesses and other organizations, personal

FIGURE 3-26
TV, videos, and movies are commonly watched online.

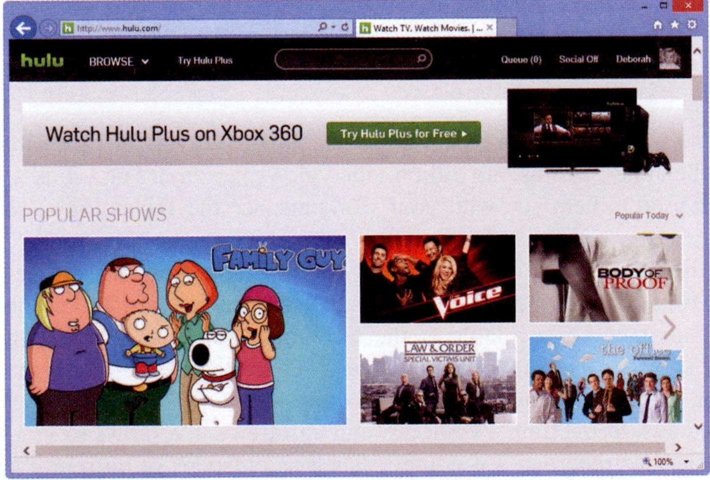

ONLINE TV AND MOVIES
TV shows and movies can be watched online for free via a variety of Web sites.

VIDEO-ON-DEMAND
Rented or purchased TV shows and movies can be delivered to your computer, TV, or mobile device.

>**Online music.** Music played or obtained via the Web. >**Online video.** Video watched or downloaded via the Web.

TECHNOLOGY AND YOU

High-Tech Workouts

Got a smartphone or media tablet? You now have a personal trainer. From apps that remind you when it's time to work out, to apps that use the accelerometer on your smartphone to chart your workout progress, to apps that provide you with a personal video workout, mobile video workouts are hot.

A leader in the area of mobile video workouts is *PumpOne*, which offers mobile personal training (see the accompanying illustration). Video workouts are available on demand in a variety of areas, such as strength training, weight loss, toning, overall conditioning, cardio, flexibility, and sports conditioning. Workouts are streamed to the appropriate device, range from 10 minutes to over an hour, and can be purchased on an unlimited basis or subscribed to on a month-to-month basis (selected workouts are free). Other options include the ability to share workouts with others and ask questions of a personal trainer.

Other popular high-tech workout tools include dumbbells that attach to a Wii remote and nunchuk to add resistance training to Wii Fit workouts; wristbands and watches that track your pace, distance, time, and calories burned on a run and that can upload this data in order to chart your programs online; and scales that record your weight and BMI and then upload this data to a Web site so you can view your weight history via a computer or smartphone.

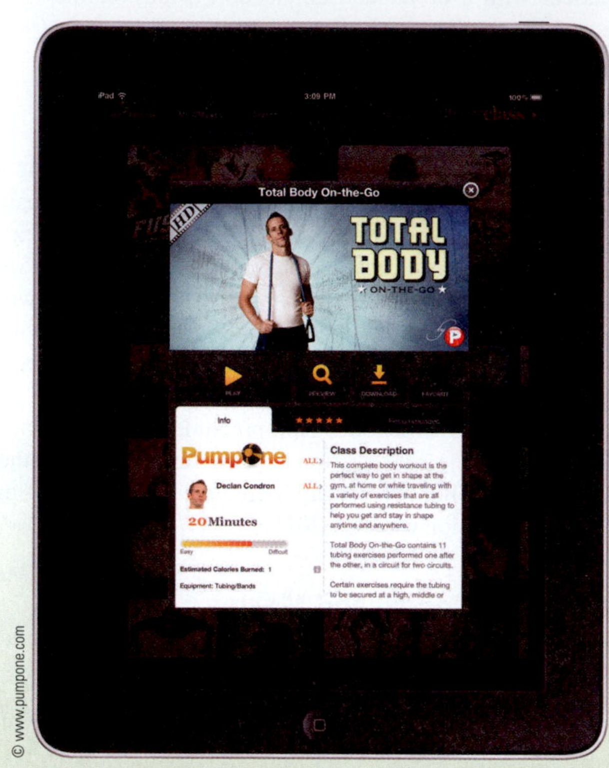

A PumpOne iPad video workout.

> **TIP**
>
> Research shows that overall streaming video usage is climbing rapidly and the trend of delivering TV and movie content to consumers wherever they are and to whatever device they prefer to use is expanding to traditional TV services, such as via the new *TV Everywhere* option available from some TV providers.

videos posted to blogs and social networking pages, and videos shared via YouTube) are widely available (YouTube alone streams one billion video views per day). For a look at how online video can be used to help you with your workouts, see the Technology and You box.

Another option is **online TV** and **online movies**. Both are available from wireless providers, TV networks, and third-party Web sites. TV shows and movies can be watched *live*, which means they are available at the time they are being aired (such as news broadcasts and sporting events) or they can be downloaded or viewed at the user's convenience. For example, many wireless providers offer *mobile TV*, which delivers live sports, live news, primetime TV shows, and children's TV shows to your smartphone. A wide variety of recorded TV content (such as episodes of current TV shows after they have been aired) is also available through the respective television network Web sites for viewing online. Both TV shows and movies are available through a number of Web sites, such as *Hulu* (shown in Figure 3-26), *TV.com*, *Xfinity TV*, and

>**Online TV.** Live or recorded TV shows available via the Web. >**Online movies.** Feature films available via the Web.

Zap2It. In addition, YouTube and the *Internet Movie Database* (*IMDb*) have full-length TV shows and movies that visitors can watch for free, and Amazon has thousands of TV shows and movies that *Amazon Prime* members can stream at no charge to their Kindles and other devices. A new trend is the development of TV shows that are only available online (such as the recent seasons of *Arrested Development* that are only available on Netflix and Hulu, and the recent revival of cancelled soap operas, like *All My Children* and *One Life to Live*, that are only available via the Web). Typically, online TV and online movies are streaming media, in which the video plays from the server when it is requested. Consequently, you need an Internet connection in order to view the video.

While much of the online TV, videos, and movies already mentioned are available free of charge (one exception is mobile TV, which is often available on a subscription basis), renting movies and TV shows that are delivered to your device at your request—referred to as **video-on-demand (VOD)**—is another option. VOD can be ordered through an individual's cable or satellite TV company or, more commonly today, through a cloud VOD provider such as *CinemaNow*, *iTunes*, *BLOCKBUSTER OnDemand*, or *Amazon Instant Video*). Rentals typically cost $4.99 or less; purchasing a movie costs around $15. In either case, the movies are streamed or downloaded to a computer, to a DVR or other device (such as a digital media player, a Blu-ray player, or a gaming console) that is connected to your TV, or to a smartphone or media tablet (refer again to Figure 3-26). Rented movies can usually be viewed only for a limited time; some services allow movies downloaded to a computer to be transferred to a portable digital media player or other mobile device during the allowable viewable period. One popular VOD option is *Netflix*, which offers unlimited video streaming to a TV, gaming console, computer, or mobile device for $8 per month.

With the arrival of today's smart TVs, TV shows and movies can now be delivered via the Internet directly to your television, along with other features such as interactive polls related to the TV show being viewed (as shown in Figure 3-5 earlier in this chapter), or *widgets* or *gadgets*—small pieces of current information such as sport scores, news headlines, or product information.

TIP

To view streaming video without it appearing choppy, Internet service that delivers a minimum download speed of 1.5 Mbps is recommended.

TIP

According to a recent Sandvine report, 33% of peak downstream Internet traffic in the United States is attributed to Netflix.

Online Gaming

Online gaming refers to games played over the Internet. Many sites—especially children's Web sites—include games for visitors to play. There are also sites whose sole purpose is hosting games that can be played online. Some of the games are designed to be played alone or with just one other person. Others, called *online multiplayer games*, are designed to be played online against many other online gamers. Online multiplayer games (such as *Doom*, *EverQuest*, *Final Fantasy*, and *City of Heroes*) are especially popular in countries, such as South Korea, that have readily available high-speed Internet connections and high levels of Internet use in general. Internet-enabled gaming consoles (such as recent versions of the PlayStation, Xbox, and Wii consoles) and portable gaming devices (such as the Sony PSP and Nintendo 3DS) that have built-in Internet connectivity can also be used for multiplayer online gaming. Online gaming is also associated quite often with *Internet addiction*—the inability to stop using the Internet or to prevent extensive use of the Internet from interfering with other aspects of one's life. Internet addiction is a growing concern and is discussed in more detail in Chapter 7.

TIP

An emerging trend is *gamification*; that is, using gaming elements (like the ability to earn points or rewards) in a non-entertainment context, such as for customer and employee engagement.

>**Video-on-demand (VOD).** The process of downloading movies and television shows, on demand, via the Web. >**Online gaming.** Playing games via the Web.

Online News, Reference, and Information

There is an abundance of news and other important information available through the Internet. The following sections discuss some of the most widely used news, reference, and information resources.

News and Reference Information

News organizations, such as television networks, newspapers, and magazines, nearly always have Web sites that are updated on a continual basis to provide access to current local and world news, as well as sports, entertainment, health, travel, politics, weather, and other news topics (see the *ABC News* Web site in Figure 3-27). Many news sites also have searchable archives to look for past articles, although some require a fee to view back articles. Once articles are displayed, they can typically be saved, printed, or sent to other individuals via e-mail. A growing trend is for newspapers and magazines to abandon print subscriptions and to provide Web-only service—primarily for cost reasons. Although some subscribers miss the print versions, there are some advantages to digital versions, such as the ability to easily search through content in some digital publications. Other online news resources include news radio programs that are broadcast over the Internet, as well as the wide variety of news video clips available through many Web sites.

Online news is commonly read on home or business computers, as well as on smartphones and media tablets. However, reading full news articles on a small device is sometimes difficult and, consequently, has resulted in the development of news apps (such as *Summly*, recently acquired by Yahoo!) that summarize the news you want to see, such as by news sources or by topics, for easier reading on your mobile device. News can also be delivered via headlines displayed on smart TVs, as well as via an app (such as the Windows 8 *News* live tile) that can be clicked to display that news story.

Reference sites are designed to provide users access to specific types of useful information. For example, reference sites can be used to generate maps (see the *MapQuest* Web site in Figure 3-27), check the weather forecast, look up the value of a home, or provide access to encyclopedias, dictionaries, ZIP Code directories, and telephone directories. One potential downside to the increased availability of online reference sites is use by criminals. For instance, one California lawmaker has introduced a bill requiring mapping sites to blur out details of schools, churches, and government buildings after being informed that some terrorists have used these maps to plan bombings and other attacks.

FIGURE 3-27
Online news and reference Web sites.

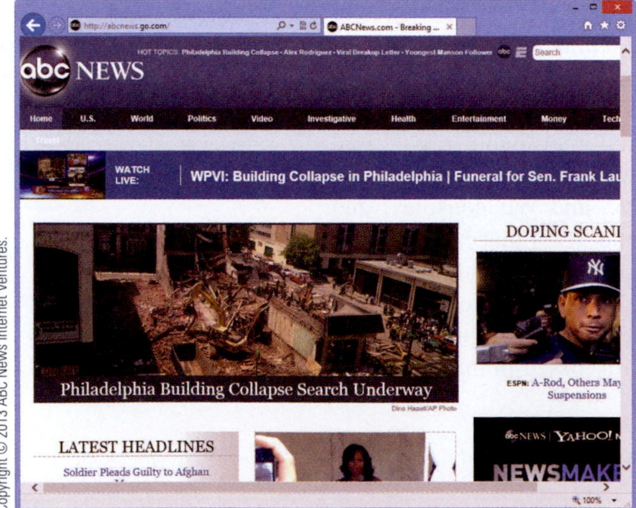

NEWS SITES
News organizations typically update their sites several times per day to provide access to the most current news and information.

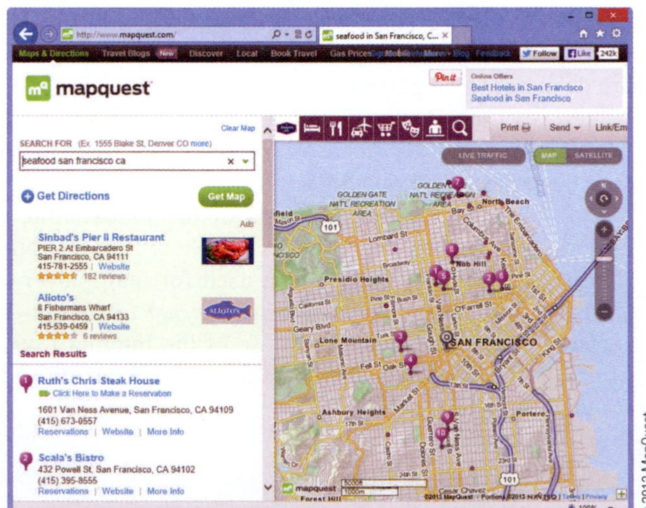

REFERENCE SITES
Reference Web sites provide access to specific types of useful information, such as the maps and driving directions available via this Web site.

Portal Pages, RSS Feeds, and Podcasts

Portal Web pages are Web pages designed to be selected as a browser's home page and used as a launching pad to access other Web pages. Portal pages (such as the *MSN* page for Windows 8 shown in Figure 3-28) typically include search capabilities, news headlines, weather, and other useful content, and can often be customized by users to display their requested content. Once a portal page is customized, the specified information is displayed each time the user visits the portal page. Popular portals include *My Yahoo!*, *MSN*, and *AOL.com*.

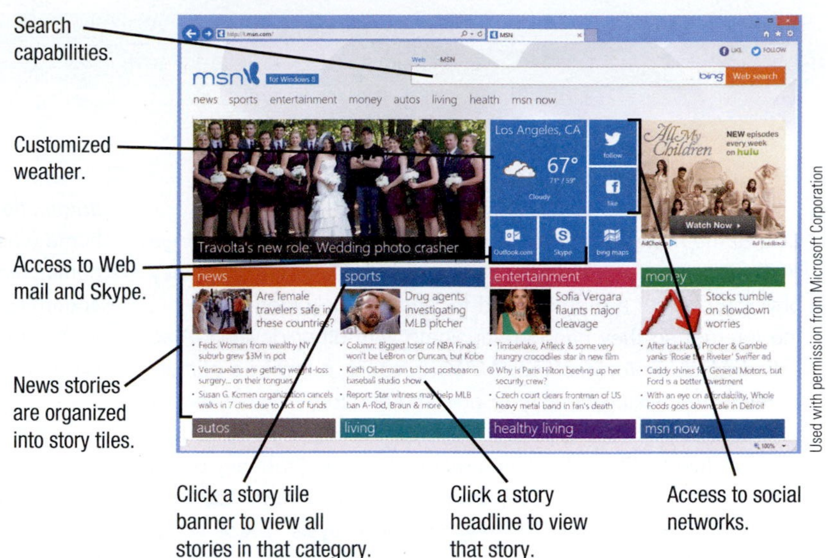

Search capabilities.
Customized weather.
Access to Web mail and Skype.
News stories are organized into story tiles.
Click a story tile banner to view all stories in that category.
Click a story headline to view that story.
Access to social networks.

Used with permission from Microsoft Corporation

FIGURE 3-28
Portal pages. Portal pages can contain a wide variety of customized news and information.

RSS (Really Simple Syndication) is an online tool designed for delivering news articles, *blogs* (discussed shortly), and other content regularly published to a Web site. Provided the content has an associated *RSS feed*, individuals can *subscribe* (usually for free) to that feed and then the content will be delivered as it becomes available. You can subscribe to an RSS feed by clicking a *subscribe* link on the associated Web page to add the feed content to your browser *feed list*; if you are using an *RSS reader* (such as *Feedly* shown in Figure 3-29), you can typically search for new feeds using that program. To view the feed content, either select that feed from your browser's feed list (such as on the *Feeds* tab in the Favorites list in Internet Explorer) or click the appropriate link in your RSS reader. RSS readers often allow you to organize your feed into categories, as shown in Figure 3-29. In either case, as new content for the subscribed feed becomes available, it will be accessible via the feed links. In the future, we will likely see RSS feeds delivered directly to watches, refrigerators, and other consumer devices that have a display screen.

FIGURE 3-29
RSS readers. RSS feeds (right) can often be organized into categories (left).

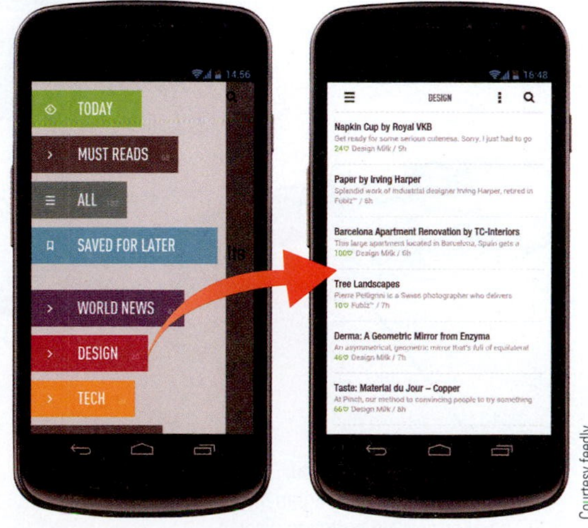

Courtesy feedly

Another Web resource that can provide you with useful information is a **podcast**—a recorded audio or video file that can be downloaded via the Internet. The term *podcast* is derived from the iPod portable digital media player (the first widely used device for playing digital audio files), although podcasts today can also be listened to using a computer or mobile phone.

Podcasting (creating a podcast) enables individuals to create self-published, inexpensive Internet radio broadcasts in order to share their knowledge, express their opinions on particular subjects, or share original poems, songs, or short stories with interested individuals. Originally created and distributed by individuals, podcasts are now also being created and distributed by businesses. For instance, some commercial radio stations are making portions of their broadcasts available via podcasts, and a growing number of news sites and corporate sites now have regular podcasts available. In fact, some view podcasts as the new and improved radio because it is an easy way to listen to your favorite radio broadcasts on your own schedule. Podcasts are also used for educational purposes. Podcasts are typically uploaded to the Web on a regular basis, and RSS feeds can be used to notify subscribers when a new podcast is available.

>**Portal Web page.** A Web page designed to be designated as a browser home page; typically can be customized to display personalized content.
>**RSS (Really Simple Syndication).** A tool used to deliver selected Web content to subscribers as the content is published to a Web site.
>**Podcast.** A recorded audio or video file that can be played or downloaded via the Web.

TREND

The Internet of Things (IoT)

One of the hottest Internet topics today is the *Internet of Things* (*IoT*). The Internet of Things refers to a world where everyday physical objects are connected to, and uniquely identifiable on, the Internet so they can communicate with other devices. Also called *Machine-to-Machine* (*M2M*) because it involves primarily machines talking directly to one another, the IoT is expected to greatly impact our lives and the way we get information and control objects. The IoT will be created by turning formerly dumb objects into smart devices (using sensors and other technology) that can send data to a system for analysis. These smart devices can range from sensors in your shoes, to smart fitness devices, to healthcare monitors, to home automation systems, to smart farm equipment, to smart freeways and traffic lights. These smart devices will communicate with each other (such as over low-power *Bluetooth Smart* technology) to, in theory, provide advantages such as making our lives more convenient, saving us money, and providing us with better healthcare and other services. Businesses will benefit from getting feedback from equipment (being notified when a machine in the field needs service or refilling, for instance, without an employee having to physically monitor it), being able to automate more processes, and getting faster and more accurate feedback about point-of-sale purchases.

One example of a personal application of IoT is *home automation*—enabling the appliances and other devices in your home (such as your alarm system, door locks, and sprinklers) to communicate with you and each other so the devices operate according to your stated preferences or observed habits, as well as be able to give you the power to control devices remotely via your smartphone, as discussed in Chapter 8. Fitness systems are another example. For instance, the *Nike+ FuelBand* uses a sports-tested accelerometer to track your daily activity—including running, walking, dancing, and basketball (professional basketball player Kevin Durant is wearing a *Nike+* FuelBand in the accompanying photo)—in steps, time of day, and calories burned. It converts your activity into *NikeFuel*, a universal measurement of activity, and syncs the data with your PC or mobile device. You can set a personal goal for yourself (and monitor your progress toward that goal by viewing the lights on the edge of the band, as well as by looking at your stats on your PC or phone). You can also share your data with others via Facebook and Twitter. Other Nike+ products can be used for more sports-specific tracking, such as for running (via the *Nike+ SportWatch GPS*) or basketball (via sensors embedded in the soles of the *Nike+ Basketball* shoes). While the IoT is larger than just home automation and *wearable* technology, these two initial IoT applications may be the ones that impact individuals the most.

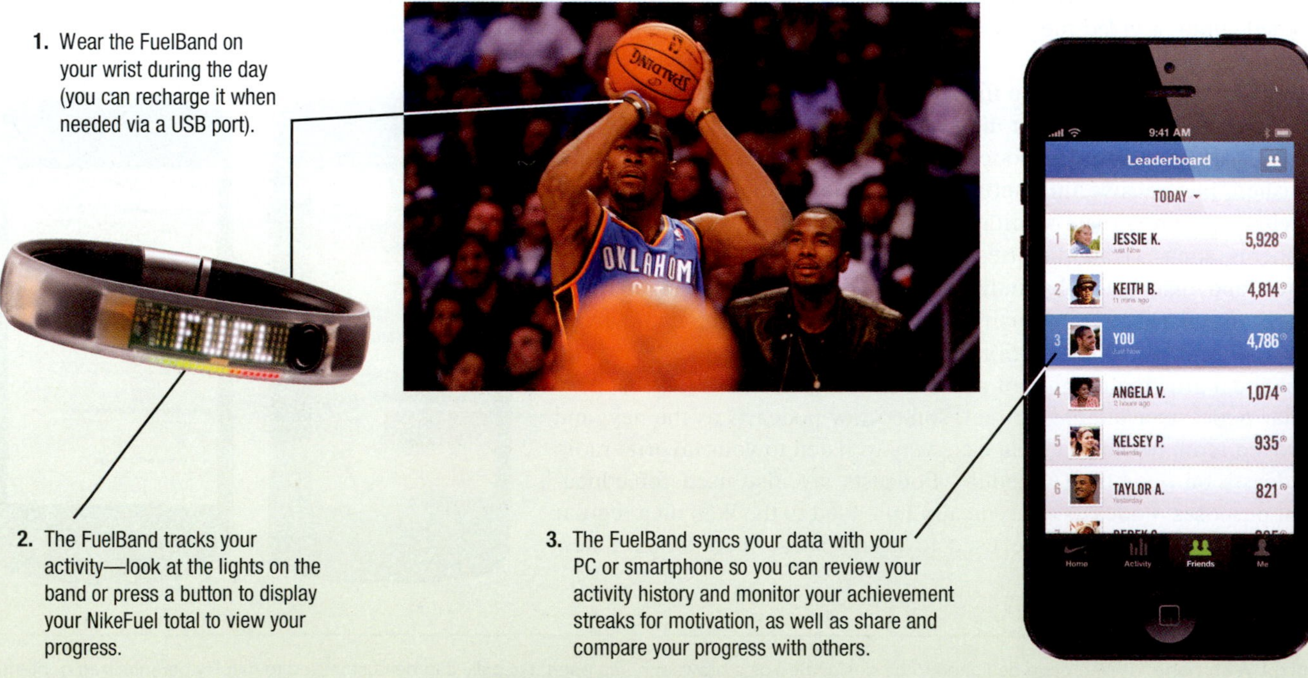

1. Wear the FuelBand on your wrist during the day (you can recharge it when needed via a USB port).
FUEL
9:41 AM
Leaderboard
TODAY
1 JESSIE K. 5,928
2 KEITH B. 4,814
3 YOU 4,786
4 ANGELA V. 1,074
5 KELSEY P. 935
6 TAYLOR A. 821
Home
Activity
Friends
Me
2. The FuelBand tracks your activity—look at the lights on the band or press a button to display your NikeFuel total to view your progress.
3. The FuelBand syncs your data with your PC or smartphone so you can review your activity history and monitor your achievement streaks for motivation, as well as share and compare your progress with others.

Courtesy Nike Inc.

How the Nike+ FuelBand works.

Product, Corporate, Government, and Other Information

The Web is a very useful tool for locating product and corporate information. Manufacturer and retailer Web sites often include product specifications, instruction manuals, and other information that is useful to consumers before or after they purchase a product. There are also numerous consumer review sites (such as *Epinions.com*) to help purchasers evaluate their options before buying a product online or in a physical store; many online stores (such as Amazon.com) also include customer reviews on product pages. For investors and consumers, a variety of corporate information is available online, from both company Web sites and sites (such as *Hoovers.com*) that offer free or fee-based corporate information. For a look at an emerging Internet trend that is beginning to impact both business and individuals—the *Internet of Things* (*IoT*)—see the Trend box.

Courtesy FactCheck.org

FIGURE 3-30

FactCheck.org. This Web site can be used to check the accuracy of political statements.

Government information is also widely available on the Internet. Most state and federal agencies have Web sites to provide information to citizens, such as government publications, archived documents, forms, and legislative bills. You can also perform a variety of tasks, such as downloading tax forms and filing your tax returns online. In addition, many cities, counties, and states allow you to pay your car registration fees, register to vote, view property tax information, or make an appointment to renew your driver's license online.

There is also a wide variety of information available from various organizations, such as nonprofit organizations, conservation groups, political parties, and more. For instance, many sites dedicated to energy conservation and saving the environment have emerged over the past few years to bring awareness to this issue, and there are numerous online resources for learning the positions of political candidates and other information important to voters. For example, the nonpartisan *FactCheck.org* Web site shown in Figure 3-30 is dedicated to monitoring the factual accuracy of what is being said by major U.S. political candidates and elected officials and reporting it, in an attempt to reduce the level of deception and confusion in U.S. politics.

Online Education and Writing

Online education—using the Internet to facilitate learning—is a rapidly growing Internet application. The Internet can be used to deliver part or all of any educational class or program; it can also be used to supplement or support traditional education. In addition, many high school and college courses use Web content—such as online syllabi, schedules, discussion boards, podcasts, and tutorials—as required or suggested supplements. For example, the Web site that supplements this book contains

ASK THE EXPERT

Courtesy of IHG

Nick Ayres, Manager, Social Marketing, IHG

How important is it for a business to have a social media presence today?

Today, customers across every industry and geography expect brands to meet them where they are. Social media has become table stakes for doing business in the 21st century and is no longer a "nice to have" marketing tool.

A social media footprint that spans the right social channels is an important step toward meeting these expectations. Importantly, however, this social media footprint is only the first step because its primary relevance comes in its ability to deliver a mechanism by which we can activate a robust customer engagement and dialog strategy.

Ultimately, we at IHG win when we find ways to deliver seamless, interactive, and dynamic hotel brand experiences—both on and offline—whether it's an InterContinental® resort or a city-center Holiday Inn® hotel, as that is increasingly what our customers expect and deserve. And while this is no small task, we believe success in this arena can produce a sustainable competitive advantage.

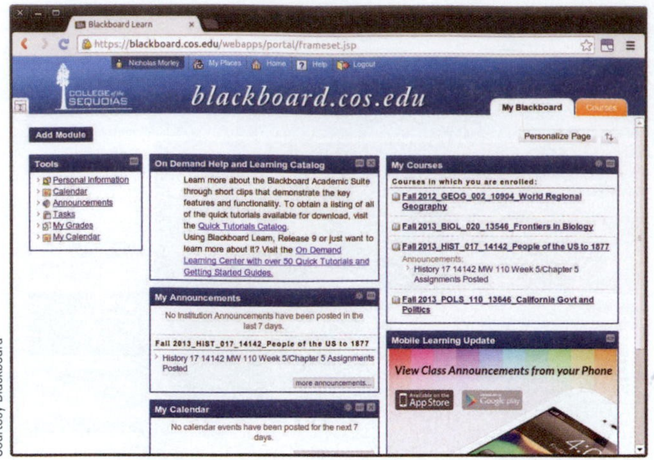

Courtesy Blackboard

FIGURE 3-31
Blackboard. This learning management system can be used to view and complete assignments, view grades and announcements, and more.

an online study guide, online quizzes, online hands-on labs, Web links, downloadable audio and video podcasts, streaming videos, and other online resources for students taking a course that uses this textbook. There are also Web-based *learning management systems* (such as *Blackboard*, shown in Figure 3-31) that are often used to deliver course content, manage assignments and grades, and more; and the use of *student response systems*—where students use a special device or their mobile phone to respond to surveys or review questions during in-class lectures is growing. The next few sections take a look at some of the most widely used online education applications.

Web-Based Training and Distance Learning

The term **Web-based training** (**WBT**) refers to any instruction delivered via the Web. It is commonly used for employee training, as well as for delivering instruction in an educational setting. **Distance learning** occurs whenever students take classes from a location—often home or work—which is different from the one where the delivery of instruction takes place. Distance learning today typically includes Web-based training or other online learning tools (and so is also called *online learning* and *e-learning*) and is available through many high schools, colleges, and universities, as well as organizations that provide professional certifications. Distance learning can be used to learn just one task or new skill; it can also be used to complete an *online course* or an entire degree online via an accredited college or university. Typically the majority of distance learning coursework is completed over the Internet via class Web pages, YouTube videos, Webinars, podcasts, discussion groups, e-mail, and learning management systems like Blackboard (refer again to Figure 3-31), although schools might require some in-person contact, such as sessions for orientation and testing.

The biggest advantage of Web-based training and distance learning is that they are typically experienced individually and at the user's own pace. Online content for Web-based training components is frequently customized to match the pace of each individual user and can be completed at the user's convenience. Web-based content can be updated as needed and online content and activities (such as exercises, exams, and animations) typically provide immediate feedback to the student. One disadvantage is the possibility of technological problems—because students need a working device and Internet connection to access the material, they cannot participate if they have no access to a computer or an appropriate mobile device, or if their device, their Internet connection, or the Web server hosting the material goes down. Another concern among educators is the lack of face-to-face contact, and security issues—such as the difficulty in ensuring that the appropriate student is completing assignments or taking exams. Some possible solutions for this latter concern are discussed in the next section.

TIP

Some distance learning classes today use *synchronous* or *live online learning*, where students and instructors are online at the same time; this has the benefit of encouraging interaction, questions and answers, and other types of instant feedback.

TIP

Online courses that have no tuition and are open to anyone via the Internet are sometimes referred to as *Massive Open Online Courses* (*MOOCs*).

Online Testing

In both distance learning and traditional classes, *online testing*—which allows students to take tests via the Internet—is a growing trend. Both objective tests (such as those containing multiple choice or true/false questions) and performance-based exams (such as those given in computer classes to test student mastery of software applications) can be administered and taken online. For instance, there are *SAM* (*Skills Assessment Manager*) tests available for use

>**Web-based training (WBT).** Instruction delivered on an individual basis via the Web. >**Distance learning.** A learning environment in which the student is physically located away from the instructor and other students; commonly, instruction and communications take place via the Web.

in conjunction with this textbook to test both Microsoft Office software skills and computer concepts. Typically online tests are graded automatically, providing fast feedback to the students, as well as freeing up the instructor's time for other activities. One recent debate focuses on the use of computers to automatically grade essay tests after "learning" how to grade them by reviewing essay exams that the instructor scored.

One challenge for online testing is ensuring that an online test is taken by the appropriate individual and in an authorized manner in order to avoid cheating. Some distance learning programs require students to go physically to a testing center to take the test or to find an acceptable test proctor (such as an educator at a nearby school or a commanding officer for military personnel). Other options are using smart cards, fingerprint scans, and other means to authenticate students taking an online exam from a remote location. For instance, one secure testing solution being used at a number of schools nationwide to enable students to take online tests from their remote locations while still ensuring the integrity of the exams is the *Remote Proctor PRO* system shown in Figure 3-32. The Remote Proctor PRO device first authenticates the individual taking the test via a fingerprint scan, and then captures real-time audio and video during the exam. The device's camera points to a reflective ball, which allows it to capture a full 360-degree image of the room, and the recording is uploaded to a server so it can be viewed by the instructor from his or her location. The Remote Proctor PRO software locks down the computer so that it cannot be used for any purpose not allowed during the test (such as performing an Internet search). It also flags suspicious behavior (such as significant noises or movements) in the recording so that the instructor can review those portions of the recording to see if any unauthorized behavior (such as leaving the room or making a telephone call) occurred during the testing period.

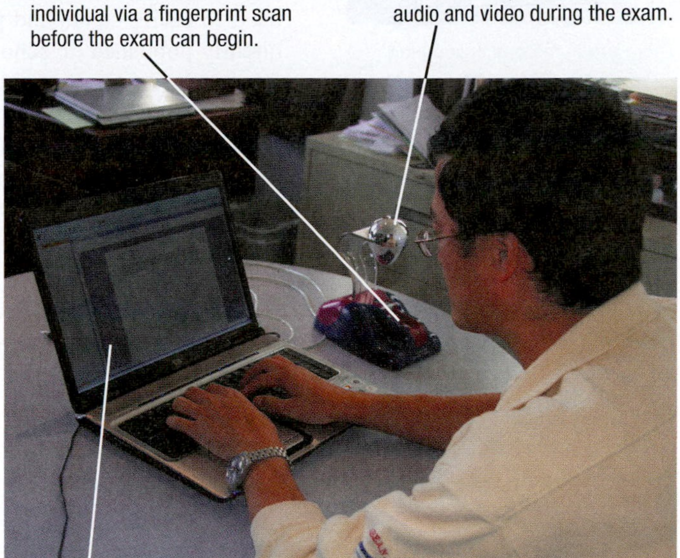

Courtesy Software Secure, Inc.

FIGURE 3-32 **Secure online testing.**

Blogs, Wikis, and Other Types of Online Writing

Some types of online writing, such as e-mail, instant and text messaging, and social networking updates, were discussed earlier in this chapter. A few additional types of online writing are discussed next.

A **blog**—also called a *Web log*—is a Web page that contains short, frequently updated entries in chronological order, typically as a means of expression or communication (see the food blog shown in Figure 3-33). In essence, a blog is an online personal journal accessible to the public that is usually created and updated by one individual. Blogs are written by a wide variety of individuals—including ordinary people, as well as celebrities, writers, students, and experts on particular subjects—and can be used to post personal commentary, research updates, comments on current events, political opinions, celebrity gossip, travel diaries, television show recaps, and more.

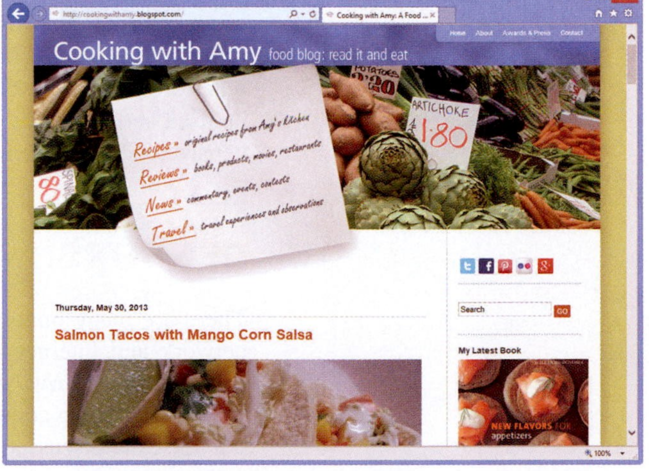

Courtesy Amy Sherman

FIGURE 3-33 **Blogs.** Allow individuals to post entries to an online personal journal.

>Blog. A Web page that contains short, frequently updated entries in chronological order, typically by just one individual.

TIP

There are numerous online blog directories—such as Technorati and Tumblr—to help you find blogs that meet your interests.

Blogging software, which is available via blogging sites such as Blogger.com, is often used to easily create and publish blogs and blog updates to the Web. Blogs are also frequently published on school, business, and personal Web sites. Blogs are usually updated frequently, and entries can be posted via computers, e-mail, and mobile devices. Blogs often contain text, photos, and video clips. With their increased use and audiences, bloggers and the *blogosphere* (the complete collection of blogs on the Internet) are beginning to have increasing influence on businesses, politicians, and individuals today. One new ethical issue surrounding blogging relates to bloggers who are paid to blog about certain products. Although some Web sites that match up bloggers with advertisers require that the blogger reveal that he or she receives payment for "sponsored" posts, some believe that commercializing blogging will corrupt the blogosphere. Others, however, view it as a natural evolution of word-of-mouth advertising.

Another form of online writing sometimes used for educational purposes is the **wiki**. Wikis, named for the Hawaiian phrase *wiki wiki* meaning *quick*, are a way of creating and editing collaborative Web pages quickly and easily. Similar to a blog, the content on a wiki page can be edited and republished to the Web just by pressing a Save or Submit button. However, wikis are intended to be modified by others and so are especially appropriate for collaboration, such as for class Web pages or group projects. To protect the content of a wiki from sabotage, the entire wiki or editing privileges for a wiki can be password protected.

Courtesy Wikipedia

FIGURE 3-34
Wikis. Wikis, such as the Wikipedia collaborative online encyclopedia shown here, can be edited by any authorized individual.

One of the largest wikis is *Wikipedia* (shown in Figure 3-34), a free online encyclopedia that contains over 25 million articles written in 287 languages, is updated by volunteer contributors, and is visited by more than half a billion individuals every month. While most Wikipedia contributors edit articles in a responsible manner, there are instances erroneous information being added to Wikipedia pages intentionally. As with any resource, visitors should carefully evaluate the content of a Wikipedia article before referencing it in a report, Web page, or other document, as discussed earlier in this chapter.

An **e-portfolio**, also called an *electronic portfolio* or *digital portfolio*, is a collection of an individual's work accessible through a Web site. Today's e-portfolios are typically linked to a collection of student-related information, such as résumés, papers, projects, and other original works. Some e-portfolios are used for a single course; others are designed to be used and updated throughout a student's educational career, culminating in a comprehensive collection of information that can be used as a job-hunting tool.

CENSORSHIP AND PRIVACY ISSUES

There are many important societal issues related to the Internet. One important issue—network and Internet security—is covered in Chapter 4. Two other important issues—*censorship* and *privacy*—are discussed next, in the context of Internet use. Other societal issues—including computer security, ethics, health, and the environment—related to computer use are discussed in further detail in Chapters 5, 6, and 7.

>**Wiki.** A collaborative Web page that is designed to be edited and republished by a variety of individuals. >**E-portfolio.** A collection of an individual's work accessible via the Web.

Censorship

The issue of Internet censorship affects all countries that have Internet access. In some countries, Internet content is filtered by the government, typically to hinder the spread of information from political opposition groups, to filter out subjects deemed offensive, or to block information from sites that could endanger national security. Increasingly, some countries are also blocking information (such as blogs and personal Web pages) from leaving the country, and have occasionally completely shut down Internet access to and from the country during political protests to stop the flow of information in and out of that country. For instance, all Internet and cell phone service was shut down in Egypt for about one week in 2011 because of mounting political unrest in that country.

In the United States, the First Amendment to the U.S. Constitution guarantees a citizen's right to free speech. This protection allows people to say things to others without fear of arrest. But how does the right to free speech relate to potentially offensive or indecent materials available over the Internet where they might be observed by children or by people who do not wish to see them? There have been some attempts in the United States and other countries to regulate Internet content—what some would view as *censorship*—in recent years, but the courts have had difficulty defining what is "patently offensive" and "indecent" as well as finding a fair balance between protection and censorship. For example, the *Communications Decency Act*, which was signed into law in 1996, made it a criminal offense to distribute patently indecent or offensive material online in order to protect children from being exposed to inappropriate Web content. In 1997, however, the Supreme Court overturned the portion of this law pertaining to indecent material on the basis of free speech, making this content legal to distribute via the Internet and protecting Web sites that host third-party content from being liable for that content.

Another example of legislation designed to protect children from inappropriate Web content is the *Children's Internet Protection Act* (*CIPA*). CIPA requires public libraries and schools to implement Internet safety policies and technologies to block children's access to inappropriate Web content in order to receive certain public funds. While this law was intended to protect children, it was fought strenuously by free speech advocacy groups and some library associations on the basis that limiting access to some Internet content violates an individual's First Amendment rights to free speech. While CIPA was ruled unconstitutional by a federal court in 2002, the Supreme Court reversed the lower court decision in 2003 and ruled that the law is constitutional because the need for libraries to prevent minors from accessing obscene materials outweighs the free speech rights of library patrons and Web site publishers. However, the Court also modified the law to require a library to remove the technologies for an adult library patron at the patron's request.

One technology commonly used to conform to CIPA regulations, as well as by parents and employees, is **Internet filtering**—the act of blocking access to particular Web pages or types of Web pages. It can be used on home computers or mobile devices by individuals to protect themselves from material they would view as offensive or by parents to protect their children from material they feel is inappropriate. It is also commonly used by employers to keep employees from accessing non-work-related sites, by some ISPs and search sites to block access to potentially objectionable materials, and by many schools and libraries to control the Web content that children are able to view in order to be in compliance with CIPA. Internet filtering typically restricts access to Web pages that contain offensive language, sex/pornography, racism, drugs, or violence

>**Internet filtering.** Using a software program or browser option to block access to particular Web pages or types of Web pages.

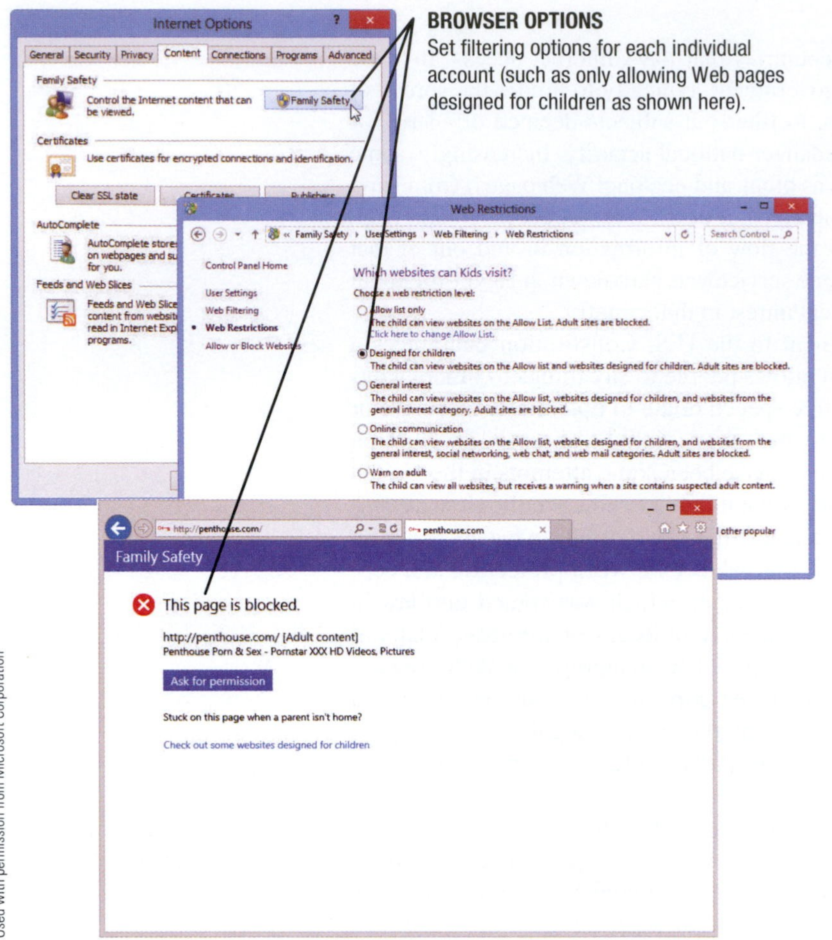

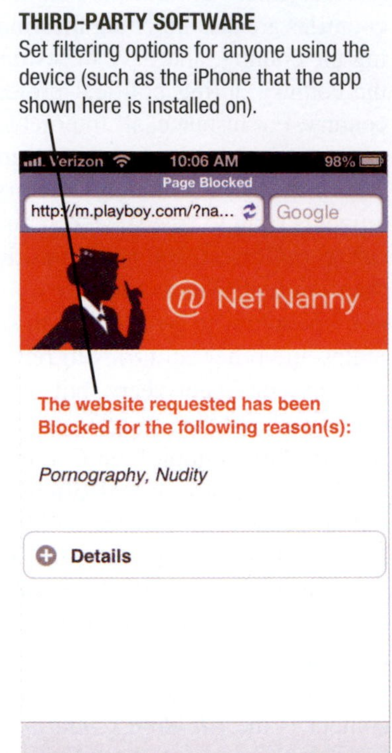

FIGURE 3-35
Internet filtering.

(based on either the keywords contained on each site or a database of URLs containing restricted content). It can also be used to block access to specific sites (such as social networking sites, YouTube, or eBay), as well as to restrict the total number of hours or the time of day that the Internet can be used.

Most browsers include some Internet filtering options. For instance, Internet Explorer's *Family Safety* options (see Figure 3-35) can be used to filter the Web sites displayed for specific users of a particular computer (although blocked Web sites can be viewed if the user knows the administrator password). More comprehensive Internet filtering can be obtained with stand-alone filtering programs, such as *NetNanny* (also shown in Figure 3-35) or *Safe Eyes* for parents, or *Netsweeper* for schools and businesses.

Web Browsing Privacy

Privacy, as it relates to the Internet, encompasses what information about individuals is available, how it is used, and by whom. As more and more transactions and daily activities are being performed online, there is the potential for vast amounts of private information to be collected and distributed without the individual's knowledge or permission. Therefore, it is understandable that public concern regarding privacy and the Internet is on the rise. Although personal privacy is discussed in more detail in Chapter 5, a few issues that are of special concern to Internet users regarding Web browsing privacy and e-mail privacy are discussed in the next few sections.

Cookies

Many Web pages today use **cookies**—small text files that are stored on your hard drive by a Web server—to identify return visitors and their preferences. Some cookies are *session based* (which means they are erased when you close your browser) and about half of *persistent cookies* (those that are stored on your hard drive) are *first-party cookies*. First-party cookies belong to the Web site you are visiting and are only read by that site. So, while some individuals view cookies as a potential invasion of privacy, they can provide some benefits to consumers. For example, cookies can enable a Web site to remember preferences for customized Web site content (such as on a portal page), as well as to save a shopping cart or remember a site password. Some Web sites also use cookies to keep track of which pages on their Web sites each person has visited in order to recommend products on return visits that match that person's interests. A use of cookies that is more objectionable to some is the use of *third-party cookies* (cookies placed on your hard drive by a company other than the one associated with the Web page that you are viewing—typically a Web advertising company). Third-party cookies target advertisements to Web site visitors based on their activities on the site (such as products viewed or advertisements clicked).

The information stored in a cookie file typically includes the name of the cookie, its expiration date, and the domain that the cookie belongs to. In addition, a cookie contains either personal information that you have entered while visiting the Web site or an ID number assigned by the Web site that allows the Web site's server to retrieve your personal information from its database. Such a database can contain two types of information: *personally identifiable information (PII)* and *non-personally identifiable information (Non-PII)*. Personally identifiable information is connected with a specific user's identity—such as his or her name and address—and is typically given during the process of ordering goods or services. Non-personally identifiable information is anonymous data—such as which product pages were viewed or which advertisements located on the site were clicked—that is not directly associated with the visitor's name or another personally identifiable characteristic.

Cookies stored on your computer's hard drive can be looked at, if desired, although sometimes deciphering the information contained in a cookie file is difficult. Internet Explorer users can view and/or delete cookies and other temporary files by using Internet Explorer's Internet Options dialog box (see Figure 3-36) and selecting *Delete* in the *Browsing history* section on the General tab to delete all temporary files or *Settings* to have the option to view cookie files. The Privacy tab in this dialog box (also shown in Figure 3-36) can be used to

FIGURE 3-36
Browser cookie management in Internet Explorer.

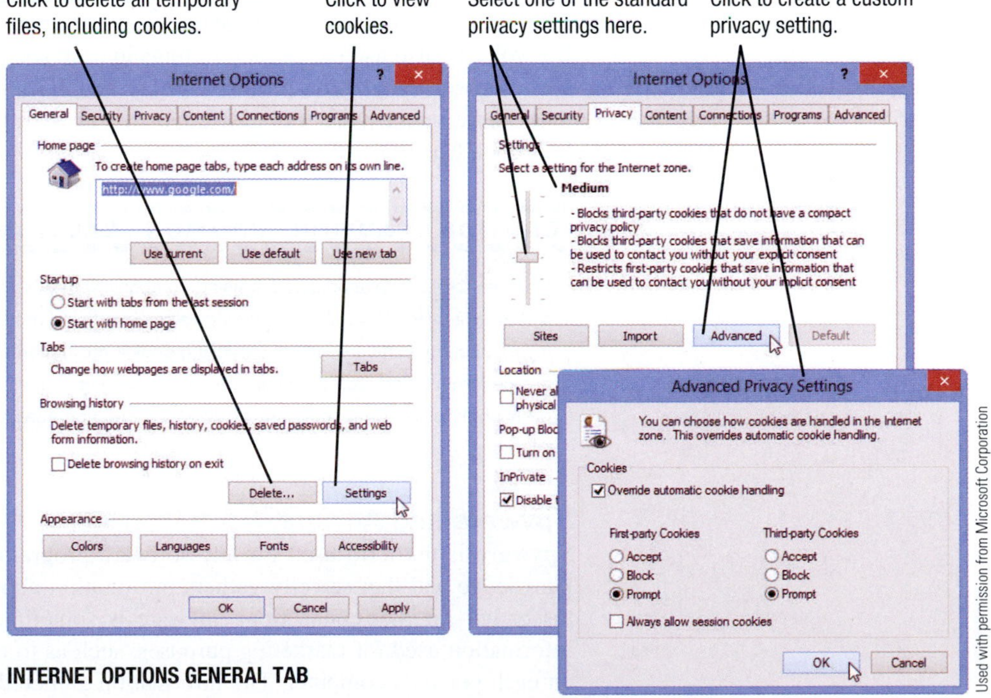

>**Cookie.** A small file stored on a user's hard drive by a Web server; commonly used to identify personal preferences and settings for that user.

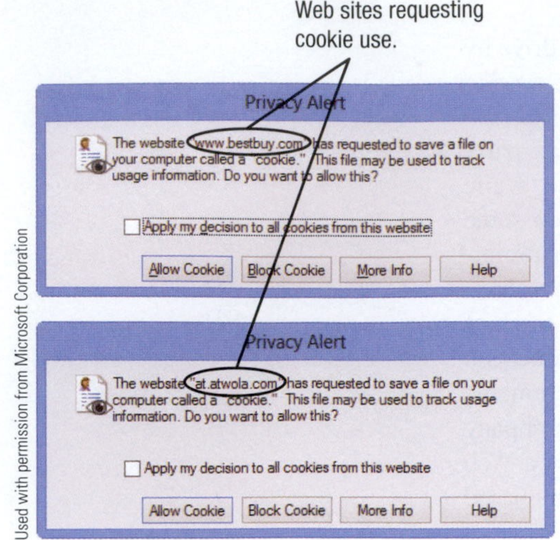

FIGURE 3-37
Cookie prompts.
After selecting the "Prompt" option in the cookie settings, you will have to accept or reject each cookie request.

specify which type of cookies (if any) are allowed to be used, such as permitting the use of regular cookies, but not third-party cookies or cookies using personally identifiable information. A growing trend (such as with Apple's Safari browser) is to not allow third-party cookies at all.

Turning off cookies entirely might make some features—such as a shopping cart—on some Web sites inoperable. The *Medium High* privacy option in Internet Explorer is a widely used setting because it allows the use of regular cookies but blocks many types of third-party cookies. Users who want more control over their cookies can choose to accept or decline cookies as they are encountered in most browsers. Although this option interrupts your Web surfing almost continually, it is interesting to see the cookies generated from each individual Web site. For example, the two cookie prompts shown in Figure 3-37 were generated while visiting the BestBuy.com Web site. Although the top cookie request is from the BestBuy.com Web site directly, the other is a third-party cookie from an online marketing company. An alternative to managing cookies within your browser is using third-party *cookie management software*.

Another alternative is the *private browsing* option available with many Web browsers, including Internet Explorer, Chrome, and Safari. As discussed more in Chapter 5, this option allows you to browse the Web without leaving any history (including browsing history, form data, cookies, usernames, and passwords) on the computer you are using. Private browsing is useful for individuals using school, library, or other public computers to visit password-protected sites, research medical information, or perform other tasks that the user may prefer to keep private. Individuals using a computer to shop for gift or other surprises for family members who share the same computer may find the feature useful, as well.

Another Web privacy issue is the privacy of social media data. The best preventative measure is to not post anything online that you would not want the general public to view. But you can also use the privacy settings in each social network that you utilize to specify who can see what in your profile. For instance, Facebook allows you to specify what content can be seen by the "Public" (anyone) and what can only be seen by "Friends" (your Facebook friends).

CAUTION CAUTION CAUTION CAUTION CAUTION CAUTION CAUT

Cookies (typically placed by advertising companies) that attempt to track your activities across a Web site or the Web sites belonging to an advertising network are referred to as *tracking cookies*. If your security software includes tracking cookie protection, be sure it is enabled to avoid these cookies from being stored on your computer. Setting your browser's privacy settings to block third-party cookies can offer you some additional protection against tracking cookies.

Spyware and Adware

Spyware is the term used for any software program that is installed without the user's knowledge and that secretly gathers information about the user and transmits it through his or her Internet connection. Spyware is sometimes used to provide advertisers with information used for marketing purposes, such as to help select advertisements to display on each person's computer. The information gathered by the spyware software is usually not associated with a person's identity. But spyware is a concern for privacy advocates

>**Spyware.** A software program that is installed without the user's permission and that secretly gathers information to be sent to others.

because it is typically installed without a user's direct knowledge (such as at the same time another program is installed, often when a program is downloaded from a Web site or a P2P service) and conveys information about a user's Internet activities. Spyware can also be used by criminals to retrieve personal data stored on your computer for use in criminal activities, as discussed in more detail in Chapter 4.

Unfortunately, spyware use is on the rise and can affect the performance of a computer (such as slowing it down or causing it to work improperly), in addition to its potential security risks. And the problem will likely become worse before it gets any better. Some spyware programs—sometimes referred to as *stealthware*—are getting more aggressive, such as delivering ads regardless of the activity you are doing on your computer, changing your browser home page or otherwise altering your browser settings (referred to as *browser hijacking*), and performing other annoying actions. The worst spyware programs rewrite your computer's main instructions—such as the Windows registry—to change your browser settings back to the hijacked settings each time you reboot your computer, undoing any changes you may have made to your browser settings.

A related type of software is *adware*, which is free or low-cost software that is supported by on-screen advertising. Many free programs that can be downloaded from the Internet include some type of adware, which results in on-screen advertising. The difference between spyware and adware is that adware typically does not gather information and relay it to others via the Internet (although it can), and it is not installed without the user's consent. Adware might, however, be installed without the user's direct knowledge because many users do not read licensing agreements before clicking OK to install a new program. When this occurs with a program that contains adware, the adware components are installed without the user's direct knowledge.

Both spyware and adware can be annoying and use up valuable system resources, in addition to revealing data about individuals. As discussed in detail in Chapter 4, *firewalls* and *antispyware programs* can be used to protect against spyware.

E-Mail Privacy

Many people mistakenly believe that the e-mail they send and receive is private and will never be read by anyone other than the intended recipient. Because it is transmitted over public media, however, only *encrypted* (electronically scrambled) e-mail can be transmitted safely, as discussed in Chapter 4. Although unlikely to happen to your personal e-mail, *nonencrypted* e-mail can be intercepted and read by someone else. Consequently, from a privacy standpoint, a nonencrypted e-mail message should be viewed more like a postcard than a letter (see Figure 3-38).

It is also important to realize that your employer and your ISP have access to the e-mail you send through those organizations. Businesses and ISPs typically archive (keep copies of) e-mail messages that travel through their servers and are required to comply with subpoenas from law enforcement agencies for archived e-mail messages.

FIGURE 3-38
You cannot assume e-mail messages are private, unless they are encrypted.

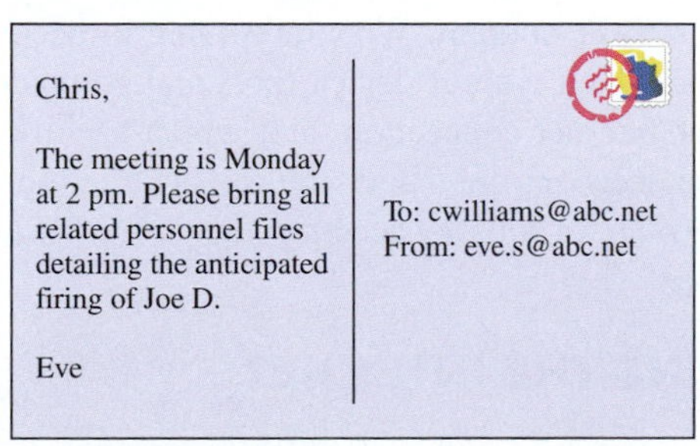

REGULAR (NONENCRYPTED E-MAIL) = POSTCARD

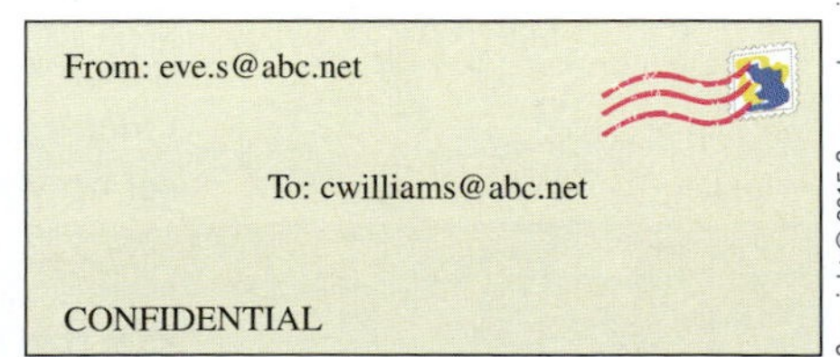

ENCRYPTED E-MAIL = SEALED LETTER

SUMMARY

EVOLUTION OF THE INTERNET

Chapter Objective 1:
Discuss how the Internet evolved and what it is like today.

The origin of the **Internet**—a worldwide collection of interconnected networks that is accessed by millions of people daily—dates back to the late 1960s. At its start and throughout its early years, the Internet was called **ARPANET**. It was not until the development of the **World Wide Web (WWW)** that public interest in the Internet began to soar. Most companies have Web sites today and consider the Web to be an indispensable business tool. While the Web is a very important and widely used Internet resource, it is not the only one. Over the years, *protocols* have been developed to download files, send e-mail messages, and perform other tasks, in addition to using Web pages. Today, the term *Internet* has become a household word and, in many ways, has redefined how people think about computers and communications. The next significant improvement to the Internet infrastructure may be the result of projects such as *Internet2*.

Chapter Objective 2:
Identify the various types of individuals, companies, and organizations involved in the Internet community and explain their purposes.

The Internet community is made up of individual *users*; companies, such as **Internet service providers (ISPs)**, **Internet content providers**, **application service providers (ASPs)**, *infrastructure companies*, and a variety of software and hardware companies; the government; and other organizations. Virtually anyone with a computer with communications capability can be part of the Internet, either as a user or supplier of information or services. **Web services** are self-contained business functions that operate over the Internet.

Because the Internet is so unique in the history of the world—and it remains a relatively new and ever-changing phenomenon—several widespread myths about it have surfaced. Three such myths are that the Internet is free, that it is controlled by some central body, and that it is synonymous with the World Wide Web.

GETTING SET UP TO USE THE INTERNET

Chapter Objective 3:
Describe device and connection options for connecting to the Internet, as well as some considerations to keep in mind when selecting an ISP.

Most Internet connections today are **direct connections** (always connected to the Internet), though some are **dial-up connections** (which need to dial up and connect to the Internet to provide access). Dial-up connections are typically **conventional dial-up Internet access**; common types of direct Internet connections include **cable**, **DSL (Digital Subscriber Line)**, **satellite**, **fixed wireless**, **mobile wireless**, and **broadband over fiber (BoF)**—also called **fiber-to-the-premises (FTTP)**—**Internet access**. Individuals can also connect to the Internet via a **Wi-Fi hotspot**. When preparing to become connected to the Internet, you need to decide which type of device (personal computer or mobile phone, for instance), which type of Internet connection, and which specific Internet service provider to use. Once all these decisions are made, you can acquire the proper hardware and software and set up your system for Internet access.

SEARCHING THE INTERNET

Chapter Objective 4:
Understand how to search effectively for information on the Internet and how to cite Internet resources properly.

Search sites are Web sites that enable users to search for and find information on the Internet. They typically locate pages using a **keyword search** (in which the user specifies **keywords** for the desired information)—a **search engine** retrieves the list of matching Web pages from a database. A **directory search** (in which the user selects categories corresponding to the desired information) is another possibility. Search site databases are generally maintained by automated *spider* programs.

There are a variety of search strategies that can be used, including typing phrases instead of single keywords; using *Boolean operators*; trying the search at multiple search sites; and using *synonyms*, *variant word forms*, *wildcards*, and *field searches*. Once a list of links to Web pages matching the search criteria is displayed, the hits need to be evaluated for their relevancy. If the information found on a Web page is used in a paper, report, or other original document, the source should be credited appropriately.

BEYOND BROWSING AND E-MAIL

Chapter Objective 5:
List several ways to communicate over the Internet, in addition to e-mail.

The Internet can be used for many different types of activities in addition to basic Web browsing and e-mail exchange. Common types of online communications include **instant messaging** or **IM** (also commonly referred to as **chat**) and **text messaging** (sending real-time typed messages via a computer or mobile phone, respectively), **Twittering** (sending short status updates via Twitter), **forums** (online locations where people post messages on a particular topic for others to read and respond to), **Web conferences** (real-time meetings taking place via the Web that typically use video cameras and microphones to enable participants to see and hear each other), and **Webinars** (seminars presented over the Web). **Social networking sites** (part of the collection of **social media** available today) also allow the members of an online community to communicate and exchange information. **Voice over Internet Protocol** (**VoIP**) refers to making voice telephone calls over the Internet.

Chapter Objective 6:
List several useful activities that can be performed via the Web.

Common Web activities for individuals include a variety of consumer *e-commerce* activities, such as **online shopping**, **online auctions**, **online banking**, and **online investing**. When performing any type of financial transaction over the Internet, it is very important to use only *secure* Web pages.

Online entertainment applications include **online gaming**, downloading music files and other types of **online music**, and **online TV**, **online movies**, and other types of **online video**. Selecting and receiving TV shows and movies via the Web is called **video-on-demand** (**VOD**). A wide variety of news, reference, government, product, and corporate information are available via the Web as well. News, reference, and search tools are commonly found on **portal Web pages**; **RSS** (**Really Simple Syndication**) feeds can be used to deliver current news, **podcasts**, and other Web content to individuals as it becomes available.

Online education options include **Web-based training** (**WBT**) and **distance learning**. *Online testing* can be used for both objective and performance-based exams and can be secured by a variety of means. Online writing includes **blogs** (Web pages that contain frequently updated entries by individuals), **wikis** (Web pages designed to be created and edited by multiple individuals), and **e-portfolios** (collections of an individual's work).

CENSORSHIP AND PRIVACY ISSUES

Chapter Objective 7:
Discuss censorship and privacy and how they are related to Internet use.

Among the most important societal issues relating to the Internet are *censorship* and *privacy*. Web content is not censored as a whole, but **Internet filtering** can be used by parents, employers, educators, and anyone wishing to prevent access to sites they deem objectionable on computers for which they have control. *Privacy* is a big concern for individuals, particularly as it relates to their Web activity. **Cookies** are typically used by Web sites to save customized settings for that site and can also be used for advertising purposes. Another item of possible concern is **spyware** (software installed without the user's permission that sends information to others). Unless an e-mail message is *encrypted*, it should not be assumed to be completely private.

REVIEW ACTIVITIES

KEY TERM MATCHING

a. cookie

b. dial-up connection

c. direct connection

d. distance learning

e. Internet

f. keyword

g. podcast

h. search engine

i. social media

j. World Wide Web (WWW)

Instructions: Match each key term on the left with the definition on the right that best describes it.

1. ______ A learning environment in which the student is physically located away from the instructor and other students; commonly, instruction and communications take place via the Web.

2. ______ A type of Internet connection in which the computer or other device is connected to the Internet continually.

3. ______ A small file stored on a user's hard drive by a Web server; commonly used to identify personal preferences and settings for that user.

4. ______ A software program used by a search site to retrieve matching Web pages from a search database.

5. ______ A type of Internet connection in which the computer or other device must dial up and connect to a service provider's computer via telephone lines before being connected to the Internet.

6. ______ A recorded audio or video file that can be played or downloaded via the Web.

7. ______ A word typed in a search box on a search site to locate information on the Internet.

8. ______ The collection of social networking sites and other communications channels used to transmit or share information with a broad audience.

9. ______ The collection of Web pages available through the Internet.

10. ______ The largest and most well-known computer network, linking millions of computers all over the world.

SELF-QUIZ

Instructions: Circle **T** if the statement is true, **F** if the statement is false, or write the best answer in the space provided. **Answers for the self-quiz are located in the References and Resources Guide at the end of the book**.

1. T F When the Internet was first developed, it was called Mosaic.

2. T F On the Internet, an *access provider* and a *content provider* are essentially the same thing.

3. T F With a direct connection, you need only open your browser to start your Internet session.

4. T F A Wi-Fi hotspot is used to provide Internet access to individuals via a wireless connection.

5. T F A Webinar is a Web site designed to allow individuals to easily create and publish blogs.

6. ______ is a type of always-on broadband Internet service that transmits data over standard telephone lines but does not tie up your phone line.

7. With a(n) ______ search, keywords are typed into the search box; with a(n) ______ search, users select categories to find matching Web pages.

8. A(n) ______ is a Web site (such as Facebook) designed to enable a community of individuals to communicate and exchange information.

9. With a(n) ________, people bid on products over the Internet, and the highest bidder purchases the item.
10. Match each Internet application to its possible situation, and write the corresponding number in the blank to the left of each situation.
    - a. ________ To communicate with a friend in a different state.
    - b. ________ To pay only as much as you specify for an item purchased through the Internet.
    - c. ________ To pay a bill without writing a check.
    - d. ________ To find Web pages containing information about growing your own Bonsai trees.

1. Online banking
2. E-mail
3. Internet searching
4. Online auction

EXERCISES

1. Match each type of Internet access to its description, and write the corresponding number in the blank to the left of each description.
    - a. ________ A common type of home broadband connection; does not use standard phone lines.
    - b. ________ Provides access to the Internet via a very fast fiber-optic network.
    - c. ________ Accesses the Internet via standard phone lines and ties up your phone; the maximum speed is 56 Kbps.

    1. Conventional dial-up
    2. BoF
    3. Cable

2. What would each of the following searches look for?
    - a. hot AND dogs ________________
    - b. snorkel* ________________
    - c. text: "Internet privacy" domain:*.gov ________________
3. List three different sets of keywords that could be used to search for information on how to maintain a trumpet.
4. Explain the difference between a blog, a wiki, and a podcast.
5. List one advantage and one disadvantage of the use of Web site cookies.

DISCUSSION QUESTIONS

1. Twittering became virtually an overnight sensation, but some question its usefulness. Do you want to know the routine activities your friends (or other individuals you choose to follow) are doing during the day? Is it useful information to tweet that your bus is stuck in traffic or having a bad day? Do you follow anyone on Twitter or tweet regularly? Why or why not? Because Twitter updates have to be very short, some may think that twittering on the job does not take up enough time to be a concern, but what about the distraction factor? Should employers allow employees to use Twitter, Facebook, and other popular online activities during work hours? Why or why not?
2. Some courtrooms today are becoming high-tech, such as using videoconferencing systems to allow defendants and witnesses to participate in proceedings from remote locations. Allowing defendants to participate remotely from the jail facility saves travel time and expense, as well as eliminates any risk of flight. Remote testimony from witnesses can save both time and money. But, could having defendants and witnesses participate remotely affect the jury's perspective? If the videoconference takes place via the Internet, can it be assured that proceedings are confidential? Do you think the benefits of these systems outweigh any potential disadvantages?

PROJECTS

HOT TOPICS

1. **Social Network Addiction** As discussed in the chapter, social networks (such as Facebook and Google+) are very popular with individuals. However, it has become apparent recently that some individuals are moving from casual social networking use to compulsive or addictive behavior.

   For this project, investigate either Facebook addiction or Internet addiction. How common is it? What are some of the warning signs? Is there an actual medical disorder associated with it? If so, what is it and how is it treated? Find one example in a news or journal article of a person who was "addicted" to using a social networking site or other online activity—why was their behavior considered addictive? Were they able to modify their behavior? Have you ever been concerned about becoming addicted to any Internet activities? At the conclusion of your research, prepare a one-page summary of your findings and opinions and submit it to your instructor.

SHORT ANSWER/ RESEARCH

2. **Online Travel Planning** Planning and booking travel arrangements online is a very popular Internet activity today and there are a number of sites that can be used.

   For this project, review two popular travel sites, such as Expedia.com and Travelocity.com, to see what services they offer and how easy it is to locate the information needed to plan and book a flight via those sites. Select a destination and use one of the sites to obtain a quote for a particular flight on a particular day. Next, go to the Web site for the airline of the flight and use the site to obtain a quote for the same flight. Is there a difference in price or flight availability? Could you make a reservation online through both sites? Would you feel comfortable booking an entire vacation yourself online, or are there services that a travel agent could provide that you feel would be beneficial? Do you think these sites are most appropriate for making business travel plans or vacation plans, or are they suited to both? At the conclusion of your research, prepare a one-page summary of your findings and submit it to your instructor.

HANDS ON

3. **Web Searching** Search sites can be used to find Web pages containing specific information, and there are strategies that can be used to make Web searching an efficient and useful experience.

   For this project, go to the Google search site and perform the following searches, then submit your results and printouts to your instructor. (Note: Some of the answers will vary from student to student.)

   a. Search for *rules*. How many pages were found? What is the name of the first page in the list of hits? Next, search for *backgammon rules*. How many pages were found? Use the hits to find a picture of how a backgammon board is initially set up, then, print that page.
   b. Search to find a recipe for Buffalo Chicken Wings; a map of where your house, apartment, or dorm is located; and the ZIP Code for 200 N. Elm Street, Hinsdale, IL, and print the pages containing this information.
   c. Go to the Advanced Search option. Use the form fields to perform a search for Web pages that contain all of the words *hiking trails Sierras*, do not contain the word *horse*, and have the domain *.gov*. After the hits are displayed, record the actual search phrase that is listed in the search box along with the name and URL of the first page displayed in the list of hits.

ETHICS IN ACTION

4. **Paid Bloggers** Blogs are traditionally online personal journals where the blogger expresses his or her opinion on desired topics. Unlike professional journalists, bloggers typically post because they want to, not because they have been hired to do so. However, as discussed in the chapter, bloggers are increasingly being paid or "sponsored" to blog. Is this ethical? If a blogger is paid to post his or her honest opinion about a product or service, does that lessen the credibility of that post? Does it change your opinion if the blogger reveals that it is a sponsored blog? If you based a purchase on a review posted in a blog that you later found out was sponsored, would you feel misled? How, if at all, do sponsored posts affect the blogosphere as a whole?

   For this project, form an opinion about the ethical ramifications of paid blogging and be prepared to discuss your position (in class, via an online class discussion group, in a class chat room, or via a class blog, depending on your instructor's directions). You may also be asked to write a short paper expressing your opinion.

PRESENTATION/ DEMONSTRATION

5. **Advanced Search** Most search sites today include advanced features to help you more efficiently find the information you are searching for.

   For this project, select one search site (such as Google or Bing) and research the advanced search options the site supports. How does the advanced search work—do you have to type special symbols or is there a form that can be used? What operators does the site support? Are you able to search for only pages that were recently updated? Are you able to find pages that link to a specified Web page? Can you search for specified file types, such as images or videos? Do you find the advanced search options for your selected site useful? Share your findings and opinions with the class in the form of a short presentation. The presentation should not exceed 10 minutes and should make use of one or more presentation aids, such as a whiteboard, handouts, or a computer-based slide presentation (your instructor may provide additional requirements). You may also be asked to submit a summary of the presentation to your instructor.

BALANCING ACT

6. **In a Cyber War, Is it Ethical to Kill Enemy Hackers?** Cyber wars are heating up. Foreign governments (particularly China) are continually being accused of trying to hack into the computer systems of both the U.S. government and high-tech companies. Cybersecurity is a very important issue today and is a source of ongoing discussion between countries such as the United States and China. For instance, cybersecurity was high on the agenda for the meeting between President Obama and Chinese President Xi Jinping in 2013 following a government report that found nearly 40 Pentagon weapons programs and almost 30 other defense technologies were compromised by cyber intrusions from China. And, earlier that year, a cybersecurity firm linked a secret Chinese military unit to years of cyberattacks against U.S. companies. While China's government denies any involvement and the countries are not officially at war, how do actual wars and cyber wars differ? Is a country hacking into another country's computer systems an act of war? If so, should those hackers be fair targets for retaliation? Just as the military is permitted to kill enemy soldiers attacking its country or its citizens, should they also kill enemy hackers? Is cyber warfare any less of an actual conflict than ground or air-based physical combat? What about computer programmers that control the drones and missles used in combat—are they fair targets?

   Pick a side on this issue, form an opinion and gather supporting evidence, and be prepared to discuss and defend your position in a classroom debate or in a 1–2 page paper, depending on your instructor's directions.

expert insight on... Software

Courtesy Microsoft, Inc.

Microsoft

Stephen Rose is the Senior Product Marketing and Community Manager for the Windows Commercial team at Microsoft. Before joining Microsoft, he was the Senior Tech Correspondent for *Fast Company Magazine* and an IT consultant. He has been a Microsoft Certified Systems Engineer and Microsoft Certified Trainer for 20 years, as well as a two-time Microsoft Most Valuable Professional (MVP). Stephen has a Bachelor of Arts degree and holds multiple technical certifications, including MCSE, MCP+I, MCT, MCTIP, A+, Net+, Security+, Linux+, Project+, and PMI.

A conversation with STEPHEN ROSE

Senior Product Marketing and Community Manager, Windows Commercial, Microsoft

". . . The fact that people want their data to synch across multiple devices from the cloud is a huge game changer."

My Background . . .

It's funny how things work out. I received a bachelor's degree in Film and Video production from Columbia College in Chicago in the late '80s. By 1996, I was burned-out and decided to follow my passion for computers and IT by becoming a technical trainer with New Horizons. Within two years I got my MCT and MCSE, and I started my own IT consulting company that designed, built, and managed software and services for companies worldwide (including many Fortune 500 companies) for 15 years. I'm now the Senior Product Marketing and Community Manager for the Windows Commercial team at Microsoft. There are 22.6 million IT pros in the world and my job is to help support them within the workplace. I oversee and manage the Windows content on Microsoft TechNet, as well as on a number of forums, newsletters, and blogs. I also speak at conferences, roundtables, and the North American and European Springboard Series Tours.

It's Important to Know . . .

Apps are moving to the cloud. While individuals have used Web mail and other cloud products for some time, businesses are now moving into the cloud, which will dramatically change the business model for many companies. With Web-based apps, virtualized desktops, and more, the computer is becoming just a vessel to connect you to the Internet and your data. Understanding the cloud, as well as where and when it makes sense to use it, is key to being a successful IT pro.

Software is not always a one-size-fits-all situation. Apps will need to run on many different form factors, such as phones, tablets, and touch-based devices, in addition to laptops and desktops. And these devices are not interchangeable. In addition, an overblown app on a device without a keyboard can be hard to use—if an app is difficult to use, no one will adopt it.

Computers are inherently secure. It is the choices that users make (such as clicking on links in e-mails and downloading music, movies, and software illegally) that make them unsecure. If users use their best judgment when surfing the Web, they will be safer. If something sounds too good to be true, it usually is. At Microsoft, we are adding many new features to our operating system and browser to help users make smart decisions.

How I Use this Technology . . .

I travel around the world and need my computing resources as I travel. One of my favorite features in Windows 8 is Direct Access, which automatically connects me to my company intranet without having to log into a secure VPN connection with tokens and pin numbers. For instance, I recently sat down at a Starbucks in Prague, turned on my Windows 8 laptop, and within seconds I was not only connected to the Wi-Fi network but also to my key internal Web sites. From Prague to Redmond in a matter of seconds without doing anything but turning on my PC. It is a seamless experience. As I have heard from so many end users over the years, "I don't care how it works. I just want it to work." I also use several laptops, so products like OneNote and Sharepoint are key to ensuring that all my data is on multiple devices and synched automatically.

What the Future Holds . . .

The cloud is one of the major technologies changing our future. It is going to dramatically change how we do business and how we perceive data. The physical PC is no longer part of the equation and the idea of "my data anywhere on the planet from any computer" is very powerful. Not storing data locally reduces risk, lowers costs, and adds more productivity via flexibility. In addition, cloud computing—along with new form factors, the need for social media accessibility, the emergence of location-aware applications, and the increased availability of app stores—have changed how we view devices. The lines between tablets, smartphones, and PCs are already blurring. With the addition of system on a chip (SoC), there will be an increase in the amount and types of devices that the end user is impacted by.

"... technology shapes us but, like any tool, it's how we leverage it and use it for the better that is important."

Cloud computing will also impact software development. The fact that people want their data to synch across multiple devices from the cloud is a huge game changer. Knowing HTML5 will be critical in the development of apps located in the cloud. HTML5 will also have a big impact on end users.

Tablets and smartphones are currently replacing laptops for many tasks and I expect that trend to continue in the future. These smart devices allow us to be more informed on many aspects of our life. They allow us to be more nimble and to take advantage of opportunities that 10 years ago were unheard of.

My Advice to Students . . .

Remember that technology shapes us but, like any tool, it's how we leverage it and use it for the better that is important.

Discussion Question

Stephen Rose believes that cloud computing will impact both individuals and businesses and change how we perceive data and do business. Think about the computing and communications tasks you use today. What is the benefit of being able to perform them via the cloud? Are there any disadvantages? Do you currently use multiple devices to access your data and apps? If so, are the data and apps stored in the cloud, on each device, or both? If not, would the ability to access your data and apps via any device, anywhere, be an advantage in your life? Would a cloud-based world change how you use data or apps on a daily basis? If a person or business decides not to utilize the cloud, will this be a disadvantage for that person or business? Why or why not? Be prepared to discuss your position (in class, via an online class discussion group, in a class chat room, or via a class blog, depending on your instructor's directions). You may also be asked to write a short paper expressing your opinion.

>For more information about Microsoft, visit www.microsoft.com. For resources for Windows and other Microsoft software, visit www.microsoft.com/springboard and windowsteamblog.com/windows/b/springboard. Follow the Springboard Series on TechNet via Twitter @MSSpringboard.

chapter 4

Network and Internet Security

After completing this chapter, you will be able to do the following:

1. Explain why computer users should be concerned about network and Internet security.
2. List several examples of unauthorized access and unauthorized use.
3. Explain several ways to protect against unauthorized access and unauthorized use, including access control systems, firewalls, and encryption.
4. Provide several examples of computer sabotage.
5. List how individuals and businesses can protect against computer sabotage.
6. Discuss online theft, identity theft, spoofing, phishing, and other types of dot cons.
7. Detail steps an individual can take to protect against online theft, identity theft, spoofing, phishing, and other types of dot cons.
8. Identify personal safety risks associated with Internet use.
9. List steps individuals can take to safeguard their personal safety when using the Internet.
10. Discuss the current state of network and Internet security legislation.

outline

OVERVIEW

As discussed in the last few chapters, networks and the Internet help many of us be more efficient and effective workers, as well as add convenience and enjoyment to our personal lives. However, there is a downside, as well. The widespread use of home and business networks and the Internet increases the risk of unauthorized computer access, theft, fraud, and other types of computer crime. In addition, the vast amount of business and personal data stored on computers accessible via company networks and the Internet increases the chances of data loss due to crime or employee errors. Some online activities can even put your personal safety at risk, if you are not careful.

This chapter looks at a variety of security concerns stemming from the use of computer networks and the Internet in our society, including unauthorized access and use, computer viruses and other types of sabotage, and online theft and fraud. Safeguards for each of these concerns are also covered, with an explanation of precautions that can be taken to reduce the chance that these security problems will happen to you. Personal safety issues related to the Internet are also discussed, and the chapter closes with a look at legislation related to network and Internet security. ■

WHY BE CONCERNED ABOUT NETWORK AND INTERNET SECURITY?

From a *computer virus* making your computer function abnormally, to a *hacker* using your personal information to make fraudulent purchases, to someone harassing you online in a discussion group, a variety of security concerns related to computer networks and the Internet exist. Many Internet security concerns today can be categorized as **computer crimes**. Computer crime—sometimes referred to as *cybercrime*—includes any illegal act involving a computer. Many computer crimes today are committed using the Internet or another computer network and include theft of financial assets or information, manipulating data (such as grades or account information), and acts of sabotage (such as releasing a computer virus or shutting down a Web server). Cybercrime is an important security concern today. It is a multibillion-dollar business that is often performed by seasoned criminals. In fact, according to the FBI, organized crime organizations in many countries are increasingly turning to computer crime to target millions of potential victims easily, and *phishing attacks* and other *Internet scams* (discussed shortly) are expected to increase in reaction to the recent troubled economy. These and other computer crimes that are carried out via the Internet or another computer network are discussed in this chapter. Other types of computer crime (such as using a computer to create counterfeit currency or make illegal copies of a DVD) are covered in Chapter 5.

TIP

According to a recent Norton Cybercrime Report, the total cost of cybercrime is now estimated to be $110 billion per year worldwide and nearly $21 billion in the United States alone with an average loss of $290 per person.

>**Computer crime.** Any illegal act involving a computer.

With some security concerns, such as when a spyware program changes your browser's home page, the consequence may be just an annoyance. In other cases, such as when someone steals your identity and purchases items using your name and credit card number, the consequences are much more serious. And, with the growing use of wireless networks, social media, cloud computing, mobile computing, and individuals accessing company networks remotely—paired with an increasing number of security and privacy regulations that businesses need to comply with—network and Internet security has never been more important. Consequently, all computer users should be aware of the security concerns surrounding computer network and Internet use, and they should take appropriate precautions. The most common types of security risks related to network and Internet use, along with some corresponding precautions, are discussed throughout this chapter.

UNAUTHORIZED ACCESS AND UNAUTHORIZED USE

Unauthorized access occurs whenever an individual gains access to a computer, mobile device, network, file, or other resource without permission—typically by *hacking* into the resource. **Unauthorized use** involves using a computing resource for unauthorized activities. Often, they happen at the same time, but unauthorized use can occur when a user is authorized to access a particular computer or network but is not authorized for the particular activity the user performs. For instance, while a student may be authorized to access the Internet via a campus computer lab, some use—such as viewing pornography—would likely be deemed off-limits. If so, viewing that content from a school computer would be considered unauthorized use. For employees of some companies, checking personal e-mail or visiting personal Facebook pages at work might be classified as unauthorized use.

Unauthorized access and many types of unauthorized use are criminal offenses in the United States and many other countries. They can be committed by both *insiders* (people who work for the company whose computers are being accessed) and *outsiders* (people who do not work for that company). Whether or not a specific act constitutes unauthorized use or is illegal depends on the circumstances, as well as the specific company or institution involved. To explain acceptable computer use to their employees, students, or other users, many organizations and educational institutions publish guidelines for behavior, often called *codes of conduct* (see Figure 4-1). Codes of conduct typically address prohibited activities, such as playing games, installing personal software, violating copyright laws, causing harm to computers or the network, and snooping in other people's files.

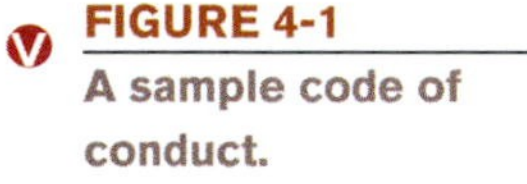

FIGURE 4-1
A sample code of conduct.

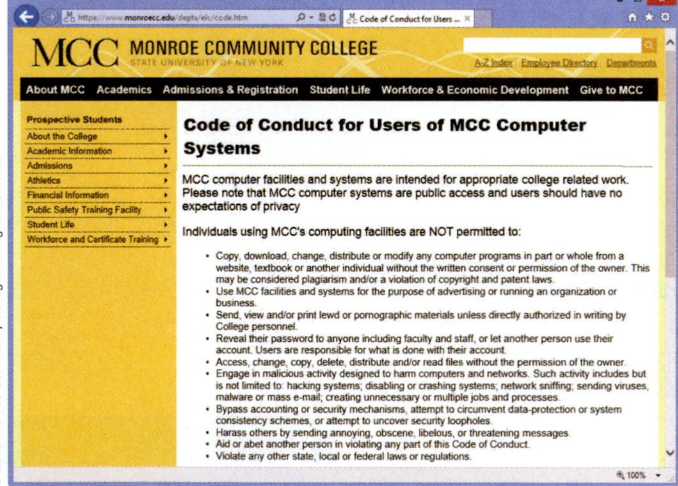

Hacking

Hacking refers to the act of breaking into a computer or network. It can be performed in person by hacking into a computer the *hacker* has physical access to, but it is more often performed via the Internet or another network. Unless authorized (such as when a company hires a *professional hacker* to test the security of its system), hacking in the United States and many other countries is a crime.

>Unauthorized access. Gaining access to a computer, mobile device, network, file, or other resource without permission. **>Unauthorized use.** Using a computing resource for unapproved activities. **>Hacking.** Using a computer to break into another computer system.

Typically, the motivation for hacking is to steal data, sabotage a computer system, or perform some other type of illegal act. In particular, the theft of consumer data (such as credit card numbers) has increased dramatically over the past several years—more than 1,600 data breaches were discovered in 2012. Some of the most notable recent breaches include the 2013 theft of prepaid debit card numbers, which were then programmed with large balances and used in simultaneous ATM withdrawals by a gang of hackers and which resulted in a $45 million global heist; the 2012 theft of 3.6 million Social Security numbers, along with names, addresses, credit card numbers, and other sensitive information, from the South Carolina Department of Revenue computer system; and the 2012 *Zappos.com* data breach, which resulted in hackers gaining access to the names, addresses, phone numbers, and the last four digits of credit card numbers of 24 million customers. Another growing trend is to hack into a computer and "hijack" it for use in an illegal or unethical act, such as taking over an individual's computer, spying via a webcam, generating spam, or hosting pornographic Web sites. Hackers are also increasingly aiming attacks at very specific individuals, such as product designers and other individuals who have access to valuable corporate data.

TIP

According to a recent study, the total cost per data breach in the United States is $5.4 million—the highest of any country.

TIP

A number of recent data breaches have been performed by the *hacktivist* group *Anonymous*.

In addition to being a threat to individuals and businesses, hacking is also considered a very serious threat to national security in the United States. The increased number of systems that are controlled by computers and are connected to the Internet, along with the continually improving abilities of hackers, has led to an increased risk of *cyberterrorism*—where terrorists launch attacks via the Internet. Current concerns include attacks by individual terrorists, as well as by other countries, against the computers controlling vital systems; vital systems include the nation's power grids, banks, and water filtration facilities, as well as computers related to national defense, the airlines, and the stock market. In fact, President Obama and Chinese President Xi Jinping began serious discussion about cybersecurity in 2013 following a government report that found nearly 40 Pentagon weapons programs and almost 30 other defense technologies were compromised by cyber intrusions from China. President Obama has declared that "cyber threat is one of the most serious economic and national security challenges we face as a nation."

Today, hackers often gain access via a wireless network. This is because wireless networks are widely used and they are easier to hack into than wired networks. In fact, it is possible to gain access to a wireless network just by being within range (about 100 to 300 feet, depending on the Wi-Fi standard being used) of a wireless access point, unless the access point is sufficiently protected. Although security features are built into wireless routers and other networking hardware, they are typically not enabled by default. As a result, many wireless networks belonging to businesses and individuals are left unsecured. Securing a Wi-Fi network is discussed shortly.

ASK THE EXPERT

Courtesy ACM

acm

Moshe Vardi, Rice University, Co-Chair of the ACM Globalization and Offshoring of Software Taskforce

Is there a national security risk to outsourcing/offshoring software development?

Offshoring magnifies existing risks and creates new and often poorly understood threats. When businesses offshore work, they increase not only their own business-related risks (e.g., intellectual property theft) but also risks to national security and to individuals' privacy. While it is unlikely these risks will deter the growth of offshoring, businesses and nations should employ strategies to mitigate the risks. Businesses have a clear incentive to manage these new risks to suit their own interests, but nations and individuals often have little awareness of the exposures created. For example, many commercial off-the-shelf (COTS) systems are developed offshore, making it extremely difficult for buyers to understand all of the source and application code in the systems. This creates the possibility that a hostile nation or nongovernmental hostile agent (such as a terrorist or criminal) could compromise these systems. Individuals are also often exposed to loss of privacy or identity theft due to the number of business processes being offshored today and managed under laws that are much less restrictive than in most developed countries.

War Driving and Wi-Fi Piggybacking

Unauthorized use of a Wi-Fi network is called **war driving** or **Wi-Fi piggybacking**, depending on the location of the hacker at the time. War driving typically involves driving in a car with a portable device looking for unsecured Wi-Fi networks to connect to. Wi-Fi piggybacking refers to accessing someone else's unsecured Wi-Fi network from the hacker's current location (such as inside his or her home, outside a Wi-Fi hotspot location, or near a local business). Both war driving and Wi-Fi piggybacking are ethically—if not legally—questionable acts. They can also lead to illegal behavior, such as individuals deciding to use data (credit card numbers, for instance) they run across while war driving for fraudulent purposes, as was the case with two men who illegally accessed a Lowe's wireless network during a war drive and later decided to steal credit card numbers via that network. War driving and Wi-Fi piggybacking can also have security risks, both for the hacker and the owner of the Wi-Fi network that is being used. For instance, they both risk the introduction of computer viruses (either intentionally or unintentionally) and unauthorized access of the data located on their computers. In addition, the owner may experience reduced performance or even the cancellation of his or her Internet service if the ISP limits bandwidth or the number of computers allowed to use a single Internet connection.

In some countries, such as the UK, the laws are clear that unauthorized access of a Wi-Fi connection is illegal. In the United States, federal law is not as clear, although some states (such as Michigan) have made using a Wi-Fi connection without permission illegal. In fact, a Michigan man was found guilty, fined, and sentenced to community service in 2007 for using the free Wi-Fi service offered to customers at a local café because he was using the service from his parked car located on the street outside the café to check his e-mail on a regular basis. And, at the time of this writing, Google was being accused, via a privacy class-action lawsuit, of collecting and storing private data (including e-mails, usernames, passwords, and documents) from unsecured home Wi-Fi networks in the United States and Europe while capturing data for its Street View mapping system.

Advocates of war driving and Wi-Fi piggybacking state that, unless individuals or businesses protect their access points, they are welcoming others to use them. Critics compare that logic to that of an unlocked front door—you cannot legally enter a home just because the front door is unlocked. Some wireless network owners do leave their access points unsecured on purpose and some communities are creating a collection of wireless access points to provide wireless Internet access to everyone in that community. However, it is difficult—if not impossible—to tell if an unsecured network is that way intentionally, unless the hotspot information states that it is a free public Wi-Fi hotspot. To help you locate public Wi-Fi hotspots, a number of services are available, such as browser-based mapping applications and smartphone apps that identify free and fee-based hotspots for a specific geographical location (see the Wi-Fi Finder app in Figure 4-2). Mobile apps have the advantage of automatically determining your geographical location to display information about hotspots in your current geographical area.

FIGURE 4-2
Wi-Fi finders. Online mapping services and smartphone apps can show you the available Wi-Fi hotspots for a particular geographic area.

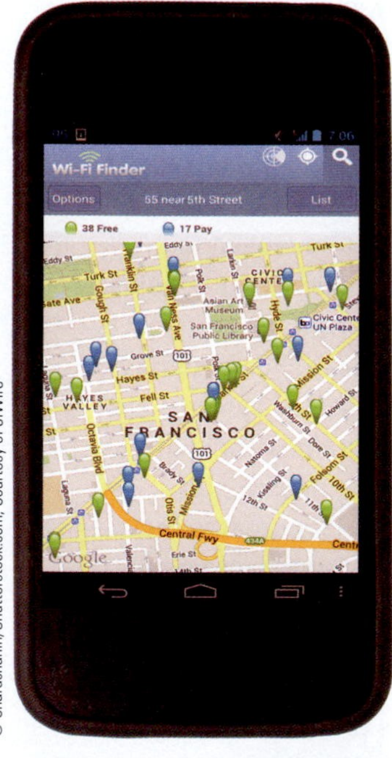

Some feel the ethical distinction of using an unsecured wireless network is determined by the amount of use, believing that it is acceptable to borrow someone's Internet connection to do a quick e-mail check or Google search, but that continually using a neighbor's Internet connection to avoid paying for your own is crossing over the line. Others feel that allowing outsiders to share an Internet connection is acceptable use, as long as the subscriber does not charge the outsider for that access. Still others believe that an Internet connection is intended for use only by the subscriber and that sharing it with others is unfair to the subscriber's ISP. This issue is beginning to be addressed by the courts and ISPs, and some answers regarding the legality of "Wi-Fi borrowing" and

>**War driving.** Driving around an area with a Wi-Fi-enabled computer or mobile device to find a Wi-Fi network to access and use without authorization. >**Wi-Fi piggybacking.** Accessing an unsecured Wi-Fi network from your current location without authorization.

Internet connection sharing will likely be forthcoming in the near future. However, the ethical questions surrounding this issue may take longer to resolve.

Interception of Communications

Instead of accessing data stored on a computer via hacking, some criminals gain unauthorized access to data, files, messages, VoIP calls, and other content as it is being sent over the Internet. For instance, *unencrypted* (unsecured) messages, files, logon information, and more sent over a wireless network (such as while using a public Wi-Fi hotspot or over an unsecured home or business Wi-Fi network) can be captured and read by anyone within range using software designed for that purpose. Once intercepted, the data can be used for unintended or fraudulent purposes.

Although it is unlikely that anyone would be interested in intercepting personal e-mail or text messages sent to friends and relatives, proprietary corporate information and sensitive personal information (such as credit card numbers and Web site logon information) is at risk if it is sent unsecured over the Internet or over a wireless home or corporate network. The widespread use of wireless networks with both home and office computers, as well as with smartphones and other portable devices, has opened up new opportunities for data interception. For instance, the data on mobile devices with Bluetooth capabilities enabled can be accessed by other Bluetooth devices that are within range and any sensitive data stored on a smartphone can be accessed by a hacker if the phone is connected to an unsecured Wi-Fi network. With an increasing number of smartphone owners storing sensitive data (such as passwords for online banking and social networking sites, and credit card account numbers) on their devices (and less than half of owners securing their mobile devices with a *password*, according to one estimate), the risk of that data being intercepted is increasing.

A relatively recent trend is criminals intercepting credit and debit card information during the card verification process; that is, intercepting the data from a card in real time as a purchase is being authorized. Often, this occurrs via *packetsniffing* software installed at payment terminals (such as restaurant cash registers or gas station credit/debit card readers) by hackers—the packetsniffing software gathers data during transactions and then sends it to the hackers, who may then use it for fraudulent purposes.

PROTECTING AGAINST UNAUTHORIZED ACCESS AND UNAUTHORIZED USE

The first step in protecting against unauthorized access and unauthorized use of a computer system is controlling access to an organization's facilities and computer networks to ensure that only authorized individuals are granted access. In addition, steps need to be taken to ensure that authorized individuals access only the resources that they are supposed to access.

Access Control Systems

Access control systems are used to control access to facilities, devices, computer networks, company databases, Web site accounts, and other assets. They can be *identification systems*, which verify that the person trying to access the facility or system is listed as an authorized user, and/or *authentication systems*, which determine whether or not the person attempting access is actually who he or she claims to be. In businesses, access control systems are often integrated into a comprehensive *identity management* (*IDM*) *system* designed to manage users' access to enterprise systems, such as to grant them secure and appropriate access to the systems they are allowed to access in as convenient a manner as possible. An emerging trend is to use *single sign-on* (*SSO*) systems that grant employees access to a number of secure resources with a single authentication. The three most common types of access control systems are discussed next, followed by a discussion of additional considerations for controlling access to wireless networks. Some emerging control systems are discussed in the Trend box later in this chapter.

TIP

To prevent a hacker from obtaining your logon info from an unused (*zombie*) online account, delete your old accounts if you are no longer going to use them.

I'm A Current Online Customer

Email Address janedoe@aol.com

Password: •••••••••
(Password is case sensitive.)

log in

FIGURE 4-3
Passwords.
Passwords are used to log on to computers, networks, Web sites, and other computing resources.

Possessed Knowledge Access Systems

A **possessed knowledge access system** is an identification system that requires the individual requesting access to provide information that only the authorized user is supposed to know. *Passwords* and *cognitive authentication systems* fall into this category.

Passwords, the most common type of possessed knowledge, are secret words or character combinations associated with an individual. They are typically used in conjunction with a *username* (often a variation of the person's first and/or last names or the individual's e-mail address). Username/password combinations are often used to restrict access to networks, computers, Web sites, routers, and other computing resources—the user is granted access only after supplying the correct information. While usernames and e-mail addresses are not secret, passwords are and, for security purposes, typically appear as asterisks or dots as they are being entered so they cannot be viewed (see Figure 4-3). For some applications (such as ATM machines), a *PIN* or *personal identification number*—a secret combination of numeric digits selected by the user—is used instead of a password. Numeric passwords are also referred to as *passcodes*. Instead of traditional passwords, some systems (such as Windows 8 devices and smartphone *lock screens*) can use *picture passwords*—typically gestures or patterns drawn on top of an image, such as a grid of dots or a photograph.

One of the biggest disadvantages of password-based systems is that any individual possessing the proper password will be granted access to the system because the system recognizes the password, regardless of whether or not the person using the password is the authorized user, and passwords can be guessed or deciphered by a hacker or a hacker's computer easily if secure password selection strategies are not applied. For example, many hackers are able to access networking hardware and databases because the system administrator passwords for those resources are still the default passwords (the ones assigned during manufacturing) and so are commonly known; some insiders gain unauthorized access to systems using passwords written down on sticky notes attached to a user's monitor. In addition, passwords can be forgotten. Consequently, it is important to select passwords that are *strong passwords* but are also easy to remember without writing them down. Strong passwords are passwords that are at least eight characters long; use a combination of letters, numbers, and symbols; and do not form words found in the dictionary or that match the username that the password is associated with. Some strategies for creating strong passwords are listed in Figure 4-4.

A growing trend in possessed knowledge access systems is the use of *cognitive authentication systems* instead of, or

FIGURE 4-4
Strategies for creating strong passwords.

PASSWORD STRATEGIES
Make the password at least eight characters and include both uppercase and lowercase letters, as well as numbers and special symbols.
Choose passwords that are not in a dictionary—for instance, mix numbers and special characters with abbreviations or unusual words you will remember but that do not conform to a pattern a computer can readily figure out.
Do not use your name, your kids' or pets' names, your address, your birthdate, or any other public information as your password.
Determine a *passphrase* that you can remember and use corresponding letters and symbols (such as the first letter of each word) for your password. For instance, the passphrase "My son John is five years older than my daughter Abby" could be used to remember the corresponding strong password "Msji5yotMd@".
Develop a system using a basic password for all Web sites plus site-specific information (such as the first two letters of the site and a number you will remember) to create a different password for each site, but still ones you can easily remember. For instance, you can combine your dog's name with the site initials followed by a number that is significant to you to form a password such as "RoverAM27" for Amazon.com.
Do not keep a written copy of the password in your desk or taped to your monitor. If you need to write down your password, create a password-protected file on your computer that contains all your passwords or use a password manager program.
Use a different password for your highly sensitive activities (such as online banking or stock trading) than for other Web sites. If a hacker determines your password on a low-security site (which is easier to break into), he or she can use it on an account containing sensitive data if you use the same password on both accounts.
Change your passwords frequently—at least every 6 months.

>**Possessed knowledge access system.** An access control system that uses information only the individual should know to identify that individual.
>**Password.** A secret combination of characters used to gain access to a computer, computer network, or other resource.

in conjunction with, usernames and passwords. Cognitive authentication systems use information that an individual should know or can remember easily. Some systems use personal information about the individual (such as his or her city of birth, first school attended, or amount of home mortgage) that was pulled from public databases or the company database and the individual must supply the correct answer in order to be granted access. Other systems (such as the password recovery systems used by many secure Web sites to verify individuals when they forget their password) allow the individual to supply answers to questions when the account is created and then the individual can supply those answers again for authentication purposes when needed.

CAUTION CAUTION CAUTION CAUTION CAUTION CAUTION CAUT

Don't select answers for the cognitive authentication questions used in the password recovery process of many Web sites that a hacker may be able to guess based on information found on your Facebook page or other online source. Instead, supply answers that you can remember but that also follow secure password rules. For instance, if your dog's name is Spot, you could enter *MDN1s$pOT* as the answer to a question about your pet's name and remember it as "My dog's name is Spot."

Possessed knowledge systems are often used in conjunction with the *possessed object access systems* and *biometric access systems* that are discussed next. Using two different methods to authenticate a user is called **two-factor authentication**. Typically, the methods used are some type of possessed knowledge (something you know) along with either a *possessed object* (something you have) or a *biometric feature* (something you are). Two-factor authentication adds an additional level of security to an access control system because hackers are much less likely to be able to gain access to two different required factors. One emerging type of two-factor authentication uses a conventional username/password combination in conjunction with a *soft token* (an electronic object available via something you already carry with you, such as a smartphone or credit card, instead of using a *hard token*, such as a *USB key token*). A soft token can be generated by a mobile app or by pressing a button on a credit card; it can also be sent via text message. A soft token supplies a *one-time password* (*OTP*), which must be entered in conjunction with your username/password in order to log on to the account. Two-factor authentication systems are common in many countries and their use is growing in the United States. For instance, many banks offer two-factor authentication for online and mobile banking, and it is an option for Google, Twitter, and Facebook users. In Facebook, for example, once two-factor authentication (called *Login Approvals*) is enabled, you will see the security code screen shown in Figure 4-5 whenever you log in with your Facebook logon information using a new browser or device; you will need to enter the OTP sent to your phone before you will be logged into your Facebook account. The disadvantage of two-factor authentication for businesses is that only one individual can access the account, unless the site (like Facebook) supports multiple users for a single account.

FIGURE 4-5
Facebook two-factor authentication. The first time you log on with a new device, you must supply the OTP sent to your mobile phone in addition to your conventional username/password combination.

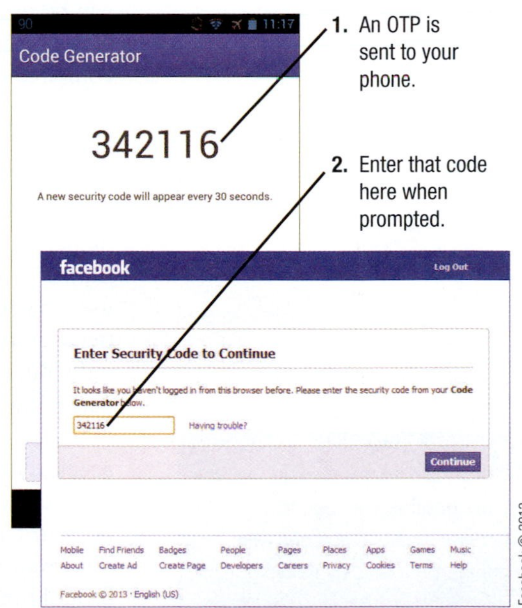

TIP

To enable Facebook Login Approvals, go to your *Security Settings* on that site.

Possessed Object Access Systems

Possessed object access systems use physical objects for identification purposes and they are frequently used to control access to facilities (called *physical access*) and computer systems (called *logical access*). Common types of possessed objects are smart

>**Two-factor authentication.** Using two different methods to authenticate a user. >**Possessed object access system.** An access control system that uses a physical object an individual has in his or her possession to identify that individual.

Photos by HID Global Corporation

PHYSICAL ACCESS
The object (in this case a mobile phone containing an appropriate microSD card) is read by a reader to provide access to a facility.

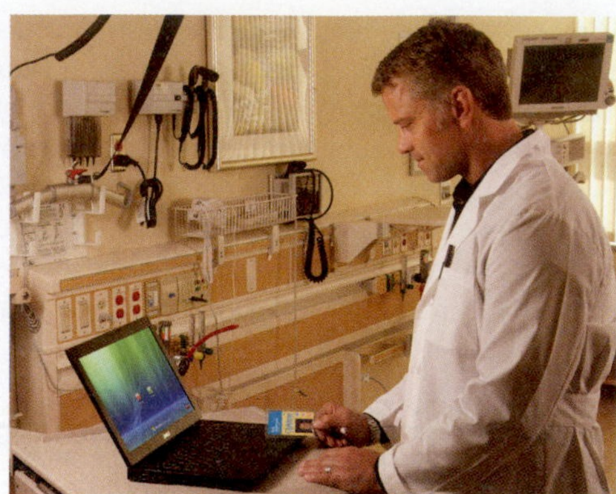

LOGICAL ACCESS
The object (in this case a smart card employee badge) is read by a reader (this reader is integrated into the computer) to provide access to that computer system.

FIGURE 4-6
Possessed objects. Can grant access to both facilities and computer resources (including computers, networks, and Web sites).

cards, RFID-encoded badges, magnetic cards, and smartphones that are swiped through or placed close to a reader to be read (see Figure 4-6)—emerging options include the use of an *NFC-enabled ring* or a Bluetooth app (as discussed in Chapter 8) to automatically lock and unlock your devices when they are within range. Possessed objects also include *USB security keys* or *tokens* (USB flash drives that are inserted into a computer to grant access to a network, to supply Web site usernames and passwords, or to provide other security features), access cards, smartphones, and other devices used to supply the OTPs used to log on to Web sites. An emerging option is integrating OTP capabilities into the hardware of devices, such as laptops that include Intel *Identity Protection Technology (IPT)*, in order to automatically authenticate the devices being used to log on to participating Web sites.

One disadvantage of using possessed objects is that they can be lost or, like passwords, can be used by an unauthorized individual if that individual has possession of the object. This disadvantage can be overcome by using a second factor, such as a username/password combination or a fingerprint or other type of *biometric* data.

Biometric Access Systems

Biometrics is the study of identifying individuals using measurable, unique physiological or behavioral characteristics. **Biometric access systems** typically identify users by a particular unique biological characteristic (such as a fingerprint, a hand, a face, veins, or an iris), although personal traits are used in some systems. For instance, some systems today use *keystroke dynamics* to recognize an individual's unique typing pattern to authenticate the user as he or she types in his or her username and password; other systems identify an individual via his or her voice, signature, or gait. Because the means of access (usually a part of the body) cannot typically be used by anyone other than the authorized individual, biometric access systems can perform both identification and authentication. Biometric access systems are used for both physical and logical access (see Figure 4-7).

To identify and authenticate an individual, biometric access systems typically use a biometric reader (such as a *fingerprint reader, finger* or *palm vein reader*, or a *hand geometry reader*) to identify an individual based on his or her fingerprint, veins, or hand image, or a digital camera to identify an individual based on his or her face or iris, in conjunction with software and a database. The system matches the supplied biometric data with the biometric data that was stored in the database when the individual was enrolled in the system and authenticates the individual if the data matches. To speed up the process, many biometric access systems require users to identify themselves first (such as by entering a username or swiping a smart card), and then the system uses that identifying information to verify that the supplied biometric data matches the identified person.

TIP

Cuts or other changes to a finger may prevent access via a fingerprint reader. To avoid this problem, be sure to enroll more than one finger, if possible, whenever you are being set up in a system that uses a fingerprint reader—any of the registered fingers may be used for access.

>**Biometric access system.** An access control system that uses one unique physical characteristic of an individual (such as a fingerprint, a face, veins, or a voice) to authenticate that individual.

Biometric access systems are used to control access to secure facilities (such as corporate headquarters and prisons); to log users on to computers, networks, and secure Web sites (by using an external reader or camera or one built into the computer); to punch employees in and out of work; and to confirm consumers' identities at ATM machines and check-cashing services. Biometric readers are also increasingly being built into smartphones, external hard drives, USB flash drives, and other hardware to prevent unauthorized use of those devices.

In addition to being used to control access to computers, networks, and other resources, biometrics are an important part of the systems used by law enforcement agencies and the military to identify individuals. For instance, the border control systems in many countries use biometrics to identify citizens, travelers, criminal suspects, and potential terrorists, and biometric identification systems are used extensively by law enforcement agencies and the military in areas of conflict. For example, the Egyptian Hospital at Bagram Airfield in Afghanistan uses biometrics (fingerprints and iris scans—see Figure 4-7) to identify and track the records of incoming patients. In addition, *face recognition systems* (biometric systems that use cameras and a database of photos to attempt to identify individuals as they walk by the cameras) are used in many airports and other public locations to help identify known terrorists and criminal suspects.

Photo by HID Global Corporation

FINGERPRINT READERS
Typically used to protect access to work facilities or computers, to log on to secure Web sites, for law enforcement identification, and to pay for products or services.

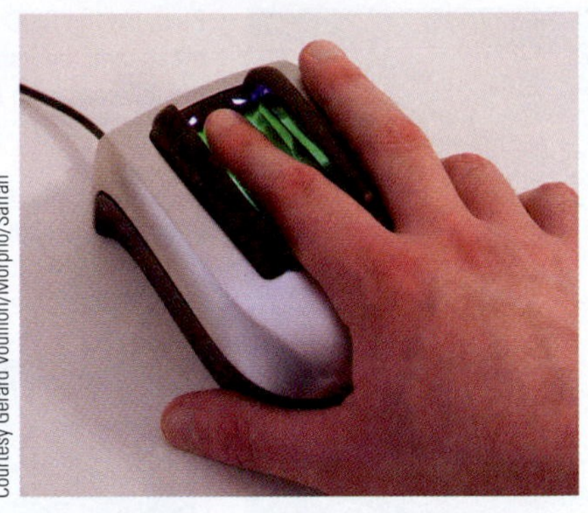

Courtesy Gérard Vouillon/Morpho/Safran

VEIN READERS
Beginning to replace hand geometry readers to control access to facilities (such as government offices, prisons, and military facilities) and to punch in and out of work.

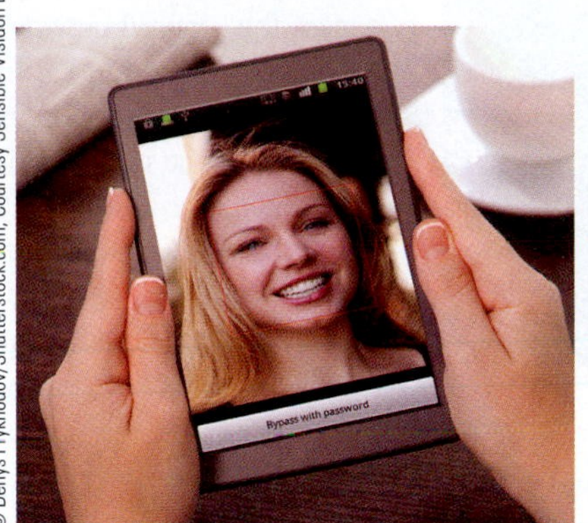

© Denys Prykhodov/Shutterstock.com; Courtesy Sensible Vision Ltd

FACE RECOGNITION SYSTEMS
Typically used to control access to highly secure areas, to identify individuals for law enforcement purposes, and to log on to devices or apps, as shown here.

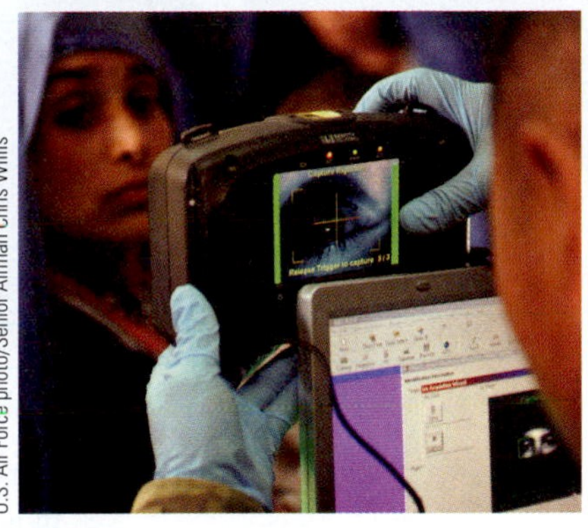

U.S. Air Force photo/Senior Airman Chris Willis

IRIS RECOGNITION SYSTEMS
Typically used to control access to highly secure areas and by the military, such as to identify Afghan patients as shown here.

FIGURE 4-7
Types of biometric access and identification systems.

Biometric access systems are very accurate. In fact, the odds of two different individuals having identical irises is 1 in 10^{78} and the statistical probability of two different irises being declared a match are 1 in 1.2 million—even identical twins (who have the same DNA structure) have different fingerprints and irises. Systems based on biological characteristics (such as a person's iris, hand geometry, face, or fingerprint) tend to be more accurate than those based on a personal trait (such as a person's voice or written signature) because biological traits do not change, but physical traits might change (such as an individual's voice, which might be affected by a cold, or a written signature, which might be affected by a broken wrist). In addition, biometric characteristics cannot be lost (like an access card), cannot be forgotten (like a password), and do not have to be pulled out of a briefcase or pocket (like an access card or other type of possessed object).

The primary disadvantages of biometric access systems are that much of the necessary hardware and software is expensive, and the data used for authentication (such as a fingerprint or an iris image) cannot be reset if it is compromised. In addition, fingerprint and hand geometry systems typically require contact with the reader device (which some users might object to)—vein systems (that use infrared LED light in conjunction with a digital camera to identify individuals based on the veins in their fingers or palms) can be contactless systems.

TIP
Fingerprint biometrics is an integral part of Windows 8.1, supporting both *touch* and *swipe fingerprint readers* for a variety of authentication functions.

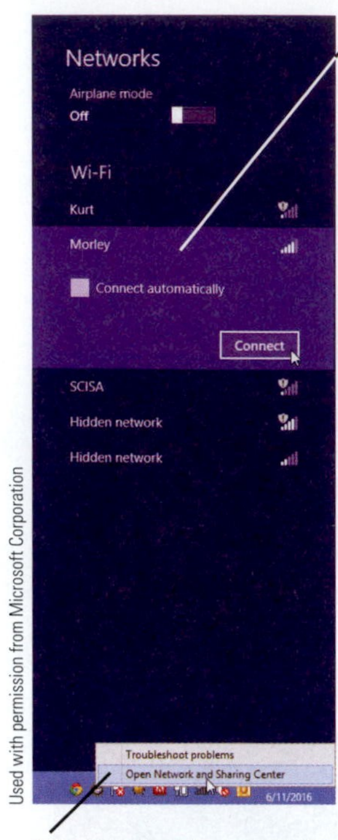
Networks
Airplane mode
Off
Wi-Fi
Kurt
Morley
Connect automatically
Connect
SCISA
Hidden network
Hidden network
Troubleshoot problems
Open Network and Sharing Center
6/11/2016
Because the SSID is being broadcast, the user can select the network from the list.
If the SSID isn't broadcast, the user must add the network manually by using its SSID in order to log on.

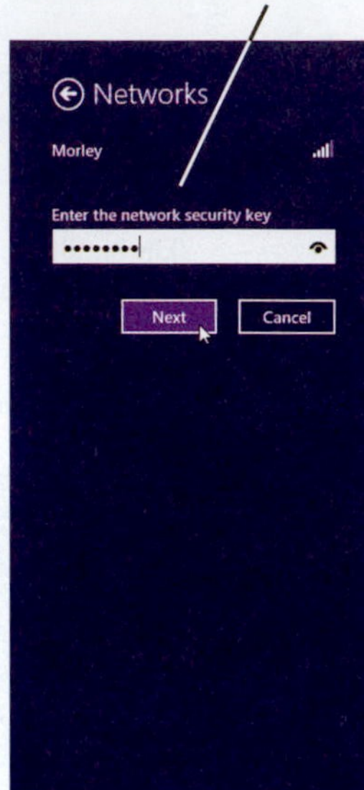
The user must supply the appropriate network key or passphrase in order to connect to the network.
Networks
Morley
Enter the network security key
Next
Cancel

FIGURE 4-8
Accessing a Wi-Fi network. To access a secure network, the appropriate passphrase must be supplied.

Controlling Access to Wireless Networks

As already discussed, wireless networks—such as Wi-Fi networks—are less secure, in general, than wired networks. There are Wi-Fi security procedures, however, that can be used to protect against unauthorized use of a wireless network and to *encrypt* data sent over the network so that it is unreadable if it is intercepted. The original Wi-Fi security standard was *WEP* (*Wired Equivalent Privacy*). WEP is now considered insecure and has been replaced with the more secure *WPA* (*Wi-Fi Protected Access*) and the even more secure *WPA2* standards. However, Wi-Fi security features only work if they are enabled. Most Wi-Fi hardware today is shipped with the security features either switched off or enabled with a *default password* that is public knowledge; many network owners never change the default settings, leaving those networks unsecured.

To protect against unauthorized access, Wi-Fi network owners should secure their networks by changing the router or access point settings to enable one of the encryption standards and to assign a *network key* or *passphrase* (essentially a password) that must be supplied in order to access the secured network. In addition, the name of the network (called the *SSID*) can be hidden from view by switching off the SSID broadcast feature. While hiding the network name will not deter serious hackers, it may reduce the number of casual war drivers or neighbors accessing the network. Once a network is secured, users who want to connect to that network need to either select or supply the network SSID name (depending on whether or not the SSID is being broadcast) and then enter the network key assigned to that network (see Figure 4-8). For an overview of how you can secure your wireless home router, see the How It Works box.

Firewalls, Encryption, and Virtual Private Networks (VPNs)

In addition to the access control systems just discussed, there are a number of other tools that can be used to prevent access to an individual computer or to prevent data from being intercepted in an understandable form during transit. These tools are discussed next.

Firewalls

A **firewall** is a security system that essentially creates a barrier between a computer or a network and the Internet in order to protect against unauthorized access. Firewalls are typically two-way, so they check all incoming (from the Internet) and outgoing (to the Internet) traffic and allow only authorized traffic to pass through the firewall. *Personal firewalls* are software programs designed to protect home computers from hackers attempting to access those computers through their Internet connections. All computers with direct Internet connections (such as DSL, cable, satellite, or fixed wireless Internet access) should use a firewall (computers using dial-up Internet access only are relatively safe from hackers). Personal firewalls can be stand-alone programs (such as the free *ZoneAlarm* program or the free *Comodo Firewall* program shown in Figure 4-9); they are also built into many operating systems (such as the *Windows Firewall* program). Many routers, modems, and other pieces of networking hardware also include built-in firewall capabilities to help secure the networks these devices are used with. Firewalls designed to protect business networks may be software-based, hardware-based, or a combination of the two. They can typically be used both to prevent network access by hackers and other outsiders, as well as to control employee Internet access.

TIP

If a legitimate application installed on your computer needs to access the Internet but cannot, check your firewall settings—you may need to unblock that program.

>**Firewall.** A collection of hardware and/or software intended to protect a computer or computer network from unauthorized access.

HOW IT WORKS

Securing a Wireless Home Router

If you have a home wireless network, it is important to secure it properly so it cannot be used by unauthorized individuals. To open your router's configuration screen to check or modify the security settings, type the IP address assigned to that device (such as 192.168.0.1—check your router's documentation for its default IP address and username) in your browser's Address bar. Use the default password to log on the first time, and then change the password using the configuration screen to prevent unauthorized individuals from changing your router settings. To secure the router, enter the network name (SSID) you want to have associated with the router, select the appropriate security mode (such as WPA or WPA2) to be used, and then type a secure passphrase to be used in order to log on to the network.

For additional security, *MAC (Media Access Control) address filtering* can be used to allow only the devices whose network adapter MAC addresses you enter into your router's settings access to the network. While MAC address filtering should not be considered an alternative to using WPA or WPA2 encryption, it does add another layer of protection. Other precautions include designating specific times (such as when you are away from home) that the router will deny access to any device, and reducing the strength of the wireless signal if its current strength reaches farther than you need.

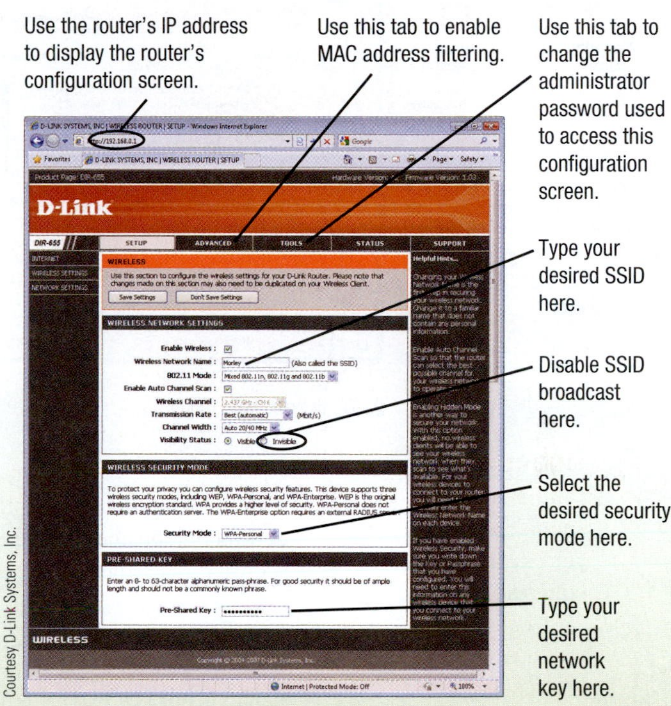

Use the router's IP address to display the router's configuration screen.
Use this tab to enable MAC address filtering.
Use this tab to change the administrator password used to access this configuration screen.
Type your desired SSID here.
Disable SSID broadcast here.
Select the desired security mode here.
Type your desired network key here.
D-Link
SETUP
ADVANCED
TOOLS
STATUS
SUPPORT
WIRELESS NETWORK SETTINGS
WIRELESS SECURITY MODE
PRE-SHARED KEY
WIRELESS

Courtesy D-Link Systems, Inc.

Configuring a home router.

Firewalls work by closing down all external *communications port addresses* (the electronic connections that allow a computer to communicate with other computers) to unauthorized computers and programs. While business firewalls are set up by the network administrator and those settings typically cannot be changed by end users, individuals may choose to change the settings for their personal firewall. For example, the user can choose to be notified when any application program on the computer is trying to access the Internet, to specify the programs that are allowed to access the Internet, or to block all incoming connections temporarily. In addition to protecting your computer from outside access, firewall programs also protect against any spyware, computer viruses, or other malicious programs located on your computer that are designed to send data from your computer

FIGURE 4-9
A personal firewall.

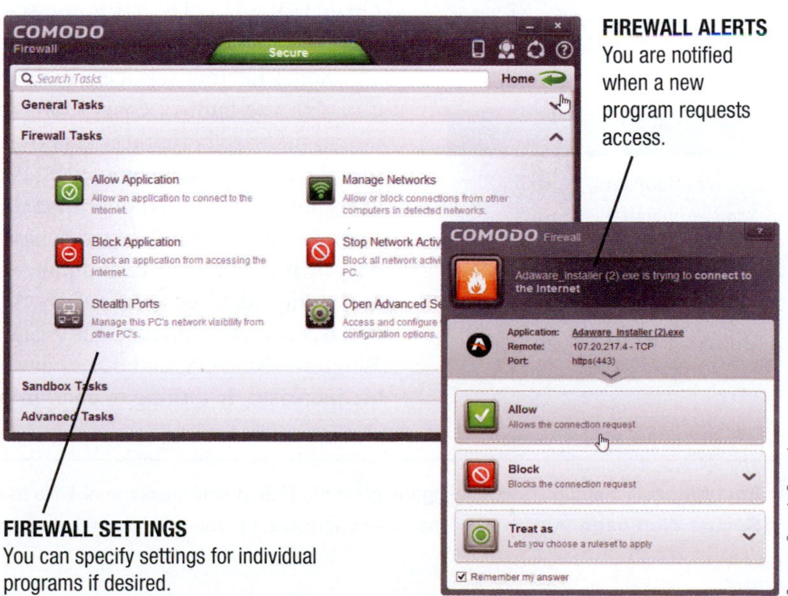

FIREWALL ALERTS

You can specify settings for individual programs if desired.

Stop Network Activity

Courtesy Comodo Group, Inc.

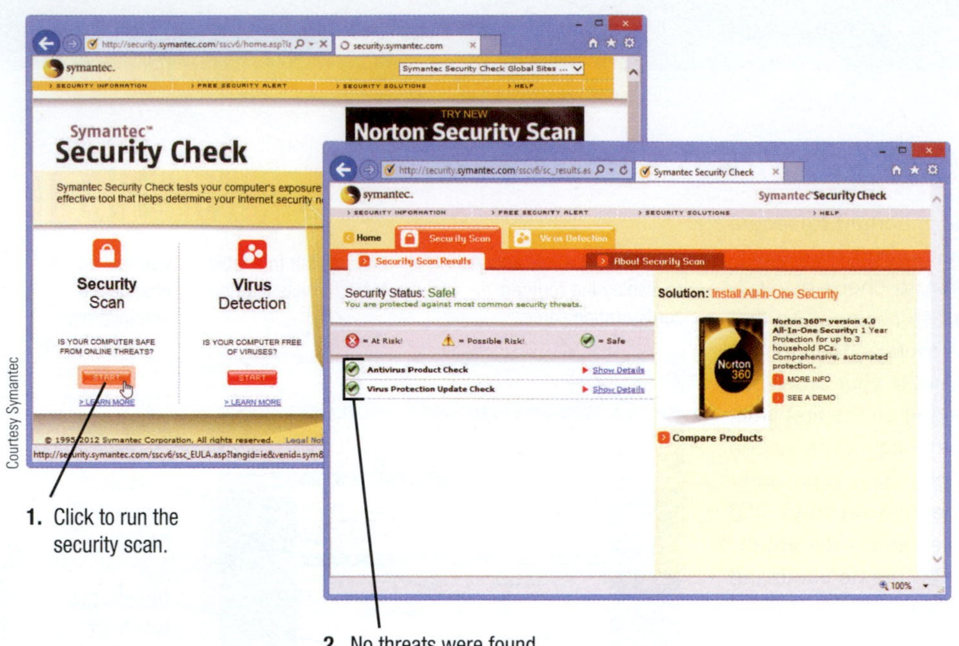

Courtesy Symantec

FIGURE 4-10
Online security scans can check your system for vulnerabilities.

(such as credit card numbers, Web site passwords, and other sensitive data stored on your hard drive) to a hacker at the hacker's request.

A related type of security system increasingly being used by businesses today and included in many security suites is an *intrusion prevention system* (*IPS*). Whereas a firewall tries to block unauthorized traffic, an IPS continuously monitors and analyzes the traffic allowed by the firewall to try to detect possible attacks as they are occurring. If an attack is in progress, IPS software can immediately block it.

After installing and setting up a firewall (and an IPS if needed), individuals and businesses should test their systems to determine if vulnerabilities still exist. Individuals can use online security tests—such as the *Symantec Security Check* shown in Figure 4-10 or the tests at Gibson Research's *ShieldsUP!* site—to check their computers; businesses may want to hire an outside consultant to perform a comprehensive security assessment.

Encryption

Encryption is a way of temporarily converting data into a form, known as a *cipher*, which is unreadable until it is *decrypted* (unscrambled) in order to protect that data from being viewed by unauthorized individuals. As previously discussed, secure Wi-Fi networks use encryption to secure data that is transferred over the network. **Secure Web pages** use encryption so that sensitive data (such as credit card numbers) sent via the Web page is protected as it travels over the Internet. The most common security protocols used with secure Web pages are *Secure Sockets Layer* (*SSL*) and *Extended Validation Secure Sockets Layer* (*EV SSL*). The URL for Web pages using either form of SSL begins with *https:* instead of *http:*.

TIP

An emerging encryption standard that may eventually replace SSL is *Transport Layer Security* (*TLS*).

TIP

Sensitive information (such as credit card numbers, account numbers, and Web site passwords) should only be entered on secure Web pages to prevent that data from being intercepted by a criminal.

Some Internet services, such as *Skype* (for VoIP calls) and *Hushmail* (for Web-based e-mails), use built-in encryption. Encryption can also be added manually to a file or an e-mail message before it is sent over the Internet to ensure that the content is unreadable if the file or message is intercepted during transit. In addition to securing files during transit, encryption can be used to protect the files stored on a hard drive so they will be unreadable if opened by an unauthorized person (such as if a hacker accesses a file containing sensitive data or if a computer containing sensitive files is lost or stolen). Increasingly, computers and storage devices (particularly those used with portable computers) are *self-encrypting*; that is, encrypting all data automatically and invisibly to the user, as discussed in Chapter 5. Windows, Mac OS, and other current operating systems support encryption and businesses are increasingly turning to encryption to prevent data loss if a data breach should occur.

>**Encryption.** A method of scrambling the contents of an e-mail message or a file to make it unreadable if an unauthorized user intercepts it.
>**Secure Web page.** A Web page that uses encryption to protect information transmitted via that Web page.

The two most common types of encryption in use today are *public key encryption* (often used with content being transmitted over the Internet, such as secure Web pages and encrypted e-mail) and *private key encryption* (most often used to encrypt files or the content of a hard drive or other device). **Private key encryption**, also called *symmetric key encryption*, uses a single secret *private key* (essentially a password) to both encrypt and decrypt the file or message. It is often used to encrypt files stored on an individual's computer because the individual who selects the private key is likely the only one who will need to access those files. Private key encryption can also be used to send files securely to others, provided both the sender and recipient agree on the private key that will be used to access the file. Private key encryption capabilities are incorporated into a variety of programs today, including Microsoft Office, the WinZip file compression program, and Adobe Acrobat (the program used to create PDF files). To encrypt a document in Microsoft Word 2013, for instance, you select *Info* on the FILE tab, click *Protect Document* and select *Encrypt with Password*, type the desired password (private key) when prompted, and then save the file. To open that document again (or any copies of the file, such as those sent via e-mail), the password assigned to that file must be entered correctly.

Public key encryption, also called *asymmetric key encryption*, utilizes two encryption keys to encrypt and decrypt documents. Specifically, public key encryption uses a pair of keys (a private key and a *public key*) that are related mathematically to each other and have been assigned to a particular individual. An individual's public key is not secret and is available for anyone to use, but the corresponding private key is secret and is used only by the individual to whom it was assigned. Documents or messages encrypted with a public key can only be decrypted with the matching private key.

Public/private key pairs are generated by the program being used to perform the encryption or they are obtained via the Internet through a *Certificate Authority*, such as VeriSign or Thawte. Once obtained, encryption keys are stored in your browser, e-mail program, and any other program with which they will be used—this is typically done automatically for you when you obtain your key pairs. Obtaining a business public/private key pair usually requires a fee, but free key pairs for personal use are available through some Certificate Authorities. If a third-party encryption program is used (such as *Pretty Good Privacy* or *PGP*), the program typically takes care of obtaining and managing your keys for you.

To send someone an encrypted e-mail message or file using public key encryption, you need his or her public key. If that person has previously sent you his or her public key (such as via an e-mail message), it was likely stored by your e-mail program in your address book or contacts list, or by your encryption program in a central key directory used by that program. In either case, that public key is available whenever you want to send that person an encrypted document. If you do not already have the public key belonging to the individual to whom you want to send an encrypted e-mail or file, you will need to request it from that individual. Once the recipient's public key has been used to encrypt the file or e-mail message and that document is received, the recipient uses his or her private key to decrypt the encrypted contents (see Figure 4-11).

To avoid the need to obtain the recipient's public key before sending that person an encrypted e-mail, *Web-based encrypted e-mail* can be used. Web-based encrypted e-mail works similarly to regular Web-based e-mail (in which e-mail is composed and viewed on a Web page belonging to a Web-based e-mail provider), but Web-based encrypted e-mail systems use secure Web servers to host the Web pages that are used to compose and read e-mail messages. Some Web-based encrypted e-mail systems—such as the popular free *Hushmail* service that automatically encrypts all e-mail sent through the

TIP

Both Facebook and Twitter allow you to encrypt your connections—enable this option when you are using a public Wi-Fi hotspot to protect your account from hackers.

>**Private key encryption.** A type of encryption that uses a single key to encrypt and decrypt the file or message. >**Public key encryption.** A type of encryption that uses key pairs to encrypt and decrypt the file or message.

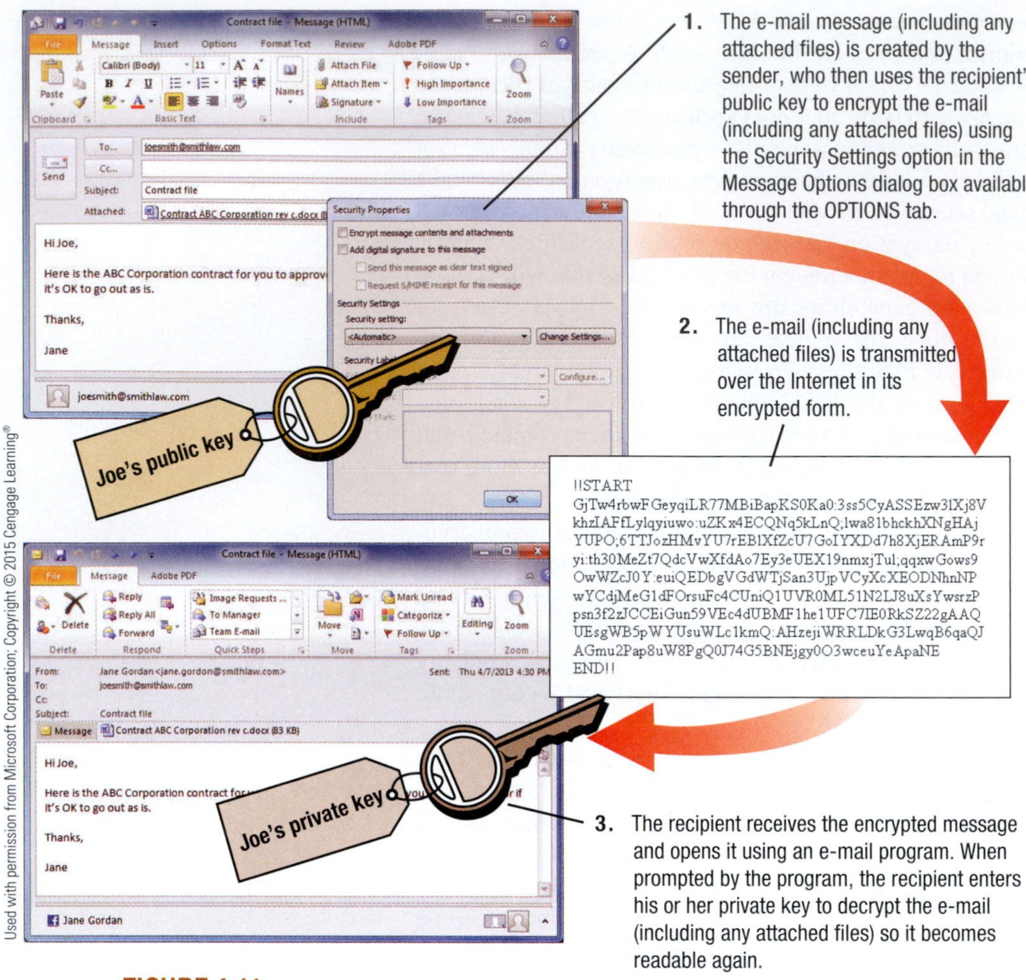

1. The e-mail message (including any attached files) is created by the sender, who then uses the recipient's public key to encrypt the e-mail (including any attached files) using the Security Settings option in the Message Options dialog box available through the OPTIONS tab.
Joe's public key
2. The e-mail (including any attached files) is transmitted over the Internet in its encrypted form.
Joe's private key
3. The recipient receives the encrypted message and opens it using an e-mail program. When prompted by the program, the recipient enters his or her private key to decrypt the e-mail (including any attached files) so it becomes readable again.

FIGURE 4-11 Using public key encryption to secure an e-mail message in Microsoft Outlook.

service—require both the sender and recipient to have accounts. Others require only the sender to have an account and the recipient is sent an e-mail containing instructions regarding how to view the message on a secure Web page.

There are various strengths of encryption available; the stronger the encryption, the more difficult it is to crack. Older 40-bit encryption (which can only use keys that are 40 bits or 5 characters long) is considered *weak encryption* and is no longer supported by Windows. Stronger encryption includes *strong 128-bit encryption* (which uses 16-character keys) and *military-strength 2,048-bit encryption* (which uses 256-character keys), although not without some objections from law enforcement agencies and the government because they state that terrorists routinely use encryption methods to communicate.

Virtual Private Networks (VPNs)

While e-mail and file encryption can be used to transfer individual messages and files securely over the Internet, a **virtual private network (VPN)** is designed to be used when a continuous secure channel over the Internet is needed. A VPN provides a secure private tunnel from the user's computer through the Internet to another destination and is most often used to provide remote employees with secure access to a company network. VPNs use encryption and other security mechanisms to ensure that only authorized users can access the remote network and that the data cannot be intercepted during transit. Because it uses the Internet instead of an expensive private physical network, a VPN can provide a secure environment over a large geographical area at a manageable cost. Once a VPN is set up, the user just needs to log on (such as with a username/password combination or a security token) in order to use the VPN.

VPNs are often used by both businesses and individuals at public Wi-Fi hotspots to prevent data interception when connecting to the Internet via the hotspot. While businesspeople will typically use a VPN set up by their companies, individuals can create *personal VPNs* using software designed for that purpose. This software automatically encrypts all inbound and outbound Internet traffic, including Web pages, e-mail messages, IMs, VoIP calls, and

TIP

Unless it is absolutely necessary and you are using a VPN, do not perform sensitive transactions (such as shopping or banking) at a public hotspot.

>Virtual private network (VPN). A private, secure path over the Internet that provides authorized users a secure means of accessing a private network via the Internet.

so forth, and also acts as a personal firewall. Using a personal VPN at a public hotspot can help individuals from becoming the victim of a hacker or an *evil twin*—a fake Wi-Fi hotspot set up to look like a legitimate hotspot.

Additional Public Hotspot Precautions

The precautions already discussed (such as using firewall software, secure Web pages, VPNs, and encryption) are a good start for protecting against unauthorized access and unauthorized use at a public Wi-Fi hotspot. However, there are additional precautions individuals can use to avoid data (both that which is on their devices and that which is being sent over the Internet) from being compromised. These precautions are listed in Figure 4-12.

PUBLIC HOTSPOT PRECAUTIONS

- Turn off automatic connections and pay attention to the list of available hotspots to make sure you connect to a legitimate access point (not an evil twin).
- Use a personal firewall to control the traffic going to and coming from your device and temporarily use it to block all incoming connections.
- Use a virtual private network (VPN) to secure all activity between your device and the Internet.
- Only enter passwords, credit card numbers, and other data on secure Web pages using a VPN.
- If you're not using a VPN, encrypt all sensitive files before transferring or e-mailing them.
- If you're not using a VPN, avoid online shopping, banking, and other sensitive transactions.
- Turn off file sharing so others can't access the files on your hard drive.
- Turn off Bluetooth and Wi-Fi when you are not using them.
- Disable *ad hoc* capabilities to prevent another device from connecting to your device directly without using an access point.
- Use antivirus software and make sure your operating system and browser are up to date.

FIGURE 4-12 Sensible precautions for public Wi-Fi hotspot users.

Sensible Employee Precautions

While only about 20% of business security breaches are committed by insiders (according to a recent Data Breach Investigations Report), they are responsible for the majority (66.7%) of exposed records. In addition, these breaches are typically malicious in nature, with an employee deliberately performing the act (though other times the breach occurs because the employee makes a mistake, such as losing a portable computer or removable storage medium, or inadvertently providing access to sensitive data). In either case, employers should be cautious. Some suggestions to avoid security breaches by employees are listed next.

Screen Potential New Hires Carefully

Employers should carefully investigate the background of all potential employees. Some people falsify résumés to get jobs. Others may have criminal records or currently be charged with a crime. One embarrassing mistake made by Rutgers University was to hire David Smith, the author of the *Melissa* computer virus, as a computer technician when he was out on bail following the arrest for that crime.

Watch for Disgruntled Employees and Ex-Employees

The type of employee who is most likely to commit a computer crime is one who has recently been terminated or passed over for a promotion, or one who has some reason to want to "get even" with the organization. Limiting access for each employee to only the resources needed for his or her job (referred to as the *Principle of Least Privilege*) and monitoring any attempts to access off-limit resources can help prevent some types of problems, such as unauthorized access of sensitive files, unintentional damage like deleting or changing files inadvertently, or sabotage like deleting or changing company files intentionally. In addition, it is vital that whenever an employee leaves the company for any reason, all access to the system for that individual (username, password, e-mail address, and so forth) should be removed immediately. For employees with high levels of system access, simultaneously removing access while the termination is taking place is even better. Waiting even a few minutes can be too late because just-fired employees have been known to barricade themselves in their office immediately after being terminated in order to change passwords, sabotage records, and perform other malicious acts. For example, on the day he was fired, one computer programmer at Fannie Mae embedded malicious code into a routine program on his company laptop before turning it in. The code, designed to destroy all data (including financial, securities, and mortgage information), was transmitted to nearly 5,000 Fannie Mae servers. The code was discovered before it was executed and the man was sentenced to more than three years in prison for computer intrusion.

INSIDE THE INDUSTRY

Securing BYOD

One growing trend today is *BYOD* or *Bring Your Own Device* (where students or employees bring their own smartphones, media tablets, or other devices to use instead of using issued devices—see the accompanying photo). Some businesses view BYOD as a cost-effective way of supplying employees with the devices they want to use; many IT departments view BYOD as a potential security nightmare. But it's here and not going away—research firm Gartner predicts that about half the world's companies will no longer provide computing devices to their employees by 2017.

BYOD is also changing the way many individuals perceive their work—no longer as a place, but as an activity that is independent of both location and specific technology. Consequently, it makes sense (and is more convenient) for individuals to carry with them at all times the devices that allow them to perform both work and personal functions as needed. For businesses, however, that brings the challenge of managing those devices. Disadvantages of BYOD from a company perspective include the risk of a *malware* infection via a BYOD device, as well as the potential exposure of company data via unsecured or lost personal devices or personal cloud storage systems (sometimes referred to as *Bring Your Own Cloud* or *BYOC*). Potential disadvantages from the employee perspective include having company-mandated restrictions on their personal devices (such as not using certain applications or cloud services and agreeing to allow the company to erase or reset the device remotely if it is lost or stolen), as well as the employer having access to personal data or activities performed via the phone. In addition, space on the device may be tied up for company data or apps that are used only for work.

While some companies use mobile device management (MDM) software to control the use of personal devices with corporate networks, one emerging solution is to completely separate the business and personal use of the device. For instance, software that supports *sandboxing* or *containerization* can create an isolated virtual environment on the user's device within which corporate data and applications can safely reside. With this method, the company would mandate control policies for just that portion of the device. An option for Windows 8 Enterprise companies is to use the *Windows To Go* feature, which uses a bootable USB flash drive to create a complete, managed Windows 8 environment on whatever device the USB flash drive is plugged into. Consequently, employees can use the Windows To Go environment on their personal devices at work, and then shut down the Windows To Go environment after work to use their devices as solely personal devices.

Develop Policies and Controls

All companies should develop policies and controls regarding security matters. As already mentioned, employees should be granted the least amount of access to the company network that they need to perform their job. Employees should be educated about the seriousness and consequences of hacking, data theft, and other computer crimes, and they should be taught what to do when they suspect a computer crime has been committed. Employees should also be instructed about proper device usage policies—such as whether or not downloading software on company devices is allowed, whether or not employees are responsible for updating their devices, and the types of removable storage media that may be used with company devices—in order to avoid inadvertently creating a security problem. Policies for removing computers and storage media containing sensitive data from the premises should also be implemented, enforced, and updated as needed, and sensitive documents should be shredded when they are no longer needed.

Employees who work from home or otherwise access the company network via the Internet also need to be educated about security policies for remote access and the proper precautions that need to be taken. These precautions include keeping their operating system and security software up to date and using only encrypted storage devices (such as self-encrypting USB flash drives) when transporting documents between work and home.

In addition, telecommuting workers and outside contractors should not be allowed to have peer-to-peer (P2P) software on computers containing company documents because data is increasingly being exposed through the use of P2P networks. For instance, classified data about the U.S. presidential helicopter discovered on a computer in Iran was traced back to a P2P network and the computer of a military contractor in Maryland; and the Social Security numbers and other personal data belonging to about 17,000 current and former Pfizer workers were once leaked onto a P2P network after an employee installed unauthorized P2P software on a company notebook computer provided for use at her home.

Use Software to Manage Employee Devices and Prevent Data Leaks

As employees are increasingly bringing portable devices (such as smartphones and USB flash drives) that can interact with business networks to the office, the challenge of securing these *BYOD* (*Bring Your Own Device*) devices (and the company network) has grown. While some companies prohibit all portable devices and others allow only company-issued portable devices so they can ensure appropriate security measures (such as encryption, password protection, and the ability to wipe the device clean remotely if it is lost or stolen) are implemented, the use of BYOD is growing, as discussed in the Inside the Industry box.

> **TIP**
>
> Deploying a centrally managed security solution to all endpoints (all user devices connected to the company network) is referred to as *endpoint security*.

To protect against employees copying or sending confidential data to others either intentionally or accidentally, *data-leakage* (also called *data-loss*) *prevention systems* can be used. Data-leakage prevention systems are available as software and/or hardware systems, and have a range of capabilities, but the overall goal is to prevent sensitive data from exposure. For instance, some systems control which devices (such as USB flash drives and smartphones) can be connected to an employee's computer in order to prevent sensitive data from being taken home inadvertently or intentionally. *Mobile device management* (*MDM*) *software* (see Figure 4-13) goes one step further by including other protections, such as specifying what apps and Web sites can be used with the device, protecting against unauthorized access and *malware*, facilitating remote access (to update software or erase a lost device, for instance), and locating a lost or stolen device. Other data-leakage prevention systems—sometimes also called *outbound-content monitoring systems*—scan all outgoing communications (e-mail, transferred files, and so forth) for documents containing Social Security numbers, intellectual property, and other confidential information and block them if they might contain prohibited content. Some can also continually scan network devices to locate documents containing sensitive data to ensure that sensitive files are not on the computer of an employee who should not have access to them. For even stronger protection of confidential company documents, *enterprise rights-management software*, which encrypts confidential documents and limits functions such as printing, editing, and copying the data to only authorized users with the appropriate password, can be used.

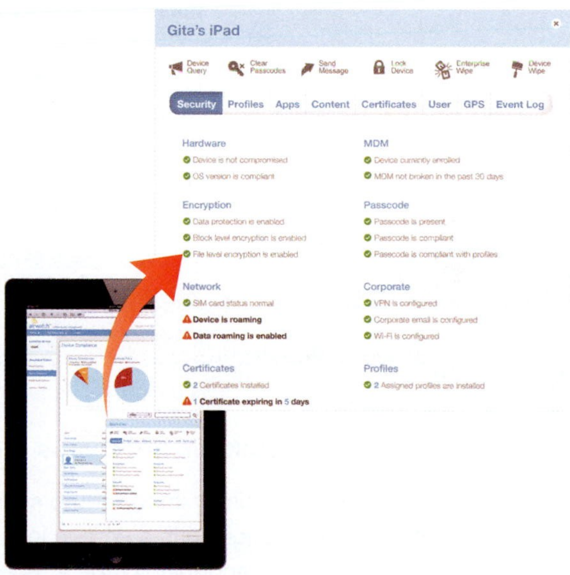

FIGURE 4-13
Mobile device management (MDM) software. Secures and manages the mobile devices used in an organization.

Ask Business Partners to Review Their Security

In this networked economy, many organizations provide some access to internal resources for business partners. If those external companies are lax with their security measures, however, attacks through the business partners' computers (such as via an employee or hacker) are possible. Consequently, businesses should make sure that their business partners maintain adequate security policies and controls. Regulations increasingly require businesses to ensure that adequate controls are in place to protect stored data. This impacts outside companies—such as business partners and *outsourcing companies* (outside vendors for specific business tasks)—if they have access to sensitive corporate data. Companies that utilize cloud computing also need to ensure that the cloud vendor's security and privacy policies match the company's requirements.

COMPUTER SABOTAGE

Computer sabotage—acts of malicious destruction to a computer or computer resource—is another common type of computer crime today. Computer sabotage can take several forms, including launching a *computer virus* or a *denial of service (DoS) attack*, altering the content of a Web site, or changing data or programs located on a computer. A common tool used to perform computer sabotage is a *botnet*, discussed next. Computer sabotage is illegal in the United States, and acts of sabotage are estimated to cost individuals and organizations billions of dollars per year, primarily for labor costs related to correcting the problems caused by the sabotage, lost productivity, and lost sales.

> **TIP**
>
> A group of major U.S. ISPs recently committed to work together to combat three major cybersecurity threats, including bots; the FCC predicts this effort will have a significant positive effect on Internet security.

Botnets

A computer that is controlled by a hacker or other computer criminal is referred to as a **bot** or *zombie computer*; a group of bots that are controlled by one individual and can work together in a coordinated fashion is called a **botnet**. Millions of U.S. computers are part of a botnet—in 2013, one operation alone (*Operation b54*) performed by Microsoft working with the FBI cut the communications among 1,462 *Citadel* botnets (one of the largest botnets in existence and responsible for about half a billion dollars in losses) and their 5 million or more infected computers. Criminals (called *botherders*) are increasingly creating botnets to use for computer sabotage, such as to spread *malware* and to launch *denial of service (DoS) attacks*, discussed shortly. Botherders also often sell their botnet services to send spam and launch Internet attacks on their clients' behalf, as well as to steal identity information, credit card numbers, passwords, corporate secrets, and other sensitive data, which are then sold to other criminals or otherwise used in an illegal manner. Bots are also used to perform *click fraud*—automatically clicking on Internet ads to increase the fees that a company must pay.

Computer Viruses and Other Types of Malware

Malware is a generic term that refers to any type of malicious software. Malware programs are intentionally written to perform destructive acts, such as damaging programs, deleting files, erasing an entire hard drive, or slowing down the performance of a computer. This damage can take place immediately after a computer is *infected* (that is, the malware software is installed) or it can begin when a particular condition is met. A malware program that activates when it detects a certain condition, such as when a particular keystroke is pressed or an employee's name is deleted from an employee file, is called a *logic bomb*. A logic bomb that is triggered by a particular date or time is called a *time bomb*.

Writing a computer virus or other type of malware or even posting the malware code on the Internet is not illegal, but it is considered highly unethical and irresponsible behavior. Distributing malware, on the other hand, is illegal, and virus writers who release their malware are being vigorously prosecuted. Malware can be very costly in terms of the labor costs associated with removing the viruses and correcting any resulting damage, as well as the cost of lost productivity of employees. One type of malware often used by computer

> **ASK THE EXPERT**
>
> 
>
> Courtesy Symantec
>
> **Marian Merritt,** Internet Safety Advocate, Symantec Corporation
>
> **Does a smartphone need virus protection?**
>
> Yes, it is increasingly important to secure your smartphone. Begin with a screen lock passcode to protect against snooping. Tape a recovery phone number to the back of the phone so a finder can contact you. Install or enable tracking software to enable you to locate or lock a lost or stolen phone. And get mobile security software to keep you from installing bad apps or clicking on a dangerous link.

>**Computer sabotage.** An act of malicious destruction to a computer or computer resource. >**Bot.** A computer that is controlled by a hacker or other computer criminal. >**Botnet.** A group of bots that are controlled by one individual. >**Malware.** Any type of malicious software.

criminals to send sensitive data secretly from infected computers to the criminal—spyware—was discussed in Chapter 3. The most common other types of malware are discussed next.

TIP

It is common practice for all types of malware to be referred to generically as "viruses," even though some may not technically be computer viruses.

Computer Viruses

One type of malware is the **computer virus**—a software program that is installed without the permission or knowledge of the computer user, that is designed to alter the way a computer operates, and that can replicate itself to infect any new media it has access to. Computer viruses are often embedded into program or data files (often games, videos, and music files downloaded from Web pages or shared via a P2P service). They are spread whenever the infected file is downloaded, is transferred to a new computer via an infected removable storage medium, or is e-mailed to another computer (see Figure 4-14). Viruses can also be installed when a recipient clicks a link in an e-mail message (often in an unsolicited e-mail message that resembles a legitimate e-mail message that normally contains a link, such as an electronic greeting card e-mail that contains a link to view the card); runs a Web app that either contains a virus or exploits a vulnerability in Java, Flash, or another common Web technology; or clicks a link in a message posted on a social networking site like Facebook. Viruses have also been found embedded in photos of bogus Craigslist items sent to potential buyers. Regardless of how it is obtained, once a copy of the infected file reaches a new computer it typically embeds itself into program, data, or system files on the new computer and remains there, affecting that computer according to its programmed instructions, until it is discovered and removed.

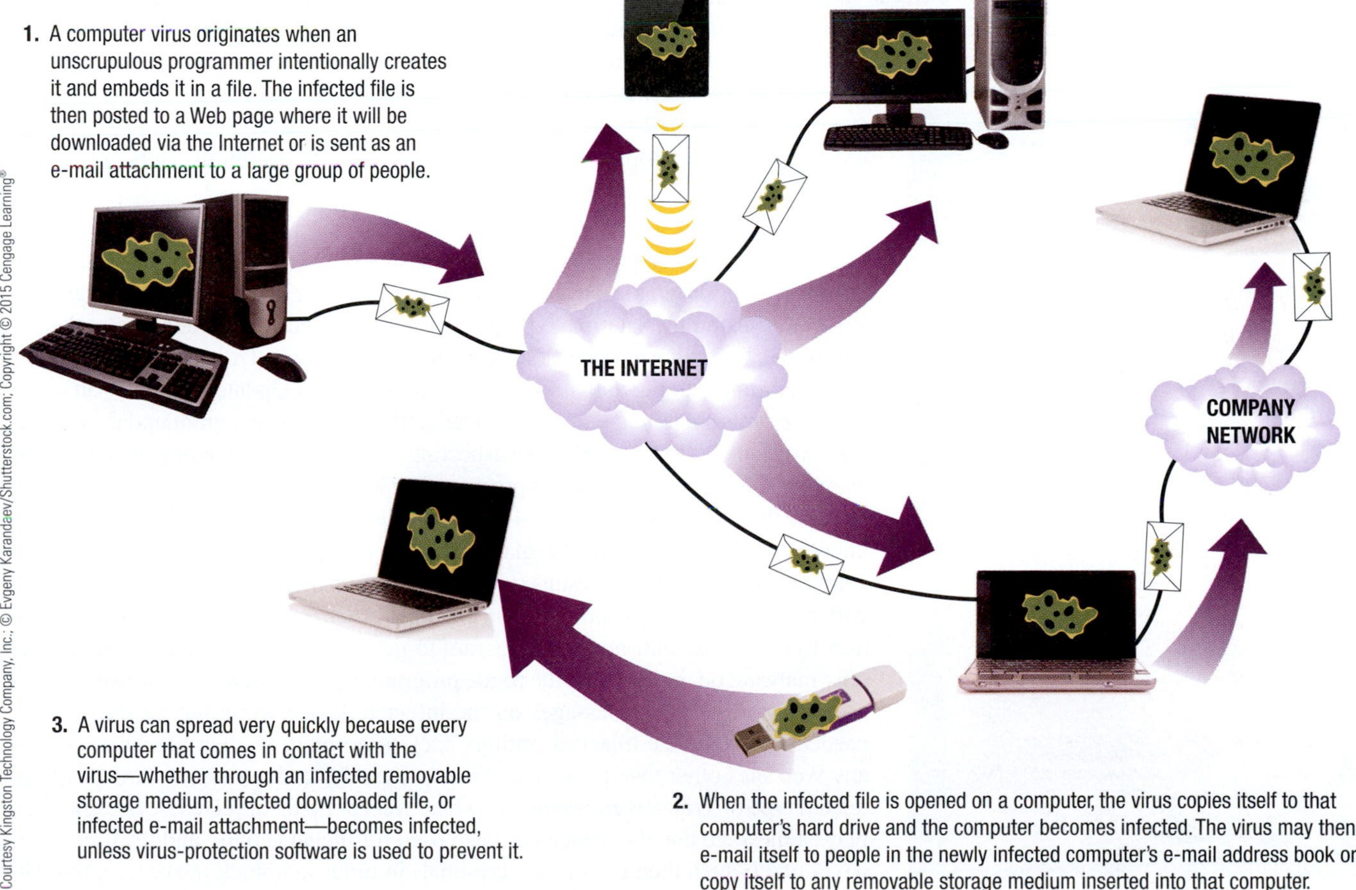

1. A computer virus originates when an unscrupulous programmer intentionally creates it and embeds it in a file. The infected file is then posted to a Web page where it will be downloaded via the Internet or is sent as an e-mail attachment to a large group of people.
THE INTERNET
COMPANY NETWORK
2. When the infected file is opened on a computer, the virus copies itself to that computer's hard drive and the computer becomes infected. The virus may then e-mail itself to people in the newly infected computer's e-mail address book or copy itself to any removable storage medium inserted into that computer.
3. A virus can spread very quickly because every computer that comes in contact with the virus—whether through an infected removable storage medium, infected downloaded file, or infected e-mail attachment—becomes infected, unless virus-protection software is used to prevent it.

FIGURE 4-14
How a computer virus or other type of malicious software might spread.

>**Computer virus.** A software program installed without the user's knowledge and designed to alter the way a computer operates or to cause harm to the computer system.

Computer Worms

Another common form of malware is the **computer worm**. Like a computer virus, a computer worm is a malicious program that is typically designed to cause damage. Unlike a computer virus, however, a computer worm does not infect other computer files on the infected computer in order to replicate itself; instead, it spreads by creating copies of its code and sending those copies to other computers via a network. Often, the worm is sent to other computers as an e-mail attachment. Usually after the infected e-mail attachment is opened by an individual, the worm inflicts its damage and then automatically sends copies of itself to other computers via the Internet or a private network, typically using addresses in the e-mail address book located on the newly infected computer. When those e-mail messages and their attachments are opened, the new computers become infected and the cycle continues. Because of its distribution method, a worm can spread very rapidly. For instance, the *Mydoom* worm (which was released in 2004 and is considered one of the fastest spreading worms ever) spread so rapidly that, at one point, one out of every 10 e-mails contained the worm, and the persistent *Conficker* worm has infected a total of more than 12 million computers since it was released in 2008 and it is still active today.

TIP

The *Stuxnet* worm, detected in 2010 and widely believed to have been created by the United States and Israel, reportedly destroyed 1,000 centrifuges in nuclear facilities located in Iran—the first instance of malware being used to cause physical damage to a facility.

Typically, worms do not require any action by the users (such as opening an e-mail attachment) to infect their computers. Instead, a worm scans the Internet looking for computers that are vulnerable to that particular worm and sends a copy of itself to those computers to infect them. Other worms just require the user to view an infected e-mail message or insert an infected removable storage medium (such as a USB flash drive) into the computer in order to infect the computer. Still other worms are specifically written to take advantage of newly discovered *security holes* (vulnerabilities) in operating systems and e-mail programs. Worms and other types of malware that are designed to take advantage of a security hole and are released at a time when no security patch to correct the problem is available are referred to as *zero-day attacks*. Unfortunately, as malware writing tools become more sophisticated, zero-day attacks are becoming more common.

FIGURE 4-15
Rogue anti-malware apps. These programs try to trick victims into purchasing subscriptions to remove nonexistent malware supposedly installed on their devices.

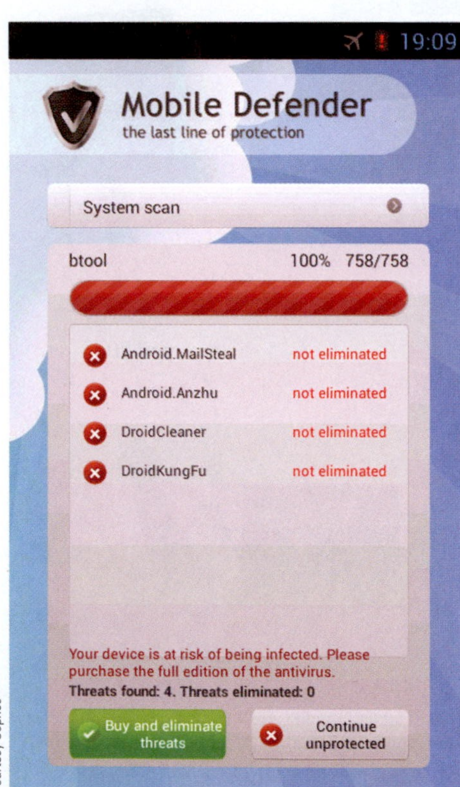

Courtesy Sophos

Trojan Horses

A **Trojan horse** is a type of malware that masquerades as something else—usually an application program (such as what appears to be a game or utility program). When the seemingly legitimate program is downloaded or installed, the malware part of the Trojan horse infects the computer. Many recent Trojan horses masquerade as normal ongoing activities (such as the Windows Update service or an *anti-malware program* telling you to download a file containing program updates) when they are installed to try to trick unsuspecting users into downloading another malware program or buying a useless program. For instance, after a *rogue anti-malware app* like the one shown in Figure 4-15 is installed (usually without the user's direct knowledge or permission), the malware takes over the device displaying bogus warning messages or scan results (see Figure 4-15) indicating the device is infected with malware. The rogue program (an example of *scareware*) typically prompts the user to buy a fake anti-malware program to get rid of the "malware." Usually the only malware on the device is the rogue program, but it is often very intrusive (such as displaying constant messages on the infected device while hiding the options needed to change the hijacked settings back to normal), it often blocks access to any Web sites other than its own, and it is extremely hard to remove. An emerging related type of Trojan is *ransomware*, which freezes up the infected device and displays a message that the device has been used for illegal activity and the user must pay a fine (which then goes to the criminal) in order to unlock the device, though

>**Computer worm.** A malicious program designed to spread rapidly to a large number of computers by sending copies of itself to other computers.
>**Trojan horse.** A malicious program that masquerades as something else.

paying the fine doesn't necessarily result in the device being returned to a usable state. Other *rogue apps* are spreading through social networks like Facebook and Twitter, primarily in the form of fake offers (such as for a free iPad) that request access to your social network information when you click the link—if granted, the scammer can then post that and additional scams (and collect information about others) via your account.

Unlike viruses and worms, Trojan horses cannot replicate themselves. Trojan horses are usually spread by being downloaded from the Internet, though they may also be sent as an e-mail attachment, either from the Trojan horse author or from individuals who forward it, not realizing the program is a Trojan horse. Some Trojan horses today act as spyware and are designed to find sensitive information about an individual (such as a Social Security number or a bank account number) or about a company (such as corporate intellectual property like mechanical designs, electronic schematics, and other valuable proprietary information) located on infected computers and then send that information to the malware creator to be used in illegal activities. One emerging type of Trojan horse is called a *RAT* (*Remote-Access Trojan*). RATs are typically installed via small files obtained from an Internet download, such as free software, games, or electronic greeting cards. Once installed, RATs are designed to record every keystroke made on the infected computer and then send the sensitive information they recorded (such as account numbers and passwords) to criminals.

Mobile Malware

In addition to computers, malware also can infect smartphones, media tablets, printers, and other devices that contain computing hardware and software. While more than 90% of today's mobile malware (according to a recent report) is spread via malicious links, smartphones with Bluetooth capabilities can also be infected just by being within range of an infected device. Some *mobile malware* is designed to be a nuisance by changing icons or otherwise making the device more difficult to use, but most (including half of mobile malware created in 2012) is designed to steal information or track the movement or activities of the user. Still other malware is money-oriented, such as malware that is designed to steal credit card data located on a smartphone and malware that places calls or sends text messages to premium rate numbers owned by the thief (for which the owner of the device is charged)—sometimes called *chargeware*. According to IBM, more malware will continue to be directed to smartphones and other devices—such as cars—that contain embedded computers as those devices continue to incorporate more software components and, consequently, become more vulnerable to malware. And mobile malware is getting more sophisticated—in 2013, Kaspersky Lab discovered the first ever Android malware app designed to infect any PCs or other devices the phone connects to. While the app was removed from Google Play, several thousand users had already downloaded it.

TIP

About 94% of mobile malware today is written for Android phones (though Apple devices are still vulnerable).

Denial of Service (DoS) Attacks

A **denial of service (DoS) attack** is an act of sabotage that attempts to flood a network server or Web server with so many requests for action that it shuts down or simply cannot handle legitimate requests any longer, causing legitimate users to be denied service. For example, a hacker might set up one or more computers to request nonexistent information continually or to *ping* (contact) a server continually with a request to send a responding ping back to a false return address. If enough useless traffic is generated, the server has no resources left to deal with legitimate requests (see Figure 4-16). An emerging trend is DoS attacks aimed at mobile wireless networks. These attacks typically involve repeatedly establishing and releasing connections with the goal of overloading the network to disrupt service.

TIP

The 2013 DDoS attacks on The Spamhaus Project created a staggering 300 Gbps of traffic.

>**Denial of service (DoS) attack.** An act of sabotage that attempts to flood a network server or a Web server with so much activity that it is unable to function.

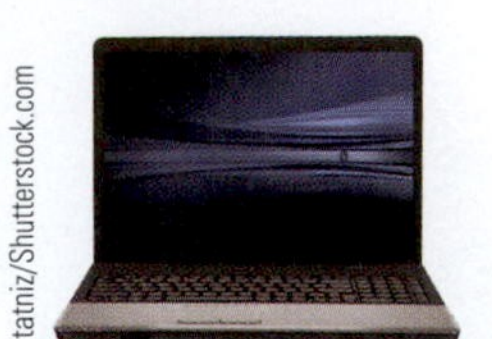
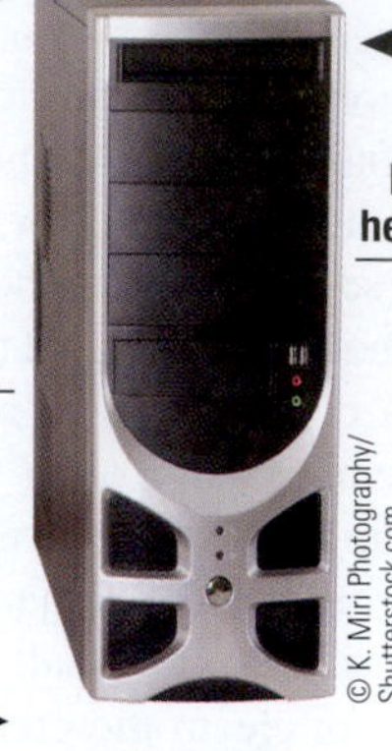

1. Hacker's computer sends several simultaneous requests; each request asks to establish a connection to the server but supplies false return information. In a distributed DoS attack, multiple computers send multiple requests at one time.
Hello? I'd like some info...
2. The server tries to respond to each request but can't locate the computer because false return information was provided. The server waits for a short period of time before closing the connection, which ties up the server and keeps others from connecting.
I can't find you, I'll wait and try again...
3. The hacker's computer continues to send new requests so, as a connection is closed by the server, a new request is waiting. This cycle continues, which ties up the server indefinitely.
Hello? I'd like some info...
HACKER'S COMPUTER
WEB SERVER
Hello? I'd like some info...
I'm busy, I can't help you right now.
LEGITIMATE COMPUTER
4. The server becomes so overwhelmed that legitimate requests cannot get through and, eventually, the server usually crashes.
© tatniz/Shutterstock.com
© K. Miri Photography/Shutterstock.com
© tatniz/Shutterstock.com

FIGURE 4-16
How a denial of service (DoS) attack might work.

DoS attacks today are often directed toward popular or controversial sites and typically are carried out via multiple computers (referred to as a *distributed denial of service attack* or *DDoS attack*). DDoS attacks are typically performed by botnets created by hackers; the computers in the botnet participate in the attacks without the owners' knowledge. Because home devices today typically use direct Internet connections but tend to be less protected than school and business computers, hackers are increasingly targeting home devices for botnets used in DDoS attacks and other forms of computer sabotage.

Denial of service attacks can be very costly in terms of business lost (such as when an e-commerce site is shut down), as well as the time and expense required to bring the site back online. Networks that use VoIP are particularly vulnerable to DoS attacks since the real-time nature of VoIP calls means their quality is immediately affected when a DoS attack slows down the network.

Data, Program, or Web Site Alteration

Another type of computer sabotage occurs when a hacker breaches a computer system in order to delete data, change data, modify programs, or otherwise alter the data and programs located there. For example, a student might try to hack into the school database to change his or her grade; a hacker might change a program located on a company server in order to steal money or information; or a disgruntled or former employee might perform a vengeful act, such as altering programs so they work incorrectly, deleting customer records or other critical data, or randomly changing data in a company's database. Like other forms of computer sabotage, data and program alteration is illegal.

Data on Web sites can also be altered by hackers. For instance, social media accounts are being increasingly targeted by hackers. In 2013, for instance, the Associated Press Twitter account was hacked and used to tweet that the president had been injured by explosions at the White House—the stock market tumbled in response. It is also becoming more common for hackers to compromise legitimate Web sites and then use those sites to perform malware attacks. Typically, a hacker alters a legitimate site to display an official-looking message that informs the user that a particular software program must be downloaded, or the hacker posts a rogue banner ad on a legitimate site that redirects the user to a malware site instead of the site for the product featured in the banner ad. According to a report by security company Websense, more than half of the Web sites classified as malicious are actually legitimate Web sites that have been compromised.

PROTECTING AGAINST COMPUTER SABOTAGE

One of the most important protections against computer sabotage is using *security software*, and ensuring that it is kept current.

Security Software

To protect against becoming infected with a computer virus or other type of malware, all computers and other devices used to access the Internet or a company network in both homes and offices should have **security software** installed. Security software typically includes a variety of security features, including a firewall, protection against spyware and bots, and protection against some types of *online fraud*, discussed shortly. Some also include a spam filter, parental controls, password managers, diagnostic software, and backup features; mobile security software also often includes *antitheft software*, discussed in more detail in Chapter 5. One of the most important components of security software is **antivirus software**, which protects against computer viruses and other types of malware.

Like most security software components, antivirus software typically runs continuously whenever the computer is on to perform real-time monitoring of the computer and incoming e-mail messages, instant messages, Web page content, and downloaded files, in order to prevent malicious software and other threats from executing. Many antivirus programs also automatically scan any devices as soon as they are connected to a USB port in order to guard against infections from a USB flash drive, a portable digital media player, or other USB device. Antivirus software helps prevent malware from being installed on your devices because it deletes or *quarantines* (safely isolates) any suspicious content (such as potentially infected e-mail attachments, downloaded files, or apps) as they arrive; regular full system scans can detect and remove any viruses or worms that find their way onto your computer (see Figure 4-17).

According to a recent Panda Security report, there are approximately 125 million malware threats in existence, and about 27 million new malware strains were discovered in 2012 alone. Consequently, it is vital that you keep your security software up to date. Security software is usually set up to download new *threat definitions* automatically from its associated Web site on a regular basis, as often as several times per day—a very important precaution. Most fee-based security

TIP

To ensure you have the latest security updates for your antivirus program, enable *automatic updates*.

TIP

According to a recent Harris Interactive survey, less than one-third of users have security software installed on their mobile devices, compared to 91% on their laptops.

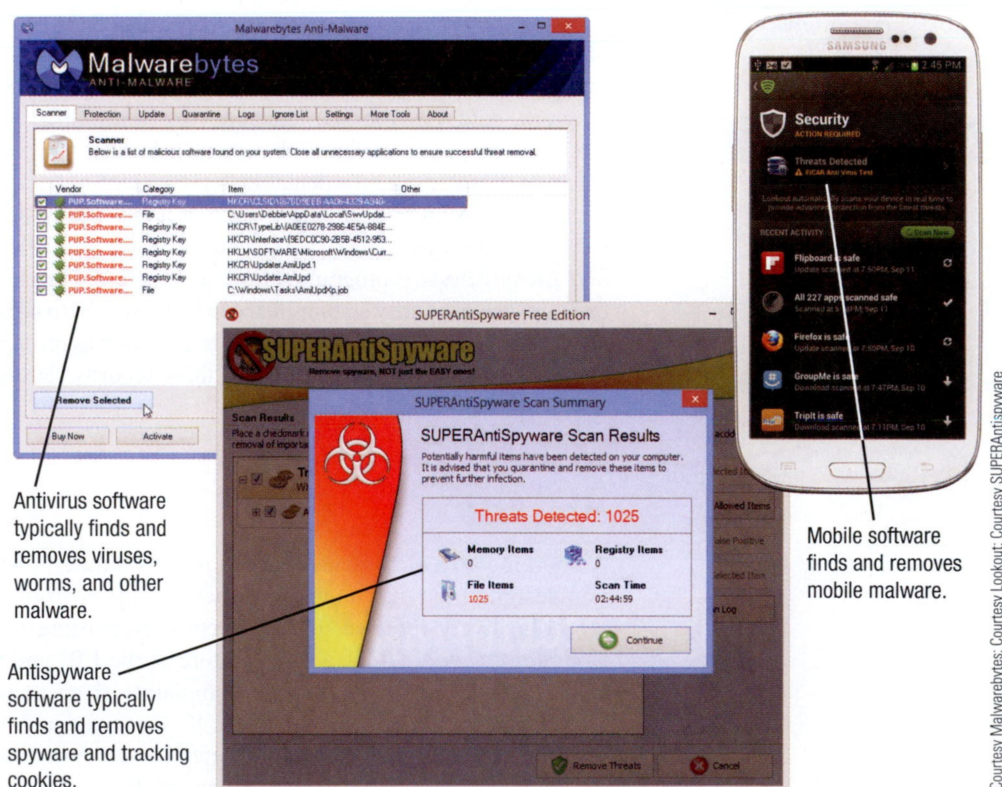
Malwarebytes Anti-Malware
Malwarebytes
ANTI-MALWARE
SUPERAntiSpyware Free Edition
SUPERAntiSpyware Scan Summary
SUPERAntiSpyware Scan Results
Threats Detected: 1025
Security
Antivirus software typically finds and removes viruses, worms, and other malware.
Antispyware software typically finds and removes spyware and tracking cookies.
Mobile software finds and removes mobile malware.
Courtesy Malwarebytes; Courtesy Lookout; Courtesy SUPERAntispyware

FIGURE 4-17
Security software. Different security programs will typically find different types of malware.

>Security software. Software, typically a suite of programs, used to protect your computer against a variety of threats. **>Antivirus software.** Software used to detect and eliminate computer viruses and other types of malware.

VIRUS-PREVENTION STRATEGIES

Use antivirus software to check incoming e-mail messages and files, and download updated virus definitions on a regular basis.

Limit the sharing of flash memory cards, USB flash drives, and other removable storage media with others.

Only download files from reputable sites.

Only open e-mail attachments that come from people you know and that do not have an executable file extension (such as .exe, .com, .bat, or .vbs); double-check with the sender before opening an unexpected, but seemingly legitimate, attachment.

For any downloaded file you are unsure of, upload it to a Web site (such as VirusTotal.com) that tests files for viruses before you open them.

Keep the preview window of your e-mail program closed so you will not view messages until you determine that they are safe to view.

Regularly download and install the latest security patches available for your operating system, browser, Java and other plug-ins, and e-mail programs.

Avoid downloading files from P2P sites.

FIGURE 4-18
Sensible precautions can help protect against computer virus infections.

TIP

If you suspect your computer is infected with a malware program that your regular antivirus software cannot detect or remove, try a software program that specializes in removing hard-to-remove malware, such as the free *Malwarebytes Anti-Malware* program shown in Figure 4-17.

software comes with a year of access to free updates; users should purchase additional years after that to continue to be protected or they should switch to a free antivirus program, such as *AVG Free*, that can be updated regularly at no cost. Schools and businesses should also ensure that students and employees connecting to the campus or company network with personal devices are using up-to-date antivirus software so they will not infect the network with malware inadvertently. Some colleges now require new students to go through a *quarantine process*, in which students are not granted access to the college network until they complete a security process that checks their computers for security threats, updates their operating systems, and installs antivirus software. Some additional virus-prevention strategies are listed in Figure 4-18.

Many ISPs and Web mail providers today also offer some malware protection to their subscribers. Typically, antivirus software scans all incoming e-mail messages at the mail server level to filter out messages containing a virus. If a message containing a virus is detected, it is usually deleted and the recipient is notified that the message contained a virus and was deleted. App stores can help remove a contaminated app when one is identified (by removing the app from the store and remotely wiping the app from phones), though that won't undo any damage already done to the phone by the malware.

Other Security Precautions

Individuals and businesses can protect against some types of computer sabotage (such as program, data, or Web site alteration) by controlling access to their computers and networks, as discussed earlier in this chapter. Intrusion protection systems can help businesses detect and protect against denial of service (DoS) attacks; some personal security software includes intrusion protection as well. For additional protection against spyware, rogue antivirus programs, and other specialized malware, specialized security programs (such as the *SUPERAntispyware* program shown in Figure 4-17) can be used. In addition, most Web browsers have security settings that can be used to help prevent programs from being installed on a computer without the user's permission, such as prompting the user for permission whenever a download is initiated. Enabling these security settings is a wise additional precaution.

ONLINE THEFT, ONLINE FRAUD, AND OTHER DOT CONS

A booming area of computer crime involves online fraud, theft, scams, and related activities designed to steal money or other resources from individuals or businesses—these are collectively referred to as **dot cons**. According to a report by the *Internet Crime Complaint Center* (*IC3*), a joint venture of the FBI and the National White Collar Crime Center that receives cybercrime complaints from consumers and reports them to the appropriate law enforcement agency, IC3 received and processed more than 24,000 complaints per month in 2012 with reported losses more than 8% higher than in 2011. Some of the most common types of dot cons are discussed next.

>**Dot con.** A fraud or scam carried out through the Internet.

TREND

Beyond Fingerprint Readers—Digital Tattoos and More

Think passwords—even the newer types of passwords that use pictures or patterns instead of characters—are ho-hum? Well, you're in luck. A number of new alternatives that can be used to protect access to your device or log on to your Web sites are about to become available.

One option that Google is developing uses *facial gestures*, such as unlocking your phone by smiling or winking at it. Instead of using a static image (as with face recognition, which has been circumvented on phone unlocking systems by using a photograph of the authorized user), this new technology includes a "Liveness Check" where the user has to prove that he or she is alive and not a photo by blinking. In addition, the system requires a match of a facial landmark (such as an eye, mouth, or nose) in two different but related facial gestures (such as smiling and not smiling).

Two other more unusual alternatives recently demonstrated by Motorola are *electronic tattoos* and *authentication pills*. The tattoos (called *Biostamps* and originally developed for remote medical monitoring of patients) contain flexible electronic circuits that are attached to the wearer's skin (see the accompanying photo) using a rubber stamp and which then can be covered with a spray-on bandage for additional waterproofing if needed. The pills (called the *Proteus Digital Health pill* and already approved by the U.S. FDA for medication monitoring) are swallowed and then send signals from the stomach. Both devices already work with smartphones and researchers propose that both technologies could be adapted to become authentication systems, automatically logging individuals on to their phones or computers and to secure Web sites. The downside is that both systems are temporary and would have to be replaced on a regular basis, which could lead to hackers stealing additional tattoos and pills not yet used and circumventing whatever activation system is in place or even kidnapping individuals to use their bodies to log in to secure systems.

Next up? *Thought-based authentication* where you can automatically log on to your wearable devices using only your brainwaves.

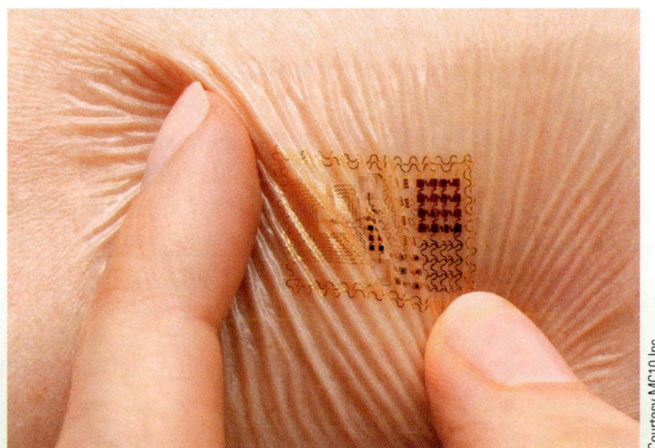
Courtesy MC10 Inc.

Theft of Data, Information, and Other Resources

Data theft or *information theft* is the theft of data or information located on or being sent from a computer. It can be committed by stealing an actual computer (as discussed in more detail in Chapter 5); it can also take place over the Internet or a network by an individual gaining unauthorized access to that data by hacking into the computer or by intercepting the data in transit. (For a look at some emerging biometric systems that may soon be used to help protect access to your PC and your Web sites, see the Trend box.) Common types of data and information stolen via the Internet or another network include customer data (such as Web site passwords or credit card information) and proprietary corporate information. As previously discussed, data breaches today frequently result in stolen customer and credit card data. Stolen consumer data is often used in fraudulent activities, such as *identity theft*, as discussed shortly.

Money is another resource that can be stolen via a computer. Company insiders sometimes steal money by altering company programs to transfer small amounts of money—for example, a few cents' worth of bank account interest—from a very large number of transactions to an account controlled by the thieves. This type of crime is sometimes called *salami shaving*. Victims of salami-shaving schemes generally are unaware that their funds have been accessed because the amount taken from each individual is very small. However, added together, the amounts can be substantial. Another example of monetary theft performed via computers involves hackers electronically transferring money illegally from online bank accounts, traditional bank accounts, credit card accounts, or accounts at online payment services (such as *PayPal*).

Identity Theft, Phishing, Social Media Hacks, and Pharming

A growing dot con trend is obtaining enough information about an individual to perform fraudulent financial transactions. Often, this is carried out in conjunction with *identity theft*; techniques frequently used to obtain the necessary personal information to commit identity theft are *phishing*, *spear phishing*, *social media hacking*, and *pharming*.

> **TIP**
>
> To help prevent identity theft, do not include your Social Security number on your résumé or any other document posted online.

> **TIP**
>
> At an estimated $388 billion per year, identity theft is approaching the illegal drug business in revenue.

Identity Theft

Identity theft occurs when someone obtains enough information about a person to be able to masquerade as that person—usually to buy products or services in that person's name (see Figure 4-19). Typically, identity theft begins when a thief obtains a person's name, address, and Social Security number, often from a discarded or stolen document (such as a preapproved credit card application that was sent in the mail), from information obtained via the Internet (such as from a résumé posted online), or from information located on a computer (such as on a stolen computer or hacked server, or information sent from a computer via a computer virus or spyware program installed on that computer). The thief may then order a copy of the individual's birth certificate, obtain a "replacement" driver's license, make purchases and charge them to the victim, and/or open credit or bank accounts in the victim's name.

Assuming the thief requests a change of address for these new accounts after they are opened, it may take quite some time—often until a company or collections agency contacts the victim about overdue bills—for the victim to become aware that his or her identity has been stolen. Although identity theft often takes place via a computer today, information used in identity theft can also be gathered from trash dumpsters, mailboxes, and other locations. Other commonly used techniques are *skimming* and *social engineering*. Skimming involves stealing credit card or debit card numbers by using an illegal device attached to a credit card reader or an ATM machine that reads and stores the card numbers (and used in conjunction with a hidden camera to capture ATM PIN numbers) to be retrieved by the thief at a later time. Social engineering involves pretending—typically via phone or e-mail—to be a bank officer, potential employer, or other trusted individual in order to get the potential victim to supply personal information. Today, social engineering schemes often use social media to obtain the needed information and gain the trust of a victim. Because of this, *social engineering tests* are often included when a company runs a security evaluation of its company and employees, as discussed in Chapter 5.

FIGURE 4-19 How identity theft works.

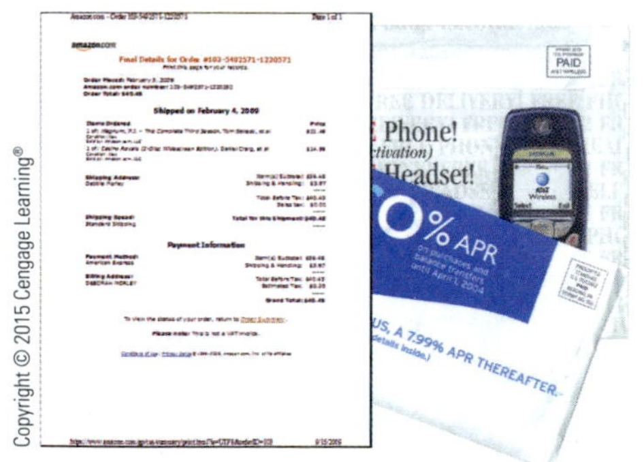

1. The thief obtains information about an individual from discarded mail, employee records, credit card transactions, Web server files, or some other method.

2. The thief makes purchases, opens new credit card accounts, and more in the victim's name. Often, the thief changes the address on the account to delay discovery.

3. The victim usually finds out by being denied credit or by being contacted about overdue bills generated by the thief. Clearing one's name after identity theft is time consuming and can be very difficult and frustrating for the victim.

>**Identity theft.** Using someone else's identity to purchase goods or services, obtain new credit cards or bank loans, or otherwise illegally masquerade as that individual.

Unfortunately, identity theft is a very real danger to individuals today. According to the Federal Trade Commission (FTC), millions of Americans have their identity stolen each year and identity theft has topped the list of consumer complaints for 13 straight years. Identity theft can be extremely distressing for victims, can take years to straighten out, and can be very expensive. Some identity theft victims, such as Michelle Brown, believe that they will always be dealing with their "alter reality" to some extent. For a year and a half, an identity thief used Brown's identity to obtain over $50,000 in goods and services, to rent properties—even to engage in drug trafficking. Although the culprit was eventually arrested and convicted for other criminal acts, she continued to use Brown's identity and was even booked into jail using Brown's stolen identity. As a final insult after the culprit was in prison, U.S. customs agents detained the real Michelle Brown when she was returning from a trip to Mexico because of the criminal record of the identity thief. Brown states that she has not traveled out of the country since, fearing an arrest or some other serious problem resulting from the theft of her identity, and estimates she has spent over 500 hours trying to correct all the problems related to the identity theft.

ASK THE EXPERT

Courtesy Symantec

Marian Merritt, Internet Safety Advocate, Symantec Corporation

What is the single most important thing computer users should do to protect themselves from online threats?

The single most important step to protect computer users from online threats is to make sure their Internet security solution is current and up to date. There are several all-in-one security solutions available, such as Symantec's Norton 360, which combine PC security, antiphishing capabilities, backup, and tuneup technologies.

It's also pivotal to maintain a healthy wariness when receiving online communications. Do not click on links in suspicious e-mails or instant messages (IMs). These links will often direct you to sites that will ask you to reveal passwords, PINs, or other confidential data. Genuine organizations or institutions do not send such e-mails, nor do they ask for confidential data (like your Social Security number) for ordinary business transactions. If you're unsure whether or not an e-mail is legitimate, type the URL directly in your browser or call the institution to confirm they sent you that e-mail. Finally, do not open attachments in e-mails of questionable origin because they may contain viruses.

Phishing and Spear Phishing

Phishing (pronounced "fishing") is the use of a *spoofed* communications (typically an e-mail message, such as one appearing to come from eBay, PayPal, Google, Bank of America, or another well-known legitimate organization, but is actually sent from a phisher) to trick the recipient into revealing sensitive personal information (such as Web site logon information or credit card numbers). Once obtained, this information is used in identity theft and other fraudulent activities. A phishing e-mail typically looks legitimate and it contains links in the e-mail that appear to go to the Web site of the legitimate business, but these links go to the phisher's Web site that is set up to look like the legitimate site instead—an act called *Web site spoofing*. Phishing e-mails are typically sent to a wide group of individuals and usually include an urgent message stating that the individual's credit card or account information needs to be updated and instructing the recipient of the e-mail to click the link provided in the e-mail in order to keep the account active. If the victim clicks the link and supplies the requested information via the spoofed site, the criminal gains access to all information provided by the victim, such as account numbers, credit card numbers, and Web site passwords. Phishing attempts can occur today via IM, text messages (called *smishing*), fake messages sent via eBay or Facebook, Twitter tweets, pop-up security alert windows, and phone calls, in addition to e-mail. Phishers also frequently utilize spyware; typically

>**Phishing.** The use of spoofed communications (typically e-mail messages) to gain credit card numbers and other personal data to be used for fraudulent purposes.

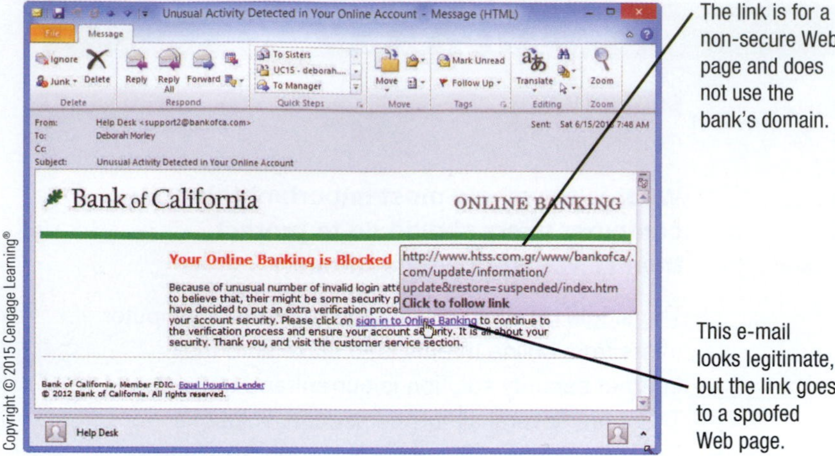

FIGURE 4-20
Phishing. Phishing schemes typically use legitimate-looking e-mails to trick users into providing private information.

clicking the link in the phishing e-mail installs the spyware on the victim's computer, and it will remain there (transmitting passwords and other sensitive data to a phisher) until it is detected and removed.

To fool victims into using the spoofed Web site, phishing e-mails and the spoofed Web sites often look legitimate (see Figure 4-20). To accomplish this, phishers typically use copies of the spoofed organization's logo and other Web site content from the legitimate Web site. For spoofed banking Web pages and other pages where the victim would expect to see a secure Web page, some criminals use a secure connection between the victim and the criminal's server so the Web page looks secure with an *https:* in the Address bar. The domain name of the legitimate company (such as *ebay* for an eBay phishing page) is also often used as part of the URL of the phishing link (such as a URL starting with the text *ebay* even though the URL's domain is not ebay.com) to make it appear more legitimate. Other phishing schemes use a technique called *typosquatting*, which is setting up spoofed Web sites with addresses slightly different from legitimate sites. For example, a spoofed Web site using the URL www.amazom.com might be used to catch shoppers intending to reach the Amazon.com Web site located at www.amazon.com in hopes that customers making this error when typing the URL will not notice it and will supply logon information via the spoofed site when they arrive.

Another recent trend is the use of more targeted, personalized phishing schemes, known as **spear phishing**. Spear phishing e-mails are directly targeted to a specific individual and typically appear to come from an organization or a person that the targeted individual has an association with. They also often include personalized information (such as the potential victim's name, employer, and other information frequently found on social networking sites and other public resources) to make the spear phishing e-mails seem even more legitimate. Some attacks use spoofed logon pages for social networking sites to obtain an individual's logon information and password. Because many individuals use the same logon information for a variety of sites, once a scammer has a valid username/password combination, he or she can try it on a variety of common e-commerce sites, such as shopping sites, online banking sites, and online payment services like PayPal.

TIP

Spear phishing attacks are expected to increase as a result of the Epsilon data breach, which exposed names and e-mail addresses of individuals along with businesses that they patronize, such as banks, hotels, and stores.

Spear phishers also target employees of selected organizations by posing as someone within the company, such as a human resource or technical support employee. These spear phishing e-mails often request confidential information (such as logon IDs and passwords) or direct the employee to click a link to supposedly reset his or her password. The goal for corporate spear phishing attacks is usually to steal intellectual property, such as software source code, design documents, or schematics. It can also be used to steal money. For instance, in one recent case, a grocery store chain received fraudulent e-mails that appeared to come from two approved suppliers. The e-mails instructed the grocery store chain to send future payments to new bank accounts listed in the e-mail—the grocery store chain deposited more than $10 million into two fraudulent bank accounts before the scam was discovered.

Social Media Hacks

The use of phishing e-mails declined dramatically in 2012, as thieves appeared to shift to other online communications, such as social networks, according to a recent Symantec

>**Spear phishing.** A personalized phishing scheme targeted at an individual.

Internet Security Threat Report. In addition to obtaining information from social networks that can be used in phishing schemes, **social media hacks** can provide phishers with social media logon information that can be used by the phishers to log on to the victim's account and then *hijack* it—posting comments or sending messages containing phishing links (posing as the victim) to the victim's friends, who are much more likely to click on the links because they appear to come from a friend. In addition to individuals' social networking accounts being hacked, business accounts have been recent targets as well. For example, the Twitter accounts of several businesses (including Burger King and Jeep) were hacked in 2013 and erroneous information posted (Burger King being purchased by McDonald's was one tweet made by the hackers). While hacking into a business's social media account and hijacking it temporarily is often a public embarrassment, sometimes (like when the stock market dipped after the recent AP Twitter hack that there was an explosion at the White House), the consequences of business social media hacking are more severe.

Pharming and Drive-By Pharming

Pharming is another type of scam that uses spoofing—specifically spoofed domain names used to obtain personal information for use in fraudulent activities. With pharming, the criminal reroutes traffic intended for a commonly used Web site to a spoofed Web site set up by the pharmer. Sometimes pharming takes place via malicious code sent to a computer via an e-mail message or other distribution method. More often, however, it takes place via changes made to a *DNS server*—a computer that translates URLs into the appropriate IP addresses needed to display the Web page corresponding to a URL. This type of pharming can take place at one of the 13 *root DNS servers* (the DNS servers used in conjunction with the Internet), but it more often takes place at a *company DNS server* (the DNS server for that company used to route Web page requests received via company Web site URLs to the appropriate company server). After hacking into a company DNS server (typically for a company with a commonly used Web site), the pharmer changes the IP addresses used in conjunction with a particular company URL (called *DNS poisoning*) so any Web page requests made via the legitimate company URL is routed (via the company's poisoned DNS server) to a phony spoofed Web page located on the pharmer's Web server. So, even though a user types the proper URL to display the legitimate company Web page in his or her browser, the spoofed page is displayed instead.

Because spoofed sites are set up to look like the legitimate sites, the user typically does not notice any difference, and any information sent via that site is captured by the pharmer. To avoid suspicion, some pharming schemes capture the user's account name and password as it is entered the first time on the spoofed site, and then display a password error message. The spoofed site then redirects the user back to the legitimate site where he or she is able to log on to the legitimate site, leaving the user to think that he or she must have just mistyped the password the first time. But, by then, the pharmer has already captured the victim's username and password and can use that information to gain access to the victim's account.

A recent variation of pharming is *drive-by pharming*. The goal is still to redirect victims to spoofed sites; however, the pharmer accomplishes this by changing the victim's designated DNS server (which often belongs to the individual's ISP and is specified in the victim's router settings) to the pharmer's DNS server in order to direct the victim to spoofed versions of legitimate Web sites when the victim enters the URLs for those sites. Typically, the pharmer uses malicious JavaScript code placed on a Web page to changes the victim's DNS settings to use the pharmer's DNS server; this change can only occur on a router in which the default administrator password was not changed.

TIP

In 2013, the Department of Homeland Security began recommending disabling Java on Web browsers due to security flaws; while not possible for all users, try it—if your Web sites function fine without it, leave it disabled.

>**Social media hack.** The act of accessing someone else's social media account to make changes to the content or to perform an activity as that individual. >**Pharming.** The use of spoofed domain names to obtain personal information in order to use that information in fraudulent activities.

Online Auction Fraud

Online auction fraud (sometimes called *Internet auction fraud*) occurs when an online auction buyer pays for merchandise that is never delivered, or that is delivered but it is not as represented. It can also occur when an online buyer receives the proper items but falsely claims that they never arrived. Like other types of fraud, online auction fraud is illegal, but similar to many types of Internet cons, prosecution is difficult for online auction fraud because multiple jurisdictions are usually involved. Although most online auction sites have policies that suspend sellers with a certain number of complaints lodged against them, it is very easy for those sellers to come back using a new e-mail address and identity.

Other Internet Scams

There is a wide range of other scams that can occur via Web sites or unsolicited e-mails. The anonymity of the Internet makes it very easy for con artists to appear to be anyone they want to be, including a charitable organization or a reputable-looking business. Common types of scams include loan scams, work-at-home cons, pyramid schemes, bogus credit card offers and prize promotions, and fraudulent business opportunities and franchises. These offers typically try to sell potential victims nonexistent services or worthless information, or they try to convince potential victims to voluntarily supply their credit card details and other personal information. Some scammers hack into a system to obtain e-mail addresses to use as targets for a scam that is based on something those indviduals have in common in order to increase the odds of a potential victim falling for the scam. Others send messages to a potential victim impersonating a distant friend or old classmate (typically found via a social networking site) and requesting money (such as by saying they are traveling out of the country and were just robbed).

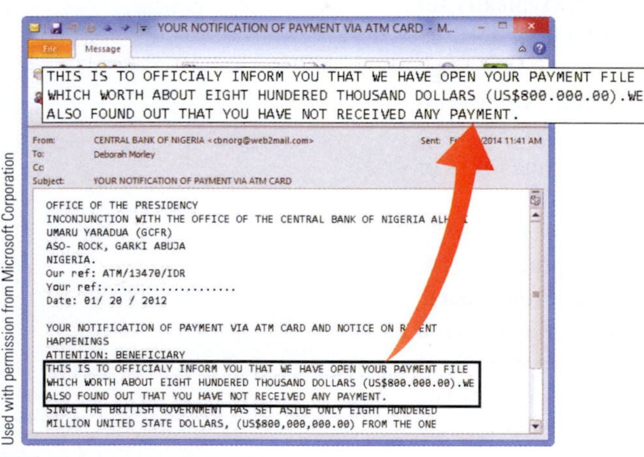

FIGURE 4-21
A Nigerian letter fraud e-mail.

One ongoing Internet scam is the *Nigerian letter fraud* scheme. This scheme involves an e-mail message that appears to come from the Nigerian government and that promises the potential victim a share of a substantial amount of money in exchange for the use of the victim's bank account. Supposedly the victim's bank account information is needed to facilitate a wire transfer (but the victim's account is emptied instead) and/or up-front cash is needed to pay for nonexistent fees (but that is kept by the con artist). The scams often change to fit current events, such as the war in Iraq or a recent natural disaster. However, the scams always involve a so-called fortune that is inaccessible to the con artist without the potential victims' help (see Figure 4-21) and the victims always lose any money they provide.

Other schemes involve con artists who solicit donations for charitable organizations after disasters and other tragic events, but who keep the donations instead. Another common scam involves setting up a pornographic site that requires a valid credit card, supposedly to prove that the visitor is an adult, but which is then used for credit card fraud. A relatively new type of scam involves posting fake job listings on job search sites to elicit personal information (such as Social Security numbers) from job seekers. An even more recent twist is to hire individuals through online job sites for seemingly legitimate positions involving money handling (such as bookkeeping or accounting positions), but then use those individuals—often without their knowledge—to facilitate Internet auction scams and other monetary scams.

>**Online auction fraud.** When an item purchased through an online auction is never delivered after payment, or the item is not as specified by the seller.

PROTECTING AGAINST ONLINE THEFT, ONLINE FRAUD, AND OTHER DOT CONS

In a nutshell, the best protection against many dot cons is protecting your identity; that is, protecting any identifying information about you that could be used in fraudulent activities. There are also specific precautions that can help protect against online theft, identity theft, online auction fraud, and other types of dot cons, as discussed next. With any dot con, it is important to act quickly if you think you have been a victim. For instance, you should work with your local law enforcement agency, credit card companies, and the three major consumer credit bureaus (*Equifax*, *Experian*, and *TransUnion*) to close any accessed or fraudulent accounts, place fraud alerts on your credit report, and take other actions to prevent additional fraudulent activity while the fraud is being investigated.

Arrests and prosecutions by law enforcement agencies may also help cut down on cybercrimes. Prosecution of online scammers has been increasing and sentences are not light. For instance, two Romanian citizens were recently sentenced for their involvement in a phishing scheme (the first time the United States has sentenced a foreigner for phishing)—one received 80 months in federal prison; the other received 27 months.

TIP

When using a public computer, always log out of your accounts at the end of your session to make sure the next user won't have access to them.

Protecting Against Data and Information Theft

Businesses and individuals can both help to prevent some types of data and information theft. For instance, businesses should use good security measures to protect the data stored on their computers. Individuals should be vigilant about protecting their private information by sending sensitive information via secure Web servers only and not disclosing personal information—especially a Social Security number or a mother's maiden name—unless it is absolutely necessary and they know how the information will be used and that it will not be shared with others. In addition, individuals should never give out sensitive personal information to anyone who requests it over the phone or by e-mail—businesses that legitimately need bank account information, passwords, or credit card numbers will not request that information via phone or e-mail. Encrypting computers and other hardware containing sensitive information, so it will not be readable if the hardware is lost or stolen, is another important precaution.

Protecting Against Identity Theft, Phishing, Social Media Hacks, and Pharming

Some precautions already discussed (such as disclosing your personal information only when necessary and only via secure Web pages) can help reduce your risk of identity theft. So can using security software (and keeping it up to date) to guard against malware that can send information from your computer or about your activities (the Web site passwords that you type, for example) to a criminal. In addition, to prevent someone from using the preapproved credit card offers and other documents containing personal information that are mailed to you, shred them before throwing them in the trash. To prevent the theft of outgoing mail containing sensitive information, don't place it in your mailbox—mail it at the post office or in a USPS drop box.

To avoid phishing schemes, never click a link in an e-mail message to go to a secure Web site—always type the URL for that site in your browser (not necessarily the URL shown in the e-mail message) instead. Phishing e-mails typically sound urgent and often contain spelling and grammatical errors—see Figure 4-22 for some tips to help

FIGURE 4-22 Tips for identifying phishing e-mail messages.

A PHISHING E-MAIL OFTEN . . .

Tries to scare you into responding by sounding urgent, including a warning that your account will be cancelled if you do not respond, or telling you that you have been a victim of fraud.

Asks you to provide personal information, such as your bank account number, an account password, credit card number, PIN number, mother's maiden name, or Social Security number.

Contains links that do not go where the link text says it will go (point to a hyperlink in the e-mail message to view the URL for that link to see the actual domain being used—a phisher would have to use a URL like microsoft.phisher.com, not microsoft.com).

Uses legitimate logos from the company the phisher is posing as.

Appears to come from a known organization, but one you may not have an association with.

Appears to be text or text and images but is actually a single image; it has been created that way to avoid being caught in a spam filter (a program that sorts e-mail based on legitimate e-mail and suspected spam) because spam filters cannot read text that is part of an image in an e-mail message.

Contains spelling or grammatical errors.

TIPS FOR AVOIDING IDENTITY THEFT

Protect your Social Security number—give it out only when necessary.

Be careful with your physical mail and trash—shred all documents containing sensitive data.

Secure your computer—update your operating system and use up-to-date security (antivirus, antispyware, firewall, etc.) software.

Be cautious—never click on a link in an e-mail message or respond to a too-good-to-be-true offer.

Use strong passwords for your computer and online accounts.

Verify sources before sharing sensitive information—never respond to e-mail or phone requests for sensitive information.

Be vigilant while on the go—safeguard your wallet, smartphone, and portable computer.

Watch your bills and monitor your credit reports—react immediately if you suspect fraudulent activity.

Use security software or browser features that warn you if you try to view a known phishing site.

FIGURE 4-23
Tips to reduce your risk of identity theft.

you recognize phishing e-mails. Remember that spear phishing schemes may include personalized information (such as your name)—do not let that fool you into thinking the phishing e-mail is legitimate. If you think an unsolicited e-mail message requesting information from you may be legitimate (for instance, if the credit card you use to make an automatic payment for an ongoing service is about to expire and you receive an e-mail message asking you to update your credit card information), type the URL for that site in your browser to load the legitimate site and then update your account information. To prevent a drive-by pharming attack, all businesses and individuals should change the administrator password for routers, access points, and other networking hardware from the default password to a strong password. Individuals can also change the DNS server for their router to one (such as *OpenDNS*) that uses filtering to block malicious sites and protect against pharming attempts.

TIP

You can order your free credit reports online quickly and easily via Web sites like *AnnualCreditReport.com.*

Keeping a close eye on your credit card bills and credit history is also important to make sure you catch any fraudulent charges or accounts opened by an identity thief as soon as possible. Make sure your bills come in every month (some thieves will change your mailing address to delay detection), and read credit card statements carefully to look for unauthorized charges. Be sure to follow up on any calls you get from creditors, instead of assuming it is just a mistake. Most security experts also recommend ordering a full credit history on yourself a few times a year to check for accounts listed in your name that you did not open and any other problems. The *Fair and Accurate Credit Transactions Act* (*FACTA*) enables all Americans to get a free copy of their credit report, upon request, each year from the three major consumer credit bureaus. Ideally, you should request a report from one of these bureaus every four months to monitor your credit on a regular basis. These reports contain information about inquiries related to new accounts requested in your name, as well as any delinquent balances or other negative reports. For another tool that you can use to help detect identity theft—*online financial alerts*—see the Technology and You box. You can also use browser-based *antiphishing* tools and *digital certificates* to help guard against identity theft and the phishing and pharming schemes used in conjunction with identity theft, as discussed next. Some additional tips for minimizing your risk of identity theft are listed in Figure 4-23.

Antiphishing Tools

Antiphishing tools are built into many e-mail programs and Web browsers to help notify users of possible phishing Web sites. For instance, some e-mail programs will disable links in e-mail messages identified as questionable, unless the user overrides them; most recent browsers warn users when a Web page associated with a possible phishing URL is requested (see Figure 4-24); and antiphishing capabilities are included in many recent security suites.

In addition, some secure Web sites are adding additional layers in security to protect against identity thieves. For example, some online banking sites analyze users' habits to look for patterns that vary from the norm, such as accessing accounts online at an hour unusual for that individual or a higher than normal level of online purchases. If a bank suspects the account may be compromised, it contacts the owner for verification. Bank of America and some other financial institutions have also added an additional step in their logon process—displaying an image or word preselected by the user and stored on the bank's server—to prove

FIGURE 4-24
Unsafe Web site alerts.

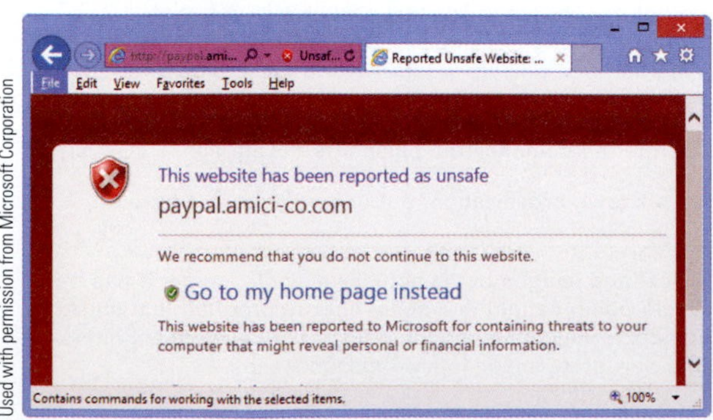

TECHNOLOGY AND YOU

Online Financial Alerts

Want to know ASAP when a transaction that might be fraudulent is charged to your credit card or deducted from your checking account? Well, *online financial alerts* might be the answer.

Many online banking services today allow users to set up e-mail alerts for credit card and bank account activity over a certain amount, low balances, and so forth. For individuals wishing to monitor multiple accounts, however, online money management aggregator services (such as *Mint.com*) make it easier. Once you have set up a free Mint.com account with your financial accounts (including credit cards and checking, savings, and PayPal accounts) and their respective passwords, you can see the status of all your accounts through the Mint.com interface. You can also set up alerts for any of the accounts based on your desired criteria, such as any fee charged or an unusual transaction (see the accompanying photo). The alerts are sent to you via e-mail or text message, depending on your preference, to help notify you as soon as possible if a suspicious activity occurs. And timeliness is of the essence, because the sooner identity theft is discovered, the less time the thief has to make additional fraudulent transactions. For security purposes, Mint.com doesn't store online banking usernames and passwords; instead, a secure online financial services provider is used to connect Mint.com to the appropriate financial institutions to update your activity. In addition, the Mint.com Web site cannot be used to move money out of or between financial accounts—it can be used only to view information.

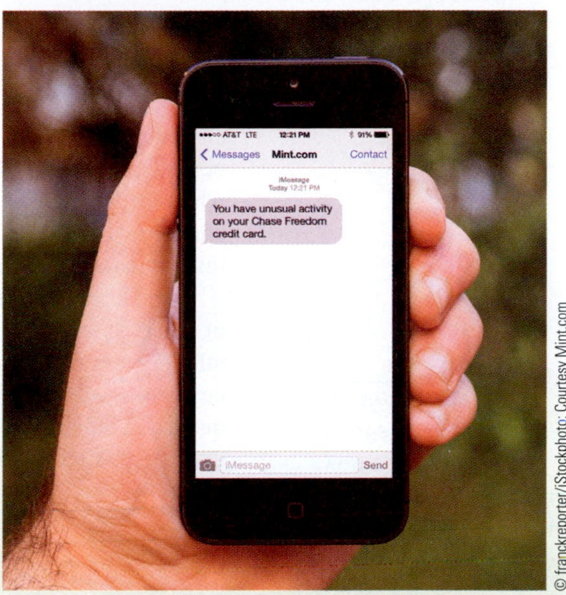

© franckreporter/iStockphoto; Courtesy Mint.com

to the user that the site being viewed is the legitimate (not a phishing) site. In addition, if the system does not recognize the computer that the user is using to log on to the system, the user is required to go through an authentication process (typically by correctly answering cognitive authentication questions) before being allowed to access the system via that computer. The questions used are specifically designed to be "out of wallet" questions—easy for the individual to answer but difficult for hackers to guess the correct answer or find in a stolen wallet. Bank of America is also one bank offering customers the option of adding the use of one-time passwords (autogenerated by a security token sent via text message to the individual's mobile phone, as in Figure 4-5) to their online banking logon procedure.

TIP

Facebook, Google, Microsoft, and other major technology companies are in the process of developing a new *DMARC* (*Domain-based Message Authentication, Report, and Conformance*) specification expected to make it easier to detect phishing e-mails using spoofed domains.

Digital Certificates and Digital Signatures

The purpose of a **digital certificate** (also called a **digital ID**) is to authenticate the identity of an individual or organization. Digital certificates are granted by Certificate Authorities and typically contain the name of the person, organization, or Web site being certified along with a certificate serial number and an expiration date. Digital certificates also include a public/private key pair. In addition to being used by the certificate holder to encrypt files and e-mail messages (as discussed earlier in this chapter), these keys and the digital certificate are used with secure Web pages to guarantee the Web pages are secure and actually belong to the stated organization (so users can know for sure who their credit

>**Digital certificate.** A group of electronic data that can be used to verify the identity of a person or organization; includes a key pair that can be used for encryption and digital signatures (also called a **digital ID**).

A red address bar (not shown) would indicate a problem with the site's digital certificate.

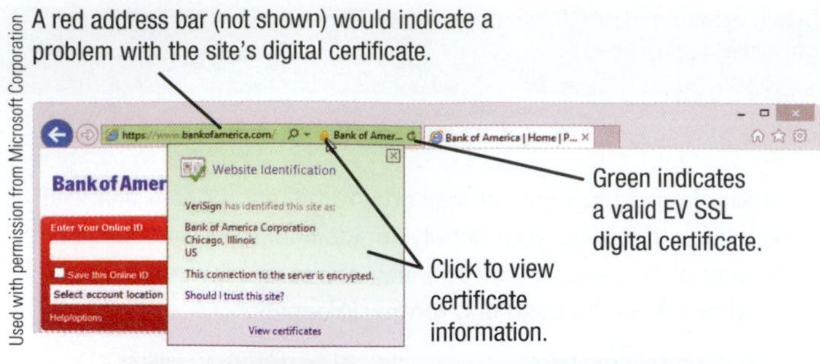

Green indicates a valid EV SSL digital certificate.

Click to view certificate information.

Used with permission from Microsoft Corporation

FIGURE 4-25

EV SSL certificates. The browser's Address bar reflects information about the digital certificate being used.

card number or other sensitive data is really being sent to in order to protect against some online scams).

Secure Web sites can obtain either a normal *SSL digital certificate* or a newer *Extended Validation (EV) SSL digital certificate* that was developed to provide consumers with a higher level of trust while online. While both digital certificates require an application process, the verification process to obtain an EV SSL digital certificate is more thorough, requiring the use of reputable third-party sources to verify that the company has the right to use the Web site domain name in question and that the business requesting the certificate is authorized to do so. With both types of certificates, individuals can click the secure Web page icon in their browser window to view that site's digital certificate in order to ensure that the certificate is valid and issued to the company associated with the Web site being viewed. If an EV SSL certificate is used, however, additional information is displayed when the Web site is viewed in an EV-compliant browser, such as recoloring the Address bar green to indicate a site using a valid EV SSL certificate and displaying certificate information in the *Security Status bar* to the right of the Address bar, as shown in Figure 4-25.

The keys included in a digital certificate can also be used to authenticate the identity of a person sending an e-mail message or other document via a **digital signature**. To digitally sign an e-mail message or other document, the sender's private key is used and that key, along with the contents of the document, generates a unique digital signature; consequently, a digital signature is different with each signed document. When a digitally signed document is received, the recipient's computer uses the sender's public key to verify the digital signature. Because the document is signed with the sender's private key (that only the sender should know) and the digital signature will be deemed invalid if even one character of the document is changed after it is signed, digital signatures guarantee that the document was sent by a specific individual and that it was not tampered with after it was signed.

Individuals can obtain a free digital certificate for personal use from several Certificate Authorities (such as *Comodo*). Once you obtain one, you will need to install it on your computer (Windows users can use the *Certificates* option on the Content tab in the Internet Properties dialog box available through the Control Panel), and then you can use the digital signature option in your e-mail program (such as Microsoft Outlook, see Figure 4-26) to sign all or just selected messages. At this time, most Web mail programs (such as Gmail and Outlook.com) do not support the use of digital signatures.

FIGURE 4-26

Digitally signing an e-mail message in Microsoft Outlook.

1. Get a digital ID and then install it.

Free Email Certificate
Sign up now!

Format Text Review
Encrypt
Permission
Sign
Permission

2. Use the appropriate option in your e-mail program to sign your e-mail messages.

3. The recipient can click an option in the message to view your digital signature.

Courtesy Comodo Group, Inc.; Used with permission from Microsoft Corporation

Protecting Against Online Auction Fraud and Other Internet Scams

The best protection against many dot cons is common sense. Be extremely cautious of any unsolicited e-mail messages you receive and realize that if an offer sounds too good to be true, it probably is. You should also be cautious when dealing with individuals online through auctions and other person-to-person activities. Before bidding on an auction item, check out the feedback rating of the seller to see comments written by other auction sellers and buyers as well as the sellers' return policy. Always pay for auctions and other online purchases using a credit card or an online payment service (such as PayPal) that accepts credit card payments so you can dispute the

>**Digital signature.** A unique digital code that can be attached to a file or an e-mail message to verify the identity of the sender and guarantee the file or message has not been changed since it was signed.

transaction through your credit card company, if needed. Using an online payment service that bills the charge to your credit card, instead of allowing the seller to charge your credit card, has the extra advantage of keeping your credit card information private. In addition, some auction sites and online payment services offer free buyer protection against undelivered items or auction items that are significantly different from their description. For instance, most eBay purchases paid for via PayPal have at least $200 of buyer protection coverage at no additional cost. For expensive items, consider using a reputable *escrow service*, which allows you to ensure that the merchandise is as specified before your payment is released to the seller.

PERSONAL SAFETY ISSUES

In addition to being expensive and inconvenient, cybercrime can also be physically dangerous. Although most of us may not ordinarily view using the Internet as a potentially dangerous activity, cases of physical harm due to Internet activity do happen. For example, children and teenagers have become the victims of pedophiles who arranged face-to-face meetings by using information gathered via e-mail, online games, social networking sites, or other online sources. There are also a growing number of incidents in which children are threatened by classmates via e-mail, social media posts, or text messages. Adults have fallen victim to unscrupulous or dangerous individuals who misrepresent themselves online, and the availability of personal information online has made it more difficult for individuals to hide from people who may want to do them harm, such as abused women trying to hide from their abusive husbands. Two of the most common ways individuals are harassed online—*cyberbullying* and *cyberstalking*—are discussed next.

Cyberbullying and Cyberstalking

Children and teenagers bullying other children or teenagers via the Internet—such as through e-mail, a text message, a social networking site, a blog, or other online communications method—is referred to as **cyberbullying**. Unfortunately, cyberbullying is common today—it affects more than one-half of all U.S. teenagers, according to a recent report. Cyberbullying can take place via direct online communications (such as with an e-mail or a text message), as well as via more subtle means. For instance, there have been cases of students posting videos on YouTube of other students being bullied or shown in compromising situations, as well as cases of individuals hacking into a student's social networking account and changing the content on the student's pages to harass that student. Unfortunately, there are also several instances where teenagers have committed suicide because of cyberbullying, which have prompted many states and schools to look at harassment statutes and bullying policies. Several antibullying campaigns have been initiated by school districts and government organizations (see Figure 4-27) and most states have implemented new laws or amended existing harassment laws to address electronic harassment. And Web sites (along with the individuals or companies responsible for them) that provide the means for the harassment may also be at risk for prosecution. In Italy, three Google executives were given suspended jail terms for ignoring a parent's request to remove a video of a boy being bullied, and at the time of this writing, Italian prosecutors were investigating whether to sue Facebook for not removing harrassing messages that led to a teenage girl's suicide.

Courtesy National Crime Prevention Council

FIGURE 4-27
An anti-cyberbullying Web banner.

While incidents of online harrassment between adults can be referred to as *cyberharassment*, repeated threats or other malicious behavior that poses a credible threat of harm carried out online between adults is referred to as **cyberstalking**. Cyberstalkers sometimes find their victims online; for instance, someone who makes a comment on a

>**Cyberbullying.** Children or teenagers bullying other children or teenagers via the Internet. >**Cyberstalking.** Repeated threats or harassing behavior between adults carried out via e-mail or another Internet communications method.

social networking site that the cyberstalker does not like, or bloggers who are harassed and threatened because of their blogging activities. Other times, the attack is more personal, such as employers who are stalked online by ex-employees who were fired or otherwise left their position under adverse conditions, and celebrities who are stalked online by fans.

Cyberstalking typically begins with online harassment—such as sending harassing or threatening e-mail messages or unwanted files to the victim, posing as the victim in order to sign the victim up for pornographic or otherwise offensive e-mail newsletters, publicizing the victim's home address and telephone number, or hacking into the victim's social networking pages to alter the content. Cyberstalking can also lead to offline stalking and possibly physical harm to, and sometimes even the death of, the victim. While there are as yet no specific federal laws against cyberstalking, all states have made it illegal (and it is being increasingly prosecuted), and some federal laws do apply if the online actions include computer fraud or another type of computer crime, suggest a threat of personal injury, or involve sending obscene e-mail messages. Many cyberstalkers are not caught, however, due in part to the anonymity of the Internet, which assists cyberstalkers in concealing their true identities.

Online Pornography

A variety of controversial and potentially objectionable material is available on the Internet. Although there have been attempts to ban this type of material from the Internet, they have not been successful. For example, the *Communications Decency Act*, signed into law in 1996—which made it a criminal offense to distribute patently indecent or offensive material online—was ruled unconstitutional in 1997 by the U.S. Supreme Court. However, like its printed counterpart, online pornography involving minors is illegal. Because of the strong link they believe exists between child pornography and child molestation, many experts are very concerned about the amount of child pornography that can be found and distributed via the Internet. They also believe that the Internet makes it easier for sexual predators to act out, such as by striking up "friendships" with children online and convincing these children to meet them in real life. And this can have devastating consequences, as it did for a 13-year-old girl from Connecticut who was strangled to death in 2002 by a 25-year-old man she met originally online and eventually in person.

PROTECTING AGAINST CYBERBULLYING, CYBERSTALKING, AND OTHER PERSONAL SAFETY CONCERNS

The growing increase in attention to cyberbullying and cyberstalking is leading to more efforts to improve safeguards for children. For instance, social networking sites have privacy features that can be used to protect the private information of their members. In addition, numerous states in the United States have implemented cyberbullying and cyberstalking laws. While there is no surefire way to protect against cyberbullying, cyberstalking, and other online dangers completely, some common-sense precautions can reduce the chance of a serious personal safety problem occurring due to online activities.

TIP

Search for yourself using search sites and online telephone books to see what personal information is available about you on the Internet.

Safety Tips for Adults

It is wise to be cautious and discreet online—especially in online profiles, Twitter tweets, forums, and other online locations where individuals communicate with strangers. To protect yourself against cyberstalking and other types of online harassment, use gender-neutral, nonprovocative identifying names, such as *jsmith*, instead of *janesmith* or *iamcute*. Be careful about the types of photos you post of yourself online and do not reveal personal information—such as your real name, address, or telephone number—to people you meet online. In addition, do not respond to any insults or other harassing comments you may receive online. You may also want to request that your personal information be removed from online directories—especially those associated with your e-mail address or other online identifiers.

TIP

Both adults and children should avoid including personal information on their social networking pages that could be used by an online stalker.

Safety Tips for Children and Teens

Most experts agree that the best way to protect children from online dangers is to stay in close touch with them as they explore the Internet. Parents should monitor their children's computer and mobile phone activities, and children and teenagers should be told which activities are allowed, which types of Web sites are off-limits, and why. In addition, it should be made clear that they are never to reveal personal information about themselves online without a parent's permission. They should also be instructed to tell a parent (or teacher if at school) if an individual ever requests personal information or a personal meeting, or threatens or otherwise harasses the child, via any type of online communications medium. Older children should also be cautioned about sending compromising photos of themselves or sexually explicit messages to others—a growing practice referred to as *sexting*. Part of the problem is that many young people don't realize they lose control of photos and other compromising content once that information has been sent to others. The issue is also complicated by *sextortion*—where someone who sees a teen's explicit photo in a text message or on the Internet threatens to expose the teen's behavior unless the teen sends more explicit photos. Sexting can result in child pornography charges being filed against teens, though some states are passing legislation to make it illegal but have lesser charges for a minor's first offense.

TIP

One controversial bill under consideration is *CISPA* (*Cyber Intelligence Sharing and Protection Act*), which would allow for voluntary information sharing between private companies and the government in the event of a cyber attack.

NETWORK AND INTERNET SECURITY LEGISLATION

Although new legislation is introduced frequently to address new types of computer crimes, it is rarely passed due to differences in opinion regarding the balance of protection vs. civil liberties. In addition, there are both domestic and international jurisdictional issues because many computer crimes affect businesses and individuals located in geographic areas other than the one in which the computer criminal is located, and hackers can make it appear that activity is coming from a different location than it really is. Nevertheless, computer crime legislation continues to be proposed and computer crimes are being prosecuted. A list of selected federal laws concerning network and Internet security is shown in Figure 4-28.

FIGURE 4-28
Computer network and Internet security legislation.

DATE	LAW AND DESCRIPTION
2004	**Identity Theft Penalty Enhancement Act** Adds extra years to prison sentences for criminals who use identity theft (including the use of stolen credit card numbers) to commit other crimes.
2003	**CAN-SPAM Act** Implements regulations for unsolicited e-mail messages.
2003	**Fair and Accurate Credit Transactions Act (FACTA)** Amends the Fair Credit Reporting Act (FCRA) to require that the three nationwide consumer reporting agencies (Equifax, Experian, and TransUnion) provide consumers, upon request, a free copy of their credit report once every 12 months.
2003	**PROTECT Act** Includes provisions to prohibit virtual child pornography.
2003	**Health Insurance Portability and Accountability Act (HIPAA)** Includes a Security Rule that sets minimum security standards to protect health information stored electronically.
2002	**Homeland Security Act** Includes provisions to combat cyberterrorism, including protecting ISPs against lawsuits from customers for revealing private information to law enforcement agencies.
2002	**Sarbanes-Oxley Act** Requires archiving a variety of electronic records and protecting the integrity of corporate financial data.
2001	**USA PATRIOT Act** Grants federal authorities expanded surveillance and intelligence-gathering powers, such as broadening the ability of federal agents to obtain the real identity of Internet users, intercept e-mail and other types of Internet communications, follow online activity of suspects, expand their wiretapping authority, and more.
1998	**Identity Theft and Assumption Deterrence Act of 1998** Makes it a federal crime to knowingly use someone else's means of identification, such as name, Social Security number, or credit card, to commit any unlawful activity.
1997	**No Electronic Theft (NET) Act** Expands computer piracy laws to include online distribution of copyrighted materials.
1996	**National Information Infrastructure Protection Act** Amends the Computer Fraud and Abuse Act of 1984 to punish information theft crossing state lines and to crack down on network trespassing.
1984	**Computer Fraud and Abuse Act of 1984** Makes it a crime to break into computers owned by the federal government. This act has been regularly amended over the years as technology has changed.

SUMMARY

WHY BE CONCERNED ABOUT NETWORK AND INTERNET SECURITY?

Chapter Objective 1: Explain why computer users should be concerned about network and Internet security.

There are a number of important security concerns related to computers and the Internet. Many of these are **computer crimes**. Because computers and networks are so widespread and many opportunities for criminals exist, all computer users should be aware of the risks of using networks and the Internet so they can take appropriate precautions.

UNAUTHORIZED ACCESS AND UNAUTHORIZED USE

Chapter Objective 2: List several examples of unauthorized access and unauthorized use.

Two risks related to networks and the Internet are **unauthorized access** and **unauthorized use**. **Hacking** is using a computer to break into a computer. **War driving** and **Wi-Fi piggybacking** refer to the unauthorized use of an unsecured Wi-Fi network. Data can be intercepted as it is transmitted over the Internet or a wireless network.

PROTECTING AGAINST UNAUTHORIZED ACCESS AND UNAUTHORIZED USE

Chapter Objective 3: Explain several ways to protect against unauthorized access and unauthorized use, including access control systems, firewalls, and encryption.

Access control systems are used to control access to a computer, network, or other resource. These include **possessed knowledge access systems** that use **passwords** or other types of possessed knowledge; **possessed object access systems** that use physical objects; and **biometric access systems** that identify users by a particular unique biological characteristic, such as a fingerprint. Passwords should be *strong passwords*; **two-factor authentication** systems that use multiple factors are more effective than single-factor systems.

To protect wireless networks, they should be secured; **firewalls** protect against unauthorized access. Sensitive transactions should be performed only on **secure Web pages**; sensitive files and e-mails should be secured with **encryption. Public key encryption** uses a private key and matching public key; **private key encryption** uses only a private key. A **virtual private network (VPN)** can be used to provide a secure remote connection to a company network, as well as to protect individuals at public Wi-Fi hotspots. Employers should take appropriate precautions with current and former employees to limit the risk of unauthorized access and use, as well as accidental exposure of sensitive information.

COMPUTER SABOTAGE

Chapter Objective 4: Provide several examples of computer sabotage.

Computer sabotage includes **malware** (**computer viruses**, **computer worms**, and **Trojan horses** designed to cause harm to computer systems), **denial of service (DoS) attacks** (designed to shut down a Web server), and data and program alteration. Computer sabotage is often performed via the Internet, increasingly by the **bots** in a **botnet**.

PROTECTING AGAINST COMPUTER SABOTAGE

Chapter Objective 5: List how individuals and businesses can protect against computer sabotage.

Protection against computer sabotage includes using appropriate access control systems to keep unauthorized individuals from accessing computers and networks, as well as using **security software**. In particular, **antivirus software** protects against computer viruses and other types of malware. It is important to keep your security software up to date.

ONLINE THEFT, ONLINE FRAUD, AND OTHER DOT CONS

There are a variety of types of theft, fraud, and scams related to the Internet—collectively referred to as **dot cons**—that all Internet users should be aware of. Data, information, or money can be stolen from individuals and businesses. A common crime today is **identity theft**, in which an individual poses as another individual—typically to steal money or make purchases posing as the victim. The information used in identity theft is often gathered via **phishing**, **spear phishing**, **social media hacking**, and **pharming**. **Online auction fraud** is another common dot con.

Chapter Objective 6:
Discuss online theft, identity theft, spoofing, phishing, and other types of dot cons.

PROTECTING AGAINST ONLINE THEFT, ONLINE FRAUD, AND OTHER DOT CONS

To protect against identity theft, individuals should guard their personal information carefully. To check for identity theft, watch your bills and credit history. When interacting with other individuals online or buying from an online auction, it is wise to be conservative and use a credit card whenever possible. To avoid other types of dot cons, be very wary of responding to unsolicited offers and e-mails, and steer clear of offers that seem too good to be true. Never click a link in an e-mail message to update your personal information. To verify a Web site, a **digital certificate** (also called a **digital ID**) can be used. To verify the sender of a document, a **digital signature** can be used. Digital certificates include key pairs that can be used to both digitally sign documents and to encrypt files.

Chapter Objective 7:
Detail steps an individual can take to protect against online theft, identity theft, spoofing, phishing, and other types of dot cons.

PERSONAL SAFETY ISSUES

There are also personal safety risks for both adults and children stemming from Internet use. **Cyberbullying** and **cyberstalking**—online harassment that frightens or threatens the victim—is more common in recent years, even though most states have passed laws against it. Cyberbully is a growing risk for children, as are the risks of potential exposure to online pornography and other materials inappropriate for children, as well as the growing *sexting* and *sextortion* trends.

Chapter Objective 8:
Identify personal safety risks associated with Internet use.

PROTECTING AGAINST CYBERBULLING, CYBERSTALKING, AND OTHER PERSONAL SAFETY CONCERNS

To protect their personal safety, adults and children should be cautious in online communications. They should be wary of revealing any personal information or meeting online acquaintances in person. To protect children, parents should keep a close watch on their children's online activities, and children should be taught never to reveal personal information to others online without a parent's consent.

Chapter Objective 9:
List steps individuals can take to safeguard their personal safety when using the Internet.

NETWORK AND INTERNET SECURITY LEGISLATION

The rapid growth of the Internet and jurisdictional issues have contributed to the lack of network and Internet security legislation. However, computer crime legislation continues to be proposed and computer crimes are actively prosecuted.

Chapter Objective 10:
Discuss the current state of network and Internet security legislation.

REVIEW ACTIVITIES

KEY TERM MATCHING

a. computer virus

b. denial of service (DoS) attack

c. dot con

d. encryption

e. firewall

f. hacking

g. identity theft

h. password

i. phishing

j. Trojan horse

Instructions: Match each key term on the left with the definition on the right that best describes it.

1. ________ A collection of hardware and/or software intended to protect a computer or computer network from unauthorized access.

2. ________ A fraud or scam carried out through the Internet.

3. ________ A malicious program that masquerades as something else.

4. ________ A method of scrambling the contents of an e-mail message or a file to make it unreadable if it is intercepted by an unauthorized user.

5. ________ A secret combination of characters used to gain access to a computer, computer network, or other resource.

6. ________ A software program installed without the user's knowledge and designed to alter the way a computer operates or to cause harm to the computer system.

7. ________ An act of sabotage that attempts to flood a network server or a Web server with so much activity that it is unable to function.

8. ________ The use of spoofed communications (typically e-mail messages) to gain credit card numbers and other personal data to be used for fraudulent purposes.

9. ________ Using a computer to break into another computer system.

10. ________ Using someone else's identity to purchase goods or services, obtain new credit cards or bank loans, or otherwise illegally masquerade as that individual.

SELF-QUIZ

Instructions: Circle **T** if the statement is true, **F** if the statement is false, or write the best answer in the space provided. **Answers for the self-quiz are located in the References and Resources Guide at the end of the book.**

1. **T F** A computer virus can only be transferred to another computer via a storage medium.

2. **T F** An access control system that uses passwords is a possessed knowledge access system.

3. **T F** Using a password that is two characters long is an example of two-factor authentication.

4. **T F** Secure Web pages use encryption to securely transfer data sent via those pages.

5. **T F** Cyberstalking is the use of spoofed e-mail messages to gain credit card numbers and other personal data to be used for fraudulent purposes.

6. Driving around looking for a Wi-Fi network to access is referred to as ________.

7. ________ access control systems use some type of unique physical characteristic of a person to authenticate that individual.

8. A(n) ________ can be used at a Wi-Fi hotspot to create a secure path over the Internet.

9. A(n) ________ can be added to a file or an e-mail message to verify the identity of the sender and guarantee the file or message has not been changed.

10. Match each computer crime to its description, and write the corresponding number in the blank to the left of the description.

    a. ________ A person working for the Motor Vehicle Division deletes a friend's speeding ticket from a database.

    b. ________ An individual does not like someone's comment on a message board and begins to send that individual harassing e-mail messages.

    c. ________ An individual sells the same item to 10 individuals via an online auction site.

    d. ________ A person accesses a computer belonging to the IRS without authorization.

    1. Online auction fraud
    2. Hacking
    3. Data or program alteration
    4. Cyberstalking

EXERCISES

1. Write the appropriate letter in the blank to the left of each term to indicate whether it is related to unauthorized access (U) or computer sabotage (C).

   a. ________ Time bomb   c. ________ Malware   e. ________ War driving

   b. ________ DoS attack   d. ________ Wi-Fi piggybacking

2. Is the password *john1* a good password? Why or why not? If not, suggest a better password.

3. Supply the missing words to complete the following statements regarding public/private key pairs.

   a. With an encrypted e-mail message, the recipient's ________ key is used to encrypt the message, and the recipient's ________ key is used to decrypt the message.

   b. With a digital signature, the sender's ________ key is used to sign the document, and the sender's ________ key is used to validate the signature.

4. To secure files on your computer so they are unreadable to a hacker who might gain access to your computer, what type of encryption (public key or private key) would be the most appropriate? Explain.

5. List two precautions you can take to protect against someone hacking your social media accounts.

DISCUSSION QUESTIONS

1. The term *hacktivism* is sometimes used to refer to the act of hacking into a computer system for a politically or socially motivated purpose. While some view hacktivists no differently than they view other hackers, hacktivists contend that they break into systems in order to bring attention to political or social causes. Is hacktivism a valid method of bringing attention to specific causes? Why or why not? Should hacktivists be treated differently from other types of hackers when caught?

2. According to security experts, several worms released in past years contain more than just the virus code—they contain code to remove competing malware from the computers they infect and messages taunting other virus writers. The goal seems to be not only to gain control of an increasing number of infected machines—a type of "bot war" to build the biggest botnet—but also to one-up rivals. If this trend continues, do you think it will affect how hackers and other computer criminals will be viewed? Will they become cult heroes or be viewed as dangerous criminals? Will continuing to increase prosecution of these individuals help or hurt the situation?

PROJECTS

HOT TOPICS

1. **Wi-Fi Hotspot Safety** As mentioned in the chapter, it is possible to inadvertently connect to an evil twin instead of the legitimate Wi-Fi hotspot you intended to connect to and, even if you are connected to a legitimate hotspot, any data you send unsecured via the hotspot can be intercepted by a criminal. In either case, if a thief intercepts your credit card number, Web site passwords, or other sensitive data, it can be used for identity theft and other criminal activities.

   For this project, research these and any other possible risks you can think of related to using a Wi-Fi hotspot. For each risk, identify a possible precaution that can be taken to guard against that risk. If you have ever used a Wi-Fi hotspot, were you at risk? Knowing what you do now, would you take any different precautions the next time you use one? Is it possible to surf safely using a Wi-Fi hotspot? What about activity performed via your smartphone wireless provider—is that safe? At the conclusion of your research, prepare a one-page summary of your findings and opinions and submit it to your instructor.

SHORT ANSWER/ RESEARCH

2. **New Viruses** Unfortunately, new computer viruses and other types of malware are released all the time. In addition to malware targeted toward computers, there is also mobile malware targeted to smartphones, media tablets, and other Internet-enabled devices.

   For this project, identify a current virus or worm (most security companies, such as Symantec and McAfee, list the most recent security threats on their Web sites) and answer the following questions: When was it introduced? What does it do? How is it spread? Is it targeted to computers or mobile devices? How many devices have been affected so far? Is there an estimated cost associated with it? Is it still in existence? At the conclusion of your research, prepare a one-page summary of your findings and submit it to your instructor.

HANDS ON

3. **Virus Check** There are several Web sites that include a free virus check, as well as other types of diagnostic software.

   For this project, locate a free virus check (such as one available from Microsoft or from a company that makes antivirus software) and run the free virus check. NOTE: If you are on a school computer, only run online checks, not downloaded programs. If the check takes more than 10 minutes and there is an option to limit the check to a particular drive and folder, redo the check but scan only part of the hard drive (such as the Documents folder) to save time. After the virus scan is completed, print the page displaying the result. Did the program find any viruses or other security threats? At the conclusion of this task, submit your printout with any additional comments about your experience to your instructor.

ETHICS IN ACTION

4. **Teaching Computer Viruses** Some college computer classes include instruction on writing computer viruses. At one university, precautions for containing code created during this course include allowing only fourth-year students to take the course, not having a network connection in the classroom, and prohibiting the removal of storage media from the classroom. Do you think these precautions are sufficient? Should writing virus code be allowed as part of a computer degree curriculum? Some believe that students need to know how viruses work in order to be able to develop antivirus software; however, the antivirus industry disagrees, and most antivirus professionals were never virus writers. Is it ethical for colleges to teach computer virus writing? Is it ethical for students to take such a course? Will teaching illegal and unethical acts (such as writing virus code) in college classes help to legitimize the behavior in society? Would you feel comfortable taking such a course? Why or why not?

   For this project, form an opinion about the ethical implications of writing virus code in college classes and be prepared to discuss your position (in class, via an online class discussion group, in a class chat room, or via a class blog, depending on your instructor's directions). You may also be asked to write a short paper expressing your opinion.

PRESENTATION/ DEMONSTRATION

5. **Virus Hoaxes** In addition to the valid reports about new viruses found in the news and on antivirus software Web sites, reports of viruses that turn out to be hoaxes abound on the Internet. In addition to being an annoyance, virus hoaxes waste time and computing resources. In addition, they may eventually lead some users to routinely ignore all virus warning messages, leaving them vulnerable to a genuine, destructive virus.

   For this project, visit at least two Web sites that identify virus hoaxes, such as the Symantec or McAfee Web sites and Snopes.com. Explore the sites to find information about recent virus hoaxes, as well as general guidelines for identifying virus hoaxes and other types of online hoaxes. Share your findings with the class in the form of a short presentation. The presentation should not exceed 10 minutes and should make use of one or more presentation aids, such as a whiteboard, handouts, or a computer-based slide presentation (your instructor may provide additional requirements). You may also be asked to submit a summary of the presentation to your instructor.

BALANCING ACT

6. **Is Mobile Banking More Secure than Online Banking?** You may have used your smartphone to pay a bill or deposit a check. While becoming common today, it is still newer than traditional online banking performed via a computer and so does not have as long of a track record. While banks are continually upgrading their security systems in response to new threats and technologies, is the security of online and mobile banking equal? Some consider traditional online banking safer because it has been tested longer, is used with computers that may have better security software installed, and is performed via home computers that are not as likely to be lost or misplaced as mobile devices. Others view mobile banking as safer because individuals tend to have their phones with them at all times and so can be notified more quickly of security breaches, GPS information can be used to identify transactions that occur in a different physical location from the registered location of the phone (and therefore might be fraudulent), and mobile banking accounts are often associated with a single phone. Mobile banking can be performed via a Web app, mobile Web site, or text messaging. Is one method safer than the other? How do the risks associated with mobile banking compare with the risks associated wtih traditional online banking? Would you feel safer using one or the other? Why?

   Pick a side on this issue, form an opinion and gather supporting evidence, and be prepared to discuss and defend your position in a classroom debate or in a 1–2 page paper, depending on your instructor's directions.

expert insight on...

Networks and the Internet

Courtesy McAfee

Greg Hampton is the Vice President of Product Management for the Network Security team at McAfee. Before joining McAfee, Hampton served as the Vice President of Marketing at Clearswift Corporation, an e-mail and Web security company based in the UK. He was also a founder and the CEO of a Silicon Valley start up for delivering network management solutions. Greg has a Bachelor of Arts degree in Economics and brings a broad range of enterprise software experience to the company.

A conversation with GREG HAMPTON

Vice President, Product Management, McAfee

". . . protect your identity and your online reputation—it will keep you and your data safe and will improve your career prospects."

My Background . . .

I am the Vice President of Product Management for Network Security at McAfee. In product management, our role is to ensure that our product roadmap is forward looking, and to help connect users with engineers so that we can build outstanding products that meet user needs. I became involved with product management when I was a general manager for a high tech company overseeing its Canadian and Latin American operations and I was asked to oversee a newly acquired company. In the process, I was exposed to the role of product management and developed an interest in it. I have found my experiences in sales management and marketing roles at high tech companies directly applicable and useful to my current position. In addition, pursuing my Bachelor of Arts degree was invaluable. It helped me develop an interest in and the skills needed to be able to learn new ideas in new areas, which is essential for individuals who work in the world of high tech.

It's Important to Know . . .

How the Internet and other networks work. Because the Internet is so integrated into our society today, it is important for people to understand the basic functions of the Internet—how it connects devices and resources, how people access it, how data is stored, and what the cloud is—so that they may understand how best to use and secure this resource in both their personal and professional lives.

That it is essential to protect your identity. Online theft, identity theft, and other privacy and security risks impact what we call our "identity." Protecting identities is a unique area of security that is important because it touches each of us personally—as employees, as students, and as individuals. In the digital world, you are your digital identity. What is associated with your digital identity becomes associated with you—and that could impact your finances, your legal standing, and your career.

Passwords alone are not an adequate security control. Today, most of our digital identities are protected by passwords. Unfortunately, a simple username and password is easy to break. What's worse, many of us use the same username and password over and over again so once one account—say, an online e-mail account—is breached, all other accounts (such as your bank account) using that same combination are then directly accessible. To make matters worse, the password policies often implemented to help prevent this (such as using a unique strong password for every account, changing them every few months, and telling people not to save them anywhere) increases these habits. Implementing better controls, such as two-factor and biometric authentication (e.g. voice and facial recognition used with our LiveSafe cloud storage product), is both safer and easier to use!

How I Use this Technology . . .

Because my job involves collecting requirements for Internet Security software and appliances, I use this knowledge and these solutions daily in my professional life. But I also use them in my personal life. For example, I use antivirus protection for all of my devices and I use two-factor or strong authentication to protect my financial and personal e-mail accounts.

What the Future Holds . . .

> *". . . a simple username and password is easy to break"*

Today in our connected society, our identity is our most valuable and our most vulnerable link. And our society will continue to become more connected. The Internet of Things (IoT) is moving beyond mobile devices and networked cars to wearable devices, household items, medical devices, and other items we use in our daily lives. In the near future, we will be connected in ways we're just beginning to imagine. As this happens, it will become increasingly important that we—as individuals, students, and a business community—continue to watch the trends around identity protection; how trust relationships are established between people, systems, data and applications; and the laws and governance for personal privacy.

Already, the most vulnerable link in our networks today is our identity, and it will become more vulnerable in the even more connected future. And, as the consumerization of IT increases the pressure to move business tools and applications to the cloud, businesses will be more challenged than ever to securely grant remote, mobile, and highly social business users and their identities easy access while not compromising their security—especially as the lines between the personal and professional continue to blur. To address these challenges, McAfee, Intel, and other companies are actively developing solutions like McAfee One Time Password and McAfee LiveSafe for businesses and consumers that use technologies like multi-factor authentication, which combines passwords with other methods like biometrics, smartphones, chips in our devices like Intel Identity Protection Technology (IPT), or other physical objects.

In the future, we can expect to see accelerated movement toward these solutions and technologies as we leave our weak and difficult-to-keep-track-of passwords behind.

My Advice to Students . . .

Protect yourself by implementing multi-factor authentication and strong passwords—today. And all of us, particularly students, should be careful of what we publish in social media. You can expose yourself to risk by sharing too much data about where you live, who you know, and what you are doing. If you share too much information, it can also impact your online reputation. Employers are increasing their scrutiny of social presence when considering job applicants and you don't want something you say or post online to hurt your job prospects in the future.

So, protect your identity and your online reputation—it will keep you and your data safe, and will improve your career prospects.

Discussion Question

Greg Hampton stresses the importance of protecting your digital identity. Think about the systems that contain personal data about you. How would you feel if those systems were breached and your information was stolen? Does your viewpoint change if the information was monetary (such as credit card information) versus private information (such as grades or health information)? What security precautions, if any, do you think should be imposed by laws? Are organizations that hold your personal data morally responsible for going beyond the minimum requirements? Be prepared to discuss your position (in class, via an online class discussion group, in a class chat room, or via a class blog, depending on your instructor's directions). You may also be asked to write a short paper expressing your opinion.

>For more information about McAfee, visit www.mcafee.com. For information about specific security issues and solutions, visit www.mcafee.com/identity and blogs.mcafee.com.

Device

chapter 5

Computer Security and Privacy

After completing this chapter, you will be able to do the following:

1. Explain why all computer users should be concerned about computer security.
2. List some risks associated with hardware loss, hardware damage, and system failure, and understand ways to safeguard a computer against these risks.
3. Define software piracy and digital counterfeiting, and explain how they can be prevented.
4. Explain what information privacy is and why computer users should be concerned about it.
5. Describe some privacy concerns regarding databases, electronic profiling, spam, and telemarketing, and identify ways individuals can protect their privacy.
6. Discuss several types of electronic surveillance and monitoring, and list ways individuals can protect their privacy.
7. Discuss the status of computer security and privacy legislation.

outline

ckup Now!

OVERVIEW

The increasing use of computers in our society today has many advantages. It also, however, opens up new possibilities for problems (such as data loss due to a system malfunction or a disaster), as well as new opportunities for computer crime (such as hardware theft, software piracy, and digital counterfeiting). In addition, our networked society has raised a number of privacy concerns. Although we can appreciate that sometimes selected people or organizations have a legitimate need for some types of personal information, whenever information is provided to others there is the danger that the information will be misused. For instance, facts may be taken out of context and used to draw distorted conclusions, or private information may end up being distributed to others without one's consent or knowledge. And, with the vast amount of sensitive information stored in databases accessible via the Internet today, privacy is an enormous concern for both individuals and businesses.

Chapter 4 discussed security risks related to network and Internet use. This chapter looks at other types of computer-related security concerns, as well as the computer-related privacy concerns facing us today. First, we explore hardware loss, hardware damage, and system failure, and the safeguards that can help reduce the risk of a problem occurring due to these security concerns. Next, software piracy and digital counterfeiting are discussed, along with the steps that are being taken to prevent these computer crimes. We then turn to privacy topics, including possible risks to personal privacy and precautions that can be taken to safeguard one's privacy. The chapter closes with a summary of legislation related to computer security and privacy. ■

WHY BE CONCERNED ABOUT COMPUTER SECURITY?

Today, there are a number of security concerns surrounding computers and related technology that all individuals should be concerned about, including having your computer stolen, losing a term paper because the storage medium your paper was stored on becomes unreadable, losing your smartphone containing your entire contact list and calendar, or running the risk of buying pirated or digitally counterfeited products. The most common security risks and computer crimes (including hacking, computer viruses, identity theft, and cyberbullying) that take place via networks and the Internet were discussed in Chapter 4, along with their respective precautions. While these concerns are extremely important today, there are additional computer security issues that are not related specifically to networks and the Internet. These computer security concerns, along with some precautions that users can take to reduce the risks of problems occurring due to these security concerns, are discussed in the next few sections.

TIP

New security risks are revealed all the time. For instance, it was recently discovered that data from some unencrypted smart meters can be accessed from nearly 1,000 feet away, enabling would-be burglars to monitor homes to see if they are occupied based on electricity usage within the homes.

HARDWARE LOSS, HARDWARE DAMAGE, AND SYSTEM FAILURE

Hardware loss can occur when a personal computer, USB flash drive, mobile device, or other piece of hardware is stolen or is lost by the owner. Hardware loss, as well as other security issues, can also result from *hardware damage* (both intentional and accidental) and *system failure*.

TIP

According to Norton research, 35% of people worldwide have lost a smartphone and the person who finds a lost phone will more often than not look through the photos and private information stored on a found phone, even when they intend to return it.

Hardware Loss

One of the most obvious types of hardware loss is **hardware theft**, which occurs when hardware is stolen from an individual or from a business, school, or other organization. Computers, printers, mobile phones, and other hardware can be stolen during a break-in; portable computers and mobile devices are also frequently stolen from cars, as well as from restaurants, airports, hotels, and other public locations. Although security experts stress that the vast majority of hardware theft is done for the value of the hardware itself, corporate executives and government employees may be targeted for computer theft for the information contained on their computers. In fact, *C-level attacks* (attacks aimed at C-level executives, such as CEOs and CIOs) are rapidly growing as executives are increasingly using e-mail and storing documents on their computers and mobile devices, as well as traveling more with these devices. And even if the data on a device is not the primary reason for a theft, any unencrypted sensitive data stored on the stolen device is at risk of being exposed or used for fraudulent purposes, and this is happening at unprecedented levels today.

Hardware loss also occurs when hardware is being transported in luggage or in a package that is lost by an airline or shipping company or when hardware is stolen during transit (for example, two thieves recently used forklifts to steal two pallets containing 3,600 iPads from a JFK cargo building); it can also occur when an individual misplaces or otherwise loses a piece of hardware. With the vast number of portable devices that individuals carry with them today (such as portable computers, media tablets, mobile phones, and USB flash drives), this latter type of hardware loss is a growing concern—by one estimate, 70 million mobile phones are lost annually in the United States alone. While lost hardware may be covered by insurance and the data stored on a lost or stolen device may not be used in a fraudulent manner, having to replace the hardware and restore the data—or, worse yet, losing the data entirely if it was not backed up—is still a huge inconvenience. If any sensitive data (such as Social Security numbers, Web site passwords, or credit card data) was contained on the lost hardware, individuals risk identity theft; in fact, one study revealed that 80% of users store information that could be used for identity theft on their mobile phones. Businesses hosting sensitive data that is breached have to deal with the numerous issues and potential consequences of that loss, such as notifying customers that their personal information was exposed (as required by nearly all of the states in the United States), responding to potential lawsuits, and trying to repair damage to the company's reputation.

TIP

According to one recent study, data breaches cost U.S. companies nearly $200 per compromised personal record.

Hardware Damage

Computer hardware often consists of relatively delicate components that can be damaged easily by power fluctuations, heat, dust, static electricity, water, and abuse. For instance, fans clogged by dust can cause a computer to overheat, dropping a device will often break it, and spilling a drink on a keyboard or leaving a mobile phone in the pocket of your jeans while they go through the wash will likely damage or ruin it. In addition to accidental damage, computers and other hardware can also be intentionally damaged by burglars, vandals, disgruntled employees, and other individuals who have access to the hardware.

TIP

To avoid future problems, some damaged landline telephone lines (such as those on the East Coast damaged by Hurricane Sandy) are being replaced with fixed wireless systems, such as Verizon's *Voice Link* system.

System Failure and Other Disasters

Although many of us may prefer not to think about it, **system failure**—the complete malfunction of a computer system—and other types of computer-related disasters do happen. From accidentally deleting a file to having your computer just stop working, computer problems can be a huge inconvenience, as well as cost you a great deal of time and money. When the system contains your personal documents and data, it is a problem; when it

>**Hardware theft.** The theft of computer hardware. >**System failure.** The complete malfunction of a computer system.

contains the only copy of your company records or controls a vital system—such as a nuclear power plant—it can be a disaster.

System failure can occur because of a hardware problem, software problem, or computer virus. It can also occur because of a natural disaster (such as a tornado, fire, flood, or hurricane), sabotage, or a terrorist attack. The terrorist attack on the New York City World Trade Center Twin Towers on September 11, 2001, illustrated this all too clearly. When the Twin Towers collapsed, nearly 3,000 people were killed and hundreds of offices—over 13 million square feet of office space—were completely destroyed; another 7 million square feet of office space was damaged (see Figure 5-1). In addition to the devastating human loss, the offices located in the WTC lost their computer systems—including all the equipment, records, and data stored at that location. The ramifications of these system failures and the corresponding data loss were felt around the world by all the businesses and people connected directly or indirectly to these organizations.

Courtesy of Verizon Communications

FIGURE 5-1
System destruction. The 9/11 attacks killed nearly 3,000 people and destroyed hundreds of business offices, including critical cables located in this Verizon office adjacent to Ground Zero.

Protecting Against Hardware Loss, Hardware Damage, and System Failure

To protect against hardware loss, hardware damage, and system failure, a number of precautions can be taken, as discussed next.

Door and Computer Equipment Locks

Locked doors and equipment can be simple deterrents to computer theft. For instance, doors to facilities should be secured with door locks, alarm systems, and whatever other access control methods (such as the possessed object and biometric access systems discussed in Chapter 4) are needed to make it difficult to gain access to hardware that might be stolen. In addition, employees should be trained regarding the proper procedures for ensuring visitors only have access to the parts of the facility that they are authorized to access. To evaluate their employees and security procedures, some companies use *social engineering tests*, also known as *vulnerability assessments*. For instance, these tests check whether or not employees will click a phishing e-mail message or give out sensitive information in response to a phishing telephone call, will grant a potential thief physical access to the facility, or will plug a USB flash drive found in the office or parking lot (and potentially containing malware planted by a hacker) into their computers. To perform a social engineering test, one company (TraceSecurity) has engineers that typically impersonate pest control workers or fire inspectors in order to gain entry to server rooms and other locations where they can then access sensitive data and equipment. They sometimes precede their visit with a spoofed internal e-mail to office employees, such as announcing an upcoming pest inspection and requesting employees grant the pest control workers full access to check for infestation. Once at the office, TraceSecurity personnel attempt to talk their way into the building and into a room that allows access to the company network. As proof of access, they tag equipment with TraceSecurity stickers (see Figure 5-2), take photographs of the documents and data they were able to access, and sometimes even remove hardware from the building (assuming the business requests this and has granted the appropriate permission). The business then receives a report detailing which tests employees passed and failed, as well as recommendations for precautions that should be taken.

FIGURE 5-2
Social engineering tests. The red and white stickers mark equipment accessed during a TraceSecurity test.

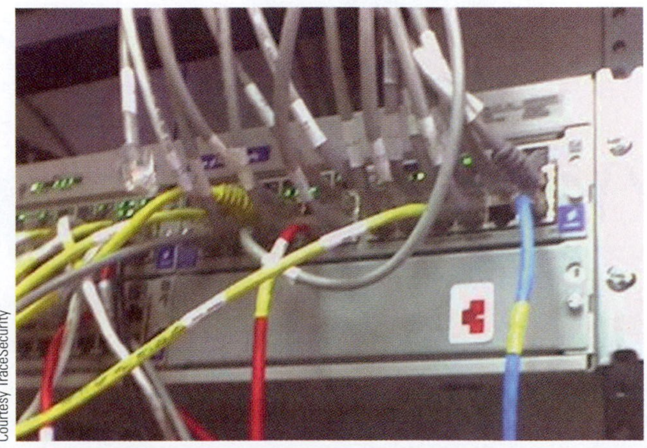

Courtesy TraceSecurity

To secure computers and other hardware to a table or other object that is difficult to move, *cable locks* can be used. Cable locks are frequently used to secure computers, media tablets, monitors, external hard drives, and other hardware found in schools and

TREND

Self-Healing Devices

Imagine being able to drop your phone or laptop without worrying about permanently damaging it. Or not having to worry about getting scratches on a touch screen. Well, you may be in luck in the near future. While protective cases and screen protectors have been available for quite some time, researchers are now going a step further by working on ways for your device to heal itself when damaged. For example, researchers at the University of Southern Mississippi in Hattiesburg recently announced a new type of plastic that mimics our skin's ability to repair itself. When the plastic is scratched or cracked, it breaks the tiny molecular links in the material, which results in that area turning red. When the plastic is exposed to light or temperature changes, it reforms—or "repairs"—itself.

Another example is the *Scratch Shield* iPhone case developed by Nissan and shown in the accompanying photograph. This case uses a special paint that can slowly return to its original state after being damaged, such as when the case receives scratches or even deep cuts. Small scratches can heal in as little as an hour; deeper scratches can take up to a week. While the paint was developed initially for use with Nissan and Infiniti cars, this iPhone case is currently being tested and may be available in the near future.

Courtesy Nissan

This Scratch Shield case from Nissan can repair itself when scratched.

TIP

iPad security cases are increasingly being used with iPads in retail environments so they can be securely used by employees and/or customers.

businesses. They are also used by college students, business travelers, and other individuals while on the go to temporarily secure their portable devices when they are not being used. To facilitate using a computer lock, most computers today come with a *security slot*—a small opening built into the system unit case designed for computer locks (see Figure 5-3). If a security slot is not available, *cable anchors* (which attach to a piece of hardware using industrial strength adhesive and which contain a connector through which the cable lock can be passed) or special *security cases* (which enclose a device and attach to a cable lock—refer again to Figure 5-3) can be used. Computer locks are available in key and number or letter combination versions.

As an additional precaution with portable computers, *laptop alarm software* that emits a very loud alarm noise if the computer is unplugged, if USB devices are removed, or if the computer is shut down without the owner's permission can be used. In addition to physically securing computers, it is also extremely important for businesses to ensure that employees follow security protocols related to portable storage media such as signing in and out portable hard drives, USB flash drives, and other storage media if required, and keeping those devices locked up when they are not in use. An emerging option for protecting mobile devices from physical damage—*self-healing devices*—is discussed in the Trend box.

FIGURE 5-3
Cable locks secure computers and other hardware.

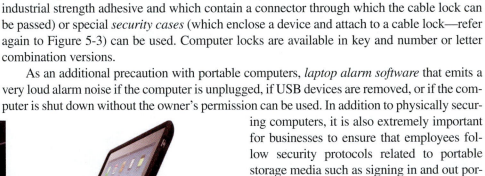

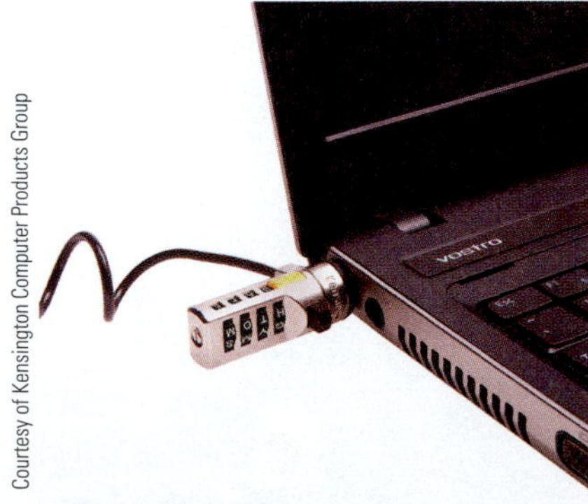

Courtesy of Kensington Computer Products Group

NOTEBOOK LOCKS
This combination cable lock connects to the security slot built into the notebook computer.

SECURITY CASES
This iPad security case/stand encloses the iPad and secures it via a keyed cable lock.

Encryption and Self-Encrypting Hard Drives

As discussed in Chapter 4, encryption can be used to prevent a file from being readable if it is intercepted or viewed by an unauthorized individual. To protect the data on an entire computer in case it is lost or stolen, **full disk encryption (FDE)** can be used. FDE systems encrypt everything stored on the drive (the operating system, application programs, data, temporary files, and so forth) automatically without any user interaction, so users don't have to remember to encrypt sensitive documents and the encryption is always enabled. To access a hard drive that uses FDE (often referred to as a **self-encrypting hard drive**), a username and password, biometric characteristic, or other authentication control is needed.

While self-encrypting hard drives are used most often with portable computers (in fact, the U.S. federal government is in the process of implementing FDE on all government-owned portable computers and mobile devices), they are also used with desktop computers and servers. Because FDE requires no user input to enable it and all files are encrypted automatically, these systems provide an easy way to ensure all data is protected, provided strong passwords are used in conjunction with the encryption system so the system cannot be easily hacked. Devices using *hardware encryption* with *hardware authentication*, where both the encryption and authentication systems are built into hardware (such as the device itself or a microSD card) instead of using software, are even more secure against hackers. Encrypted devices are used today by individuals, as well as businesses. In addition, businesses, such as law firms, are beginning to use encryption systems with their mobile phones in order to protect client-related voice calls and text messages.

Encryption can also be used to protect the data stored on removable media, such as flash memory cards and USB flash drives; a strong password, a biometric feature, or a PIN number (such as is used with the device shown in Figure 5-4) provides access to the data on the drive. Many encrypted devices allow multiple users to be registered as authorized users (by assigning each individual a password or registering his or her fingerprint image, for instance); some allow a portion of the device to be designated as unencrypted for nonsensitive documents, if desired. Many businesses today are requiring that all desktop computers, portable computers, portable storage devices, and mobile phones issued to employees be encrypted in order to protect against a data breach.

ASK THE EXPERT

Courtesy SONIC

Craig Miller, Chief Information Officer, Sonic, America's Drive-In

If the computers or software supporting the order entry system in one of your restaurants fails, can the restaurant still process orders?

Even in this age of dependency on technology, SONIC drive-in locations can continue to run should our point-of-sales (POS) system not function. Each drive-in is equipped with a crash kit that includes guest tickets for order taking, menus for pricing reference, and a "tax chart" so that crew members can manually take orders. SONIC crew members also have specific steps that our Operations team has set out for them to follow. Our main focus is to ensure guest satisfaction remains high, even if our system goes down.

LOK-IT Secure Flash Drive®

FIGURE 5-4
Encrypted devices.
The data on this encrypted USB flash drive cannot be accessed until the user enters the appropriate PIN.

Device Tracking Software and Antitheft Tools

Some software tools are not designed to prevent hardware from being stolen; instead, they are designed to aid in its recovery. This can be beneficial because, according to FBI statistics, 1 in 10 newly-purchased laptops will be stolen within 12 months and only 3% will be recovered. One software tool that can be used to help increase the chances of a stolen or lost device being recovered is *device tracking software*. When a device with tracking

>**Full disk encryption (FDE).** A technology that encrypts everything stored on a storage medium automatically, without any user interaction.
>**Self-encrypting hard drive.** A hard drive that uses full disk encryption (FDE).

HOW IT WORKS

Self-Destructing Devices

When a business or an individual is less concerned about recovering a stolen device than about ensuring the data located on the device is not compromised, devices that self-destruct upon command are a viable option. Available as part of some device tracking apps, as well as stand-alone utilities, *kill switch* capabilities destroy the data on a device (typically by overwriting preselected files multiple times, rendering them unreadable) when instructed—see the example in the accompanying illustration. Kill switches built into device tracking systems are typically activated by the customer or by the tracking company upon customer request when the device is determined to be lost or stolen. Once the kill switch is activated, all data on the device is erased the next time it connects to the Internet or when another predesignated remote trigger is activated (such as a certain number of unsuccessful logon attempts). Users of some cloud services can also use those services to remotely wipe their mobile devices when needed.

Kill switch technology is also beginning to be built into some USB flash drives and hard drives. For example, some encrypted hard drives automatically delete the encryption key (which leaves the data unaccessible) after a specific number of unsuccessful password entry attempts. Not quite *Mission Impossible*, but when hardware containing sensitive data is stolen (which could impact an individual's personal privacy or a business's legal liability, reputation, and bottom line), kill switch technology could save the day.

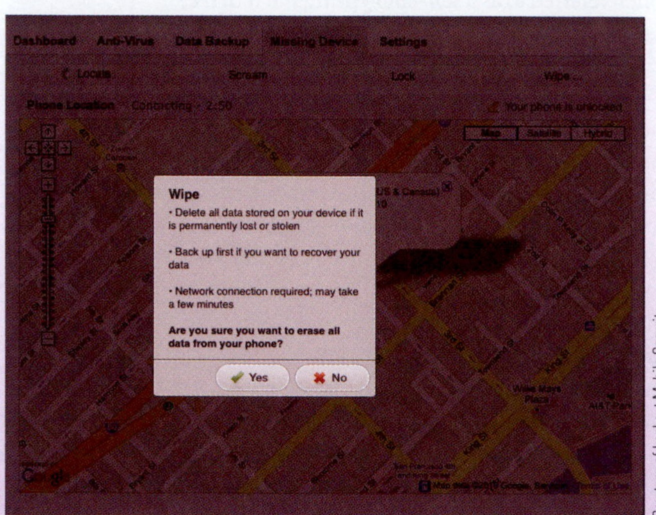

Courtesy of Lookout Mobile Security

FIGURE 5-5
Device tracking software.

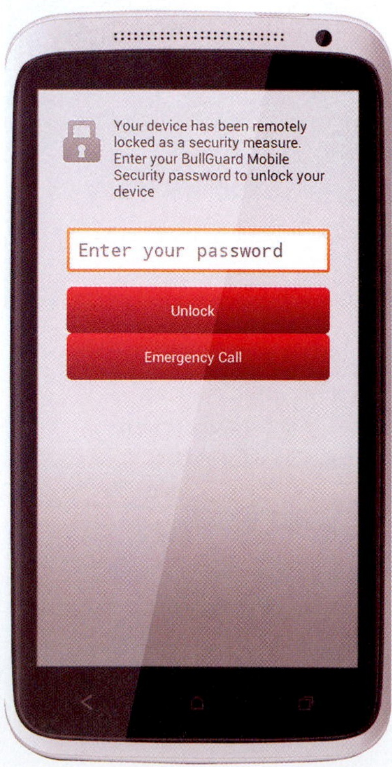

Courtesy Bullguard

software installed is reported lost or stolen, the tracking software sends information about the location of the device, typically determined by GPS or the nearest Wi-Fi network, to the tracking software company on a regular basis when the device is connected to the Internet so that information can be provided to law enforcement agencies to help them recover the device. Some tracking software can even take video or photos of the person using the stolen device (via the device's video camera) to help identify and prosecute the thief.

Most tracking software is available on a subscription basis; to protect itself, most tracking software can also survive operating system reinstallations and hard drive reformats. Some can also display a message on the screen when the device is lost or stolen. This message might be a plea to return the device for a reward or simply a message like "THIS DEVICE IS STOLEN" in a big bright banner on the desktop or lock screen to call attention to the fact that the device is stolen. Another common option is the ability to *remotely lock* the device and display a message that the device is locked and won't function without the appropriate password (see one example in Figure 5-5). A feature included in many device tracking programs is a *kill switch*—a technology that causes the device to self-destruct, as discussed in the How It Works box. A different type of kill switch that federal prosecutors are urging smartphone manufacturers to implement as part of the 2013 *Secure Our Smartphones (SOS) Initiative* is technology that would make all stolen smartphones inoperable, on any network, anywhere in the world, even if the SIM card is removed. This push is due to growing crime—including murder—related to smartphone theft. In fact, one in every three robberies nationwide involves a stolen mobile phone.

Another antitheft tool is the use of *asset tags* on hardware and other expensive assets. These labels usually identify the owner of the asset and are designed to be permanently attached to the asset. Some tags are designed to be indestructible; others are *tamper evident labels* that change their appearance if someone (such as a thief) tries to remove them. For instance, some labels have a printed message hidden underneath the label that is etched into the surface of the device and is exposed when the label is removed. Both of these features alert a potential buyer to the fact that the item is likely stolen.

MOBILE COMPUTING PRECAUTIONS

- Install and use encryption, antivirus, antispyware, and firewall software.
- Secure computers with boot passwords; set your mobile phone to autolock the screen after a short period of time and require a passcode to unlock it.
- Use only secure Wi-Fi connections and disable Wi-Fi and Bluetooth when they are not needed.
- Never leave usernames, passwords, or other data attached to your computer or inside its carrying case.
- Use a plain carrying case to make a portable computer less conspicuous.
- Keep an eye on your devices at all times, especially when going through airport security.
- Avoid setting your devices on the floor or leaving them in your hotel room; use a cable lock to secure the device to a desk or other object whenever this is unavoidable.
- Back up the data stored on the device regularly, but don't carry the backup media with your device and don't store unencrypted sensitive data on your device.
- Consider installing tracking or kill switch software.

FIGURE 5-6
Common-sense precautions for portable computer and mobile device users.

Additional Precautions for Mobile Users

With the increased use of smartphones and other mobile devices today, securing these devices against theft and unauthorized use is becoming increasingly more important. Businesses today often utilize *mobile device management* (*MDM*) software to manage the various mobile devices used by their employees. For instance, MDM software can control the apps installed or available on a device, or disable the camera while on the premises if cameras are not allowed. In addition, the software typically includes device tracking software to remotely lock down or wipe a lost or stolen phone, display a message on the phone containing instructions for returning the device, display the current location of the device on a map (using GPS coordinates), and/or overrule volume settings to play a loud sound to help the owner locate the phone if it is nearby. Another option is a *wireless tether* system that ties your phone to a key fob in order to sound an alarm and lock the phone if the phone and key fob become further away than the specified allowable distance. However, to avoid losing the device in the first place or to prevent someone from accessing the data stored on the device, other precautions should be used.

While on the go, the best antitheft measure is common sense. For example, you should never leave a portable computer or mobile device unattended in a public location (keep it in your line of sight or in physical contact at all times so it cannot be stolen without you noticing). When staying in a hotel, take your computer with you, use a cable lock to secure it to a piece of furniture, or lock it in a hotel safe (many hotel rooms today have room safes large enough to hold a portable computer) when you leave your hotel room for the day. Other sensible precautions include using a plain carrying case to make a portable computer less conspicuous and labeling your portable computer (and other portable devices and hardware that you take with you on the go) with your contact information so a lost or stolen device can be returned to you when it is recovered. One additional possibility for protecting data while on the road is using cloud services to store all data online or on the company server instead of on your device—if no data is stored on the device, then there is no data that can be directly compromised if the device is lost or stolen. In addition, mobile users should disable wireless connections when they are not needed and enable password protection for accessing the device. These precautions are summarized in Figure 5-6.

FIGURE 5-7
Protective cases.

MOBILE PHONES

MEDIA TABLETS

Courtesy of OtterBox

Proper Hardware Care

Proper care of hardware can help to prevent serious damage to a computer system. The most obvious precaution is to not harm your hardware physically, such as by dropping a device, knocking a piece of hardware off a desk, or jostling a desktop computer's system unit. *Protective cases* (see Figure 5-7) can be used

© iStockPhoto.com/aijohn784

RUGGED LAPTOPS

Courtesy Xplore Technologies Corp.

RUGGED TABLETS

Courtesy Kyocera

RUGGED PHONES

FIGURE 5-8
Ruggedized devices.

to help protect portable devices against minor abuse. These cases are usually padded or made from protective material to prevent damage due to occasional bumps and bangs; they typically also have a thin protective layer over the device's display to protect against scratches. Some protective cases are water resistant to protect the device from rain or dust damage. There are also neoprene *laptop sleeves* available to protect portable computers from scratches and other damage when they are carried in a conventional briefcase or bag.

TIP

Some devices today look conventional but have some rugged features, such as the Sony *Xperia Tablet Z* media tablet and the Kyocera *Hydro* smartphone that can withstand being under 1 meter (about 3 feet) of water for up to 30 minutes.

For users who need more protection than a protective case can provide, **ruggedized devices** are available (see Figure 5-8). These devices are designed to withstand much more physical abuse than conventional devices and range from *semirugged* to *ultrarugged*. For instance, semirugged devices typically have a more durable case and are spill-resistant. Rugged and ultrarugged devices go a few steps further—they are designed to withstand falls from three feet or more onto concrete, extreme temperature ranges, wet conditions, and use while being bounced around over rough terrain in a vehicle. Many rugged devices are also cooled without fans to avoid bringing dust into the circuitry; some are designed to be used in bright sunlight and while wearing gloves. Ruggedized devices are used most often by individuals who work out of the office, such as field workers, construction workers, outdoor technicians, military personnel, police officers, and firefighters.

FIGURE 5-9
Surge suppressors and uninterruptible power supplies (UPSs).

Courtesy of Schneider Electric

SURGE SUPPRESSOR

UPS

To protect hardware from damage due to power fluctuations, it is important for all users to use a **surge suppressor** (see Figure 5-9); the surge suppressor should be used to connect a computer and other hardware whenever they are plugged into a power outlet. When electrical power spikes occur, the surge suppressor prevents them from harming your devices. For the best protection, surge suppressors should be used with all the powered components that have a wired connection to the computer (such as a monitor or printer). There are small surge suppressors designed for use while on the go, and others designed for business and industrial use.

Users who want their desktop computers to remain powered up when the electricity goes off should use an **uninterruptible power supply (UPS)**, which contains a built-in battery (see Figure 5-9). The length of time that a UPS can power a system depends on the type and

>Ruggedized device. A device (such as a portable computer or mobile phone) that is designed to withstand much more physical abuse than its conventional counterpart. **>Surge suppressor.** A device that protects hardware from damage due to electrical fluctuations. **>Uninterruptible power supply (UPS).** A device containing a built-in battery that provides continuous power to a computer and other connected components when the electricity goes out.

number of devices connected to the UPS, the power capacity of the UPS device (typically measured in watts), and the age of the battery (most UPS batteries last only 3 to 5 years before they need to be replaced). Most UPS devices also protect against power fluctuations. UPSs designed for use by individuals usually provide power for a few minutes to keep the system powered up during short power blips, as well as to allow the user to save open documents and shut down the computer properly in case the electricity remains off. Industrial-level UPSs typically run for a significantly longer amount of time (such as a few hours), but not long enough to power a facility during an extended power outage such as those that happen periodically in some parts of the United States due to winter storms, summer rotating blackouts, and other factors. To provide longer-term power during extended power outages, as well as to provide continuous power to facilities (such as hospitals, nuclear power plants, and business data centers) that cannot afford to be without power for any period of time, *generators* can be used.

TIP

Use surge suppressors to protect all of your sensitive electronics, such as televisions and gaming consoles in addition to computers, from electrical fluctuations.

Dust, heat, static electricity, and moisture can also be dangerous to hardware, so be sure not to place your devices in direct sunlight or in a dusty area. Small handheld vacuums made for electrical equipment can be used periodically to remove the dust from the keyboard and from inside the system unit of a computer, but be very careful when vacuuming inside the system unit. Also, be sure the system unit has plenty of ventilation, especially around the fan vents. To help reduce the amount of dust that is drawn into the fan vents, raise your desktop computer several inches off the floor. You should also avoid placing a portable computer on a soft surface, such as a couch or blanket, to help prevent overheating (*notebook cooling stands* can be used to provide air circulation when a soft surface must be used). To prevent static electricity from damaging the inside of your computer when installing a new expansion card, RAM, or other internal device, turn off the power to the computer and unplug the power cord from the computer before removing the cover from the system unit. Wearing an antistatic wristband is an additional good precaution. Unless your computer is ruggedized (like the one shown in Figure 5-10), do not get it wet or otherwise expose it to adverse conditions. Be especially careful with mobile phones and other mobile devices when you are near water (such as a swimming pool, lake, or large puddle) so you do not drop them into the water (more than 50% of the phones received by one data recovery firm are water damaged).

FIGURE 5-10
Proper hardware care. Unless your computer is ruggedized (such as the one shown here), keep it out of the heat, cold, rain, water, and other adverse conditions.

Courtesy General Dynamics Itronix

Both internal and external magnetic hard drives also need to be protected against jostling or other excess motion that can result in a *head crash*, which occurs when a hard drive's read/write heads actually touch the surface of a hard disk. Unless your portable computer contains a solid-state drive instead of a magnetic hard drive, it is a good idea to turn off the computer, hibernate it, or put it into standby mode before moving it because magnetic hard drives are more vulnerable to damage while they are spinning. In addition, storage media—such as flash memory cards, hard drives, CDs, and DVDs—are all sensitive storage media that work well over time, as long as appropriate care is used. Don't remove a USB storage device (such as a USB flash drive or USB hard drive) when it is being accessed—use the *Safely Remove Hardware and Eject Media* icon in the system tray on a Windows computer to stop the device before unplugging it to avoid data loss and damage to the device. Keep CDs and DVDs in their protective *jewel cases* and handle them carefully to prevent fingerprints and scratches on the data sides of the discs (usually the bottom, unprinted side on a single-sided disc). A *screen protector* (a thin plastic film that covers the display screen of a smartphone or other mobile device) can be used to protect the displays of pen-based and touch devices.

For more tips on how to protect your desktop or portable computer, see the Technology and You box. Many of these tips apply to smartphones, media tablets, and other mobile devices as well.

TECHNOLOGY AND YOU

Protecting Your PC

All computer users should take specific actions to protect their computers. In this world of viruses, worms, hackers, spyware, and "buggy" (error-prone) software, it pays to be cautious. Although safeguards have been covered in detail throughout this book, some specific precautionary steps all computer users should follow are summarized in this box.

Step 1: Protect your hardware.
Be sure to plug all components of your computer system (such as the system unit, monitor, printer, and scanner) into a surge suppressor. Be careful not to bump or move the computer when it is on. Don't spill food or drink onto the keyboard or any other piece of hardware. Store your flash memory cards and CDs properly. If you need to work inside the system unit, turn off the computer and unplug it before touching any component inside the system unit. When taking a portable computer on the road, never leave it unattended, and be careful not to drop or lose it.

Step 2: Install and use security software.
Install a good security program and set it up to scan your system on a continual basis, including checking all files and e-mail messages before they are downloaded to your computer. To detect the newest viruses and types of malware, keep your security program up to date (have it automatically check for and install updates) and use a personal two-way firewall program to protect your computer from unauthorized access via the Internet, as well as to detect any attempts by spyware to send data from your computer to another party. For additional protection, enable file sharing only for files and folders that really need to be accessed by other users. Run an antispyware program—such as Ad-Aware or Spybot Search & Destroy—on a regular basis to detect and remove spyware.

Step 3: Back up regularly.
Once you have a new computer set up with all programs installed and the menus and other settings the way you like them, create a full backup so the computer can be restored to that configuration in case of a major problem with your computer or hard drive. Be sure also to back up your data files on a regular basis. Depending on how important your documents are, you may want to back up all of your data every night, or copy each document to a removable storage medium after each major revision. If you use local (instead of Web-based) e-mail, periodically back up the folder containing your e-mail, such as the *Outlook.pst* file used to store Microsoft Outlook mail. To facilitate data backup, keep your data organized using folders (such as storing all data files in a main folder called "Data"). For an even higher level of security, use *continuous data protection (CDP)* in conjunction with an external hard drive or an online backup service (see the iDrive CDP program in the accompanying illustration)—if your main hard drive ever becomes unstable and needs to be reformatted or replaced, you can restore your computer using the backup. If an online backup service is not used, backup media should be stored in a location that is different from the location where your computer is stored, such as in a different building or in a fire-resistant safe.

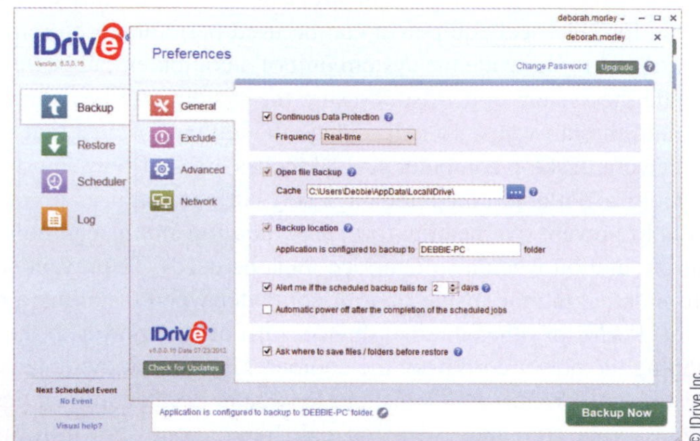

Continuous data protection (CDP) protects your data on an ongoing basis.

Step 4: Update your operating system, browser, and e-mail program regularly.
Most companies that produce operating systems, Web browsers, or e-mail programs regularly post updates and patches—small programs that take care of software-specific problems or bugs, such as security holes—on their Web sites regularly. Some programs include an option within the program to check online for updates; for other programs, you will need to go to each manufacturer's Web site directly to check for any critical or recommended updates. For any programs—such as Windows and most antivirus and firewall programs—that have the option to check for updates automatically, enable that option.

Step 5: Test your system for vulnerabilities.
There are several free tests available through Web sites to see if your computer's ports are accessible to hackers or if your computer is infected with a virus or spyware. These tests, such as the one on the Symantec Web site shown in Figure 4-10 in Chapter 4 or the ShieldsUP! test available on the Gibson Research Web site, should be run to check for any remaining vulnerabilities once you believe your antivirus software, firewall, and any other protective components you are using are set up correctly.

Backups and Disaster Recovery Plans

As mentioned in Chapter 1, creating a *backup* means making a duplicate copy of important files so that when a problem occurs (such as a hard drive failure or a stolen computer), you can restore those files using the backup copy. Data to be backed up includes company files, personal documents, photos, e-mail messages, and any other files that are important and the owner of the files would miss if they were lost. Backups can be performed for personal computers, servers, mobile phones, and other devices that contain important data. Backing up a smartphone often involves syncing the data to a cloud account or a computer.

Businesses should make backups of at least all new data on a regular basis (at least once per day) and include data located on both company computers and employer-issued smartphones. Individuals should make backups of important documents as they are created and back up the rest of their data periodically. Businesses and individuals that utilize cloud computing should also back up important data stored online.

After a backup is performed, the backup media used needs to be secured so that it will be intact when it is needed. If backup media is stored in-house, it should be placed in a fire-resistant safe; however, it is even better to store backup media in a different physical location or in the cloud. For instance, many businesses today use *online backup services* or *data storage companies* that store their backup media at a secure remote location; businesses can request their backups stored at a data storage facility be returned whenever they are needed. To secure the data on the backup media while it is in transit and being stored, as well as data stored in the cloud, the data should be encrypted.

For an even higher level of security than a scheduled backup, *continuous data protection* (*CDP*) can be used. A CDP backup system backs up data in real time as it changes so that data can be recovered from any point in time (even just a few minutes ago) with no data loss, and recovery can be as fast as five minutes after a failure. Although expensive when used with large quantities of data, it is one of the best ways to ensure that company data is protected. In addition to business data, CDP is beginning to be used by individuals to safeguard their data (one online CDP backup service is shown in the Technology and You box). For extra protection against data loss due to a natural disaster or other geographic-specific risk, businesses should use cloud providers that are in a physical location that is different from the company's location.

To supplement backup procedures, businesses and other organizations should have a **disaster recovery plan** (also called a *business continuity* plan)—a plan that spells out what

ASK THE EXPERT

Courtesy of DriveSavers Data Recovery www.drivesavers.com

Mike Cobb, Director of Engineering, DriveSavers Data Recovery

Of the hard drives sent to you for recovery, what is the most common type of problem you see and is there a way that problem can be prevented?

We often receive hard drives that have severe media damage. That means that the read/write heads have come in contact with the platters and scraped off portions of the surface and data. This often occurs because the hard drive was left powered on after the problem occurred. The platters inside a drive spin at high speed, so a great deal of damage can occur in a very short period of time as the heads bounce around and create more debris. Eventually the damage becomes too great for even a professional data recovery company to overcome.

The best rule of thumb to prevent the loss of critical data is to back up religiously and to verify that the backup is really backing up the critical files. In addition, if a hard drive exhibits any sign of failure including unusual noises (such as repetitive clicking or grinding) and if the data is irreplaceable and has not been backed up recently, the best solution is to immediately shut down the computer and then seek the assistance of a professional data recovery company like DriveSavers.

TIP

Be sure backup generators and servers are located in an appropriate location; for example, they should not be in a basement or in any locations prone to flooding. As an extra precaution, consider moving primary servers or installing remote backup servers in regions of the country that don't have the same risk factors as the company's location.

>**Disaster recovery plan.** A written plan that describes the steps a company will take following the occurrence of a disaster.

> **TIP**
>
> Be sure to also back up important nonelectronic documents in your life, such as birth certificates, tax returns, passports, and so forth, by making copies of them and storing the copies in a safe place.

> **TIP**
>
> If you use Web mail and don't automatically download new messages to your computer, be sure to back up your Web mail frequently (such as by using *Gmail Backup* if you are a Gmail user) to avoid losing your mail if the Web mail service is disrupted.

the organization will do to prepare for and recover from a disruptive event, such as a fire, natural disaster, terrorist attack, power outage, or computer failure. Disaster recovery plans should include information about who will be in charge immediately after the disaster has occurred, what alternate facilities and equipment (including computers and mobile devices) can be used, where backup media is located, the priority of getting each operation back online, disaster insurance coverage information, emergency communications methods, and so forth. If a *hot site*—an alternate location equipped with the computers, cabling, desks, and other equipment necessary to keep a business's operations going—is to be used following a major disaster, it should be set up ahead of time, and information about the hot site should be included in the disaster recovery plan. Businesses that host their e-mail on site should also consider making arrangements with an *emergency mail system provider* to act as a temporary mail server if the company mail server is not functioning. Copies of the disaster recovery plan should be located off site, such as at an appropriate employee's house or at the office of an associated organization located in a different city.

It is important to realize that disaster recovery planning isn't just for large businesses. In fact, disasters such as a fire or computer malfunction can cause a small company to go out of business if its data is not backed up. Measures as straightforward as backing up data daily and storing the backups in a fire-resistant safe at the owner's house with a plan regarding how that data can be quickly reinstated on a new system or otherwise used for business continuity can go a long way in protecting a small business. Companies that are evaluating cloud computing services should find out what types of outages are to be expected (such as for regular maintenance) and what type of advance notice will be sent regarding these outages, as well as what types of disaster recovery services (such as switching to alternate servers if the main servers go down) are available.

The importance of a good disaster recovery plan was made obvious following the collapse of the World Trade Center Twin Towers in 2001. Minutes after the first airplane hit the towers, corporate executives, disaster recovery firms, and backup storage companies began arranging for employees and backup data to be moved to alternate sites. Employees at the data storage company Recall Corporation spent the day of the attack gathering backup tapes belonging to clients located in and near the attacks, using barcode readers to locate the needed 30,000 tapes out of the 2 million in their secure storage facility. Bond trader Cantor Fitzgerald, which lost 700 employees and all the equipment and data located in its WTC offices, relocated to a prearranged hot site where employees received backup tapes the day after the attack, and it was able to begin trading the next morning. Although Cantor Fitzgerald—like the other organizations and businesses located in the WTC—suffered enormous human loss, good disaster recovery planning enabled Cantor Fitzgerald to restore the records containing client accounts and portfolios completely, avoiding an additional economic disaster related to this tragedy.

> **TIP**
>
> The piracy of and ethical use of digital music and movies are discussed in detail in Chapter 6.

SOFTWARE PIRACY AND DIGITAL COUNTERFEITING

Instead of stealing an existing computer program, object, or other valuable that belongs to someone else, *software piracy* and *digital counterfeiting* involve creating duplicates of these items, and then selling them or using them as authentic items.

Software Piracy

Software piracy, the unauthorized copying of a computer program, is illegal in the United States and many other—but not all—countries. Because of the ease with which computers can create exact copies of a software program, software piracy is a widespread problem.

>**Software piracy.** The unauthorized copying of a computer program.

According to a recent study by research firm IDC, at least one-third of all software is counterfeit. In addition, 78% of pirated software has spyware attached to it and consumers visiting Web sites to obtain (typically stolen) activation keys for counterfeit software have a 36% chance of being infected with malware in the process. The study also estimates that the total annual cost to businesses of dealing with malware from counterfeit software exceeds $110 billion, and consumers worldwide will waste 1.5 billion hours each year dealing with the malware resulting from countefeit software.

Software piracy can take many forms, including individuals making illegal copies of programs to give to friends, businesses installing software on more computers than permitted in the program's *end-user license agreement* or *EULA* (see Figure 5-11), computer retailers installing unlicensed copies of software on computers sold to consumers, and large-scale operations in which the software and its packaging are illegally duplicated and then sold as supposedly legitimate products. Pirated software—as well as pirated music CDs and movie DVDs—are commonly offered for sale at online auctions; they can also be downloaded from some Web sites and peer-to-peer file sharing services. Creating and distributing pirated copies of any type of *intellectual property* (such as software, music, e-books, and movies) is illegal. Intellectual property is discussed in more detail in Chapter 6.

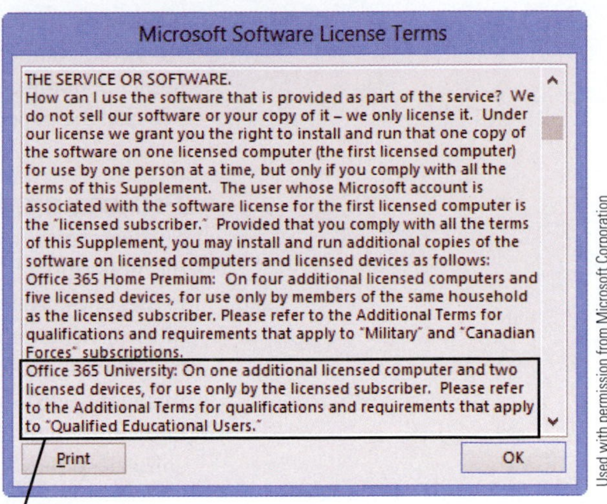

This software can be installed on one primary computer, one additional computer, and two additional devices to be used by a single user.

Used with permission from Microsoft Corporation

FIGURE 5-11
An end-user license agreement (EULA). Specifies the number of computers on which the software can be installed and other restrictions for use.

Digital Counterfeiting

The availability of high-quality, full-color imaging products (such as scanners, color printers, and color copiers) has made **digital counterfeiting**—creating counterfeit copies of items (such as currency and other printed resources) using computers and other types of digital equipment—easier and less costly than in the recent past. The U.S. Secret Service estimates that more than 60% of all counterfeit money today is produced digitally—up from 1% in 1996.

With digital counterfeiting, the bill (or other item to be counterfeited) is either color-copied or it is scanned into a computer and then printed. In addition to counterfeiting currency, other items that are digitally counterfeited include fake business checks, credit cards, printed collectibles (such as baseball cards or celebrity autographs), and fake identification papers (such as corporate IDs, driver's licenses, passports, and visas)—see Figure 5-12.

Counterfeiting is illegal in the United States and is taken very seriously. For creating or knowingly circulating counterfeit currency, for instance, offenders can face up to 15 years in prison for each offense. In spite of the risk of prosecution, counterfeiting of U.S. currency and other documents is a growing problem both in the United States and in other countries. Although the majority of counterfeit currency is produced by serious criminals (such as organized crime, gangs, and terrorist organizations), the Secret Service has seen an increase in counterfeiting among high school and college students. This is attributed primarily to the ease of creating counterfeit bills—although not necessarily high-quality counterfeit bills—using digital technology. Because the paper used with real U.S. bills is very expensive and cannot legally be made by paper mills for any other purpose and because U.S. bills contain a number of other characteristics that are difficult to reproduce accurately, as discussed in more

FIGURE 5-12
Digitally counterfeited documents.

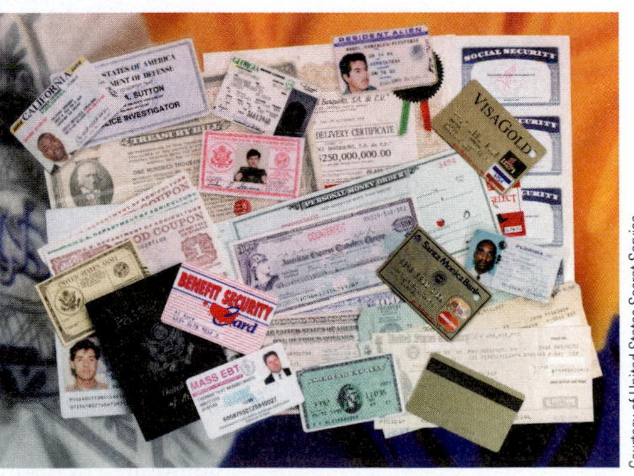

Courtesy of United States Secret Service

>**Digital counterfeiting.** The use of computers or other types of digital equipment to make illegal copies of currency, checks, collectibles, and other items.

detail shortly, the majority of the counterfeit money made by amateurs is easily detectable. However, counterfeit bills made by bleaching genuine small denomination bills and printing higher denominations on them that don't include special security features are harder to detect because the paper used is authentic.

Protecting Against Software Piracy and Digital Counterfeiting

Software piracy and digital counterfeiting affect individuals, as well as businesses and the government. For instance, some software companies charge higher prices and have less money available for research and development because of the losses from software pirates, which ultimately hurts law-abiding consumers. In addition, individuals and businesses that unknowingly accept counterfeit currency lose the face value of that currency if it is identified as counterfeit while it is in their possession, and they risk legal issues if they knowingly pass the counterfeit bills on to others. Some tools currently being used to curb software piracy and digital counterfeiting are discussed next.

Software Antipiracy Tools

One tool the software industry is using in an attempt to prevent software piracy is education. By educating businesses and consumers about the legal use of software and the possible negative consequences associated with breaking antipiracy laws, the industry hopes to reduce the use of illegal software. To counteract piracy performed because of time or convenience issues, many software companies offer consumers the option of downloading software and, therefore, giving them a legal option for obtaining software that is as fast and convenient as downloading a pirated version. Some software manufacturers have launched extensive public relations campaigns—such as including information on their Web sites, in product information, and in ads—to inform consumers what software piracy is, and why they should not commit it or buy pirated software.

Another antipiracy tool is requiring a unique activation code (often called a *registration code*, an *activation key*, or a *product key*) before the software can be installed (for commercial software) or before certain key features of a program are unlocked (for shareware or demo software). Typically the activation code is included in the product packaging (for software purchased on CD or DVD) or is displayed on the screen or sent to the user via e-mail once payment is made (for downloaded software). A related tool is checking the validity of a software installation before upgrades or other resources related to the program can be accessed. For instance, Microsoft checks a user's Windows installation before the user is allowed to download software from Microsoft's Web site (such as templates or updates for Microsoft Office)—if their operating system is identified as invalid, users cannot download the resources. The goal of these techniques is to make pirated software unusable enough so that individuals will buy the licensed software.

Other antipiracy techniques used by software companies include watching online auction sites and requesting the removal of suspicious items, as well as buying pirated copies of software via Web sites and then filing lawsuits against the sellers. The increase in actions against individuals who illegally sell or share software (and other types of digital content, such as music and movies) may also help reduce piracy and encourage individuals to obtain legal copies of these products. The inclusion of malware in counterfeit software may also help with detection. For example, Microsoft recently settled 3,265 software piracy cases worldwide—the majority of the cases were reported to Microsoft by customers unhappy with the included malware or because the software didn't work correctly. In addition, Microsoft continually finds and requests the removal of URLs that are related to the distribution of pirated software from search sites.

One new option for software vendors is incorporating code into their programs that is designed to inform the vendor when pirated copies of its software are being used or when its software is being used in another manner that violates the terms of the software license. For instance, commercial software that contains the newest version of V.i Labs *CodeArmor Intelligence* software is designed to detect and report products in use that have been tampered with (such as products whose licensing features have been disabled and then resold as legitimate products), as well as products that are being used with more computers than allowed by the software license. Once piracy is detected, information about the infringement is sent to the software vendor's piracy dashboard. This information includes identifying data about the user of the pirated software (such as the business's domain name or IP address and a link to its location on Google Maps—see Figure 5-13) that can be used to help the vendor contact the business to give them the opportunity to come into license compliance before pursuing any legal actions. It also provides the vendor with useful data about the overall state of piracy of their products in order to help the company make appropriate business decisions regarding the distribution channels and the safeguards used with its products.

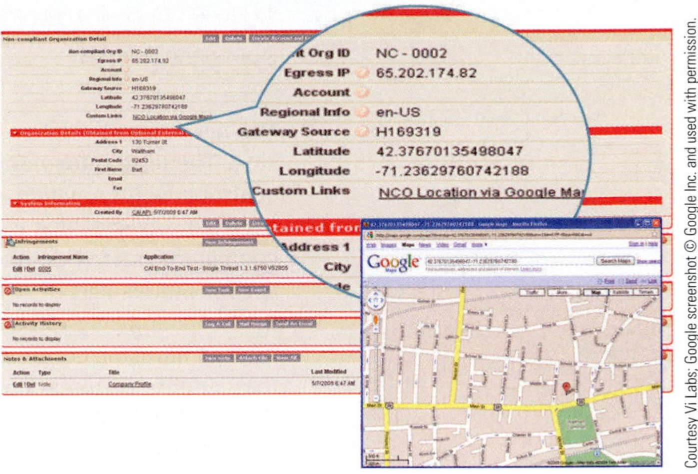

Courtesy Vi Labs; Google screenshot © Google Inc. and used with permission.

FIGURE 5-13
Antipiracy software.

Digital Counterfeiting Prevention

To prevent the counterfeiting of U.S. currency, the Treasury Department releases new currency designs every 7 to 10 years. These new designs (such as the new $100 bill released in 2013 and shown in Figure 5-14) contain features (such as *microprinting, watermarks*, a *security thread*, a *security ribbon, color-shifting ink,* and *raised printing*) that make the new currency much more difficult to duplicate than older currency. Because the watermarks, security thread, and security ribbon are embedded in the paper, counterfeiters are unable to duplicate those features when creating counterfeit bills either from scratch or by bleaching the ink out of existing lower-denomination bills and reprinting them with higher denominations. Consequently, counterfeit copies of bills using the new designs are easy to detect just by holding them up to the light and looking for the proper watermark, security thread, or security ribbon, or by feeling for the raised printing. In addition, hardware and software companies that have adopted the *counterfeit deterrence system* (*CDS*) developed by the *Central Bank Counterfeit Deterrence Group* (*CBCDG*) help to deter the use of digital counterfeiting of currency. For instance, some hardware and software will not allow images of currency to be printed and many color copiers print invisible codes on copied documents, making counterfeit money copied on those machines traceable.

Prevention measures for the counterfeiting of other types of documents—such as checks and identification cards—include using RFID tags, *digital watermarks*, and other difficult-to-reproduce content. As discussed in more detail in Chapter 6, a digital watermark is a subtle alteration that is not noticeable when the work is viewed or played but that can be read using special software to authenticate or identify the owner of the item. Finally, educating consumers about how the appearance of fake products differs from that of authentic products is a vital step in the ongoing battle against counterfeiting.

TIP

The new $100 bill also includes a large gold *100* on the back to help visually-impaired individuals identify the denomination.

FIGURE 5-14
Anticounterfeiting measures used with U.S. currency.

SECURITY THREAD
Embedded in the paper and contains *USA* and *100s*; glows pink when placed in front of an ultraviolet light.
SECURITY RIBBON
Woven into the paper and displays bells and then *100s* when the bill is moved.
MICROPRINTING
Extremely small print that is very difficult to reproduce appears in three different locations on the front of the bill (on the jacket collar, around the black space containing the watermark, and along the golden quill), though it is hard to see without a magnifying glass.
COLOR-SHIFTING INK
Changes the number *100* in the lower-right corner and the bell in the inkwell from copper to green as the bill is tilted.
WATERMARK
A Benjamin Franklin watermark located to the right of the portrait is visible when the bill is held up to the light.

Photo courtesy of U.S. Department of the Treasury

WHY BE CONCERNED ABOUT INFORMATION PRIVACY?

Privacy is usually defined as the state of being concealed or free from unauthorized intrusion. The term **information privacy** refers to the rights of individuals and companies to control how information about them is collected and used. The problem of how to protect personal privacy—that is, how to keep personal information private—existed long before computers entered the picture. For example, sealing wax and unique signet rings were used centuries ago to seal letters, wills, and other personal documents to guard against their content being revealed to unauthorized individuals, as well as to alert the recipient if such an intrusion occurred while the document was in transit. But today's computers, with their ability to store, duplicate, and manipulate large quantities of data—combined with the fact that databases containing our personal information can be accessed and shared via the Internet—have added a new twist to the issue of personal privacy. Another new twist is the increased ability of *electronic surveillance* tools used by some government and law enforcement agencies.

As discussed in Chapters 3 and 4, one concern of many individuals is the privacy of their Web site activities and e-mail messages. Cookies and spyware are possible privacy risks, and e-mail and other documents can be read if intercepted by another individual during transit unless they are encrypted. For businesses and employees, there is the additional issue of whether or not Web activities, e-mail, and instant messages sent through a company network are private. In addition, businesses need to make sure they comply with privacy laws regarding the protection and the security of the private information they store on their servers. Recently, there has been an unprecedented number of high-profile data breaches—some via hacking and other network intrusions discussed in Chapter 4, and others due to lost or stolen hardware, or carelessness with papers or storage media containing Social Security numbers or other sensitive data. Because every data breach occurring today is a risk to information privacy, protecting the data stored in databases today is an important concern for everyone. Other privacy concerns are *spam* and other marketing activities, electronic surveillance, and *electronic monitoring*. These concerns, along with precautions that can be taken to safeguard information privacy, are discussed throughout the remainder of this chapter.

ASK THE EXPERT

Courtesy of EFF

Jillian York, Director for International Freedom of Expression, Electronic Frontier Foundation (EFF)

What are the biggest Internet-related privacy risks for individuals today?

With Internet use on the rise globally, the latest threats to privacy come both from companies looking to capitalize on user data and from governments seeking to track citizens' conversations and movements. But although Internet users have good reason to be concerned about the privacy practices of corporations like Google, I believe the biggest threat facing them today is surveillance by government agencies, such as the United States' National Security Agency (NSA). The mass surveillance conducted by such agencies means that all of us are being spied on, whether or not we're suspected of committing a crime. It is all too easy for governments to abuse this type of power. Even if you think you have nothing to hide, your privacy is being invaded on a daily basis by governments and by big business. To try to protect yourself, minimize the amount of personal data stored on your devices, encrypt your data and use secure passwords, and use privacy-enhancing browsing tools and settings.

>**Privacy.** The state of being concealed or free from unauthorized intrusion. >**Information privacy.** The rights of individuals and companies to control how information about them is collected and used.

DATABASES, ELECTRONIC PROFILING, SPAM, AND OTHER MARKETING ACTIVITIES

There are marketing activities that can be considered privacy risks or, at least, a potential invasion of privacy. These include *databases, electronic profiling*, and *spam*.

Databases and Electronic Profiling

Information about individuals can be located in many different databases. For example, most educational institutions have databases containing student information, most organizations use an employee database to hold employee information, and most physicians and health insurance providers maintain databases containing individuals' medical information. If these databases are adequately protected from hackers and other unauthorized individuals and if the data is not transported on a portable computer or other device that may be vulnerable to loss or theft, then these databases do not pose a significant privacy concern to consumers because the information can rarely be shared without the individuals' permission. However, the data stored in these types of databases is not always sufficiently protected and has been breached quite often in the past. Consequently, these databases, along with two other types of databases—*marketing databases* and *government databases*—that are typically associated with a higher risk of personal privacy violations and are discussed next, are of growing concern to privacy advocates.

Marketing databases contain marketing and demographic data about people, such as where they live and what products they buy. This information is used for marketing purposes, such as sending advertisements that fit each individual's interests (via regular mail or e-mail) or trying to sign people up over the phone for some type of service. Virtually anytime you provide information about yourself online or offline—for example, when you subscribe to a magazine, fill out a sweepstakes entry or product registration card, or buy a product or service using a credit card—there is a good chance that the information will find its way into a marketing database.

TIP

Judges and police investigators made 37,196 requests to Microsoft for end-user data in the first half of 2013 alone.

Marketing databases are also used in conjunction with Web activities, such as social media activity and searches performed via some personalized search services. For instance, the data stored on Facebook, MySpace, Google+, and other social networking sites can be gathered and used for advertising purposes by marketing companies, and the activities of users of personalized search services (where users log in to use the service) can be tracked and that data can be used for marketing purposes. And Google, with its vast array of services that collect enormous amounts of data about individuals, worries many privacy advocates. For instance, Google may have data stored about your search history (Google search site), browsing history (Google Chrome), e-mail (Gmail), appointments (Google Calendar), telephone calls (Google Voice), photos (Picasa Web Albums), shopping history (Google Checkout), and friends and activities (Google+). While Google allows users to *opt out* of collecting some data (such as by not signing into a service) and states that the data stored on separate servers is not combined, the vast amount of collected data is a concern to some.

TIP

To download a copy of your data stored within Google products, use the *Google Takeout* service.

Other emerging privacy concerns center on location-based services and reward apps. Location-based services, such as Foursquare, use the GPS information from your smartphone to provide services such as enabling you to meet up with friends who are close to your current location or allowing you to *check in* to the businesses that you frequent to share your location with others or participate in marketing activities. For example, reward apps, such as shopkick, offer you rewards or discounts for checking into participating businesses. While

>Marketing database. A collection of data about people that is stored in a large database and used for marketing purposes.

popular with many individuals, there is concern about location information being used inappropriately (such as by stalkers and home burglars), as well as if and for how long location data is stored. In addition, some of these apps (such as Foursquare) can tie into other social networks, such as Facebook or Twitter, so your friends on those social networks can access your location information even if they are not your friend on the location app.

Information about individuals is also available in **government databases**. Some information, such as Social Security earnings and income tax returns, is confidential and can legally be seen only by authorized individuals. Other information—such as birth records, marriage certificates, and divorce information, as well as property purchases, assessments, liens, and tax values—is available to the public, including to the marketing companies that specialize in creating marketing databases. One emerging government database application is the creation of a *national ID system* that links driver's license databases across the country. Although controversial, this system is mandated by the *Real ID Act* that was passed in 2005, which also requires states to meet new federal standards for driver's licenses and other identification cards (such as the inclusion of a barcode or other machine-readable technology that can be used in conjunction with the ID database). The emerging *Federal Services Data Hub* database that will be used to connect healthcare insurance exchanges with numerous federal databases containing Social Security, IRS, and other personal data of Americans in order to share data has also been controversial due to security and privacy concerns.

In the past, the data about any one individual was stored in a variety of separate locations, such as at different government agencies, individual retail stores, the person's bank and credit card companies, and so forth. Because it would be extremely time consuming to locate all the information about one person from all these different places, there was a fairly high level of information privacy. Today, however, most of an individual's data is stored on computers that can communicate with each other, and some *database search services* are available online for free or for a fee (see some examples in Figure 5-15). Although often

FIGURE 5-15
A variety of searchable databases are available via the Internet.

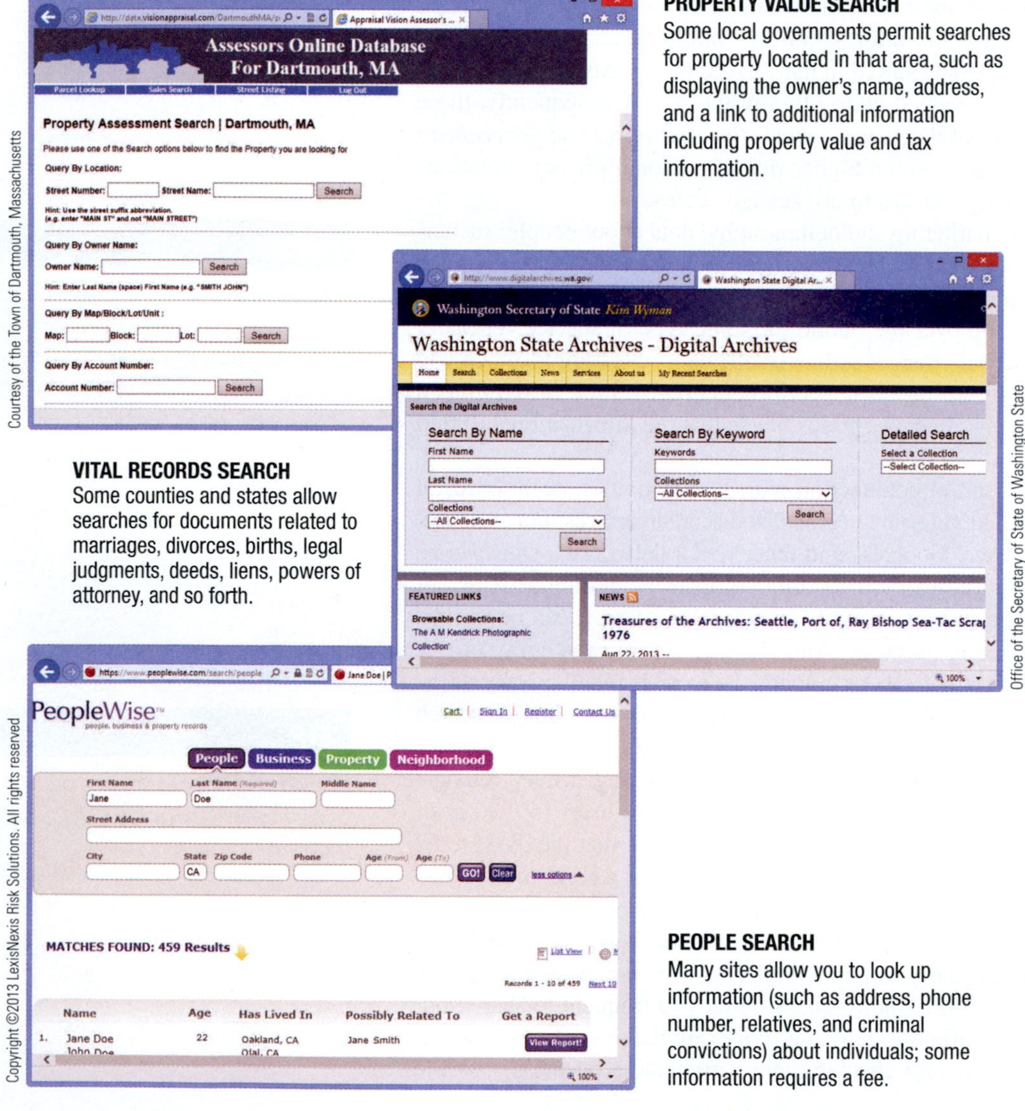
Assessors Online Database
For Dartmouth, MA
Property Assessment Search | Dartmouth, MA
PROPERTY VALUE SEARCH
Some local governments permit searches for property located in that area, such as displaying the owner's name, address, and a link to additional information including property value and tax information.
Washington State Archives - Digital Archives
Search By Name
Search By Keyword
Detailed Search
VITAL RECORDS SEARCH
Some counties and states allow searches for documents related to marriages, divorces, births, legal judgments, deeds, liens, powers of attorney, and so forth.
PeopleWise
People
Business
Property
Neighborhood
MATCHES FOUND: 459 Results
PEOPLE SEARCH
Many sites allow you to look up information (such as address, phone number, relatives, and criminal convictions) about individuals; some information requires a fee.

>**Government database.** A collection of data about people that is collected and maintained by the government.

When you make an electronic transaction, information about who you are and what you buy is recorded, usually in a database.

Databases containing the identities of people and what they buy are sold to marketing companies.

The marketing companies add the new data to their marketing databases; they can then reorganize the data in ways that might be valuable to other companies.

The marketing companies create lists of individuals matching the specific needs of companies; the companies buy the lists for their own marketing purposes.

FIGURE 5-16
How electronic profiling might work.

this ability to search online databases is an advantage—such as checking the background of a potential employee or looking up a misplaced phone number—it does raise privacy concerns. In response to the increased occurrence of identity theft (discussed in detail in Chapter 4), some local governments have removed birth and death information from their available online database records.

Collecting in-depth information about an individual is known as **electronic profiling**. Marketing companies often use data acquired from a variety of sources—such as from product and service purchases that are tied to personally identifiable information, as well as from public information like property values, vehicle registrations, births, marriages, and deaths—to create electronic profiles of individuals for marketing purposes. Electronic profiles are generally designed to provide specific information and can include an individual's name, current and previous addresses, telephone number, marital status, number and age of children, spending habits, and product preferences. The information retrieved from electronic profiles is then sold to companies upon request to be used for marketing purposes (see Figure 5-16). For example, one company might request a list of all individuals in a particular state whose street addresses are considered to be in an affluent area and who buy baby products. Another company might request a list of all SUV owners in a particular city who have not purchased a car in five years. Still another company may want a list of business travelers who fly to the East Coast frequently.

Most businesses and Web sites that collect personal information have a **privacy policy** (see the Facebook privacy policy in Figure 5-17) that discloses how the personal information you provide will be used. As long as their actions do not violate their privacy policy, it is legal for businesses to sell the personal data that they collect. There are some

FIGURE 5-17
Privacy policies. Web site privacy policies explain how your personal information might be used.

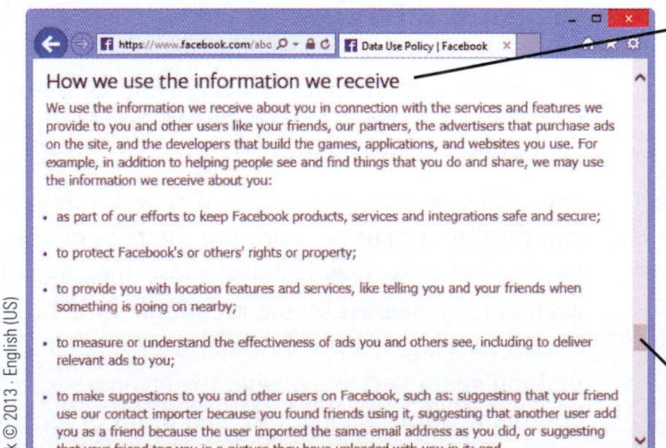

This section explains how your information may be used, such as to provide location services and to make suggestions based on Facebook activity.

Scroll to read other sections of the policy that explain how the data may be shared, how long it is kept, and more.

>Electronic profiling. Using electronic means to collect a variety of in-depth information about an individual, such as name, address, income, and buying habits. **>Privacy policy.** A policy, commonly posted on a company's Web site, that explains how personal information provided to that company will be used.

problems with privacy policies, however, such as the fact that they are sometimes difficult to decipher and the reality that most people do not take the time to read them before using a site. In addition, many businesses periodically change their privacy policies without warning, requiring consumers to reread privacy policies frequently or risk their personal information being used in a manner that they did not agree to when the information was initially provided. Some companies notify customers by e-mail when their privacy policies change but, more commonly, they expect customers to check the current policy periodically and notify the business if any new actions are objectionable.

Spam and Other Marketing Activities

Spam refers to unsolicited e-mail sent to a large group of individuals at one time. The electronic equivalent of junk mail (see Figure 5-18), spam is most often used to sell products or services to individuals. Spam is also used in phishing schemes and other dot cons and is sent frequently via botnets, as discussed in Chapter 4 (the text message spam shown in Figure 5-18 is an example of a phishing spam message). A great deal of spam involves health-related products (such as medicine or weight loss systems), counterfeit products (such as watches and medicine), pornography, and new—and often fraudulent—business opportunities and stock deals. Spam can also be generated by individuals forwarding e-mail messages they receive (such as jokes, recipes, or notices of possible new privacy or health concerns) to everyone in their address books. In addition to spam, most individuals receive marketing e-mails either from companies they directly provided with their e-mail addresses or from other companies that acquired their e-mail addresses from a third party to whom that information was provided (such as from a partner site or via a purchased mailing list). While these latter types of marketing e-mail messages do not technically fit the definition of spam because they were permission-based, many individuals consider them to be spam. Spam can also be sent via IM (called *spim*); via text message (called *mobile phone spam* or *SMS spam*); to Facebook, MySpace, Google+, and Twitter pages and via other social networking communications methods; via phone calls; and to fax machines.

FIGURE 5-18
Examples of spam.

E-MAIL SPAM

TEXT MESSAGE SPAM

While e-mail spam is decreasing as a result of better *spam filters* and other protections (discussed shortly), it is still a problem (Kasperkey Labs recently estimated that more about 72% of all e-mail messages are now spam). At best, spam is an annoyance to recipients and can slow down a mail server's delivery of important messages. At worst, spam can disable a mail network completely, or it can cause recipients to miss or lose important e-mail messages because those messages have been caught in a spam filter or were accidentally deleted by the recipient while he or she was deleting a large number of spam e-mail messages. Most Internet users spend several minutes each day dealing with spam, making spam very expensive for businesses in terms of lost productivity, consumption of communications bandwidth, and drain of technical support. Spam sent to a mobile phone (either via text message or e-mail) is also expensive for end users that have a limited data or text message allowance.

TIP

According to the Pew Internet & American Life Project, 69% of individuals who use text messaging on their mobile phones receive spam—25% said they face problems with spam texts at least weekly.

>**Spam.** Unsolicited, bulk e-mail sent over the Internet.

One of the most common ways of getting on a spam mailing list is by having your e-mail address entered into a marketing database, which can happen when you sign up for a free online service or use your e-mail address to register a product or make an online purchase. Spammers also use software to gather e-mail addresses from Web pages, online posts, and social networking sites. Many individuals view spam as an invasion of privacy because it arrives on computers without permission and costs them time and other resources (bandwidth, mailbox space, and hard drive space, for instance).

Most spam is legal, but there are requirements that must be adhered to in order for it to be legal. For instance, the *CAN-SPAM Act of 2003* established requirements (such as using truthful subject lines and honoring remove requests) for commercial e-mailers, as well as specified penalties for companies and individuals that break the law. While the *CAN-SPAM Act* has not reduced the amount of spam circulated today, it has increased the number of spammers prosecuted for sending spam. In fact, several spammers have been convicted in recent years. They have either been fined or sent to prison, and more are awaiting trial. For instance, one spammer was ordered to pay $230 million to MySpace for spamming MySpace users and another was ordered to pay Facebook a record $873 million for spamming its members.

TIP

When posting your e-mail address online, write it so individuals can read it, but spiders and other automated programs cannot, such as writing *johndoe at xyz.com* instead of *johndoe@xyz.com.* To send you an e-mail, individuals will just need to substitute the @ sign for the word "at" and the spaces surrounding it.

Protecting the Privacy of Personal Information

There are a number of precautions that can be taken to protect the privacy of personal information. Safeguarding your e-mail address and other personal information is a good start. You can also surf anonymously, *opt out* of some marketing activities, and use filters and other tools to limit your exposure to spam. Businesses also need to take adequate measures to protect the privacy of information stored on their servers and storage media. These precautions are discussed next.

Safeguard Your E-Mail Address

Protecting your e-mail address is one of the best ways to avoid spam. One way to accomplish this is to use one private e-mail address for family, friends, colleagues, and other trusted sources, and use a *disposable* or **throw-away e-mail address**—such as a second address obtained from your ISP or a free e-mail address from Yahoo! Mail, AOL Mail, Outlook.com, or Gmail (see Figure 5-19)—for online shopping, signing up for free offers, forums, product registration, and other activities that typically lead to junk e-mail. Although you will want to check your alternate e-mail address periodically (to check for online shopping receipts or shipping notifications, for instance), this precaution can prevent a great deal of spam from getting to your regular e-mail account.

Another advantage of using a throw-away e-mail address for only noncritical applications is that you can quit using it and obtain a new one if spam begins to get overwhelming or too annoying. To help with this, some ISPs (such as EarthLink) provide disposable anonymous e-mail addresses to their subscribers—e-mail messages sent to a subscriber's anonymous address are forwarded to the subscriber's account until the disposable address is deleted by the subscriber. Consequently, individuals can easily change disposable addresses when they

FIGURE 5-19
Free e-mail accounts. Can be used for throw-away e-mail addresses.

Click to create a free account.

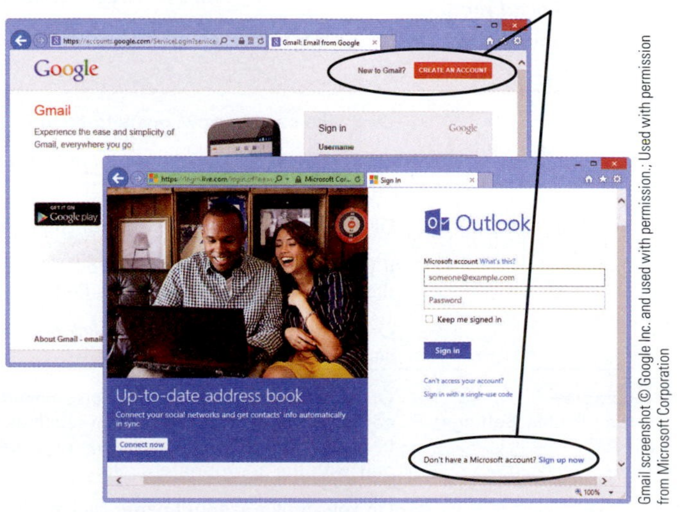

>Throw-away e-mail address. An e-mail address used only for nonessential purposes and activities that may result in spam; the address can be disposed of and replaced if spam becomes a problem; also called a *disposable e-mail address.*

TIP

If you only need an e-mail address for a very short period of time (such as to receive a confirmation for registering for a free online service), use a *temporary disposable e-mail address*, such as the ones available through *10 Minute Mail* that are valid for only 10 minutes.

begin to receive too much spam or when the disposable address is no longer needed. There are also *anonymous e-mail services* (such as the one provided by *Anonymous Speech*) that allow users to route e-mail messages (and other Web activities if desired) using an anonymous domain. These services typically range from free to about $75 per year.

To comply with truth-in-advertising laws, an *unsubscribe e-mail address* included in an unsolicited e-mail must be a working address. If you receive a marketing e-mail from a reputable source, you may be able to unsubscribe by clicking the supplied link or otherwise following the unsubscribe instructions. Because spam from less-legitimate sources often has unsubscribe links that do not work or that are present only to verify that your e-mail address is genuine—a very valuable piece of information for future use—many privacy experts recommend never replying to or trying to unsubscribe from any spam.

Be Cautious of Revealing Personal Information

In addition to protecting your real e-mail address, protecting your personal information is a critical step toward safeguarding your privacy. Consequently, it makes sense to be cautious about revealing your private information to anyone. Privacy tips for safeguarding personal information include the following:

TIP

Don't forget that once you post content on a Web site or send it via e-mail, you cannot control how long it will "live" in digital form. Be very careful about the personal information you post and send to avoid the possibility of that information creating problems for you in the future.

- Read a Web site's privacy policy (if one exists) before providing any personal information. If the Web site reserves the right to share your information unless you specifically notify them otherwise, it is best to assume that any information you provide will eventually be shared with others—do not use the site if that is unacceptable to you.
- Avoid putting too many personal details on your Web site or on a social networking site. Although complete anonymity would defeat the purpose of using a social network, it is a good idea to be careful about what content you post and who can view it. If you would like to post photos or other personal documents on a Web site for friends and family members to see, use a photo sharing site that allows you to restrict access to your photos (such as *Flickr, Snapfish*, or *Fotki*). Avoid using location-based services that share your location information with strangers. For more tips related to how to protect your privacy on social networking sites, see Figure 5-20.
- When you sign up for free trials or other services that may result in spam, use your throw-away e-mail address.
- Consider using privacy software, such as *Privacy Guardian*, to hide your personal information as you browse the Web so it is not revealed and your activities cannot be tracked by marketers. Also check the privacy settings of the cloud services that you use to see what control you have over what personal data is collected and shared. For instance, Google users can use the *Google Dashboard* to control the privacy settings of Google services.
- Just because a Web site or registration form asks for personal information, that does not mean you have to give it. Supply only the required information and if you are asked for more personal information than you are comfortable providing, look for an alternate Web site for the product or information you are seeking. As a rule of thumb, do not provide an e-mail address (or else use a throw-away address) if you do not want to receive offers or other e-mail from that company.

FIGURE 5-20 Social media privacy tips.

Facebook (use Privacy Settings)	Limit who can see your posts to *Friends* only.
	Limit who can look you up to *Friends* or *Friends of Friends* only.
	Disable search engines linking to your timeline.
	If you allow friends to post on your timeline, enable the settings to review the posts first.
	On your profile's *About* page, click each section and limit viewing to *Friends* only.
Google+ (use Profile Settings)	Organize your contacts into *circles* based on the content you will share with them (such as work, friends, and family) and then post or share content only with the appropriate circle.
	On your profile's *About* page, click each section and limit viewing to *Your circles* only.
Twitter (use Account Settings)	Enable *Tweet privacy* so only those who you approve will receive your tweets.
	Keep location information disabled so your location won't be added to your tweets.

- If you are using a public computer (such as at a school, a library, or an Internet café), be sure to remove any personal information and settings stored on the computer during your session. You can use browser options to delete this data manually from the computer before you leave (use the *Browsing history* option on the General tab of the Internet Options dialog box in Internet Explorer to delete this data). To prevent the deleted data from being recovered, run the Windows Disk Cleanup program on the hard drive, making sure that the options for Temporary Internet Files and the Recycle Bin are selected during the Disk Cleanup process. An easier option is using the *private browsing* mode offered by some browsers, such as Internet Explorer's *InPrivate* or Chrome's *Incognito* modes (see Figure 5-21), that allow you to browse the Web without leaving any history (such as browsing history, temporary Internet files, form data, cookies, usernames, and passwords) on the computer you are using. In either case, be sure to log out of any Web sites you were using before leaving the computer.

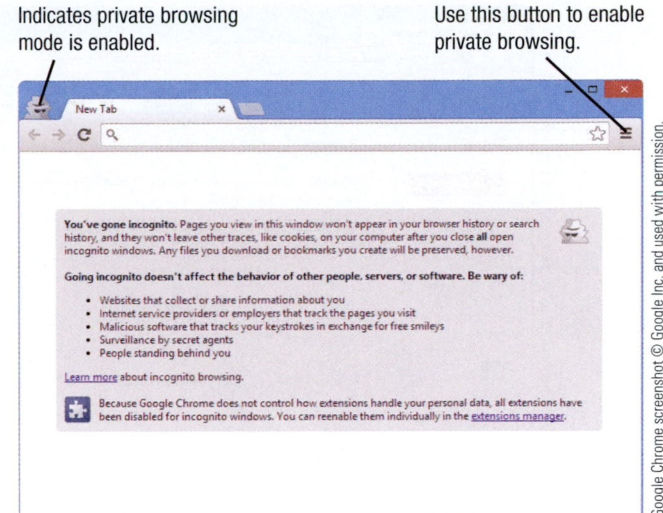

FIGURE 5-21
Private browsing can protect your Web-surfing privacy at public computers.

Use Filters and Opt Out

While keeping your personal information as private as possible can help to reduce spam and other direct marketing activities, *filtering* can also be helpful. Some ISPs automatically block all e-mail messages originating from known or suspected spammers so those e-mail messages never reach the individuals' mailboxes; other ISPs flag suspicious e-mail messages as possible spam, based on their content or subject lines, to warn individuals that those messages may contain spam. To deal with spam that makes it to your computer, you can use an **e-mail filter**—a tool for automatically sorting your incoming e-mail messages. E-mail filters used to capture spam are called **spam filters**. Many e-mail programs have built-in spam filters that identify possible spam and either flag it or move it to a Spam or Junk E-mail folder. Individuals can typically change the spam settings used in their e-mail program to indicate the actions that should be taken with suspected spam. In addition, they can create e-mail filters in their e-mail program, or they can use third-party filtering software to customize their spam filtering further. Many spam filters can also "learn" what each user views as spam based on the user identifying e-mail messages that were classified incorrectly (either spam messages placed in the Inbox or legitimate messages placed in the Spam folder) by the spam filter. The user typically provides this information by clicking a button such as *Report Spam* or *Not Spam* when the message is selected; the spam filter uses this input to classify messages from that sender correctly in the future. Businesses can set up spam filters in-house, but they are increasingly turning to dedicated *antispam appliances* to filter out spam without increasing the load on the company e-mail server.

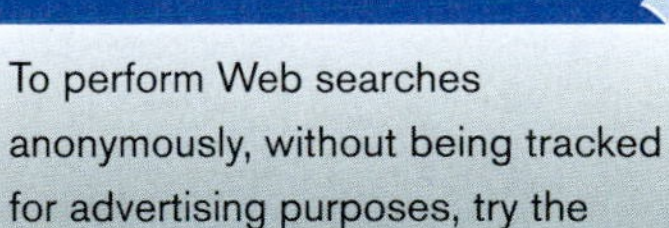
TIP

To perform Web searches anonymously, without being tracked for advertising purposes, try the *DuckDuckGo* search site.

Custom e-mail filters are used to route messages automatically to particular folders based on stated criteria. For example, you can specify that e-mail messages with keywords frequently used in spam subject lines (such as *free, porn, opportunity, last chance, weight, pharmacy*, and similar terms) be routed into a folder named *Possible Spam*, and you can specify that all e-mail messages from your boss's e-mail address be routed into an *Urgent*

>**E-mail filter.** A tool that automatically sorts your incoming e-mail messages based on specific criteria. >**Spam filter.** An e-mail filter used to redirect spam from a user's Inbox.

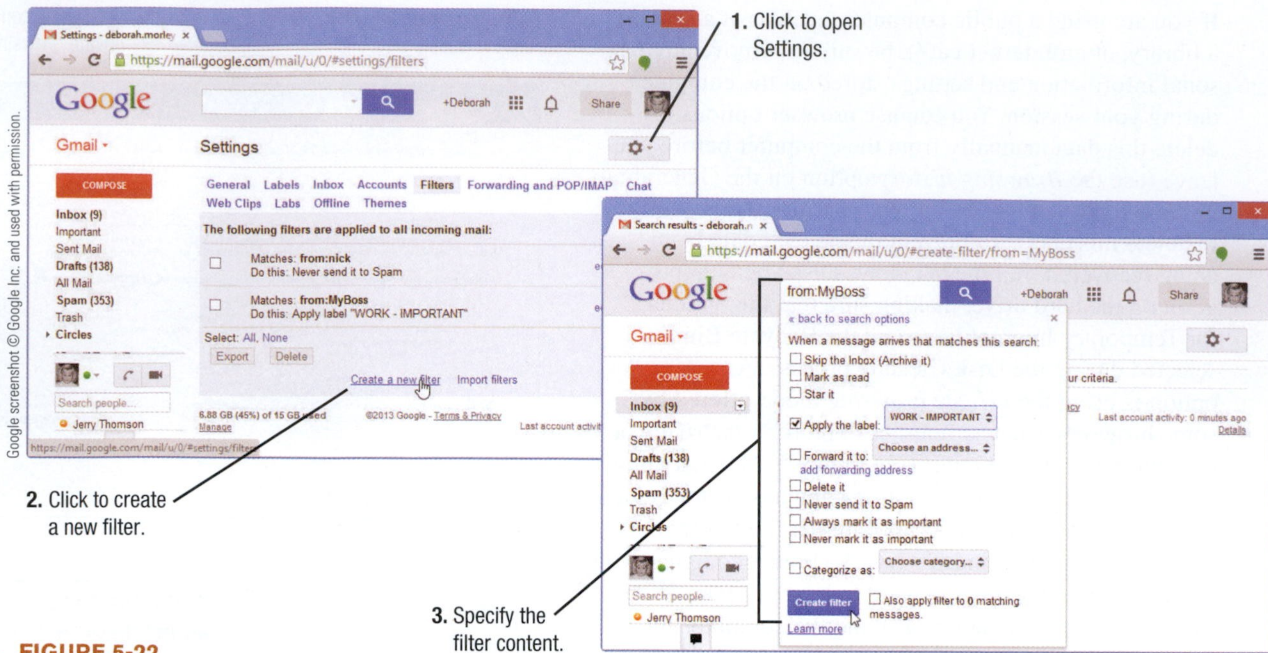
1. Click to open Settings.
2. Click to create a new filter.
3. Specify the filter content.
Google screenshot © Google Inc. and used with permission.

FIGURE 5-22 **Creating a Gmail filter.**

FIGURE 5-23 **Mobile spam filtering.** Can detect both spam texts and spam calls.

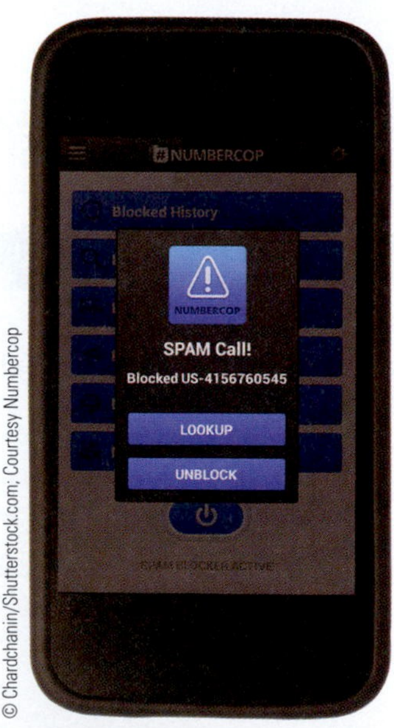
NUMBERCOP
SPAM Call!
Blocked US-4156760545
LOOKUP
UNBLOCK
© Chardchanin/Shutterstock.com; Courtesy Numbercop

folder. Filtering can help you find important messages in your Inbox by preventing it from becoming cluttered with spam. However, you need to be sure to check your Possible Spam or Junk E-mail folder periodically to locate any e-mail messages mistakenly filed there—especially before you permanently delete those messages. Creating a new e-mail filter in Gmail is shown in Figure 5-22.

Mobile users who receive Web-based e-mail via smartphones can use the filters available via their Web mail provider to filter out spam. There are also some *mobile spam apps* available to detect or block spam sent via text message or voice calls (see one example in Figure 5-23).

Another alternative for reducing the amount of spam you receive is to **opt out**. *Opting out* refers to following a predesignated procedure to remove yourself from marketing lists, or otherwise preventing your personal information from being obtained by or shared with others. By opting out, you instruct companies you do business with (such as your bank, insurance company, investment company, or an online store) not to share your personal information with third parties. You can also opt out of being contacted by direct and online marketing companies.

To opt out from a particular company or direct marketing association, you can contact them directly—many organizations include opt-out instructions in the privacy policies posted on their Web sites. For Web sites that use registered accounts for repeat visitors, opt-out options are sometimes included in your personal settings and can be activated by modifying your personal settings for that site. Opt-out instructions for financial institutions and credit card companies are often included in the disclosure statements that are periodically mailed to customers; they can also often be found on the company's Web site.

To assist consumers with the opt-out process, there are a number of Web sites, such as the *Center for Democracy and Technology* and the *PrivacyRightsNow!* Web sites, which provide opt-out tools for consumers. For example, some sites help visitors

>**Opt out.** To request that you be removed from marketing activities or that your information not be shared with other companies.

create opt-out letters that can be sent to the companies in order to opt out. For online marketing activities, organizations—such as the *Network Advertising Initiative* (*NAI*)—have tools on their Web sites to help consumers opt out of online targeted ads. Typically, this process replaces an advertiser's marketing cookie with an *opt-out cookie*. The opt-out cookie prevents any more marketing cookies belonging to that particular advertiser from being placed on the user's hard drive as long as the opt-out cookie is present (usually until the user deletes the opt-out cookie file, either intentionally or unintentionally). You can also use the *tracking protection* options available with some browsers; for example, the Internet Explorer tracking protection is enabled using the *Safety* settings. Once enabled (see Figure 5-24), it will send a "do not track" indicator to Web sites, which will then display generic ads instead of targeted ads. This process may become easier and more automatic in the future if proposed *Do Not Track* legislation becomes a reality.

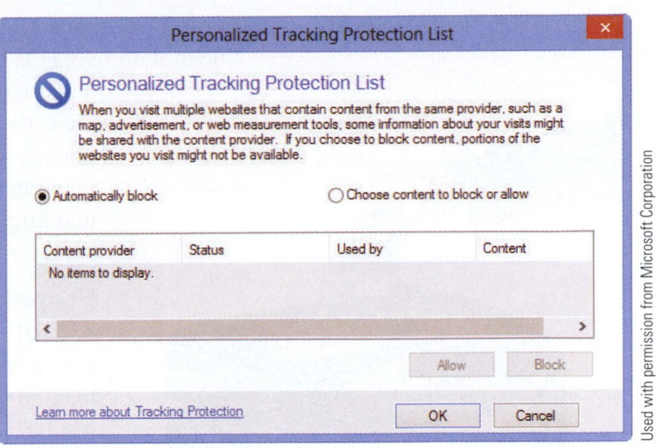

FIGURE 5-24
Enabling tracking protection in Internet Explorer.

At the present time, opting-out procedures are confusing and time consuming, and they do not always work well. Consequently, some privacy groups are pushing to change to an *opt-in* process, in which individuals would need to **opt in** (request participation in) to a particular marketing activity before companies can collect or share any personal data (as is the case in the European Union). In fact, Walmart recently changed its privacy policy to share information with third parties only if customers opt in. However, the general practice in the U.S. business community today is to use your information as allowed for by each privacy policy unless you specifically opt out.

TIP

Google recently paid $22.5 million to settle a lawsuit regarding its alleged circumventing of Do Not Track technologies connected to the Safari Web browser.

Secure Servers and Otherwise Protect Personal Information

Any business that stores personal information about employees, customers, or other individuals must take adequate security measures to protect the privacy of that information. As discussed in Chapter 4, secure servers and encryption can protect the data stored on a server; firewalls and access systems can protect against unauthorized access. To prevent personal information from being sent intentionally or inadvertently via e-mail, organizations can use e-mail encryption systems that automatically encrypt or block e-mail messages containing certain keywords. For instance, some hospitals use encryption systems that scan all outgoing e-mail messages and attachments and then automatically encrypt or block all messages that appear to contain patient-identifiable information, such as a Social Security number, medical record number, patient name, or medical term like "cancer." The recipient of an encrypted e-mail message typically receives a link to a secure Web site to log in and view the encrypted e-mail message. Similar systems are used by banks and other businesses. Businesses also need to be very careful with papers, portable hard drives, and other media that contain personal data. For instance, many recent data breaches have occurred because of carelessness, such as papers containing personal information being found in dumpsters, lost in transit, or faxed to the wrong individual.

TIP

Register both your landline and mobile phone numbers with the *National Do Not Call Registry* by going to www.donotcall.gov to prevent telemarketing calls from companies you do not have a business relationship with.

Ensuring that the private data stored by a business is adequately protected is increasingly the responsibility of a *chief privacy officer* (*CPO*)—a rapidly growing new position in business today. Typically, CPOs are responsible for ensuring privacy laws are complied with, identifying the data in a company that needs to be protected, developing policies to

>**Opt in.** To request that you be included in marketing activities or that your information be shared with other companies.

protect that data, and responding to any incidents that occur. Another issue that must be dealt with by CPOs is the changing definition of what information is regarded as personal and, therefore, needs to be safeguarded. For instance, some privacy advocates view the IP address of computers and the location information of mobile phones to be personal data. As protecting new types of information becomes integrated into privacy laws, these laws impact companies that store or utilize that information.

Courtesy Fellowes, Inc.

FIGURE 5-25
Media disposal. When disposing of CDs, DVDs, and other storage media, the media should be shredded to ensure the information on the media is destroyed.

Properly Dispose of Hardware Containing Data

A final consideration for protecting the privacy of personal information for both individuals and businesses is protecting the information located on paper documents and hardware (such as old backup media, used CDs, obsolete computers, and old mobile phones) that are to be disposed of. Papers, CDs, DVDs, and other media containing sensitive data should be shredded (see Figure 5-25), and the hard drives of computers to be disposed of should be *wiped*—overwritten several times using special *disk-wiping* or *disk-erasing* software—before they are sold or recycled. Unlike the data on a drive that has merely been erased or even reformatted (which can still be recovered), data on a properly wiped drive is very difficult or impossible to recover.

Wiping is typically viewed as an acceptable precaution for deleting sensitive data (such as Web site passwords and tax returns) from hard drives and other storage media belonging to individuals, as well as for storage media to be reused within an organization. However, before disposing of storage media containing sensitive data, businesses should consider physically destroying the media, such as by shredding or melting the hardware. To help with this process, *data destruction services* can be used, as discussed in the Inside the Industry box. To ensure that all hardware containing business data is properly disposed of, it is important for all businesses today to develop and implement a policy (often called a *media sanitization* or *data destruction policy*) for destroying data that is no longer needed.

TIP

Be sure to remove personal data from any device containing a hard drive before disposing of it, including gaming consoles, portable digital media players, and cars with entertainment system hard drives.

CAUTION CAUTION CAUTION CAUTION CAUTION CAUTION CAUT

When upgrading your mobile phone, be careful not to expose the personal data stored on your old phone to others. Before disposing of or recycling it, be sure to reset your mobile phone to its factory settings to clear all personal data from the phone.

ELECTRONIC SURVEILLANCE AND MONITORING

There are many ways electronic tools can be used to watch individuals, listen in on their conversations, or monitor their activities. Some of these tools—such as devices used by individuals to eavesdrop on wireless telephone conversations—are not legal for individuals to use. Other products and technologies, such as the GPS devices that are built into some cars so they can be located if they are stolen or the monitoring ankle bracelets used for offenders sentenced to house arrest, are used solely for law enforcement purposes. GPS technology can also be used by law enforcement agencies to track criminal suspects but, according to a 2012 U.S. Supreme Court ruling, only with a search warrant. Still other electronic tools, such as *computer monitoring software, video surveillance* equipment, and *presence technology*, discussed next, can often be used legally by individuals, by businesses in conjunction with *employee monitoring*, and by law enforcement agencies.

INSIDE THE INDUSTRY

Data Killers

With the vast amount of sensitive and classified data stored on personal and business devices today, disposing of those devices or removing the data from those devices so they can be reused is an important issue. In particular, business computers tend to contain a wide variety of sensitive data that needs to be removed if the hard drive containing that data needs to be disposed of or will be reused by another employee. *Data destruction services* are designed for this purpose.

Data destruction ranges from purging the data (such as wiping a magnetic hard drive clean or *degaussing* (demagnetizing) the drive so the data cannot be restored) to destroying the drive physically. The level of destruction needed depends on the type of drive (SSDs cannot be as reliably erased as magnetic hard drives), the type of data being deleted, and where the hardware will go next. For instance, purging might be appropriate for personal hard drives being sold and for business hard drives that will be reused within the company, but all business hard drives that will no longer be used within the company and that contain sensitive data should be physically destroyed.

While data destruction can be performed by in-house personnel, there are also external data destruction services (such as *Data Killers*) designed for this purpose. Such services typically can purge, degauss, or shred hard drives and other media, depending on the customer's preference. Once a hard drive has been shredded (see the accompanying photo), it is virtually impossible for any data to be recovered from the pieces. However, for extra security, magnetic drives containing extremely sensitive data can be degaussed and then shredded. To ensure drives are not lost or compromised in transit, most data destruction companies offer secure transportation to the destruction facility using tamper-proof locked cases, and will provide signed and dated Certificates of Purging or Certificates of Destruction, when requested. Some even offer destruction on site, if the customer desires. Purged hard drives are returned to the customer; shredded hard drives are typically recycled.

Courtesy of Data Killers

Hard drive before (left) and after (right) shredding.

Computer Monitoring Software

Computer monitoring software is used specifically for the purpose of recording keystrokes, logging the programs or Web sites accessed, or otherwise monitoring someone's computer activity; some programs also have apps that can be used to monitor media tablet and smartphone activity. These programs are typically marketed toward parents (to check on their children's online activities), spouses (to determine if a spouse is having an affair, viewing pornography, or participating in other activities that are unacceptable to the other spouse), law enforcement agencies (to collect evidence against suspected criminals), or employers (to ensure employees are using company computers and time only for work-related or otherwise approved activities). Computer monitoring programs can keep a log of all computer keystrokes performed on a computer, record the activities taking place (such as the amount of time spent on and tasks performed via the Web or installed software), take screenshots of the screen at specified intervals, and more (see Figure 5-26). Computer monitoring software designed for businesses also typically provides a summary of the

>**Computer monitoring software.** Software that can be used to record an individual's computer usage, such as capturing images of the screen, recording the actual keystrokes used, or creating a summary of Web sites and programs accessed.

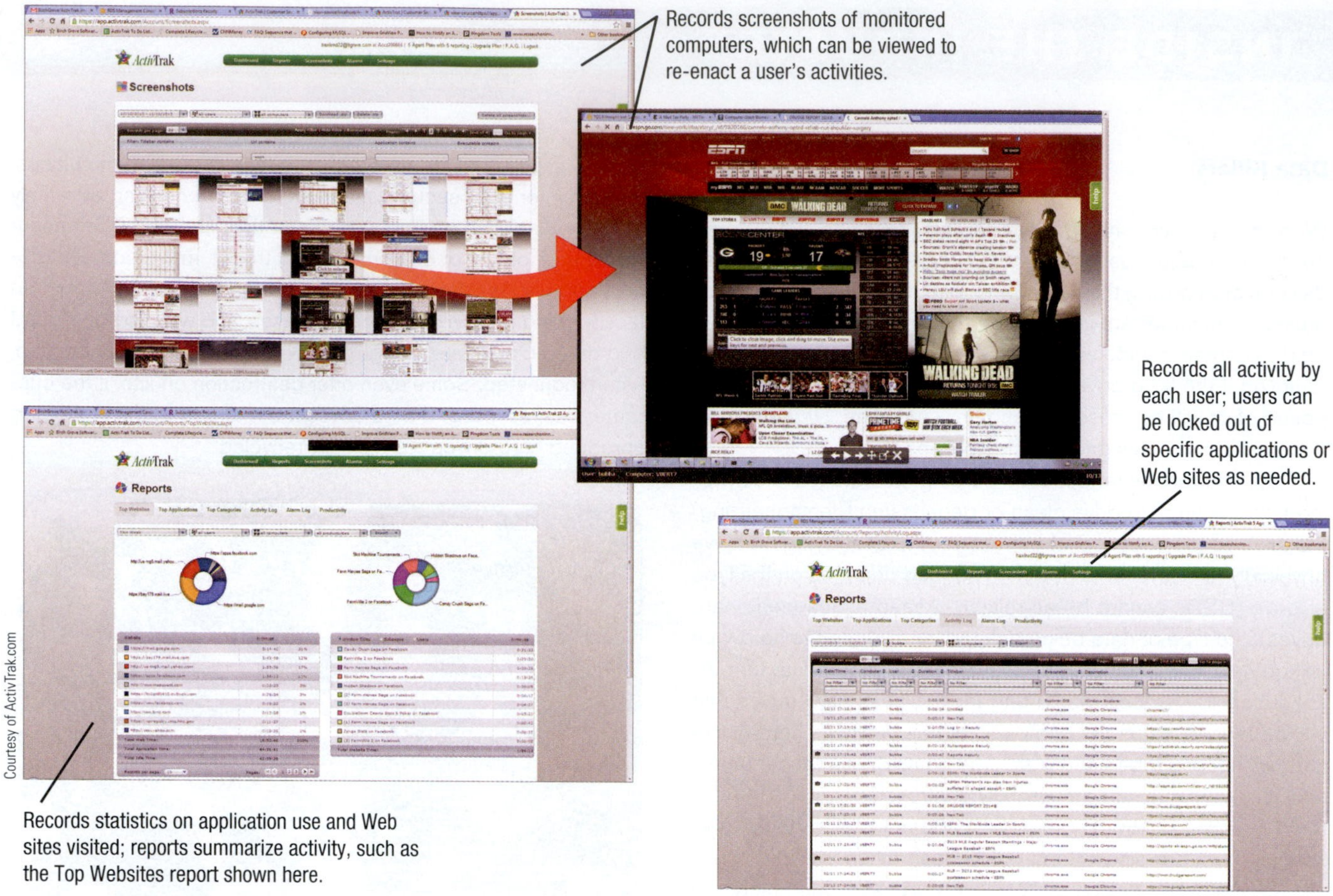

Records screenshots of monitored computers, which can be viewed to re-enact a user's activities.

Records all activity by each user; users can be locked out of specific applications or Web sites as needed.

Records statistics on application use and Web sites visited; reports summarize activity, such as the Top Websites report shown here.

Courtesy of ActivTrak.com

FIGURE 5-26
Computer monitoring software. Can be used to monitor employee computer activity, as shown here.

activities (such as the programs used or the Web sites visited) performed on all company computers (refer again to Figure 5-26). In addition, some computer monitoring software can block specific Web sites, as well as notify a designated party (such as the parent or computer administrator) if the individual using the computer being monitored uses specified keywords (such as inappropriate language for children or terms referring to company secrets for employees) or visits a Web site deemed inappropriate.

Although it is legal to use computer monitoring software on your own computer or on the computers of your employees, installing it on other computers without the owners' knowledge to monitor their computer activity is usually illegal. A growing illegal use of computer monitoring software is the use of a *keystroke logging system* by hackers. A keystroke logging system is typically software-based, but it can also be implemented via a small device that is installed between the system unit and the keyboard of a computer. In either case, it is used to record all keystrokes performed on the computer in order to capture usernames, passwords, and other sensitive data entered into the computer via the keyboard. Keystroke logging software can be installed on an individual's computer via malware, or it can be installed on public computers in person if the proper precautions are not taken. For instance, in 2008, a Colombian man pled guilty to installing keystroke logging software on computers located in hotel business centers and Internet cafés around the world; the software collected the personal information he needed to access the bank, payroll, brokerage, and other financial accounts of over 600 individuals. He was sentenced in mid-2009 to nine years in prison and ordered to pay $347,000 in restitution.

In addition to computer monitoring products designed for individuals and businesses, there are also computer monitoring programs available for use only by law enforcement and other government agencies. Like wiretapping, electronic monitoring of computer activity requires a court order or similar authorization to be legal (although the *USA PATRIOT Act* does allow the FBI to conduct a limited form of Internet surveillance first, such as to capture e-mail addresses or IP addresses used with traffic going to or coming from a suspect's computer). With proper authorization and cooperation from a suspect's ISP, law enforcement agencies can use computer monitoring software to intercept files and e-mail messages sent to or from a suspect's computer. If the documents are encrypted, keystroke logging software can be used to record e-mail messages and documents before they are encrypted, as well as to record the private keys used to encrypt messages and files. As recent disclosures have revealed, the U.S. *National Security Agency* (*NSA*) routinely accesses and monitors Web activity (including e-mail messages, Skype calls, cloud documents, browsing activity, and other Web-related communications). In fact, the *Wall Street Journal* recently reported that the NSA has the capacity to reach about 75% of all U.S. Internet communications and NSA officials recently announced that this surveillance has helped to stop more than 50 terrorist plots since 9/11. One tool supposedly used to collect this data is referred to as *PRISM*; the huge new data center being built to house this data is referred to as the *Utah Data Center*.

Video Surveillance

The idea of **video surveillance** is nothing new. Many retail stores, banks, office buildings, and other privately owned facilities that are open to the public routinely use closed-circuit security cameras to monitor activities taking place at those facilities for security purposes. In recent years, however, video surveillance has been expanded to a number of additional public locations (such as streets, parks, airports, sporting arenas, subway systems, and so forth) in many cities in the United States and other countries for law enforcement purposes (worldwide, two of the most monitored cities are London and New York City). These cameras are typically located outside and attached to or built into fixtures, such as lamp posts (see Figure 5-27), or attached to buildings. Video surveillance cameras are also commonly installed in schools in the United States and other countries to enable administrators to monitor both teacher and student activities and to have a record of incidents as they occur. A snapshot of a live video feed from a camera installed at a university in Oregon is shown in Figure 5-27.

Public video surveillance systems are often used in conjunction with face recognition technology to try to identify known terrorists and other criminals, to identify criminals when their crimes are caught on tape, and to prevent crimes from occurring. Video surveillance data is proving to be valuable to police for catching terrorists and other types of criminals, and it is routinely used to identify the individuals and cars used in attacks; this benefit is expected to increase as video

FIGURE 5-27
Examples of public video surveillance.

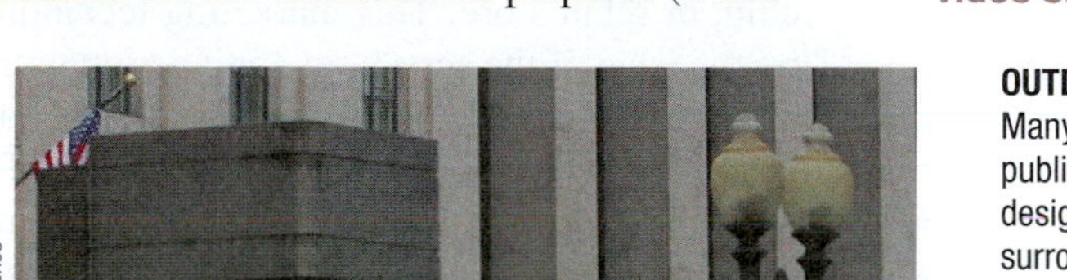

Image source EPIC.org project Observing Surveillance

OUTDOOR SURVEILLANCE
Many cameras placed in public locations are designed to blend into their surroundings to be less intrusive, such as the camera inside this light fixture on a Washington, D.C., street.

INDOOR SURVEILLANCE
Many cameras are placed inside businesses, schools, and other locations; a snapshot from a video camera located at a university in Oregon is shown here.

Courtesy University of Oregon

>**Video surveillance.** The use of video cameras to monitor activities of individuals, such as employees or individuals in public locations, for work-related or crime-prevention purposes.

surveillance moves to high definition. For example, video surveillance systems helped police identify six of the attackers in the deadly 2013 Westgate Mall attack in Kenya. Some public video surveillance systems are also beginning to be used in conjunction with software to try to identify suspicious behavior (such as an unattended bag or a truck circling a skyscraper) and alert authorities to these possible threats before they do any damage.

Many privacy advocates object to the use of video surveillance and face recognition technology in public locations; their concerns are primarily based on how the video captured by these systems will be used. Privacy advocates also have doubts about the usefulness of these systems in protecting citizens against terrorism. They also object to the fact that, unlike private security video that is typically viewed only after a crime has occurred, the images from many public video cameras are watched all the time. In addition, networks of police video cameras that feed into a central operations center allow the observation of innocent people and activities on a massive scale. Some privacy advocates also fear being under perpetual police surveillance and the eventual expansion of these security surveillance systems, such as using them to look for "deadbeat dads" or for other applications not vital for national security. However, law enforcement agencies contend that face recognition systems and public video surveillance are no different from the many private video surveillance systems in place today in a wide variety of public locations, such as in retail stores and banks. They view this technology as just one more tool to be used to protect the public, similar to scanning luggage at the airport.

An emerging privacy issue related to public video cameras is their use with the display screens used to project advertisements in public places, such as a mall, health club, or retail store. This marketing technique uses tiny video cameras embedded in or on the edge of the screen, in conjunction with software, to identify characteristics of the individual looking at the screen (such as gender and approximate age) in order to display advertising content targeted to each viewer. The video cameras can also be used to determine if the displayed ads are reaching the intended demographic. Similar technology is used with some in-store mannequins to analyze shopper characteristics to help stores adjust in-store displays accordingly. While still in the infancy stage, this advertising tool is expected to be more prominent in the near future. To alleviate privacy concerns, developers state that no images are ever stored and individuals are not personally identified—only their characteristics. However, the idea of targeted advertisements based on physical appearance is a concern for some privacy advocates.

A related privacy concern is the inclusion of imaging capabilities in many mobile devices today, such as mobile phones (see Figure 5-28), media tablets, and Google Glass. Although digital cameras in mobile devices are increasingly being used to help law enforcement (such as being used by citizens to take photos of crimes as they are being committed) and camera functions are included for personal enjoyment and convenience, some fear that the ubiquitous nature of mobile phones will lead to increased privacy violations. In fact, some athletic clubs have banned mobile phones entirely to protect the privacy of their members while working out and in the dressing rooms. Many YMCAs, city parks and recreation departments, and other recreational facilities have banned camera phone use in locker rooms and restrooms to protect the privacy of both children and adults. Camera phones are also being banned by some schools to prevent cheating, by many courthouses to prevent witness or jury intimidation, and by many research and production facilities to prevent corporate espionage. Google Glass has the additional issue of the user being able to take photos and record videos in an even more subtle manner than with a mobile phone. Legally speaking, people typically have few rights to privacy in public places, but many believe that new technology—such as camera phones and Google Glass—will require the law to reconsider and redefine what is considered to be a public place and where citizens can expect to retain particular aspects of personal privacy.

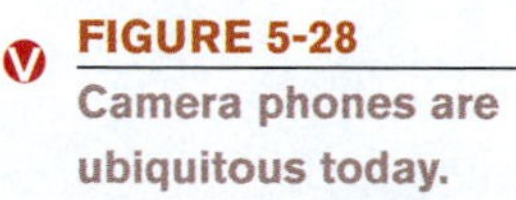

FIGURE 5-28
Camera phones are ubiquitous today.

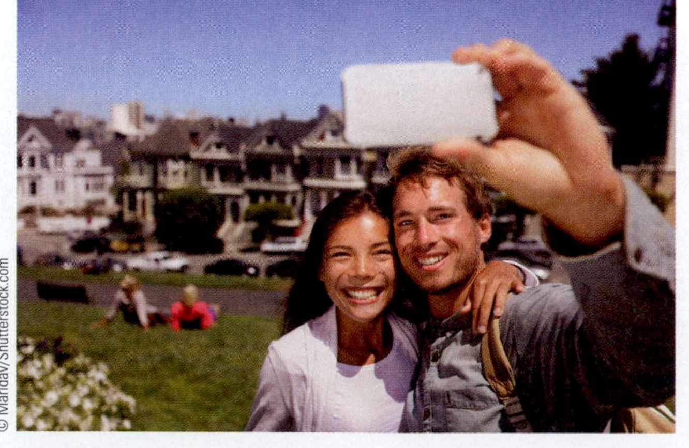

Employee Monitoring

Employee monitoring refers to companies recording or observing the actions of employees while on the job. With today's technology, employee monitoring is very easy to perform, and much of it can be done through the use of computers. Common employee monitoring activities include screening telephone calls, reviewing e-mail, and tracking computer and Internet usage; with the growing inclusion of video cameras in computers and monitors today, employee monitoring via webcams may become more prominent in the near future. Although many employees feel that being watched at work is an invasion of their personal privacy, it is legal and very common in the United States. According to the American Management Association (AMA), the vast majority of all U.S. companies use some type of electronic surveillance with their employees, and it is common for employers to discipline employees for misuse of e-mail or the Internet at work. Typically, the primary reason is to monitor Internet usage for legal liability, but monitoring employee productivity is another motivating factor. Many employers are finding that some employees waste large amounts of time on social networking sites and other Web activities. While access to these sites is frequently blocked by employers, many believe a better alternative is identifying employees who abuse their Internet access and then dealing with those employees directly. This can be accomplished using the computer monitoring software discussed in a previous section.

For monitoring the physical locations of employees, video cameras (such as video surveillance cameras or webcams) can be used, but another possibility is the use of smart or RFID-enabled ID cards (sometimes called *proximity cards*). While these cards are most often used for access control—such as to facilitate access to a building or computer network, to automatically lock an employee's computer when he or she gets a certain distance away from it (to eliminate the problem of nosy coworkers), and to automatically unlock the computer when the employee returns (to eliminate the need for passwords)—they can also be used to track the physical location of employees. There are also *proximity apps* that use the Bluetooth connection on your smartphone, media tablet, or other Bluetooth-enabled mobile device to lock or unlock your computer based on the phone's physical location (your phone needs to be within Bluetooth range of the computer in order for the computer to be unlocked)—see the *Keycard app* in Figure 5-29. Other types of employee monitoring systems designed for tracking an employee's location are location-based systems, such as those systems that track an employee via his or her smartphone or those that notify the employer if the employee's company vehicle exits a prescribed work area. GPS monitoring systems are discussed in more detail in Chapter 8.

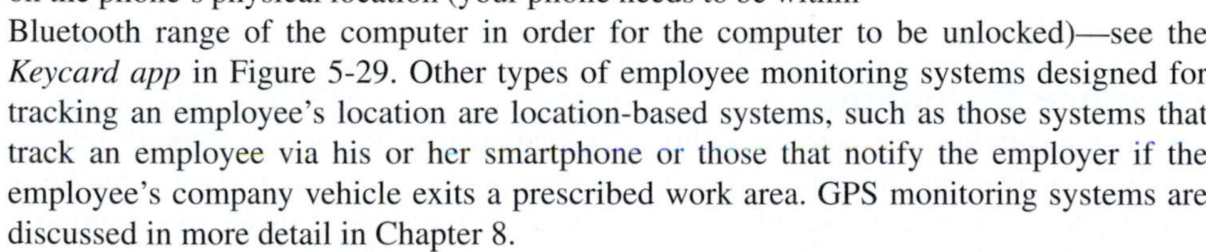

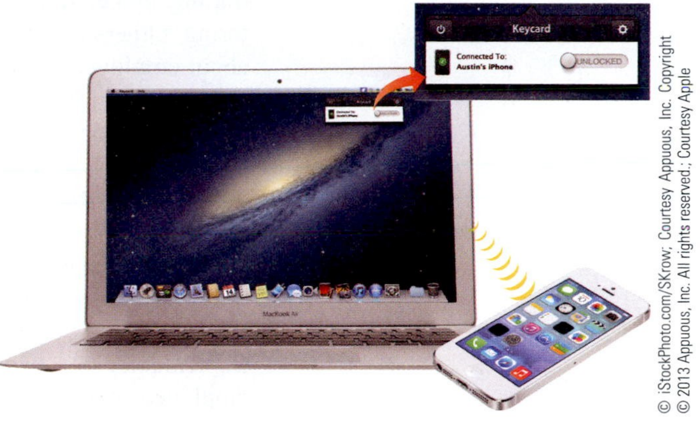

FIGURE 5-29
Proximity apps.
This app locks and unlocks your computer automatically as your iPhone moves in and out of range.

Although some employees may view workplace monitoring as an invasion of their personal privacy, employers have several valid reasons for monitoring employee activities, such as security concerns, productivity measurement, legal compliance, and legal liability. For example, management has a responsibility to the company (and to its stockholders, for publicly held corporations) to make sure employees do the jobs that they are being paid to do. If any employees are spending too much time away from their desks chatting with other employees, answering their personal e-mail, or placing bids at online auctions, the company has the right to know and the responsibility to stop that misuse of company time and resources. For example, there have been many instances of employees viewing

>**Employee monitoring.** Observing or reviewing employees' actions while they are on the job.

pornography, downloading pirated movies or music, watching live sports video feeds—even running their own businesses—on company time and computers. In addition, the company needs to protect itself against lost business (due to employee incompetence or poor client skills, for example) and lawsuits (such as from employees when offensive e-mail messages are circulated within the office or when an employee includes statements that defame another business or reveal private information in a company blog). In addition, government regulations—such as the *Sarbanes-Oxley Act*, which requires publicly traded companies to keep track of which employees look at sensitive documents—may require it. However, some employees object to being monitored and some privacy advocates feel that some types of employee monitoring cross the line between valid employee monitoring and an invasion of privacy.

Comprehensive employee monitoring systems can be expensive; however, many companies view the cost as insignificant compared with the risk of a potential multimillion-dollar lawsuit. It is becoming increasingly common for U.S. firms to face sexual harassment and/or racial discrimination claims stemming from employee e-mail and Internet use and lawsuits can be costly—Chevron was once ordered to pay female employees $2.2 million to settle a sexual harassment lawsuit stemming from inappropriate e-mails sent by male employees.

To reduce cost and objections from employees, some businesses have found employee training and education to be an effective and cost-efficient alternative to continuous monitoring. Others use statistical-analysis software to detect unusual patterns in data collected about employee computer usage, and then use the reports to investigate only the employees and situations indicated as possible problems. Regardless of the techniques used, it is wise for businesses to inform employees about their monitoring practices (including what activities may be monitored and how long records of that monitoring will be archived), although they are not required by law in the United States at the current time to do so. However, bills have been introduced in several states in the United States that would prohibit employee monitoring without employee notification and some countries—such as in the European Union—are much more limiting with respect to the types of employee monitoring that can be performed without active notification. In addition, legislation has been implemented or is being considered in several states to prevent employers from implanting employees with RFID chips without the employee's consent in order to prevent employers from requiring that chips be implanted into employees for monitoring purposes, security access, or other work-related functions.

Presence Technology

Presence technology refers to the ability of one computing device (a desktop computer, portable computer, or smartphone, for example) on a network (such as the Internet or a mobile phone network) to identify another device on the same network and determine its status. It can be used to tell when someone on the network is using his or her computer or mobile device, as well as the individual's availability for communications; that is, whether or not the individual is able and willing to take a voice or video call or respond to an IM at the present time. For example, when an employee at a company utilizing presence technology (sometimes called *presence management* in a business context) has a question that needs answering, he or she can check the directory displayed on his or her computer or mobile device to see which team members are available, regardless of where those team members are physically located. The employee can then call an available team member or send an instant message. Presence technology is expected to be used eventually

TIP

The ability of a device to share status information (including presence and location information) across a network is a form of *context-aware computing*.

>**Presence technology.** Technology that enables one computing device (such as a computer or mobile device) to locate and identify the current status of another device on the same network.

on company Web pages so that visitors—usually potential or current customers—can see which salespeople, service representatives, or other contacts are currently available. Another possible application is including dynamic presence buttons in e-mail messages—the presence button would display one message (such as "I'm online") if the sender is online at the time the e-mail message is read, and a different message (such as "I'm offline") if the sender is not online at that time.

Presence technology today can be implemented via software, as well as by GPS, RFID, or other technology. For instance, IM software indicates the current status of each buddy on an individual's contact list (based on each buddy's signed-in status) and chat tools (such as in Facebook) reveal which of your contacts are currently online. In addition, the presence technology built into many mobile devices today enables individuals to see when a contact is available (see Figure 5-30). The GPS capabilities integrated in many smartphones today also allow you to keep track of your friends' physical locations, such as by using the Buddy Beacon or GyPSii application to view their current locations on a map. The GPS capabilities built into smartphones can also be used by law enforcement to determine the location of a phone (such as one belonging to a missing individual or a criminal) when needed.

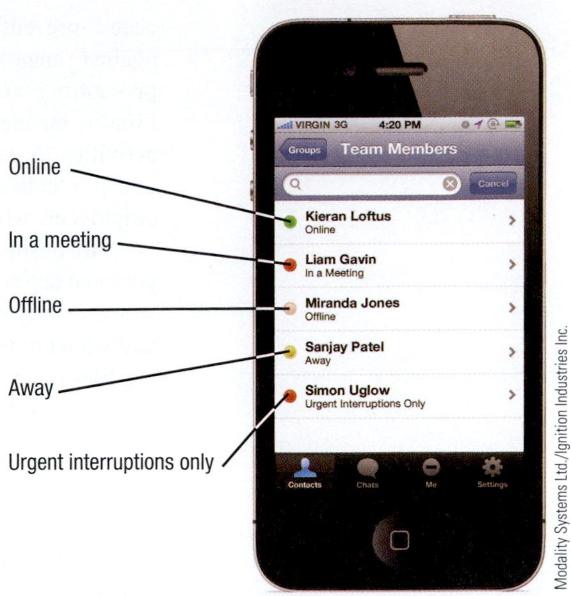

FIGURE 5-30
Presence technology. Presence icons indicate the status of individual contacts.

While some aspects of presence technology are useful and intriguing, such as being able to tell that a loved one's flight arrived safely when you notice that his or her smartphone is on again, knowing if a friend or colleague is available for a phone call before dialing the number, or identifying the location of your children at any point in time, privacy advocates are concerned about the use of this technology. They are concerned about presence technology being used to target ads and information to individuals based on their current physical location (such as close to a particular restaurant at lunchtime) and other activities that they view as potential privacy violations. In addition, there are concerns about location data being archived and how that archived data may be used.

Protecting Personal and Workplace Privacy

There are not many options for protecting yourself against computer monitoring by your employer or the government, or against video surveillance systems. However, businesses should take the necessary security measures (such as protecting the company network from hackers, monitoring for intrusions, and using security software) to ensure that employee activities are not being monitored by a hacker or other unauthorized individual. Individuals should also secure their home computers to protect against keystroke logging or other computer monitoring software that may be inadvertently installed via an electronic greeting card, game, or other downloaded file, and that is designed to provide a hacker with account numbers, passwords, and other sensitive data that could be used in identity theft or other fraudulent activities. *Antispyware software*, such as the programs discussed in Chapter 4, can be used to detect and remove some types of illegal computer monitoring and spyware software. To prevent location data associated with your smartphone from being available to strangers, change the privacy settings of the services you use to limit location data to specific friends, if that option is available. If you don't use location-based services frequently, turn off the GPS feature on your phone until you need it, if possible.

The Employer's Responsibilities

To protect the personal privacy of their employees and customers, businesses and organizations have a responsibility to keep private information about their employees, the company, and their customers safe. Strong security measures, such as firewalls and access-prevention methods for both computer data and facilities, can help to protect against unauthorized access by hackers. Businesses and organizations should take precautions against both intentional and accidental breaches of privacy by employees. Finally, businesses and organizations have the responsibility to monitor their employees' activities to ensure workers are productive. In general, businesses must maintain a safe and productive workplace environment and protect the privacy of their customers and employees, while at the same time ensure the company is not vulnerable to lawsuits.

All businesses should have an *employee policy* that informs employees about what personal activities (if any) are allowed during company time or on company equipment, as well as about what company communications (such as e-mail messages and blog postings) and what employee activities (such as Web surfing, e-mail, telephone calls, and downloading files to an office computer) may be monitored. Employee policies are usually included in an employee handbook or posted on the company intranet.

The Employees' Responsibilities

Employees have the responsibility to read a company's employee policy when initially hired and to review it periodically to ensure that they understand the policy and do not violate any company rules while working for that organization. In addition, because at-work activities may legally be monitored by an employer, it is wise—from a privacy standpoint—to avoid personal activities at work. From reading the organization's employee policy, an employee can determine if any personal activities are allowed at all (such as checking personal e-mail during the lunch hour), but it is safer to perform personal activities at home, regardless. Be especially careful with any activity, such as sending a joke via e-mail to a coworker, that might be interpreted as harassment. For personal phone calls, employees should use their mobile phones during their lunch hour or a rest break.

COMPUTER SECURITY AND PRIVACY LEGISLATION

The high level of concern regarding computer security and personal privacy has led state and federal legislators to pass a variety of laws since the 1970s. Internet privacy is viewed as one of the top policy issues facing Congress today, and numerous bills have been proposed in the last several years regarding spam, telemarketing, spyware, online profiling, and other very important privacy issues (such as the *Do-Not-Track Online Act of 2013* recently introduced in the U.S. Congress and the *Consumer Privacy Bill of Rights* unveiled recently by the Obama Administration). However, despite a renewed interest in privacy legislation, due at least in part to the recent leak of NSA surveillance operations, Congress has had difficulty passing new legislation. There are several reasons for this, including that it is difficult for the legal system to keep pace with the rate at which technology changes, and there are jurisdictional issues because many computer crimes affect businesses and individuals located in geographic areas other than the one in which the computer criminal is located. In addition, privacy is difficult to define and there is a struggle to balance freedom of speech with the right to privacy.

Another issue is weighing the need to implement legislation versus the use of voluntary methods to protect computer security and personal privacy. For instance, the *Child Online Protection Act* (*COPA*) has been controversial since it was passed in 1998, and, in fact, it has never been implemented. This legislation prohibited making pornography or any other content deemed harmful to minors available to minors via the Internet. This law was blocked by the U.S. Supreme Court several times, based on the likelihood that it violates the First Amendment and that less-restrictive alternatives (such as Internet filtering) can be used instead to prevent the access of inappropriate materials by minors. A list of selected federal laws related to computer security and privacy are shown in Figure 5-31.

DATE	LAW AND DESCRIPTION
2009	**American Recovery and Reinvestment Act** Requires HIPAA covered entities to notify patients and/or customers when protected health information has been compromised.
2006	**U.S. SAFE WEB Act of 2006** Grants additional authority to the FTC to help protect consumers from spam, spyware, and Internet fraud and deception.
2005	**Real ID Act** Establishes national standards for state-issued driver's licenses and identification cards.
2005	**Junk Fax Prevention Act** Requires unsolicited faxes to have a highly visible opt-out notice.
2003	**CAN-SPAM Act** Implements regulations for unsolicited e-mail messages and lays the groundwork for a federal Do Not E-Mail Registry.
2003	**Do Not Call Implementation Act** Amends the Telephone Consumer Protection Act to implement the National Do Not Call Registry.
2003	**Health Insurance Portability and Accountability Act (HIPAA)** Includes a Security Rule that sets minimum security standards to protect health information stored electronically.
2002	**Sarbanes-Oxley Act** Requires archiving a variety of electronic records and protecting the integrity of corporate financial data.
2001	**USA PATRIOT Act** Grants federal authorities expanded surveillance and intelligence-gathering powers, such as broadening the ability of federal agents to obtain the real identity of Internet users and to intercept e-mail and other types of Internet communications.
1999	**Financial Modernization (Gramm-Leach-Bliley) Act** Extends the ability of banks, securities firms, and insurance companies to share consumers' non-public personal information, but requires them to notify consumers and give them the opportunity to opt out before disclosing any information.
1998	**Child Online Protection Act (COPA)** Prohibits online pornography and other content deemed harmful to minors; has been blocked by the Supreme Court.
1998	**Children's Online Privacy Protection Act (COPPA)** Regulates how Web sites can collect information from minors and communicate with them.
1998	**Telephone Anti-Spamming Amendments Act** Applies restrictions to unsolicited, bulk commercial e-mail.
1991	**Telephone Consumer Protection Act** Requires telemarketing companies to respect the rights of people who do not want to be called.
1988	**Computer Matching and Privacy Protection Act** Limits the use of government data in determining federal-benefit recipients.
1988	**Video Privacy Protection Act** Limits disclosure of customer information by video-rental companies.
1986	**Electronic Communications Privacy Act** Extends traditional privacy protections governing postal delivery and telephone services to include e-mail, mobile phones, and voice mail.
1984	**Cable Communications Policy Act** Limits disclosure of customer records by cable TV companies; extended in 1992 to include companies that sell wireless services.
1974	**Education Privacy Act** Stipulates that, in both public and private schools that receive any federal funding, individuals have the right to keep the schools from releasing information such as grades and evaluations of behavior.
1974	**Privacy Act** Stipulates that the collection of data by federal agencies must have a legitimate purpose.
1970	**Fair Credit Reporting Act** Prevents private organizations from unfairly denying credit and provides individuals the right to inspect their credit records.
1970	**Freedom of Information Act** Gives individuals the right to inspect data concerning them that is stored by the federal government.

FIGURE 5-31
Federal legislation related to computer security and privacy.

SUMMARY

WHY BE CONCERNED ABOUT COMPUTER SECURITY?

Chapter Objective 1:
Explain why all computer users should be concerned about computer security.

There are a number of important security concerns related to computers, such as having your computer stolen, losing data, and running the risk of buying pirated or digitally counterfeited products online. All computer users should be aware of possible security risks and the safeguards they can implement to prevent security problems because these problems can cost them time and money, as well as be an inconvenience.

HARDWARE LOSS, HARDWARE DAMAGE, AND SYSTEM FAILURE

Chapter Objective 2:
List some risks associated with hardware loss, hardware damage, and system failure, and understand ways to safeguard a computer against these risks.

Hardware loss (perhaps as a result of **hardware theft** or lost hardware), hardware damage (both intentional and unintentional), and **system failure** are important concerns. System failure can occur because of a hardware problem, or it can be the result of a natural or man-made disaster. To protect against hardware theft, door and equipment locks can be used. To protect against accidental hardware damage, **surge suppressors**, **uninterruptible power supplies** (**UPSs**), proper storage media care, and precautions against excess dust, heat, and static electricity are important. **Ruggedized devices** can be used when necessary. To protect against data loss, backups are essential for both individuals and businesses—most businesses should also develop a **disaster recovery plan** for natural and man-made disasters. Encryption can be used to protect individual files and the content of data stored on a storage medium. **Full disk encryption** (**FDE**) and **self-encrypting hard drives** can be used to encrypt all the content located on a hard drive automatically.

SOFTWARE PIRACY AND DIGITAL COUNTERFEITING

Chapter Objective 3:
Define software piracy and digital counterfeiting, and explain how they can be prevented.

Software piracy (the unauthorized copying of a computer program) and **digital counterfeiting** (creating fake copies of currency and other resources) are illegal in the United States. They cost manufacturers billions of dollars each year, and some of these costs are passed on to law-abiding consumers. Various tools, such as consumer education, holograms, and software activation procedures, can be used to prevent software piracy. Many businesses are also aggressively pursuing software pirates in court in an attempt to reduce piracy. The government has various methods in place to prevent digital counterfeiting of currency, such as using difficult-to-reproduce materials and features like *security threads* and *watermarks*.

WHY BE CONCERNED ABOUT INFORMATION PRIVACY?

Chapter Objective 4:
Explain what information privacy is and why computer users should be concerned about it.

Privacy issues affect the lives of everyone. A number of important **privacy** concerns are related to computers and the Internet. For instance, **information privacy** refers to the rights of individuals and companies to control how information about them is collected and used. Other common concerns include the privacy of Web site activities and e-mail messages, as well as the high number of security breaches on systems that contain personal information. Businesses need to be concerned with protecting the privacy of the personal information they store because data breaches violate the privacy of their customers. In addition, data breaches are costly, and they can result in lawsuits and damaged reputations.

DATABASES, ELECTRONIC PROFILING, SPAM, AND OTHER MARKETING ACTIVITIES

The extensive use of **marketing databases** and **government databases** is of concern to many privacy organizations and individuals. Information in marketing databases is frequently sold to companies and other organizations; information in some government databases is available to the public. Some public information can be retrieved from databases via the Web. **Electronic profiling** is the collection of diverse information about an individual. An organization's **privacy policy** addresses how any personal information submitted to that company will be used. Another privacy issue that individuals need to be concerned about centers on the vast amount of **spam** (unsolicited bulk e-mail) that occurs today.

Chapter Objective 5: Describe some privacy concerns regarding databases, electronic profiling, spam, and telemarketing, and identify ways individuals can protect their privacy.

Protecting your e-mail address is one of the best ways to avoid spam. A **throw-away e-mail address** can be used for any activities that may result in spam; your permanent personal e-mail address can then be reserved for communications that should not result in spam. Before providing any personal information via a Web page, it is a good idea to review the Web site's privacy policy to see if the information will be shared with other organizations. Consider whether or not the Web site is requesting too much personal information, and only provide the required data. Do not provide personal details in chat rooms and personal Web sites. Unless you do not mind spam or are using a throw-away e-mail address, avoid completing online forms, such as those used to enter sweepstakes.

E-mail filters can be used to manage an individual's e-mail; **spam filters** are used to identify possible spam. To reduce the amount of spam, junk mail, online ads, and telemarketing calls received, an individual can **opt out** of marketing activities. It's possible that future marketing activities will require individuals to **opt in** in order to participate.

Individuals and businesses should be cautious when disposing of old hardware, such as hard drives and CDs, that contain sensitive data. Minimally, hard drives to be reused should be *wiped* clean; CDs, DVDs, and other media to be disposed of should be shredded.

ELECTRONIC SURVEILLANCE AND MONITORING

Computer monitoring software that can record an individual's computer use is viewed as a privacy violation by some, as is the increased use of **video surveillance** in public locations. Although it is allowed by law, some employees view **employee monitoring** (such as monitoring computer use, telephone calls, and an individual's location using a smart ID card or video surveillance) as an invasion of their privacy. **Presence technology**—the ability of one device on a network to know the status of another device on that network—allows users of computers, mobile phones, and other communications devices to determine the availability of other individuals before contacting them.

Chapter Objective 6: Discuss several types of electronic surveillance and monitoring, and list ways individuals can protect their privacy.

To protect the privacy of employees and customers, businesses have a responsibility to keep private information about their employees, the company, and their customers safe. Firewalls, password-protected files, and encryption can help secure this information. Businesses have the responsibility to monitor employee activities in order to ensure that employees are performing the jobs they are being paid to do, are not causing lost business, and are not leaving the company open to lawsuits. To inform employees of allowable activities, an *employee policy* or code of conduct should be developed and distributed to employees. For the highest level of privacy while at the workplace, employees should perform only work-related activities on the job.

COMPUTER SECURITY AND PRIVACY LEGISLATION

Although computer security and privacy are viewed as extremely important issues, legislating these issues is difficult due to ongoing changes in technology, jurisdictional issues, and varying opinions. Some legislation related to computer security has been enacted; new legislation is being considered on a regular basis.

Chapter Objective 7: Discuss the status of computer security and privacy legislation.

REVIEW ACTIVITIES

KEY TERM MATCHING

Instructions: Match each key term on the left with the definition on the right that best describes it.

a. digital counterfeiting

b. disaster recovery plan

c. full disk encryption (FDE)

d. information privacy

e. presence technology

f. software piracy

g. spam

h. surge suppressor

i. system failure

j. uninterruptible power supply (UPS)

1. ________ A device containing a built-in battery that provides continuous power to a computer and other connected components when the electricity goes out.

2. ________ A device that protects hardware from damage due to electrical fluctuations.

3. ________ A written plan that describes the steps a company will take following the occurrence of a disaster.

4. ________ Technology that enables one computing device (such as a computer or mobile device) to locate and identify the current status of another device on the same network.

5. ________ The complete malfunction of a computer system.

6. ________ The rights of individuals and companies to control how information about them is collected and used.

7. ________ A technology that encrypts everything stored on a storage medium automatically, without any user interaction.

8. ________ The unauthorized copying of a computer program.

9. ________ The use of computers or other types of digital equipment to make illegal copies of currency, checks, collectibles, and other items.

10. ________ Unsolicited, bulk e-mail sent over the Internet.

SELF-QUIZ

Instructions: Circle **T** if the statement is true, **F** if the statement is false, or write the best answer in the space provided. **Answers for the self-quiz are located in the References and Resources Guide at the end of the book.**

1. T F As long as a business owns one legal copy of a software program, it can install that program on as many computers as desired without fear of retribution.

2. T F Electronic profiling is the act of using electronic means to collect a variety of in-depth information about an individual, such as name, address, income, and buying habits.

3. T F Encryption can be used for privacy purposes, in addition to security purposes.

4. T F One way of safeguarding your e-mail address is to use a single e-mail address for all online activity, including personal e-mail and online shopping.

5. T F Very few major U.S. companies monitor the online activities of their employees.

6. A(n) ________ plan can help a business get operational again following a fire, an act of sabotage, or a similar disaster.

7. Color copying money is an example of ________.

8. An e-mail ________ can be used to route suspected spam automatically into an e-mail folder.

9. If you ________, you are requesting that you be removed from marketing activities or that your information not be shared with other companies; if you ________, you are requesting to participate.

10. Match each precaution with the security risk it is designed to protect against, and write the corresponding number in the blank to the left of each security risk.

a.	________ Digital counterfeiting	**1.** Encryption
b.	________ Hardware theft	**2.** Surge suppressor
c.	________ Privacy breach	**3.** Security thread
d.	________ System damage	**4.** Proximity app
e.	________ Unauthorized computer access	**5.** Cable lock

EXERCISES

1. Match each privacy risk with its related phrase, and write the corresponding number in the blank to the left of each phrase.

a.	________ Throw-away e-mail address	**1.** Employee monitoring
b.	________ Computer monitoring software	**2.** Video surveillance
c.	________ Riding public transportation	**3.** Spam

2. Supply the missing words to complete the following statements.
   a. ________ refers to all content on a storage medium being encrypted automatically.
   b. ________ refers to the ability to locate the current status of an individual via a network.
3. List two precautions that can be taken while traveling with a portable computer to guard against its theft.
4. Explain the purpose of an uninterruptible power supply (UPS) and how it differs in function from a surge suppressor.
5. Think of one computer-related security or privacy risk you have encountered recently. Describe the risk and list at least one precaution that could be taken to minimize that risk.

DISCUSSION QUESTIONS

1. Some privacy controversies stem from the fact that individuals are automatically included instead of having to opt in. For instance, with several new Facebook features over the past few years members were automatically enrolled when the feature was introduced until the member opted out. Should all online marketing activities be on an opt-in basis? How would you feel if your online activities (such as your online purchases) were shared with others without your consent? Does it make a difference if the activities are linked to your identity or anonymous? Facebook was once ordered to pay $9.5 million ($6.5 million of which was used to fund a privacy foundation) in response to a lawsuit related to its Beacon advertising program that was eventually abandoned due to user privacy complaints—is this justified?
2. Spam is increasingly being filtered by ISPs and e-mail programs, and pop-up blockers can block many Web page advertisements. If this trend continues and these activities are no longer viable marketing activities, what will the long-term effect be? Will free Web content begin to disappear? Is paying Internet users to receive spam or view Web ads a viable option? Just as with television, some amount of advertising is typically necessary in order to support free content. What do you think is the optimal balance for the Web?

PROJECTS

HOT TOPICS

1. **Electronic Health Records (EHRs)** The use of electronic health records (EHRs) is growing rapidly. Proponents view EHRs as a means to deliver better care more efficiently. However, some privacy advocates are concerned about the possible security breaches of servers containing digital private medical information.

   For this project, research the current use of EHRs. What are the benefits? Are EHRs widely used? Are you concerned about your medical history being stored on a computer that, potentially, could be accessed by a hacker or other unauthorized individual? Do you think the risk of a privacy breach is higher with EHRs as compared with the records contained in conventional paper file folders? At the conclusion of your research, prepare a one-page summary of your findings and opinions and submit it to your instructor.

SHORT ANSWER/ RESEARCH

2. **E-Voting** E-voting—casting ballots online or via an electronic e-voting machine—has been surrounded by controversy. Concerns include the accuracy and security of e-voting machines, the ability of online voting systems to prevent someone from voting as another individual and to protect the privacy of votes cast electronically, and the ability to perform an accurate recount.

   For this project, research the current status of e-voting. Have universal standards been developed for all e-voting machines used in the United States or is that decision made on a state-by-state basis? What security measures are being used with e-voting and online voting systems to ensure they cannot be hacked and that only the registered voter is permitted to cast his or her vote? Form an opinion about the use of e-voting machines and online voting. Would you be comfortable casting your vote via an e-voting machine? How about online? At some point, do you think online voting will become the norm? If so, how would you suggest handling individuals who have no Internet access available to them on Election Day? At the conclusion of your research, submit your findings and opinions to your instructor in the form of a short paper, no more than two pages in length.

HANDS ON

3. **Browser Privacy Settings** There are a variety of settings in a Web browser that pertain to privacy, such as cookie, cache, and history settings.

   For this project, find a computer (either your own or one in a school computer lab or at your local public library) on which you are permitted to change the Internet options (ask permission first if you are not sure if these actions are allowed) and perform the following tasks:

   a. Open Internet Explorer and use the *Internet Options* option on the Tools menu or button to check the current settings on the General and Privacy tabs. Using the General tab, delete your browsing history (temporary files, history, cookies, saved passwords, and Web form information).

   b. Visit at least five different Web sites to build a history and cookie list. You may want to go to an e-commerce site and add items to your shopping cart (but don't check out) or personalize a portal page, such as MSNBC.com or My Yahoo!.

   c. Display your history list. Are the Web sites you visited listed? Use the Browsing history Settings button on the Internet Options dialog box to view the temporary files, including your cookie files. Were new cookies added during your session? If so, are they all from the Web sites you visited, or are any of them third-party cookies?

   d. Delete all temporary Internet files, sign out of any personalized pages, and close the browser window. Prepare a short summary of your work to submit to your instructor.

ETHICS IN ACTION

4. **Security Camera Networks** As discussed in the chapter, live surveillance cameras are being used at an increasing number of public locations. Some view this as a valid crime prevention tool; others think it is an invasion of privacy. Is it ethical for businesses to use video cameras to record customers' activities? If so, for what purposes? Does the government have the responsibility to use every means possible to protect the country and its citizens? Or do citizens have the right not to be watched in public? One objection stated about these systems is "It's not the same as a cop on the corner. This is a cop on every corner." What if it were a live police officer at each public video camera location instead of a camera? Would that be more acceptable from a privacy standpoint? If people do not plan to commit criminal acts in public, should they be concerned that law enforcement personnel may see them? Does the risk of being recorded deter some illegal or unethical acts?

   For this project, form an opinion about the ethical ramifications of public video surveillance and be prepared to discuss your position (in class, via an online class discussion group, in a class chat room, or via a class blog, depending on your instructor's directions). You may also be asked to write a short paper expressing your opinion.

PRESENTATION/ DEMONSTRATION

5. **Privacy Policy Flip-Flops** Although a company's privacy policy may look acceptable when you read it before submitting personal information to that company, there is no guarantee that the policy will not be changed.

   For this project, locate three different privacy policies on Web sites, analyze them, and compare them. Do the policies specify what personal information might be shared and with whom? Do the organizations reserve the right to change their policies at a later time without notice? If so, will they try to notify consumers? Do any of the policies allow for any sharing of data to third-party organizations? If so, is the data personally identifiable, and can customers opt out? Form an opinion regarding a company's right to change its privacy policy and the impact such a change may have on customer loyalty. Share your findings with the class in the form of a short presentation. The presentation should not exceed 10 minutes and should make use of one or more presentation aids, such as a whiteboard, handouts, or a computer-based slide presentation (your instructor may provide additional requirements). You may also be asked to submit a summary of the presentation to your instructor.

BALANCING ACT

6. **Should the Government Be Allowed to Prevent Web Site Tracking?** The proposed *Do-Not-Track Online Act of 2013* has rekindled the debate surrounding tracking Web site activity for advertising purposes. Though the law, if enacted, wouldn't prohibit tracking, it would require the FTC to establish standardized mechanisms that people could use to have their Web browser tell Web sites and other online entities if they agree to tracking activities. Advocates of do-not-track provisions argue that they just want to protect privacy. Companies with Web sites (particularly small- and medium-sized businesses) state they depend on ad networks and other online resources to connect with potential customers and do-not-track provisions may create a hardship. If tracking provisions are enabled, should consumers be required to opt in to marketing activities or to opt out of them? Who should make the regulations—technology companies? Consumers? The government? Are you concerned that some Web sites track your browsing activities to display relevant ads and offers or do you like the customization provided by the tracking? Is voluntary compliance with standards developed by the industry sufficient or does this issue require legislation? If you use social media, how does Web site tracking compare with the information you share via your social networking sites in terms of loss of privacy? If tracking were illegal unless a consumer opts in, would you? Why or why not?

   Pick a side on this issue, form an opinion and gather supporting evidence, and be prepared to discuss and defend your position in a classroom debate or in a 1–2 page paper, depending on your instructor's directions.

expert insight on...

Web-Based Multimedia and E-Commerce

Courtesy eBay. The eBay logo is a trademark of eBay Inc.

Jim Griffith, aka "Griff," is the Dean of eBay Education, a roving eBay ambassador, an eBay spokesperson, the host of eBay Radio, and the author of *The Official eBay Bible*. An enthusiastic eBay buyer and seller since 1996, Griff spends nearly all his waking hours teaching others how to use eBay effectively, safely, and profitably, and spreading the word about eBay across print, radio, and TV. Griff has worked for eBay for 17 years.

A Conversation with JIM GRIFFITH

Dean of eBay Education, eBay

> "*. . . the most valuable asset for any business, online or offline, is the customer.*"

My Background . . .

Although I have many roles at eBay, my most public role—Dean of eBay Education—is unique, slightly unorthodox, and best understood in the context of my history with the company. I was originally a user on eBay in the very early days (1996) and spent a lot of time assisting other buyers and sellers on eBay's one chat board. My posts came to the attention of eBay founder Pierre Omidyar who offered me a job as eBay's first customer support rep. I continued to be an active member of the eBay community along with my new duties at the time, which included assisting and teaching buyers, sellers, and eBay employees how to use eBay. Over time, I also became an eBay spokesperson, lead instructor of our eBay University program, author of *The Official eBay Bible* (now in its third edition), and host of eBay Radio.

In addition to the obvious knowledge of the eBay Web site, our policies, and the basics of business, the skills that proved to be most critical during my seventeen-year tenure at eBay (and I should say I am still refining them) would be diplomacy, empathy, civility, and a strong sense of self-deprecating humor.

It's Important to Know . . .

The basic principles behind successful e-commerce are no different than those behind traditional offline commerce. For example, the most valuable asset for any business, online or offline, is the customer. This is especially true for e-commerce where the competition for customers is fierce. Although the technologies and transaction experience for the Web and for traditional retail are markedly different, the standard, tried-and-true business basics (such as business planning, inventory procurement and management, customer acquisition and management, and marketing) are as crucial to e-commerce as they are to traditional business.

The importance of an easy-to-use, well-designed, and appealing Web site. All of the inventory in the world is for naught if the buyer cannot search through it and purchase it with ease.

Online commerce technologies are constantly changing. What is cutting edge today will soon be passé. Anyone who makes his or her living online absolutely must stay on top of all online marketplace technology advances and adopt and implement them as necessary. As an example, the recent explosion in the popularity and adoption of social networking sites like Twitter and Facebook have created an entire new field of online business called "Social Commerce." Consumers in general—and online consumers in particular—are much more business and technology savvy than they were a mere 5 years ago. Demanding consumers will have little or no patience for online businesses that do not provide the best possible shopping experience.

How I Use this Technology . . .

Besides working for eBay, I am an avid consumer and seller online. I make at least one online purchase a day and I always have a selection of items up for sale (on eBay). My online e-commerce activity along with my job of instructing and assisting buyers and sellers to navigate and utilize eBay and PayPal requires an extensive working knowledge of and familiarity with our own Web sites (eBay and PayPal).

> *"Anyone who makes his or her living online absolutely must stay on top of all online marketplace technology advances . . ."*

What the Future Holds . . .

The Internet revolution has in many ways changed the nature of human commerce forever. The most important impact of the Internet revolution has been the empowerment of the consumer. Never before has the buyer had so much control over the direction of the marketplace. This will only increase as time goes on, and the businesses that acknowledge this new reality and plan accordingly are the ones that will survive and thrive.

In the future, more brick-and-mortar business owners will adopt the Internet as a primary or secondary channel for their businesses. In addition, more small businesses will start up solely on the Internet as the cost of entry into the online marketplace continues to drop and the gap in the costs of starting an online and offline business continues to grow. This will lead to even more choices for the online consumer, who will continue to exert increasing service demands and pricing pressure on online sellers.

However, as the Internet becomes more a part of our day-to-day lives, the idea of the Internet as a unique environment will start to disappear, especially as access to the Internet becomes cheaper and more widespread (for example, embedded in appliances, cell phones, media devices, and even the walls of our homes!). Just like technologies before it (such as telegraph, telephone, radio, and television), we will soon take the Internet for granted as it matures and eventually becomes completely entwined within the matrix of our daily lives.

My Advice to Students . . .

Unless you're interested in pursuing a career in computer science, engineering, or programming, an academic study of the inner workings of the Internet or computers will not be a requirement for a career in an Internet-based industry. However, Internet companies will have an ever-increasing demand for inventive product marketing personnel, product designers, and intellectual property attorneys.

That said, whatever career you pursue, never forget that the direction of online commerce (and the world in general) is toward more control in the hands of the individual. Adjust your career path accordingly!

Discussion Question

Jim Griffith views the online buyer as an extremely influential part of the e-commerce marketplace. Think of online purchases you have made. How did your buying decision differ from shopping locally? What factors influenced your final decision? How does the increased number of online sources for products impact the online marketplace? Do consumers have more influence over online stores than over brick-and-mortar stores? Why or why not? If you were starting a business, would you have an e-commerce presence? A brick-and-mortar presence? Both? Be prepared to discuss your position (in class, via an online class discussion group, in a class chat room, or via a class blog, depending on your instructor's directions). You may also be asked to write a short paper expressing your opinion.

>For more information on eBay, visit www.ebay.com. For more information about e-commerce, read *FutureShop* by Daniel Nissanoff, and for more information about effective, safe, and successful buying or selling on eBay, refer to *The Official eBay Bible* by Jim "Griff" Griffith.

chapter 6

Intellectual Property Rights and Ethics

After completing this chapter, you will be able to do the following:

1. Understand the different types of intellectual property rights and how they relate to computer use.
2. Explain what is meant by the term *ethics*.
3. Provide several examples of unethical behavior in the use of intellectual property and in computer-related matters.
4. Explain what computer hoaxes and digital manipulation are and how they relate to computer ethics.
5. Understand how ethics can impact business practices and decision making.
6. Discuss the current status of legislation related to intellectual property rights and ethics.

outline

Masterfile

OVERVIEW

While computers and related technology add convenience and enjoyment to our daily lives, they also can make it easier to perform some types of illegal or unethical acts. For example, computers can be used to launch computer viruses, create high-quality illegal copies of software programs and music CDs, and copy information from a Web page and present it as original work. However, just because technology enables us to do something, does that make it right? Is legality the only measuring stick, or are there some acts that are legal but still morally or ethically wrong? Is there only one set of ethics, or can ethics vary from person to person? This chapter continues where Chapter 5 left off by exploring computer-related societal issues. Two important issues—intellectual property rights and ethics—are discussed in this chapter; other societal issues are included in Chapter 7.

The chapter begins with a look at a legal issue that all computer users should be aware of—intellectual property rights. The specific types of intellectual property rights are discussed, along with examples of the types of property that each right protects. Next is a discussion of ethics, including what they are and a variety of ethical issues surrounding computer use by individuals and businesses. Topics include the ethical use of copyrighted material, ethical uses of resources and information, unethical use of digital manipulation, ethical business practices and decision making, and the impact of cultural differences with respect to ethics and business decisions. The chapter closes with a look at legislation related to the issues discussed in this chapter. ■

INTELLECTUAL PROPERTY RIGHTS

Intellectual property rights are the legal rights to which the creators of *intellectual property*—original creative works—are entitled. Intellectual property rights indicate who has the right to use, perform, or display a creative work and what can legally be done with that work. In addition, intellectual property rights determine how long the creator retains rights to the property and other related restrictions. Examples of intellectual property include music and movies; paintings, computer graphics, and other works of art; poetry, books, and other types of written works; symbols, names, and designs used in conjunction with a business; architectural drawings; and inventions. Intellectual property rights can be claimed by individuals or by companies or other organizations. The three main types of intellectual property rights are *copyrights, trademarks*, and *patents*. Copyrights, trademarks, and patents are issued by individual countries; U.S. intellectual property rights are discussed in more detail next.

>**Intellectual property rights.** The legal rights to which creators of original creative works (such as artistic or literary works, inventions, corporate logos, and more) are entitled.

Copyrights

A **copyright** is a form of protection available to the creator of an original artistic, musical, or literary work, such as a book, movie, software program, song, or painting. It gives the copyright holder the exclusive right to publish, reproduce, distribute, perform, or display the work. The *1976 Copyright Act* extends copyright protection to nonpublished works, so, immediately after creating a work in some type of material form (such as on paper, film, videotape, or a digital storage medium), the creator automatically owns the copyright of that work. Consequently, the creator is entitled to copyright protection of that work and has the right to make a statement, such as "Copyright © 2014 John Smith. All rights reserved." Although works created in the United States after March 1, 1989, are not required to display a copyright notice in order to retain their copyright protection, displaying a copyright statement on a published work (see Figure 6-1) reminds others that the work is protected by copyright law and that any use must comply with copyright law. Only the creator of a work (or his or her employer if the work is created as a *work for hire*; that is, within the scope of employment) can rightfully claim copyright. Copyrights can be registered with the *U. S. Copyright Office*. Although registration is not required for copyright protection, it does offer an advantage if the need to prove ownership of a copyright ever arises, such as during a copyright-infringement lawsuit. Most countries offer some copyright protection to works registered in other countries.

© 2014 Course Technology, Cengage Learning

ALL RIGHTS RESERVED. No part of this work covered by the copyright herein may be reproduced, transmitted, stored or used in any form or by any means graphic, electronic, or mechanical, including but not limited to photocopying, recording, scanning, digitizing, taping, Web distribution, information networks, or information storage and retrieval systems, except as permitted under Section 107 or 108 of the 1976 United States Copyright Act, without the prior written permission of the publisher.

BOOK COPYRIGHT NOTICES

© 2013 Pinterest. All rights reserved.

WEB SITE COPYRIGHT NOTICES

FIGURE 6-1

Copyright statements. Are often included on books, Web sites, and other original copyrighted works.

Anyone wanting to use copyrighted materials must first obtain permission from the copyright holder and pay any required fee. One exception is the legal concept of *fair use*, which permits limited duplication and use of a portion of copyrighted material for specific purposes, such as criticism, commentary, news reporting, teaching, and research. For example, a teacher may legally read a copyrighted poem for discussion in a poetry class, and a news crew may videotape a small portion of a song at a concert to include in a news report of that concert. Copyrights apply to both published and unpublished works and remain in effect until 70 years after the creator's death. Copyrights for works registered either by an organization or as anonymous works last 95 years from the date of publication or 120 years from the date of creation, whichever is shorter. One emerging issue is the *termination rights* granted to musicians and songwriters in the *1976 Copyright Act*—if they originally gave music rights to their publisher, they can request those rights back after 35 years (because the law went into effect in 1978, the first set of rights became eligiable for termination in 2013).

TIP

The first copyright termination victor was Victor Willis, the lead singer of the Village People, who, in 2013, was granted control of his share of the copyright to *YMCA* and other songs he wrote in the late 1970s.

It is important to realize that purchasing a copyrighted item (such as a book, painting, or movie) does not change the copyright protection afforded to the creator of that item. Although you have purchased the right to use the item, you cannot legally duplicate it or portray it as your own creation. Some of the most widely publicized copyright-infringement issues today center around individuals illegally distributing copyright-protected content (particularly music, movies, and e-books) via the Internet, as discussed later in this chapter.

To protect their rights, some creators of digital content (such as art, music, photographs, and movies) use **digital watermarks**—a subtle alteration of digital content that is not noticeable when the work is viewed or played but that identifies the copyright holder. For instance, the digital watermark for an image might consist of slight changes to the brightness of a specific pattern of pixels that are imperceptible to people but are easily read by software. Digital watermarks can also be made visible, if desired, such as to add the name of a company or Web site URL to a photo being posted online, or to inform individuals that the photo is copyrighted and should not be used elsewhere.

>**Copyright.** The legal right to sell, publish, or distribute an original artistic or literary work; it is held by the creator of a work as soon as it exists in physical form. >**Digital watermark.** A subtle alteration of digital content that is not noticeable when the work is viewed or played but that identifies the copyright holder.

Digital watermarks can be added to images, music, video, TV shows, e-books, and other digital content found online or distributed in digital form to identify their copyright holders, their authorized distributors, and other important information. Digital watermarks are typically added with software and, as shown in Figure 6-2, are usually invisible until they are read with appropriate software (such as Adobe Photoshop or a proprietary reader). The purpose of digital watermarking is to give digital content a unique identity that remains intact even if the work is copied, edited, compressed, or otherwise manipulated. For instance, movies sent to movie theaters typically include a digital watermark that can be used to trace a pirated movie back to the theater where the pirated movie was created in order to help authorities locate and prosecute the criminal. Some digital watermark services also offer search services that continually scan the Web to locate digitally watermarked images and notify the copyright holder when those images are found. Because of the vast amount of copyrighted content distributed via the Internet today, the market for digital watermarking technology is growing rapidly. For a look at a new application for digital watermarking—linking rich media to published content—see the Inside the Industry box.

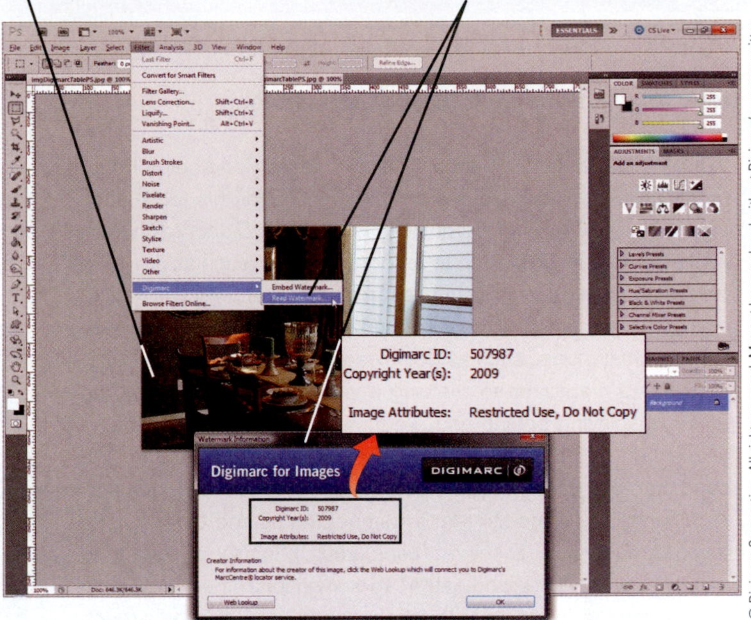

FIGURE 6-2
Digital watermarks.

Another rights-protection tool used with digital content is **digital rights management (DRM) software**. DRM software is used to control the use of a work. For instance, DRM software used in conjunction with business documents (called *enterprise rights management*) can protect a sensitive business document by controlling usage of that document, such as by limiting who can view, print, or copy it. DRM software used with digital content (such as movies, e-books, and music) downloaded or streamed via the Internet can control whether or not a downloaded file can be copied to another device, as well as make a video-on-demand movie or a rented e-book unviewable after the rental period expires.

Trademarks

A **trademark** is a word, phrase, symbol, or design (or a combination of words, phrases, symbols, or designs) that identifies and distinguishes one product or service from another. A trademark used to identify a service is also called a *service mark*. Trademarks that are claimed but not registered with the *U.S. Patent and Trademark Office* (*USPTO*) can use the mark ™; nonregistered service marks can use the symbol ℠. The symbol ® is reserved for registered trademarks and service marks. Trademarks for products usually appear on the product packaging with the appropriate trademark symbol; service marks are typically used in the advertising of a service because there is no product on which the mark can be printed. Trademarked words and phrases—such as iPod®, Chicken McNuggets®, Google Docs™, and FedEx Office℠—are widely used today. Trademarked logos (see Figure 6-3) are also common. Trademarks last 10 years, but they can be renewed as many times as desired, as long as they are being used in commerce.

In addition to protecting the actual trademarked words, phrases, or logos, trademark law also protects domain names that match a company's trademark, such as Amazon.com and Lego.com. There have been a number of claims of

FIGURE 6-3
Examples of trademarked logos.

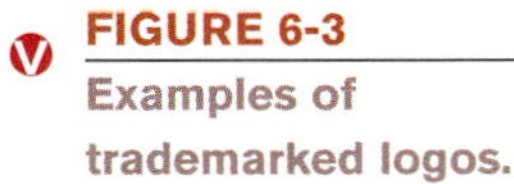

>**Digital rights management (DRM) software.** Software used to protect and manage the rights of creators of digital content, such as art, music, photographs, and movies. >**Trademark.** A word, phrase, symbol, or design that identifies goods or services.

INSIDE THE INDUSTRY

New Applications for Digital Watermarking

While digital watermarks are still used to identify and help protect digital content from misuse, new applications for this technology are emerging. One such technology is *Digimarc Discover*™, which enables your mobile device to recognize media (such as newspapers, magazines, product packaging, television shows, and music) in your immediate surroundings to provide you with online content linked to that media, such as downloading a coupon for a product shown in a magazine ad, viewing a video related to a magazine article, displaying pricing and product information corresponding to a product's packaging, and viewing band information for the song currently being played over a restaurant's sound system.

Available as a mobile app for smartphones and other mobile devices, Digimarc Discover uses your phone's camera and microphone to "look and listen" to surrounding media. An app recognizes the digital watermarks embedded in the media (such as in the textbook shown in the accompanying illustration), and then the appropriate options for the available online content and services are displayed on the phone (such as a virtual tour of the Colosseum, historical photos and other information, or prices for upcoming flights to Rome).

This emerging digital watermarking application enables publishers, advertising agencies, and other companies to make a variety of rich media available to customers without having to give up valuable space in print publications or product packaging (as is required with a QR code or other code that needs to be displayed on the printed media in order to be functional).

online trademark infringement in recent years, particularly those involving domain names that contain, or are similar to, a trademark. For instance, several celebrities—such as Madonna and Tracy Morgan—have fought to be given the exclusive right to use what they consider their rightful domain names (Madonna.com and TracyMorgan.com, respectively). Other examples include Twitter's complaint against an organization using the domain name *twitter.org*, RadioShack's objection to a private individual using *shack.com* for the Web site of his design business, and Microsoft being accused by British Sky Broadcasting Group of trademark infringement with its SkyDrive service.

While businesses and individuals can file lawsuits to recover a disputed domain name, a faster and less-expensive option is to file a complaint with a dispute resolution provider, such as the *World Intellectual Property Organization* (*WIPO*). WIPO is a specialized agency of the United Nations and attempts to resolve international commercial disputes about intellectual property between private parties. This includes domain name disputes; in fact, WIPO has resolved more than 27,000 domain name dispute cases since it was formed. Complainants pay a filing fee to start the resolution process, and then WIPO has the power to award the disputed domain name to the most appropriate party. If the domain name was acquired with the intent to profit from the goodwill of a trademark belonging to someone else (such as by generating revenue from Web site visitors intending to go to the trademark holder's Web site or by trying to sell the domain name to the trademark holder at an inflated price) or to otherwise abuse a trademark, the act of acquiring that domain name is deemed to be **cybersquatting** and the

>**Cybersquatting.** The act of registering a domain name with the intent to profit from the goodwill of a trademark belonging to someone else.

trademark holder generally prevails. If the current domain name holder has a legitimate reason for using that name and does not appear to be a cybersquatter, however, WIPO may allow the holder to continue to use that domain name. For instance, WIPO ruled that TracyMorgan.com and twitter.org were confusingly similar to the actor's name and the trademark owned by Twitter, respectively, and that neither owner of the disputed domain names had a legitimate interest in their respective domain name, so WIPO transferred the disputed domain names to Tracy Morgan and Twitter, respectively. However, the owner of the design business (whose last name is Shackleton and whose nickname is "Shack") was allowed to keep the shack.com domain name because it was ruled that he had a legitimate interest in that name. In the SkyDrive case, Microsoft was not accused of cybersquatting but did lose the case and, therefore, must rebrand its SkyDrive service, unless it reaches an agreement with Sky to purchase use of the trademark. The *Anticybersquatting Consumer Protection Act*, which was signed into law in 1999, makes cybersquatting illegal and it allows for penalties up to $100,000 for each willful registration of a domain name that infringes on a trademark.

TIP

Trademarks and patents are territorial, so companies and individuals wanting trademark or patent protection in multiple countries should apply for a trademark or patent in all of those countries.

Many recent cybersquatting cases deal with *typosquatting*—registering a domain name that is similar to a trademark or domain name but that is slightly misspelled in hopes that individuals will accidentally arrive at the site when trying to type the URL of the legitimate site. These sites often contain pay-per-click advertising used to generate revenue for the typosquatter; they can also be phishing sites that use spoofed Web pages to try to obtain sensitive information from visitors, or they can redirect visitors to sites for competing products or services. To prevent typosquatting and to protect their brands and other trademarks, many companies register variations of their domain names proactively. For instance, Verizon has registered more than 10,000 domain names related to its three most visible brands (Verizon, VZ, and FiOS). If a cybersquatter is causing enough damage to warrant it, companies can file a lawsuit against the cybersquatter. For instance, Verizon once sued a company for unlawfully registering 663 domain names that were either identical or confusingly similar to Verizon trademarks. In late 2008, Verizon was awarded more than $33 million in that case—the largest cybersquatting judgment to date. Another form of cybersquatting involves individuals not affiliated with a company opening social media accounts using the company's brand names or variations of its brand names—typically either to use the account to sell pirated goods posing as the legitimate company, or in hopes the company will pay them to relinquish control of the accounts.

FIGURE 6-4

Patents. The patent shown here is for a new e-book menu system.

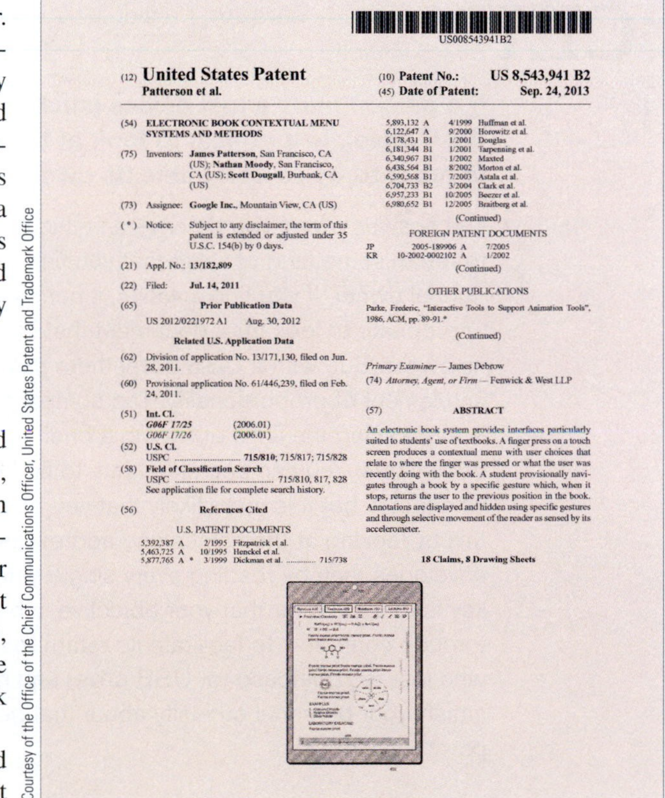

US008543941B2

(12) **United States Patent**
Patterson et al.

(10) **Patent No.: US 8,543,941 B2**
(45) **Date of Patent: Sep. 24, 2013**

(54) **ELECTRONIC BOOK CONTEXTUAL MENU SYSTEMS AND METHODS**

(75) Inventors: **James Patterson**, San Francisco, CA (US); **Nathan Moody**, San Francisco, CA (US); **Scott Dougall**, Burbank, CA (US)

(73) Assignee: **Google Inc.**, Mountain View, CA (US)

(*) Notice: Subject to any disclaimer, the term of this patent is extended or adjusted under 35 U.S.C. 154(b) by 0 days.

(21) Appl. No.: **13/182,809**

(22) Filed: **Jul. 14, 2011**

(65) **Prior Publication Data**

US 2012/0221972 A1 Aug. 30, 2012

Related U.S. Application Data

(62) Division of application No. 13/171,130, filed on Jun. 28, 2011.

(60) Provisional application No. 61/446,239, filed on Feb. 24, 2011.

(51) **Int. Cl.**
G06F 17/25 (2006.01)
G06F 17/26 (2006.01)

(52) **U.S. Cl.**
USPC **715/810**; 715/817; 715/828

(58) **Field of Classification Search**
USPC 715/810, 817, 828
See application file for complete search history.

(56) **References Cited**

U.S. PATENT DOCUMENTS

5,392,387 A 2/1995 Fitzpatrick et al.
5,463,725 A 10/1995 Henckel et al.
5,877,765 A * 3/1999 Dickman et al. 715/738
5,893,132 A 4/1999 Huffman et al.
6,122,647 A 9/2000 Horowitz et al.
6,178,431 B1 1/2001 Douglas
6,181,344 B1 1/2001 Tarpenning et al.
6,340,967 B1 1/2002 Maxted
6,438,564 B1 8/2002 Morton et al.
6,590,568 B1 7/2003 Astala et al.
6,704,733 B2 3/2004 Clark et al.
6,957,233 B1 10/2005 Beezer et al.
6,980,652 B1 12/2005 Braitberg et al.

(Continued)

FOREIGN PATENT DOCUMENTS

JP 2005-189906 A 7/2005
KR 10-2002-0002102 A 1/2002

(Continued)

OTHER PUBLICATIONS

Parke, Frederic, "Interactive Tools to Support Animation Tools", 1986, ACM, pp. 89-91.*

(Continued)

Primary Examiner — James Debrow
(74) *Attorney, Agent, or Firm* — Fenwick & West LLP

(57) **ABSTRACT**

An electronic book system provides interfaces particularly suited to students' use of textbooks. A finger press on a touch screen produces a contextual menu with user choices that relate to where the finger was pressed or what the user was recently doing with the book. A student provisionally navigates through a book by a specific gesture which, when it stops, returns the user to the previous position in the book. Annotations are displayed and hidden using specific gestures and through selective movement of the reader as sensed by its accelerometer.

18 Claims, 8 Drawing Sheets

Courtesy of the Office of the Chief Communications Officer, United States Patent and Trademark Office

Patents

Unlike copyrights (which protect artistic and literary works) and trademarks (which protect a company's logo and brand names), a **patent** protects inventions by granting exclusive rights of an invention to its inventor for a period of 20 years. A patented invention is typically a unique product, but it can also be a process or procedure that provides a new way of doing something or that offers a new technical solution to a problem. Like trademarks, U.S. patents are issued by the U.S. Patent and Trademark Office (USPTO). A recent patent issued to Google for a new e-book menu system is shown in Figure 6-4.

The number of patent applications, particularly those related to computer and Internet products, has skyrocketed in recent

>**Patent.** A form of protection for an invention that can be granted by the government; gives exclusive rights of an invention to its inventor for 20 years.

years. In the United States, patents have also been granted for Internet business methods and models, such as Priceline.com's name-your-own-price business model and Amazon.com's one-click purchase procedure. One controversial patent granted to Google in 2013 is for "pay-for-gaze" advertising—a business model for charging advertisers according to the number of views an ad receives via a "head mounted gaze tracking device" (speculated to be Google Glass). When a product or business model is patented, no other organization can duplicate it without paying a royalty to the patent holder or risking prolonged patent litigation. Patent issues sometimes interfere with a company's new products or services and tech companies are regularly sued for patent infringement. For instance, Apple has been sued in several patent infringement lawsuits related to its iPhone, Microsoft has claimed that Linux infringed on many of its patents, and Marvell Technology was recently ordered to pay $1.17 billion for infringing on disk drive patents held by Carnegie Mellon University.

Patents can be difficult, expensive, and time consuming to obtain. However, companies routinely seek patents for new inventions (IBM was awarded 6,478 patents in 2012 and has been the patent leader for 20 years). Patents can also be very lucrative; consequently, businesses have been acquired, at least in part, for their patents, and patents are sometimes purchased outright. For example, Microsoft recently agreed to pay AOL $1 billion for 800 undisclosed technology patents.

ETHICS

The term **ethics** refers to standards of moral conduct. For example, telling the truth is a matter of ethics. An unethical act is not always illegal, although it might be, but an illegal act is usually viewed as unethical by most people. For example, purposely lying to a friend is unethical but usually not illegal, while perjuring oneself in a courtroom as a witness is both illegal and unethical. Whether or not criminal behavior is involved, ethics guide our behavior and play an integral role in our lives.

Much more ambiguous than the law, ethical beliefs can vary widely from one individual to another. Ethical beliefs may also vary based on one's religion, country, race, or culture. In addition, different ethical standards can apply to different areas of one's life. For example, *personal ethics* guide an individual's personal behavior and *business ethics* guide an individual's workplace behavior. **Computer ethics** relate to an individual's computer use and are significant today because the proliferation of computers and mobile devices in the home and workplace provides more opportunities for unethical acts than in the past. The Internet also makes it easy to distribute information that many individuals would view as unethical

ASK THE EXPERT

CEI **Dr. Ramon C. Barquin,** President, Computer Ethics Institute

Courtesy of Computer Ethics Institute

If a person finds a lost device (such as a USB flash drive), is it ethical to look at the contents in order to try to determine its owner?

The answer is yes, you do have an ethical obligation to return something of value that you find to its rightful owner. If you find a wallet, it certainly is appropriate to look for a document that identifies its owner. But, with a USB drive, there has to be an element of proportionality. The comparison here is more along the lines of finding a briefcase full of documents. You can and should try to find the person who lost it, but it is more likely that you could do this by looking at the names and addresses on the envelopes than by reading every single letter. The key is to remember that your objective in browsing through content is to facilitate its return to the person who lost the briefcase (or USB drive) and not to satisfy your personal curiosity about that person's private affairs.

>**Ethics.** Overall standards of moral conduct. >**Computer ethics.** Standards of moral conduct as they relate to computer use.

TECHNOLOGY AND YOU

Virtual Currency—Real or Not?

While Second Life, World of Warcraft, and other virtual worlds only exist in cyberspace, there is nothing virtual about the money being made. For instance, in 2006, Ailin Graef became the first virtual world millionaire when her Second Life assets (measured in the virtual currency *Linden dollars*) topped $1 million in U.S. dollars.

But Linden dollars and *World of Warcraft gold* aren't the only *digital currency* (electronic money passed between parties without traditional banking or money transfer systems) in town. For instance, digital gift cards like *Facebook Credits* and *Nintendo Points* can be used to purchase games and apps on Facebook or for Nintendo devices, respectively, and *Amazon Coins* can be used to purchase content for Kindle Fire devices. And one of the most prominent digital currencies, *Bitcoins* (see the accompanying photo), can be used to make purchases in numerous online games and at some online retailers.

One issue surrounding the growing use of digital currency is whether or not it is a real currency and, as such, is subject to existing laws. For instance, the U.S. Commodity Futures Trading Commission is considering whether virtual currency (such as Bitcoin) should be subject to its rules and Bitcoin and several online payment entities (including mobile payment processor Square) were issued cease and desist letters from states for failing to have proper licensing for money transmission. However, a federal judge may have ended the controversy in 2013 with an opinion issued in a fraud case related to a Bitcoin-based Ponzi scheme worth millions of dollars. The defendant challenged the fraud charges on the basis that Bitcoins do not meet the definition of currency—the judge disagreed and ruled that Bitcoin is a currency or form of money, in the same way that gold and silver are commodities that are recognized as money.

Another issue is the taxability of virtual profits. When virtual goods are cashed out for actual cash, it's clear that the profits should be reported as taxable income. But what about taxing virtual profits that never leave the virtual world? This issue is complicated by the fact that goods or services obtained through barter or as prizes are taxable in the United States under current law, and the fact that virtual transactions have real-world value. While the IRS has not yet specifically addressed the issue of whether or not virtual income is taxable in the United States before it is exchanged for real-life money and/or for goods or services, the issue is being looked into. Some countries have already made that decision, such as Australia, which implemented taxes on virtual income in late 2006, and South Korea, which has a *value-added tax* (*VAT*) on individuals with virtual income over a certain amount. Whether the United States and other countries will follow suit remains to be seen.

Courtesy Casascius

These physical Bitcoins each have a unique code that can be used to retrieve virtual Bitcoins online.

(such as computer viruses and spyware), as well as to distribute copies of software, movies, music, and other digital content in an illegal and, therefore, unethical manner.

Whether at home, at work, or at school, individuals encounter ethical issues every day. For example, you may need to make ethical decisions such as whether or not to accept a relative's offer of a free copy of a downloaded song or movie, whether or not to have a friend help you take an online exam, whether or not to upload a photo of your friend to Facebook without asking permission, whether or not to post a rumor on a campus gossip site, or whether or not to report as taxable income the virtual money you make online, as discussed in the Technology and You box.

As an employee, you may need to decide whether or not to print your child's birthday party invitations on the office color printer, whether or not to correct your boss if he or she gives you credit for another employee's idea, or whether or not to sneak a look at information that technically you have access to but have no legitimate reason to view. IT employees, in particular, often face this latter ethical dilemma because they typically have both access and the technical ability to retrieve a wide variety of personal and professional information about other employees, such as their salary information, Web-surfing history, and e-mail.

TIP

Social networks have introduced new ethical dilemmas, such as whether or not businesses have the right to reprimand employees over social networking activity and whether or not school districts have the right to limit communications teachers have with students via social networks.

Businesses also deal with a variety of ethical issues in the course of normal business activities—from determining how many computers on which a particular software program should be installed; to identifying how customer information should be obtained, used, and shared; to deciding business practices. **Business ethics** are the standards of conduct that guide a business's policies, decisions, and actions.

Ethical Use of Copyrighted Material

Both businesses and individuals should be very careful when copying, sharing, or otherwise using copyrighted material to ensure that the material is used in both a legal and an ethical manner. Common types of copyrighted material encountered on a regular basis include software, books, Web-based articles, music, e-books, and movies. Software ownership rights were discussed in Chapter 2; the rest of these topics are covered next.

TIP

For a review of how to cite online material properly, refer to Figure 3-16 in Chapter 3.

Books and Web-Based Articles

Copyright law protects print-based books, newspaper articles, e-books, Web-based articles, and all other types of literary material. Consequently, these materials cannot be reproduced, presented as one's own original material, or otherwise used in an unauthorized manner. Students, researchers, authors, and other writers need to be especially careful when using literary material as a resource for papers, articles, books, and so forth, to ensure the material is used appropriately and is properly credited to the original author. To present someone else's work as your own is **plagiarism**, which is both a violation of copyright law and an unethical act. It can also get you fired, as some reporters have found out the hard way after faking quotes or plagiarizing content from other newspapers. Some examples of acts that would normally be considered plagiarism or not considered plagiarism are shown in Figure 6-5.

With the widespread availability of online articles and fee-based online term paper services, some students might be tempted to create their papers by copying and pasting excerpts of online content into their documents to pass off as their original work. But these students should realize that this is plagiarism, and instructors can usually tell when a paper is created in this manner. There are also online resources instructors can use to test the originality of student papers; the results of one such test are shown in Figure 6-6. Most colleges and universities have strict consequences for plagiarism, such as automatically failing the assignment or course, or being expelled from the institution. As Internet-based plagiarism continues to expand to younger and younger students, many middle schools and high schools are developing strict plagiarism policies as well.

FIGURE 6-5
Examples of what is and what is not normally considered plagiarism.

PLAGIARISM	NOT PLAGIARISM
A student including a few sentences or a few paragraphs written by another author in his essay without crediting the original author.	A student including a few sentences or a few paragraphs written by another author in his essay, either indenting the quotation or placing it inside quotation marks, and crediting the original author with a citation in the text or with a footnote or endnote.
A newspaper reporter changing a few words in a sentence or paragraph written by another author and including the revised text in an article without crediting the original author.	A newspaper reporter paraphrasing a few sentences or paragraphs written by another author without changing the meaning of the text, including the revised text in an article, and crediting the original author with a proper citation.
A student copying and pasting information from various online documents to create her research paper without crediting the original authors.	A student copying and pasting information from various online documents and using those quotes in her research paper either indented or enclosed in quotation marks with the proper citations for each author.
A teacher sharing a poem with a class, leading the class to believe the poem was his original work.	A teacher sharing a poem with a class, clearly identifying the poet.

>**Business ethics.** Standards of moral conduct that guide a business's policies, decisions, and actions. >**Plagiarism.** Presenting someone else's work as your own.

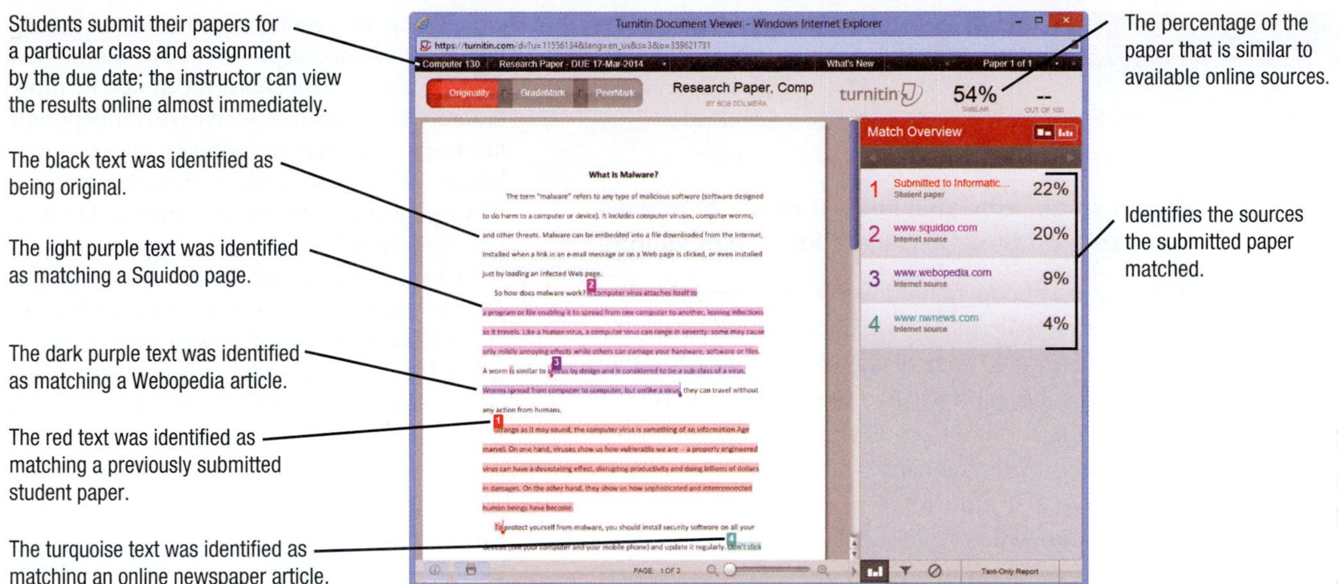
Students submit their papers for a particular class and assignment by the due date; the instructor can view the results online almost immediately.
The black text was identified as being original.
The light purple text was identified as matching a Squidoo page.
The dark purple text was identified as matching a Webopedia article.
The red text was identified as matching a previously submitted student paper.
The turquoise text was identified as matching an online newspaper article.
The percentage of the paper that is similar to available online sources.
Identifies the sources the submitted paper matched.
Turnitin Document Viewer - Windows Internet Explorer
Research Paper, Comp
turnitin
54%
Match Overview
1 Submitted to Informatic... Student paper 22%
2 www.squidoo.com Internet source 20%
3 www.webopedia.com Internet source 9%
4 www.nwnews.com Internet source 4%
What Is Malware?

Courtesy of iParadigms LLC

FIGURE 6-6
Results of an online originality test.

Music

There have been many issues regarding the legal and ethical use of music over the past few years. The controversy started with the emergence and widespread use of *Napster* (the first P2P music sharing site that facilitated the exchange of music files from one Napster user's computer to another). Many exchanges via the original Napster service violated copyright law and a flood of lawsuits from the music industry eventually shut down Napster and other P2P sites that were being used to exchange copyright-protected content illegally. Additional issues arose with the introduction of recordable and rewritable CD and DVD drives, portable digital media players, mobile phones, and other devices that can be used to duplicate digital music. Some issues regarding the legal and ethical use of digital music have been resolved over the years. For instance, downloading a music file from a P2P site without compensating the artist and record label is a violation of copyright law and an unethical act; so is transferring legally obtained songs to a storage medium to sell or give to others. Today's wide availability of music stores and other onlines sources for legal music downloads and streaming (see the *Spotify* app in Figure 6-7) give individuals a legal alternative for obtaining digital music quickly and easily. However, illegal music exchanges are still taking place and law enforcement agencies, as well as the Recording Industry Association of America (RIAA), are pursuing individuals who violate music copyrights. For instance, the RIAA won its first lawsuit against an individual in late 2007 when a young woman was found guilty of sharing music online and was ordered to pay a total of $222,000 to record companies. At a new trial in 2009, the verdict was the same but the award was increased to $1.92 million—$80,000 per downloaded song.

Once an MP3 file or audio CD has been obtained legally, however, most experts agree that it falls within the fair use concept for an individual to transfer those songs to a CD, computer, portable digital media player, or mobile phone, as long as it is for personal, noncommercial use and does not violate a user agreement. In the past, songs downloaded from some online music stores included DRM controls, which prevented the songs from being copied to other devices. While this helped prevent the illegal copying of downloaded songs from one user to another, it also prevented users from transferring legally downloaded music from one of their devices to another. In response to user protests, many music stores today offer their songs in the universal (and DRM-free) MP3 format so they can be played on a wide range of devices.

One long-standing controversy related to digital music is the issue of royalties. While conventional radio stations pay licensing fees to air music, they have been battling record

FIGURE 6-7
Music apps. Allow you to legally listen to music on demand on your devices.

14:47
Justin Timberlake
Mirrors
Hide
THE 20/20
EXPERIENCE
2:23
8:04

Courtesy Spotify

ASK THE EXPERT

Rhapsody **David Rosenberg,** Vice President, Legal and Business Affairs, Rhapsody International Inc.

Courtesy of Rhapsody International

How can an individual know if music or movies available via the Internet are legal to download?

Distribution of copyrighted works (including music and movies) without permission from the copyright owners is illegal. The best way to determine whether music available for download is authorized is to evaluate the source—is the Web site from which you want to download the music reputable? What do the terms of use state? If the Web site has a license from the copyright owner to distribute the musical content, the copyright owner is likely being paid and the download is legal. A good legitimacy test is if you either have to pay a fee or view advertisements in order to obtain the music. If the Web site appears to be "too good to be true," there is a strong likelihood that it is not authorized to distribute the music and you could be held personally liable for copyright infringement.

companies for years over whether or not the broadcasters should pay a royalty each time a song is aired—especially for songs recorded before 1972, which is when federal copyright law began to protect recordings (songs recorded before 1972 are protected only under state law, to varying degrees). At the time of this writing, for example, *Sirius XM Radio* was being sued by several record labels for using pre-1972 songs without paying for them. Another current lawsuit (against *Vimeo*) focuses on the liability of content hosts for posts that include copyrighted content without permission. While Vimeo argues that it is protected by the *safe harbor provision* included in the *Digital Millennium Copyright Act (DMCA)*, the lawsuit argues that Vimeo should not be protected because it should have known about the copyright infringement.

E-Books

The popularity of e-books (for example, sales for e-books at Amazon.com surpassed print books in 2011) has resulted in legal and ethical issues similar to those found in the digital music industry, as well as a rapid increase in piracy. In fact, some e-books have been shared or downloaded illegally more than 100,000 times within the first few days of an e-book release.

Movies

Since 1984, when Disney and Universal sued Sony to stop production of the *Betamax* (the first personal VCR), concern about movie piracy has increased dramatically. The lawsuit was eventually decided in Sony's favor—the Supreme Court upheld the consumers' rights to record shows for convenience (called *time shifting*), as long as it was for personal use. As a result of this decision, VCR use became commonplace. Interestingly, in direct contrast to the views held by the entertainment industry in 1984, videos have been credited with boosting Hollywood's revenues tremendously over the years. Nevertheless, the entertainment industry continues to be concerned about the ability of consumers to make copies of movies—especially today, because digital content can be duplicated an unlimited number of times without losing quality. The Motion Picture Association of America (MPAA) estimates that losses due to movie piracy worldwide exceed $18 billion per year.

FIGURE 6-8
Amazon Instant Video. Allows you to legally download (buy) or stream (rent) movies and TV shows to your TV, computer, or mobile device.

Courtesy Amazon

There are many online services that can be used to download or stream movies, TV shows, and similar content (one example is shown in Figure 6-8). To prevent individuals from making unauthorized copies of feature films purchased on DVDs or downloaded via the Internet, many of these items contain copy protection or some other form of DRM. Movie pirates, however, can often circumvent copy protection with software and other tools in order to duplicate the movies and create illegal copies. Pirated copies of movies are also often created today by videotaping them with a camcorder during a prerelease screening or on the opening day of a movie. This practice has resulted in a vast number of movies becoming illegally available on DVDs and via the Internet at about the same time they arrive in theaters. As a result, Congress passed the *Family Entertainment and Copyright Act of 2005*, which makes transmitting or recording a movie during a performance at a U.S. movie theater illegal. To help identify and prosecute a "cammer," most movie studios now embed invisible digital watermarks in each print released to a theater, as discussed earlier in this chapter. The information contained in these watermarks can be used to identify the location where the movie was recorded once a bootleg copy of a movie is discovered.

The access to both authorized and unauthorized copies of movies via the Internet, as well as the widespread use of DVRs and DVD players today, create new legal and ethical dilemmas for individuals. If one individual records a television show and then shares it with a friend via the Internet or a DVD disc, does that go beyond the concept of fair use? If you run across a Web site from which you can download a copy of a movie not yet out on DVD, are you legally at risk if you make the download? What if you watch the movie once and then delete it—are you still in the wrong? What if you download a video-on-demand movie and then share it with a friend? Is that any different, legally or ethically, from sharing a movie rented from a brick-and-mortar video store with a friend before you return it? What about the *placeshifting* products on the market, such as the *Slingbox*, that enable you to watch recorded content away from home using your portable computer or mobile device? If you use such a product to transfer a movie or TV show obtained through your cable or satellite TV connection to another location, are you rebroadcasting that content or simply placeshifting it? What if you send the content to another individual to watch via his or her computer—is that legal?

While the answers to these questions have yet to be unequivocally decided, distributing bootleg copies of movies via the Internet is both illegal and unethical. There have been many local, state, and federal operations in the United States and other countries in recent years focused on targeting online piracy of copyrighted software, movies, music, and games. To help remind individuals that piracy is illegal, the FBI introduced the *FBI Anti-Piracy Warning Seal* (see Figure 6-9) designed to be used in conjunction with movie DVDs, music CDs, and other intellectual properties that are commonly pirated. Today, this seal is often printed on product packaging and it is displayed with additional piracy warnings when many DVD movies are played.

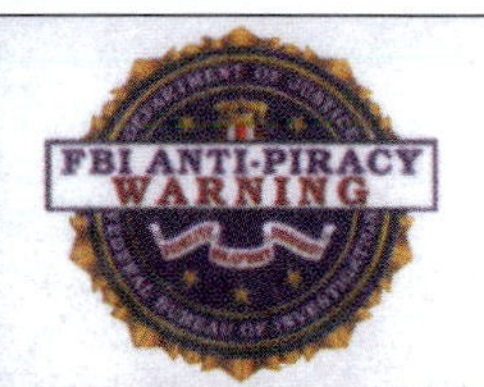

Federal Bureau of Investigation. Used with permission.

FIGURE 6-9
The FBI Anti-Piracy Warning Seal.

The MPAA also recently began pursuing civil litigation against movie pirates. The organization is concentrating mainly on the individuals who create illegal DVDs, but prosecution of individuals who upload movies to be shared via the Internet is also occurring. To catch people who are sharing movies illegally on the Internet, the MPAA uses special software that monitors file sharing networks to find copyrighted movies and then identifies the responsible individual by using the IP address of the computer being used to share the movie. Members of the movie industry also hire special firms, such as Irdeto, that specialize in monitoring P2P networks, Web sites, and other Internet resources in order to identify their clients' copyrighted material (such as documents, graphics, music, or movie files) that is being misused on the Internet. When a firm finds a client's file that is being shared illegally, the firm can issue an infringement notice to the violator via his or her ISP. The firm also typically collects any data that might be needed in case the client (the copyright holder) decides to pursue legal action.

To prevent the sharing of movies that have been downloaded legally (such as video-on-demand movie rentals and movies purchased in downloadable form), many downloaded movies include DRM controls. For instance, DRM controls can be used to prevent the movie from being copied to another medium or they can allow the movie to be used only for a specified period of time (such as a 24-hour period beginning when the movie first starts to play). Consumers have some objections to the current movie DRM systems, similar to the objections they have with music DRM systems. In response, some services (such as TiVo) now allow consumers to transfer content to other devices for convenience. For a look at *Digital Copy*—an option for taking your legally purchased movies with you on your computer or mobile device—see the How It Works box.

HOW IT WORKS

Digital Copy Movies

Did you ever want to take a copy of a DVD movie you own with you on your portable digital media player or smartphone but didn't want to pay to download a second digital copy of the movie? Well, now you can, with *Digital Copy.*

A growing trend in movie delivery available from most major movie studios (including Twentieth Century Fox, Warner Brothers, Sony Pictures, and Disney), Digital Copy allows individuals who purchase a DVD or Blu-Ray Disc movie that supports Digital Copy to copy the movie to both a computer and a mobile device, such as a portable digital media player, media tablet, or smartphone (some also allow you to copy to a specific gaming device, such as a Sony PSP for Sony Digital Copy movies). The DVD package typically includes two discs—a conventional DVD disc containing the movie that can be played in a computer DVD drive or a DVD player as usual, and a Digital Copy disc that can be used to install the movie on a computer and mobile device. Some Digital Copy movies allow you to download the digital copy instead of using a disc.

The general procedure for installing a Digital Copy movie is shown in the accompanying illustration. While the process varies some from studio to studio, you typically follow these steps: First, insert the Digital Copy disc into your computer's DVD drive. Next, use the menus (supplying the activation code contained inside the movie case when prompted) to copy the movie to the iTunes or Windows Media Player library on your computer. (Which library you use depends on the type of mobile device the movie will be copied to, as discussed shortly, and iTunes users will need to log in to their account in order to activate the movie.) After the movie is installed in the library on your computer, the Digital Copy disc is no longer needed to play the movie from the library on your computer, and you can use the sync process to transfer the movie to one mobile device.

While Digital Copy movies can only be transferred to devices supported by the library being used (such as iPods, iPhones, and iPads for iTunes users and devices that support DRM Windows Media .wmv files for Windows Media Player users), for users with devices that work seamlessly with the Digital Copy process, Digital Copy gives you an easy offline option for taking your movies with you while on the go.

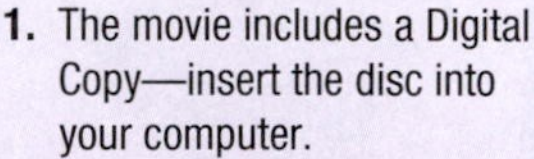

1. The movie includes a Digital Copy—insert the disc into your computer.

Cloudy With a Chance of Meatballs is available on Blu-ray Disc™ from Sony Pictures Home Entertainment

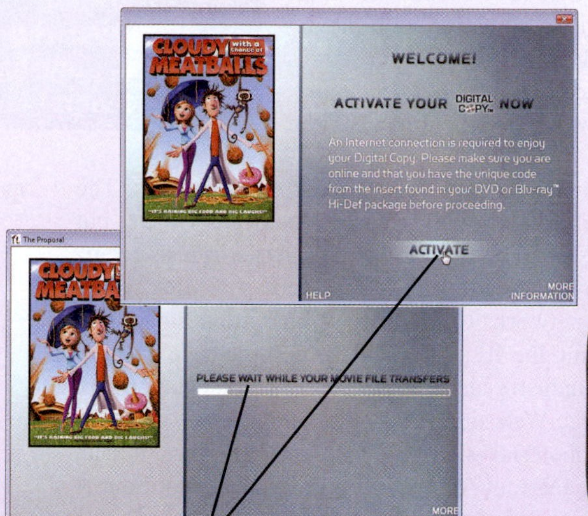

2. Follow the on-screen instructions to activate your Digital Copy and transfer the movie to your computer and mobile device.

© Chardchanin/Shutterstock.com

3. The movie can be played on your mobile device, as well as on your computer.

Ethical Use of Resources and Information

A variety of resources (such as school computers, company computers, and equipment) and types of information (such as customer or employee information) can be used in an unethical manner. For example, some employees use company computers for personal use, some students perform dishonest acts while completing assignments or taking exams, and some job applicants provide erroneous or misleading information during the application or interview process.

Ethical Use of School or Company Resources

What is considered proper and ethical use of school or company resources may vary from school to school or company to company. To explain what is allowed, many schools and businesses have policies that specify which activities are allowed and which are forbidden. Often, these policies are available as a written **code of conduct** that is included in a student or employee handbook. They are also often available online via an organization's intranet or Web site (a code of conduct was shown in Figure 4-1 in Chapter 4). Policies can vary; for example, one school may allow the use of school computers to download software and another school may not, and one business may allow limited use of the office photocopier or printer for personal use while another may forbid it. As a result, all students and employees should find out what is considered ethical use of resources at their school or place of business, including what types of computer and Internet activities are considered acceptable, and what personal use (if any) of resources, such as computers, printers, photocopiers, telephones, and fax machines, is allowed. To enforce its policies, businesses may use employee monitoring, which was discussed in Chapter 5.

Another code widely used by various industries and organizations is a **code of ethics**. Codes of ethics (see the IEEE code of ethics in Figure 6-10) summarize the moral guidelines adopted by a professional society or other organization. They typically address such issues as honesty, integrity, proper use of intellectual property, confidentiality, and accountability. So, while codes of conduct usually address specific activities that can and cannot be performed, codes of ethics cover broader ethical standards of conduct.

Although employees are typically forbidden from revealing confidential or proprietary information to outsiders, a dilemma exists when that information is related to an illegal, an unethical, or a dangerous activity involving the business. Employees who reveal wrongdoing within an organization to the public or to authorities are referred to as *whistle-blowers*. These individuals have varying degrees of protection from retaliation (such as being fired) for whistle-blowing. The type and extent of protection depends on the kind of wrongdoing and the organization involved, as well as the state in which the company and employee are located. The *Sarbanes-Oxley Act* (also called the *Corporate Responsibility Act* and signed into law in mid-2002) provides federal protection for whistle-blowers who report alleged violations of Securities and Exchange Commission rules or any federal law relating to shareholder fraud.

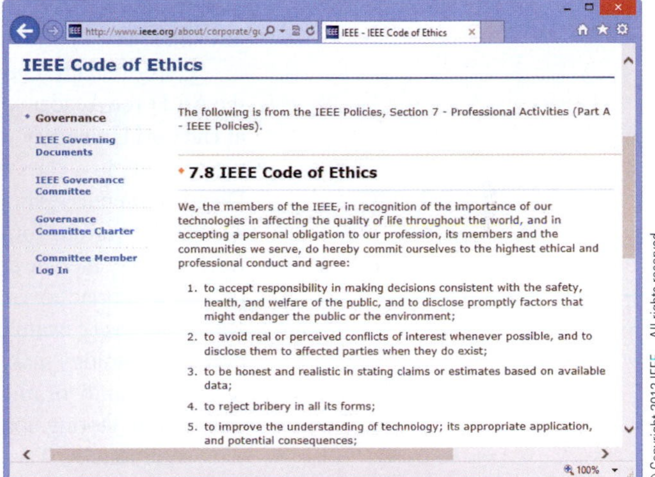

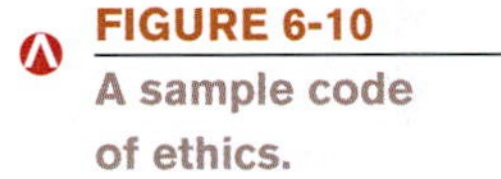
FIGURE 6-10
A sample code of ethics.

Ethical Use of Employee and Customer Information

While a business may be legally bound by such restrictions as employee confidentiality laws, union contracts, and its customer privacy policy, there are gray areas inside which ethical decisions need to be made. For example, should an ISP comply with a request from a government for customer e-mail records or the identity of a customer matching an IP address? Should a company use marketing data that was mined from individuals' social networking sites? Or should a business share or sell customer information, even if it is legal to do so? This latter decision is one that many businesses have struggled with, especially in challenging economic times when a quick source of revenue gained from selling customer data is tempting. Although some businesses have succumbed to this temptation and have sold their customer lists, others believe that any short-term

>**Code of conduct.** A policy, often for a school or business, that specifies allowable use of resources, such as computers and other equipment.

>**Code of ethics.** A policy, often for an organization or industry, that specifies overall moral guidelines adopted by that organization or industry.

> **TIP**
>
> Be sure to get authorization from your employer for any business-related social media accounts you set up and be sure it is clear who will own and control the account if you ever leave the company.

gains achieved through ethically questionable acts will adversely affect customer loyalty and will ultimately hurt the business in the long run. An emerging issue is who owns an employee's work-related social media accounts. There have been several lawsuits surrounding this issue, such as an employee who took company Twitter followers with him to a new company and an employee who discovered that her employer was posting tweets from her account when she was in the hospital. It is expected that soon social media laws will be developed to resolve these types of issues.

To prepare future employees for these types of decisions, most business schools incorporate business ethics into their curriculum. For example, the *Giving Voice to Values (GVV)* business school curriculum, created by the Aspen Institute and Yale School of Management and being piloted at over 50 institutions, focuses on ethical implementation of values-based leadership.

Cheating and Falsifying Information

Just as the Internet makes it easier for individuals to plagiarize documents, computers, mobile devices, and the Internet also make it easier for individuals to cheat on assignments or exams, or to perform other similar unethical acts.

Unfortunately, cheating at all levels is rampant today. Recently, for instance, 78 cadets at the Air Force Academy were accused of cheating on an online calculus test, about 70 students at Harvard University were required to withdraw from school for one year after nearly half of the students in a class were suspected of cheating on a take-home final exam, and three San Diego elementary schools lost their standardized API scores for two years after teachers were accused of various forms of cheating during the state tests. Acts of cheating commonly performed today include creating a paper from material plagiarized from Web sites, storing notes on a smartphone to view during a test, texting answers to another student during a test, or taking photos of exam questions to pass on to a student taking the test at a later time. In addition to technology making it easier to cheat, it also may make it feel less like cheating. During one recent study of middle and high school students, for instance, about 25% of the students didn't think storing notes on a mobile phone or texting during an exam constituted cheating.

Traditionally, it was typically weaker students who cheated to prevent failing a course or an exam. Today, however, studies have shown that honor students and others with higher GPAs are more likely to cheat, possibly due to the increased competition and pressure to succeed—according to Donald McCabe of Rutgers University, "Students have told me over the years they have to get the job done, and they don't care how." But whether they realize it or not, students who choose to cheat are cheating themselves of an education. They are also being unfair to honest students by possibly altering the grading curve. Widespread cheating can also have a negative impact on society, such as when underprepared employees enter the workforce.

To explain to students what behavior is expected of them, many schools are developing *academic honor codes*. Research has shown that having an academic honor code effectively reduces cheating. For example, one McCabe study found that cheating on tests on campuses with honor codes is typically one-third to one-half less than on campuses that do not have honor codes, and the level of cheating on written assignments is one-quarter to one-third lower. To bring attention to their honor codes, some schools encourage incoming students to sign their honor codes upon admission. For instance, all Penn State Smeal College of Business students are invited to sign the school's honor code publicly (see Figure 6-11); it was signed by about 3,000 people in 2013. Regardless of whether or not students choose to sign the honor code, they are required to abide by it.

FIGURE 6-11 **Academic honor codes.** Students at Smeal College of Business sign the honor code during the first week of classes.

Courtesy Matthew Ross of the Smeal College of Business

Like academic cheating, lying on a job application or résumé is more common than most of us may think it is. The practice of providing false information in an attempt to look more qualified for a job, sometimes referred to as *résumé padding*, is both dishonest and unethical. It is also widespread. In a recent study by employment screening service

HireRight, 69% of the companies surveyed reported catching a job candidate lying on his or her résumé. In addition to being unethical, providing false information to a potential employer can have serious consequences—many companies have a policy that lists termination as the appropriate action for employees who were hired based on falsified résumés or applications. Being blacklisted from an industry or being sued for breach of contract are also possibilities. Résumé writers should remember that background checks are easily available online, which means credentials are easy to check and verify. Even if individuals believe they will not be caught, applicants should not embellish their résumés or job applications to any extent because it is an unethical thing to do. Another recent ethical issue surrounding IT employees is cheating on IT certification exams. Copies of certification questions and entire certification exams are available for purchase online, and some Web sites offer the services of "gunmen" (usually located in Asia) who will take certification tests for individuals for a fee. In response, companies that offer IT certifications are looking at the security of their testing processes to try to put a stop to this new type of cheating.

There are personal situations that may tempt some individuals to provide inaccurate information, such as when writing online dating profiles, participating in chat rooms, or in other situations when individuals may wish to appear to be someone different from who they really are. There are differing opinions about how ethical these actions are—some individuals believe that it is a person's right to portray himself or herself in any way desired; others feel that any type of dishonesty is unethical.

TIP

When looking for a distance learning program, be sure to check the school's accreditation because some human resources departments view college degrees from online diploma mills or other nonaccredited organizations as another form of résumé padding.

Computer Hoaxes and Digital Manipulation

Most people realize that information in print media can, at times, be misleading and that photos can be manipulated. Information found on the Internet may also be inaccurate, misleading, or biased. Some of this type of information is published on Web pages; other information is passed on via e-mail. Two types of computer-oriented misinformation include computer hoaxes and digital manipulation.

Computer Hoaxes

A **computer hoax** is an inaccurate statement or story—such as the "fact" that flesh-eating bacteria have been found in banana shipments or that Applebee's will send you a gift certificate for forwarding an e-mail—spread through the use of computers. These hoaxes are sometimes published on Web pages, but they are more commonly spread via e-mail or social media. Common computer hoax subjects include nonexistent computer viruses, serious health risks, impending terrorist attacks, chain letters, and free prizes or giveaways. Inaccurate information posted online just to be misleading can also be considered a computer hoax. E-mail hoaxes are written with the purpose of being circulated to as many people as possible. Some are started as experiments to see how fast and how far information can travel via the Internet; others originate from a joke or the desire to frighten people. Similar to spam, e-mail hoaxes can be annoying, waste people's time, bog down e-mail systems, and clog users' Inboxes. Because computer hoaxes are so common, it is a good idea to double-check any warning you receive by e-mail or read on a Web site before passing that warning on to another person, regardless of how realistic or frightening the information appears to be (sites like the one shown in Figure 6-12 can help you research potential hoaxes).

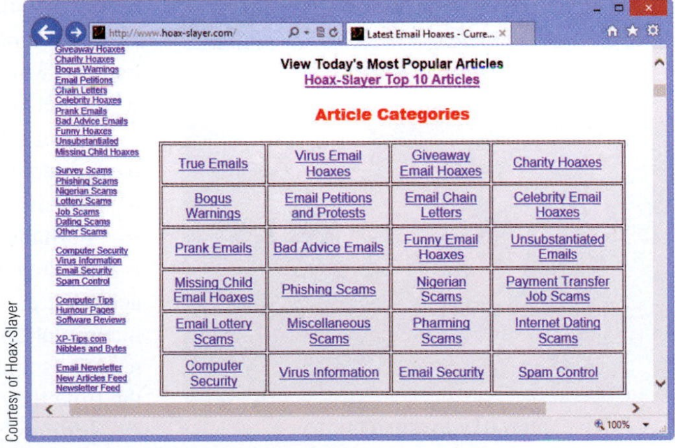

Courtesy of Hoax-Slayer

FIGURE 6-12

Hoax-Slayer. This is one site that can be used to research possible computer hoaxes.

>**Computer hoax.** An inaccurate statement or story spread through the use of computers.

Digital Manipulation

Computers make it very easy to copy or modify text, images, photographs, music, and other digital content. In addition to being a copyright concern, **digital manipulation** (digitally altering digital content) can be used to misquote individuals, repeat comments out of context, retouch photographs—even create false or misleading photographs—and so is an ethical concern, as well. While there are some beneficial, ethical, noncontroversial applications of digital manipulation (such as aging photos of missing children to show what they may look like at the present time, or altering photos of wanted criminals or suspects to show possible alternate appearances for law enforcement purposes), the matter of altering photos for publication purposes is the subject of debate. Some publications and photographers see no harm in altering photographs to remove an offending item (such as a telephone pole behind someone's head), to remove red-eye or otherwise make someone look a little more attractive, to illustrate a point, or to increase circulation; others view any change in content as unethical and a great disservice to both the public and our history. For example, fifty years from now, will anyone know that a staged or altered photograph of a historical event was not an actual depiction of the event?

Although manipulation of photographs has occurred for quite some time in tabloids and other publications not known as being reputable news sources, there have been several incidents of more reputable news publications using digitally altered photographs in recent years. Many of these became known because the unaltered photograph was used in another publication at about the same time. One of the most widely publicized cases occurred in 1994, just following the arrest of O. J. Simpson. While *Newsweek* ran Simpson's mug shot unaltered, *TIME* magazine darkened the photograph, creating a more sinister look and making Simpson's skin color appear darker than it actually is. This photo drew harsh criticism from Simpson supporters who felt the photograph made him appear guilty, the African-American community who viewed the alteration as an act of racial insensitivity, and news photographers who felt that the action damaged the credibility not only of that particular magazine but also of all journalists.

FIGURE 6-13
Digital manipulation. The digitally manipulated photo (bottom) added sleeves and a higher neckline to the real photo (top) of Michelle Obama.

ORIGINAL PHOTO

DIGITALLY ALTERED PHOTO

Chris Pizzello/Invision/AP

A more recent example is the case of a one-time Pulitzer Prize finalist who resigned from a Toledo, Ohio, newspaper after it was discovered that he had submitted for publication nearly 80 doctored photos in just the 14 weeks prior to his resignation, including one sports photo of a basketball game with a digitally added basketball placed in midair. Other recent instances of digitally manipulated images being printed in news media include a photo of an Iranian missile test that appeared in many newspapers but that contained a digitally added missile to replace one that did not fire during the test; a photo of a Boston Marathon bombing victim that appeared in the New York *Daily News* but that was edited to make the victim's injuries appear less severe than they were; and an altered photo of Michelle Obama at the 2013 Academy Awards—instead of showing the real sleeveless, scoop neck gown she wore, Iran's Far news agency added sleeves and a higher neckline to the photo that is posted on its Web site (see Figure 6-13).

Perhaps the most disturbing thing about known alterations such as these is that some may never have been noticed and, consequently, may have been accepted as true representations. Adding to the problem of unethical digital manipulation is that, unlike film cameras, digital cameras don't have photo negatives that could be used to show what photographs actually looked like at the time they were taken. Although some publications allow the use of "photo illustrations," others have strict rules about digital manipulation—especially

>**Digital manipulation.** The alteration of digital content, usually text or photographs.

TREND

Social Commerce

Social commerce—the use of social networking sites (such as Facebook, Twitter, and Pinterest) and other social media to promote online sales—is huge. At perhaps the simplest level, posts by individuals about buying products or Liking Facebook pages may influence their friends' purchases both online and offline. You can also buy gifts within Facebook for your friends and you can use a service such as *SellPin* to sell products on Pinterest. Businesses can create custom *Amazon Pages* and use *Amazon Posts* to put content on their Amazon and Facebook pages simultaneously, as well as place ads on social networking sites to generate traffic to their Web site or social media pages. Facebook also allows ads to be targeted to specific individuals, such as individuals in a specific geographical area who like cycling. To help determine relevant ads for each person, individual ads can be hidden by the user (and then different targeted ads appear in their place). A new feature is the ability to include downloadable apps in Facebook ads.

A more recent social commerce option includes offering goods and services for sale within social networking sites. Dubbed *F-commerce* and *F-stores*, the number of businesses and individuals selling real goods and real services inside Facebook is increasing (see one example in the accompanying illustration). Products can either be sold directly within Facebook or the Facebook page can contain a link that brings the visitor to the appropriate Web page to purchase that item when the link is clicked.

Another impact of social media on e-commerce is the social aspect. In addition to the word-of-mouth effect, businesses can also harness social networking information located in an individual's social networking profile or Facebook page. And the use of *social media monitoring* companies and tools to analyze social media activity related to a particular business is a fast-growing market.

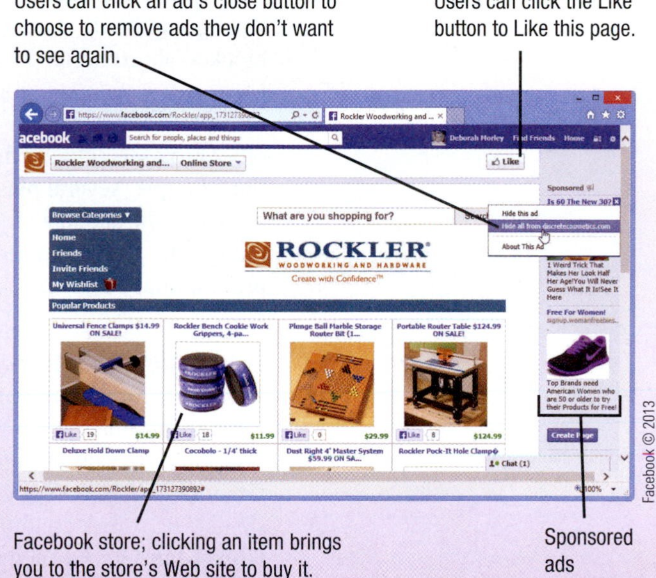
Users can click an ad's close button to choose to remove ads they don't want to see again.
Users can click the Like button to Like this page.
ROCKLER
WOODWORKING AND HARDWARE
Facebook store; clicking an item brings you to the store's Web site to buy it.
Sponsored ads

for news photojournalists. For instance, the *LA Times* fired a staff photographer covering the war in Iraq when he combined two of his photographs into one to convey a point better.

Ethical Business Practices and Decision Making

Most businesses must make a variety of ethics-related business decisions, such as whether or not to sell a product or service that some may find offensive or objectionable; how to best utilize social media, such as whether or not to utilize services that mine social networking sites for personal data for marketing purposes or whether or not to place targeted ads on social networking sites (see the Trend box for a look at the impact of social media on e-commerce); whether or not to install video cameras in the workplace for monitoring purposes; or whether or not to perform controversial research. In addition, corporate integrity, as it relates to accounting practices and proper disclosure, is a business ethics topic that has come to the forefront recently.

TIP

The widespread use of social media has also led to a new ethics dilemma in the medical field—whether or not to use social networking sites to evaluate patient behaviors that affect treatment, such as the recent incident of a liver transplant team finding a photo that a transplant candidate had posted on his Twitter feed that showed him drinking, which contradicted his claims of sobriety.

Fraudulent Reporting and Other Scandalous Activities

Following the large number of corporate scandals occurring since 2002, business ethics have moved into the public eye. The scandals, such as the ones surrounding executives at Enron, Tyco International, and WorldCom, involved lies, fraud, deception, and other illegal and unethical behavior. This behavior forced both Enron and WorldCom into bankruptcy proceedings. When asked to comment on the scandals, 3Com Chief Executive Officer Bruce Claflin said on CNBC, "I would argue we do not have an accounting problem—we have an ethics problem."

In reaction to the scandals, Congress passed the *Sarbanes-Oxley Act of 2002*. This law includes provisions to improve the quality of financial reporting, independent audits, and accounting services for public companies; to increase penalties for corporate wrongdoing; to protect the objectivity and independence of securities analysts; and to require CEOs and CFOs to vouch personally for the truth and fairness of their company's disclosures. Businesses need to keep current laws in mind, as well as the businesses' ethical standards, when preparing financial reports, press releases, and other important documents that represent a company's position.

Ethically Questionable Business Decisions

One ethical issue a business may run into is whether or not to implement a business process or decision that is ethically questionable. For example, Google and Microsoft are in an ongoing battle about Microsoft's decision to offer its own YouTube app (which Google blocked shortly after its release because the app violated Google's terms of service), and Microsoft is facing a possible $7 billion fine for its decision not to display a screen that would enable European Union Windows users to choose between Internet Explorer and other browsers. Other ethically questionable business decisions relate to customer privacy. For example, several plastic surgeons have been sued recently for posting pre-op and post-op photos of patients on their Web sites; in one current case, the photos were posted even though the patient signed a statement that she did not give consent to use her photos for promotional purposes.

Ethically Questionable Products or Services

Another ethical issue a business may run into is whether or not to sell products or services that some people find objectionable. For example, the eBay Web site states that it prohibits the sale of some controversial or sensitive items, in addition to illegal items. For instance, it will not allow items that promote or glorify hatred; violence; or racial, sexual, or religious intolerance. Consequently, it bans Nazi propaganda materials, Ku Klux Klan (KKK) memorabilia, crime scene and morgue photographs, and letters and belongings of notorious criminals, even though sellers may legally be able to sell such items elsewhere.

Another ethical decision for businesses that allow individuals to upload content to their Web sites (such as social networking sites, wikis, classified ad sites, forums, and photo or video sharing sites) is how (if at all) they should monitor the content posted on their sites. For instance, YouTube relies on the user community to flag videos that might be inappropriate for some viewers (such as the Saddam Hussein execution video posted on YouTube shortly after that execution took place); videos that remain flagged as age-restricted first display a warning screen and viewers need to verify that they are over 18 by logging in to their YouTube account before they can view the video. In another example, Craigslist has been under fire for years for numerous crimes (including rape, murder, prostitution, and attempted baby-selling) that have occurred via ads posted on its site and, recently, police investigators announced that they believe Facebook pages are being used by terrorists to recruit young people in Indonesia.

ASK THE EXPERT

Courtesy Dice

Shravan Goli, President, Dice

What is the biggest mistake that applicants for technology-oriented jobs make today?

Mistakes can be made at every step of the process: Résumé and application, HR interview, and interviewing with hiring managers. If there is a consistent mistake, it's not understanding the audience for each step. When applying for a position, for example, it's important to understand the company and its plans for the future and incorporate that into the application. In the HR interview, tech professionals should highlight their business and soft skills, and not over emphasize technical skills. The last step is the tech interview. Technologists tend to want each step to be the tech interview, but it's really only the last step in the process.

In response, Craigslist has eliminated its adult services category and Facebook says it removes any reported content that promotes terrorism or contains direct statements of hate and disables the account.

Companies that do business in more than one country also have global considerations to address. For instance, a Brazilian court once ordered YouTube to shut down access to a racy video clip of a Brazilian celebrity and her boyfriend on the beach, even though YouTube is a U.S. company. Cultural issues such as these are discussed in more detail shortly.

Another decision is the need for age verification. To protect children from predators, many states are pushing social networking sites, such as MySpace and Facebook, to implement age-verification systems. Age-verification procedures also benefit the adults who use these sites so they know they are acting appropriately with other members. Businesses that offer products or services that are inappropriate for children (such as alcohol, tobacco, adult movies and video games, pornography, online gambling, and even movie previews) also need to make decisions regarding access; for example, the types of safeguards they need to provide in order to ensure children do not have access to these products and services. They also need to determine if the company is required legally, or just ethically, to provide these safeguards. This is especially significant for businesses with an e-commerce presence. In a conventional store, individuals can be asked to show an ID to prove they are of the required age before they are allowed to buy tobacco products, alcohol, pornographic materials, and other products that cannot legally be sold to minors. But, during an online transaction, it is much more difficult to verify that a buyer is the required age.

To comply with state and federal laws, as well as to protect themselves from potential litigation, Web sites selling or providing adult products and services should implement adequate age-verification procedures. Some sites require visitors to click a statement declaring they are the required age or to enter a valid credit card number before accessing or purchasing adult-only content or products. However, these precautions can be bypassed easily by underage visitors. Other sites require proof of age at delivery, which is a safer precaution for physical goods purchased online and is required by law in some states for certain types of shipments. Even safer is using an *online age- and identity-verification service*, such as Veratad (which verifies individuals based on comparing submitted personal information with public records from trusted sources) or Jumio (which verifies individuals by capturing and validiating an official document such as a driver's license or passport—see Figure 6-14).

The decisions about which products or services to offer online and offline are important—and sometimes difficult—ethical decisions for businesses to make. Typically, these decisions are based on the company's overall corporate mission and desired public image. Consequently, some businesses may choose not to sell adult-only content at all. Others may decide to sell it via the Internet only in conjunction with a third-party age- and identity-verification service, or to sell those products or services online but require an adult to sign for the items when they are delivered. Still other businesses may feel that a warning statement or similar precaution on their Web sites is all that is needed, and that it is the parents' responsibility to make sure their children do not purchase illegal or inappropriate items or view adult-only content via the Internet.

FIGURE 6-14
Online age- and identity-verification services. This service uses a smartphone app that scans a customer's official document to verify he or she is the required age for a transaction.

Workplace Monitoring

As discussed in Chapter 5, the majority of businesses in the United States today monitor employees to some extent. Although businesses have the right and responsibility to ensure that employees are productive and that company resources are not being abused, many believe that businesses also have an ethical responsibility to inform employees of any monitoring that takes place. This is especially true in countries other than the United States, such as in the European Union where companies are much more limited in what types of monitoring they can do legally without notifying employees. One related issue that is occurring during the hiring process is social media scrutiny. While it is not unusual or viewed as unethical for a company to view the public information an applicant posts online, some hiring managers are asking applicants to log on to their social media accounts during interviews in order for the manager to review the content, and some require applicants and employees to be Facebook friends with their human resources liasions—which is considered by many to cross the ethical line.

FIGURE 6-15
Cultural considerations.
In some countries, bootleg copies of music CDs and movie DVDs are sold openly.

Cultural Considerations

With today's global economy, businesses also need to be sensitive to the ethical differences that may exist among different businesses located in the same country, as well as among businesses located in different countries. Ethics are fundamentally based on values, so when beliefs, laws, customs, and traditions vary among businesses, the ethics associated with those businesses will likely differ as well.

Ethical decisions need to be made whenever a business practice or product is legal or socially acceptable in one country but not in another. For instance, an individual may be able to purchase a bootleg copy of a software program, music CD, or movie (see Figure 6-15) in person or online from vendors in countries where copies of these types of items are legal or where copyright law is not strongly enforced. This raises the question of ethical responsibility. Is it the individual's responsibility not to make these types of unethical purchases, even if technology makes it possible? What legal and ethical responsibility do online auction sites and other businesses that may unknowingly facilitate illegal transactions have to ensure that customers do not have access to products or services that are illegal in their customers' locations?

In addition to legal issues, organizations conducting business in other countries should also take into consideration the ethical standards prevalent in the countries with which they do business. Factors such as gender roles, religious beliefs, and cultural customs should be considered and respected when corresponding, negotiating, and otherwise interacting with businesses located in other countries. For example, some cultures may require a handshake or other ritual that is impossible to carry out online in order to close a deal. In this case, while the terms of the deal may be carried out online, the deal itself would need to be closed in person. Businesses should also be careful not to offend individuals from other countries or other cultures that they do business with. Some straightforward questions acceptable in the United States—such as a request to verify certain numbers or double-check a source—may be viewed as an insult in some cultures. And in some countries, you can be arrested for some types of social media posts, such as the man who is currently serving two years in prison in Kuwait for posting an insulting tweet about the country's ruler.

To prepare students properly to succeed in our global economy, some business schools include diversity and cross-cultural training in their curriculum. Similarly, some international organizations arrange for their employees to have such training prior to traveling out of the country.

TIP

When exchanging e-mails with individuals in other countries, especially business e-mails, avoid trying to add humor to your messages. Humor can be difficult to translate to other languages and cultures, and it can be misinterpreted if read at a later time, such as during an audit or legal proceeding.

CAUTION CAUTION CAUTION CAUTION CAUTION CAUTION CAUT

When purchasing goods from another country, it is important to realize that the laws regarding the sale of products, as well as the laws regarding the privacy of personal information supplied to a vendor during a transaction, vary from one country to another. Avoid purchasing questionable goods online and avoid providing personal information to any Web site in a country that may have lax privacy laws—as a minimum, be sure to read the privacy statements for any Web site carefully before you provide them with any personal information you do not want to be shared with others.

RELATED LEGISLATION

There have been several new laws over the past decade or so (see Figure 6-16) attempting to revise intellectual property laws to reflect digital content and the Internet. For instance, the *Family Entertainment and Copyright Act of 2005* makes it illegal to transmit or record a movie being shown at a movie theater. Other recent laws related to intellectual property include the *U.S. Anticybersquatting Consumer Protection Act of 1999*, which makes domain name cybersquatting illegal; the *Copyright Term Extension Act*, which adds 20 years to the existing copyright terms; and the *Digital Millennium Copyright Act* (*DMCA*), which makes it illegal to circumvent antipiracy measures built into digital media and devices. Other laws, such as ones to increase the penalties for illegally sharing music and movies via the Internet, are proposed on a regular basis.

Legislation regarding ethics has been more difficult to pass—or to keep as law once it has passed. For example, as discussed in Chapter 3, the *Communications Decency Act* that was signed into law in 1996 and made it a criminal offense to distribute patently indecent or offensive material online was eventually declared unconstitutional on the basis of free speech. The courts so far have had difficulty defining what is "patently offensive" and "indecent," as well as finding a fair balance between protection and censorship. Consequently, very few ethically oriented laws have been passed in recent years. Some exceptions are the *Children's Online Privacy Protection Act* (*COPPA*), which regulates how Web sites can collect information from minors, and the *Sarbanes-Oxley Act* (*Corporate Responsibility Act*), which includes provisions to improve the quality of financial reporting and increases penalties for corporate wrongdoing.

FIGURE 6-16
Federal legislation related to intellectual property rights and ethics.

DATE	LAW AND DESCRIPTION
2005	**Family Entertainment and Copyright Act** Makes it illegal to transmit or record a movie being shown at a movie theater.
2002	**Sarbanes-Oxley Act** Requires archiving a variety of electronic records and protecting the integrity of corporate financial data. Also requires CEOs and CFOs to vouch personally for the truth and fairness of their company's disclosures.
2001	**Child Internet Protection Act (CIPA)** Requires public libraries and schools to use filtering software to block access to certain Web content in order to receive public funds.
1999	**U.S. Anticybersquatting Consumer Protection Act of 1999** Amends the Lanham Act of 1946 to extend trademark protection to domain names and makes cybersquatting illegal.
1999	**Digital Theft Deterrence and Copyright Damages Improvement Act of 1999** Amends federal copyright law to increase statutory and additional damages a court may award for copyright infringement.
1998	**Digital Millennium Copyright Act (DMCA)** Makes it illegal to circumvent antipiracy measures built into digital media and devices.
1998	**Children's Online Privacy Protection Act (COPPA)** Regulates how Web sites can collect information from minors and communicate with them.
1998	**Copyright Term Extension Act** Extends the duration of copyright in a work created on or after January 1, 1978 by 20 years.
1997	**No Electronic Theft (NET) Act** Expands computer antipiracy laws to include distribution of copyrighted material over the Internet and sets penalties for willfully infringing a copyright for purposes of commercial advantage or private financial gain.
1996	**Communications Decency Act** Makes it a criminal offense to distribute patently indecent or offensive material online. Was declared unconstitutional by the U.S. Supreme Court in 1997.
1976	**Copyright Act of 1976** Gives the owner of a copyright the exclusive right to publish, reproduce, distribute, perform, or display the work.
1946	**Lanham Act (Trademark Act of 1946)** Allows the registration of trademarks for commercial purposes and prohibits the use, reproduction, or limitation of registered trademarks.

SUMMARY

INTELLECTUAL PROPERTY RIGHTS

Chapter Objective 1:
Understand the different types of intellectual property rights and how they relate to computer use.

Intellectual property rights specify how *intellectual property*, such as original music compositions, drawings, essays, software programs, symbols, and designs, may be lawfully used. **Copyrights** protect the creators of original artistic or literary works and are granted automatically once a work exists in a physical medium. A copyright can be registered, which provides additional protection should infringement occur. The copyright symbol © can be used to remind others that content is copyrighted; **digital watermarks** can be incorporated into digital content so that the copyright information can be viewed, even if the work is altered. **Digital rights management** (**DRM**) **software** can be used to protect the rights of creators and to manage digital content, such as art, music, photographs, and movies.

Trademarks are words, phrases, symbols, or designs that identify an organization's goods or services and can be either claimed (and use the symbol ™ or ℠) or registered (and use the symbol ®). In addition to logos and text-based phrases, domain names are also protected by trademark law. Registering a domain name with the intent to profit from someone else's trademark is called **cybersquatting**. **Patents** grant an exclusive right to an invention for 20 years. In addition to products, processes and procedures may be patented as well.

ETHICS

Chapter Objective 2:
Explain what is meant by the term *ethics*.

Chapter Objective 3:
Provide several examples of unethical behavior in the use of intellectual property and in computer-related matters.

Ethics are standards of moral conduct. *Personal ethics* guide one's personal life, **business ethics** provide the standards of conduct guiding business decisions, and **computer ethics** provide the standards of conduct with respect to computers and computer use. Computer ethics have taken on more significance in recent years because the increased use of computers in the home, in the workplace, and at school provides more opportunities for unethical behavior than in the past.

Both businesses and individuals need to make ethical decisions on a regular basis. Today one of the most important ethical concerns regarding computers is using someone else's property in an improper way. Books, music, movies, and other types of intellectual property are protected by copyright law, but they are still often used in an illegal or unethical manner. Presenting someone else's work as your own is referred to as **plagiarism**, which is illegal and unethical. Plagiarism can be performed by both students and employees, although it can be detected and usually has grave academic or professional consequences.

Movies and music also qualify for copyright protection. The practice of individuals sharing movies and music via the Internet has been a primary source of legal and ethical copyright debates. There has been increased prosecution against those individuals illegally distributing copyright-protected works, as well as end users, in the hopes of reducing this type of piracy. Legal alternatives, such as legal online music stores and video-on-demand (VOD) services, may help reduce illegal activity related to copyright-protected works.

It is becoming increasingly common for businesses and schools to establish **codes of conduct** to address what behavior is considered ethical and unethical at that particular organization. Students and employees should refer to these codes, if they exist, to become familiar with the behaviors viewed as ethical and unethical for that particular school or business. Some organizations and industries publish **codes of ethics** listing overall standards of conduct, such as honesty, fairness, confidentiality, and more.

Businesses need to determine how they will use employee and customer information, based on both legal and ethical guidelines. Because computers make it easier to plagiarize and cheat on assignments and exams, students need to make an ethical decision regarding their behavior. Some job applicants choose to supply erroneous or misleading information on their applications or résumés in hope of gaining an advantage. This action is unethical and can result in job termination at many organizations if this deception is discovered at a later time.

Chapter Objective 4:
Explain what computer hoaxes and digital manipulation are and how they relate to computer ethics.

A **computer hoax** is an inaccurate statement or story spread through the use of computers, often by e-mail. It is a good idea to make sure questionable information is not a computer hoax before passing the information on to others. **Digital manipulation** is the use of computers to modify something in digital form, usually text or a photograph. While digitally altering photographs sometimes has a positive or an ethically acceptable use—such as aging photos of missing children—the use of digital manipulation on photographs published in newspapers and magazines is more controversial and is viewed as highly unethical by many people.

Chapter Objective 5:
Understand how ethics can impact business practices and decision making.

Ethics are highly intertwined with determining business practices and making business decisions. Decisions, such as which financial information to publicize, which products or services to provide, which safeguards (if any) to establish with products or services that are illegal for minors or objectionable to some individuals, and whether or not to monitor employees, all require ethical consideration.

Because ethics are fundamentally based on values, different types of businesses may have different ethics. Furthermore, ethics and moral standards may vary from country to country and from culture to culture. In addition to legal considerations, businesses with global connections should consider the prevailing ethical standards of all countries involved when making business decisions.

RELATED LEGISLATION

Chapter Objective 6:
Discuss the current status of legislation related to intellectual property rights and ethics.

There are numerous laws in place to protect intellectual property. For example, there are laws relating to trademark and copyright terms, and there are a number of laws protecting various types of intellectual property, such as the *U.S. Anticybersquatting Consumer Protection Act of 1999*, which applies patent law to domain names, and the *Family Entertainment and Copyright Act of 2005*, which makes it illegal to record a movie as it is being shown in a movie theater. Because moral and ethical standards are more difficult to agree on, ethical legislation is slower in coming. However, some laws (such as the *Children's Online Privacy Protection Act* or *COPPA*) have been implemented.

REVIEW ACTIVITIES

KEY TERM MATCHING

a. business ethics

b. computer ethics

c. computer hoax

d. copyright

e. digital manipulation

f. digital watermark

g. intellectual property rights

h. patent

i. plagiarism

j. trademark

Instructions: Match each key term on the left with the definition on the right that best describes it.

1. ________ A form of protection for an invention that can be granted by the government; gives exclusive rights of an invention to its inventor for 20 years.

2. ________ An inaccurate statement or story spread through the use of computers.

3. ________ A subtle alteration of digital content that is not noticeable when the work is viewed or played, but that identifies the copyright holder.

4. ________ A word, phrase, symbol, or design that identifies goods or services.

5. ________ Presenting someone else's work as your own.

6. ________ Standards of moral conduct as they relate to computer use.

7. ________ Standards of moral conduct that guide a business's policies, decisions, and actions.

8. ________ The alteration of digital content, usually text or photographs.

9. ________ The legal right to sell, publish, or distribute an original artistic or literary work; it is held by the creator of a work as soon as it exists in physical form.

10. ________ The rights to which creators of original creative works (such as artistic or literary works, inventions, corporate logos, and more) are entitled.

SELF-QUIZ

Instructions: Circle **T** if the statement is true, **F** if the statement is false, or write the best answer in the space provided. **Answers for the self-quiz are located in the References and Resources Guide at the end of the book.**

1. T F All unethical acts are illegal.

2. T F Changing the background behind a television newscaster to make it appear that he or she is reporting on location instead of from inside the television studio would be an example of digital manipulation.

3. T F Patents are used to protect artistic works, such as music or books.

4. T F Copying a song from a CD you own to your computer to create a custom music CD for personal use is normally considered fair use.

5. T F Résumé padding or lying on a job application would be viewed as unethical by most employers.

6. A software program would be protected by ________ law, while a corporate logo would be protected by ________ law.

7. Turning in a copy of a poem you found on a Web site as your original composition for a poetry class assignment is an example of ________.

8. ________ software is used to protect and manage the rights of creators of digital content, such as by allowing a digital music file to be copied a limited number of times.

9. The overturning by the U.S. Supreme Court of the________ Act, which made it illegal to distribute patently indecent or offensive material online, is considered a landmark decision for free speech advocates.

10. Match each term to its description or example, and write the corresponding number in the blank to the left of each description or example.

a. ________ What the symbol © stands for.

b. ________ Can vary from another's depending on his or her values, culture, and so forth.

c. ________ A warning about a nonexistent virus spread via e-mail.

d. ________ A subtle alteration of digital content that identifies the copyright holder.

1. Computer hoax
2. Copyright
3. Digital watermark
4. Ethics

EXERCISES

1. For each of the following situations, write the appropriate letter—E (ethical) or U (unethical)—in the blank to the right of the situation to indicate how most individuals would view the act.

Situation	**Type of Situation**
a. A teenager rips a new CD she just bought and e-mails the MP3 files to all her friends.	________
b. A photographer combines two of his photographs to create a new composite artistic piece.	________
c. A physician incorporates another doctor's research into her journal article submission, including the researcher's name and article in her submission.	________

2. Match each term with its related example, and write the corresponding number in the blank to the left of each example.

a. ________ Copying and pasting Web page text without recognizing the source.

b. ________ Online age-verification systems.

c. ________ Service marks.

1. Plagiarism
2. Intellectual property rights
3. Business ethics

3. Assume that you have created a Web site to display your favorite original photographs. Is the site and/or your photographs protected by copyright law? Why or why not?

4. Explain the difference between a copyright and a trademark.

5. Under what circumstances might a business need to consider cultural differences when creating a Web site? List at least two examples.

DISCUSSION QUESTIONS

1. There are research services available online that can be used by students preparing term papers. Is the use of these services ethical? Is the use of programs to detect plagiarism by instructors ethical? How can the problem of plagiarism and other forms of cheating at schools today be resolved? Whose responsibility is it to ensure students do not cheat themselves out of a proper education?

2. While the Web contains a vast amount of extremely useful information, some content can be harmful. Think about suicide Web sites that explain in detail how to kill oneself, Web sites that broadcast the beheadings by terrorists, and Web sites that explain how to build bombs. If a Web site instructs visitors how to perform an illegal act, should the site's creators be criminally liable if a visitor carries out those instructions? Who, if anyone, is responsible for preventing potentially harmful information from being shared via the Web? Is there any Internet content that you believe a government has the right or obligation to censor? If so, what? Where should the line between freedom of speech and national or personal safety be drawn?

PROJECTS

HOT TOPICS

1. **Ethics and Virtual Worlds** As discussed in the chapter, there are a number of ethical issues surrounding virtual worlds, such as whether or not virtual money is real currency and whether individuals should pay taxes on profits earned in a virtual world.

   For this project, consider some of the ethical issues discussed in the chapter (such as reporting income from virtual world activities to the IRS, using online age-verification systems to enable Web site visitors to access age-restricted areas, the possibility that someone could pose as another individual online, and the ability to portray oneself differently than who you really are) and think about how these virtual world issues relate to real world decisions. Select one issue and research it to find out its current status and to form an opinion on that issue, including what you think is the ethical thing to do with respect to this issue, what you think the majority of individuals do with respect to this issue, the potential ramifications of this issue, and any changes you think are needed in the future. At the end of your research, prepare a one-page summary of your findings and opinions and submit it to your instructor.

SHORT ANSWER/ RESEARCH

2. **Copyright Registration** Think of an original creation (paper, poem, photograph, or song) to which you believe you are entitled copyright protection and assume that you would like to register a copyright for your creation.

   For this project, research how you would obtain a copyright for your chosen creation. Visit the U.S. Copyright Office Web site (search for it using a search site) and determine the necessary procedure for registration, the required paperwork, and the necessary fee. Use the information located on the site to make sure your creation is entitled to copyright protection, then find the appropriate online registration form (if one is available online). If possible, open and print just one page of the form. From the site, also determine what notice you will receive once your copyright claim has been recorded and how long it will take to receive it. Prepare a short summary of your findings to submit to your instructor, stapled to the single page of the appropriate application if you were able to print it.

HANDS ON

3. **Ethical Web Images** Many Web sites have free or low-cost clip art, photos, or other images available for use on personal or business newsletters, reports, or other printed documents, as well as on Web pages. Use of other images located on Web pages, however, may be restricted.

   For this project, use a search site to find a Web site that offers free images. Determine the types of images and file formats available, as well as if there are any restrictions for use. Next, use the Google Images feature to search for an image you might want to use on a personal Web site or social networking page. Can you tell from the Web page on which the image is located if you are allowed to use that image? If so, is there a fee for its use? If no information is available on the Web page, is there contact information that you could use to request permission to use the image? Are similar images available for free or for a nominal fee online? If so, is the fee reasonable enough for use on a personal Web page? At the conclusion of your research, form an opinion about the availability of free or low-cost images online and the ethical and legal use of Web page images and make a recommendation for individuals looking for images to use on personal Web pages. Prepare a short summary of your findings and recommendations and submit it to your instructor.

ETHICS IN ACTION

4. **Net Neutrality and Your ISP** The term *net neutrality* refers to the equality of data as it is transferred over the Internet. For instance, the data from an individual and the data from Microsoft are treated the same. A recent controversy surrounding the cable giant Comcast brought up the possibility of ISPs interfering with the delivery of Internet data. According to complaints by customers, Comcast has been blocking the use of P2P sites like BitTorrent to download movies, music, and other large files. Comcast, like most ISPs, includes a statement in its terms of service that allows it to use tools to "efficiently manage its networks" in order to prevent those customers using a higher than normal level of bandwidth from interfering with the access of other customers. However, the Comcast issue was considered by many to be a blatant net neutrality issue—blocking access to multimedia from sources other than its own cable sources. Do you think the actions taken by Comcast were ethical? Does an ISP have a right to block selected Internet traffic? Why or why not? Was there a more ethical way Comcast could have handled the problem of some users consuming a higher than normal level of bandwidth?

For this project, form an opinion about the ethical ramifications of ISPs blocking selected Internet traffic and be prepared to discuss your position (in class, via an online class discussion group, in a class chat room, or via a class blog, depending on your instructor's directions). You may also be asked to write a short paper expressing your opinion.

PRESENTATION/ DEMONSTRATION

5. **Your Domain** As mentioned in the chapter, domain names are protected by trademark law.

For this project, select a domain name you would like to use for a fictitious Web site. Visit at least two domain name registration Web sites (GoDaddy.com and Register.com, for instance) to determine how you would register your domain name and the registration cost. Which top-level domains (such as .com or .biz) would you be able to use for your Web site? Use a lookup feature available on a registration site to see if your chosen domain name is available. If not, keep trying variations of that name until you find an appropriate available domain name. Would the available name be easy for customers to remember? Next, select a well-known company and search for its domain name, as well as a few variations of that name. Are the names available, registered to the company, or registered to a different entity? If a different entity, do you think it might be cybersquatting? Share your findings with the class in the form of a short presentation. The presentation should not exceed 10 minutes and should make use of one or more presentation aids, such as a whiteboard, handouts, or a computer-based slide presentation (your instructor may provide additional requirements). You may also be asked to submit a summary of the presentation to your instructor.

BALANCING ACT

6. **Is It Ethical to Post Compromising Photos or Videos of Others?** Posting photos and videos on Facebook, YouTube, and other social media is an everyday activity for many individuals. When you post a photo of just yourself or of others who are aware that the content is going online, it isn't controversial. But what if the photo or video is less than flattering or shows the individual in a compromising position? Is it OK to post the content without asking the individual first? What if you post it but don't tag the individual so he or she isn't identified—does that make a difference? What if you don't tag the person but someone else does—is it your fault for posting the content originally? What if the individual knows you are posting it but then regrets it later—should you remove the item? What if a photo or video you post causes someone else a problem (such as an angry parent or a partner, or a lost job opportunity)? Is it ever ethical to post potentially compromising photos or videos of others online? Why or why not?

Pick a side on this issue, form an opinion and gather supporting evidence, and be prepared to discuss and defend your position in a classroom debate or in a 1–2 page paper, depending on your instructor's directions.

expert insight on...
Systems

Stuart Feldman is a past President of ACM and is a Vice President of Engineering at Google. He is a Fellow of the IEEE, a Fellow of the ACM, and serves on a number of government advisory committees. He is a recipient of the 2003 ACM Software System Award for creating a seminal piece of software engineering known as Make, a tool for maintaining computer software. Stuart has a Ph.D. in Mathematics from MIT and an honorary doctorate from the University of Waterloo.

A Conversation with STUART FELDMAN

Past President of ACM and Vice President, Engineering, Google

"The types of data to be managed are also shifting—most is now visual, audio, unstructured, or executable."

My Background . . .

I am one of the original computer brats—I learned to program on a vacuum tube machine in the early 1960s as a kid at a summer course. I was enthralled by computer programming, and the ability to create programs that did new and surprising things.

Throughout my computer career, I've worked as a computer science researcher at Bell Labs, as a research manager and software architect at Bellcore, and as Vice President for Computer Science at IBM Research. I am now a Vice President at Google (and responsible for engineering activities at Google's offices in the eastern parts of the Americas and in Asia, as well as some specific products). I was also President of ACM (Association for Computing Machinery)—the largest computing society in the world. Overall, my career has been spent in research and engineering at very high-tech companies, working on the cutting edge of computing. It's fun and exciting.

It's Important to Know . . .

The world of data has shifted radically. I can remember when a megabyte was a lot of information. Today, tens of gigabytes fit on a thumb drive, a few terabytes fit on an inexpensive disk, and large companies manage petabytes—and even exabytes. The types of data to be managed are also shifting—most is now visual, audio, unstructured, or executable. We still access data and information on desktop computers, but more often on portable devices—laptops, phones, and tablets.

Programming languages last a long time. While most programmers write in dynamic languages (such as Ruby, Python, and JavaScript) today, FORTRAN programs are still being written and Java and the C family are still very healthy. Even more people do programming without thinking about it by editing spreadsheet formulas and fancy Web pages. We will almost certainly see this continue—a hard core of experts supporting basic systems and tools, and millions (soon billions) of people doing occasional programming and customization.

The impact of systems on society is tremendous. System capabilities have made enormous increases in efficiency possible, and have also opened up new types of business and social activities. Think about how finance has changed—how often do you go into a bank or brokerage today?—and about how you look up information and find people. Also, think about how personal communication and expectations shifted from sending letters with a stamp, to sending e-mail, to staying in touch incessantly with others via texting, blogging, and various social networks. Perhaps our attention span has shrunk, but our ability to reach out has increased. Information systems support globalization and rapid business change—sharing of information, shifting of jobs, and the creation of new jobs and whole new types of careers.

How I Use this Technology . . .

I spend a lot of time writing papers and presentations, so I use Google Docs and Microsoft Office applications—both complex systems that maintain data and perform reliably—to create documents and collaborate with others. I keep my digital information in the cloud and carry a smartphone or tablet everywhere to maintain contact with information and communications. I use secure, integrated financial systems when I perform online financial transactions and I use the Web dozens of times a day for research, communications, personal interactions, shopping, and amusement.

What the Future Holds . . .

The cost of computing, measured in cost of instructions executed or information stored or transmitted, will continue to drop. In addition, the value of information and knowledge that is encapsulated in computer programs and online services will increase: once something is in code, it can be used and replicated at low incremental cost. This will continue to drive our digitization and automation of activities.

> "Big Data analysis and computing in the cloud aren't buzzwords, they are increasingly common paths to results."

There will also be the increasing ability to do massive amounts of computing for enormous numbers of users and to apply computing resources to problems that were too expensive to address just a few years ago. Big Data analysis and computing in the cloud aren't buzzwords, they are increasingly common paths to results. This will be facilitated by the increased use of integration, as well as by dynamic languages and the increased use of Web standards.

There will be new service computing models, ranging from enterprise integration to service industries like Google search tools and remote medical advice. Mobile apps have become a great way to connect information and enhance interactions, and they are a new source of revenue for developers. For program development, we see increasing agility—shifting from waterfall and rigid development methods to more exploratory, agile methods with fast trials and iterations. Verification and testing will continue to be essential—lives and jobs frequently depend on systems today.

Perhaps the biggest shifts will come from our increasing dependence on information and access, the risks when things go wrong, and the possibilities of new applications that can improve our lives. For instance, as information arrives and can be examined more easily, we can do a better job of managing our health, our activities, and our personal interactions.

My Advice to Students . . .

IT jobs, computer applications, programming languages, approaches to system development, and business needs are always changing. The best preparation for a long and successful career is to understand the fundamentals of computing deeply, and be able to apply them to new situations. You need to become expert in some area—such as a programming language, a methodology, or an environment—but you also must always be prepared to learn new technologies and gain new expertise, as well as to learn what people want to do with computers.

Discussion Question

Stuart Feldman points out how our expectations for the systems we use today have shifted—for example, we demand faster communications and information retrieval. What are your expectations when you send an e-mail message or post a photo or video on a social network? Do you expect an immediate response? Are you disappointed if you don't get immediate feedback? How does instant access to communications, news, personal status, and other timely information affect our society today? Be prepared to discuss your position (in class, via an online class discussion group, in a class chat room, or via a class blog, depending on your instructor's directions). You may also be asked to write a short paper expressing your opinion.

>For access to Google search tools and applications, visit www.google.com. There are some excellent papers available at research.google.com. For more information about ACM or to access the ACM Digital Library, visit www.acm.org.

chapter 7

Health, Access, and the Environment

After completing this chapter, you will be able to do the following:

1. Understand the potential risks to physical health resulting from the use of computers.
2. Describe some possible emotional health risks associated with the use of computers.
3. Explain what is meant by the term *digital divide*.
4. Discuss the impact that factors such as nationality, income, race, education, and physical disabilities may have on computer access and use.
5. List some types of assistive hardware that can be used by individuals with physical disabilities.
6. Suggest some ways computer users can practice *green computing* and properly dispose of obsolete computer equipment.
7. Discuss the current status of legislation related to health, access, and the environment in relation to computers.

outline

OVERVIEW

Computers have unarguably changed the way many of us work and live. We typically use them at work to assist with job-related tasks; at home to shop, pay bills, correspond with others, watch TV, and more; and on the go to keep in touch with others and get the information we need at any given time. While our extensive use of computers often makes daily tasks easier, it also can cause serious health and emotional problems, and it can have a negative impact on the environment. In addition, although computer use is becoming almost mandatory in our society, many believe that access to technology is not equally available to all individuals.

The chapter begins with a look at health-oriented concerns, including the impact computers may have on a user's physical and emotional health, as well as strategies individuals can use to lessen those risks. Next, we turn to the issue of equal access, including a discussion of the digital divide and how other factors—such as gender, age, and physical disabilities—may affect computer access and use. We then look at the potential impact of computers on our environment and some ways of lessening that impact. The chapter closes with a look at legislation related to the issues discussed in this chapter. ■

COMPUTERS AND HEALTH

Despite their many benefits, computers can pose a threat to a user's physical and mental well-being. *Repetitive stress injuries* and other injuries related to the workplace environment are estimated to account for one-third of all serious workplace injuries and cost employees, employers, and insurance companies in lost wages, healthcare expenses, legal costs, and workers' compensation claims. Other physical dangers (such as heat burns and hearing loss) can be associated with computers and related technology, and there are some concerns about the long-term effect of using computers and other related devices. *Stress, burnout, computer/Internet addiction*, and other emotional health problems are more difficult to quantify, although many experts believe computer-related emotional health problems are on the rise. While researchers are continuing to investigate the physical and emotional risks of computer use and while researchers are working to develop strategies for minimizing those risks, all computer users should be aware of the possible effects of computers on their health, and what they can do today to stay healthy.

TIP

Many mobile phones today contain nickel, which can cause an allergic reaction in 10–20% of the population. If you get an itchy rash on one side of your face, use the speakerphone, a headset, or a protective cover on your phone and check with your doctor about a possible nickel allergy.

Physical Health

Common physical conditions caused by computer use include eyestrain, blurred vision, fatigue, headaches, backaches, and wrist and finger pain. Some conditions are classified as **repetitive stress injuries (RSIs)**, in which hand, wrist, shoulder, or neck pain is caused

>**Repetitive stress injury (RSI).** A type of injury, such as carpal tunnel syndrome, that is caused by performing the same physical movements over and over again.

by performing the same physical movements over and over again. For instance, extensive keyboard and mouse use has been associated with RSIs, although RSIs can be caused by non-computer-related activities, as well. One RSI related to the repetitive finger movements made when using a keyboard is **carpal tunnel syndrome (CTS)**—a painful and crippling condition affecting the hands and wrists. CTS occurs when the nerve in the *carpal tunnel* located on the underside of the wrist is compressed. An RSI associated with typing on the tiny keyboards commonly found on smartphones and other mobile devices is **DeQuervain's tendonitis**—a condition in which the tendons on the thumb side of the wrists are swollen and irritated. Another physical condition is *computer vision syndrome (CVS)*—a collection of eye and vision problems associated with computer and mobile device use. The most common symptoms are eyestrain or eye fatigue, dry eyes, burning eyes, light sensitivity, blurred vision, headaches, and pain in the shoulders, neck, or back. Eyestrain and CVS are growing more common as individuals are increasingly reading content on the small displays commonly built into smartphones and other mobile devices. Other conditions related to mobile device use include *gorilla arm* (a term coined by Apple's Steve Jobs to refer to the arm fatigue associated with the prolonged vertical use of a touch screen) and *iPad shoulder* (a term used to refer to the shoulder and neck injuries that people who look down at a tablet in their laps are at risk for).

TIP

To avoid gorilla arm, use an external keyboard if you need to do much typing while your touch screen computer or media tablet is in a stand.

TIP

A recent study found that hearing loss among U.S. teens is up 30%—and experts predict hearing loss will continue to rise because of unsafe use of personal audio devices.

Some recent physical health concerns center around the heat from devices commonly held in the hands or lap. For instance, studies have indicated that the peak temperature on the underside of a typical notebook computer can exceed 139° Fahrenheit and an iPad can reach 116° Fahrenheit when performing CPU-intensive tasks. Consequently, manufacturers now warn against letting any part of a notebook touch your body, and a variety of *laptop desks* or notebook cooling stands are available for those occasions when your lap must be used as your work surface.

Another growing physical health concern is noise-induced hearing loss, mainly due to playing music on mobile devices with the volume turned up high and to the earbud headsets typically used with these devices that deliver sound directly into the ear. In addition, people often listen to the music stored on these devices while they are on the go; as a result, they may increase the volume in an attempt to drown out outside noise, further posing a risk to their hearing. To protect against hearing loss, experts suggest a 60/60 rule, which means using earbuds for only about 60 minutes per day with the volume less than 60% of the device's maximum volume. For extended use, *noise reduction headphones* that help block out external noise to allow listeners to hear music better at lower volumes can help, as can using over-the-ear-headphones instead of earbuds and using an external speaker whenever possible.

Another danger is text messaging while driving. There have been many cases of texting-related car accidents, including many fatalities, and nearly 25% of all auto collisions in 2011 involved mobile phones. According to an AT&T study, 49% of commuters and 43% of teens admit to texting while driving. Currently, 41 states in the United States have laws against texting while driving and 12 have laws against using a handheld mobile phone while driving. While some feel these laws are a step in the right direction, studies have found that using a mobile phone with a hands-free device still distracts drivers. One possible solution is using a service or an app (see Figure 7-1) that disables a mobile

FIGURE 7-1
Safe driving apps. Restrict mobile phone use when the car is in motion.

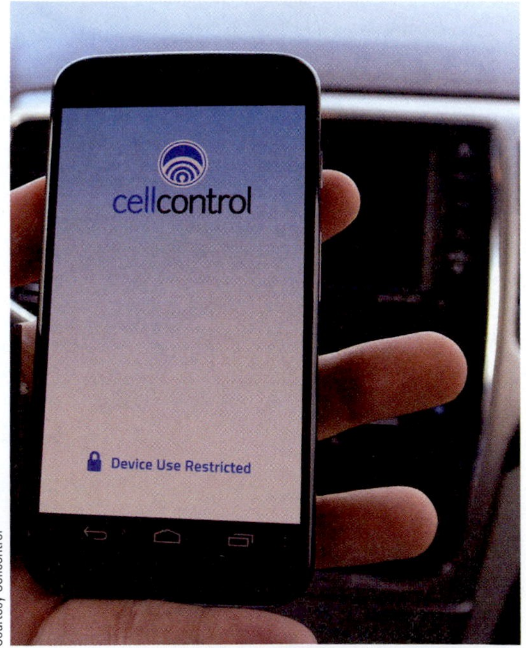

Courtesy Cellcontrol™

>**Carpal tunnel syndrome (CTS).** A painful and crippling condition affecting the hands and wrists that can be caused by computer use.
>**DeQuervain's tendonitis.** A condition in which the tendons on the thumb side of the wrist are swollen and irritated.

phone when the car is in motion. These services and apps are most commonly used by parents to protect their children and by employers to protect their employees as well as reduce their liability in case of an accident. Typically, the service or app responds to all incoming calls and texts to state that the owner is driving; passengers can request an override from the administrator of the service or app (typically the parent or employer). For safety reasons, virtually all services and apps permit outgoing 911 calls. In addition, the U.S. Department of Transportation is requesting that automakers incorporate features in new cars to reduce driver smartphone use, such as disabling smartphones that are paired with the car when the car is in motion or including a proximity sensor that sets off an alarm (similar to a seatbelt reminder) whenever the driver uses a phone.

An additional health concern is the possible risks due to the radiation emitted from wireless devices, such as mobile phones, Wi-Fi and Bluetooth devices, wireless peripherals, and so forth. Mobile phones, in particular, have been studied for years because of their close proximity to the user's head. The results of the studies have been conflicting, with many experts believing that the possible health risks (such as cancer and brain tumors) due to wireless technology have been exaggerated, and others believing the risks are very real. It is difficult to study the long-term possible effects of having a cell phone close to your body because cell phone usage is constantly changing and has not been widespread for enough years for a long-term study. However, until more conclusive research results are available, some health officials recommend keeping the device away from your head as much as possible, such as by using the speakerphone mode or a Bluetooth headset, or by texting instead of talking. In addition, parents may want to limit the amount of time their children spend on a mobile phone.

TIP

Many states have stricter laws for specific categories of drivers; for instance, 37 states ban mobile phone use by novice drivers and 18 states prohibit it by school bus drivers.

TIP

Do not text someone that you know is driving; in addition to endangering them, you may also be legally liable if they crash, according to a recent decision by three New Jersey judges.

CAUTION CAUTION CAUTION CAUTION CAUTION CAUTION CAUT

When using a mobile phone while on the go (to text or to make voice calls, with or without a headset), be sure to be aware of your surroundings. A recent study revealed that participants crossing a virtual street while having a phone conversation took 25% longer to cross and were much more likely to get virtually run over than participants not talking on a phone. To avoid collisions with cars and other objects, be sure to pay attention as you walk and keep the volume down low enough to hear surrounding sounds like car horns and sirens.

What Is Ergonomics?

Ergonomics is the science of fitting a work environment to the people who work there. It typically focuses on making products and workspaces more comfortable and safe to use. With respect to computer use, it involves designing a safe and effective workspace, which includes properly adjusting furniture and hardware and using *ergonomic hardware* when needed. A proper work environment—used in conjunction with good user habits and procedures—can prevent many physical problems caused by computer use. A proper work environment is important for anyone who works on a computer or mobile device, including employees using a computer, media tablet, or smartphone on the job, individuals using one of these devices at home, and children doing computer activities or texting while at home or at school.

>**Ergonomics.** The science of fitting a work environment to the people who work there.

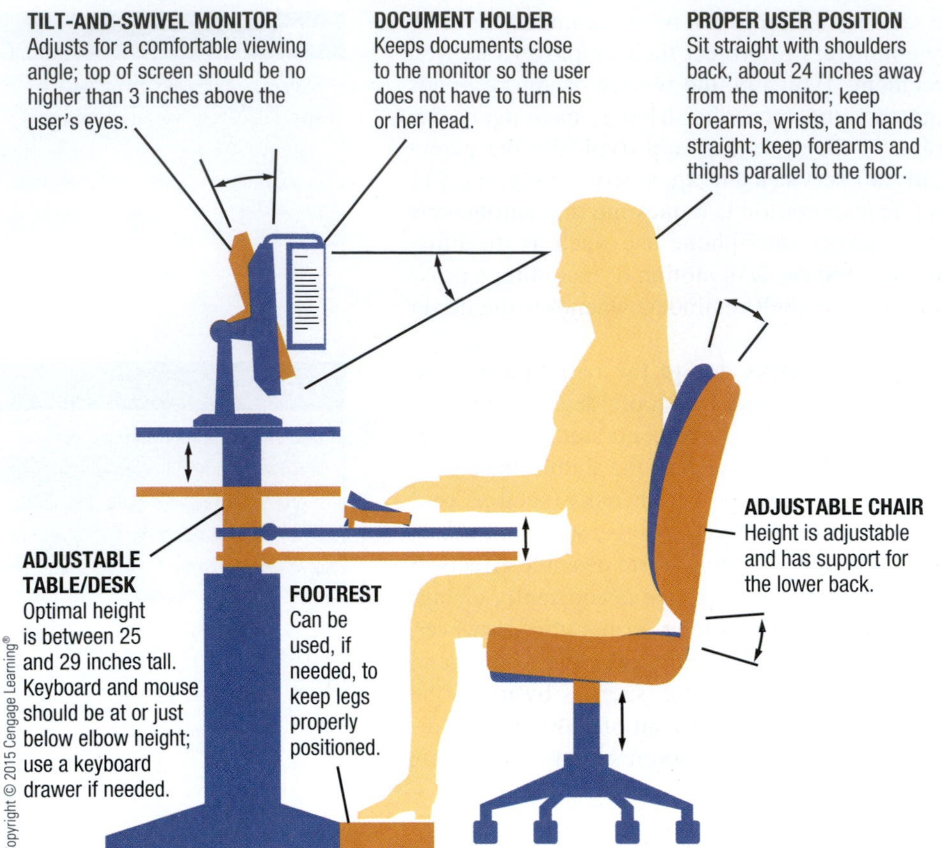

TILT-AND-SWIVEL MONITOR
Adjusts for a comfortable viewing angle; top of screen should be no higher than 3 inches above the user's eyes.
DOCUMENT HOLDER
Keeps documents close to the monitor so the user does not have to turn his or her head.
PROPER USER POSITION
Sit straight with shoulders back, about 24 inches away from the monitor; keep forearms, wrists, and hands straight; keep forearms and thighs parallel to the floor.
ADJUSTABLE CHAIR
Height is adjustable and has support for the lower back.
ADJUSTABLE TABLE/DESK
Optimal height is between 25 and 29 inches tall. Keyboard and mouse should be at or just below elbow height; use a keyboard drawer if needed.
FOOTREST
Can be used, if needed, to keep legs properly positioned.

FIGURE 7-2
Ergonomic workspace design.

Workspace Design

The design of a safe and an effective computer workspace—whether it is located at work, home, or school—includes the placement and adjustment of all the furniture and equipment involved, such as the user's desk, chair, computing device, and peripheral devices such as a keyboard and monitor. Workspace lighting or glare from the sun also needs to be taken into consideration. Proper workspace design can result in fewer injuries, headaches, and general aches and pains for computer users. Businesses can reap economic benefits from proper workspace design, such as fewer absences taken by employees, higher productivity, and lower insurance costs. For example, when one government department in New Jersey installed ergonomically correct workstations in its offices, computer-related health complaints fell by 40% and doctor visits dropped by 25% in less than one year.

Proper placement and adjustment of furniture is a good place to start when evaluating a workspace from an ergonomic perspective (see Figure 7-2). The desk should be placed where the sun and other sources of light cannot shine directly onto the screen or into the user's eyes. The monitor should be placed directly in front of the user about an arm's length away, the top of the screen should be no more than 3 inches above the user's eyes once the user's chair is adjusted, and a *document holder* should be used for individuals who refer to written documents frequently while working on their computers in order to minimize the movement of looking between a document and the monitor. The desk chair should be adjusted so that the keyboard is at, or slightly below, the height at which the user's forearms are horizontal to the floor (there are also special *ergonomic chairs* that can be used, when desired). A footrest should be used, if needed, to keep the user's feet flat on the floor once the chair height has been set. The monitor settings should be adjusted to make the screen brightness match the brightness of the room and to have a high amount of contrast; the screen should also be periodically wiped clean of dust. An emerging trend is workspaces that allow the user to stand while working (see Figure 7-3).

FIGURE 7-3
Standing desks.

The workspace design principles just discussed and illustrated in Figure 7-2 apply to users of desktop computers, portable computers, and mobile devices like media tablets. However, an ergonomic workspace is more difficult to obtain when using a portable computer or mobile device. To create a safer and more comfortable work environment, users of these devices should work at a desk and attach and use a separate keyboard and mouse whenever possible (*travel mice* and *travel keyboards*, which are smaller and lighter than conventional models, can make this easier), both at home and while traveling. The device should also be elevated whenever possible to create a better viewing angle. To help with this and with connecting peripheral devices, *docking stations* as well as *notebook* and *tablet stands* can be used. For a closer look at *tablet docks*, see the Technology and You box on page 271.

Courtesy ASUSTeK Computer Inc.

DOCKING STATIONS

Courtesy Belkin International, Inc.

TABLET STANDS

Courtesy Bluelounge

SMARTPHONE DOCKS

FIGURE 7-4
Docking stations and device stands can help create a more comfortable working environment.

While a keyboard, mouse, monitor, and printer can be connected to a portable computer directly, a **docking station** (see Figure 7-4) is designed to connect a portable computer to peripheral devices more easily—the computer connects to the docking station, and then the devices connected to the ports on the docking station can be used with that computer. Docking stations are often used in homes and offices when a portable computer is used as a primary computer—typically, the peripheral devices remain connected to the docking station and the computer is just connected and disconnected as needed. For example, the docking station shown in Figure 7-4 enables its associated dual-mode (Windows 8 and Android) tablet to be used as an all-in-one Windows 8 PC (when the tablet is docked) including all the hardware (additional RAM, a hard drive, a DVD drive, a more powerful processor, and additional ports, for instance) built into the docking station and as a fully functioning Android media tablet (when the tablet is undocked). There are also keyboard docks and folios available for media tablets (as shown in Chapter 8) that can be used when a physical keyboard is needed for those devices. A **notebook stand** or **tablet stand** (shown in Figure 7-4) is designed primarily to elevate a notebook computer or media tablet to the proper height. If the notebook or tablet stand has built-in USB ports, USB peripheral devices can be connected to the stand; if not, any peripheral devices (such as a keyboard and mouse) to be used with the device while it is inserted into the stand need to be connected directly to the device. In addition to helping with screen placement and connectivity, notebook and tablet stands also allow air to circulate around the bottom of the device. For additional cooling, some notebook stands have a built-in cooling fan that is powered (via a USB port) by the computer. Docks are also available for smartphones (refer again to Figure 7-4) and media tablets (see the Technology and You box). Some additional ergonomic tips for users of portable computers and media tablets are included in Figure 7-5.

FIGURE 7-5
Ergonomic tips for portable computer and media tablet users.

OCCASIONAL USERS	FULL-TIME USERS
Sit with the device on a table and position it for comfortable wrist posture, using a stand for tablets whenever possible. If no table or stand is available, use a laptop desk to protect your legs.	Sit with the device on a desk or table (use a notebook or tablet stand to attain the proper display screen height); use a separate keyboard and mouse.
Adjust the screen to a comfortable position so you can see the screen as straight on as possible. If you will be doing extensive touch screen work, tilt the device so it is not in a vertical position.	Elevate the device so the screen is at the proper height and distance, or connect the device to a stand-alone monitor; in either case, adjust the screen to the proper viewing angle and distance.
Bring a travel keyboard and mouse to use with the device, whenever practical.	Use a separate keyboard and mouse, either attached directly to the device or to a docking station or notebook stand.
When purchasing a new device, pay close attention to the total weight of the system if you will be using it primarily while traveling.	When purchasing a new device, pay close attention to the size and clarity of the display screen, as well as the ease of connecting the device to a docking station or stand and additional hardware.

>**Docking station.** A device designed to easily connect a portable computer to conventional hardware, such as a keyboard, mouse, monitor, and printer. >**Notebook stand.** A device that elevates the display of a notebook computer to a better viewing height; can contain USB ports to connect additional hardware (called a **tablet stand** when designed for use with a media tablet).

TIP

You can also use a USB hub as a docking station if your device has a USB port—just keep your USB devices connected to the USB hub and connect the hub to your device when you are at home.

TIP

Ergonomic techniques and devices designed to help you achieve a *neutral posture* are referring to positions when the joints are not bent or twisted and the muscles are in a resting (relaxed) position.

Some of these tips apply to smartphones as well; additional smartphone tips include limiting the duration of use, reducing keystrokes by using text shortcuts and voice input, avoiding looking down at the device excessively, and switching hands periodically.

Ergonomic Hardware

In addition to the workspace devices (adjustable chairs and tables, footrests, docking stations, device stands, laptop desks, and so on) already discussed, **ergonomic hardware** can be used to help users avoid physical problems due to extensive computer use or to help alleviate the discomfort associated with an already existing condition. Some of the most common types of ergonomic hardware are shown in Figure 7-6 and discussed next.

- *Ergonomic keyboards* use a shape and key arrangement designed to lessen the strain on the hands and wrists. They are available in both desktop and mobile versions (see Figure 7-6).
- *Trackballs* are essentially upside-down mice and *ergonomic mice* use a more ergonomically correct design; both can be more comfortable to use than a conventional mouse. The ergonomic mouse shown in Figure 7-6 is a *vertical mouse*, designed to be used in a vertical position.
- *Tablet arms* connect to a desk or to a monitor and hold a media tablet at the proper height for comfortable viewing.
- *Document holders* can be used to keep documents close to the monitor, enabling the user to see both the document and the monitor without turning his or her head.
- *Antiglare screens*—also called *privacy filters*—cover the display screen and can be used to lessen glare and resulting eyestrain. Many antiglare screens double as privacy screens, preventing others sitting next to you (such as on an airplane) from reading what is displayed on your display screen.

FIGURE 7-6 Ergonomic hardware.

DESKTOP ERGONOMIC KEYBOARDS

MOBILE ERGONOMIC KEYBOARDS

ERGONOMIC MICE

TABLET ARMS

KEYBOARD DRAWERS/TRAYS

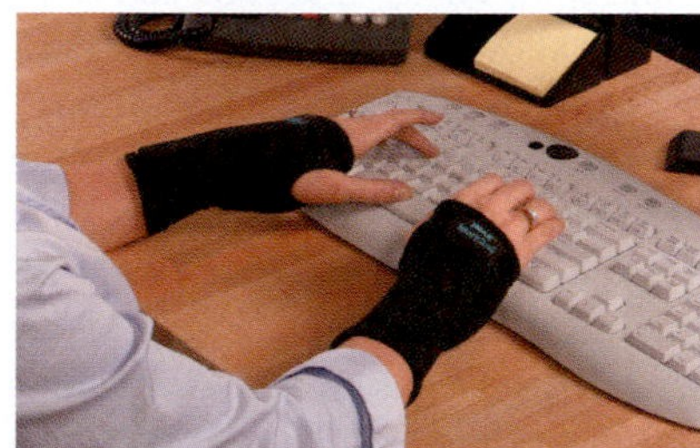

COMPUTER GLOVES

>**Ergonomic hardware.** Hardware, typically an input or output device, that is designed to be more ergonomically correct than its nonergonomic counterpart.

- *Keyboard drawers/trays* lower the keyboard so it is beneath the desk or table top, enabling the user to keep his or her forearms parallel to the floor more easily.
- *Computer gloves* support the wrists and thumbs while allowing the full use of the hands. They are designed to prevent and relieve wrist pain, including carpal tunnel syndrome, tendonitis, and other RSIs.

TIP

A recent study found that 20–30% of viruses on a glass surface like a smartphone screen will transfer to your fingertips—to be safe, don't touch your mouth or eyes while using your phone, unless you wash your hands first.

Good User Habits and Precautions

In addition to establishing an ergonomic workspace, computer users can follow a number of preventive measures while working on their computers or mobile devices (see Figure 7-7) to help avoid physical problems. Finger and wrist exercises, as well as frequent breaks in typing, are good precautions for helping to prevent repetitive hand and finger stress injuries. Using good posture and periodically taking a break to relax or stretch the body can help reduce or prevent back and neck strain. Rotating tasks—such as alternating between computer work, phone work, and paperwork every 15 minutes or so—is also a good idea. For locations where some glare from a nearby window is unavoidable at certain times of the day, closing the curtains or blinds can help to prevent eyestrain. All device users should refocus their eyes on an object in the distance for a minute or so, on a regular basis, and smartphone and mobile device users should increase font size and light level when viewing text on a small display screen. Eyeglass wearers should discuss any eye fatigue or blurriness during computer use with their eye doctors—sometimes a different lens prescription or special *computer glasses* can be used to reduce eyestrain while working on a computer. Computer glasses are optimized for viewing in the intermediate zone of vision where a computer monitor usually falls; that is, closer than glasses designed for driving and farther away than glasses designed for reading.

FIGURE 7-7

Good user habits. These preventative measures can help avoid discomfort while working on a computer or mobile device.

CONDITION	PREVENTION
Wrist/arm/ hand soreness and injury	➤ Use a light touch on a keyboard and touch screen. ➤ Rest and gently stretch your fingers and arms every 15 minutes or so. ➤ Keep your wrists and arms relaxed and parallel to the floor when using a keyboard. ➤ When using a touch screen for extended periods of time, place the device more horizontally than vertically. ➤ When using a device with a small keyboard, type short messages, take frequent breaks, and use a separate keyboard whenever possible. ➤ Use an ergonomic keyboard, ergonomic mouse, computer gloves, and other ergonomic devices if you begin to notice wrist or hand soreness.
Eyestrain	➤ Cover windows or adjust lighting to eliminate glare. ➤ Rest your eyes every 15 minutes or so by focusing on an object in the distance (at least 20 feet away) for one minute and then closing your eyes for an additional minute. ➤ Make sure your display's brightness and contrast settings are at an appropriate level and the display is placed at an appropriate distance from your eyes. ➤ Use a larger text size or lower screen resolution, if needed. You should be able to read your display screen from three times the distance at which you normally sit.
Sore or stiff neck	➤ Use good posture; never hunch over a keyboard or device. ➤ Place your display and any documents you need to refer to while using your device directly in front of you. ➤ Adjust your display to a comfortable viewing angle with the top of the screen no higher than 3 inches above your eyes. ➤ Use a headset if you spend a significant amount of time on the phone; never prop a phone between your face and shoulders.
Backache; general fatigue	➤ Use good posture and adjust your chair to support your lower back; use an ergonomic chair, if needed. ➤ Use a footrest, if needed, to keep your feet flat on the floor. ➤ Walk around or stretch briefly at least once every hour. ➤ Alternate activities frequently. ➤ When traveling, bring lightweight devices and carry only the essentials with you.
Ringing in the ears; hearing loss	➤ Turn down the volume when using headphones (you should be able to hear other people's voices). ➤ Wear over-the-ear-headphones instead of earbuds. ➤ Limit the amount of time you use headphones or earbuds. ➤ Use external speakers instead of headphones when possible.
Leg discomfort or burns	➤ Use a laptop desk, cooling stand, or other barrier between a portable computer and your legs when using a computer on your lap.

Emotional Health

The extensive use of computers and mobile devices in the home and office in recent years has raised new concerns about emotional health. Factors such as financial worries, feelings of being overworked, being unable to relax, and information overload often produce emotional stress. Decades of research have linked stress to a variety of health concerns, such as heart attacks, stroke, diabetes, and weakened immune systems. Workers who report feeling stressed incur more healthcare costs—according to the American Institute of Stress, stress costs U.S. employers more than $300 billion each year in healthcare, missed work, and stress-reduction services provided to employees.

For many individuals, computer use or computer-related events are the cause of, or at least partially contribute to, the stress that they experience. Another emotional health concern related to computer use is addiction to the Internet or another technology.

© iStockphoto.com/jacomstephens

POLICE OFFICERS

Courtesy of DE SANTOS

RESTAURANT SERVERS

Courtesy American Airlines

AIRLINE PASSENGERS

© iStockphoto.com/AzmanL

FIELD WORKERS

FIGURE 7-8

Ever-growing computer use. Many jobs and tasks that did not require computer use in the past require it today.

Stress of Ever-Changing Technology

When computers were first introduced into the workplace, workers needed to learn the appropriate computer skills if their jobs required computer use. Airline agents, for example, had to learn to use computer databases. Secretaries and other office employees needed to learn to use word processing and other office-related software, and customer service representatives needed to learn how to use e-mail. Today, many people entering the workforce are aware of the technology skills they will need to perform the tasks associated with their chosen professions. However, as computers and mobile devices have become continually more integrated into our society, jobs that did not require the use of a computer or a mobile device in the recent past frequently require it today, and individuals are increasingly required to use a computer in day-to-day activities (see Figure 7-8). And, at the rapid pace that technology keeps changing, many workers must regularly learn new skills to keep up to date. For example, they may need to upgrade to a new version of a software program, learn how to use a new software program, or learn how to use a new mobile device feature or app. Although some find this exciting, the ongoing battle to stay current with changing technology creates stress for many individuals.

Impact of Our 24/7 Society

One benefit of our communications-oriented society is that one never has to be out of touch. With the use of smartphones, media tablets, and portable computers, as well as the ability to access e-mail and company networks from virtually anywhere, individuals can be available around the clock, if needed. Although the ability to be in touch constantly is an advantage for some people under certain conditions, it can also be a source of stress. For example, employees who feel that they are "on call" 24/7 and cannot ever get away from work may find it difficult to relax during their downtime (see Figure 7-9). Others (about 54% of employees, according to managers in a recent Harris Interactive study, and 95% of senior IT professionals, according to expert estimates) are expected to be available to do some work while on vacation. In either case, individuals may feel like they are always "on the job" with no time to recharge, which can affect their personal lives, emotional health, and overall well-being. Finding a balance between work time and personal time is important for good emotional health. There is also concern about the increasing use of smartphones, media tablets, and other devices with bright screens in bed.

FIGURE 7-9

Our 24/7 society.

© iStockphoto.com/asiseeit

TECHNOLOGY AND YOU

Tablet Docks

Notebook computer docking stations for use in the home or office have been available for several years. These docking stations make it easier for users to connect their portable computers to hardware (such as a second monitor, a wired printer, or a wired network connection) that stays behind at the home or office. In response to the unprecedented popularity of mobile devices today, new docking options are becoming available. For example, *tablet docks* are emerging to help tablet users with productivity in addition to mobility.

Some tablet docks are designed primarily as a stand to hold the device for easier, hands-free viewing. But, increasingly, tablet docks are including a keyboard for easier data entry; these types of docks typically include a special *docking port* to connect the tablet to the dock. Tablet docks can also have additional functionality, including ports to connect peripheral devices (such as a mouse or an additional monitor) to the tablet. Some tablet docks include a second battery to extend the battery life of the device; others incorporate battery-charging capabilities into the dock so the device can be recharged while it is docked. Some tablets—such as the detachable hybrid notebook-tablet computers discussed in Chapter 1 and the media tablet shown in the accompanying photo—are sold as a package with both the tablet and dock included for flexibility. Stand-alone docks are also available for iPads and other tablets that do not come with a dock.

Up next: Docks for your mobile phone.

Courtesy ASUSTeK Computer Inc.

In addition to being a distraction (particularly for children and teenagers), studies indicate the light from these devices can disrupt sleep.

Information Overload

Although the amount of information available through the Internet is a great asset, it can also be overwhelming at times. When you combine Internet information with TV and radio news broadcasts; newspaper, journal, and magazine articles; and phone calls, voice mail messages, and faxes, some Americans are practically drowning in information. The amount of e-mail received each day by some individuals and organizations is almost unfathomable. For example, the U.S. Senate receives millions of e-mail messages each day, and one study found that workers in small- to medium-sized businesses in the United States spend half of their workday dealing with e-mail messages. Several strategies can be used to avoid becoming completely overwhelmed by information overload.

For efficiently extracting the information you need from the vast amount of information available over the Internet, good search techniques are essential. Perhaps the most important thing to keep in mind when dealing with information overload is that you cannot possibly read everything ever written on a particular subject. At some point in time when performing Internet research, the value of additional information decreases and, eventually, it is not worth your time to continue the search. Knowing when to quit a search or when to try another research approach is an important skill in avoiding information overload.

Efficiently managing your incoming e-mail is another way to avoid information overload. Tools for managing e-mail can help alleviate the stress of an overflowing Inbox, as well as cut down the amount of time you spend dealing with your online correspondence. As discussed in Chapter 5, e-mail filters can be used to route messages automatically into specific folders (such as suspected spam into a Spam folder) based on criteria you set.

TIP

For a review of how to perform efficient and effective Internet searches, refer again to Chapter 3.

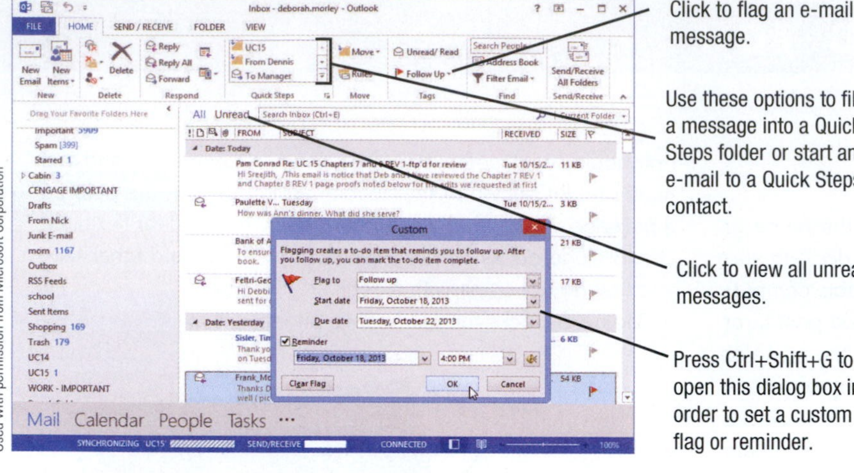
Click to flag an e-mail message.
Use these options to file a message into a Quick Steps folder or start an e-mail to a Quick Steps contact.
Click to view all unread messages.
Press Ctrl+Shift+G to open this dialog box in order to set a custom flag or reminder.
Used with permission from Microsoft Corporation

FIGURE 7-10
E-mail reminder flags can help you organize your Inbox.

When you go through your Inbox, first delete any messages that you don't need to read (such as advertisements that didn't get sent to your Spam folder) and then you can concentrate on the messages remaining in your Inbox. If you need to follow up on a message at a later time, flag it so you don't have to worry about forgetting to follow up at the appropriate time. Many e-mail programs, such as Microsoft Outlook, allow you to flag messages, as well as to add a reminder alarm so you will be reminded automatically when it is time to respond. As shown in Figure 7-10, Outlook also has *Quick Steps* available on the HOME tab (which allows you to file messages in a specific folder quickly, start a new message to a particular contact, or perform any other routine tasks that you specify with a single click), as well as the ability to view all unread messages quickly. Because it can take up to 25 minutes after an interruption to concentrate fully again on a task, productivity training companies advise treating e-mail like physical mail and opening it only a limited number of times per day. To help avoid the temptation of checking e-mail more frequently, close your e-mail program, turn off your new e-mail alert notifier, or mute your speakers so you do not hear new messages arrive. You may also wish to turn off notifications of texts and social networking updates on your smartphone and just check it periodically for updates. For a closer look at an emerging trend that may help your smartphone assist you more efficiently—*augmented reality*—see the How It Works box.

TIP

View your Inbox as a temporary location only; after reading an e-mail message, immediately delete it, flag it, or file it in an e-mail folder to keep your Inbox clean.

Burnout

Our heavy use of computers, combined with information overload and 24/7 accessibility via technology, can lead to **burnout**—a state of fatigue or frustration brought about by overwork. Burnout is often born from good intentions—when, for example, hardworking people try to reach goals that, for one reason or another, become unrealistic. Early signs of burnout include a feeling of emotional and physical exhaustion, no longer caring about a project that used to be interesting or exciting, irritability, feelings of resentment about the amount of work that needs to be done, and feeling pulled in many directions at once.

When you begin to notice the symptoms of burnout, experts recommend reevaluating your schedule, priorities, and lifestyle. Sometimes, just admitting that you are feeling overwhelmed is a good start to solving the problem. Taking a break or getting away for a day can help put the situation in perspective. Saying no to additional commitments and making sure that you eat properly, exercise regularly, and otherwise take good care of yourself are also important strategies for coping with and alleviating both stress and burnout.

ASK THE EXPERT

Dice

Courtesy Dice

Shravan Goli, President, Dice

What is the hottest IT-oriented job today and what do you expect it to be in the future?

"Big data" positions now and in the future. There will always be more data to mine, as well as the business need to use data for insights that drive performance. Gartner found that 42% of IT leaders have invested in big data technology or plan to within a year. It's still early for companies and talent, which means that opportunities abound.

>**Burnout.** A state of fatigue or frustration usually brought on by overwork.

HOW IT WORKS

Augmented Reality

Augmented reality refers to overlaying computer-generated images on top of real-time images. Some of the earliest applications were industrial, such as displaying wiring diagrams on top of the actual wiring of an airplane or other item via a headset. Today, augmented reality is going mobile—being used with smartphones, as well as other mobile devices. To accomplish this, content is displayed over the images seen through the smartphone's camera and displayed on the smartphone. The content is typically based on the user's location (determined by the phone's GPS), the video feed from the smartphone's camera, a digital compass, and other data obtained from the smartphone. Displaying this information requires a *mobile AR browser* or an appropriate *mobile AR app*.

Some initial mobile augmented reality apps designed for consumers include overlaying home listing information (such as pricing and photos) over the video images displayed as a phone is pointing at houses in a neighborhood, displaying information (such as real-time game stats and player information) as a phone is pointing at a sporting event, and displaying activity opportunities (such as restaurant, movie, museum, or shopping information) as a phone is pointing at a business district (see the accompanying illustration). Travelers can use apps designed to overlay directions on top of a street map corresponding to what the camera sees, as well as apps to display sightseeing information as the camera is pointing at a historical building, a statue, or another landmark. Mobile augmented reality can also work indoors, such as identifying displays, concession stands, restrooms, and more at conventions or displaying exhibit information at museums.

Emerging mobile augmented reality opportunities for businesses include displaying the exact physical location of a business and relevant information or ads when an individual points his or her phone in the vicinity of the business. Information displayed could include room photos and pricing (for hotels), dining room photos and menus (for restaurants), or merchandise photos and specials (for stores). And augmented reality is moving beyond smartphones to glasses (such as *Google Glass*) and, eventually, it is expected to work in three dimensions, with devices that will be able to recognize objects and understand their physical properties.

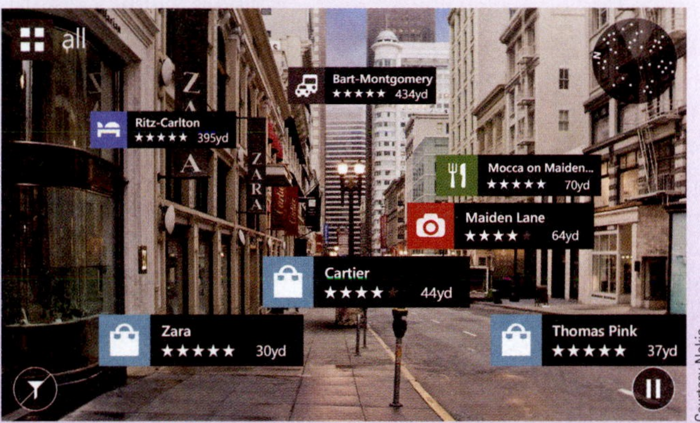

Courtesy Nokia

Internet and Technology Addiction

When an individual's use of the Internet interferes with normal living and causes severe stress to family and other loved ones, it is referred to as **Internet addiction** (also called *Internet dependency, Internet compulsivity, cyberaddiction,* and *technology addiction*, depending on the technology being used). Addictive behavior can include compulsive use of the Internet, a preoccupation with being online, lying about or hiding Internet activities, and an inability to control the behavior. According to Dr. Kimberly Young, an expert on Internet addiction and the director of the Center for Internet Addiction Recovery in Pennsylvania, Internet addiction is a compulsive behavior that completely dominates the addict's life (see Figure 7-11 for Dr. Young's list of Internet addiction symptoms). Studies suggest that one in eight Americans suffer from problematic Internet use; in China, Taiwan, and Korea, it is estimated to be at least 30% of the population. Internet addiction is considered a serious disorder and is being considered for inclusion as a new diagnosis in the upcoming revision of the *Diagnostic and Statistical Manual of Mental Disorders* (*DSM-V*).

>**Internet addiction.** The problem of overusing, or being unable to stop using, the Internet.

Do you feel preoccupied with the Internet (think about the previous online activity or anticipate the next online session)?
Do you feel the need to use the Internet with increasing amounts of time in order to achieve satisfaction?
Have you repeatedly made unsuccessful efforts to control, cut back, or stop Internet use?
Do you feel restless, moody, depressed, or irritable when attempting to cut down or stop Internet use?
Do you stay online longer than originally intended?
Have you jeopardized or risked the loss of a significant relationship, job, educational, or career opportunity because of the Internet?
Have you lied to family members, a therapist, or others to conceal the extent of involvement with the Internet?
Do you use the Internet as a way of escaping from problems or of relieving a dysphoric mood (e.g., feelings of helplessness, guilt, anxiety, depression)?

Courtesy of Dr. Kimberly Young, Director of the Center for Internet Addiction Recovery

FIGURE 7-11

Signs of Internet addiction. You may be addicted to the Internet if you answer "yes" to at least five of these questions.

Originally, Internet addiction sufferers were stereotyped as younger, introverted, socially awkward, computer-oriented males. However, with the increased access to computers and the Internet today, this stereotype is no longer accurate. Internet addiction can affect anyone of any age, race, or social class and can take a variety of forms. Some individuals become addicted to e-mailing or text messaging. Others become compulsive online shoppers or online gamblers, or become addicted to social media activities. Still others are addicted to cybersex, cyberporn, or online gaming, or struggle with real-world relationships because of virtual relationships. Currently, *Internet sex addiction* to chat rooms and online pornography are the most common forms of Internet addiction.

Like other addictions, addiction to using a computer, the Internet, texting, or other technology may have significant consequences, such as relationship problems, job loss, academic failure, health problems, financial consequences, loss of custody of children, and even suicide. There is also growing concern about the impact of constant use of technology among teenagers. In addition to texting and posting to Facebook, many teens are taking these devices to bed with them, raising concerns about sleep deprivation and its consequences, such as concentration problems, anxiety and depression, and unsafe driving. Internet addiction is also increasingly being tied to crime and even death in countries (such as China and South Korea) that have high levels of broadband Internet access. For instance, Internet addiction is blamed for much of the juvenile crime in China, a number of suicides, and several deaths from exhaustion by players unable to tear themselves away from marathon gaming sessions.

Internet addiction is viewed as a growing problem worldwide. Both China and South Korea have implemented military-style boot camps to treat young people identified as having Internet addiction, and the growing number of Internet-addicted youth prompted the Chinese government to ban minors from Internet cafés. In the United States, there are a number of inpatient treatment centers that treat Internet addiction, such as the reSTART program in the state of Washington and the Internet Addiction Recovery and Treatment Program at the Bradford Regional Medical Center in Pennsylvania—the first hospital-based Internet addiction treatment and recovery program in the United States.

ASK THE EXPERT

Courtesy Strike Fighter Weapons School Pacific, NAS Lemoore

Tony Onorati, Former Naval Aviator and Former Commanding Officer, Strike Fighter Weapons School Pacific, NAS Lemoore

What computer experience is needed to be a U.S. Navy pilot?

While no computer experience is necessarily required to enter flight school, failure to have a solid knowledge of the Windows operating system will put the candidate well behind his/her contemporaries when they finally do reach the fleet as a pilot. All the tactical planning tools for preflight preparation, navigation, ordnance delivery, and mission planning, as well as all aircraft-specific publications, manuals, and training, are all computer based. For the FA-18 Hornet, all mission data is created on the computer, copied to a mission computer card, and plugged into the jet where it is downloaded into the aircraft's computer for use in flight. Becoming a naval aviator without computer skills is like entering flight school without ever having flown before—it can be done but it places you well behind the power curve.

Many experts believe that while Internet addiction is a growing problem, it can be treated, similar to other addictions, with therapy, support groups, and medication. Research to investigate its impact, risk factors, and treatment possibilities, as well as investigate treatment differences among the various types of technology abuse, is ongoing. New studies are also looking at the overall impact of technology and how its overuse or abuse may also impact people's lives in order to identify other potential problems and possible solutions.

ACCESS TO TECHNOLOGY

For many, a major concern about the increased integration of computers and technology into our society is whether or not technology is accessible to all individuals. Some believe there is a distinct line dividing those who have access and those who do not. Factors such as age, gender, race, income, education, and physical abilities can all impact one's access to technology and how one uses it.

The Digital Divide

The term **digital divide** refers to the gap between those who have access to information and communications technology and those who do not—often referred to as the "haves" and "have nots." Typically, the digital divide is thought to be based on physical access to computers, the Internet, and related technology. Some individuals, however, believe that the definition of the digital divide goes deeper than just access. For example, they classify those individuals who have physical access to technology but who do not understand how to use it or are discouraged from using it in the "have not" category. Groups and individuals trying to eliminate the digital divide are working toward providing real access to technology (including access to up-to-date hardware, software, Internet, and training) so that it can be used to improve people's lives. In addition to access to computers and the Internet, digital divides related to other technologies may exist as well. For instance, one recent study found that hospitals that primarily serve low-income patients are less likely to have adopted electronic health records (EHRs) and other safety-related technologies (such as clinical decision supports and electronic medication lists) than hospitals with more affluent patients.

TIP

Many people today—regardless of income level—view having a mobile phone as a necessity, not a luxury.

The digital divide can refer to the differences between individuals within a particular country, as well as to the differences between countries. Within a country, use of computers and related technology can vary based on factors such as age, race, education, and income.

The U.S. Digital Divide

Although there is disagreement among experts about the current status of the digital divide within the United States, there is an indication that it is continuing to shrink. As discussed in Chapter 3, more than 80% of the U.S. adult population are Internet users, using the Internet at work, home, school, or another location. Free Internet access at libraries, school, and other public locations, as well as the availability of low-cost computers and low-cost or free Internet access in many areas today, has helped Internet use begin to approach the popularity and widespread use of telephones and TVs, and has helped it become more feasible for low-income families today than in the past. In general, however, according to recent reports by the Pew Internet & American Life Project, individuals with a higher level of income or a higher level of education are more likely to go online, and younger individuals are more likely to be online than older Americans. Some overall demographic data about Internet use in the United States is shown in Figure 7-12. Similar trends occur with digital divide statistics for other technologies, such as smartphone use.

TIP

While the digital divide involves more than just Internet use (it can relate to any type of technology necessary to succeed in our society), the growing amount of Internet use is an encouraging sign that the digital device is shrinking.

>**Digital divide.** The gap between those who have access to technology and those who do not.

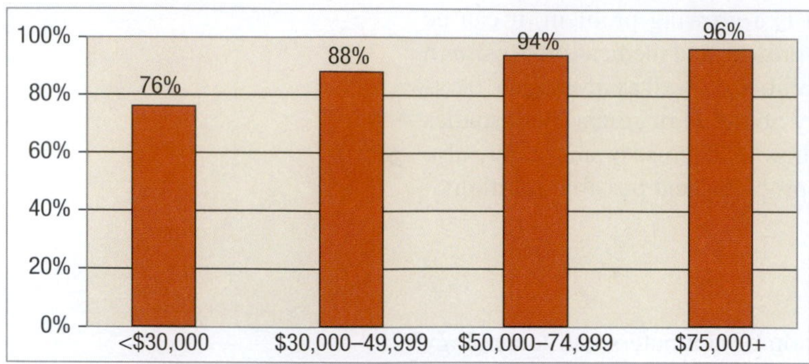

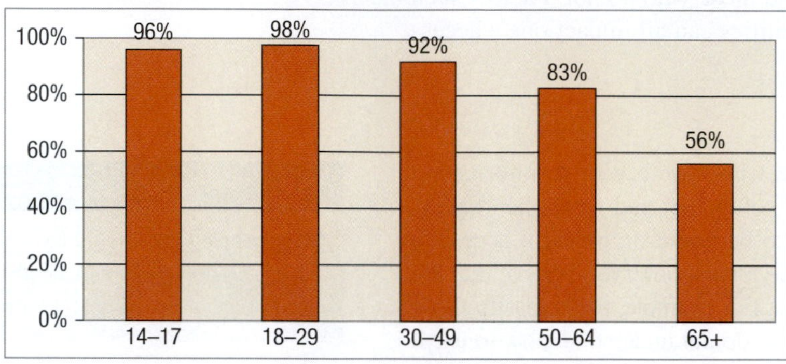

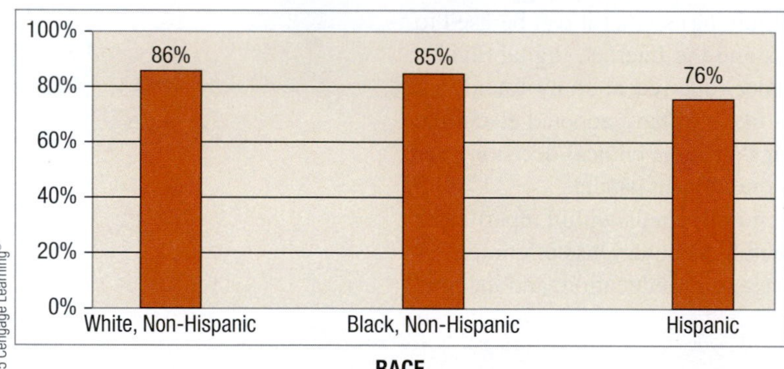

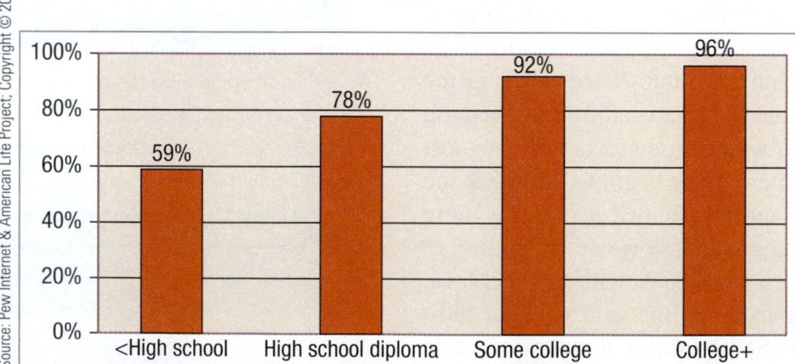

FIGURE 7-12

Key U.S. Internet use statistics. Shows the percent of individuals in each category who use the Internet.

Because the United States is such a technologically advanced society, reducing—and trying to eliminate—the digital divide is extremely important to ensure that all citizens have an equal chance to be successful in this country. Although there has been lots of progress in that direction, more work still remains. For instance, the Navajo Nation (a sovereign tribal nation with more than 250,000 citizens living across 27,000 square miles in New Mexico, Arizona, and Utah) has lagged significantly behind the rest of the United States in terms of technology. Many schools lack computers and Internet access, many residents have to drive seven or eight miles over roads impassable during rain or snow storms to reach the nearest telephone, and even some government entities within the Navajo Nation have dial-up or no Internet access. However, this is slowly changing as a result of the *Internet to the Hogan* project—a project designed to end the digital divide in the Navajo Nation. It will first provide Internet to tribal colleges and other central locations, which will be extended to community-based chapter houses, and then to schools, medical clinics, hospitals, firehouses, and homes.

Many individuals view technology as essential for all Americans today. For instance, students need access to devices and Internet resources to stay informed and be prepared for further education and careers. As already discussed, most jobs in the United States require some sort of computer or Internet use. And the Internet is becoming an increasingly important resource for older Americans, particularly for forming decisions about health and healthcare options. However, it is important to realize that not all individuals want to use computers or go online. Just as some people choose not to have televisions, mobile phones, or other technologies, some people—rich or poor—choose not to have a computer or go online. Sometimes this is a religious decision; at other times, it is simply a lifestyle choice.

The Global Digital Divide

While the digital divide within a country is about some individuals within that country having access to technology and others not having the same access, the global digital divide is about some countries having access to technology and others not having the same level of access. It is becoming increasingly important for all countries to have access to information and communications technology in order to be able to compete successfully in our global economy. The global digital divide is perhaps more dramatic than the U.S. digital divide. According to InternetWorldStats.com, more than 2.4 billion people globally are online—only about 34% of the world's population. With more than 78% of its population online, North America is the leading world region in Internet users; with only 15.6% of its population online, Africa has one of the lowest percentages of Internet users.

For some, it is difficult to imagine how computers and the Internet would benefit the world's hungry or the 1.2 billion people in the world without access to reliable electricity. Others view technology as a means to bridge the global digital divide. For instance, mobile phones and computers with solar-rechargeable batteries can be used in developing countries for education and telemedicine. A variety of wireless Internet projects that are designed to bring wireless Internet to remote areas of the world are also helping to bridge the gap. These projects provide Internet access to rural schools and homes, as well as provide services (such as telemedicine) to remote villages that would not otherwise have those services available.

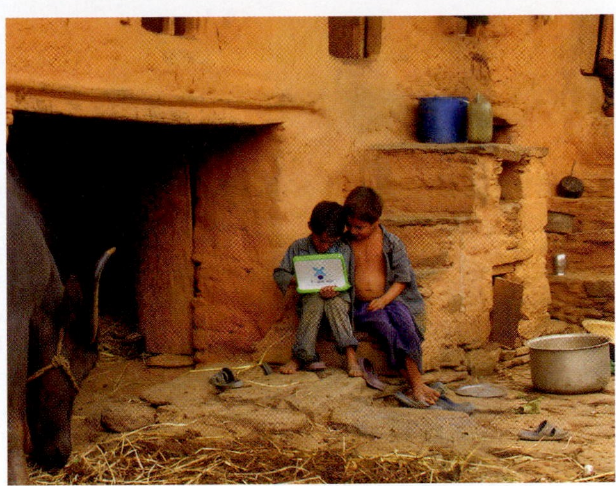

Courtesy One Laptop Per Child

FIGURE 7-13
The OLPC XO laptop.

For personal computer use, new products are emerging that could help lessen the global digital divide. Perhaps the most widely known project in this area is the *One Laptop Per Child* (*OLPC*) project. The goal of OLPC is to ensure that every child in the world has access to a rugged, low-cost, low-power connected laptop (see Figure 7-13) in order to provide them with access to new channels of learning, sharing, and self-expression. The current model of the *XO laptop* developed by OLPC is the *XO-4 Touch*.

The XO laptop is made of thick plastic for durability with a display that can be viewed in direct sunlight and the rubber keyboard is sealed to keep out dirt and water. The XO is very energy-efficient, and it can be charged via an electrical outlet, as well as from a car battery, foot pedal, or pull string. It is Linux-based and includes a Wi-Fi adapter, flash memory slot, built-in video camera, microphone, touchpad, 7.5-inch touch screen, accelerometer, keyboard, and USB ports; has 1 or 2 GB of RAM; and uses 4 or 8 GB of flash memory for storage. More than 2 million children and teachers in Latin America (plus another 500,000 in Africa and the rest of the world) have been provided with an XO laptop. According to OLPC, making it possible for students in developing countries to have a laptop will greatly impact their education, as well as society as a whole. They believe that by empowering children to educate themselves, a new generation will ultimately be better prepared to tackle the other serious problems (poverty, malnutrition, disease) facing their societies. An Android tablet version—the *XO Tablet* shown in Figure 7-14—recently became available; it is being distributed to schools with underprivileged children in the United States and is also available to the general public.

FIGURE 7-14
The $129 XO tablet.

Courtesy One Laptop Per Child

Assistive Technology

Research has found that people with disabilities tend to use computers and the Internet at rates below the average for a given population. Part of the reason may be that some physical conditions—such as visual impairment or limited dexterity—make it difficult to use a conventional computer system. That is where **assistive technology**—hardware and software specially designed for use by individuals with physical disabilities—fits in. While assistive technology is not currently available to help with all types of computer content (primarily streaming video and other multimedia content increasingly found on Web pages), there has been much improvement in assistive technology in recent years. In addition, researchers are continuing to develop additional types of assistive technology, such as *multimedia accessibility tools* to help individuals with visual impairments better

TIP

There are also assistive devices designed for elderly individuals, such as smartphones with large, easy to read and press keys.

>**Assistive technology.** Hardware and software specifically designed for use by individuals with physical disabilities.

Courtesy DynaVox Mayer-Johnson

FIGURE 7-15
AAC systems help individuals with speech disabilities communicate with others.

control and experience Web-based multimedia. This growth in assistive technology is due in part to demands by disabled individuals and disability organizations for equal access to computers and Web content, as well as *Section 508* of the *Rehabilitation Act* (which requires federal agencies to make their electronic and information technology accessible to people with disabilities) and the *Americans with Disabilities Act* (*ADA*) (which requires companies with 15 or more employees to make reasonable accommodations for known physical or mental limitations of otherwise qualified individuals). In order to be accessible to users of assistive technology, Web pages need to assign *alt tags* (text-based descriptions) to Web page images and use meaningful text-based hyperlinks—such as *How to Contact Us* instead of *Click Here*.

To help provide individuals with physical disabilities equal access to technology, assistive input and output devices—such as *Braille keyboards*, specialized pointing devices, and *screen readers*—are available for personal computers, as well as some smartphones and other mobile devices. In addition, there are apps and devices designed to assist people with disabilities with day-to-day tasks. For example, mobile apps can identify the price, name, and other data about a product once a product label is scanned with a smartphone camera; talking GPS devices can guide blind or low-vision individuals; and *augmentative and alternative communication* (*AAC*) tablets (see Figure 7-15) can help people who are unable to use verbal speech to communicate with others.

Assistive Input Systems

Assistive input devices allow for input in a nontraditional manner (see Figure 7-16). For example, *Braille keyboards*, large-print keyboards, or conventional keyboards with Braille or large-print key overlays are available for visually impaired computer users. *Keyguards*—metal or plastic plates that fit over conventional keyboards—enable users with limited hand mobility to more easily press the keys on a keyboard. *One-handed keyboards* are designed to be used with only one hand, and speech recognition systems allow data and commands to be input hands-free. *Switches*—hardware devices that can be activated with hand, foot, finger, or face movement, or with sips and puffs of air—can also be used to input data and commands. Some conventional input devices can also be used for assistive purposes, such as scanners, which—if they have optical character recognition (OCR) capabilities—can input printed documents as text that can be enlarged on the screen or read aloud.

TIP

Assistive hardware is also used by the general population, such as voice input systems for voice commands and input and head pointing systems for gaming and virtual reality (VR) applications.

Assistive pointing devices can be used to move and select items; they can also be used to enter text-based data when used in conjunction with an on-screen keyboard. Examples include *foot-controlled mice*, *head pointing systems* that control the on-screen pointer using head movement, and *eye tracking systems* that allow users to select items on screen using only their gaze. For example, the eye tracking system shown in Figure 7-16 connects to nearly any Windows 8 device and translates eye gazes to Windows 8 touch commands.

FIGURE 7-16
Assistive input devices.

Courtesy of Hooleon Corporation

BRAILLE KEYBOARDS
The keys on this keyboard contain Braille overlays.

Courtesy of Matias Corporation

ONE-HANDED KEYBOARDS
Each key on this half keyboard contains two letters (one set for the keys on the right half of the keyboard and one set for the left half) so all keys can be reached with one hand.

Courtesy Tobii Technology AB

EYE TRACKING SYSTEMS
Cameras track the user's eye movements, which are used to select icons and other objects on the screen.

Courtesy of Freedom Scientific

SCREEN READER SOFTWARE

Courtesy HumanWare

BRAILLE DISPLAYS

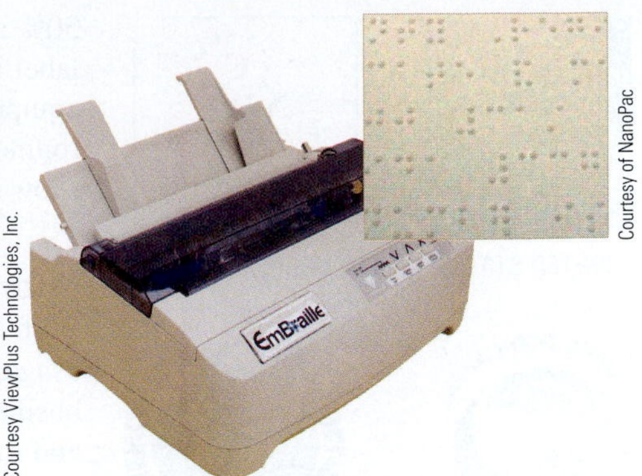

Courtesy ViewPlus Technologies, Inc.

Courtesy of NanoPac

BRAILLE PRINTERS

FIGURE 7-17
Assistive output devices.

Assistive Output Systems

Some examples of *assistive output devices* that can be used by blind and other visually impaired individuals are shown in Figure 7-17. A *screen reader* is a software program that reads aloud all text information available via the computer screen, such as instructions, menu options, documents, and Web pages. *Braille displays* are devices that can be attached to conventional computers or mobile devices and that continuously convert screen output into Braille form. *Braille printers* (also called *Braille embossers*) print embossed output in Braille format on paper instead of, or in addition to, conventional ink output.

Some operating systems also include accessibility features. For instance, recent versions of Windows and Mac OS include a screen reader, on-screen keyboard, speech recognition capabilities, and settings that can be used to magnify the screen, change text size and color, convert audio cues into written text, and otherwise make the computer more accessible.

ENVIRONMENTAL CONCERNS

The increasing use of computers in our society has created a variety of environmental concerns. The amount of energy used to power personal computers, servers, and computer components, as well as the heat generated by computing equipment, is one concern. Another is our extensive use of paper, CDs, and other disposables, and how much of it ends up as trash in landfills. The hazardous materials contained in computer equipment or generated by the production of computers and related technology, as well as the disposal of used computing products, are additional concerns. With an increasing amount of attention being focused on energy usage and carbon emissions, businesses and individuals are paying more attention to energy costs and their *carbon footprint* (the amount of carbon dioxide produced to support activities), as well as the carbon footprints of their suppliers and business partners.

Green Computing

The term **green computing** refers to the use of computers in an environmentally friendly manner. Minimizing the use of natural resources, such as energy and paper, is one aspect of green computing. In 1992, the U.S. Environmental Protection Agency (EPA) introduced **ENERGY STAR** as a voluntary labeling program designed to identify and promote energy-efficient products to reduce greenhouse gas emissions. Computers and monitors were among the first labeled products; an ENERGY STAR-qualified computer will use between

>**Green computing.** The use of computers in an environmentally friendly manner. >**ENERGY STAR.** A program developed by the Environmental Protection Agency (EPA) to encourage the development of energy-saving devices.

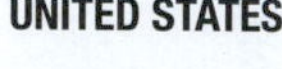
UNITED STATES

EUROPEAN UNION

KOREA

BRAZIL

AUSTRALIA

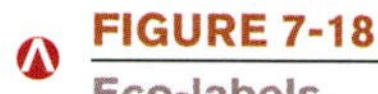
FIGURE 7-18
Eco-labels.

U.S. Environmental Protection Agency, ENERGY STAR program; Courtesy of the European Commission; General Courtesy of Korea Environmental Labeling Association (KELA); Courtesy of ABNT - ASSOCIAÇÃO BRASILEIRA DE NORMAS TÉCNICAS; Courtesy Good Environmental Choice Australia

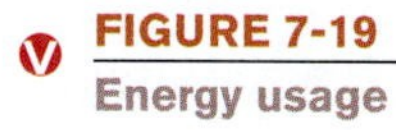
FIGURE 7-19
Energy usage monitors.

Courtesy P3 International Corporation

30% and 65% less energy, depending on how it is used. Today, the ENERGY STAR label (see Figure 7-18) appears on office equipment, residential heating and cooling equipment, major appliances, lighting, home electronics, and more. **Eco-labels**—environmental performance certifications—are also used in other countries; Figure 7-18 show some examples.

Energy Consumption and Conservation

With the high cost of electricity today and the recent increase in data center energy usage, power consumption and heat generation by computers are key concerns for businesses today. Today's faster and more powerful computers tend to use more energy and run hotter than computers from just a few years ago, which leads to greater cooling costs. Servers, in particular, are power hungry, so consolidating servers (such as by the use of virtualization) is a common energy-saving tactic used by businesses today (for example, AOL recently decommissioned nearly 10,000 servers and saved about $5 million total, with $1.65 million of the savings attributed to energy savings). Other strategies include powering down computers when they are not in use, using desktop virtualization, and utilizing cloud computing. Green computing can have tremendous financial benefits. In fact, the EPA estimates that even a 10% reduction in energy consumption by U.S. data centers would save enough energy to power up to 1 million homes per year and save U.S. businesses $740 million annually.

In response to the growing emphasis on green computing today, hardware manufacturers are working to develop more energy-efficient personal computers, servers, microprocessors, storage systems, displays, power supplies, motherboards, and other computer components. Some energy-saving features found on computer hardware today include devices (such as computers and printers) that can go into very low-power sleep mode when not in use, low-power-consumptive chips and boards, high-efficiency power supplies, energy-efficient flat-panel displays, liquid cooling systems, and CPUs that power up and down on demand. The energy savings by using more energy-efficient hardware can be significant. For instance, moving to an LED flat-panel display instead of a conventional LCD display saves around 12% in energy consumption.

While ENERGY STAR-qualified computers deliver substantial energy savings over conventional computers, computers can still draw quite a bit of power when they are in these modes—particularly with a screen saver enabled. Because of this, it is important for businesses, schools, and individuals to power down computers manually or automatically (using software or power-saving settings) when they are not in use to save power. Mobile phone manufacturers are also working to reduce the environmental impact of their products, such as displaying reminders on mobile phones to unplug them from their chargers when they are fully charged because chargers can draw up to five watts per hour even if nothing is plugged into them. Other devices that draw power when they are turned off (sometimes called *energy vampires*) include computers, home electronics, and home appliances. In fact, it is estimated that the average U.S. household spends $100 per year powering devices that are turned off or in stand-by mode. To determine how much power a device is using, you can use a special device like the *Kill a Watt* shown in Figure 7-19. This device displays the amount of power (in kilowatts or dollar value) any device plugged into it is currently using. To save on vampire power costs, unplug your devices when you are not using them (you can connect your electronic devices to a power strip and just switch off the power at the power strip to make this process easier). However, don't cut the power to any device (such as a wireless router, DVR, or cable box) that will need to be active to perform a needed

>**Eco-label.** A certification, usually by a government agency, that identifies a device as meeting minimal environmental performance specifications.

function. *Smart power strips* that turn off outlets on the strip when it senses those devices aren't being used and *smart charging stations* that recharge USB devices and shut off when the devices are fully charged are other power-saving alternatives.

Alternate Power

In addition to more energy-efficient hardware, other possibilities for greener computing are being developed, such as alternate power sources for computers and mobile devices. For instance, *solar power* is a growing alternative for powering electronic devices, including mobile phones and portable computers. With solar power, *solar panels* convert sunlight into direct current (DC) electricity, which is then stored in a battery.

Although it has been expensive to implement in the past, improvements in solar technology are making its use more feasible for a greater number of individuals. Today's solar panels are typically *thin-film solar panels*, which are created by printing nanoparticles onto rolls of thin, flexible panels and which cost a fraction of the cost of earlier generations. Much of the current research is working to develop what is viewed as the next generation of solar cells—very low cost *printable photo voltaic cells* (*PVCs*) that are printed using nanocrystal-based "ink" and may reduce the cost to an even more competitive level. To encourage this development, Harvard University recently released a list of 20,000 organic compounds that may be viable replacements for silicon. As the flexibility of solar manufacturing increases and the price decreases, solar panels are becoming available for an increasing number of applications. For instance, solar panels are built into the covers of some computer and tablet cases, and portable solar panels can be attached to backpacks and other items (see Figure 7-20). As also shown in this figure, hand-powered chargers can be used with portable computers, smartphones, and other mobile devices. While currently these devices are most often used wherever dependable electricity is not available, such as in developing countries and while outdoors, *transparent solar panels* are in the research stage and are expected to eventually be built into the screens of smartphones, tablets, and other devices to charge those devices on a continual basis—they may even be built into car sunroofs and the windows of buildings. For a look at other emerging options for powering your devices, see the Trend box.

Solar power can be also used to power more permanent computer setups. For instance, some Web hosting companies in the United States (including Solar Energy Host and AISO.Net) are now 100% solar powered and the solar panels that cover most of the rooftops at Google's Mountain View, California, headquarters power 30% of the energy needs for that complex. Solar power plants are also being implemented (for example, Apple is building a new solar power plant in Reno to continue working toward its goal of all data centers using 100% renewable energy), and some experts predict that many buildings in the future will be *solar buildings* with solar cells integrated into the rooftop, walls, and windows of the building to generate electricity.

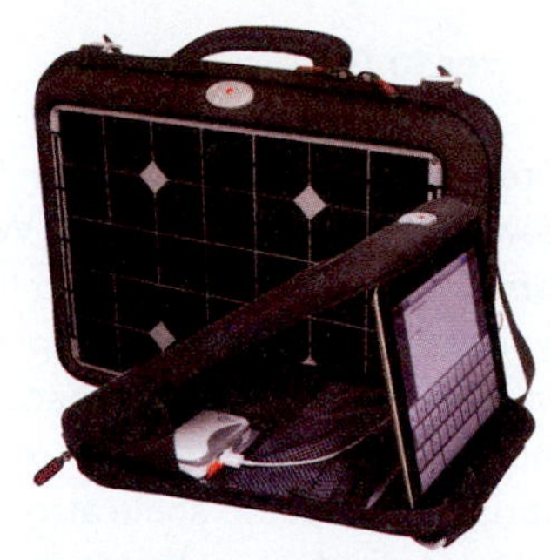

Courtesy Voltaic Systems, Inc.

SOLAR COMPUTER AND TABLET BAGS

Courtesy Voltaic Systems, Inc.

SOLAR-POWERED CHARGERS

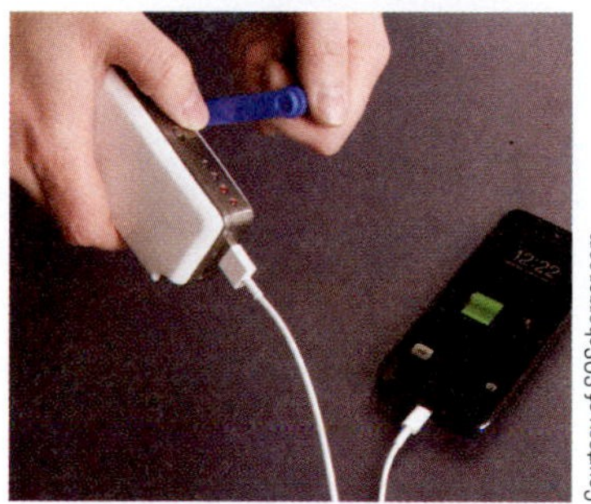

Courtesy of SOScharger.com

HAND-POWERED CHARGERS

FIGURE 7-20

Alternate power.

Can be used to power smartphones, portable digital media players, GPS devices, portable computers, and other devices.

Green Components

In addition to being more energy-efficient, computers today are being built to run quieter and cooler, and they are using more recyclable hardware and packaging. Many computer manufacturers are also reducing the amount of toxic chemicals being used in personal computers. For instance, Dell bans the use of some hazardous chemicals, such as cadmium and mercury; has reduced the amount of lead used in several desktop computers; and meets the European Union requirement of being completely lead-free for all electronics shipped to the EU. Some mobile phones are also going green, being made out of recycled plastics, including solar panels to charge the phone's battery, and including a pedometer and other apps to calculate the volume of CO_2 emissions you have avoided by not driving.

TREND

Power to Go

Tired of your smartphone or laptop battery running out of power at inopportune times? Well, there are several new *portable power devices* lining up to save the day. Some devices, typically the size of a smartphone, consist of a power pack with built-in cables to connect your various devices. Most of these power packs can be recharged via a USB cable and portable computer; some also can be plugged into a wall outlet for super fast recharging. An option geared toward commuters is the *PowerCup power inverter* that is shaped like a large portable coffee container so it fits nicely in a car cup holder. The PowerCup connects to the car via the car's 12-volt power outlet and can power up to two regular devices (such as a laptop or DVD player) using standard AC plugs, as well as one USB-powered device (such as a smartphone).

One unique option (shown in the accompanying photo) is the *PowerTrekk* device, which uses *fuel cell* technology to create the energy needed (fuel cells produce electricity using a chemical reaction). This pocket-sized device connects to any mobile device with a USB connection (such as a smartphone, digital media player, or media tablet) to provide nearly instant power to the device (the charger uses replaceable hydrogen fuel pucks and water—one puck charges approximately one smartphone).

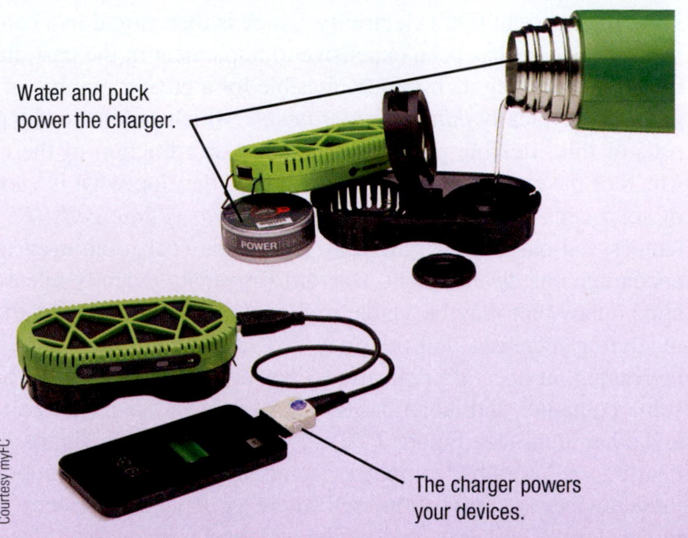

Water and puck power the charger.
The charger powers your devices.

Courtesy myFC

Recycling and Disposal of Computing Equipment

Another environmental concern is the amount of trash—and sometimes toxic trash—generated by computer use. One concern is paper waste. Despite the increase in the use of electronic forms, electronic signatures, e-books, online newspapers and magazines, and online bill pay, it appears that the so-called *paperless office* that many visionaries predicted has not yet arrived. Instead, research indicates that global paper use has grown more than sixfold since 1950, and one-fifth of all wood harvested in the world today ends up as paper. The estimated number of pages generated by computer printers worldwide is almost one-half billion a year—an amount that would stack more than 25,000 miles high. One possible solution for the future (e-paper) is discussed in the Inside the Industry box. There are also utilities, such as *GreenPrint* and *PrintWhatYouLike.com*, designed to reduce paper consumption. These utilities eliminate images, blank pages, and other non-critical content located on documents and/or Web pages in order to print just the necessary content on the least number of pages possible.

In addition to paper-based trash, computing refuse includes electronic hardware such as used toner cartridges, obsolete or broken computers and peripherals, and discarded CDs, DVDs, and other storage media. Mobile phones that are discarded when individuals upgrade their phones or switch providers—as well as new disposable consumer products, such as disposable digital cameras—also add to the alarming growth of **e-waste** (also called *e-trash*) generated today.

>**E-waste.** Electronic waste or trash, such as discarded computer components.

INSIDE THE INDUSTRY

E-Paper

Electronic paper (*e-paper*) is a technology used with flat panel display devices that attempts to mimic the look of ordinary printed paper. The purpose of an *Electronic Paper Display* (*EPD*) is to give the user the experience of reading from paper, while providing them with the ability to update the information shown on the device electronically. EPDs display content in high-contrast, so they can be viewed in direct sunlight. They also require much less electricity than other types of displays because they don't require a backlight and they don't require power to maintain the content shown on the display—they only require power to change the content. Because the content stored in an EPD can be erased when it is no longer needed and then replaced with new content, EPDs are more environmentally friendly than conventional paper documents. An additional benefit is portability; an *e-reader* (such as the Amazon *Kindle* and the Barnes & Noble *Nook,* shown in the accompanying photograph), for instance, can hold thousands of books stored in electronic format in a device about the size of a paperback novel. In fact, with an e-reader, you could carry a small library in your backpack. New e-books are transferred to the e-reader via a flash memory card or a wireless (typically Wi-Fi or 3G) download. E-readers today typically have color displays and many support Web browsing, apps, and other functions in addition to displaying e-books.

E-paper is also widely used for *e-signs*, which look like ordinary paper signs but their text can be changed wirelessly. Their low power consumption means that e-signs can run off battery power for an extended period of time, even with moving data. Some e-signs don't even require a battery; instead, the wireless signal used to transmit data to the display is strong enough to update the sign content. Other retail applications currently on the market include e-paper shelf price tags that can communicate electronically with the store's database so the current price is always displayed, e-paper displays on wristwatches and USB flash drives, and destination displays on trains.

E-paper technology used with fabric, plastic, metal, and other materials is in development and is expected to be used to enable keyboards to be printed on military uniform sleeves, light switches to be printed onto wallpaper, and radio circuitry and controls to be printed onto clothing and other everyday objects. It may also allow e-paper to be used on billboards, T-shirts, and even paint for easy redecorating, as well as regular-sized e-paper that can be inserted into a special computer printer to be printed electronically and then reused over and over. One improvement that has already occurred is the incorporation of touch and pen input with e-paper displays. For instance, both touch and pen input can be used with many e-readers today to flip the "pages" of the book and otherwise control the device, as well as to make notes on the pages or highlight passages of text.

So how does e-paper work? It is based on a display technology called *electrophoretic*, which was invented and is now manufactured and marketed by E Ink® Corporation. An electrophoretic display contains *electronic ink*—essentially charged ink that consists of millions of tiny beads or *microcapsules* about half the diameter of a human hair. For monochrome displays, these beads contain positively charged white particles and negatively charged black particles suspended in a clear fluid. When voltage is applied to the beads (through the circuitry contained within the display), either the white or the black particles rise to the top and the opposite colored particles are pulled to the bottom of the bead, depending on the polarity of the charge applied. Consequently, the beads in each pixel appear to be either white or black (see the accompanying illustration) and remain in that state until another transmission changes the pattern. Color e-ink displays work in a similar manner but typically include a color filter to make the images appear in color.

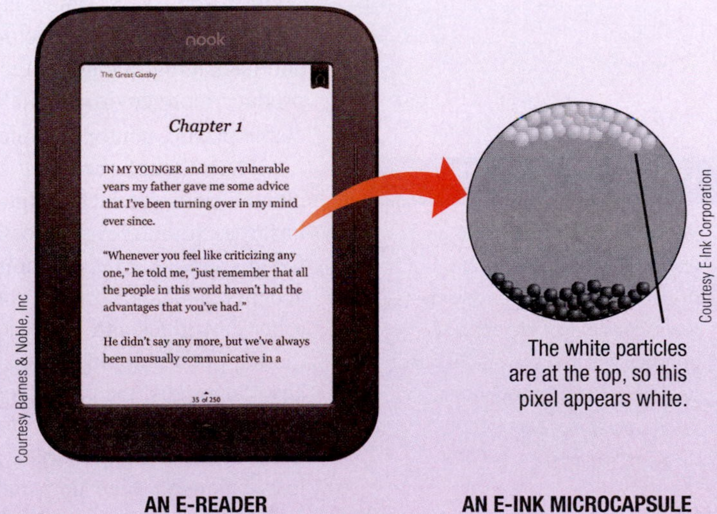

Courtesy Barnes & Noble, Inc

Courtesy E Ink Corporation

AN E-READER **AN E-INK MICROCAPSULE**

FIGURE 7-21
E-waste. E-waste is often exported to developing countries.

Compounding the problem of the amount of e-waste generated today is the fact that computers, mobile phones, and related hardware contain a variety of toxic and hazardous materials. For instance, a single desktop computer may contain up to 700 different chemical elements and compounds, many of which (such as arsenic, lead, mercury, and cadmium) are hazardous and expensive to dispose of properly.

A global concern regarding e-waste is where it all eventually ends up. Much of it ends up in municipal landfills that are not designed for toxic waste. And, even worse, the majority of all computer equipment sent to recyclers in developed countries (at least 80%, according to most estimates) ends up being exported to developing countries (such as China, India, and Nigeria) with more lax environmental standards, legislation, or enforcement than in the United States. Much of the e-waste exported to these countries is simply dumped into fields or processed with primitive and dangerous technologies that release toxins into the air and water. Unaware of the potential danger of these components, rural villagers are often employed to try to repair equipment or reclaim metals or plastic (see Figure 7-21)—hardware that cannot be repaired or reclaimed is often burned or treated with acid baths to try to recover precious metals but such processes release very dangerous pollutants. Activists believe unchecked exportation by the United States and other countries—such as England, Japan, Australia, and Canada—has been going on for at least 10 years. The primary reason for exporting e-waste is cost—proper disposal of a computer in the United States costs between $5 and $10, compared with $1 or less in third-world countries. Another reason is that U.S. states are increasingly banning dangerous computing equipment—such as CRT monitors—from landfills.

While it is difficult—or, perhaps, impossible—to reverse the damage that has already occurred from e-waste, many organizations are working to develop ways to protect people and the environment from future contamination. For instance, the *Basal Action Network* has worked with industry leaders to create the *eStewards Certification program* designed to help individuals and organizations locate responsible electronics recyclers, and *Clean Production Action* and *Greenpeace* have created programs to push hardware manufacturers to stop using toxic chemicals in their products. Some countries have environmental regulations (such as Europe's regulations that require manufacturers to avoid use of toxic substances and that forbid exporting hazardous wastes to developing countries). In Europe, Japan, and increasingly in some U.S. states, laws are based on the policy of *extended producer responsibility* (*EPR*), where manufacturers are responsible for the entire life cycle of their products and packaging, including recycling. In response, computer manufacturers are beginning to produce more environmentally friendly components, such as system units made from recyclable plastic, nontoxic flame-retardant coatings, and lead-free solder on the motherboard.

TIP

When donating old computers and equipment to nonprofit organizations, be sure to verify the organizations are actually nonprofit—some scammers pose as nonprofit organizations to obtain equipment for free that they then resell for a profit.

Even though recycling computer equipment is often difficult because of toxic materials and poor product designs, proper recycling is essential to avoid pollution and health hazards. Some recycling centers will accept computer equipment, but many charge a fee for this service. Many computer manufacturers have voluntary take-back programs that will accept obsolete or broken computer equipment from consumers at a minimal cost. Expired toner cartridges and ink cartridges can sometimes be returned to the manufacturer (using the supplied shipping label included with some cartridges) or exchanged when ordering new cartridges; the cartridges are then *recharged* (refilled) and resold. Cartridges that cannot be refilled can be sent to a recycling facility. In addition to helping to reduce e-waste in landfills, using recharged printer cartridges saves the consumer money because they are less expensive than new cartridges. Other computer components—such as CDs, DVDs, USB flash drives, and hard drives—can also be recycled through some organizations, such as *GreenDisk*. GreenDisk accepts shipments of all types of storage media (plus printer cartridges, mobile phones, mice, notebook computers, chargers, and more) for a modest charge; it reuses salvageable items and recycles the rest. There are also recycling programs for mobile phones. These programs typically refurbish and sell the phones; many organizations donate a portion of the proceeds to nonprofit organizations.

In lieu of recycling, older equipment that is still functioning can be used for alternate purposes (such as for a child's computer, a personal Web server, or a DVR), or it can be donated to schools and nonprofit groups. Some organizations accept and repair donated equipment and then distribute it to disadvantaged groups or individuals in need of the hardware. In the United States, for instance, *Operation Homelink* refurbishes donated computers and sends them to families of U.S. military personnel deployed overseas, who then use the computers to communicate with the soldiers via e-mail, social networks, and video calls (for instance, the family of the soldier about to be deployed to Afghanistan and shown in Figure 7-22 will use this refurbished laptop to communicate with him while he is overseas).

Courtesy Operation Homelink

FIGURE 7-22 Operation Homelink.

For security and privacy purposes, data stored on all computing equipment should be completely removed before disposing of that equipment so that someone else cannot recover the data stored on that device. As discussed in Chapter 5, hard drives should be wiped clean (not just erased) using special software that overwrites the data on the drive several times to ensure it is completely destroyed; storage media that cannot be wiped (such as rewritable DVDs) or that contain very sensitive data (such as business hard drives being discarded) should be shredded. The shredded media is then typically recycled.

Consumers and companies alike are increasingly recognizing the need for green computing, including end-of-life reuse and recycling. Support for nationwide legislation is growing, and manufacturers are seeing the economic and social advantages of producing more easily recyclable and less toxic hardware. So, even though there is a long way to go before e-waste stops being an environmental and health hazard, it is encouraging that the trend is moving toward creating a safer and less-wasteful environment.

RELATED LEGISLATION

There has been some legislation related to health, access, and the environment in the past few years. For instance, many states make it illegal to use a mobile phone without a hands-free system while driving in an attempt to cut down on the number of accidents due to distracted drivers. The most significant recent legislation regarding accessibility has been the 1998 amendment to *Section 508* of the *Rehabilitation Act* requiring federal agencies to make their electronic and information technology (including Web sites) accessible to people with disabilities. While there are currently no federal U.S. computer recycling laws, federal agencies are required to purchase energy-efficient electronic products. In addition, some federal laws (such as the *Sarbanes-Oxley Act* and *HIPAA*) have established privacy and data protection standards for companies disposing of computer hardware that contains specific types of data, and some states have implemented laws related to e-waste.

ASK THE EXPERT

GreenDisk

Courtesy GreenDisk, Inc.

David Beschen, President, GreenDisk Inc.

How large of a problem is e-waste today and what can we do about it?

According to a 2010 EPA report, over 5 million tons of e-waste were in storage in the United States and another 2.5 million tons were prepped for end-of-life but only 25% of those devices were recycled. Many of these devices contained some of the worst toxins on earth, as well as things we do not want "recycled," such as private information belonging to the individuals and businesses that used the devices.

Properly recycling e-waste is important to the environment, our health, and our privacy. It keeps our electronic waste out of landfills (and our garages). However, in our experience at GreenDisk, people simply do not know what to do with their obsolete technology and they have no sense of urgency to do anything with it. And, unfortunately, current e-waste solutions are neither easy to use nor well promoted. Consequently, we need to keep inventing products that use recycled materials, keep implementing incentives to promote recycling among both the producers and the end users, and keep our old technology heading into recycle bins (and, even better, into our new stuff).

SUMMARY

COMPUTERS AND HEALTH

Chapter Objective 1: Understand the potential risks to physical health resulting from the use of computers.

Since the entry of computers into the workplace and their increased use in our society, they have been blamed for a variety of physical ailments. **Carpal tunnel syndrome** (**CTS**), **DeQuervain's tendonitis**, and other types of **repetitive stress injuries** (**RSIs**) are common physical ailments related to computer use; *computer vision syndrome* (*CVS*), eyestrain, fatigue, backaches, and headaches are additional possible physical risks. Conditions related to mobile device use include *gorilla arm* and *iPad shoulder*; there are also concerns about the heat from these devices, noise-induced hearing loss, and the dangers of texting while driving.

Ergonomics is the science of how to make a computer workspace, hardware, and environment fit the individual using it. Using an ergonomically correct workspace and **ergonomic hardware** (such as *ergonomic keyboards, ergonomic mice, document holders, antiglare screens, keyboard drawers, wrist supports,* and *computer gloves*) can help avoid or lessen the pain associated with some RSIs. In addition, all users should use good posture, take rest breaks, alternate tasks, and take other common-sense precautions. For portable computers, **docking stations** can be used to allow easy connections to more ergonomically correct hardware, and **notebook stands** or **tablet stands** can be used to elevate a notebook computer or tablet, respectively, so its display screen can be set at an ergonomically correct height, in order to create more ergonomically correct workspaces.

Chapter Objective 2: Describe some possible emotional health risks associated with the use of computers.

In addition to physical health issues, the extensive use of computers and related technology in the home and office has raised concerns about emotional side effects of computer use. The *stress* of keeping up with ever-changing technology, layoffs, always being in touch, fear of being out of touch, information overload, and **burnout** are all possible emotional problems related to computer use. Taking a break, reevaluating your schedule, and taking good care of yourself can help you avoid or reduce the stress that these problems may cause. To manage all the digital information you encounter, good search techniques, e-mail filters, and other tools can be used.

Internet addiction (also referred to as *Internet dependency, Internet compulsivity*, *cyberaddiction*, and *technology addiction*) refers to not being able to stop using computers, the Internet, or other technology. Many experts believe it is a growing problem and is most prominent in countries with high levels of broadband Internet access. It can affect users of any age and is treated similarly to other addictions.

ACCESS TO TECHNOLOGY

Chapter Objective 3: Explain what is meant by the term *digital divide.*

The **digital divide** refers to the gap between those who have access to computers and communications technology and those who do not. Although the term *digital divide* normally refers to physical access to technology, its "have not" category is sometimes thought to include not only those who do not have access to technology, but also those who have physical access to technology but who do not understand it or are discouraged from using it. There can be a digital divide within a country or between countries. Globally, the digital divide separates countries with access to technology from those without access to technology.

Chapter Objective 4: Discuss the impact that factors such as nationality, income, race, education, and physical disabilities may have on computer access and use.

In the United States, studies show that the digital divide may be lessening, as people of every income, education, race, ethnicity, and gender continue to go online at increased rates. However, individuals living in low-income households or having little education still trail the national average for computer use. While the United States has a high number of Internet users, continuing to reduce the digital divide is important to ensure all citizens have an equal chance of being successful.

There are several programs designed to bring computers, Internet access, and technology to developing countries, such as the *One Laptop Per Child (OLPC) project*. Research suggests that people with disabilities tend to use computers and the Internet at rates lower than the average population. Part of the reason may be because some types of conventional hardware—such as keyboards and monitors—are difficult to use with some types of physical conditions. **Assistive technology** includes hardware and software that makes conventional computer systems easier for users with disabilities to use.

Examples of *assistive input devices* include *Braille keyboards*, *keyguards*, voice input systems, *switches*, *foot-controlled mice*, *head pointing systems*, and *eye-tracking systems*. *Assistive output devices* include *screen readers*, *Braille displays*, and *Braille printers*. In order to be compatible with screen readers and other assistive devices, Web pages need to use features, such as *alt tags* for Web page images and descriptive text-based hyperlinks. There are also apps and devices designed to assist people with disabilities with day-to-day tasks.

Chapter Objective 5:
List some types of assistive hardware that can be used by individuals with physical disabilities.

ENVIRONMENTAL CONCERNS

Many people worry about the environmental issues related to computer use, such as high energy use and the massive amount of paper computer users consume. **Green computing** refers to using computers in an environmentally friendly manner. It can include using environmentally friendly hardware (such as devices approved by an **eco-label** system like the **ENERGY STAR** certification used in the United States), as well as using procedures (such as consolidating servers and using power management features to place devices into standby or sleep mode when not in use) to reduce energy consumption. Environmentally friendly computers (such as those that run quieter and cooler, use more recyclable hardware and packaging, and contain fewer hazardous chemicals) are now on the market, and alternate-powered hardware (such as computer bags and other hardware with built-in solar panels, solar chargers, and hard-powered chargers) is becoming available.

Chapter Objective 6:
Suggest some ways computer users can practice *green computing* and properly dispose of obsolete computer equipment.

In addition to practicing green computing when buying and using computer equipment, discarded equipment should be reused whenever possible. Computer equipment that is still functioning may be able to be donated and refurbished for additional use, and toner and ink cartridges can often be refilled and reused. Hardware that cannot be reused should be recycled if possible, or properly disposed of if not recyclable so that it does not end up as hazardous **e-waste** in landfills. Recycling programs and initiatives may help obsolete products be disposed of in a more environmentally friendly manner.

For security and privacy purposes, storage media containing personal or sensitive data should be disposed of properly, such as wiped or shredded before being reused or recycled.

RELATED LEGISLATION

There are some laws in place to help protect our health, access to technology, and the environment. The most significant legislation regarding accessibility is the 1998 amendment to the *Rehabilitation Act* requiring federal agencies to make their electronic and information technology accessible to people with disabilities. While there are currently no U.S. computer recycling laws, federal agencies are required to purchase energy-efficient products. In the United States, some federal regulations and state laws impact the disposal of computer hardware. In addition, some federal laws (such as the *Sarbanes-Oxley Act* and *HIPAA*) have established privacy and data protection standards for companies disposing of computer hardware that contains specific types of data. Some states have implemented laws related to e-waste.

Chapter Objective 7:
Discuss the current status of legislation related to health, access, and the environment in relation to computers.

REVIEW ACTIVITIES

KEY TERM MATCHING

a. assistive technology

b. carpal tunnel syndrome (CTS)

c. DeQuervain's tendonitis

d. digital divide

e. docking station

f. eco-label

g. ergonomic hardware

h. green computing

i. Internet addiction

j. notebook stand

Instructions: Match each key term on the left with the definition on the right that best describes it.

1. _______ A certification, usually by a government agency, that identifies a device as meeting minimal environmental performance specifications.

2. _______ A condition in which the tendons on the thumb side of the wrist are swollen and irritated.

3. _______ A device designed to easily connect a portable computer to conventional hardware, such as a keyboard, mouse, monitor, and printer.

4. _______ A device that elevates the display of a notebook computer to a better viewing height; can contain USB ports to connect additional hardware.

5. _______ A painful and crippling condition affecting the hands and wrist that can be caused by computer use.

6. _______ Hardware and software specifically designed for use by individuals with physical disabilities.

7. _______ Hardware, typically an input or output device, that is designed to be more ergonomically correct than its nonergonomic counterpart.

8. _______ The gap between those who have access to technology and those who do not.

9. _______ The use of computers in an environmentally friendly manner.

10. _______ The problem of overusing, or being unable to stop using, the Internet.

SELF-QUIZ

Instructions: Circle **T** if the statement is true, **F** if the statement is false, or write the best answer in the space provided. **Answers for the self-quiz are located in the References and Resources Guide at the end of the book.**

1. T F A repetitive stress injury is related to the emotional health issue of stress.

2. T F The ENERGY STAR program is an energy conservation program developed by the United States government.

3. T F Carpal tunnel syndrome can be caused by using a computer keyboard.

4. T F As computer use has become more common, the potential for stress related to computer use has decreased.

5. T F Assistive technology is hardware and software designed to help all beginning computer users learn how to use a computer.

6. The science of fitting a work environment to the people who work there is called _______ .

7. A state of fatigue or frustration usually brought on by overwork is referred to as _______.

8. The _______ can be used to describe discrepancies in access to technology by individuals within a country, as well as to compare access from country to country.

9. Craving more and more time at the computer can be an indicator of _______.

10. _______ power refers to electricity generated by the sun.

EXERCISES

1. For each of the following situations, write the appropriate letter—Y (yes) or N (no)—in the blank to the right of the situation to indicate if the act is an example of green computing.

Situation	Green Computing?
a. You adjust the power settings on your computer to never go into sleep mode.	_______
b. Your boss requires you to print all of his e-mail messages so he can read them on paper.	_______
c. You drop your old mobile phone off in a recycling box instead of throwing it in the trash.	_______

2. Match each term with its related example, and write the corresponding number in the blank to the left of each example.

a. _______ Assistive hardware	**1.** Green computing
b. _______ Server consolidation	**2.** Ergonomics
c. _______ Docking stations	**3.** Digital divide
d. _______ E-mail filters and flags	**4.** Information overload

3. List at least two assistive input or output devices designed for individuals with a visual impairment and explain the function of each.
4. List three possible negative physical effects that can result from computer use and describe one way to lessen each effect.
5. List three possible negative effects on the environment that can result from computer use and describe one way to lessen each effect.

DISCUSSION QUESTIONS

1. It is becoming increasingly common for biometric devices to be used to grant or deny access to facilities, as well as to identify consumers for financial transactions. In order to facilitate this, some data about each participant's biometric features must be stored in a database. How do you feel about your biometric characteristics being stored in a database? Does it depend on whether the system belongs to your bank, employer, school, or the government? Since biometric features cannot be reset, are you at risk using a biometric ID system? Can the use of biometric systems and other systems that require less actual use of the computer by individuals help the issue of accessibility and lessen the digital divide? If, for instance, the norm for controlling a computer was the voice, would that level the technological playing field for all individuals? Why or why not?
2. While gaming and texting are both popular pastimes, it is possible to become injured by performing these activities. For instance, some Wii users have developed tennis elbow and other ailments from some Wii Sports games and heavy texters have developed problems with their thumbs. Think of the devices you use regularly. Have you ever become sore or injured from their use? If so, was it the design of the input device being used, overuse, or both? What responsibilities do hardware manufacturers have in respect to creating safe input devices? If a user becomes injured due to overuse of a device, whose fault it is? Should input devices come with warning labels?

PROJECTS

HOT TOPICS

1. **E-Paper** The chapter Inside the Industry box discusses e-paper—an erasable, reusable alternative to traditional paper and ink. While e-paper has many societal benefits (such as reducing the use of traditional paper and ink, as well as the resources needed to create and dispose of them), it has been slow to catch on.

   For this project, research the current state of e-paper. What products are available now and what products are due out soon? When a new technology, such as e-paper, that has obvious benefits to society is developed, who (if anyone) should be responsible for making sure it gets implemented in a timely fashion? Do you think businesses or individuals will choose to use e-paper products if the only incentive is a cleaner environment? Or will there need to be economic incentives, such as savings on paper and ink surpassing the cost of e-paper? Would you be willing to switch to a new technology (such as e-paper) that is beneficial to society if it costs more than the existing technology? Is it ethical for an industry or the government to mandate the use of new technologies if they create an additional cost or inconvenience to individuals? At the conclusion of your research, prepare a one-page summary of your findings and opinions and submit it to your instructor.

SHORT ANSWER/ RESEARCH

2. **Section 508** Section 508 is a section of the Rehabilitation Act that refers to requirements for making electronic and information technology accessible to people with disabilities.

   For this project, research Section 508 and the Rehabilitation Act in general to see how the law applies to Web site design and to whom the law applies. If you were to set up a personal or small business Web site, would you be legally obligated to conform to Section 508 regulations? What types of features or modifications does a Web site need to include to be Section 508 compliant? How would one go about testing to see if a Web site was Section 508 compliant? Prepare a one-page summary of your findings and submit it to your instructor.

HANDS ON

3. **Ergonomic Workspaces** Some aspects of an ergonomic workspace, such as a comfortable chair and nonglaring light, may feel good right from the beginning. Others, such as using an ergonomic keyboard or wrist rest, may take a little getting used to.

   For this project, find at least one local store that has some type of ergonomic equipment—such as adjustable office chairs, desks with keyboard drawers, ergonomic keyboards, or notebook stands—on display that you can try out. Test each piece, adjusting it as needed, and evaluate how comfortable it seems. Next, evaluate your usual computer workspace. Are there any adjustments you should make or any new equipment you would need to acquire to make your workspace setup more comfortable? Make a note of any changes you could make for free, as well as a list of items you would need to purchase and the estimated cost. Prepare a short summary of your findings to submit to your instructor. If you made any adjustments to your regular workspace during this project, be sure to include a comment regarding whether or not you think it increased your comfort.

ETHICS IN ACTION

4. **Toxic Devices** As discussed in the chapter, computers, mobile devices, and other hardware can contain a variety of toxic and hazardous materials. Is it ethical for manufacturers to continue to use hazardous materials in their products? What if a restriction on these compounds severely limited the types of electronic equipment that could be manufactured or significantly increased the price? Is it ethical for consumers to buy products that are made of hazardous materials or are not recyclable? What efforts should be made to recycle e-waste in the United States and who is ethically responsible for the cost—the manufacturers, the consumers, or the government? Should the government require the recycling of e-waste? Should it ban the exportation of e-waste?

   For this project, form an opinion about the ethical ramifications of toxic devices and e-waste and be prepared to discuss your position (in class, via an online class discussion group, in a class chat room, or via a class blog, depending on your instructor's directions). You may also be asked to write a short paper expressing your opinion.

PRESENTATION/ DEMONSTRATION

5. **Recycle or Trash?** As mentioned in the chapter, a great deal of obsolete computing equipment eventually ends up in a landfill, even though there may be alternative actions that could be taken instead.

   For this project, research what options would be available to discard the following: (1) a 10-year-old computer that is no longer functioning, (2) a 4-year-old computer that still works but is too slow for your needs, and (3) a used-up toner cartridge for a laser printer. Check with your local schools and charitable organizations to see if they would accept any of these items. Check with at least one computer manufacturer and one recycling company to see if they would accept the computers, and, if so, what the procedure and cost would be. Check with at least one vendor selling recharged toner cartridges to see if it buys old cartridges or requires a trade-in with an order. Share your findings with the class in the form of a short presentation. Be sure to include any costs associated with the disposal options you found, as well as your recommendation for each disposal situation. The presentation should not exceed 10 minutes and should make use of one or more presentation aids, such as a whiteboard, handouts, or a computer-based slide presentation (your instructor may provide additional requirements). You may also be asked to submit a summary of the presentation to your instructor.

BALANCING ACT

6. **Is E-Hording Bad for Us?** With large amounts of storage available to us at a reasonable cost or even for free, many computers users today are sloppy about deleting e-mails, old photos, and other digital data that they may no longer want or need. The average worker alone sends and receives more than 100 e-mails per day and about 90 billion spam e-mails are sent each day. With that kind of volume, it's hard for anyone to keep a clean Inbox. But should we try? Most workers are governed by policies regarding what e-mails and documents they are allowed to delete, but what about our personal documents? Is there anything wrong with saving everything in case it might be needed again? Or does having that much clutter create unnecessary stress and waste our time? If we have the necessary storage, are we prudent to keep everything in case we need it again? Or are we just lazy?

   Pick a side on this issue, form an opinion and gather supporting evidence, and be prepared to discuss and defend your position in a classroom debate or in a 1–2 page paper, depending on your instructor's directions.

expert insight on...

Computers and Society

Courtesy of Dell Inc.

DELL

Frank Molsberry is a Technologist in Dell's Office of the CTO. Prior to his current position, he helped found Dell's Workstation Architecture and Development team and the Enterprise Architecture and Technology Group. He has over 30 years of management and engineering experience in the computer industry, a Bachelor's degree in Computer Science, and several patents in the area of computer security. Frank is a Contributor Advisor to the Trusted Computing Group Board of Directors and does regular customer briefings on security and emerging technology trends.

A conversation with FRANK MOLSBERRY

Sr. Principal Engineer and Security Technologist for Dell Inc.

"Social media and cloud-based services are seeing explosive growth, but little consideration is given to the use, security, and privacy of the personal information stored via these services . . ."

My Background . . .

I've been in the field of computer software and hardware development for over 30 years. I joined Dell in 1998 after working at IBM for 15 years. I am currently a Sr. Principal Engineer and Security Technologist in the End User Computing Office of the CTO. My focus area is on Security Architecture and Technology. In that role, I support the current engineering efforts for incorporating security hardware and software into Dell products, work with the various security technology companies to evaluate and influence current and planned offerings, and participate with standards organizations, such as the Trusted Computing Group (TCG), in the definition of future security standards.

In many cases, the subjects we focus on now (such as security) are not about stand-alone systems anymore, but instead involve an entire ecosystem of hardware devices, software applications, and the infrastructure connecting them. Because this can entail a great deal of breadth and depth of knowledge, I've found that it is important to have a "big-picture" vision and the ability to rapidly drill into the details as needed, but only to the level needed to answer the questions in front of you.

It's Important to Know . . .

The recommendations presented in these chapters are not one-time things. Managing your security and privacy needs to be a regular routine—like brushing your teeth.

Technology is a double-edged sword and can always have a dark side. As you develop new and innovative hardware or software applications, you must always look at the threats that can be brought against it and, more importantly, how the technology could be misused beyond its intended purpose. By stepping back and identifying these issues up front, the developers and users of the technology can be better prepared to combat it. Security is a mindset. In the same way you look at the features, usability, and performance of a solution, you need to specifically look at the security characteristics, as well.

We now have a global economy. The products and services you provide must consider a global culture and have the flexibility to satisfy the varying customs, rules, and requirements of a global economy.

How I Use this Technology . . .

I use all the standard precautions on my personal computer, tablet, and smartphone—such as antivirus software, antispyware software, and backing up my data—to avoid data loss. When traveling, I use a privacy screen to prevent others from viewing my work and I use encryption software to protect the data on my devices and portable media, such as USB flash drives.

What the Future Holds . . .

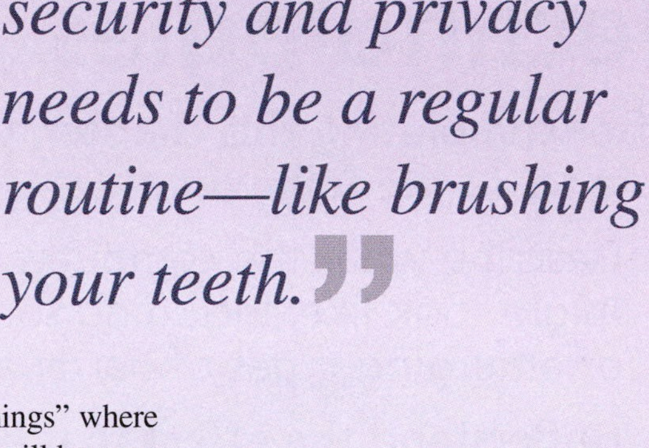
"Managing your security and privacy needs to be a regular routine—like brushing your teeth."

The next big thing is not usually a revolution as much as it is a continued progression that, when looked at over a long window of a time, shows up as a major change in technology or use model. So the trends of faster, smaller, cheaper will continue for the next decade.

The impact of security and privacy technology on society is huge. One issue is identity theft and the tremendous effort it takes to recover from it. Tasks like monitoring your credit report activity can help prevent identity theft or alert you to suspicious activity. Social media and cloud-based services are seeing explosive growth, but little consideration is given to the use, security, and privacy of the personal information stored via these services, or to what happens to it when one of these entities goes out of business. One must ask, "Can the collection of information I provide about myself online be used to compromise my identity?" And, as we move toward the "Internet of Things" where our devices will constantly communicate, authentication of people and devices will become paramount. Without a solid security architecture as the base, however, this paradigm will fail.

Methods to protect the environment from the impact of technology will continue to expand. Major manufacturers like Dell have implemented initiatives to reduce or eliminate hazardous materials like lead from their systems, and there are major programs for computer recycling and for returning consumables, such as printer cartridges. A possible development for the future is using more modular architectures, allowing the average user to easily change or upgrade the capabilities of a computer, TV, or printer without having to purchase an entirely new system.

It's important to realize that the digital divide is not new. It occurs when each new method of information communication is developed, such as with the introduction of radio and television. The continued decreases in the cost of computing, new categories of devices like tablets and hybrids, and improvements in wireless connectivity will help to close the current divide, but there may be new digital divides in the future. However, we must not lose sight of where information and communications fit in the hierarchy of needs. For those populations where the basic needs of food, clothing, and shelter are not being met, technology should help find solutions to those problems before focusing on broad access to computing resources.

My Advice to Students . . .

Computers and the ever-changing technology they are based on are just tools. It is important not to just focus on the "coolness" of something new, but the problem it is trying to solve, the user experience, and the barriers to adoption.

Discussion Question

Frank Molsberry believes that developers must look at how new products could be misused. Think about a few recent new technologies or products. Have they been used in an illegal or unethical manner? What responsibility, if any, does a developer have if its product is used inappropriately? Be prepared to discuss your position (in class, via an online class discussion group, in a class chat room, or via a class blog, depending on your instructor's directions). You may also be asked to write a short paper expressing your opinion.

>For more information on Dell, visit www.dell.com. For security information, visit www.trustedcomputinggroup.org and searchsecurity.techtarget.com. For a summary of many online tech news sites, visit www.dailyrotation.com.

chapter 8

Emerging Technologies

After completing this chapter, you will be able to do the following:

1. Describe what the computer of the future might look like, including some examples of emerging types of hardware.
2. Understand the effect that emerging computer technologies, such as nanotechnology, quantum computers, and optical computers, may have on the computer of the future.
3. Name some emerging wired and wireless networking technologies.
4. Explain what is meant by the term *artificial intelligence* (AI) and list some AI applications.
5. List some new and upcoming technological advances in medicine.
6. Name some new and upcoming technological advances in the military.
7. Discuss potential societal implications of emerging technologies.

outline

OVERVIEW

No study of computers would be complete without a look to the future. The rapid technological advancements that we've seen in the last few decades have been extraordinary, but some believe the best is yet to come. New advances are being made all the time in areas such as computer hardware, Internet applications, and networking technologies. In general, technology is continuing to become more user-friendly and more integrated into our daily lives, and that trend is expected to continue. For instance, imagine the following scenario: You walk up to your locked front door and gain access simply by touching the doorknob or speaking your name. When you enter a room, the lights, stereo system, and digital artwork on the walls change automatically to reflect your preferences. Your refrigerator and pantry keep up-to-the-moment inventories of their contents, and your closet automatically selects outfits for you based on the weather and your schedule for the day. Sounds like something out of a science fiction movie, doesn't it? Yet, all the technologies just mentioned are either already available or in development.

Many of us are excited to see what new applications and technological improvements the future will bring, as well as how computers, the Internet, and other technologies will evolve. However, our enthusiasm for this progress should be balanced with the understanding that some future applications may not turn out the way we expect or may actually have a negative impact on society. One of the biggest challenges in an era of rapidly changing technologies is evaluating the potential impact of new technology and trying to ensure that new products and services do not adversely affect our security, privacy, and safety.

This chapter focuses on some of the emerging technologies that are already beginning to impact our lives. Topics include the computer of the future, emerging networking technologies, artificial intelligence (AI), and technological advances in medicine and in the military. The chapter closes with a discussion of the societal implications of emerging technologies. ■

THE COMPUTER OF THE FUTURE

While the exact makeup of future computers is anyone's guess, it is expected that they will keep getting smaller, faster, more powerful, and more user-friendly, and that they will eventually use voice, touch, gestures, and other alternative input methods more than keyboards and mice. Portable computers and mobile devices will continue to be used as primary computing devices at home and work, as well as while on the go. Tomorrow's home and business computers will likely not even look like today's computers—instead they may be built into walls, desks, appliances, and perhaps even jewelry and clothing. In addition to their changing appearance, computers are expected to keep converging with other devices and to continue to take on multiple roles to serve our personal needs, as well as to control our household or office environment. Computers in the future may also be able to offer multisensory output—enabling users to see, hear, feel, taste, and smell output—and they will likely become even more environmentally friendly.

Some examples of emerging new hardware are discussed next, followed by a discussion of some technologies that may change the overall makeup of computers in the future—namely, *nanotechnology*, *quantum computers*, and *optical computers*.

TIP

Google's new *Handwrite* feature allows you to use your finger to write out search queries on the device's screen in order to perform a mobile search more quickly than using an on-screen keyboard, and it is likely more accurate than using voice input. To use the Handwrite feature, just write your search terms anywhere on the Google home page displayed on your smartphone or tablet screen.

ASK THE EXPERT

Courtesy TabletKiosk

Martin Smekal, President and Founder, TabletKiosk

What do you expect to be the optimal input device of the future?

The launch of Apple's iPad has brought unprecedented awareness of the tablet form factor and created wider market acceptance of touch screen technology. As a result, we've seen a sharp rise in companies looking to incorporate touch technology into their business solutions. The optimal device, in our opinion, will offer a range of input options for total flexibility—multiple touch input options, digital inking for handwriting recognition, voice recognition, and, soon, even gesture recognition will be the norm.

Emerging Hardware

The overall size and appearance of computers seem to change on a continual basis. We now have fully functioning personal computers that are small enough to fit in a pocket or be worn on the body. Technologies are continuing to be developed to make computers and computer components smaller, faster, and more capable. Some of the exciting emerging input, processing, output, and storage hardware and technologies are discussed next.

Emerging Input Devices

Because of the increasing amount of data entered into mobile devices today, these devices often have a keyboard or can be inserted into a *keyboard dock* or *keyboard folio* (see Figure 8-1) when a keyboard is needed. New input methods for mobile devices include tiny keyboards (such as on smart watches) that automatically zoom in on the part of the keyboard you touch to allow you to touch a larger key for your final selection, and the *Swype* app used with on-screen keyboards to supply input by continuously dragging through the letters in a word to spell that word (refer again to Figure 8-1). In addition, voice input and speech recognition capabilities are increasingly being incorporated into computers, smartphones, car navigation systems, and other devices to enable hands-free input. Specialty speech recognition systems are frequently used to control robots and other electronic equipment, such as those used by surgeons during surgical procedures. Touch, pen, and *gesture* input is beginning to be used with personal computers and is becoming the norm for mobile devices. The use of gesture input started with motion-sensitive gaming controllers, such as the *Wii Remote* and the *Xbox Kinect*. Today, gesture input is also used to detect gestures made in conjunction with large screen interactive advertising displays and it may soon be incorporated into computers of the future (see the Trend box).

One new trend in the area of touch input is the *table PC*—a large screen computer either built into a table or designed to be used on a table (such as the 27-inch table PC shown in Figure 8-1) and that allows multi-touch input from multiple users. Table PCs can be used by several individuals at once to play games together, work together on a project, participate in an interactive museum display together, and so forth.

FIGURE 8-1
Examples of emerging input devices.

Courtesy Logitech

KEYBOARD FOLIOS

Courtesy Nuance

SWIPE APP

Courtesy Lenovo

TABLE PCS

TREND

Perceptual Computing

In the 2002 futuristic movie *Minority Report*, Tom Cruise changes the images on his display by gesturing with his hands. While it was fiction in the movie, it is now just about a reality. Enter the trend of *perceptual computing* where users control their devices with three dimensional (3D) gestures, voice commands, and facial expressions instead of with traditional input devices like the keyboard and mouse.

Gesture input itself isn't new—it's been used in various forms for several years with devices such as the Nintendo Wii, Xbox Kinect, and the Apple iPhone and in large screen consumer gaming and advertising applications; it is also an important component of the Windows 8 operating system. But the gesture-input systems of the future are expected to be much more sophisticated and combined with other types of input to allow users to more naturally control their computers and to allow the devices to adapt to each individual's need. For example, a computer or phone could offer to make a game easier if a player appears frustrated or could offer to turn the page on a tablet displaying a recipe if the hands of the person cooking are covered with flour.

One recent step in this direction is the *Leap 3D System* shown in the accompanying photograph. It is an iPod-sized box that connects to a computer via a USB port and creates an eight-cubic-foot 3D interactive space inside which users can swipe, grab, pinch (refer again to the photo), and move objects around as if they were using a touch screen, except that they are not actually touching the screen. And noncontact systems such as this have additional advantages, such as being able to use 3D gestures instead of just 2D gestures, avoiding the fingerprint and germ issues related to public keyboard and touch screen use, allowing for full body input, and enabling input to be performed from a slight distance (such as from a nearby chair or through a glass storefront window).

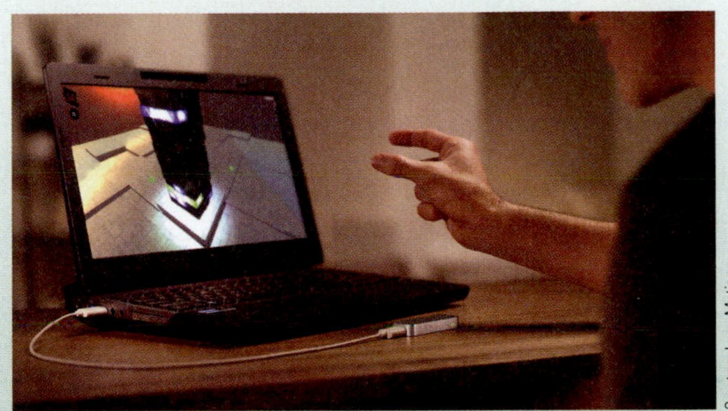

Courtesy Leap Motion

The digital camera capabilities built into most smartphones today allow for several types of emerging input applications. For instance, they allow gesture input, as well as the use of *two-dimensional (2D) barcodes* and *augmented reality applications* to retrieve and display useful information. **Two-dimensional (2D) barcodes**—such as the *QR (Quick Response) code* that represents data with a matrix of small squares—store information both horizontally and vertically and so can hold significantly more data than conventional one-dimensional barcodes. Most 2D barcodes today are designed to be used by consumers with smartphones. For instance, capturing the image of a QR barcode located on a magazine or newspaper ad, poster, or billboard with a smartphone's camera could enable the consumer's smartphone to load a Web page, dial a phone number or send a text message (to enter a contest, for example), display a video clip or photo (stored either in the code or online), download a coupon or ticket, or Like a Facebook page (see Figure 8-2). QR codes can also be used to transfer contact information to a phone or add an event to an online calendar. **Augmented reality** is another emerging smartphone application. With augmented reality, computer-generated images are overlayed on top of real-time images. Today, Web-based content is typically displayed over the images seen through a smartphone's camera and displayed on the smartphone. The content is

FIGURE 8-2
Most smartphones can read 2D barcodes.

Courtesy SPARQCode

>**Two-dimensional (2D) barcode.** A barcode that represents data with a matrix of small squares and stores information both horizontally and vertically so it can hold significantly more data than a conventional one-dimensional barcode. >**Augmented reality.** When computer generated images are overlayed on top of real-time images, such as to overlay information over the photo or video displayed on a smartphone.

typically based on the user's location (determined by the smartphone's GPS), the video feed from the smartphone's camera, a digital compass, and other data obtained from the smartphone. Displaying this information requires a *mobile AR browser* or an appropriate *mobile AR app*. Some initial mobile augmented reality apps include overlaying home listing information over the video images displayed as a phone is pointing at houses in a neighborhood, displaying stats and player information as a phone is pointing at a sporting event, and displaying activity opportunities (such as restaurant, movie, museum, or shopping information) as a phone is pointing at a business district.

For making electronic payments while on the go, use of *Near Field Communication (NFC)* technology is expected to grow in the near future. NFC uses RFID technology to facilitate communication between devices, including transferring payment information, receipts, boarding passes, and other information wirelessly between payment terminals and smartphones. Worldwide, vending machines are also increasingly going cashless, supporting only NFC, credit cards, and other electronic payment methods, instead of cash.

FIGURE 8-3
Flexible electronics.

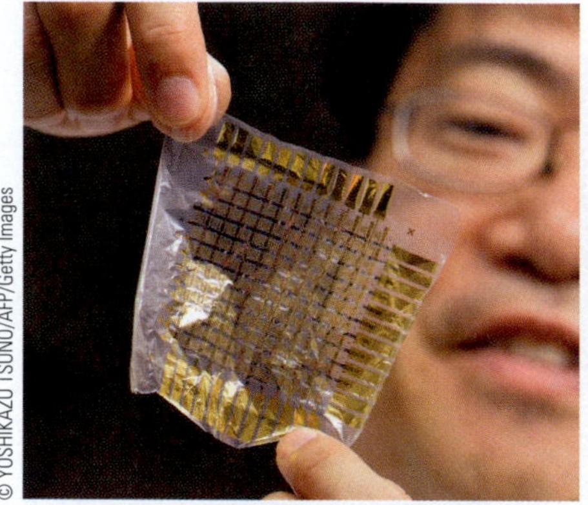

Emerging Processing Technologies

Computers and CPU manufacturers are continually working to develop ways to make computers work better, faster, more reliably, and more efficiently. For example, new designs for motherboards and CPUs are always under development, computer components are continually being built smaller so more power and capabilities can be contained in the same size package, new materials are being used, and new technologies are being developed on a continual basis. For instance, the new *USB 3.0* standard allows peripheral devices to communicate with a computer at more than 10 times the speed of USB 2.0. And, for integrating CPUs and other computer components into clothing and other flexible materials, as well as for creating flexible devices (such as the flexible smartphone screens that are expected to be available soon), *flexible electronic components* (see Figure 8-3) are needed and are currently being developed. In addition to the ability to be bent without damaging the circuitry, flexible circuits will be thinner, lighter, generate little heat, and consume significantly less energy than conventional processors.

For packing an increasing number of components onto small chips, the *three-dimensional (3D) chip* is one emerging technology. Typically, 3D chips are created by layering individual silicon wafers on top of one another, which cuts down on the surface area required. 3D chips are now being used with memory, flash memory, and CPUs. For example, recent Intel CPUs (such as third-generation Core processors) include a 3D transistor called *Tri-Gate* (see the illustration in Figure 8-4). Tri-Gate transistors provide increased performance and low voltage, making them ideal for use in small devices, such as mobile devices. In addition, Samsung recently announced the release of the world's first mass-produced 3D flash memory chip. By using a special etching technology to drill down through the chip layers to connect them electronically, Samsung plans to eventually produce chips with 24 layers.

FIGURE 8-4
3D chips. In this 3D transistor, the electrical current (represented by the yellow dots) flows on three sides of a vertical fin.

One hurdle in 3D chip development, as well as in other means of packing an increasing amount of technology into a smaller system unit, is the amount of heat generated. Because heat can damage components and cooler chips can run faster, virtually all computers today employ *fans*, *heat sinks* (small components usually made out of aluminum with fins that help to dissipate heat), or other methods to cool the CPU and system unit. Mobile device cases today aren't designed for fans and so their cooling systems typically rely on using mobile CPUs that run cooler than desktop CPUs and on adapting the speed and power of the device's components to cool the device as needed. However, as the speed and capabilities of mobile devices continue to increase, additional cooling methods may become necessary and are currently under development. *Liquid cooling systems* consist of liquid (often a water solution) filled tubes that draw heat away from processors and other critical components, and they can be designed to cool between the layers of 3D chips, as well as to cool the inside of the system unit. An emerging possibility for cooling servers is *immersion cooling* where the hardware is actually submerged into units filled with a liquid cooling solution (refer to Figure 8-5).

As demand by consumers and businesses for online software, services, and media-rich experiences continues to increase, some experts predict that *tera-scale computing*—the ability of a computer to process one trillion floating point operations per second (*teraflops*)—will eventually be more common. While supercomputers currently reach teraflop and *petaflop* (1,000 teraflops) speeds, much of today's tera-scale research is focusing on creating multi-core processors with tens to hundreds of cores used in conjunction with multithreaded hardware and software that can execute multiple streams of instructions—*threads*—at the same time in order to achieve teraflop performance. The research also includes working on developing higher-speed communications between computers, such as between Web servers and high-performance mobile devices or computers, to help facilitate high-performance cloud computing. Intel, one of the leaders in tera-scale research, has created a *teraflop processor* that contains 80 cores to test strategies for moving terabytes of data rapidly from core to core and between cores and memory. It has also developed a 20 MB *SRAM* memory chip that is attached directly to the processor in order to speed up communication between processors and memory. This design allows thousands of interconnections, which enable data to travel at more than one *terabyte per second* (*TBps*) between memory and the processor cores. It is expected that this speed will be needed to handle the terabytes of data used by applications in the near future. In fact, *exascale computers* that perform 1 million trillion calculations per second and may have as many as 100 million CPU cores are expected to appear by 2018.

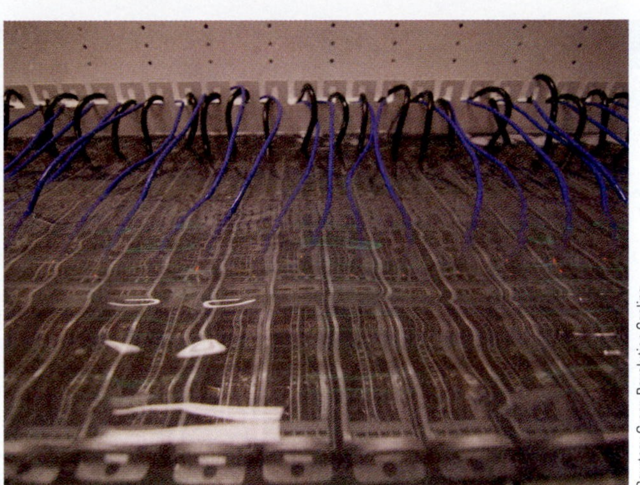

Courtesy Green Revolution Cooling

FIGURE 8-5
Immersion cooling systems. Can be used to cool servers in large data centers.

TIP

To more easily fit into the shrinking notebook and tablet PC form factor, fans the size and thickness of a credit card are in development and expected to become available before 2015.

For memory improvements, several forms of **nonvolatile RAM (NVRAM)**—that is, memory that retains its data when the power to the device is off—are either becoming available or under development. For instance, *magnetic RAM* (commonly referred to as *MRAM*) uses *magnetic polarization* rather than an electrical charge to store data, *memristor-based RAM* uses memristors (short for *memory resistors*) that change their resistance in response to current flowing through them, *NRAM* uses *carbon nanotubes* (discussed later in this chapter), and *PRAM* (*phase change random access memory*) has a special coating that changes its physical state when heat is applied (similar to the rewritable CDs and DVDs discussed in Chapter 2). The most common applications for nonvolatile RAM today include storing critical data for enterprise systems as they operate to guard against data loss and saving the data necessary to help industrial automation and robotics systems recover quickly from a power loss. Other emerging applications include "instant-on" computers and mobile devices that can be turned on and off like an electric light, without any loss of data. Another advantage of nonvolatile RAM is that it doesn't require power to retain data so, when used in mobile devices, it consumes less power, which can extend battery life. It is expected that, in the future, a form of nonvolatile RAM will replace volatile RAM, flash memory chips, and possibly even hard drives in computers. As capacities increase (Crossbar recently announced the development of a 1 TB NVRAM chip), that day may be getting closer.

>**Nonvolatile RAM (NVRAM).** Memory chips that do not lose their contents when the power to the computer is turned off.

TIP

Researchers at Intel Labs predict that much of the Internet will use realistic-looking 3D applications by 2020.

Emerging Output Devices

Some of the most recent improvements in display technology center on more versatile output devices and new flat-screen technologies. For instance, recent improvements in flat-panel display technology and graphics processing have led to several emerging *three-dimensional (3D) output devices*, including *3D display screens* for computers. While traditional 3D displays (and most 3D televisions today) require special 3D glasses, the newest 3D computer display products use filters, prisms, multiple lenses, and other technologies built into the display screen to create the 3D effect and, as a result, do not require 3D glasses. Some 3D displays resemble conventional monitors; others are shaped differently, such as the dome-shaped *Perspecta* 3D display that is used primarily for medical imaging. 3D consumer products are increasingly available as well, such as the *Nintendo 3DS* handheld gaming device.

Another emerging 3D output device is the *3D projector*. Some 3D projectors are designed to project 3D images that are viewed with 3D glasses, similar to 3D televisions. Others are designed to project actual 3D projections or *holograms*. For instance, holograms of individuals and objects can be projected onto a stage for a presentation, and hologram display devices can be used in retail stores, exhibitions, and other locations to showcase products or other items in 3D. Another emerging projection option that can be used to project content to a small audience while on the go is the *pico projector*. These pocket-sized projectors typically connect to a smartphone or portable computer to enable the device to project an image (such as a document, presentation, or movie) onto a wall or other flat surface from up to 12 feet away. Pico projectors are also beginning to be integrated directly into mobile devices (see the Samsung Beam *projector phone* shown in Figure 8-6).

TIP

NASA is preparing to launch a 3D printer into space in 2014 in order to enable astronauts to print tools, spare parts, rocket pieces, and even small satellites using spools of plastic strands.

When permanent 3D output is required, such as to print a 3D model of a new building or prototype of a new product, *3D printers* (which typically form output in layers using molten plastic during a series of passes to build a 3D version of the desired output—see Figure 8-6) can be used. 3D printers are becoming available in a variety of sizes, from personal printers for printing smartphone cases, toys, jewelry, and other personal objects to professional printers for printing working product prototypes or custom manufacturing parts. They have even begun to be used to print medical implants using FDA-approved 3D material. One issue with the increased availability of 3D printers is the risk of them being used to print dangerous or illegal items, such as working plastic guns. In fact, after a 3D-printed gun was recently demonstrated firing standard bullets, lawmakers are considering enacting legislation to ban plastic weapons created by 3D printers.

FIGURE 8-6
Some emerging output devices.

Courtesy Samsung

PICO PROJECTORS
Can be stand-alone or built into a mobile device; images from the mobile device (such as the smartphone shown here) are projected onto any surface.

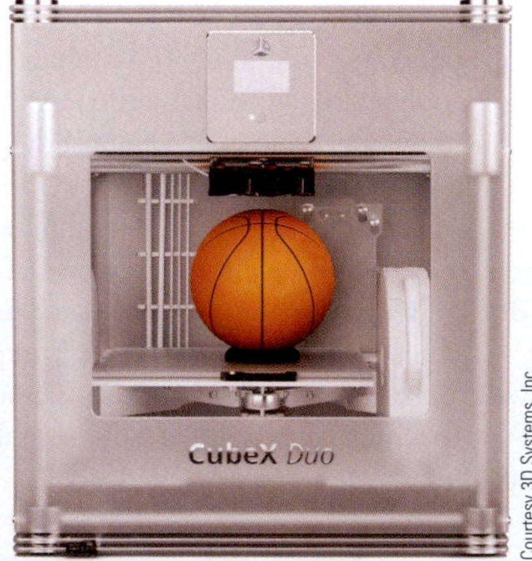

Courtesy 3D Systems, Inc.

3D PRINTERS
This printer can print objects up to the size of a standard basketball.

Courtesy ZINK Imaging

INTEGRATED PRINTERS
This printer uses no ink and is integrated into the digital camera to print digital photographs.

The capabilities of ink-jet printers are also expanding. For instance, ink-jet technology may eventually be used for dispensing liquid metals, aromas, computer chips and other circuitry, and even "printing" human tissue and other organic materials for medical purposes. In addition, printers are beginning to be integrated into other devices, such as the camera in Figure 8-6 that contains an integrated *ZINK printer*. Unlike conventional printers, ZINK printers use no ink; instead, they use special paper that is coated with special color dye crystals. Before printing, the embedded dye crystals are clear, so *ZINK Paper* looks like regular white photo paper. The ZINK printer uses heat to activate and colorize these dye crystals when a photo is printed, creating a full-color image.

For display screens used with computers, mobile devices, and other electronic devices, there are a number of technologies under development designed to create displays that are more visible, while at the same time using less energy. Some of these technologies are based on *organic light emitting diode* (*OLED*) technology. **Organic light emitting diode (OLED) displays** use layers of organic material, which emit a visible light when electric current is applied. While conventional flat-panel displays based on *LCD* (*liquid crystal display*) technology do not produce light and so require *backlighting*, OLEDs emit a visible light and, therefore, do not use backlighting. This characteristic makes OLEDs more energy efficient than LCDs and lengthens the battery life of portable devices using OLED displays. Other advantages of OLEDs are that they are thinner than LCDs, they have a wider viewing angle than LCDs and so displayed content is visible from virtually all directions, and their images are brighter and sharper than LCDs. Today, OLED displays are incorporated into many digital cameras, mobile phones, portable digital media players, *Google Glass*, and other consumer devices. They are also beginning to appear in television and computer displays and are expected to be more prominent in the near future.

Special types of OLEDs also support applications not possible with CRT or LCD technology. For instance, *flexible OLED* (*FOLED*) displays are built on flexible surfaces, such as plastic or metallic foil, and so they can roll up when not in use (see Figure 8-7). Flexible screens may also be used for integrating displays on military uniform sleeves, as well as allowing retractable wall-mounted large screen displays. *Transparent OLED* (*TOLED*) displays are transparent. The portion of the display that does not currently have an image displayed (and the entire display device when it is off) is nearly as transparent as glass, so the user can see through the screen. TOLEDs open up the possibility of displays on home windows, car windshields, helmet face shields, and other transparent items.

Another emerging flat-panel display technology is *interferometric modulator* (*IMOD*) *displays*. Designed

TIP

Another emerging option in display technology is the *USB monitor*, which connects to a computer via a USB port. Conventional monitors can also connect to a computer via a *USB display adapter*, enabling multiple monitors to be connected to a computer without requiring a new video card.

TIP

White OLED displays are in development for use with light bulbs.

FIGURE 8-7
Some emerging display technologies.

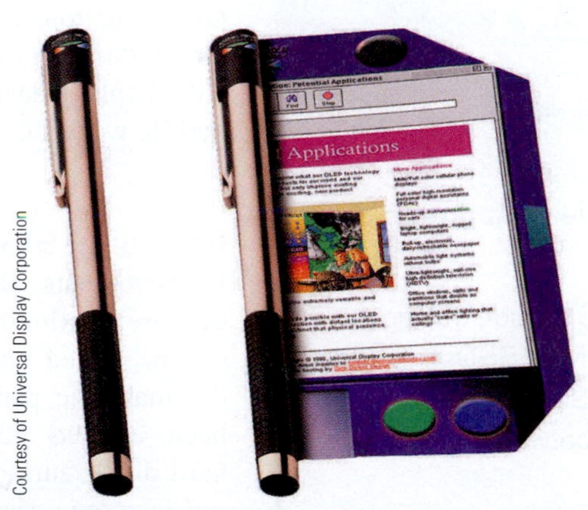

Courtesy of Universal Display Corporation

FOLEDS
Used to create flexible displays on plastic or another type of flexible material.

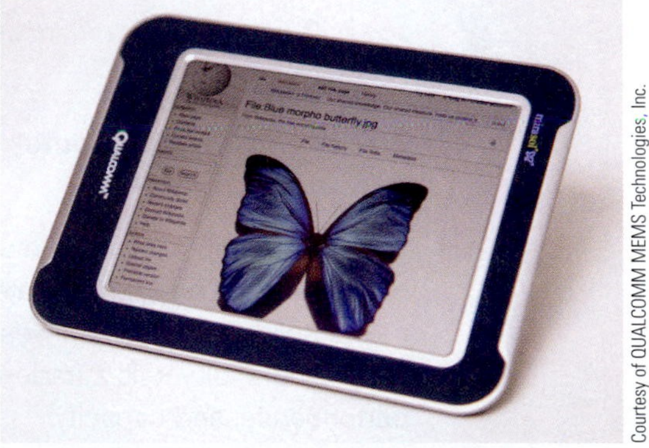

Courtesy of QUALCOMM MEMS Technologies, Inc.

IMODS
Display is bright and readable, even in direct sunlight.

>**Organic light emitting diode (OLED) display.** A type of flat-panel display that uses emissive organic material to display brighter and sharper images than LCDs.

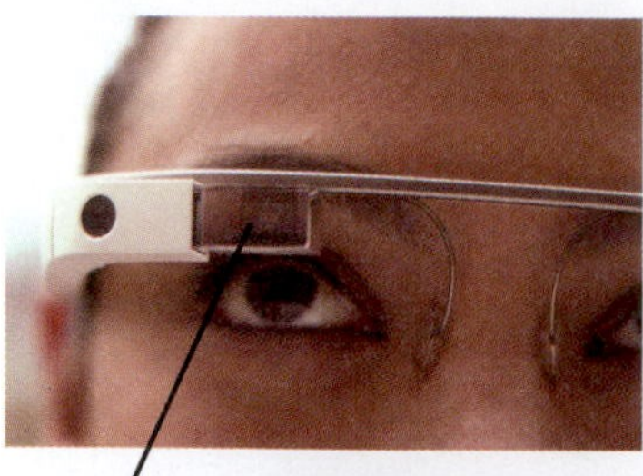
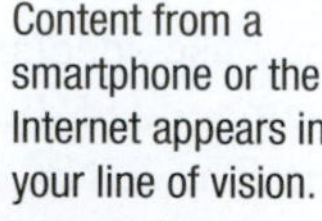

Content from a
smartphone or the
Internet appears in
your line of vision.

Display is built
into the Glass
frames.

Courtesy Google

FIGURE 8-8
Google Glass.

initially for mobile phones and other portable devices, IMOD displays use external light, such as from the sun or artificial light inside a building, to display images so images are bright and clear even in direct sunlight (refer again to Figure 8-7). And, because backlighting isn't used, power consumption is much less than what is needed for LCD displays. In fact, similar to the e-paper discussed in the Chapter 7 Inside the Industry box, devices using IMOD displays use no power unless the image changes, which means they can remain on at all times without draining the device battery. Beginning to be used with mobile devices, IMODs could eventually be used for outdoor television screens, large digital signs, and other outdoor display devices that normally consume a great deal of power.

While most displays are designed to be looked at from at least several inches away, some displays are designed to be wearable. A *wearable display* usually projects the image from a mobile device (such as a smartphone or media tablet) to a display screen built into the glasses via a wireless connection. Typically, the technology allows the user to see the image as if it is on a distant large screen display, and many wearable displays overlay the projected image on top of what the user is seeing in real time to provide augmented reality. For example, the *Google Glass* eyeglasses-based display shown in Figure 8-8 has a tiny display located where the right lens would be and users can see content projected on that screen in front of what they are seeing normally. Google Glass is typically connected (via Bluetooth) to a smartphone and then content (such as text messages, maps and directions, video calls, and Web pages) is streamed from that phone to the Google Glass display. Google Glass also has a built-in Web browser and can connect directly to a Wi-Fi hotspot when needed, has a touch-sensitive pad on the right side of the frame for input, and a bone-conductive audio output system so that audio output is heard only by the user. In addition to consumer wearable displays that have entertainment and productivity applications (such as being able to access GPS directions as needed or to monitor your e-mail during a meeting), there are also wearable displays designed for soldiers and other mobile workers.

ASK THE EXPERT

Courtesy of Seagate Technology LLC

Josh Tinker, Product Planning Manager, Seagate Technology

Should my next computer have a magnetic hard drive or an SSD?

Your storage options for a new PC include traditional hard drives (HDDs), solid-state drives (SSDs), and the newer solid-state hybrid drives (SSHDs). Selecting what is right for you is a trade-off between price, performance, and capacity.

- SSDs have maximized PC performance and very good shock resistance, but are low capacity and pricey.
- HDDs have the lowest cost and high capacity but have average performance.
- SSHDs have SSD-like performance and high capacity, but have a small price premium.

Emerging Storage Devices

Improvements in magnetic disk technology are continuing to increase the data that can be stored on hard drives. Traditionally, the magnetic particles on a hard disk have been aligned horizontally, parallel to the hard disk's surface (referred to as *longitudinal magnetic recording*). To increase capacity and reliability, most new hard drives today use *perpendicular magnetic recording* (*PMR*), in which the bits are placed upright to allow them to be closer together than is possible with a horizontal layout. For instance, PMR currently allows a recording density up to 1 *terabit per square inch* (*Tb/inch*^{2}), which results in internal hard drives with capacities up to about 4 TB of storage for a 3.5-inch hard drive, 1 TB for a 2.5-inch hard drive, and 100 GB for a 1-inch hard drive. To allow for higher capacities, new hard drive technologies are under development. For instance, *shingled magnetic recording* (*SMR*), which squeezes more data onto disks by overlapping the data tracks on them like the shingles on a roof, is expected to become available sometime in 2014 and offer increased capacities. Another option for the future is *Heat-Assisted Magnetic Recording* (*HAMR*), which uses lasers to temporarily heat the surface of the hard disks when storing data in order to pack more data onto the surface than is normally possible—it is expected to boost the storage capacity of a 3.5-inch hard drive to 60 TB by 2016.

One high-capacity storage possibility that, after many years of research and development, is just about a reality is **holographic storage**. *Holographic drives* record data onto *holographic discs* or *holographic cartridges*. To record data, the holographic drive splits the light from a blue laser beam into two beams (a *reference beam* whose angle determines the address used to store data at that particular location on the storage medium and a *signal beam* that contains the data). The signal beam passes through a device called a *spatial light modulator* (*SLM*), which translates the data's 0s and 1s into a *hologram*—a three-dimensional representation of data in the form of a checkerboard pattern of light and dark pixels. The two beams intersect within the recording medium to store the holographic image at that location (see Figure 8-9) by changing the optical density of the medium.

Data stored on a holographic medium is arranged into pages of data containing 1.5 million bits each. An entire page of data can be stored at one time in a single flash of light, so holographic storage systems are very fast. And, because the hologram goes through

TIP

Researchers recently demonstrated the ability to store data in 5D in synthetic crystals—this technology may eventually result in discs that can store 360 TB each and that are stable enough to last essentially forever.

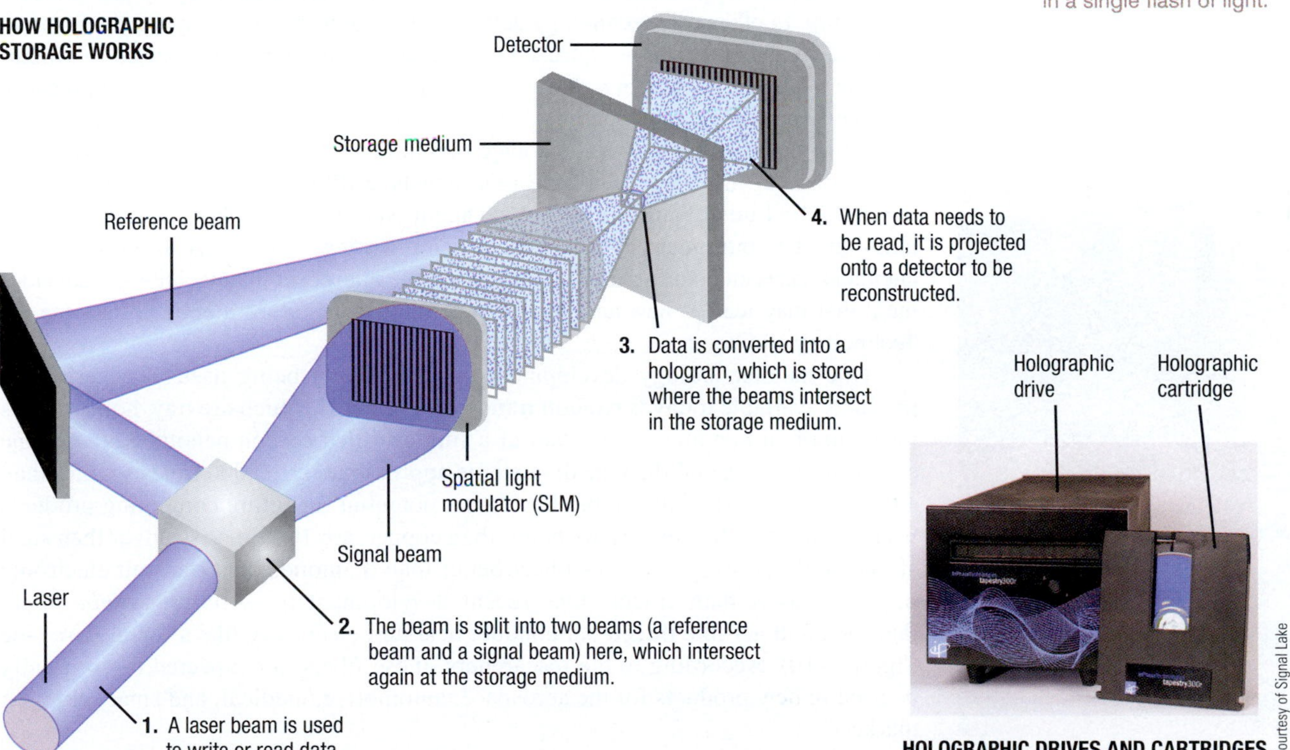
HOW HOLOGRAPHIC STORAGE WORKS
Detector
Storage medium
Reference beam
4. When data needs to be read, it is projected onto a detector to be reconstructed.
3. Data is converted into a hologram, which is stored where the beams intersect in the storage medium.
Spatial light modulator (SLM)
Signal beam
Laser
2. The beam is split into two beams (a reference beam and a signal beam) here, which intersect again at the storage medium.
1. A laser beam is used to write or read data.
Holographic drive
Holographic cartridge
HOLOGRAPHIC DRIVES AND CARTRIDGES
Courtesy of Signal Lake

FIGURE 8-9
Holographic storage. Holographic drives store more than one million bits of data in a single flash of light.

>**Holographic storage.** An emerging type of storage technology that uses multiple blue laser beams to store data in three dimensions.

the entire thickness of the medium, much more data can be stored on a holographic disc or cartridge than on a CD, DVD, or BD of the same physical size. In fact, hundreds of holograms can be stored in an overlapping manner in the same area of the medium—a different reference beam angle or position is used for each hologram so it can be uniquely stored and retrieved when needed. To read data, the reference beam projects the hologram containing the requested data onto a *detector* that reads the entire data page at one time. Holographic storage systems will initially use removable recordable holographic discs that hold 300 GB to 500 GB per disc; most systems can hold multiple discs for increased storage capacity. Holographic data storage systems are particularly suited to applications in which large amounts of data need to be stored or retrieved quickly but rarely changed, such as for business data archiving, high-speed digital video delivery, and image processing for medical, video, and military purposes.

The Impact of Nanotechnology

Although there are varying definitions, most agree that **nanotechnology** involves creating computer components, machines, and other structures that are less than 100 nanometers in size. Consequently, today's CPUs contain components that fit the definition of nanotechnology. However, some experts believe that, eventually, current technology will reach its limits. At that point, transistors and other computer components may need to be built at the atomic and molecular level; that is, starting with single atoms or molecules to construct the components. Prototypes of computer products built in this fashion include a *single atom transistor*, which is a single switch that can be turned on and off like a transistor but is made from a single organic molecule, as well as tiny nickel-based *nanodots* that would, theoretically, allow about 5 TB of data to be stored on a hard drive roughly the size of a postage stamp. In other nanotechnology developments, prototypes of tiny *nanogenerators* have been developed that can be squeezed to generate power; they are expected to eventually be able to power mobile devices with low-frequency vibrations, such as a heartbeat or a simple body movement like walking. And researchers are looking at DNA as a possible long-term high-density archiving storage option and, in fact, have already encoded a variety of data—including Shakespeare's sonnets, a JPEG photo, and an MP3 recording of Martin Luther King Jr.'s "I Have a Dream" speech—into DNA material by translating the data into binary 0s and 1s and then rewriting that data as strings of DNA's chemical bases and storing it in DNA. For a look at a recent nanotechnology development that may lead to new and improved glass on your future mobile phone, see the Technology and You box.

FIGURE 8-10
Carbon nanotubes. This light bulb is powered and held in place by two carbon nanotube fibers.

© Jeff Fitlow/Rice University

One nanotechnology development that is already being used in a variety of products available today is **carbon nanotubes (CNTs)**, which are tiny, hollow tubes made up of carbon atoms. The wall of a single-walled carbon nanotube is only one carbon atom thick and the tube diameter is approximately 10,000 times smaller than a human hair. Carbon nanotubes have great potential for future computing products because they conduct electricity better than copper, are 100 times stronger than steel at one-sixth the weight, conduct heat better than diamonds, and transmit electronic impulses faster than silicon. One recent development is *carbon nanotube fibers* that look and act like thread but conduct heat and electricity like a metal wire (see Figure 8-10). According to the researchers, these fibers are expected to eventually be used in new products for the aerospace, automotive, medical, and smart-clothing markets.

>Nanotechnology. The science of creating tiny computers and components by working at the individual atomic and molecular levels. **>Carbon nanotubes (CNTs).** Tiny, hollow tubes made of carbon atoms.

TECHNOLOGY AND YOU

"Magic" Glass

A smartphone with a non-glare, self-cleaning screen? That could be the wave of the future based on a recent development by MIT researchers. By creating nano-sized conical patterns on the surface of the glass using coating and etching techniques, the researchers were able to eliminate its reflective properties, resulting in glass that resists fogging and glare (see the accompanying illustration) and is even self-cleaning.

In addition to making it easier to use mobile devices outdoors, the technology has a host of other possible applications, such as being used for eyeglasses, televisions, car windshields, and even windows in buildings. It could also be applied to solar panels, which can lose as much as 40% of their efficiency within three months due to dust and dirt accumulating on their surfaces. But, for most people, it will likely be the possibility of a tablet or smartphone with glass that eliminates reflections and cleans itself of fingerprints that gets the most attention.

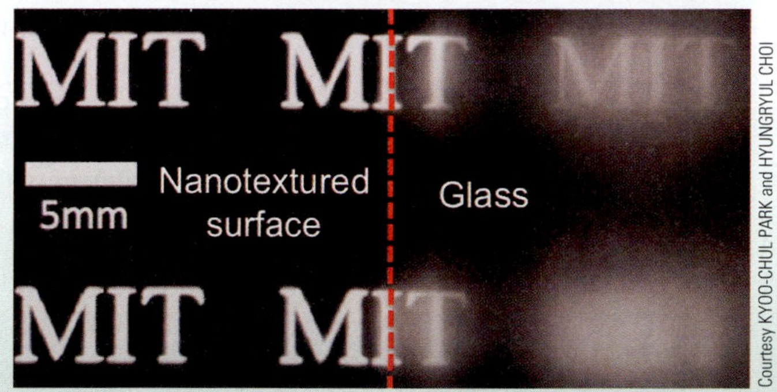

MIT "magic" glass vs. normal glass. The normal half of this piece of glass (right) can fog up and produce glare; the MIT glass half (left) remains clear.

CNT products currently on the market include lithium ion batteries, and several nanotube-based computing products—like nanotube-based display screens and memory—are currently under development. In addition, IBM researchers are experimenting with a combination of DNA molecules and carbon nanotubes to make smaller, more powerful, and more energy-efficient computer chips. Because carbon nanotubes can transmit electricity and are transparent, they are also being used for product development in the areas of TVs, solar cells, light bulbs, and other similar noncomputing applications. In addition, because of their strength and lightness for their size, carbon nanotubes are being integrated into products that benefit from those characteristics, such as automobile panels, airplanes, tennis rackets, and racing bikes. In fact, the Army recently initiated a two-year program to develop carbon nanotube products to replace conventional copper-based wires and cables in aircraft. Carbon nanotubes are also beginning to be combined with other materials, such as plastic, to increase the durability of materials used to produce other consumer items, such as surfboards.

Two recent developments are *nanofilters* that can remove contaminants from water sources and *nanosensors* that can detect cancer-causing toxins or cancer drugs inside single living cells. Possible future applications of nanotechnology include disposing of e-waste by rearranging dangerous components at the atomic level into inert substances, *nanosponges* that can enter the bloodstream and soak up toxins, improved military uniforms that protect against bullets and germ warfare, and computers and sensors that are small enough to be woven into the fibers of clothing or embedded into paint and other materials. Some of the devices generated by nanotechnology research may contain or be constructed out of organic material.

TIP

Data stored in DNA uses densities that are at least 1,000 times greater than current storage media—about 2.2 PB per gram. At that rate, if you took everything human beings have ever written (an estimated 50 PB of text) and stored it in DNA, it would weigh less than a granola bar.

Quantum and Optical Computers

Computers a few decades from now will likely use technology that is very different from the silicon chips and electronic bits and bytes we are accustomed to today. In addition to being miniature—based on nanotechnology—and likely incorporated into a variety of everyday devices, computers in the future may be *quantum* or *optical computers*.

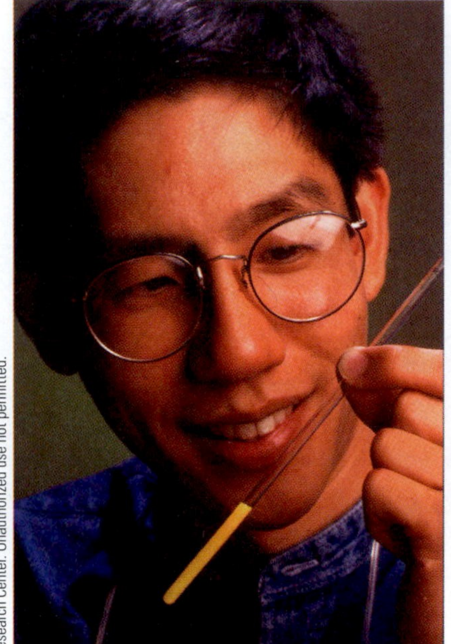

FIGURE 8-11
Quantum computers. The vial of liquid shown here contains the 7-qubit computer used by IBM researchers in 2001 to perform the most complicated computation by a quantum computer to date—factoring the number 15.

Quantum Computing

The idea of **quantum computing** emerged in the 1970s, and it has received renewed interest lately. Quantum computing applies the principles of quantum physics and quantum mechanics to computers, going beyond traditional physics to work at the subatomic level. Quantum computers differ from conventional computers in that they utilize atoms or nuclei working together as *quantum bits* or *qubits*. Qubits function simultaneously as both the computer's processor and memory, and each qubit can represent more than just the two states (one and zero) available to today's electronic bits; a qubit can even represent many states at one time. Quantum computers can perform computations on many numbers at one time, making them, theoretically, exponentially faster than conventional computers. Physically, quantum computers in the future might consist of a thimbleful of liquid whose atoms are used to perform calculations as instructed by an external device.

Even though quantum computers are still in the pioneering stage, working quantum computers do exist. For instance, in 2001 the researchers at IBM's Almaden Research Center created a 7-qubit quantum computer (see Figure 8-11) composed of the nuclei of seven atoms that can interact with each other and be programmed by radio frequency pulses. This quantum computer successfully factored the number 15—not a complicated computation for a conventional computer, but the fact that a quantum computer was able to understand the problem and compute the correct answer is viewed as a highly significant event in the area of quantum computer research. One of the obstacles to creating a fully functional quantum computer has been the inability of qubits to hold information for long periods of time. Recently, UCLA scientists developed a new technique for cooling molecules, which may be applied to future quantum computers in order to bring the molecules to the state at which they can be manipulated to store and transmit data. In addition, scientists in Australia have created a silicon quantum bit using a single atom—this development is viewed as a big step forward in the development of silicon-based quantum computers. These breakthroughs are viewed as significant steps toward the ability to create more sophisticated working quantum computers in the future.

Quantum computing is not well suited for general computing tasks but it is ideal for, and expected to be widely used in, highly data-intensive applications, such as encryption and code breaking.

Optical Computing

Optical chips, which use light waves to transmit data, are also currently in development. A possibility for the future is the **optical computer**—a computer that uses light, such as from laser beams or infrared beams, to perform digital computations. Because light beams do not interfere with each other, optical computers can be much smaller and faster than electronic computers. For instance, according to one NASA senior research scientist, an optical computer could solve a problem in one hour that would take an electronic computer 11 years to solve. While some researchers are working on developing an all-optical computer, others believe that a mix of optical and electronic components—or an *opto-electronic*

>**Quantum computing.** A technology that applies the principles of quantum physics and quantum mechanics to computers to direct atoms or nuclei to work together as quantum bits (qubits), which function simultaneously as the computer's processor and memory. >**Optical computer.** A computer that uses light, such as from laser beams or infrared beams, to perform digital computations.

computer—may be the best bet for the future. Opto-electronic technology is already being used to improve long-distance fiber-optic communications. Initial opto-electronic computer applications are expected to be applied to the area of speeding up communications between computers and other devices, as well as between computer components. In fact, IBM recently created chips that have both optical and electrical functions combined on a single silicon chip and that use standard semiconductor processes—a feat that was thought to be impossible until recently. One additional benefit of opto-electronic chips is reduced power consumption. While increased bandwidth (such as between servers, between CPU cores, or between the CPU and memory) increases power consumption using electrical connections, the impact is much less with opto-electronic chips because they move data with light instead of electricity.

FIGURE 8-12
Telepresence videoconferencing.

Students in this classroom see a life-sized projected image of the professor.
The instructor sees a projected image of these students, who appear to be seated behind the students physically located in the professor's classroom.
Courtesy Cisco Systems, Inc.

EMERGING NETWORKING TECHNOLOGIES

Improvements are being made on a continual basis to both wired and wireless networking technologies to increase speed and connectivity options for *local area networks* (*LANs*) and Internet connections, as well as to support the continued growth in Internet-based multimedia and communications applications used by computers and mobile devices that require fast, dependable connections, such as Voice over IP (VoIP), video-on-demand (VOD), video calls, mobile TV, and teleconferencing. For instance, one new improvement to videoconferencing technology to make it more closely mimic a real-time meeting environment is referred to as *telepresence videoconferencing*. Although telepresence videoconferencing setups are expensive, with travel becoming increasingly more expensive and time consuming, many businesses view videoconferencing as a viable replacement for face-to-face meetings. Telepresence videoconferencing is also used in educational settings (for instance, the system shown in Figure 8-12 is installed at the Wharton School campuses in both Philadelphia and San Francisco to hold bicoastal classes).

FIGURE 8-13
GPS-based child monitoring systems.
Allow parents to track their children in real time.

Monitoring Systems

Some emerging networking applications involve location information, such as the geobrowsing and geofencing applications discussed in the Chapter 3 How It Works box and monitoring systems that utilize GPS. For instance, *vehicle monitoring systems* are available that can be installed in cars by parents and employers to monitor the location and use of the vehicles (by teenagers or employees, respectively) using networking technology; *child monitoring systems* allow parents to monitor the physical locations of their children. Both types of monitoring systems typically record a location history; many also allow the location of a vehicle or child to be tracked in real time via a Web site or mobile app (see Figure 8-13). Some systems can even be used to set up a "virtual fence" for a child or a car or a maximum allowable car speed; the parent or employer is notified (usually via a text message) anytime the child or vehicle leaves the prescribed geographical area or exceeds the designated speed. Child monitoring systems often include additional features, such as the ability to have the child's location pushed to the parent's device at regular intervals, the ability to have the parent notified if the child is within 500 feet of a registered sex offender, and an "SOS" button that the child can press if he or she is lost or afraid. The child monitoring system shown in Figure 8-13 is also available

Locations of registered offenders.
Child's current (green) and past (red) locations.
Map
Standard
Hybrid
Courtesy Amber Alert GPS; © Chardchanin/Shutterstock.com

Courtesy Nest Labs

FIGURE 8-14
Smart thermostats. This thermostat (left) contains a variety of sensors and can be controlled remotely via a mobile app (right).

as a smartphone app for teenagers. Similar GPS systems are designed to be used to track elderly parents or by individuals who are hiking or traveling so they can be located if they become lost or injured.

Other monitoring systems are designed for use in the home. For instance, *home health monitoring systems* are designed to monitor elderly or infirm individuals (such as by taking the vital signs of the individual or prompting him or her to answer questions about food or medication consumed that day) and to notify someone if a possible problem is detected. Other home monitoring systems use *sensors*—devices that respond to a stimulus (such as heat, light, or pressure) and generate an electrical signal that can be measured or interpreted. For example, *smart door locks* allow you to unlock your front door with your smartphone and the thermostat shown in Figure 8-14 contains temperature, humidity, activity, and light sensors; can be controlled via a mobile app; and can be programmed based on your activity within the home. IBM expects to see the use of sensor technology expanding to additional areas in the future, such as nano-sized sensors embedded in paint that help manage the energy use of a building or as a coating applied to plumbing systems to detect leaks and other potential problems.

New Wireless and Cloud Applications

Improved networking technology has also created a host of new wireless networking applications. For instance, *wireless displays* connect to a computer or other device (such as to a smartphone, as in Figure 8-15) using a wireless networking connection. Once connected, either all content or selected content from the source device is displayed on the wireless display. Printers are also increasingly using a wireless connection and, if your printer has Internet access, you can print content from your smartphone, media tablet, or other mobile device to your home or office printer from any location with Internet access (refer again to Figure 8-15); you can also send printouts wirelessly to public printers, such as those located at airports, libraries, office stores, and shipping stores such as FedEx Office and the UPS Store.

TIP

It has been predicted that 50 billion devices (essentially anything with an on-off switch) will be connected to the Internet by 2020, creating the Internet of Things (IoT).

Wired Networking Standards

Ethernet is the most widely used standard for wired networks. It was invented in the mid-1970s and has continued to evolve over the years to support faster speeds. The most common Ethernet standards for LANs today are *Fast Ethernet*, which supports data transfer rates of up to 100 Mbps; *Gigabit Ethernet*, which is even faster at 1,000 Mbps (1 Gbps); and *10 Gigabit Ethernet*, which supports data transfer rates of 10 Gbps. The

FIGURE 8-15
New wireless and cloud applications.

Courtesy HTC

WIRELESS DISPLAYS

Courtesy Epson America

CLOUD PRINTING

newer *40 Gigabit Ethernet* and *100 Gigabit Ethernet* standards were ratified in 2010. Development of the even faster *400 Gigabit Ethernet* and *Terabit Ethernet* standards are currently being explored; if ratified, they are expected to be used for connections between servers, as well as for delivering video, digital X-rays and other digital medical images, and other high-speed, bandwidth-intensive Internet applications.

A relatively new Ethernet development is **Power over Ethernet (PoE)**, which allows electrical power to be sent along the cables in an Ethernet network (often referred to as *Ethernet cables*) along with data (see Figure 8-16). Consequently, the Ethernet cable, in addition to sending data, can be used to supply power to the devices on the network. PoE is most often used in business networks with remote wired devices (such as outdoor networking hardware, security cameras, and other devices) that are not located near a power outlet. Using PoE requires special hardware and devices designed for PoE; regular Ethernet-enabled devices can be powered via PoE if a special *PoE adapter*, such as the one shown in Figure 8-16, is used.

ASK THE EXPERT

D-Link Building Networks for People

Courtesy D-Link Systems, Inc.

Daniel Kelley, Vice President, Marketing, D-Link Systems, Inc.

How will the Internet of Things (IoT) affect our daily lives?

The Internet of Things (IoT) is one of the more intriguing topics on where technology is going and how it will impact almost every aspect of our daily lives. We are already seeing technology with embedded Internet connectivity emerge in things like cars, buildings, and more in order to develop a conversation between devices, the user, and the devices around them. While most IoT applications today are focused on information and entertainment, I foresee a big advancement in safety when cars are able to not only avoid traffic but also avoid accidents by getting "smarter" and having constant dialogue with other cars and the environment around them.

For easily creating wired home networks, the *Phoneline* (also called *HomePNA*) and *Powerline* (also called *HomePlug AV*) *standards* allow computers to be networked through ordinary existing telephone jacks and power outlets, respectively. As both of these standards have emerged, their speeds have increased and now both can be used to network home entertainment devices in addition to computers. The *G.hn standard* is a new standard designed as a unified worldwide standard for creating home networks over any existing home wiring—phone lines, power lines, and/or coaxial cable. It is viewed as the next-generation standard for wired home networking and it may eventually replace the Powerline and Phoneline standards. G.hn is fast—up to 1 Gbps—and G.hn adapters and other products are expected to be available soon.

FIGURE 8-16
Power over Ethernet (PoE) powers devices through an Ethernet connection.

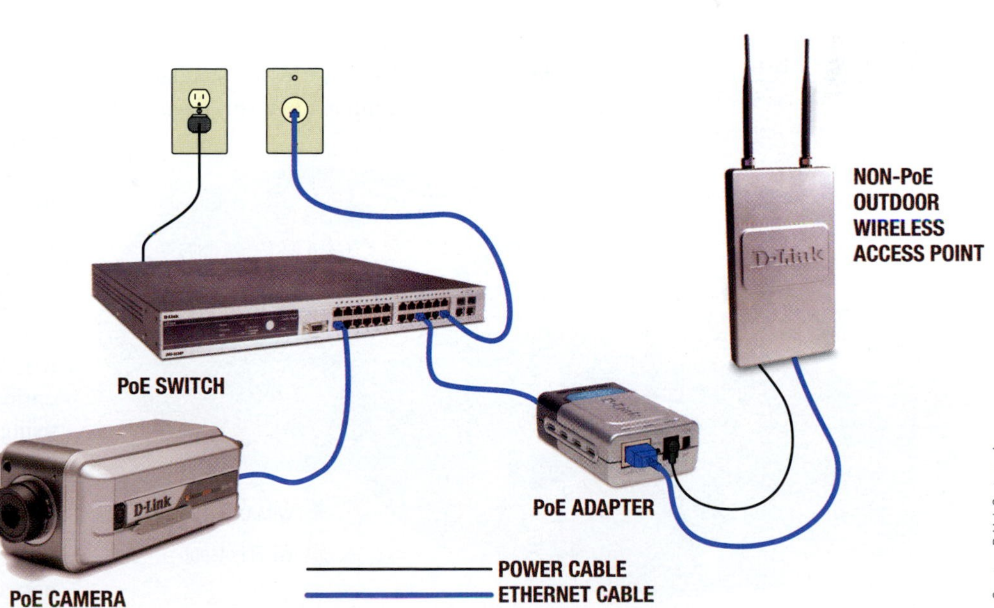

> **Power over Ethernet (PoE).** A wired networking standard that allows electrical power to be sent along with data over standard Ethernet cables.

FIGURE 8-17
Smart scales.
This scale transmits readings to a smartphone via Wi-Fi.

Wireless Networking Standards

Developed in the late 1990s, **Wi-Fi** (for *wireless fidelity*) is a family of wireless networking standards that use the IEEE standard **802.11**. Wi-Fi is the current standard for wireless networks in the home or office, as well as for public Wi-Fi hotspots. Wi-Fi capabilities are built into virtually all portable computers and mobile devices today; they are also becoming increasingly integrated into everyday products, such as printers, digital cameras, portable digital media players, external hard drives, baby monitors, gaming consoles, home audio systems, televisions—even bathroom scales (see Figure 8-17)—to allow those devices to wirelessly network with other devices or to access the Internet. Like Ethernet, the Wi-Fi standard is continually evolving to support increased speed and other capabilities. The speed of a Wi-Fi network and the area it can cover depend on a variety of factors, including the *Wi-Fi standard* and hardware being used, the number of solid objects (such as walls, trees, or buildings) between the access point and the computer or other device being used, and the amount of interference from cordless phones, baby monitors, microwave ovens, and other devices that also operate on the same radio frequency as Wi-Fi (usually 2.4 GHz). In general, Wi-Fi is designed for medium-range data transfers—typically between 100 and 300 feet indoors and 300 to 900 feet outdoors. There are a number of different versions of the 802.11 standard; the *802.11g*, *802.11n*, and *802.11ac* standards are the most widely used today. Emerging 802.11 standards under development are expected to offer increased speed, security, and other factors in the future.

While Wi-Fi is very widely used today, it does have some limitations—particularly its relatively limited range. For instance, an individual using a Wi-Fi hotspot inside a Starbucks coffeehouse will lose that Internet connection when he or she moves out of range of that network and will need to locate another hotspot at his or her next location. In addition, other wireless technologies are in development for specific purposes, such as *multimedia networking*. These emerging wireless technologies are discussed next. For a look at another emerging wireless technology—powering your hardware devices via *wireless power*—see the Inside the Industry box.

WiMAX (802.16)

WiMAX (802.16) is a series of standards designed for longer range wireless networking connections. Similar to Wi-Fi, *fixed WiMAX* (also known as *802.16a*) is designed to provide Internet access to fixed locations (sometimes called *hotzones*), but the coverage area is significantly larger (a typical hotzone radius is between 2 and 6 miles, though WiMAX can transmit data as far as 10 miles or more—see Figure 8-18). With fixed WiMAX, it is feasible to provide coverage to an entire city or other geographical area by using multiple WiMAX towers (refer again to Figure 8-18). *Mobile WiMAX* (*802.16e*) is the mobile version of the WiMAX wireless networking standard. It is designed to deliver fast wireless networking to mobile users via a mobile

FIGURE 8-18
WiMAX vs. Wi-Fi.
A WiMAX hotzone can provide service to anyone in the hotzone, including mobile users.

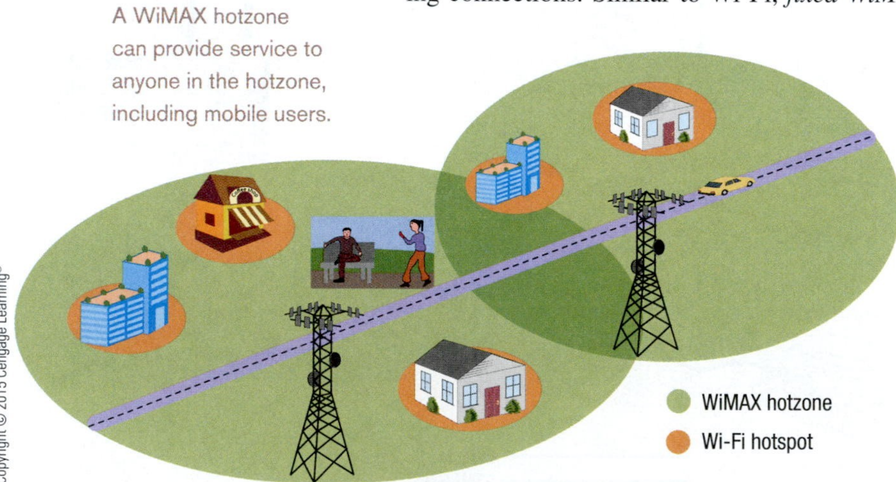

>**Wi-Fi (802.11).** A widely used networking standard for medium-range wireless networks. >**WiMAX (802.16).** A wireless networking standard that is faster and has a larger range than Wi-Fi.

INSIDE THE INDUSTRY

Wireless Power

Imagine recharging your notebook computer or mobile phone just by setting it down in the right place, or using your kitchen blender just by placing it on a countertop but not plugging it in. These scenarios are possible with *wireless power*. While wireless power products are now becoming available, one of the challenges has been creating a standard for wireless power so that multiple devices from different manufacturers can be charged at the same time using the same technology.

One company working toward this standard is Fulton Innovation. This company, along with the more than 100 other companies that are members of the *Wireless Power Consortium* (including Panasonic, Verizon Wireless, Sony, Energizer, Motorola Mobility, Nokia, and LG Electronics), supports wireless power technology that uses *magnetic induction* to transfer power wirelessly from a charging power supply device to a target device containing the appropriate receiving technology. Products meeting the consortium standard will be able to use the *Qi* (pronounced "chee") logo. Qi systems are compatible with one another (though not with competing charging systems that are also under development). They automatically adjust the power transmitted to each device being charged to meet the needs of that device, and they deactivate the charging process when the device is fully charged. Charging works with the device's regular battery (but the device needs an embedded receiver) and takes about the same time as a regular wired charger.

Assuming the Qi standard becomes the norm, virtually all devices in the future are expected to contain a built-in charging receiver; some Nokia, LG, and HTC mobile phones already include one. Several cars with Qi charging stations (see the accompanying photo) are already on the market. In the near future, charging bases are expected to be built into other objects, such as desks, kitchen countertops, restaurant tabletops, hotel nightstands, airline tray tables—basically anywhere you might normally place your devices—in order to power all your devices in all of the spaces that you use. Qi technology can also be used with household and kitchen appliances. Future wireless power applications could even include charging transmitters built into walls to power all of the devices located in the home on a continual basis, as well as into garage floors and parking lots to wirelessly recharge electric vehicles.

Because there is a cost associated with providing the wireless power, it is expected that businesses providing wireless charging services may eventually charge for these services or include a certain amount of recharge with a purchase, similar to when Wi-Fi hotspots first started appearing in public locations.

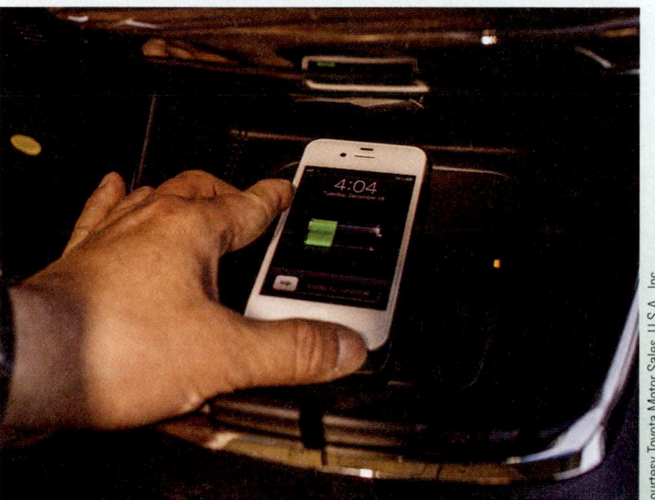

Qi wireless charging stations are available in some recent cars, such as the Toyota Avalon shown here.

phone, portable computer, or other WiMAX-enabled device. Mobile WiMAX is capable of speeds of approximately 70 Mbps, but speeds of 1 to 6 Mbps are more typical. The newest version of mobile WiMAX (*802.16m* or *WiMAX Release 2*) supports speeds up to approximately 120 Mbps.

WiMAX capabilities are beginning to be built into portable computers and other devices, and WiMAX is currently being used to provide Internet access to more than 1 billion people in about 150 countries.

TIP

If your Internet connection slows down, try *power cycling* your modem and router: Unplug the modem and router and wait for 30 seconds, plug in the modem and wait for 30 seconds, and then plug in the router.

Cellular Standards

Cellular standards have also evolved over the years to better fulfill the demand for mobile Internet, mobile multimedia delivery, and other relatively recent mobile trends. The current standards for cellular networks today in the United States and many other countries are *3G* (*third generation*) and *4G* (*fourth generation*). 3G and 4G networks are designed to support both data and voice. Users of both 3G and 4G smartphones and other mobile devices can access broadband Internet content (such as online maps, music, games, TV, videos, and more) at relatively fast speeds—typically, between 1 and 4 Mbps and 3 to 15 Mbps, respectively. Because 3G and 4G speeds are equivalent to the speeds many home broadband Internet users experience, Internet access via a 3G or 4G network is often referred to as *mobile broadband*. Virtually all wireless providers today have both a 3G and a 4G network, though 4G service may not be available in all areas. There are two primary standards for 4G networks today: the mobile WiMAX standard already discussed and *Long Term Evolution (LTE)*, supported by AT&T Wireless, Verizon Wireless, and T-Mobile. LTE is the fastest standard and the *Phase 2 LTE network* currently being implemented by AT&T is expected to double 4G speeds. While mobile WiMAX is not technically a cellular standard, it is being used by some companies (such as Sprint) to provide 4G wireless service to subscribers.

TIP

The SmartGlass app that enables you to have a second Xbox 360 screen via your smartphone or tablet can connect via either Wi-Fi or a 3G/4G cellular network.

Short-Range Wireless Standards

There are several wireless networking standards in existence or being developed that are designed for short-range wireless networking connections (for a summary of these standards and the standards already discussed, see Figure 8-19). **Bluetooth** is a wireless standard that was originally designed for very short-range (10 meters, approximately 33 feet, or less) connections, though there is no maximum range and some industrial products have a range of 300 feet. Bluetooth is designed to replace cables between devices, such as to connect a wireless keyboard or mouse to a desktop computer, to send print jobs wirelessly from a portable computer to a printer, or to connect a mobile phone to a wireless headset. The Bluetooth standard is continually evolving to be faster and to support new applications. One of the key enhancements in the newest Bluetooth specification (*Bluetooth 4.0*, also called *Bluetooth Smart*) is low energy, which enables small devices to run for years on a single button-sized battery. Consequently, Bluetooth is increasingly being used with consumer devices, such as to connect health and fitness devices to a watch or smartphone, to connect a mobile phone to a portable speaker, and to connect 3D glasses to a 3D television set.

TIP

NFC is also being used for new networking applications, such as the emerging *NFC ring* that can be used to automatically unlock assigned doors or smartphones within range of your ring finger.

Another standard that is designed to connect peripheral devices, similar to Bluetooth, but that transfers data more quickly is **wireless USB**. The speed of wireless USB depends on the distance between the devices being used, but it is approximately 100 Mbps at 10 meters (about 33 feet) or 480 Mbps at 3 meters (about 10 feet). While Bluetooth and wireless USB can be used for similar applications, it is possible they might coexist. For example, wireless USB might

FIGURE 8-19 Summary of common wireless networking standards.

CATEGORY	EXAMPLES	INTENDED PURPOSE	RANGE
Short range	Bluetooth Wireless USB	To connect peripheral devices to a mobile phone or computer.	33 feet–200 feet
	Ultra Wideband (UWB) WirelessHD (WiHD) TransferJet WiGig	To connect and transfer multimedia content between home consumer electronic devices (computers, TVs, DVD players, etc.).	1 inch–33 feet
Medium range	Wi-Fi (802.11)	To connect computers and other devices to a local area network.	100–300 feet indoors; 300–900 feet outdoors
	Wi-Fi Direct	To connect computers and other devices directly together.	600 feet
Long range	WiMAX Mobile WiMAX	To provide Internet access to a large geographic area for fixed and/or mobile users.	6 miles non-line of sight; 30 miles line of sight
	Cellular standards	To connect mobile phones and mobile devices to a cellular network for telephone and Internet service.	10 miles

>**Bluetooth.** A networking standard for very short-range wireless connections; the devices are automatically connected once they get within the allowable range. >**Wireless USB.** A wireless version of USB designed to connect peripheral devices.

be used to connect computer hardware in more permanent setups, while Bluetooth might be used in short-range mobile situations with portable computers and mobile devices.

A newer standard also designed to connect devices for short-range communications is **Wi-Fi Direct**. Wi-Fi Direct enables Wi-Fi devices to connect directly to each other, such as to transfer photos or documents or to *tether* devices to a Wi-Fi Direct device's Internet connection by creating a hotspot (see Figure 8-20), without needing any additional networking hardware. Wi-Fi Direct is not designed to replace traditional Wi-Fi networks, but it is considered a competitor to Bluetooth because it has the advantage of faster speeds (up to 250 Mbps) and a greater range (up to 600 feet).

For transferring multimedia content quickly between nearby devices (such as between televisions and DVD players, or between computers and mobile devices), a number of different standards are emerging. For instance, *Ultra Wideband* (*UWB*) transfers data at speeds from 100 Mbps at 10 meters (about 33 feet) to 480 Mbps at 2 meters (about 6.5 feet). Similar, but faster, standards include *WiGig*, which is being developed by the *Wi-Fi Alliance* and supports short-range data transfers of up to 7 Gbps, and *wirelessHD* (*WiHD*), which is backed by seven major electronics companies and is designed to transfer full-quality uncompressed high-definition audio, video, and data within a single room at speeds up to 28 Gbps. A wireless standard designed for fast transfers between devices that are extremely close together (essentially touching each other) is *TransferJet*. Developed by Sony, TransferJet is designed to transfer large files (such as digital photos, music, and video) quickly between devices as soon as they come in contact with each other (such as to transfer data between smartphones or between digital cameras, to download music or video from a consumer kiosk or digital signage system to a smartphone or other mobile device, or to transfer images or video from a digital camera to a TV or printer). At a maximum speed of 560 Mbps, TransferJet is slower than some of the other technologies, but it is fast enough to support the transfer of video files.

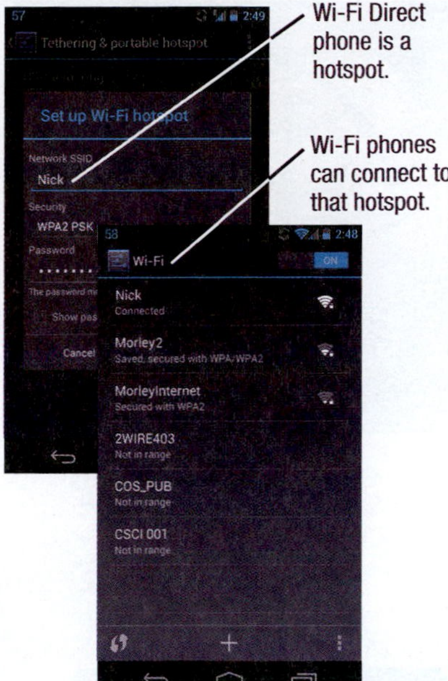

FIGURE 8-20
Wi-Fi Direct. Allows Wi-Fi devices to connect directly to one another.

ARTIFICIAL INTELLIGENCE (AI)

Although they cannot yet think completely on their own, computers and software programs have become more sophisticated, and computers are being programmed to act in an increasingly intelligent manner.

What Is Artificial Intelligence (AI)?

According to John McCarthy, who coined the term **artificial intelligence (AI)** in 1956 and is considered by many to be one of its fathers, AI is "the science and engineering of making intelligent machines." In other words, AI researchers are working to create intelligent devices controlled by intelligent software programs; in essence, machines that think and act like people and that perform in ways that would be considered intelligent if observed in human beings. In 1950, Alan Turing—one of the first AI researchers—argued that if a machine could successfully appear to be human to a knowledgeable observer, then it should be considered intelligent. To illustrate this idea, Turing developed a test—later called the *Turing Test*—in which one observer interacts electronically with both a computer and a person. During the test, the observer submits written questions electronically to both the computer and the person, evaluates the typed responses, and tries to identify which answers came from the computer and which came from the person. Turing argued that if the computer could repeatedly fool the observer into thinking it was human, then it should be viewed as intelligent.

TIP

DARPA (*Defense Advanced Research Projects Agency*) is experimenting with AI (in conjunction with computational linguistics, machine learning, and natural language technologies) to create an automated system to help analysts more efficiently evaluate and understand the connections among large volumes of text-based documents.

>**Wi-Fi Direct.** A standard for connecting Wi-Fi devices directly, without using a router or an access point. >**Artificial intelligence (AI).** When a computer performs actions that are characteristic of human intelligence.

Courtesy of Dr. Hugh Loebner

FIGURE 8-21
The Loebner Prize gold medal has yet to be awarded.

Many Turing Test contests have been held over the years, and in 1990, Dr. Hugh Loebner initiated the Loebner Prize, pledging a grand prize of $100,000 and a solid gold medal (see Figure 8-21) for the developer of the first computer whose responses to a Turing Test were indistinguishable from that of a human's responses. A contest is held every year, awarding a prize of $4,000 and a bronze medal to the developer of the most humanlike computer but, so far, the gold medal has not been awarded. However, some experts believe that a computer will pass the Turing Test within the next 20 years. Although the Turing Test is interesting and is still providing grounds for research today, many experts believe that the Turing Test provides only one possible test of computer intelligence. These experts argue that there could be different definitions of intelligence, and a machine could still be considered intelligent without knowing enough about humans to imitate one.

Some of the initial advances in AI were made in the area of game playing—namely, chess. Early chess-playing programs were easily defeated by amateur chess players. But, as computers became more powerful and AI software became more sophisticated, chess-playing programs improved significantly. In 1996, IBM's Deep Blue computer won two of six games in a chess match against then world chess champion Garry Kasparov. A landmark moment in AI history occurred in 1997 when Deep Blue beat Kasparov in a rematch, winning the match 3½ to 2½ (three of the six games ended in a draw). And in late 2006, world chess champion Vladimir Kramnik lost a match to the chess program *Deep Fritz* (see Figure 8-22)—the beginning of the end of humans being able to beat chess programs, in the opinion of some AI researchers. One reason for this is because once the human player makes a mistake, there is no hope (as there would be with a human opponent) that the computer opponent will make its own mistake at a later time to level the playing field in that game.

TIP

Self-driving cars generate 1 GB of data during each second of operation—this and other types of fast-moving data that can't easily be handled by existing data tools are referred to as *big data*.

AI Applications

Today's AI applications contain some aspect of artificial intelligence, although they tend to mimic human intelligence rather than display pure intelligence. Technological advances will undoubtedly help AI applications continue to evolve and become more intelligent and sophisticated in the future. For instance, one recent advancement is IBM's Watson supercomputer that has the ability to analyze complex questions and form answers well enough to compete with human beings on the *Jeopardy!* game show and win (see Figure 8-22)—Watson's software is now being applied to other applications, such as medical diagnosis systems and business intelligence systems. However, just as the debate about what constitutes intelligence in nonhumans will continue, so will the debate about how far we as a society should delve into the area of artificial intelligence. AI applications that exist in some form today include *intelligent agents*, *expert systems*, *neural networks*, and *robotics*. For a look at the *self-driving cars* you may be using in the future, see the How It Works box.

FIGURE 8-22
AI and game playing.

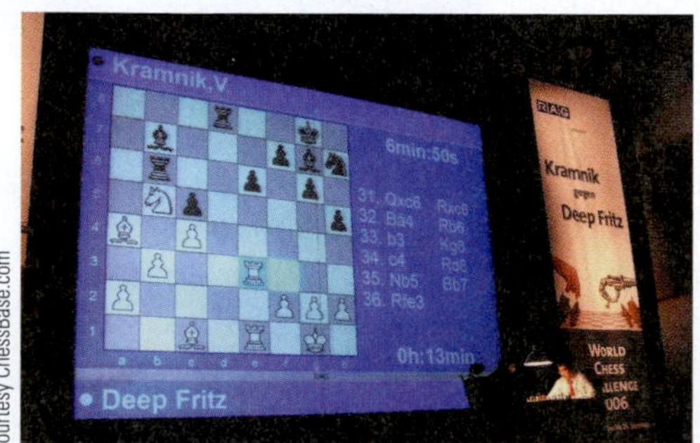

Courtesy ChessBase.com

KRAMNIK VS. DEEP FRITZ
Deep Fritz beat world champion Vladimir Kramnik 4 games to 2 in 2006.

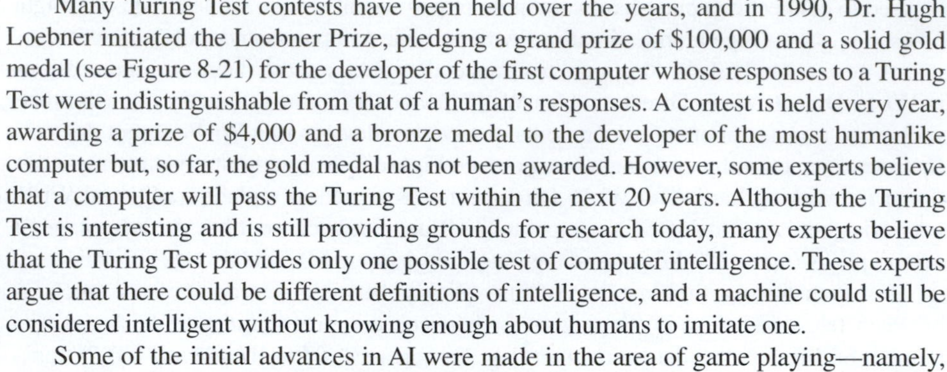

Courtesy of IBM Corporation

WATSON VS. *JEOPARDY!* CHAMPIONS
Watson easily beat both champions in 2011.

Intelligent Agents

Intelligent agents (also called *smart assistants*) are programs that perform

>**Intelligent agent.** A program that performs specific tasks to help make a user's work environment more efficient or entertaining and that typically modifies its behavior based on the user's actions.

HOW IT WORKS

Self-Driving Cars

Did you ever wish you had a car that could drive itself? Well, you're in luck—self-driving cars are here. Google's self-driving car (shown in the accompanying photo) has already logged half a million miles during testing. And, recently, California, Florida, and Nevada passed legislation allowing self-driving cars to be tested on state roads. To plan for the future, California has directed the DMV to work with other state agencies (such as highway patrol, transportation, and insurance) to determine how *autonomous vehicles* will be allowed to be used in the state once they become available. Issues include how the cars and riders should be licensed, any limitations on use for safety (such as use in school zones or bad weather), any allowable use by blind or underage individuals, how the cars will be insured if there is no driver assigned to them, how to protect the cars against hackers, and so forth.

Google autonomous cars are essentially robotic cars. They include an onboard computer, cameras, and a roof-mounted laser range finder; the data generated by these devices is combined with GPS data to enable the cars to avoid obstacles and adhere to traffic laws. Because they are analytical, aren't capable of being distracted, don't make mistakes, and can't be impaired by alcohol, drugs, or lack of sleep, Google and other autonomous vehicle promoters propose that self-driving cars are safer, in addition to making driving more enjoyable and more efficient. In addition, these vehicles could use short-range communications technology to communicate with each other to avoid collisions—by one estimate, these cars could prevent, or reduce in severity, as many as 80% of crashes involving non-impaired drivers alone.

Currently, the use of autonomous cars is in the testing phase and requires a licensed driver to be in the car, but California plans to have regulations in place within a year to prepare for autonomous cars coming on the market in the near future, once they are deemed safe. It is expected that, initially, a licensed driver will be required to be in the car. But, who knows in the future? You may be able to send your car out for pizza or to pick up a guest arriving at the airport. Only time will tell.

Courtesy Google

specific tasks to help make a user's work environment more efficient or entertaining. Typically, the agent program runs in the background until it is time for the agent to perform a task, and it usually modifies its behavior based on the user's actions or instructions. Intelligent agents are found on Web sites, as well as incorporated into software programs and mobile operating systems. Some specific types of intelligent agents include the following:

- *Application assistants*—provide help or assistance for a particular application program. Some can detect when the user might be having trouble with the program and automatically offer appropriate advice. Others add speech capabilities to common programs, such as instant messaging programs.
- *Shopping bots*—search online stores to find the best prices for specified products.
- *Entertainment bots*—provide entertainment, such as a virtual pet to take care of or an animated character to play games with.
- *Chatterbots*—carry on written "conversations" with people in a *natural language* (such as English, Spanish, French, or Japanese). Chatterbots typically respond both verbally and with appropriate facial expressions to create the illusion that the exchange is taking place between two thinking, living entities (see Figure 8-23).

Intelligent agents are expected to be an important part of the *Semantic Web*—a predicted evolution of the current Web in which all Web content is stored in formats

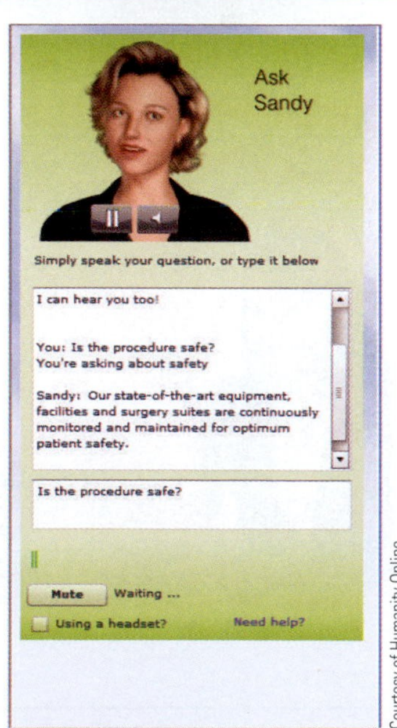

Courtesy of Humanity Online

FIGURE 8-23
A Web page chatterbot.

that are more easily read by software applications and intelligent agents so those tools can perform an increasing number of tasks. To accomplish this, the *semantics* (structure) of the data is defined in a standard manner (using tags and other identifying data). Whether or not the Semantic Web—viewed as part of the next generation *Web 3.0* by some—actually arrives, and arrives in the format in which it is now envisioned, remains to be seen.

Expert Systems

Expert systems are software programs that can make decisions and draw conclusions, similar to a human expert. Expert systems (see Figure 8-24) have two main components: a *knowledge base* (a database that contains facts provided by a human expert and rules that the expert system should use to make decisions based on those facts) and an *inference engine* (a software program that applies the rules to the data stored in the knowledge base in order to reach decisions). For instance, as shown in Figure 8-24, an expert system used to authorize credit for credit card customers would have a knowledge base with facts about customers and rules about credit authorization, such as "Do not automatically authorize purchase if the customer has exceeded his or her credit limit."

Expert systems are widely used for tasks such as diagnosing illnesses, making financial forecasts, scheduling routes for delivery vehicles, diagnosing mechanical problems, and performing credit authorizations. Some expert systems are designed to take the place of human experts, while others are designed to assist them. For instance, medical expert systems are often used to assist physicians with patient diagnoses, suggesting possible diagnoses based on the patient's symptoms and other data supplied to the expert system. Because it has access to an extensive knowledge base, the expert system may provide more possible diagnoses to the attending physician than he or she may have thought of otherwise.

When using an expert system, it is important to realize that its conclusions are based on the data and rules stored in its knowledge base, as well as the information provided by the users. If the expert knowledge is correct, the inference engine program is written correctly, and the user supplies accurate information in response to the questions posed by the expert system, the system will draw correct conclusions; if the knowledge base is wrong, the inference engine is faulty, or the user provides inaccurate input, the system will not work correctly.

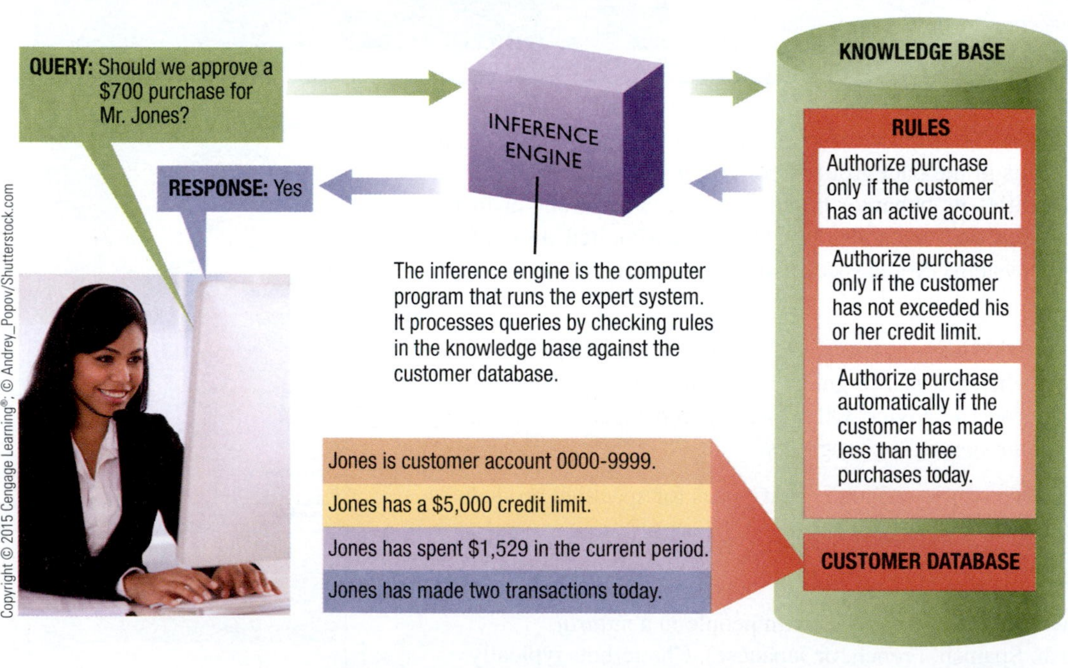
QUERY: Should we approve a $700 purchase for Mr. Jones?
RESPONSE: Yes
INFERENCE ENGINE
The inference engine is the computer program that runs the expert system. It processes queries by checking rules in the knowledge base against the customer database.
KNOWLEDGE BASE
RULES
Authorize purchase only if the customer has an active account.
Authorize purchase only if the customer has not exceeded his or her credit limit.
Authorize purchase automatically if the customer has made less than three purchases today.
CUSTOMER DATABASE
Jones is customer account 0000-9999.
Jones has a $5,000 credit limit.
Jones has spent $1,529 in the current period.
Jones has made two transactions today.
Copyright © 2015 Cengage Learning®; © Andrey_Popov/Shutterstock.com

FIGURE 8-24 An expert system at work.

Neural Networks

Artificial intelligence systems that attempt to imitate the way a human

---

>**Expert system.** A computer system that provides the type of advice that would be expected from a human expert.

brain works are called **neural networks**. Neural networks (also called *neural nets*) are networks of processors that are connected together in a manner similar to the way the neurons in a human brain are connected. They are designed to emulate the brain's pattern-recognition process in order to recognize patterns in data and make more progressive leaps in associations and predictions than conventional computer systems. Neural networks are used in areas such as handwriting, speech, and image recognition; medical imaging; crime analysis; biometric identification (see Figure 8-25); and *vision systems* that use cameras to inspect objects and make determinations—for example, the systems that check products for defects at manufacturing plants or that recognize stamps during postal processing.

Courtesy of Crossmatch

FIGURE 8-25
Neural network systems. Often used in biometric identification systems, such as to analyze fingerprints.

Robotics

Robotics is the field devoted to the study of **robots**—devices, controlled by a person or a computer, that can move and react to sensory input. Robots are widely used by the military and businesses to perform high-precision but monotonous jobs, as well as to perform tasks that are dangerous or impossible for people to perform. There are also robots designed to perform personal tasks for individuals. The appearance of robots varies depending on their purpose, such as robot arms permanently connected to an assembly line, robots built on sturdy mobile platforms designed to travel over rough terrain, robots with fins for water tasks, robots shaped like animals (such as snakes or spiders) for special climbing abilities, and robots that resemble pets or human beings for consumer applications. Robots used for medical and military applications are discussed shortly; robots used for business and consumer applications are discussed next.

Robots are used in business for a variety of purposes, such as for looking for intruders, gas leaks, and other hazards, as well as working on factory assembly lines and other monotonous tasks (see Figure 8-26). Robots are also used for mining coal, repairing oil rigs, locating survivors in collapsed mines and buildings, and other dangerous tasks. They are also used to facilitate videoconferencing and other *remote presence* applications by sitting in for a remote participant and relaying video and audio images to and from that participant. For instance, the videoconferencing robot shown in Figure 8-26 enables remote individuals to more actively participate in meetings and other face-to-face encounters from their current location. In addition, robots are used for service tasks such as search and rescue missions and fighting fires.

There are also a number of *personal robots* available or in development to assist with personal tasks. Some are primarily entertainment robots and are designed to interact with people (such as by reciting phrases, delivering messages, taking photos or video, or singing and dancing). Others, such as the toy robot shown in Figure 8-26, are designed to be toys or companions for children. Still other personal robots are designed for household tasks, such as to mow the lawn (see Figure 8-26) or clean the pool.

Household robots that can assist individuals with more complex tasks, such as putting away the dishes or picking up toys before vacuuming the living room, are a little further in the future—after robot technology improves to allow for better navigation and improved physical manipulation and after prices come down. Expected to have a more *humanoid* form than the household robots currently on the market, these future robots could be used to assist the elderly and wheelchair-bound individuals, in addition to

TIP

Some personal robots can act autonomously once they are assigned a program; others are designed to be controlled remotely—increasingly via smartphones.

> **Neural network.** An expert system in which the human brain's pattern-recognition process is emulated by the computer system.
> **Robotics.** The study of robot technology. > **Robot.** A device, controlled by a human operator or a computer, that can move and react to sensory input.

Photo courtesy of KUKA Robotics Corporation

ASSEMBLY LINE ROBOTS

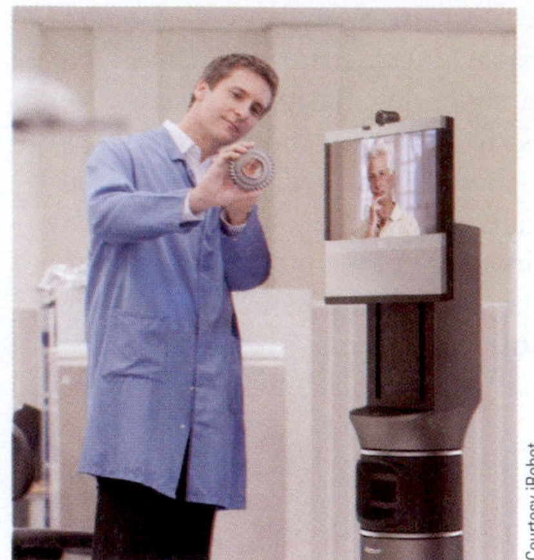
Courtesy iRobot

REMOTE PRESENCE ROBOTS

Courtesy LEGO

TOY ROBOTS

Courtesy Robomow

HELPER ROBOTS

FIGURE 8-26
Business and personal robots.

helping with household tasks. In fact, it has been reported that the South Korean government expects to have at least one robot in every South Korean household by 2020.

Many would agree that the use of robots has numerous benefits to society—such as adding convenience to our lives, replacing human beings for dangerous tasks, and, potentially, monitoring and assisting the disabled and the elderly. But some individuals are concerned that, as true artificial intelligence becomes closer to reality, a class of robots with the potential for great harm could be created. In response, several organizations—including the South Korean government and the European Robotics Research Network (EURON)—are developing standards for robots, users, and manufacturers concerning the appropriate use and development of robots. The U.S. military is also studying ways to ensure robotic soldiers can be programmed to recognize and obey international laws of war and the U.S. military's rules of engagement in order to prevent them from performing acts such as firing on a hospital or crowd of civilians, even if enemy forces are nearby. Regardless of the progress made in implementing controls on robots, the roles robots should take in our society are likely to be debated for quite some time.

TIP

You can download new apps for your personal robots at the *Robot App Store*.

CAUTION CAUTION CAUTION CAUTION CAUTION CAUTION CAUT

While some robots are designed to be durable and used in adverse conditions, remember that robotic devices are electronic. To avoid the risk of electric shock and damage to robotic devices, do not use them in the water or in other adverse conditions unless the instructions specifically state that the action is safe.

TECHNOLOGICAL ADVANCES IN MEDICINE

Technological advances in the area of medicine in the past several years include computers that can analyze test results to identify precancerous cells too small for a person to see, implanted devices that enhance the functions of a current organ (such as cochlear implants that can restore hearing), electronic monitors that detect potentially dangerous medical conditions, and digital cameras the size of a pill that are swallowed to photograph the patient's digestive tract. Other topics in the forefront of medical technology research include *brain-to-computer interfacing* (*BCI*), *telemedicine*, and *telesurgery*.

Brain-to-Computer Interfacing (BCI)

Brain-to-computer interfacing (BCI) is the process of connecting the brain with a computer, such as implanting electrodes directly into the brain or using a headset that wirelessly reads and interprets brainwaves. Medical applications of BCI—such as using it to restore lost functionality to or facilitate the communications of severely disabled individuals—are under development. For instance, after training, a severely paralyzed individual can use BCI to move a mouse, click it to type text, and perform other computer-related tasks using only his or her thoughts—raising the possibility that paralyzed individuals will someday be able to control robot assistants with their thoughts. A recent experiment went one step further—human *brain-to-brain interfacing*. In this experiment, two University of Washington researchers were located in separate labs across campus and each wore a special cap (one to read electrical brain activity and one to stimulate the motor cortex). As the first researcher played a simple video game, using only his mind to visualize his right hand hitting the "fire" button, the second researcher involuntarily moved his right hand to push the spacebar on the keyboard in front of him, as if to hit the "fire" button.

FIGURE 8-27
Examples of telemedicine applications.

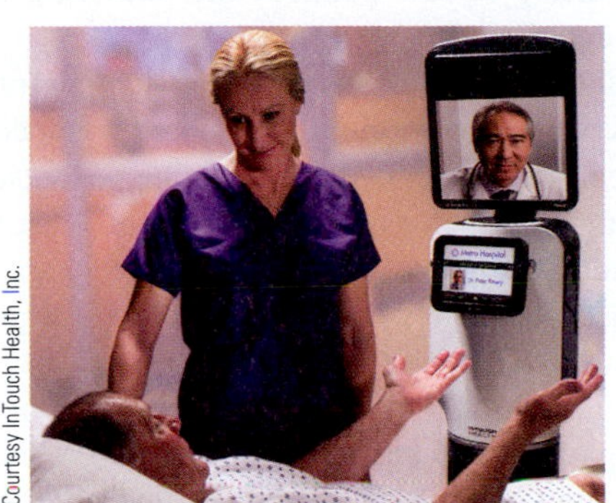

REMOTE CONSULTATIONS
Using remote-controlled teleconferencing robots, physicians can "virtually" consult with patients or other physicians in a different physical location; the robot (left photo) transmits video images and audio to and from the doctor (via his or her computer or mobile device, right photo) in real time.

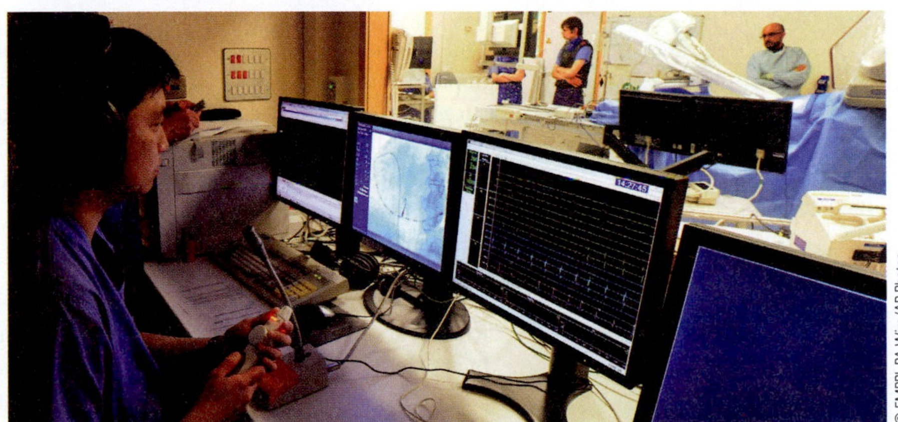

TELESURGERY
Using voice or computer commands, surgeons can perform operations (such as inserting a catheter during the heart surgery shown here) remotely via the Internet or a private network; a robotic system uses the surgeon's commands to physically operate on the patient.

Despite the potential benefits of brain interfacing, there is the concern that this technology could be misused. Medical ethicists are currently working on setting up standards and criteria to ensure that brain implant devices allow, according to medical ethicist Joseph Fins of Cornell University, ". . . patients to have control, not be under control." While the focus of brain interfacing and thought-controlled computers is bringing communications capabilities to the severely disabled, gaming applications are also under development and some researchers foresee the technology someday becoming mainstream—viewing brainwave input as the next step in the evolution of the human-computer input interface.

Telemedicine and Telesurgery

Telemedicine is the use of networking technology to provide medical information and services. At its simplest level, it includes Web sites that patients can access to contact their physicians, make appointments, view lab results, and more. However, more complex telemedicine systems (such as the examples shown in Figure 8-27) are often used to provide care to individuals who may not otherwise have access to that care, such

> **Brain-to-computer interfacing (BCI).** The process of connecting the brain with a computer, such as implanting electrodes directly into the brain or using a headset that wirelessly reads and interprets brainwaves. > **Telemedicine.** The use of networking technology to provide medical information and services.

as allowing individuals living in remote areas to consult with a specialist. For instance, physicians can use videoconferencing robots to communicate remotely with other physicians or with hospitalized patients (see Figure 8-27). Physicians can also use telemedicine to perform remote diagnosis of patients (for example, healthcare workers at rural locations, childcare facilities, and other locations can use video cameras, electronic stethoscopes, and other devices to send images and vital statistics of a patient to a physician located at a medical facility).

Another example of telemedicine is **telesurgery**—a form of *robot-assisted surgery* (where a robot controlled by a physician operates on the patient) in which at least one of the surgeons performs the operation by controlling the robot remotely over the Internet or another network (refer again to Figure 8-27). Robot-assisted surgery systems typically use cameras to give the human surgeon an extremely close view of the surgical area. As a result, robot-assisted surgery is typically more precise and results in smaller incisions than those made by a human surgeon, allowing for less invasive surgery (for example, not having to crack through the rib cage to access the heart) and resulting in less pain for the patient, a faster recovery time, and fewer potential complications.

Telemedicine has enormous potential for providing quality medical care to individuals who live in rural or underdeveloped areas and who do not have access to sufficient medical care. Telemedicine will also be necessary for future long-term space explorations—such as a trip to Mars and back that may take two years or more—because astronauts will undoubtedly need medical care while on the journey. In fact, NASA astronauts and physicians have performed telesurgery experiments in the Aquarius Undersea Laboratory 50 feet below the ocean surface to help in the development of a robotic unit that will eventually allow physicians to perform surgery remotely on patients who are in outer space. Some individuals envision the eventual use of portable robot-assisted telesurgery units in space, war zones, and other environments where access to surgeons is extremely limited.

TECHNOLOGICAL ADVANCES IN THE MILITARY

The U.S. military works on a continual basis with technological and research organizations to improve military equipment, such as weapons, protective gear for soldiers, and surveillance tools. The military is also involved in researching many of the other emerging technologies already discussed, such as nanotechnology and artificial intelligence. Two specific areas of research related to the military—*battlefield robots* and *exoskeleton systems*—are discussed next.

Battlefield Robots

Robots are used extensively by the U.S. military. For instance, **battlefield robots** are used in areas of conflict to investigate caves, buildings, trails, and other locations before soldiers enter them to make sure the locations are safe (see Figure 8-28), and to help soldiers locate and dispose of bombs, landmines, and other explosive devices. In addition to land-based robots, there are also military robots designed for underwater use, such as to detect mines or perform underwater surveillance and reconnaissance, as well as *Unmanned Aerial Vehicles* (*UAVs*) or *drones* (unmanned planes) used to take surveillance photos. Currently, military

>**Telesurgery.** A form of robot-assisted surgery in which the doctor's physical location is different from the patient's and robot's physical location; the doctor controls the robot remotely over the Internet or another network. >**Battlefield robot.** A robot used by the military to ensure that locations are safe prior to sending in soldiers.

robots are controlled remotely by soldiers, though researchers are working on more *autonomous robots* that can navigate on their own, perceiving obstacles and determining their course without continuous directions from a human operator, to accompany soldiers into combat. According to national security expert John Pike, autonomous armed robotic soldiers may become a reality as soon as 2020.

Courtesy of iRobot

BATTLEFIELD ROBOTS
Designed to investigate dangerous, hostile, or inaccessible areas prior to human entry.

Courtesy of Lockheed Martin

EXOSKELETON SYSTEMS
Designed to give soldiers enhanced mobility and endurance while carrying heavy loads.

FIGURE 8-28
Military robotic applications.

Exoskeleton Systems

Another military robotic application is the **exoskeleton suit**, whose name refers to a hard protective or supportive outer structure. Currently being researched and developed by several organizations under grants from the Defense Advanced Research Projects Agency (DARPA), exoskeleton suits are wearable battery-operated robotic systems designed to give an individual additional physical capabilities and protection. For instance, an exoskeleton suit can give a soldier the ability to run faster and carry heavier items than he or she could without the suit—up to 200 pounds at a top speed of 10 mph for the *Human Universal Load Carrier* (*HULC*) exoskeleton suit shown in Figure 8-28. Exoskeleton suits in the future may include additional capabilities, such as being made of bulletproof material that is able to solidify on demand to form a shield or turn into a medical cast if a soldier is injured. Other possible features of an exoskeleton suit include changing its color automatically for camouflage purposes; relaying information via sensors about a soldier's health, injuries, and location to field headquarters; and administering painkillers or applying pressure to a wound when directed by a physician. DARPA is also involved with the development of robotic prosthetic arms that feel, look, and perform like natural arms—these robotic arms will be used by military personnel who are injured in the line of duty.

TIP

It is expected that *personal exoskeleton suits* designed to enhance an individual's abilities (such as to help elderly or disabled individuals walk or lift things more easily) will become available within the next 10 to 15 years.

SOCIETAL IMPLICATIONS OF EMERGING TECHNOLOGY

A new computing technology usually provides many benefits because it normally would not become widely available for consumers if it was not designed to solve a problem or add convenience to our lives. However, not all advances are embraced by all individuals. For instance, security and privacy issues are areas of continual concern with emerging technologies. Potential dangers include trusting "intelligent" computers and robots so much that they become a personal safety hazard, allowing medical technology to enable people to be controlled by others, and spending resources on some areas of research and development that might be better spent elsewhere. Some people also worry that technology is advancing at such a rapid pace that we cannot possibly envision all the potential repercussions until it is too late. It is important to evaluate new and emerging technologies in terms of the entire picture—their benefits, as well as their possible risks and societal implications.

>**Exoskeleton suit.** A wearable robotic system designed to give an individual additional physical capabilities and protection.

SUMMARY

THE COMPUTER OF THE FUTURE

Chapter Objective 1: Describe what the computer of the future might look like, including some examples of emerging types of hardware.

While the exact makeup of future computers is not certain, they will likely continue to get smaller, smarter, and more user-friendly. Portable computers will continue to grow more powerful and useful; home and business computers may be built into furniture, walls, desks, and other objects. Emerging input devices include gesture-based devices; input for consumer applications that may soon become the norm include **two-dimensional (2D) barcodes**, **augmented reality**, and a variety of RFID payment systems. CPU technology is continuing to evolve and it is possible that a form of **nonvolatile RAM (NVRAM)** may eventually replace the RAM we know today. Emerging output devices include *3D display screens*, *pico projectors*, *3D projectors*, *wearable personal displays*, and displays based on variations of **organic light emitting diode (OLED) display** technology. For storage, new formats of USB flash memory drives and flash memory cards are emerging and **holographic storage** is expected to be a viable storage alternative in the near future.

Chapter Objective 2: Understand the effect that emerging computer technologies, such as nanotechnology, quantum computers, and optical computers, may have on the computer of the future.

Future computers will likely be influenced by **nanotechnology** research, which focuses on building computer components at the individual atomic and molecular levels. Both computing and noncomputing products that use **carbon nanotubes (CNTs)** are being developed. **Quantum computing** (which uses atoms or nuclei working together as quantum bits or *qubits*) and **optical computers** (which perform operations using light instead of electrical current) are in the early stages of development.

EMERGING NETWORKING TECHNOLOGIES

Chapter Objective 3: Name some emerging wired and wireless networking technologies.

Improvements are being made on a continual basis to wired and wireless networking technologies to increase speed and connectivity options, and to support an ever-growing number of new applications. Faster versions of the *Ethernet* standard are under development, and **Power over Ethernet (PoE)**—which sends both electrical power and data over Ethernet cables—is a relatively new option. For easy home networks, the *Phoneline* or *Powerline* standards can be used; a standard for delivering Internet over existing power lines *is broadband over power lines* (*BPL*).

New versions of the **Wi-Fi (802.11)** standard for wireless networks (such as for improved speed and security) are being developed on a regular basis. **Wi-Fi Direct** enables Wi-Fi devices to be connected directly, without additional hardware. **WiMAX (802.16)** is an emerging wireless standard with a greater range than Wi-Fi; *mobile WiMAX* is a version of WiMAX designed for use with mobile phones and other mobile devices. **Bluetooth** can be used for very short-range applications (such as wirelessly connecting a keyboard to a computer), though **wireless USB** is a new option. Several new wireless standards—such as *Ultra Wideband* (*UWB*) and *wirelessHD* (*WiHD*) are designed for wirelessly delivering multimedia content between computers, TVs, digital cameras, DVD players, and other consumer devices.

ARTIFICIAL INTELLIGENCE (AI)

Chapter Objective 4: Explain what is meant by the term *artificial intelligence* (AI) and list some AI applications.

When a computer performs in ways that would be considered intelligent if observed in people, this is referred to as **artificial intelligence (AI)**. Some of the earliest advances in AI were in the area of chess; the most common test for AI is the *Turning Test*. One AI application is the **intelligent agent**. Examples include *application assistants*, *search agents*, *shopping bots*, *entertainment bots*, and *chatterbots*. Intelligent agents typically act as *virtual assistants* and modify their behavior based on the user's actions. They are frequently built into application programs and operating systems and are beginning to be used on Web pages. Some—like many chatterbots—use a *natural language interface*.

Expert systems perform tasks that would otherwise be performed by a human expert, such as diagnosing medical conditions, making financial forecasts, and performing credit authorizations. Expert systems use a *knowledge base* (a database containing specific facts and rules about the expert area) and an *inference engine* (a software program used to apply rules to the data stored in the knowledge base to reach decisions).

Neural networks and *robotics* are two other areas of artificial intelligence. A neural network is an AI system that tries to imitate the way the human brain works and is typically used for pattern recognition, such as speech analysis, crime analysis, and biometric identification. **Robotics** is the study of **robots**—devices, controlled by a person or a computer, that can move and react to sensory input. Robots are commonly used for repetitive and dangerous tasks; they are also being used for household tasks, for entertainment purposes, and to assist with business and personal tasks.

TECHNOLOGICAL ADVANCES IN MEDICINE

Chapter Objective 5:
List some new and upcoming technological advances in medicine.

Technological advances in recent years include computers that analyze test results, implanted devices that assist an organ's functioning, and digital cameras that can be ingested to record images of a person's digestive tract. **Brain-to-computer interfacing (BCI)** is the process of connecting the brain with a computer, such as implanting electrodes directly into the brain or using a headset that wirelessly reads and interprets brainwaves, and may eventually enable paralyzed individuals to control robot assistants with only their thoughts. These and similar technological advances in medicine are embraced by some but are not without controversy.

Telemedicine is the use of communications technology to provide medical information and services and can take a variety of forms. One application is **telesurgery**—a form of *robot-assisted surgery* where a robot (controlled by a physician) operates on a patient. With telesurgery, the robot is controlled remotely, such as over the Internet. Robots can use smaller incisions in some types of surgeries, which results in less pain for the patient and a faster recovery period. Other forms of telemedicine include remote professional consultations and diagnosis, such as via a videoconferencing system.

TECHNOLOGICAL ADVANCES IN THE MILITARY

Chapter Objective 6:
Name some new and upcoming technological advances in the military.

Recent and expected future technological advances in the military include newly designed weapons, protective gear, and surveillance tools. Surveillance tools in the future may include an increased use of **battlefield robots** and the use of *autonomous robots* that can navigate on their own. The uniform of the future may include an **exoskeleton suit**—a wearable robotic system that not only protects the user but also gives him or her additional physical capabilities.

SOCIETAL IMPLICATIONS OF EMERGING TECHNOLOGY

Chapter Objective 7:
Discuss potential societal implications of emerging technologies.

There are many potential societal implications associated with emerging technologies, such as unexpected results, trusting "intelligent" computers and robots so much that they become a personal safety hazard, and allowing medical technology to enable people to be controlled by others. Because virtually any new technology could be used for both good and evil, we need to weigh the societal risks and benefits of emerging technologies in order to make educated and informed decisions about what we would like our lives and society to be like.

REVIEW ACTIVITIES

KEY TERM MATCHING

a. artificial intelligence (AI)

b. augmented reality

c. exoskeleton suit

d. expert system

e. nanotechnology

f. neural network

g. optical computer

h. robot

i. telemedicine

j. WiMAX (802.16)

Instructions: Match each key term on the left with the definition on the right that best describes it.

1. ________ A computer system that provides the type of advice that would be expected from a human expert.

2. ________ A computer that uses light, such as from laser beams or infrared beams, to perform digital computations.

3. ________ A device, controlled by a human operator or a computer, that can move and react to sensory input.

4. ________ A wireless networking standard that is faster and has a greater range than Wi-Fi.

5. ________ An expert system in which the human brain's pattern-recognition process is emulated by the computer system.

6. ________ A wearable robotic system designed to give an individual additional physical capabilities and protection.

7. ________ The science of creating tiny computers and components by working at the individual atomic and molecular levels.

8. ________ The use of networking technology to provide medical information and services.

9. ________ When a computer performs actions that are characteristic of human intelligence.

10. ________ When computer generated images are overlayed on top of real-time images, such as to overlay information over the photo or video displayed on a smartphone.

SELF-QUIZ

Instructions: Circle **T** if the statement is true, **F** if the statement is false, or write the best answer in the space provided. **Answers for the self-quiz are located in the References and Resources Guide at the end of the book.**

1. T F Two-dimensional (2D) barcodes can store more data than conventional one-dimensional barcodes.

2. T F Nonvolatile RAM (NVRAM) chips do not lose their contents when the power to the computer is turned off.

3. T F Computers that process data with light are referred to as quantum computers.

4. T F Wi-Fi Direct is a wireless version of USB designed to connect peripheral devices.

5. T F One advantage of robot-assisted surgery is faster recovery time.

6. In quantum computing, ________ (which can represent more than two possible states) are used instead of electronic bits.

7. Many products today use carbon ________, which are a by-product of nanotechnology research.

8. ________ is a wired networking standard that allows electrical power to be sent along with data over standard Ethernet cables.

9. A(n) ________ is an expert system in which the human brain's pattern-recognition process is emulated by the computer system.
10. A ________ robot is used by the military in combat, such as to ensure locations are safe prior to sending in soldiers.

EXERCISES

1. For the following list of emerging devices or technologies, write the appropriate letter (I, P, O, S, or C) in the space provided to indicate whether each device or technology is used for input (I), processing (P), output (O), storage (S), or communications (C).

   a. ________ WiGig
   b. ________ OLED
   c. ________ 2D barcode
   d. ________ PMR
   e. ________ NVRAM
   f. ________ IMOD

2. Supply the missing words to complete the following statements.

   a. ________ storage systems use multiple blue laser beams to store data in three dimensions.

   b. ________ is a form of robot-assisted surgery in which the doctor's physical location is different from the patient's and robot's physical location and the doctor controls the robot remotely over the Internet or another communications medium.

3. Write the number of the networking standard that best matches each of the following descriptions in the blank to the left of each description.

   a. ________ Used to create a wired home or business network.
   b. ________ Used to create a home network via existing telephone jacks.
   c. ________ Used to send power along with data over networking cables.
   d. ________ Used to connect peripheral devices to a mobile phone or computer.

   1. PoE
   2. Bluetooth
   3. Ethernet
   4. Phoneline

4. Would an OLED display or an LCD display use more battery power? Explain why.
5. Would Wi-Fi or WirelessHD be better for wirelessly networking two computers within a home? Explain.

DISCUSSION QUESTIONS

1. More and more everyday devices—including cars and other vehicles—are being controlled by computers. There are advantages, such as avoiding possible driver errors and the ability to change the speed of or reroute trains automatically to avoid collisions. But are there potential risks, as well? For example, Thailand's Finance Minister once had to be rescued from inside his limousine after the onboard computer malfunctioned, leaving the vehicle immobilized and the door locks, power windows, and air conditioning not functioning. Do you think the benefits of increased automation of devices that could put us in danger if they malfunction outweigh the risks? What types of safeguards should be incorporated into computer-controlled cars, subway trains, and other automated vehicles? What about medication dispensers and other automated medical devices?

2. Interference with wireless devices is happening much more often than in the past. For instance, unlicensed walkie-talkies used on TV sets have interfered with police radios, and British air traffic control transmissions have been interrupted by transmissions from nearby baby monitors. If devices that use unlicensed radio frequencies interfere with each other, whose fault is it? The individual for buying multiple products that use the same radio frequency? The manufacturers for not ensuring their products can switch channels as needed to use a free channel? The government for allowing unregulated airwaves? Is there a solution to this problem? Who, if anyone, should be responsible for fixing this problem?

PROJECTS

HOT TOPICS

1. **WiMAX vs. Wi-Fi** As discussed in the chapter, WiMAX and Wi-Fi are both wireless networking standards.

   For this project, research WiMAX and Wi-Fi to determine their current status and the differences between the two standards. Are they designed for the same or different purposes? Explain. How are they being used today? Home networks? Business networks? Hotspots? College campuses? Mobile phone calls? Do you think the standards will coexist in the future, or will one eventually replace the other? At the conclusion of your research, prepare a one-page summary of your findings and opinions and submit it to your instructor.

SHORT ANSWER/ RESEARCH

2. **Today's Robots** As discussed in the chapter, robots can be used today for a variety of activities in businesses and the military, as well as in the home.

   For this project, select one type of robotic device on the market today—for instance, a robotic toy, vacuum cleaner, or lawn mower; a security or manufacturing robot; a robot used by the military or NASA; a robot used by law enforcement agencies; or a robotic personal assistant—and research it. Find out what the product does, what it costs, how it is powered and controlled, and if it can be reprogrammed. What are the advantages of the robotics part of the product? Do you think this is a worthwhile or beneficial product? At the conclusion of your research, prepare a one- to two-page summary of your findings and opinions and submit it to your instructor.

HANDS ON

3. **Cloud Storage** There are a number of cloud storage services (such as ADrive, Microsoft SkyDrive, Google Drive, and Box) designed to allow individuals to back up files online and share specific files with others; specialty online storage services designed for digital photo sharing include Flickr, Photobucket, and SnapFish.

   For this project, visit at least one cloud storage site designed for backup and file exchange, and at least one site designed for digital photo sharing. You can try the sites listed above or use a search site to find alternative sites. Tour your selected sites to determine the features each service offers, the cost, the amount of storage space available, and the options for sending uploaded files to others. Do the sites password-protect your files, or are they available for anyone with an Internet connection to see? What are the benefits for using these types of storage services? Can you think of any drawbacks? Would you want to use any of the storage sites you visited? Why or why not? At the conclusion of this task, prepare a short summary of your findings and submit it to your instructor.

ETHICS IN ACTION

4. **Emotion Recognition Software** An emerging application is *emotion recognition software*, which uses camera input to try to read people's current emotion. The first expected application of such a system is for ATM machines because they already have cameras installed. Possibilities include changing the advertising display based on the customer's emotional response to displayed advertising, and enlarging the screen text if the customer appears to be squinting. Is it ethical for businesses using emotion recognition software to read the emotions of citizens without their consent? Proponents of the technology argue that it is no different than when human tellers or store clerks interpret customers' emotions and modify their treatment of the customer accordingly. Do you agree? Why or why not? Is this a worthy new technology or just a potential invasion of privacy? Would you object to using an ATM machine with emotion-recognition capabilities? Why or why not?

   For this project, form an opinion about the ethical ramifications of emotion recognition systems and be prepared to discuss your position (in class, via an online class discussion group, in a class chat room, or via a class blog, depending on your instructor's directions). You may also be asked to write a short paper expressing your opinion.

PRESENTATION/ DEMONSTRATION

5. **Wired Home Network** If you have two or more computers at home and want to share files, an Internet connection, or a printer, you will need to set up a home network. Although a wireless network is an option, wired networks still exist and new options for wired networks are emerging.

   For this project, suppose that you want to set up a wired home network. Create a scenario (real or fictitious) that describes the number of computers and other devices involved, where each item is located, and the tasks for which the network will be used. Select a wired networking option (such as Ethernet, Powerline, or Phoneline) and determine the steps and equipment necessary to implement that network for your scenario. Be sure to include the cost of the necessary hardware and how the network would be physically installed. Share your findings (including a diagram of your proposed network) with your class in the form of a presentation. The presentation should not exceed 10 minutes and should make use of one or more presentation aids, such as a whiteboard, handouts, or a computer-based slide presentation (your instructor may provide additional requirements). You may also be asked to submit a summary of the presentation to your instructor.

BALANCING ACT

6. **Should Unlicensed Drivers Be Allowed to Use Self-Driving Cars?** As discussed in the chapter, self-driving cars are getting closer to becoming a reality. While currently in the testing stage, consumer products could be on the market soon. In anticipation, states are beginning to determine regulations for these vehicles. One of the biggest questions is whether or not a licensed driver will be required to be in the vehicle. One could argue that a human driver isn't necessary once self-driving cars are declared safe and legal and not requiring one would create one new benefit—the ability of unlicensed drivers (such as visually-impaired individuals and underage children) to be safely and legally transported without the use of a licensed driver. But should these individuals be allowed to use self-driving cars? Will we ever be certain enough that autonomous cars are safe to eliminate the need for a human being to be available to take control of the car if needed? Is it discrimination if unlicensed individuals aren't allowed to use these cars? If a licensed driver is required, what if that individual is intoxicated or under the influence of drugs—should that be illegal even if the car is driving? Should autonomous cars be allowed to run errands alone, such as picking up a pizza or parking the car after the passengers get out? Would you feel comfortable being driven by an autonomous car? Why or why not?

   Pick a side on this issue, form an opinion and gather supporting evidence, and be prepared to discuss and defend your position in a classroom debate or in a 1–2 page paper, depending on your instructor's directions.

REFERENCES AND RESOURCES GUIDE

INTRODUCTION

When working on a computer or taking a computer course, you often need to look up information related to computers, smartphones, and other devices. For instance, you may need to find out when the IBM PC was first invented, you may want tips about what to consider when buying a new device, or you may want to find out more about how numbering systems work. To help you with the tasks just mentioned and more, this References and Resources Guide brings together in one convenient location a collection of technology-related references and resources.

OUTLINE

COMPUTER HISTORY TIMELINE

The earliest recorded calculating device, the abacus, is believed to have been invented by the Babylonians sometime between 500 B.C. and 100 B.C. It and similar types of counting boards were used solely for counting.

500 B.C.

Blaise Pascal invented the first mechanical calculator, called the Pascaline Arithmetic Machine. It had the capacity for eight digits and could add and subtract.

1642

Dr. John V. Atanasoff and Clifford Berry designed and built ABC (for Atanasoff-Berry Computer), the world's first electronic, digital computer.

1937

Precomputers and Early Computers

1621

The slide rule, a precursor to the electronic calculator, was invented. Used primarily to perform multiplication, division, square roots, and the calculation of logarithms, its widespread use continued until the 1970s.

1804

French silk weaver Joseph-Marie Jacquard built a loom that read holes punched on a series of small sheets of hardwood to control the weave of the pattern. This automated machine introduced the use of punch cards and showed that they could be used to convey a series of instructions.

1944

The Mark I, considered to be the first digital computer, was introduced by IBM. It was developed in cooperation with Harvard University, was more than 50 feet long, weighed almost five tons, and used electromechanical relays to solve addition problems in less than a second; multiplication and division took about 6 and 12 seconds, respectively.

Precomputers and Early Computers (before approximately 1945)

Most precomputers and early computers were mechanical machines that worked with gears and levers. Electromechanical devices (using both electricity and gears and levers) were developed toward the end of this era.

First Generation (approximately 1946–1957)

Powered by vacuum tubes, these computers were faster than electromechanical machines, but they were large and bulky, generated excessive heat, and had to be physically wired and reset to run programs. Input was primarily on punch cards; output was on punch cards or paper. Machine and assembly languages were used to program these computers.

First Generation | Second Generation | Third Generation

1947

John Bardeen, Walter Brattain, and William Shockley invented the transistor, which had the same capabilities as a vacuum tube but was faster, broke less often, used less power, and created less heat. They won a Nobel Prize for their invention in 1956 and computers began to be built with transistors shortly afterwards.

1951

The UNIVAC 1, the first computer to be mass produced for general use, was introduced by Remington Rand. In 1952, it was used to analyze votes in the U.S. presidential election and correctly predicted that Dwight D. Eisenhower would be the victor only 45 minutes after the polls closed, though the results were not aired immediately because they weren't trusted.

1957

The FORTRAN programming language was introduced.

1960

The COBOL programming language was developed by a committee headed by Dr. Grace Hopper.

1964

The first mouse was invented by Doug Engelbart.

The IBM System/360 computer was introduced. Unlike previous computers, System/360 contained a full line of compatible computers, making upgrading easier.

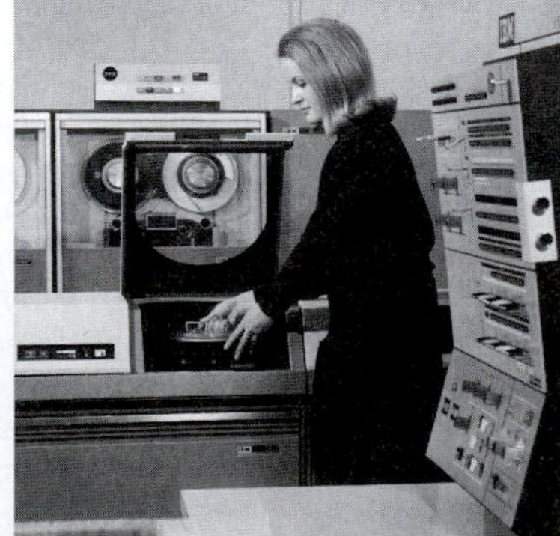

1967

The first floppy disk (8 inches in diameter) was introduced.

1968

Robert Noyce and Gordon Moore founded the Intel Corporation.

1969

UNIX was developed at AT&T's Bell Laboratories; Advanced Micro Devices (AMD) was formed; and ARPANET (the predecessor of today's Internet) was established.

IBM unbundled some of its hardware and software and began selling them separately, allowing other software companies to emerge.

Second Generation (approximately 1958–1963)

Second-generation computers used transistors instead of vacuum tubes. They allowed the computer to be physically smaller, more powerful, more reliable, and faster than before. Input was primarily on punch cards and magnetic tape; output was on punch cards and paper; and magnetic tape and disks were used for storage. High-level programming languages were used with these computers.

Third Generation (approximately 1964–1970)

The third generation of computers evolved when integrated circuits (IC)—computer chips—began being used instead of conventional transistors. Computers became even smaller and more reliable. Keyboards and monitors were introduced for input and output; magnetic disks were used for storage. The emergence of the operating system meant that operators no longer had to manually reset relays and wiring.

The first microprocessor, the Intel 4004, was designed by Ted Hoff. The single processor contained 2,250 transistors and could execute 60,000 operations per second.

1971

Bill Gates and Paul Allen wrote a version of BASIC for the Altair, the first computer programming language designed for a personal computer. Bill Gates dropped out of Harvard to form Microsoft with Paul Allen.

1975

Software Arts' Visi-Calc, the first electronic spreadsheet and business program for personal computers, was released. This program is seen as one of the reasons personal computers first became widely accepted in the business world.

1979

IBM introduced the IBM PC. This DOS-based PC used a 4.77 MHz 8088 CPU with 64 KB of RAM and quickly became the standard for business personal computers.

1981

Fourth Generation

1972

The C programming language was developed by Dennis Ritchie at Bell Labs.

Seymour Cray, called the "father of supercomputing," founded Cray Research, which would go on to build some of the fastest computers in the world.

1976

Steve Wozniak and Steve Jobs founded Apple computer and released the Apple I (a single-board computer), followed by the Apple II (a complete personal computer that became an instant success in 1977). They originally ran the company out of Jobs' parents' garage.

1980

Sony Electronics introduced the 3.5-inch floppy disk and drive.

Seagate Technology announced the first Winchester 5.25-inch hard disk drive, revolutionizing computer storage.

IBM chose Microsoft to develop the operating system for its upcoming personal computer. That operating system was PC-DOS.

1982

Intel introduced the 80286 CPU.

TIME magazine named the computer its "Machine of the Year" for 1982, emphasizing the importance of the computer in our society.

Fourth Generation (approximately 1971–present)

The fourth generation of computers began with large-scale integration (LSI), which resulted in chips that could contain thousands of transistors. Very large-scale integration (VLSI) resulted in the microprocessor and the resulting microcomputers. The keyboard and mouse are predominant input devices, though many other types of input devices are now available; monitors and printers provide output; and storage is obtained with magnetic disks, optical discs, and memory chips.

1983

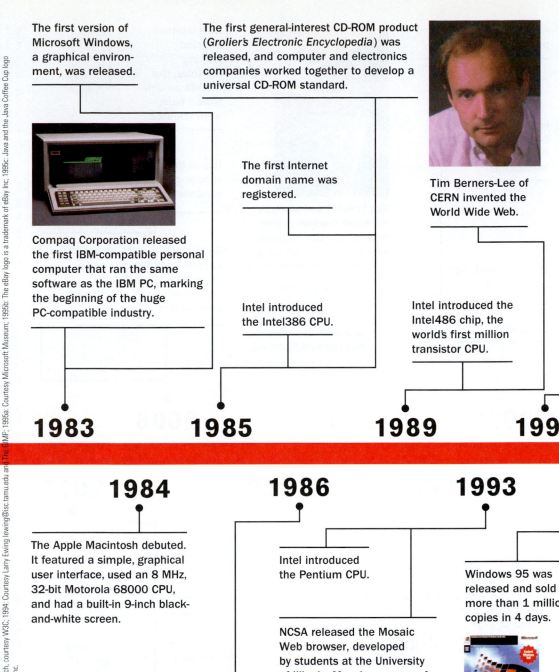

The first version of Microsoft Windows, a graphical environment, was released.

Compaq Corporation released the first IBM-compatible personal computer that ran the same software as the IBM PC, marking the beginning of the huge PC-compatible industry.

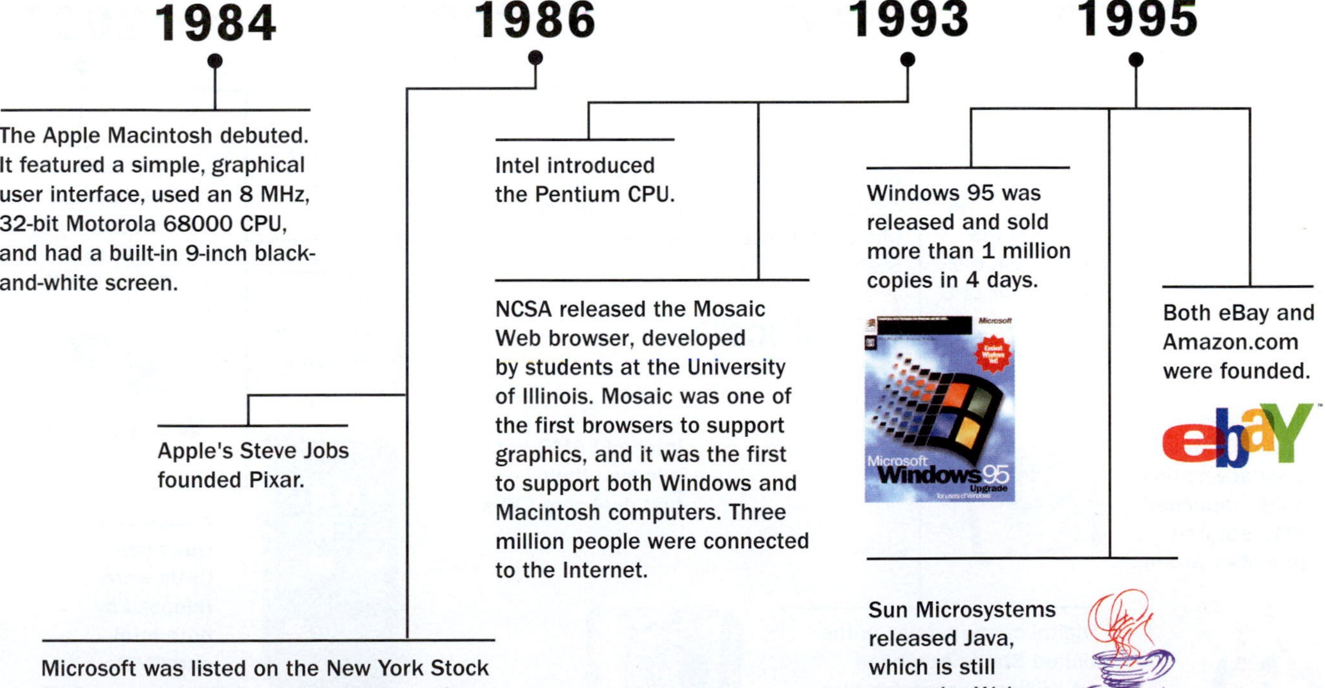

1984

The Apple Macintosh debuted. It featured a simple, graphical user interface, used an 8 MHz, 32-bit Motorola 68000 CPU, and had a built-in 9-inch black-and-white screen.

1985

The first general-interest CD-ROM product (*Grolier's Electronic Encyclopedia*) was released, and computer and electronics companies worked together to develop a universal CD-ROM standard.

The first Internet domain name was registered.

Intel introduced the Intel386 CPU.

1986

Apple's Steve Jobs founded Pixar.

Microsoft was listed on the New York Stock Exchange and began to sell shares to the public; Bill Gates became one of the world's youngest billionaires.

1989

Tim Berners-Lee of CERN invented the World Wide Web.

Intel introduced the Intel486 chip, the world's first million transistor CPU.

1993

Intel introduced the Pentium CPU.

NCSA released the Mosaic Web browser, developed by students at the University of Illinois. Mosaic was one of the first browsers to support graphics, and it was the first to support both Windows and Macintosh computers. Three million people were connected to the Internet.

1994

Linus Torvalds created Linux, which launched the open source revolution. The penguin logo/mascot soon followed.

1995

Windows 95 was released and sold more than 1 million copies in 4 days.

Both eBay and Amazon.com were founded.

Sun Microsystems released Java, which is still a popular Web programming language.

1997

The number of Internet users worldwide surpassed 100 million.

1983: Courtesy, Hewlett-Packard Company; 1989: Fabian Bachrach, courtesy W3C; 1994: Courtesy Larry Ewing lewing@isc.tamu.edu and The GIMP; 1995a: Courtesy Microsoft Museum; 1995b: The eBay logo is a trademark of eBay Inc; 1995c: Java and the Java Coffee Cup logo are trademarks or registered trademarks of Sun Microsystems, Inc.

1998

Apple released the iMac, a modernized version of the Macintosh computer. Its futuristic design helped to make this computer immensely popular.

Microsoft shipped Windows 98.

2000

The first USB flash drives were released.

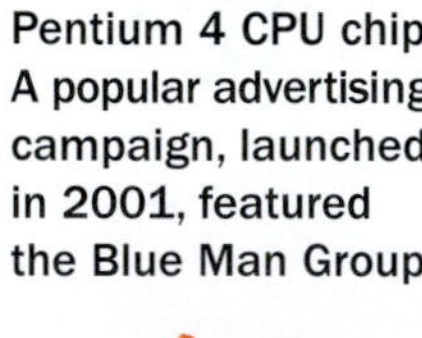

Intel introduced its Pentium 4 CPU chip. A popular advertising campaign, launched in 2001, featured the Blue Man Group.

2001

Apple introduced the iPod personal music player.

Intel's first 64-bit CPU, the Itanium, was introduced.

Microsoft released its XP line of products, including Windows XP and Office XP.

2003

AMD released the 64-bit Opteron server CPU and the Athlon 64, the first 64-bit CPU designed for desktop computer use.

Microsoft shipped the Office 2003 editions of its Microsoft Office System.

Digital camera sales in the United States exceeded 14 million, surpassing film camera sales for the first time.

2004

The Internet and wireless networks enabled people to work and communicate with others while on the go.

Spyware became a major problem; some studies indicated that over 80% of computers had spyware installed.

2005

Phishing and identity theft became household words.

Intel and AMD both released their first dual-core CPUs.

2006

New Internet-enabled gaming consoles, like the Wii console shown here, were released.

Use of the Internet for online shopping and entertainment continued to grow.

Broadband Internet access approached the norm and improvements to wireless networking (such as WiMAX) continued to be developed.

2007

Twitter was launched.

Apple released the revolutionary iPhone.

Microsoft released Windows Vista and Office 2007.

Quad-core CPUs were released by both Intel and AMD.

Netbooks were introduced.

Google introduced the Chrome Web browser.

Use of social networking sites exploded; Facebook announced it had more than 100 million users.

2008

Microsoft Office 2010

Microsoft released Office 2010, which included cloud versions for the first time.

Microsoft introduced Kinect, the first controller-free interface for a gaming console; voice and movement are used instead.

Apple released the iPad, which started a mobile tablet trend.

2010

Windows 8 Office 365 Microsoft released Windows 8, Office 2013, and Office 365.

The availability and use of Android phones and media tablets soared.

Pinterest

Pinterest became available.

facebook

Social media took off; Facebook hit 1 billion active users.

iPad mini was released.

2012

Fifth Generation

2009

Geobrowsing applications became more prominent; 4G phones became available.

Cloud computing entered the mainstream for both individuals and businesses.

Microsoft released Windows 7.

Notebooks outsold desktops.

2011

Supercomputer Watson beat human players in *Jeopardy!*.

Amazon sold more e-books than print books and released Kindle Fire, the first color e-book reader.

The first Chromebooks become available.

Apple founder Steve Jobs passed away at the age of 56.

2013

Google Glass became available.

More than half of all U.S. adults owned a smartphone; Apple released the iPhone 5s and iOS 7.

Touch computing became common with a variety of devices, including desktop PCs.

HTML5 took off and started to change the way Web pages were developed.

Fifth Generation (now and the future)

The fifth generation of computers is in its infancy stage. Today, they tend to be based on artificial intelligence and include voice and touch input. In the future, they are expected to be constructed differently, such as in the form of optical computers, tiny computers that utilize nanotechnology, and as general-purpose computers built into desks, home appliances, and other everyday devices.

GUIDE TO BUYING A PC

Before buying a new computer or other computing device, it is important to give some thought to what your needs are, including what software you want to run, any other devices with which you need to be compatible, how you might want to connect to the Internet, and how much portability is needed. This section of the References and Resources Guide explores topics related to buying a new personal computing device. ■

Analyzing Needs

When referring to a computing device, a need refers to a functional requirement that the device must be able to meet. For example, at a video rental store, a computer system must be able to enter barcodes automatically from videos or DVDs being checked in and out, identify customers with overdue movies, manage movie inventories, and do routine accounting operations. Portability is another example of a possible need. For example, if you need to take your device with you as you travel or work out of the office, you will need a portable computer or a media tablet instead of a desktop computer.

Selecting a device for home or business use must begin with the all-important question "What do I want the device to do?" Once you have determined what tasks it will be used for and the amount of portability that is needed, you can choose among the software and hardware alternatives available. Making a list of your needs in the areas discussed in the next few sections can help you get a picture of what type of system you are shopping for. If you are not really sure what you want a system to do, you should think twice about buying one—you can easily make expensive mistakes if you are uncertain about what you want a system to do. Some common decision categories are discussed next; Figure R-1 provides a list of questions that can help you define the type of device that will meet your needs.

FIGURE R-1
Questions to consider when getting ready to buy a computing device.

POSSIBLE QUESTIONS

- What tasks will I be using the device for (writing papers, accessing the Internet, watching TV, making phone and video calls, composing music, playing games, etc.)?
- Do I have an operating system preference? Are there any other devices I need my documents and storage media to be compatible with?
- How fast do I need the system to be?
- Do I need portability? If so, do I need a powerful desktop replacement notebook or will a less-powerful notebook or a media tablet suffice?
- What size screen do I need? Do I need to be able to connect to a second monitor or an HDTV set?
- What removable storage media will I need to use (such as DVDs, flash memory cards, or USB flash drives)?
- What types of Internet access will I be using (such as DSL, cable, satellite, or mobile wireless)?
- What types of networks will I need to connect to (wired, Wi-Fi, cellular)? What type of network adapter is needed to connect to those networks?
- What additional hardware do I need (scanner, printer, wireless router, digital camera, notebook stand, or tablet stand, for example)?
- What brand(s) do I prefer? When do I need the device?
- Do I want to pay extra for a better warranty (such as a longer time period, more comprehensive coverage, or on-site service)?

Application Software Decisions

Determining what functions you want the system to perform will also help you decide which software is needed. Most users start with an application suite containing a word processor, spreadsheet, and other programs—either installed or cloud software. In addition, specialty programs or apps, such as tax preparation, drawing, home publishing, reference software, games, and more, may be needed or desired.

Not all software is available for all operating systems. Consequently, if a specific piece of software is needed, that choice may determine which operating system you need to use. In addition, your operating system and application software decisions may already be made for you if your documents need to be compatible with those of another computer (such as other office computers or between a home and an office computer).

Platforms and Configuration Options

If your operating system has already been determined, that is a good start in deciding the overall platform you will be looking for—most users will choose between the PC-compatible and Apple Macintosh platforms. PC-compatible computers usually run either Windows or Linux; Apple computers almost always use Mac OS. Mobile devices typically run either Android or iOS.

Configuration decisions initially involve determining the size of the device desired (see Figure R-2). For nonportable systems, you have the choice between tower, desktop, or all-in-one configurations; in addition, the monitor size needs to be determined. Fully functioning personal computers can be notebook or tablet computers. For tablet computers, you need to decide if you will require keyboard use on a regular basis; if so, a hybrid notebook-tablet computer would be the best choice. If a powerful fully functioning computer is not required, you may decide to go with an even more portable option, such as a netbook or media tablet.

You should also consider any other specifications that are important to you, such as the size and type of internal storage (hard drive or flash memory media, for instance), types of other storage devices needed, amount of memory required, and so forth. As discussed in the next section, these decisions often require reconciling the features you want with the amount of money you are willing to spend.

Courtesy Lenovo

DESKTOPS

Courtesy Apple

NOTEBOOKS

Courtesy Lenovo

HYBRID NOTEBOOK-TABLETS

Courtesy of Samsung

MEDIA TABLETS

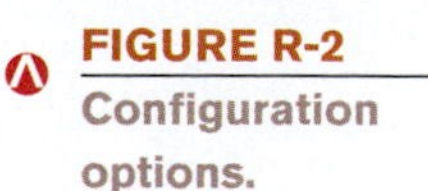
FIGURE R-2
Configuration options.

Power vs. Budget Requirements

As part of the needs analysis, you should look closely at your need for a powerful system versus your budgetary constraints. Most users do not need a state-of-the-art system. Those who do should expect to pay more than the average user. A device that was top of the line six months or a year ago is usually reasonably priced and more than adequate for most users' needs. Individuals who want a device only for basic tasks, such as using the Internet and word processing, can likely get by with an inexpensive device designed for home use.

When determining your requirements, be sure to identify the features and functions that are absolutely essential for your primary computing tasks (such as a large hard drive and lots of memory for multimedia applications, a fast video card for gaming, a fast Internet connection, a TV tuner card for individuals who want to use the computer as a TV set, and so forth). After you have the minimum configuration determined, you can add optional or desirable components, as your budget allows.

Listing Alternatives

After you consider your needs and the questions mentioned in Figure R-1, you should have a pretty good idea of the hardware and software you will need. You will also know what purchasing options are available to you, depending on your time frame (while some retail stores have systems that can be purchased and brought home the same day, special orders or some systems purchased online will take longer). The next step is to get enough information from possible vendors to compare and contrast a few alternative systems that satisfy your stated needs. Most often, these vendors are local stores (such as computer stores, warehouse clubs, and electronic stores) and/or online stores (such as manufacturer Web sites and *e-tailers*—online retailers). To compare prices and specifications for possible systems, find at least three systems that meet or exceed your needs by looking through newspaper advertisements, configuring systems online via manufacturer and e-tailer Web sites, or calling or visiting local stores. A comparison sheet listing your criteria and the systems you are considering, such as the one in Figure R-3, can help you summarize your options. Although it is sometimes very difficult to compare the prices of systems since they typically have somewhat different configurations and some components (such as CPUs) are difficult to compare, you can assign an approximate dollar value to each extra feature a system has (such as $50 for an included printer or a larger hard drive). Be sure to also include any sales tax and shipping charges when you compare the prices of each total system.

COMPONENT	EXAMPLE OF DESIRED SPECIFICATIONS	SYSTEM #1 VENDOR:	SYSTEM #2 VENDOR:	SYSTEM #3 VENDOR:
Type of device	Notebook computer			
Operating system	Windows 8			
Manufacturer	Sony or Dell			
CPU	Intel quad core			
RAM	8 GB or higher			
Hard drive	2 TB or higher			
Removable storage	Flash memory card reader			
Optical drive	Blu-ray Disc drive			
Monitor	Widescreen 17"; touch screen			
Video card and video RAM	Prefer video card and HDMI			
Keyboard/mouse	Portable USB mouse with scroll wheel			
Sound card/speakers	No preference			
Modem	None			
Networking	Wi-Fi (802.11ac); Bluetooth			
Printer	Laser if get a good package deal			
Included software	Microsoft Office 365			
Warranty	3 years min.			
Other features	3 USB ports minimum			
Price				
Tax				
Shipping				
TOTAL COST				

FIGURE R-3
Comparing computing alternatives. A checklist such as this one can help to organize your desired criteria and evaluate possible systems.

If your budget is limited, you will have to balance the system you need with extra features you may want. But do not skimp on memory or hard drive space because sufficient memory can help your programs to run faster and with fewer problems and hard drive space is consumed quickly. Often for just a few extra dollars, you can get additional memory, a faster CPU, or a larger hard drive, which is significantly cheaper than trying to upgrade any of those features later. A good rule of thumb is to try to buy a little higher system than you think you need. On the other hand, do not buy a top-of-the-line system unless you fall into the power user category and really need it. Generally, the second or third system down from the top of the line is a very good system for a much more reasonable price. Some guidelines for minimum requirements for a new computer for most home users are as follows:

- A relatively fast multi-core CPU.
- 6 GB of RAM for desktop and notebook users.
- 500 GB or more hard drive space.
- Recordable or rewritable DVD or Blu-ray Disc drive.
- Network adapter or modem for the desired type(s) of Internet access.
- Sound card and speakers; built-in webcam and microphone.
- At least 2 USB ports.
- A built-in flash memory media reader.

A LOOK AT NUMBERING SYSTEMS

As discussed in Chapter 2 of this text, a numbering system is a way of representing numbers. People generally use the *decimal numbering system* explained in Chapter 2 and reviewed next; computers process data using the *binary numbering system*. Another numbering system related to computer use is the *hexadecimal numbering system*, which can be used to represent long strings of binary numbers in a manner more understandable to people than the binary numbering system. Following a discussion of these three numbering systems, we take a look at conversions between numbering systems and principles of computer arithmetic, and then close with a look at how to perform conversions using a scientific calculator. ■

The Decimal and Binary Numbering System

The *decimal* (*base 10*) numbering system uses 10 symbols—the digits 0, 1, 2, 3, 4, 5, 6, 7, 8, and 9—to represent all possible numbers and is the numbering system people use most often. The *binary* (*base 2*) numbering system is used extensively by computers to represent numbers and other characters. This system uses only two digits—0 and 1. As mentioned in Chapter 2, the place values (columns) in the binary numbering system are different from those used in the decimal system.

The Hexadecimal Numbering System

Computers often output diagnostic and memory-management messages and identify network adapters and other hardware in *hexadecimal* (*hex*) notation. Hexadecimal notation is a shorthand method for representing the binary digits stored in a computer. Because large binary numbers—for example, 1101010001001110—can easily be misread by people, hexadecimal notation groups binary digits into units of four, which, in turn, are represented by other symbols.

The hexadecimal numbering system is also called the *base 16 numbering system* because it uses 16 different symbols. Since there are only 10 possible numeric digits, hexadecimal uses letters instead of numbers for the additional 6 symbols. The 16 hexadecimal symbols and their decimal and binary counterparts are shown in Figure R-4.

The hexadecimal numbering system has a special relationship to the 8-bit bytes of ASCII and EBCDIC that makes it ideal for displaying addresses and other data quickly. As you can see in Figure R-4, each hex character has a 4-bit binary counterpart, so any combination of 8 bits can be represented by exactly two hexadecimal characters. For example, the letter N (represented in ASCII by 01001110) has a hex representation of *4E* (see the Binary Equivalent column for the hexadecimal characters *4* and *E* in Figure R-4).

FIGURE R-4
Hexadecimal characters and their decimal and binary equivalents.

HEXADECIMAL CHARACTER	DECIMAL EQUIVALENT	BINARY EQUIVALENT
0	0	0000
1	1	0001
2	2	0010
3	3	0011
4	4	0100
5	5	0101
6	6	0110
7	7	0111
8	8	1000
9	9	1001
A	10	1010
B	11	1011
C	12	1100
D	13	1101
E	14	1110
F	15	1111

Converting Between Numbering Systems

The concept of interpreting binary numbers was discussed in Chapter 2. Specifically, to convert from binary to decimal, you need to multiply each digit of the binary number by the appropriate power of 2 for that place value, such as by 2^0 or 1 for the rightmost digit, 2^1 or 2 for the next digit, and so forth, and then add those products together. Three other types of conversions computer professionals sometimes need to make are discussed next.

Hexadecimal to Decimal

As shown in Figure R-5, the process for converting a hexadecimal number to its decimal equivalent is similar to converting a binary number to its decimal equivalent, except the base number is 16 instead of 2. To determine the decimal equivalent of a hexadecimal number (such as 4F6A, as shown in Figure R-5), multiply the decimal equivalent of each individual hex character (determined by using the table in Figure R-4) by the appropriate power of 16 and then add the results to obtain the decimal equivalent of that hex number.

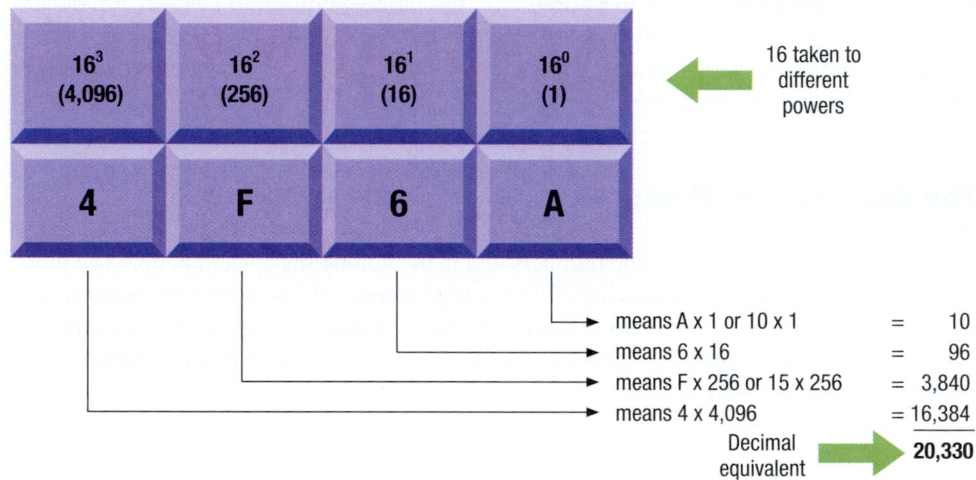

FIGURE R-5
The hexadecimal (base 16) numbering system. Each digit in a hexadecimal number represents 16 taken to a different power.

Hexadecimal to Binary and Binary to Hexadecimal

To convert from hexadecimal to binary, we convert each hexadecimal digit separately to 4 binary digits (using the table in Figure R-4). For example, to convert F6A9 to binary, we get

F	6	A	9
1111	0110	1010	1001

or 1111011010101001 in binary representation. To convert from binary to hexadecimal, we go through the reverse process. If the number of digits in the binary number is not divisible by 4, we add leading zeros to the binary number to force an even division. For example, to convert the binary number 1101101010011 to hexadecimal, we get

0001	1011	0101	0011
1	B	5	3

or lB53 in hexadecimal representation. Note that three leading zeros were added to change the initial 1 to 0001 before making the conversion.

Decimal to Binary and Decimal to Hexadecimal

To convert from decimal to either binary or hexadecimal, we can use the *remainder method*. To use the remainder method, the decimal number is divided by 2 (to convert to a binary number) or 16 (to convert to a hexadecimal number). The *remainder* of the division operation is recorded and the division process is repeated using the *quotient* as the next dividend, until the quotient becomes 0. At that point, the collective remainders (written backwards) represent the equivalent binary or hexadecimal number (see Figure R-6).

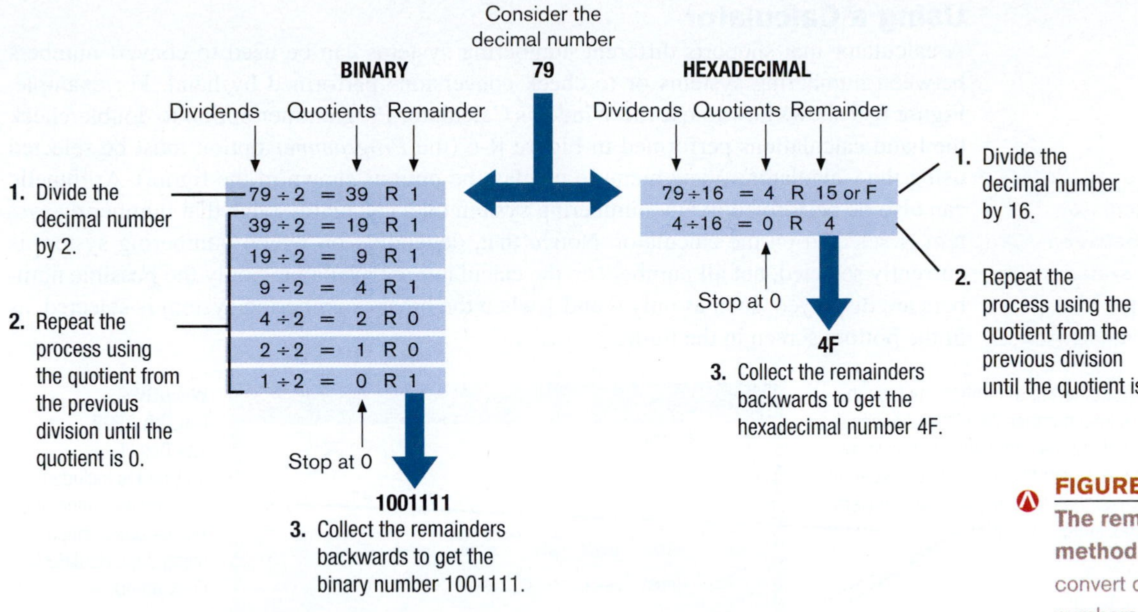
Consider the decimal number
79
BINARY
Dividends Quotients Remainder
1. Divide the decimal number by 2.
79 ÷ 2 = 39 R 1
39 ÷ 2 = 19 R 1
19 ÷ 2 = 9 R 1
9 ÷ 2 = 4 R 1
4 ÷ 2 = 2 R 0
2 ÷ 2 = 1 R 0
1 ÷ 2 = 0 R 1
2. Repeat the process using the quotient from the previous division until the quotient is 0.
Stop at 0
1001111
3. Collect the remainders backwards to get the binary number 1001111.
HEXADECIMAL
Dividends Quotients Remainder
79 ÷ 16 = 4 R 15 or F
4 ÷ 16 = 0 R 4
1. Divide the decimal number by 16.
2. Repeat the process using the quotient from the previous division until the quotient is 0.
Stop at 0
4F
3. Collect the remainders backwards to get the hexadecimal number 4F.
Copyright © 2015 Cengage Learning®

FIGURE R-6 **The remainder method.** Used to convert decimal numbers to binary or hex format.

A table summarizing all the numbering system conversion procedures covered in this text is provided in Figure R-7.

FIGURE R-7 **Summary of conversions.**

FROM BASE	TO BASE 2	TO BASE 10	TO BASE 16
2		Starting at the rightmost digit, multiply binary digits by 2^0, 2^1, 2^2, etc., respectively, and then add products.	Starting at the rightmost digit, convert each group of four binary digits to a hex digit.
10	Divide repeatedly by 2 using each quotient as the next dividend until the quotient becomes 0, and then collect the remainders in reverse order.		Divide repeatedly by 16 using each quotient as the next dividend until the quotient becomes 0, and then collect the remainders in reverse order.
16	Convert each hex digit to four binary digits.	Starting at the rightmost digit, multiply hex digits by 16^0, 16^1, 16^2, etc., respectively, and then add products.	

Computer Arithmetic

To most people, decimal arithmetic is second nature. Addition and subtraction of binary and hexadecimal numbers is not much different from the process used with decimal numbers—just the number of symbols used in each system varies. For instance, the digits in each column are added or subtracted and you carry to and borrow from the column to the left as needed as you move from right to left. Instead of carrying or borrowing powers of 10, however—as you would in the decimal system—you carry or borrow powers of 2 (binary) or 16 (hexadecimal).

Figure R-8 provides an example of addition and subtraction with decimal, binary, and hexadecimal numbers.

FIGURE R-8 **Adding and subtracting with the decimal, binary, and hexadecimal numbering systems.**

	DECIMAL	BINARY	HEXADECIMAL
Addition	1 144 + 27 171	1 1 1 100101 + 10011 111000	1 8E + 2F BD
Subtraction	3 1 144 - 27 117	0 1 0 1 100101 - 10011 10010	7 1 8E - 2F 5F

Using a Calculator

A calculator that supports different numbering systems can be used to convert numbers between numbering systems or to check conversions performed by hand. For example, Figure R-9 shows how to use the Windows Calculator Programmer option to double-check the hand calculations performed in Figure R-6 (the *Programmer* option must be selected using the Calculator's View menu to display the options shown in the figure). Arithmetic can also be performed in any numbering system on a calculator, once that numbering system is selected on the calculator. Notice that, depending on which numbering system is currently selected, not all numbers on the calculator are available—only the possible numbers are displayed, such as only 0 and 1 when the binary numbering system is selected, as in the bottom screen in the figure.

FIGURE R-9
Using a calculator to convert between numbering systems and perform arithmetic.

1. After entering a number (such as the decimal number 79 with the decimal numbering system selected as shown here), select the numbering system to which the number should be converted (hex in this example).

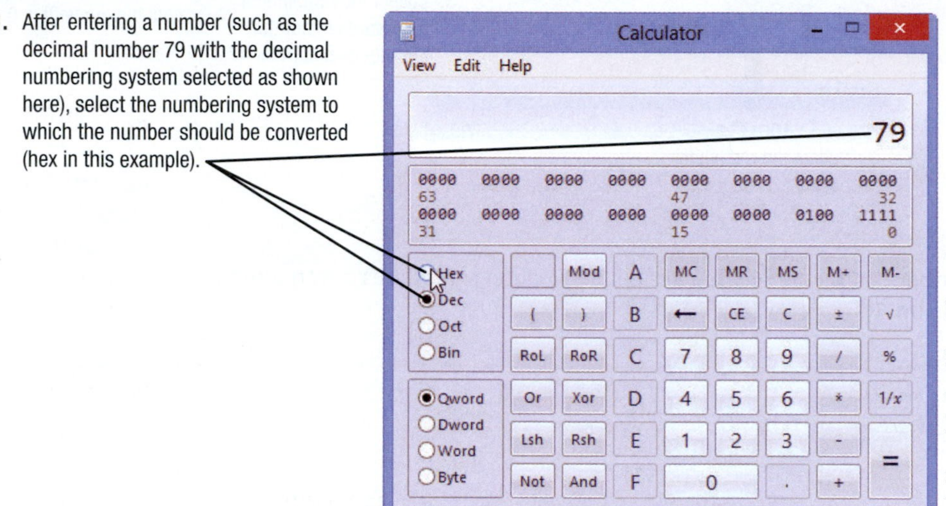

WINDOWS CALCULATOR
The Calculator program is included in Windows; select the *Programmer* option using the Calculator's View menu.

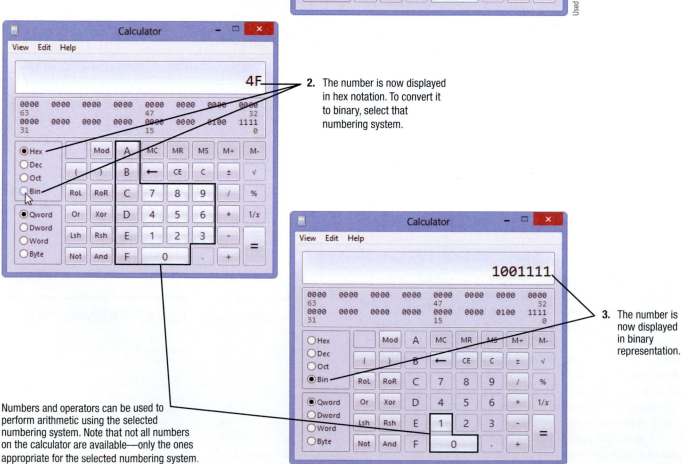

2. The number is now displayed in hex notation. To convert it to binary, select that numbering system.

3. The number is now displayed in binary representation.

Numbers and operators can be used to perform arithmetic using the selected numbering system. Note that not all numbers on the calculator are available—only the ones appropriate for the selected numbering system.

CODING CHARTS

As discussed in Chapter 2 of this text, coding systems for text-based data include ASCII and Unicode; *EBCDIC* is another coding system for text-based data that was developed primarily for use with mainframes. ■

ASCII and EBCDIC

Figure R-10 provides a chart listing the 8-digit ASCII and EBCDIC representations (in binary) for most of the symbols found on a typical keyboard.

FIGURE R-10
ASCII and EBCDIC binary codes for typical keyboard symbols.

SYMBOL	ASCII	EBCDIC	SYMBOL	ASCII	EBCDIC	SYMBOL	ASCII	EBCDIC
A	0100 0001	1100 0001	e	0110 0101	1000 0101	8	0011 1000	1111 1000
B	0100 0010	1100 0010	f	0110 0110	1000 0110	9	0011 1001	1111 1001
C	0100 0011	1100 0011	g	0110 0111	1000 0111	(	0010 1000	0100 1101
D	0100 0100	1100 0100	h	0110 1000	1000 1000	)	0010 1001	0101 1101
E	0100 0101	1100 0101	i	0110 1001	1000 1001	/	0010 1111	0110 0001
F	0100 0110	1100 0110	j	0110 1010	1001 0001	-	0010 1101	0110 0000
G	0100 0111	1100 0111	k	0110 1011	1001 0010	*	0010 1010	0101 1100
H	0100 1000	1100 1000	l	0110 1100	1001 0011	+	0010 1011	0100 1110
I	0100 1001	1100 1001	m	0110 1101	1001 0100	,	0010 1100	0110 1011
J	0100 1010	1101 0001	n	0110 1110	1001 0101	.	0010 1110	0100 1011
K	0100 1011	1101 0010	o	0110 1111	1001 0110	:	0011 1010	0111 1010
L	0100 1100	1101 0011	p	0111 0000	1001 0111	;	0011 1011	0101 1110
M	0100 1101	1101 0100	q	0111 0001	1001 1000	&	0010 0110	0101 0000
N	0100 1110	1101 0101	r	0111 0010	1001 1001	\	0101 1100	1110 0000
O	0100 1111	1101 0110	s	0111 0011	1010 0010	$	0010 0100	0101 1011
P	0101 0000	1101 0111	t	0111 0100	1010 0011	%	0010 0101	0110 1100
Q	0101 0001	1101 1000	u	0111 0101	1010 0100	=	0011 1101	0111 1110
R	0101 0010	1101 1001	v	0111 0110	1010 0101	>	0011 1110	0110 1110
S	0101 0011	1110 0010	w	0111 0111	1010 0110	<	0011 1100	0100 1100
T	0101 0100	1110 0011	x	0111 1000	1010 0111	!	0010 0001	0101 1010
U	0101 0101	1110 0100	y	0111 1001	1010 1000	|	0111 1100	0110 1010
V	0101 0110	1110 0101	z	0111 1010	1010 1001	?	0011 1111	0110 1111
W	0101 0111	1110 0110	0	0011 0000	1111 0000	@	0100 0000	0111 1100
X	0101 1000	1110 0111	1	0011 0001	1111 0001	_	0101 1111	0110 1101
Y	0101 1001	1110 1000	2	0011 0010	1111 0010	`	0110 0000	1011 1001
Z	0101 1010	1110 1001	3	0011 0011	1111 0011	{	0111 1011	1100 0000
a	0110 0001	1000 0001	4	0011 0100	1111 0100	}	0111 1101	1101 0000
b	0110 0010	1000 0010	5	0011 0101	1111 0101	~	0111 1110	1010 0001
c	0110 0011	1000 0011	6	0011 0110	1111 0110	[	0101 1011	0100 1010
d	0110 0100	1000 0100	7	0011 0111	1111 0111	]	0101 1101	0101 1010

A 0041	N 004E	a 0061	n 006E	0 0030	{ 007B	* 002A	■ 25A0	অ 0985
B 0042	O 004F	b 0062	o 006F	1 0031	| 007C	+ 002B	□ 25A1	গ 0997
C 0043	P 0050	c 0063	p 0070	2 0032	} 007D	, 002C	▲ 25B2	ে 09C7
D 0044	Q 0051	d 0064	q 0071	3 0033	~ 007E	- 002D	℅ 2105	৶ 09F6
E 0045	R 0052	e 0065	r 0072	4 0034	! 0021	. 002E	℞ 211E	څ 0685
F 0046	S 0053	f 0066	s 0073	5 0035	" 0022	/ 002F	⅓ 2153	ڴ 06B4
G 0047	T 0054	g 0067	t 0074	6 0036	# 0023	£ 20A4	⅔ 2154	ڪ 06AA
H 0048	U 0055	h 0068	u 0075	7 0037	$ 0024	Σ 2211	♕ 2655	α 03B1
I 0049	V 0056	i 0069	v 0076	8 0038	% 0025	∅ 2205	☂ 2602	β 03B2
J 004A	W 0057	j 006A	w 0077	9 0039	& 0026	√ 221A	❐ 2750	Δ 0394
K 004B	X 0058	k 006B	x 0078	[005B	' 0027	∞ 221E	❂ 2742	ϕ 03A6
L 004C	Y 0059	l 006C	y 0079	\ 005C	(0028	≤ 2264	➲ 27B2	Ω 03A9
M 004D	Z 005A	m 006D	z 007A	] 005D	) 0029	≥ 2265	♥ 2665	Ϋ 03AB

FIGURE R-11
Selected Unicode codes.

Unicode

Since consistent worldwide representation of symbols is increasingly needed today, use of Unicode is growing rapidly. Unicode can be used to represent every written language, as well as a variety of other symbols. Unicode codes are typically listed in hexadecimal notation—a sampling of Unicode is shown in Figure R-11.

The capability to display characters and other symbols using Unicode coding is incorporated into many programs. For instance, when the Symbol dialog box is opened using the INSERT tab in Microsoft Office Word, the Unicode representation (as well as the corresponding ASCII code in either decimal or hexadecimal representation) can be viewed (see Figure R-12). Some programs allow you to enter a Unicode symbol using its Unicode hexadecimal value. For instance, in Microsoft Office programs you can use the Alt+X command when the insertion point is just to the right of a Unicode hex value to convert that hex value into the corresponding symbol. For example, the keystrokes

2264Alt+X

result in the symbol corresponding to the Unicode code 2264 (the less than or equal sign ≤) being inserted into the document; entering 03A3 and then pressing Alt+X inserts the symbol shown in the Word screen in Figure R-12.

FIGURE R-12
Using Unicode.

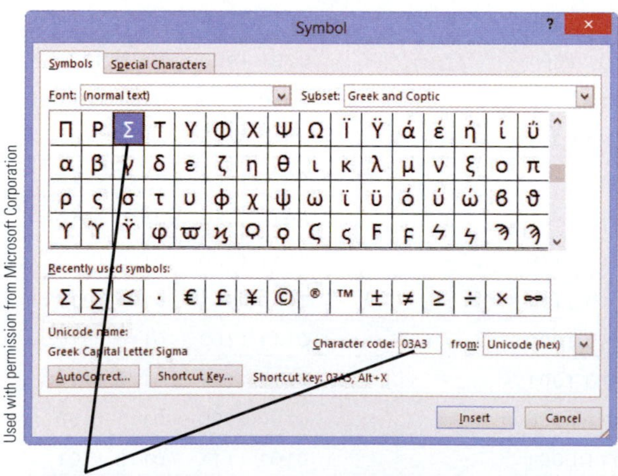

UNICODE REPRESENTATION
The Symbol dialog box shown here lists the Unicode representation of each symbol as it is selected. If preferred, the ASCII representation can be displayed.

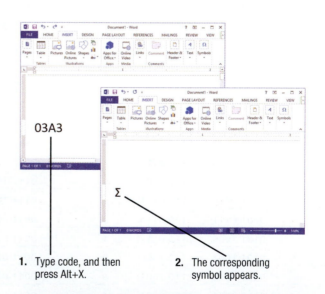

INSERTING SYMBOLS USING UNICODE
In Microsoft Office programs, typing the hexadecimal Unicode code for a symbol and then pressing Alt+X displays the corresponding symbol.

ANSWERS TO SELF-QUIZ

Chapter 1

1. T **2.** F **3.** F **4.** F **5.** T **6.** Input **7.** hybrid notebook-tablet **8.** Virtualization **9.** electronic mail or e-mail **10. a.** 4 **b.** 2 **c.** 1 **d.** 3

Chapter 2

1. T **2.** T **3.** F **4.** F **5.** T **6.** scanner, optical scanner, flatbed scanner, or portable scanner **7.** quad-core **8.** flash memory **9.** folders **10. a.** 2 **b.** 5 **c.** 1 **d.** 4 **e.** 3

Chapter 3

1. F **2.** F **3.** T **4.** T **5.** F **6.** Digital Subscriber Line or DSL **7.** keyword; directory **8.** social network or social networking site **9.** online auction **10. a.** 2 **b.** 4 **c.** 1 **d.** 3

Chapter 4

1. F **2.** T **3.** F **4.** T **5.** F **6.** war driving **7.** Biometric **8.** virtual private network or VPN **9.** digital signature **10. a.** 3 **b.** 4 **c.** 1 **d.** 2

Chapter 5

1. F **2.** T **3.** T **4.** F **5.** F **6.** disaster recovery **7.** digital counterfeiting **8.** filter **9.** opt out; opt in **10. a.** 3 **b.** 5 **c.** 1 **d.** 2 **e.** 4

Chapter 6

1. F **2.** T **3.** F **4.** T **5.** T **6.** copyright; trademark **7.** plagiarism **8.** Digital rights management (DRM) **9.** Communications Decency **10. a.** 2 **b.** 4 **c.** 1 **d.** 3

Chapter 7

1. F **2.** T **3.** T **4.** F **5.** F **6.** ergonomics **7.** burnout **8.** digital divide **9.** Internet addiction **10.** Solar

Chapter 8

1. T **2.** T **3.** F **4.** F **5.** T **6.** qubits **7.** nanotubes **8.** Power over Ethernet (PoE) **9.** neural network or neural net **10.** battlefield

INDEX

D

dictionary, 108
Digimarc Discover, 236
digital camcorder, 56
digital camera An input device that takes pictures and records them as digital images. 12, 55–56
digital certificate A group of electronic data that can be used to verify the identity of a person or organization; includes a key pair that can be used for encryption and digital signatures (also called a digital ID). 174, 175–176
digital computer, 47
Digital Copy, 243, 244
digital counterfeiting The use of computers or other types of digital equipment to make illegal copies of currency, checks, collectibles, and other items. 201–202
  prevention, 203
digital currency, 239
digital divide The gap between those who have access to technology and those who do not. 275–277
digital form, 52
digital manipulation The alteration of digital content, usually text or photographs. 248–249
Digital Millennium Copyright Act (DMCA), 242, 253
digital pen. *See* stylus
digital photo, 5
digital photo frame, 62
digital portfolio. *See* e-portfolio
digital rights management (DRM) software Software used to protect and manage the rights of creators of digital content, such as art, music, photographs, and movies. 235
digital signal, 62
digital signature A unique digital code that can be attached to a file or an e-mail message to verify the identity of the sender and guarantee the file or message has not been changed since it was signed. 176
digital still camera, 56
Digital Subscriber Line. *See* DSL (Digital Subscriber Line) Internet access
Digital Theft Deterrence and Copyright Damages Improvement Act of 1999, 253
digital video camera, 56
digital video recorder (DVR), 5
digital voice, 114
digital watermark A subtle alteration of digital content that is not noticeable when the work is viewed or played but that identifies the copyright holder. 203
digital writing, 51
digitizing tablet. *See* graphics tablet
direct connection A type of Internet connection in which the computer or other device is connected to the Internet continually. 27, 102
direct message, 113
directory. *See* folder
directory search A type of Internet search where categories are selected to locate information on the Internet. 106, 107
disaster recovery plan A written plan that describes the steps a company will take following the occurrence of a disaster. 199–200
discussion group. *See* forum
disk-erasing software, 214
disk-wiping software, 214
display device An output device that contains a viewing screen. 62–63
  Braille, 279
display screen, 12, 62
disposable e-mail address. *See* throw-away e-mail address
disposal
  e-waste, 282, 284–285
  hardware containing data, 214, 285
distance learning A learning environment in which the student is physically located away from the instructor and other students; commonly, instruction and communications take place via the Web. 5–6, 126
distributed denial of service attack (DDoS attack), 164
DL disc. *See* dual-layer (DL) disc
DMARC (Domain-based Message Authentication, Report, and Conformance), 175
DMCA. *See* Digital Millennium Copyright Act (DMCA)
DNA data storage, 305
DNS poisoning, 171
DNS server. *See* domain name system (DNS) server
Do Not Call Implementation Act, 223
Do Not Track legislation, 213
docking port, 271
docking station A device designed to easily connect a portable computer to conventional hardware, such as a keyboard, mouse, monitor, and printer. 22, 266, 267
document, 83. *See also* file; word processing software
  formatting, 82, 83
document holder, 266, 268
domain name A text-based Internet address used to uniquely identify a computer on the Internet. 28
  cybersquatting, 236–237
domain name system (DNS) server, 28, 171
Domain-based Message Authentication, Report, and Conformance. *See* DMARC (Domain-based Message Authentication, Report, and Conformance)
Do-Not-Track Online Act of 2013, 222
Doom, 121
DoS attack. *See* denial of service (DoS) attack
dot con A fraud or scam carried out through the Internet. 166–172
dot-matrix printer, 63
dots per inch (dpi), 53
double-layer disc. *See* dual-layer (DL) disc
double-sided disc, 70
download manager, 31
downward compatibility, 71
dpi. *See* dots per inch (dpi)
dragging-and-dropping, 51
drive bay, 57
drive-by pharming, 171
DRM. *See* digital rights management (DRM) software
drone, 320
Dropbox, 75
DSL (Digital Subscriber Line) Internet access Fast, direct Internet access via standard telephone lines. 78, 102, 103
DSL modem, 103
DSM-V. *See* Diagnostic and Statistical Manual of Mental Disorders (DSM-V)
dual-core CPU A CPU that contains two separate processing cores. 59
dual-layer (DL) disc, 70
DuckDuckGo search site, 211
dumb terminal, 22
Durant, Kevin, 124
DVD disc A medium capacity (typically 4.7 GB or 8.5 GB) optical disc that is often used to deliver software and movies, as well as to store user data. 12, 13, 55, 66, 69, 70
DVD drive, 12, 13, 57, 66, 69
DVD+R disc, 71
DVD-R disc, 71
DVD+R DL disc, 71
DVD-R DL disc, 71
DVD-R drive, 71
DVD-RE disc, 72
DVD-ROM (digital versatile disc read-only memory) disc, 71
DVD+RW disc, 72
DVD-RW disc, 72
DVD+RW drive, 72
DVD-RW drive, 72
DVR. *See* digital video recorder (DVR)

E

earbud, 65
earphone, 65
earthquake, 108
eBay, 118
EBCDIC. *See* Extended Binary Coded Decimal Interchange Code (EBCDIC)
e-book, 5, 242
e-book reader, 62
eco-label A certification, usually by a government agency, that identifies a device as meeting minimal environmental performance specifications. 280
e-commerce, 117
editing Changing the content of a document, such as inserting or deleting words. 82
education
  computer use in, 5–6
  online, 125–126
Education Privacy Act, 223
EHR. *See* electronic health record (EHR)
802.11. *See* Wi-Fi (802.11)
802.11ac standard, 310
802.11g standard, 310
802.11n standard, 310
802.16. *See* WiMAX (802.16)
802.16m standard, 311
Eisenhower, Dwight D., 11
e-learning. *See* distance learning
electron, 66
electronic circuit, 11
Electronic Communications Privacy Act, 223
electronic health record (EHR), 52, 76
electronic link, 283
electronic mail (e-mail) Electronic messages sent from one user to another over the Internet or other network. 4, 32–33
  addresses. *See* e-mail address
  convergence, 4
  e-mail program, 15, 16, 198
  iPad ordering system, 7
  phishing, 35, 143, 169–170, 173–175
  privacy, 133
  spam, 34–35, 204, 208–209
electronic monitoring, 204
electronic paper (e-paper), 283
Electronic Paper Display (EPD), 283
electronic pen. *See* stylus
electronic portfolio. *See* e-portfolio
electronic profiling Using electronic means to collect a variety of in-depth information about an individual, such as name, address, income, and buying habits. 207
electronic surveillance tool, 204

F